Personal
Financial Planning

Personal Financial Planning

Fifth Edition

Kwok Ho
York University

Chris Robinson
York University

Captus Press

Personal Financial Planning, Fifth Edition

Copyright © 2000–2012 by Kwok Ho, Chris Robinson and Captus Press Inc.

First edition, 1995
Fifth edition, 2012

Captus Press Inc.
Units 14 & 15, 1600 Steeles Avenue West
Concord, Ontario L4K 4M2 Canada
Telephone: (416) 736–5537   Fax: (416) 736–5793
Email: info@captus.com   Internet: www.captus.com

The names of persons and organizations in the cases, problems and examples in this book are fictitious. Any similarities to the name of an actual person, living or dead, or to an actual organization, is purely coincidental.

Library and Archives Canada Cataloguing in Publication
Ho, Kwok, 1948–
  Personal financial planning / Kwok Ho, Chris Robinson. — 5th ed.

Includes bibliographical references and index.
ISBN 978-1-55322-254-5

  1. Finance, Personal — Canada. I. Robinson, Chris, 1950– . II. Title.
HG179.H6 2012   332.02400971   C2012-904423-7

Canada We acknowledge the financial support of the Government of Canada through the Canada Book Fund for our publishing activities.

0 9 8 7 6 5 4 3 2
Printed in Canada

To my wife, Frances Chung
— Kwok Ho

To my parents, Fred and Fran Robinson
— Chris Robinson

Contents

ABOUT THE AUTHORS

List of Figures/Tables

Preface

We wrote this book to provide a thorough coverage of personal finance grounded in finance theory. No such work is widely available for use in universities and colleges, but financial institutions need people who have proper training to work with their clientele. In addition, students need to learn how to manage their own finances in an orderly way.

We have taught part-time and full-time undergraduate and MBA students at York University using this textbook. Some of our graduates have successfully completed the Certified Financial Planner® exam and work as professional planners. They find it both personally relevant and useful in their careers. We hope you will enjoy it too.

In the fifth edition we have added substantial new material in tax and retirement planning. We deleted Chapters 19 and 20, but substantially revised versions will be made available on the Captus Press website later. Interested readers can order them online. We have made many smaller changes and additions throughout the book, including new problems.

Farshad Adlgostar helped us create problems and solutions. Professor Joanne Magee reviewed the tax chapters and provided extensive advice on tax questions throughout the book. Syed Ahmed, Bob Barney, John Benson, Shawn Brayman, Trevor Chamberlain, Helena Cheung, John Churchill, Coleen Clark, Dan Collison, Esther Deutsch, Alan Goldhar, Debbie Good, Yves Groleau, Ivon T. Hughes, Ken Hopper, Jury Kopach, Franck Lerman, Craig Lilley, Simeon Ling, Jane Londerville, Maureen MacDonald, Bernice Miedzinski, Moshe Arye Milevsky, Grady Perdue, Meredith Perren, Ruth Reimer, Fred and Fran Robinson, Chris Veld, David West, Victoria Zaremba, and Xiaoyu Zhang provided helpful comments on various sections. The late Nora Campbell typed and edited about half of the manuscript of the first edition. We would like to acknowledge also the support and patience of the students on whom we have practised the ideas contained in this book and our colleagues at York University.

Chris Robinson previously wrote a private textbook in personal finance for the Institute of Canadian Bankers, in 1986–87. For the knowledge and skills that he gained from that experience, he thanks: Gilles Bernier of Laval University, his co-author; Jérôme Camus, Rosaire Couturier, Pierre Goulet, and Mark Webb, who worked for the Institute at the time.

Last, but not least, we are grateful to the staff at Captus Press who have supported us so well through every edition.

Kwok Ho
Chris Robinson
Toronto, Ontario
July 2012

CHAPTER I

Introduction

- Grinder McSnarl will lend money to Jennie Sweettooth — for a price.
- John Ross wants to be a millionaire by the time he is 40.
- Harold and Donalda Woodhaven work out their financial position.
- Rose and Andre Vino can reduce their taxes, with careful planning.
- How much life insurance should Max Brownlie buy?
- Should Jack and Jill rent or buy a condominium?
- Rose and Sam Wise want to retire with $30,000 per year.
- How much can Simona spend of her retirement nest egg each year?

Meet these people and many others throughout the book. They may be your clients in the future, or perhaps you will become them. Learn how to advise them to make the best financial decisions for their own situations.

OBJECTIVES OF THE BOOK

> ➢ *Learn the foundations of personal financial planning in a rigorous framework as the first step in providing financial counselling to others.*
>
> ➢ *Learn to manage your own family's personal finances using sound principles to help you achieve your goals in life.*

Personal finance has exploded into popular consciousness in the last decade. The Internet is full of websites on personal finance, especially investing. Gossip in chat rooms now drives share prices of small companies up and down at a dizzying rate because of amateur day traders. Every bookstore carries a wide variety of publications, from those dealing with very simple budgeting and planning to those covering complex income taxation issues that were once found only on the bookshelves of accountants and lawyers. Television programs on personal finance and consumer issues draw large ratings, and there is even one aimed specifically at teenagers and their financial concerns. Local radio stations feature financial advisors with daily tips or hotline phone-in programs. Financial institutions offer solutions to your financial planning problems, often at the touch of a computer button. Financial planning has become a rapidly expanding (and little regulated) new "profession".

What can we offer with this book that hasn't been written or said already? The advice that you receive from these popular sources is often valuable and very timely. For example, if you want to know more about Registered Retirement Savings Plans, you can be sure that the rules, issues, and investment choices will be discussed endlessly in every newspaper in the two months before the annual February deposit deadline. The same holds true for Canada Savings Bonds and the November 1 purchase deadline. And so on.

The weakness of this popular advice is that it is fragmented and relates to the specific financial product or issue in isolation. Our book builds on a coherent and consistent framework of basic finance principles to allow you to develop a complete plan or response to a personal financial situation. It requires more work and attention than does the popular "Make Your Money Grow", or "How to be a Millionaire and Retire Early", but the foundation it provides leads to sound planning.

You can use this foundation to help others manage their personal finances. Financial institutions are recognizing that they must offer much more service to their individual or retail customers, and personal financial planning is one way to do it. If you are a student interested in working for a bank, trust company, insurance company, independent financial planning company, or investment dealer, personal financial planning is a valuable part of your education. Even if you never use it with your clients, a rigorous personal financial planning education will help you meet your own goals.

We cannot make you or your client rich or secure with this book. We cannot even ensure that you don't starve. Only you can do these things. What we can do is give you the means to manage whatever money you have and can save in a rational manner, so that you have the best chance possible to realize your goals in life. All of this financial planning occurs within the context of a family unit, though the unit can be a single person or parents with four dependent children.

In the rest of this chapter we present a simple model of the *financial planning process*. We describe the contents of the book by showing how the different elements of financial planning fit into this simple model. We then go beyond the book with advice on how to keep up-to-date in financial planning, and where to go for further help in designing and implementing your plan.

A SIMPLE MODEL OF FINANCIAL PLANNING

Money won't make you happy, as many poets and singers have told us, but its absence can lead to a lot of unhappiness. Personally, we don't believe that accumulating great wealth is a sure route to a happy life. However, human society uses money as a medium of exchange and so we have to learn to manage it if we are to survive. The goals that we strive for using personal financial management are therefore financial ones, though they are simply means towards non-financial ends, like having enough to eat, a place to live, entertainment, etc.

Think of the **financial planning process** as a series of decisions on how much money you need at some future time in order to meet your goals, and how you will get that money. Goals must be in monetary terms and have some date attached to them, in order to plan for them. To reach the goal, you have two sources of money. You have some money now, which earns more money as you invest it over time. You earn money by working, and you consume some of that money as well, with the net amount being your savings. The saved money goes into the investment pot with the previous savings and earns investment income, too. If you are to meet your goals, you must arrange your affairs so that the following equation is true:

Financial goal (at time n)
= Existing savings + Investment income for n years on the existing savings
   + (Earnings − Consumption each year)
   + Investment income on the annual savings, n.[1]

---

[1] We model this process more formally in Chapter 3.

THE CONTENTS OF THE BOOK

Reprinted with permission — The Toronto Star Syndicate. © 1994 GREG HOWARD distributed by King Features Syndicate.

Every chapter in the book relates to some part of this equation. Chapters 2–7 present the fundamental tools or mechanics of personal financial management. The student must understand these techniques thoroughly and be able to apply the calculations throughout the rest of the book. Chapters 8–16 contain the elements that we combine to form the financial plan. Chapters 17–18 discuss retirement planning, which incorporates all the fundamentals and elements, directed towards the specific goal of a comfortable retirement.

Chapter 2, **Time Value of Money**, covers the basic arithmetic of finance that allows us to compare amounts of money received or paid at different times.

Chapter 3, **Setting Goals and the Financial Planning Process**, discusses how to set realistic financial goals and how to adjust your goal when it isn't realistic.

Chapter 4, **Measuring and Controlling Personal Finances**, shows you how to determine your present financial position and plan for future saving. The technique is simple financial accounting applied to personal, instead of corporate, affairs.

Chapter 5, **Family Law**, discusses the various financial planning issues that are affected by family law. The intention of this chapter is to help understand the important issues and the possible financial planning choices and consequences, not to replace legal advice.

Chapter 6, **The Life Cycle and Financial Intermediation**, puts personal finance into its context in the entire economic system. We explain how different aspects of personal finance are more important at different stages in the family life cycle. The system of financial intermediation and institutions that we use to implement our plans has evolved in our economy to meet those needs.

Chapters 7 and 8, **Personal Income Tax** and **Income Tax Planning**, provide a basic introduction to this extremely complex topic, which plays a major role in determining both the rate of return on your investments and the amount of money you save. Chapter 7 explains the basic structure of the personal tax system, focusing on the personal income tax return. Chapter 8 shows how these rules affect financial decisions, and how you must use your knowledge to minimize your taxes. Most people will find that these two chapters explain what they need to know for most situations they will encounter. What we have left out, however, is a huge field, and in some cases, the effect can be very large.

Chapter 9, **Risk Management**, is the theoretical basis for insurance, but you will see in later chapters that there are other ways to control risk as well.

Chapters 10 and 11, **Life, Health, and Disability Insurance** and **Property, Home, and Automobile Insurance**, are the principal means of financing risks that you cannot control by other means. We go into some detail on how to calculate your requirements, and the characteristics of insurance policies that you need to know to choose the right ones for your specific risk management needs.

Most families will encounter periods early in the life cycle when they need to borrow money. As well, most people use credit or charge cards as a matter of convenience. Chapter 12, **Credit and Debt Management**, provides advice on these subjects.

In the long run, we all hope that we will have positive savings, and we then have to decide how to invest them, which is the subject of Chapters 13–16. Chapter 13, **Buying a Home and Mortgage Financing**, discusses the problem of whether to rent or buy, and develops a framework for deciding which house to buy and how to go about it. Chapter 14, **Principles of Investment**, discusses in intuitive terms a topic that has generated a huge and very technical research literature in finance. Your investment decisions will determine how high your rate of return is and how risky. The factors that bear upon this decision require some study.

Theory is a necessary foundation for investment management, but you must invest your money in the real world. Chapters 15 and 16, **Types of Investments** and **Mutual Funds**, describe the different choices available to you and what sort of values and variations in rates of return you might expect from each. Financial market institutions are constantly inventing new instruments; so some of the basic characteristics described in Chapters 14 and 15 are important in order to understand how to assess innovations.

Chapter 17, **Retirement Planning**, takes us back to square one as we try to determine how much we need to live in retirement and how much our current savings pattern will provide. Thus, our goal of wealth available for retirement must equal the *present value* of all the consumption during retirement. Once we determine the desired standard of living and what it entails in wealth at retirement, we can plan how we will achieve the required savings, and how we will invest our savings.

Chapter 18, **Maturation of the Retirement Plan**, builds a risk management framework for the decision on how to organize the retirement savings and their withdrawal from the pre-retirement investment instruments. We provide an introduction to estate planning.

GOING BEYOND THIS BOOK

Keeping Up-to-Date

Warning! By the time you finish reading this book, some of the details may be obsolete! The environment of personal finance changes rapidly, and some of the structural factors, like tax rules and financial instruments, may have changed, making some of what we say incorrect or irrelevant. That is why we concentrate on fundamental finance principles, since they do not change quickly and provide a long-term basis for financial planning.

Even though the principles stay the same, the environment in which you make your decisions is changing. The level of interest rates and inflation, trends in consumer spending, and expectations about future incomes, all affect personal financial planning. Only a few years before we wrote this book, protection against inflation was a major concern. The developed Western economies enjoyed a long period of booming incomes and low inflation (1–3%) from about 1953 through the mid-1960s. Inflation started rising in 1968, and throughout the 1970s and 1980s it was the biggest single worry for financial planners, sometimes hitting double digits.

Today we find ourselves back in a world of 2% inflation. Now, however, incomes are falling, unemployment is widespread and seemingly permanent for a growing number of people. Consumer spending is declining, especially on consumer durables — refrigerators, cars, furniture — the engine of the post-War boom economy. People who thought they had secure and rising incomes for life — civil servants, teachers, doctors, auto workers, municipal workers, pulpwood cutters — have found their incomes frozen or their jobs eliminated altogether. In this scary world, security has taken on new importance, and planning for it is much different than it was in a world where inflation was higher, but everyone believed that they could outrun it. The global financial crisis of 2008 ended that dream.

Your financial plan requires constant attention in this turbulent and risky environment. Even if your personal circumstances don't seem to have changed, you are at greater financial risk than at any time since the depression of the 1930s. The principles and analytical techniques in this book should remain useful, but what you put into the analysis keeps changing.

The *Personal Financial Planner's Manual*™ is a reference source with a great deal of technical knowledge, such as family law, income tax law, retirement planning, etc. It is produced and updated as necessary, about twice a year, by the trademark owners, D.R. Gobeil and Associates (www.gobeil.ca).

The Internet has become the largest source of immediate information — so much data and changing so rapidly in form that we do not provide information on personal finance sites in the static format of a printed textbook. We warn you that the enormous quantity of data and freedom of the Internet is also risky because there is no quality control. In the next few paragraphs, the information sources we mention are moving more and more to delivery over the Web, though many publications are still produced in paper form also.

The major daily newspapers record the important economic events and provide valuable statistics in their business pages. You can track returns on your investments and changes in mortgage rates daily if you need to. If unemployment in your occupation is high, you know to make doubly sure of your safety nets just in case you, too, lose your job.

The dailies feature personal finance articles in the business sections. The specialist business newspapers carry even more coverage, sometimes in special sections — *The Globe and Mail*'s Report on Business and The Financial Post section of the *National Post* are the most widely read.

Magazines dedicated to personal finance often have somewhat short lives, but *Canadian Moneysaver* has maintained a broad and very independent stance for years, while accepting no advertising (<www.canadianmoneysaver.ca>). If you are working in the personal finance or investment field already or intend to do so, *Investment Executive* is a monthly newspaper worth reading, along with its glossy supplement, *IE Money*.

There are many other sources of financial planning advice. Investment dealers, mutual funds, banks, trust companies, insurers, credit unions, and caisses populaires are all in the financial intermediation business. One way for them to get your business is to publish newsletters and brochures providing personal finance tips. These publications vary widely in quality, since their primary purpose is to get you to buy the particular institution's offerings. The best of them are quite good, however, because these institutions have the resources to hire the best professional advisors, and the incentive to give good advice to maintain their reputation. Most of these publications are free, but you have to search a bit to find them. Their industry associations publish general interest personal finance tracts as well.

Professional accountants do a lot of personal finance work, especially on income tax. The largest public practice firms of chartered accountants (CA) and certified general accountants (CGA) publish newsletters and specific issue pamphlets that are free upon request. If you want to know how a provincial or federal budget may affect you, their post-budget analyses are useful. *CA Magazine* (monthly) has a personal finance column. The provincial and federal associations of the CAs, CGAs, and the certified management accountants (CMAs) also have some publications, mostly dealing with income taxes.

Professional and occupational associations provide useful financial information for their members through their regular magazines and special bulletins. This information can be particularly valuable since it will reflect issues specific to a given occupation. Taxes and insurance are the topics most often seen in these sources. We have seen very good material for teachers, university professors, and medical professionals, for example.

We do not recommend relying on television or radio for anything but the most general reminders about personal finance. The nature of the broadcast media does not lend itself to the careful analysis necessary for important financial decisions.

Getting Expert Help

Choosing an Advisor

Before we get into details, let us express our own preference for the type of advisors you should seek. Aside from the obvious requirement for technical competence, we look for honesty and a commitment to serve our personal finance needs as thoroughly as possible. The institution or advisor that wants to help us first, before selling us the most profitable product or service, is the one we want. We trust those who do not make extravagant claims about tax savings waiting to be seized or huge profits from _____ (fill in the latest advertised scam). If we are looking to establish a long-run relationship, say banking or an insurance policy, we want someone who has our long-run interests in mind, too.

Implementing the Plan

No matter how good this book is and how skilled you become at personal financial planning, you will need expert help to implement many aspects of your plan. If you want to invest in the stock market, you need an intermediary licensed to execute trades on your behalf. You need banks and insurance companies and their employees for the services they provide. You may be able to write a simple will and buy a house without a lawyer,[2] but you need their help with more complex transactions.

The key to dealing with these people effectively and enlisting their best services on your behalf is to know what you need. You must have a financial plan before you start buying insurance, investing in penny mines, etc. Use this book as a reference in specific areas. For example, you should determine whether you really need life insurance, how much you need, and what special characteristics should be attached to the policy *before* you visit an insurance agent. Chapter 10 shows you how to do this. Then, it is an easy matter for the agent to provide you with one or more policies meeting your requirements. The agent gets a good commission without much work, and you get what you need. If you wander into his office with only a vague idea of what you need, the easiest course of action for the agent to follow is to sell you the policy paying the largest agent's commission. Even the most experienced and honest agent may have a hard time selling you the right insurance if you don't have a financial plan.

Financial Planners

We classify them into four categories based on the way in which they are paid. "He who pays the piper calls the tune" is the old saying, and the quality of the

---

[2] Your local library or business book store has detailed guides on how to write a will, transfer property, and write and execute other basic contracts. We do not advise you either to choose or to avoid this way of saving legal fees, but we ourselves pay lawyers to do this kind of work, and stick to what we know best.

financial plan they plan for you is affected by who pays them. You should ask any financial planner how he or she is remunerated before you commit yourself. Disclosure requirements vary by jurisdiction.

Salaried employees of institutions, such as banks or trust companies, are sometimes designated as financial planners and provide advice to their customers free of charge, or for a nominal fee. The advice often consists of a computer printout from a generalized computer package, based on inputs from the customer. The only reason for this service is to sell you the particular products and services of the institution; so the advice you get is very limited in value. Sometimes, these institutions have professionally trained advisors working in private banking units where their job is to smooth the lives of the wealthiest customers. Sometimes the goodwill of these customers is worth so much to the bank that something approaching expert independent advice is rendered, but this service is not offered to everyone.

Commission planners receive their compensation in the form of fees and commissions from the sellers of services and products that they recommend. They may be employed directly by the institution (but paid by commission, not salary), act as exclusive or general agents, or simply search all opportunities in the market without allegiance to any institutions. These planners may have a little more independence, but the incentive is to steer you into the products that pay the best commissions. The commission dollars come from someone, and that someone is you. For example, whole life insurance provides the best commissions, but costs the consumer more than individual or group term insurance.

Fee-based planners receive their compensation partly in the form of a fee, usually hourly, that you pay them, and partly from commissions from the institutions. These planners are almost always independent of specific institutions, but still have incentives to choose the highest commissions. The conflict of interest is reduced, but not eliminated.

Fee-only or *fee-for-service planners* charge the client directly on an hourly basis for the time spent doing the planning. These planners earn all their income from their clients and take no commissions. The hourly fee ranges from $50 to $300.

How do you decide which one you need? In our opinion, if you want proper financial counselling and you have enough assets and difficult issues to justify the cost, the fee-only planner is the best bet. The cost of poor advice given to generate commissions or justify an employee's salary is less obvious than the independent planner's service fees, but you could lose a great deal more. If your needs are simple and don't justify the hourly fees, then the other planners will probably do a good enough job. Just as with implementation of the plan, your best bet is always to do as much of the planning yourself as you can. The cost of this book and the time spent to understand it is far less than the loss you could suffer from underinsurance or an ill-advised investment.

How do you know who is qualified to be a planner? There are few regulations governing financial planners in Canada[3] and almost anyone can hang out a shingle. Financial planners are bound by the same statutes and common law that apply to anyone selling services. They must perform their work with due care, and they cannot misrepresent their work or their qualifications. We cannot offer any sure-fire guide as to which planners will do the best work, though.

Financial Planners Standards Council (FPSC) is an umbrella group that has a mandate to provide a uniform set of educational and practice standards for personal financial planning in Canada. It was established in November of 1995, and has seven member organizations: L'institut québécois de planification financière (IQPF), Financial Advisors Association of Canada (Advocis), Canadian Institute of Financial Planning (CIFP), Canadian Institute of Chartered Accountants, Society of Management Accountants of Canada, Certified General Accountants Association of Canada, and the Credit Union Institute of Canada. FPSC licenses the trademark Certified Financial Planner® from the Financial Planning Standards Board. The CFP® designation is the most widely recognized personal finance designation in the world, and is licensed in many countries.

The FPSC sets the path to certification as a CFP in Canada:

- Complete all the FPSC-approved core curriculum courses in a qualifying educational institution.

- Pass the FPSC's Financial Planning Exam 1 (FPE1) after completing a core curriculum. FPE1 is a four-hour multiple choice exam.

- Complete at least one year of practical experience as a financial planner (may be done before or after passing FPE1).

- Complete an FPSC-approved capstone course in a qualifying educational institution. The course syllabus must include one of the comprehensive cases created by the FPSC.

- Pass the FPSC's Financial Planning Exam 2 (FPE2) after the capstone and at least one year of experience. FPE2 is a problem-based exam using small cases with constructed response templates that the candidate fills in with the answers.

- Complete a total of three years of practical experience as a financial planner.

There is more detailed information at <www.fpsc.ca/earn-certification>.

A number of universities and community colleges offer FPSC-accredited core curriculum programs and some of them offer the capstone course also. The authors' own school, the School of Administrative Studies at York University, offers an FPSC-accredited core curriculum and capstone course as part of its Bachelor

---

[3] Financial planners fall under provincial jurisdiction, and so the rules vary. Quebec is the only one to require anyone calling himself or herself a financial planner to meet certain standards of knowledge and performance.

of Administrative Studies (Honours) degree in Finance. The complete list of accredited education providers can be found at <www.fpsc.ca/core-curriculum>.

CFP licensees must undertake continuing professional education each year. The Council has developed a Code of Ethics for financial planners that includes both principles and specific rules to make the principles operational.[4] The regulatory situation does not give the Council any formal power, but with the voluntary support of so many of the players, it may well bring about a more organized and stable playing field in financial planning, which will benefit consumers.

Many other professionals have also entered this field to some extent. The most notable ones are professional accountants. Although the course of study and codes of ethics of the CA, CGA and CMA associations are not intended to deal with personal finance, the substantial expertise these professionals acquire in income tax and budgeting, and in analysis of financial problems generally, has allowed them to enter the field. Some of them practise solely in the personal finance field, and others make it an important part of their work. These are usually sole practitioners. Some of the large firms have established separate groups that deal with personal financial planning. Accountants are most qualified to deal with difficult tax issues. Although they are quite capable of becoming expert in other areas, the formal course of study does not lead them into areas like insurance and investment theory in any depth. Professional accountants charge fees at the upper end of the scale. One of the benefits of dealing with them is that their rigorous courses of study and high qualification standards provide some assurance of good-quality work. Their long-established existence within the framework of self-regulating associations with well-developed codes of ethics reduces the probability of negligence and professional misconduct.

Lawyers are frequently involved in the execution of specific parts of financial plans, like estate planning and income taxation. Few lawyers have the financial training to suit them to giving broad-based financial counselling. Other finance professionals that provide financial planning services include insurance agents, investment dealers, mutual fund salespersons, credit union advisors and trust officers.

COMPUTER SOFTWARE

There are many computer software packages in personal finance, including PlanPlus and FP Solutions (CCH-Advocis); Quicken and Mint.com provide software more oriented to cash flow analysis and forecasting. Most personal finance software programs run on Windows and are user-friendly. They can handle many of the elements of personal finance that we discuss in this book. For example, you can

---

[4] See <www.fpsc.ca/sites/fpsc.ca/files/documents/FPSC_Standards_of_Professional_Responsibility_0.pdf>.

use them to solve problems in the time value of money, mortgages, personal financial statements, cash budgets, tax return preparation, investment record-keeping, and retirement planning. The diskette icon beside a paragraph in the text or a problem at the end of a chapter indicates that *PlanPlus for Students* can be used to solve the problem; other mainstream professional planning software will also probably handle it. Appendix 2.1 demonstrates the PlanPlus solutions to some problems similar to the examples in the textbook in Chapter 2.

They can be very useful tools in the hands of a user who understands the principles of personal finance. However, they are nothing more than tools and cannot replace a sound understanding of the theory and concepts of personal finance. As the saying goes, "garbage in, garbage out." Inappropriate or uninformed use of these packages can generate only useless or even misleading financial plans. You must learn personal finance, and how computers can help, before you use them.

SUMMARY

The objective of this book is to teach you how to plan your own or other families' personal finances using sound principles of finance. Personal financial planning is a series of decisions on how to accumulate and protect the money you need to meet specified future goals. The topics you must learn to do this planning include time value of money, budgeting, goal-setting, risk management, income taxation, insurance, debt management, investment principles and practice, and retirement planning. We also suggest sources for updating your knowledge, and how you can get further help from experts if this book is not enough for your needs.

DISCUSSION QUESTIONS

1. Explain the significance of the following entries:

   financial planning process / how to choose an advisor / keeping up-to-date / know what you need / professional planners — different types

2. What are the objectives of studying personal financial management? Why study principles when all you really need to know is how to do it?

3. Name and describe briefly the elements of a financial plan. You should refer to the section on the contents of the book.

4. How would you go about selecting a personal financial advisor? The chapter offers some advice, but you should be able to say more.

5. Financial planners are largely unregulated. If they were to be regulated, it would be a provincial matter. Find out what regulations, if any, govern

financial planners in your province. The best starting point in your search is probably the government ministry handling consumer affairs.

6. Should financial planners be
   (a) unregulated;
   (b) regulated by a government department, using statutory regulations; or
   (c) required to form a self-regulating association whose power derives from a law, but which decides by vote of its members what ethical conduct and standards of performance must be followed?

7. Will this book (or any popular book on personal finance or personal investments) provide you with the clue to become rich and secure?

CHAPTER 2

Time Value of Money

▶ You want to buy a new TV set, but you haven't the money right now. The salesperson offers you a deal to pay for it over 24 months. Your bank would also give you a consumer loan to buy it. Decide which financing method to choose. See Example 2.8.

▶ Loan-shark rates aren't all that high, are they? Meet Grinder McSnarl and find out how to calculate his rates in Example 2.2.

LEARNING OBJECTIVES

> ➢ *To master completely the mechanics of the time value of money.*
> ➢ *To understand the concept of rate of return over one and many periods, and the different factors affecting the rate of return.*

This chapter teaches the most important single technique in personal financial planning — how to compare monetary amounts that you pay or receive at different times. This technique is called the **time value of money** or **interest rate mathematics**. It is the arithmetic of personal financial management, and you must become as comfortable with it as you are with basic arithmetic.

Underlying the time value of money is the concept of a rate of return. We use the rate of return to compare different investments and loans, and so we need to understand the assumptions underlying the calculations. The advertisements you see in newspapers and flyers claiming high rates of return or low interest rate charges are often misleading if you don't realize the different ways in which they can be calculated. Understanding rate of return is an essential preparation for debt and credit management and investment management.

Once you have mastered the mechanics of time value, we continue the topic of rates of return with holding period returns and multiple period rates of return. We discuss the problem of the reinvestment assumption that is inherent in any multiperiod rate of return. We then extend our discussion to the sources of differences in rates of return: *risk*, *inflation*, and *income taxes*.

In later chapters we show you how to apply the techniques in many different problems, including bond valuation, residential mortgages, and consumer loans. The traditional method uses tables of values, but we operate using a financial calculator. Such calculators are now cheaply available and everyone who wants to solve personal finance problems should own one. Separate sections will show step-by-step solutions to some problems using one specific calculator: the Texas Instruments BA Π Plus.

In the appendix to this chapter, we include step-by-step solutions to the same problems, but using PlanPlus for Students instead. You will need to learn how to use PlanPlus for Students before you attempt to replicate the answers you got with a calculator. Henceforth, we will refer to this software as PlanPlus for convenience, but you should remember that the abridged student version does not include all of the regular package's capabilities.

RATE OF RETURN — SINGLE PERIOD

Suppose you can invest in a discount bond for $909.09 today. In one year's time you will receive $1,000. A **discount bond** is an investment that pays no interest during its life; therefore, the interest you receive on it is part of the final payment. What rate of return do you earn on this bond?

First, we note that the amount you earn is $1,000 - $909.09 = $90.91. You invest $909.09 to get $90.91, so your rate of return is $90.91 ÷ $909.09 = .1000 or 10.00%. In general, if we call the rate of return k, and the cash flows at the beginning and end of the year CF_0 and CF_1, then:

$$k = \frac{CF_1 - CF_0}{CF_0}$$

$$\text{e.g., } k = \frac{\$1,000 - \$909.09}{\$909.09} = .1$$

The equation only holds for a single period with cash flows at the beginning and end of the period.

What Is a Discount Rate?

Suppose we state the previous problem a little differently. You want to invest money in a bond for one year, and you want to earn a 10% rate of return on your investment. If you have $909.09 to invest today, how much do you expect to receive at the end of one year? We already know the answer will be $1,000. That is, you earn 10% on the money you invest, and you also get the amount invested back:

$$1.1 \times \$909.09 = \$1,000 \text{ (after rounding)}$$

Finally, let's state the previous problem this way: You have some money to invest today for one year, and interest rates for one year are 10%. How much do you have to invest if you want to have $1,000 in one year? We know that the answer is $909.09. We would arrive at this by the same equation rearranged:

$$\$1,000 ÷ 1.1 = \$909.09$$

All this is very simple arithmetic, but it has several important meanings. We call the 10% interest rate the **discount rate**, which is the interest rate or rate of return that we use to equate amounts of money paid or received in different periods. We often say that the $909.09 is the value of $1,000 *discounted* at 10% for one year. The discount rate is a rate of return. The time value of money is the arithmetic with which we convert money between periods, or calculate what rate of return is implied by a given set of cash flows. Why do we care what the value of money is in different time periods?

Opportunity Cost

What do you want to do with your money today? What would you do with it tomorrow? If you spend the $909.09 on clothes today, you have the clothes and can start wearing them now. What do you give up by spending the money now? The answer is that you give up $1,000 in one year's time. The $1,000 you give up is the **opportunity cost** of your decision. We also say that the opportunity cost of money is 10%, because that is what you can earn if you don't spend the money today. Only you can decide whether you want to spend $909.09 today or have $1,000 to spend in one year. The discount rate simply tells you in monetary value the amount that you are giving up — the opportunity foregone — in order to consume now.

Another way to look at it is to call the discount rate the rate that makes us indifferent between present and future amounts (in any pattern). That is, if we use the appropriate discount rate to calculate the present value of a future amount, we don't care whether we receive the present value now or the future value at the later date.

Who decides this discount rate? How do we know what discount rate to use?

Best Alternative Available

When we decide where to invest our money, we naturally want to get as high a return as possible. In order to compare alternative investments, we must keep everything else equal. That means risk, income taxes, and the time length of the investment must be identical. We will discuss the implications of these issues later in the chapter and in other chapters, since they are very important. For now, let us accept that we are choosing between otherwise identical investments.

Suppose we observe a bank, a trust company, and a credit union, each offering us the chance to invest our money in a guaranteed investment certificate (GIC) for one year. Each one pays $1,000. To get the $1,000, we must invest $909.09 at the bank, $907 at the trust company, and $905 at the credit union. We shouldn't need to think very hard to realize that the credit union is offering the best rate, since we invest the lowest amount to realize $1,000. We can convert these offers to rates of return as we did previously. The bank is offering 10%; the trust company, 10.25%; and the credit union, 10.5%. Thus, the rate of return, or discount rate, gives us a convenient way to compare the three choices, even if the amounts to invest happen to be different.

The best alternative available provides the discount rate, then. In the previous example, the discount rate is 10.5%, because that is the highest rate we can get. We would discount all other similar investment opportunities at that rate to see if they are as good.

The best rate isn't so easily determined in practice because of different risks involved in different investments. Nonetheless, we can try to use it as a benchmark. Think of the previous example again. Suppose you also owed $900 on your credit card. If you put the money into a GIC you would have to pay interest on the credit card balance at 19.56% p.a. Clearly, the discount rate for any financial decision up to $900 should be 19.56%, since you can save that amount by paying off the credit card balance, and it is higher than the interest you can earn. Once you have paid off the balance, and any other debts, then you could use the credit union's 10.5% as the best alternative rate.

Let us now turn to the mechanics of time value of money problems.

RATE OF RETURN — MULTIPERIOD

Why Annual Rates?

When we refer to rate of return in this book, or when people refer to it in finance generally, annual rate is almost always implied. Sometimes, interest is charged or accrued for different time periods, e.g., monthly interest on a credit card debt. Since so many natural and social processes are measured at yearly intervals, finance has adopted the convention of converting discount rates/rates of return to annual rates. This conversion appears to be a simple mechanical exercise, but there are several critical issues that arise. If we are to understand the various rates quoted in the finance world, we need to look at these issues carefully.

Arithmetic and Geometric Rates of Return

Suppose we invest $100 for two years. At the end of two years, we receive $120. What rate of return did we earn?

We could start by calculating the dollar return as $20. We earned it over two years, so we divide by two to get $10 per year, which is 10% of $100.

Alternatively, we could apply the time value rules we learned in the previous section and ask: What annual discount rate compounds $100 to $120 in two years? The answer, from a calculator, is 9.5445%.

Which answer is right? This isn't an academic question, because different investment opportunities may be quoted using one or the other. Mutual funds, for example, often quote their past rates of return using the first method.

The second answer, 9.5445%, is correct, because it allows for compounding. Think of the two-year investment as two one-year investments. If the annual rate of return is 10%, then at the end of one year you have $110. After another year at 10%, you should have ($110 × 1.1) or $121. Now do the same thing with the 9.5445% rate. After one year you have $109.54. After the second year you have ($109.54 × 1.095445) or $120.

This difference still holds when we know the individual rate of return for each year, though it isn't so obvious. Suppose we want to know the average annual rate of return we earned over four years, with the following observed rates in each year:

Year	Return (%)
1990	17
1991	8
1992	2
1993	15

We could sum them and take the mean, which is 10.5%. This average is called the **arithmetic mean return**. In general, if k_t is the return in period t, the arithmetic mean is calculated as:

$$\text{Arithmetic mean return} = \sum_{t=1}^{n} \frac{k_t}{n}$$

$$= \frac{.17 + .08 + .02 + .15}{4}$$

$$= .105$$

The alternative method is to find the rate of return which would compound to the same final answer as the individual rates multiplied together. This average is called the **geometric mean return**, and it is calculated as:

$$\text{Geometric mean return} = \left[\prod_{t=1}^{n} (1 + k_t) \right]^{\frac{1}{n}} - 1$$

This equation tells us to multiply together all the factors $(1 + k_t)$ for the years and then take the nth root. For the example above, this is:

$$\sqrt[4]{(1.17 \times 1.08 \times 1.02 \times 1.15)} - 1 = 10.34\%$$

The geometric mean return is lower than or equal to the arithmetic mean return. The difference could be large. Consider a share that loses 50% of its value in one year and then doubles in the second year to return to its original price. The geometric mean return is 0, but the arithmetic mean is (–50% + 100%) ÷ 2 = 25% p.a. When the annual returns are exactly equal for every year in the sequence, the two means are equal.

We use the arithmetic mean return in analyzing investments when we want to estimate an average or expected return across different investments in the same period. For example, if we wanted to say what the average rate of return offered by bank savings deposit accounts is compared with the rate offered by trust company accounts, we would use an arithmetic mean.

Worked Example with a TI BA Π Plus Calculator

There are two methods to get the geometric mean. Each starts out with

$$1.17 \times 1.08 \times 1.02 \times 1.15 = 1.4822.$$

Then,

either	1.4822	**y^x**		.25	=	<u>1.10338</u>

or	1.4822	**FV**			
	−1	**PV**			
	4	**N**			
	CPT	**I/Y**		ans.	=	<u>10.338</u>

In future examples we will always use the first method with the **y^x** key to convert interest rates between frequencies of compounding, but both methods will always give the same answer.

COMPOUNDING MORE FREQUENTLY THAN ANNUALLY

Many loans are compounded more frequently than once a year, and this raises some interesting issues when we try to determine how to compare the discount rates. We convert the actual periodic rates to annual rates just as we do for rates over several years, and for the same reason. Virtually every form of consumer loan, including residential mortgages, is compounded more than once a year, and the loan rates that the institutions quote can be misleading if you don't know how they quote them.

Annual Percentage Rate

The **annual percentage rate (APR)** is a conventional method of quoting interest rates that ignores the compounding effect completely. The periodic rate is multiplied by the number of periods in a year. If m is the number of periods in one year and k_m is the rate of return or discount rate for one period, then:

$$APR = m \times k_m$$

This method is used for quoting rates for consumer loans, residential mortgages, corporate/commercial mortgages and other loans, and bond yields. Everyone is expected to understand the convention in the business world, although consumer protection legislation sometimes requires more explanation for non-business loans. Thus, the wording on a loan contract might read like this:

The interest rate shall be 12% (twelve per cent) per annum, compounded and payable monthly...

What this wording means is that the monthly interest rate is 1%, and it is compounded every month. You are also required to make monthly payments, rather than allowing the loan balance and interest to accumulate as is usually done when a financial institution is borrowing from you.[1]

It is certainly wrong to call this interest rate 12%, since we know that the 1% interest paid at the end of the first month could have earned interest for you for another 11 months if you hadn't had to pay it to the lender. Therefore, you have a greater cost (including the opportunity cost of paying interest early) if you pay 1% per month than if you pay 12% at the end of 12 months. In the next section we introduce the effective annual rate, which is a more reasonable procedure.

Effective Annual Rate

The conventional solution is to compound the periodic rate the number of times there are periods in the year, to arrive at the **effective annual rate (EAR)**. Using the same notation as for the APR:

$$EAR = (1 + k_m)^m - 1$$

For example, an interest rate of 1% per month has an EAR of $(1.01)^{12} - 1 = .1268$ or 12.68%. In personal finance we use the EAR as a way of converting periodic rates to a common annual basis. Some types of consumer lending require disclosure of the EAR now, but not all of them. If you are the investor, then it is your problem to calculate rates of return. Bond yields are quoted as APRs, for example, though this fact is not evident in any table of yields. We will show examples in other applications in the chapter, but first we have some specific problems for you to solve.

Worked Examples with a TI BA Π Plus Calculator

Example 2.1: You are the manager of credit card statements for the Tottery Bank Visa Card operation. Declining interest rates have led the bank to lower its monthly interest rate on unpaid balances to 1.25%. What is the APR? What is the EAR? Which rate must you disclose to cardholders?

---

[1] That is, when you deposit money in a long-term deposit at the bank, the bank is now the borrower. Most such deposits do not pay the interest periodically, but rather compound it over the life of the certificate. When the certificate matures, the bank pays you the principal and all the interest, including compounded interest on interest, for the entire term of the loan.

Answer:[2]   APR: $1.25 \times 12 = \underline{15.00\%}$
EAR: (1.0125) **y**^{x} $12 = \underline{1.1608} - 1 = \underline{16.08\%}$[3]
You must disclose the EAR to cardholders.

Example 2.2:   "Yeah, 1% a day is purty high interest, sweetheart, but I guess ya gotta have that fix of Gelato Fresca Devil's Chocolate ice cream purty quick or yer gonna get the shakes — an' I don' mean McDonald's shakes, heh, heh. So let me make it real clear. I lend you four bucks, at 1% per day, and ya pay me back $4.28 in one week. Else, I start countin' the vigorish [*ed. comment:* vigorish is interest] on the $4.28 at the same rate, except fer I give ya a day off at Christmas, heh, heh."

Grinder McSnarl operates an unofficial financial institution out of his long, black limousine. His "chauffeur" sits in the front cleaning his teeth with a switchblade. Grinder has just explained his lending terms to nine-year-old Jennie Sweettooth.
(a)   What is Grinder's compounding frequency?
(b)   What is the EAR of Grinder's loan?
(c)   If Jennie falls into his clutches and borrows $4.00 without paying it off for a whole year, how much will she then owe him?

Answer: (a)   There is a trick here. Grinder is not compounding daily, since he says she'll owe $4.28 in one week. $0.28/$4.00 is 7%, or $7 \times 1\%$, so his compounding frequency is weekly.

(b)   Since he generously charges no interest on Christmas, there are exactly 52 weeks in a standard year. Thus, EAR = 1.07 **y**^{x} $52 = \underline{33.725} - 1 = \underline{3,272.5\%}$ p.a.

(c)   Either:

–4	**PV**
52	**N**
7	**I/Y**
CPT	**FV** ans. = $\underline{\$134.90}$

or, more simply, $4 \times 33.725 = \underline{\$134.90}$.

---

[2] You can also do these operations on TI BA II Plus using the "Interest Conversion Worksheet", but we think that our method is easier, and shows more clearly the logic of the operation.

[3] Note that when you use the time value of money keys on this and most financial calculators, the answer is in % already. When you use the **y**^{x} key, the answer is in the form of 1 + a decimal. You must deduct 1 and move the decimal point two places to the right to convert to a %.

Reinvestment Rate Assumption

In the previous section we said that we would use the EAR to compare different rates. EAR, too, is just a conventionally accepted method, and it has an assumption that is not necessarily true. The assumption concerns at what rate the periodic payments are reinvested.

The APR assumes that the periodic payments are not reinvested at all. That is, the lender hides the money under his mattress until the end of the year, then adds it up and calculates the return. Clearly, this is an unreasonable assumption. Our financial system quotes rates at the APR simply as a convention, or convenience, with the implicit understanding that the opportunity cost is something greater.

The EAR assumes that the periodic payments are reinvested at the same rate as the original loan. This assumption is more reasonable, because the lending institution will have many loans of different amounts and maturities outstanding. It will lend out the repayments as part of other loans at similar rates. However, if interest rates change, then the lender will receive a rate on the reinvested payments that differs from the rate on the original loan. Then, the EAR will give the wrong rate in economic terms, although not by much.

The same analysis holds from the borrower's viewpoint. If you could hold on to those interim payments, what would be the best alternative use of them from your point of view? If it is different from the loan rate, then the effective cost to you is different from the EAR.[4]

As a practical matter, we won't worry about this problem and will continue to use the EAR as the benchmark in this book. Interest rates do not change by large amounts nor do they change very quickly in Canada, so any imprecision is small. Furthermore, when we look at a lending or investment decision before we make it, the current interest rate is our best estimate of the average anyway. Therefore, the EAR we calculate at the start of a loan or investment is a valid measure of our best estimate of what it will cost us (or earn for us).

MECHANICS OF TIME VALUE

Future and Present Value — Single Period

You deposit $100 in a caisse populaire for one year at an annual rate of interest of 4%. How much money do you have at the end of the year?

---

[4] The student will recognize that this is similar to the problem of using the internal rate of return (IRR) in corporate finance to make capital budgeting decisions. The IRR assumes that any interim cash flows to the investor can be reinvested at the IRR. If this IRR represents a positive net present value, that is, it is lower than the appropriate cost of capital for the company, then using IRR to make decisions assumes that there are an infinite number of such positive net present value projects available in which the company can reinvest its earnings. Such an assumption is clearly unwarranted.

You get back the $100, which is also called the **principal**, plus 4% of $100, or $4 in **interest**. Your total balance is thus $104. We call this amount the **future value (FV)** of $100 at 4% for one year.

We reverse the problem and ask how much the future value of $104 is worth today at a discount rate of 4%. We call the answer of $100 the **present value (PV)** of $104 at 4% for one year. That is, $104 ÷ 1.04 = $100.

We can express these two concepts in two equations, where k is the discount rate:

Future Value: $$FV = PV (1 + k)$$

Present Value: $$PV = \frac{FV}{(1 + k)}$$

e.g., $$FV = \$100 (1 + .04) = \$104$$

$$PV = \frac{\$104}{(1 + .04)} = \$100$$

In fact, there is only one equation, rearranged for whatever we want to solve. We can also solve for the discount rate if we know the PV and the FV. Note an important mathematical fact here. Most interest rate mathematics deals with (1 + discount rate). When we invest money, the money we get back is both principal and interest. If we express discount rates as (1 + discount rate), we preserve this relationship.

Now we will look at present and future values for more than one period.

Future and Present Value — Multiperiod

Compound Interest

You deposit $100 in a bank account for five years at a rate of 5% p.a., compounded annually. What does it mean to compound? At the end of the first year you have $105 in the account. If you leave the entire amount in the account, you earn $5.25 in interest in the second year. You earn $5 on the original principal, and $0.25 on the first year's interest. Each year the interest earned increases because of interest on interest. We call this method of calculation **compound interest**.[5] Every year's ending balance is (1 + discount rate) times the previous year's balance. Thus, we can extend our previous equation to get the future value of an amount invested for any period of time we want. The actual length of the

---

[5] The alternative method is called simple interest. Interest is paid only on the original balance every period, with no interest paid on any interest left with the borrower. Modern financial contracts assume compound interest.

period is whatever we want it to be. Years and months are common periods in financial contracts, but any length of time could be specified as the compounding period.

Future Value

The equation for the future value of an amount, compounded each period for t periods is:

$$FV = PV(1 + k)^t$$

Returning to the problem at the start of the section, what will the balance in the account be at the end of five years?

$$FV = \$100 \times (1.05)^5 = \underline{\$127.63}$$

Compounding means that every period, in this case every year, we multiply the principal plus interest of the previous period (i.e., the ending balance) by (1 + discount rate) to get the next ending balance. This is the same as multiplying (1 + discount rate) together five times and then multiplying by the original principal, which is what the previous equation does. We can verify the answer by doing it the long way.

FV after	one period	$100.00	×	1.05	=	$105.00
	two periods	105.00	×	1.05	=	110.25
	three	110.25	×	1.05	=	115.76
	four	115.76	×	1.05	=	121.55
	five	121.55	×	1.05	=	127.63

Present Value

The present value of a multiperiod stream is calculated by rearranging the equation for future value, just as we did in the single period case.

$$PV = \frac{FV}{(1 + k)^t}$$

Example 2.3: Your great aunt Aida promises to give you $10,000 when you turn 21. You are 16 now and a five-year GIC pays 6% p.a. How much should Aida give you today to be worth as much as the future amount?

Answer: $$PV = \frac{\$10,000}{(1.06)^5} = \$7,472.58$$

26

These two equations for future and present value are perfectly general and with them we can equate any pattern of cash flows in present and future time to any other. The $(1 + k)^n$ part of the future value equation is called the **future value interest factor (FVIF)**. Table A2 in Appendix A shows the FVIFs for $1 for a range of interest rates and numbers of periods. The $1/(1 + k)^n$ part of the present value equation is called the **present value interest factor (PVIF)**. Table A1 shows the PVIFs for $1 for a range of interest rates and numbers of periods. You can use the tables to find the PV or FV of any single amount for any interest rate and number of periods listed by multiplying the amount by the factor.

We have one shortcut method that will help us reduce the work whenever we have a series of equal payments.

Annuities

An **annuity** is any payment that is the same amount for many consecutive periods. Many pensions are paid as annuities. The rent for an apartment is an annuity until the landlord raises it. Some simple mathematical manipulation allows us to get easy formulas for annuities, instead of having to calculate a string of present or future values and add them up. We won't show the details, but in essence you add up all the FVIFs or PVIFs to get annuity factors.

One critical assumption is when the payment is made: at the beginning or the end of the period. In most finance work in North America, payments are assumed to occur at the end of the period. This is an **ordinary** or **deferred annuity**. An **annuity due** is one for which the payments are made at the beginning of the period. The formulas that follow are for deferred annuities, but the factors can be converted easily to those for annuities due simply by multiplying by $(1 + k)$. Since each payment is received one period earlier, an annuity due accumulates one more period of interest.

The **future value interest factor for an annuity (FVIFA)**, also called the sum of an annuity, is:

$$FVIFA = \frac{(1 + k)^n - 1}{k}$$

Example 2.4: You send your nephew Hezekiah $100 every Christmas for 10 years. He deposits it in a bank account earning 6%. How much does he have after the 10th gift?

Answer:

$$FVA = \left[\frac{(1.06)^{10} - 1}{.06} \right] \times \$100 = \$1,318.08$$

The **present value interest factor for an annuity (PVIFA)** is:

$$PVIFA = \frac{1 - \dfrac{1}{(1 + k)^n}}{k}$$

Example 2.5: Hezekiah comes to you and asks for the next five Christmas presents in advance. Leaving aside the difficulty of explaining time value to a child, how much should you give him to produce the same value as the annuity?

Answer:

$$PVA = \left[\frac{1 - \dfrac{1}{(1.06)^5}}{.06} \right] \times \$100 = \$421.24.[6]$$

Tables of present value and future value annuity factors are shown in Appendices A3 and A4.

Using a Financial Calculator

People have used the tables in Appendix A for time value calculations for many years, but the development of cheap financial calculators that do the same thing has rendered the tables obsolete. The calculators do it faster, with less chance for you to make an error. More important, calculators can handle any fractional interest rate and any fractional period, which the tables cannot do. The tables are also limited by practical space considerations and do not list every possible number of periods.

For the rest of this book we will assume that you are using a basic financial calculator. It will have buttons on it to enter the number of periods, the interest rate, the payment amount (for annuities), and the present and future values. It will have buttons that will compute annuities deferred and annuities due, whichever you need.

The best source of instruction is the manufacturer's instruction booklet. White provides excellent step-by-step guidance to financial problems on a variety of Sharp, Hewlett-Packard, and Texas Instrument financial calculators.[7] We cannot replace these sources, but we will show a few solutions with the steps for a Texas Instruments BA Π Plus calculator.

---

[6] He is expecting $500. If you are a parent faced with explaining time value, you might try saying that you don't have whatever amount is demanded right now, but if you put the present value into a bank account, it will grow to the desired amount.

[7] Mark A. White, *Financial Analysis with an Electronic Calculator*, 5th ed. (Boston: McGraw-Hill/Irwin, 2004).

Details to remember:

We show the operations keys you press in **boldface**, and the numbers entered in ordinary typeface, in our examples.

1. Calculators (including the BA Π Plus) usually treat percentages as numbers, not as fractions. .6% is .6 **I/Y**, NOT .006 **I/Y**. However, if you do something the long way, using $(1 + k)$ and the power key, y^x, then you express percentages as decimals, and .6% = .006.

2. Most calculators, including the BA Π Plus model we use, require either the PV or the FV to be entered as a negative number.

3. In this book we solve every problem with the frequency of compounding set to once per period. The BA Π Plus is set to a frequency of 12 times per period and you will need to reset it to follow our calculations exactly.

Worked Examples with a TI BA Π Plus Calculator

The diskette symbol will appear in the margin beside problems you can solve using PlanPlus. The appendix to this chapter contains the solutions to the following three problems, done using PlanPlus.

Example 2.6: If you deposit $5,000 in an RRSP account at a guaranteed rate of 7%, how much will you have when you retire 10 years from today?

Answer: Turn on the calculator: **ON/OFF**

Don't forget to clear the time value registers before new calculations each time: **2nd CLR TVM**.

You have a present value, a length of time it will be invested, and the interest rate. You need the future value.

−5,000	**PV**	
10	**N**	
7	**I/Y**	
CPT	**FV**	ans. <u>9,835.757</u>

Example 2.7: Your fairy godmother appears at the bedside when you are born. Into an account paying 5% interest per annum, she promises to deposit $2,000 p.a. on each birthday from your first to twenty-first, inclusive. What is the present value of her gift on the day you are born?

Answer: This is an annuity problem. Since it is paid at the end of each period, it is an ordinary or deferred annuity, and you will be using the **CPT** button. First to twenty-first inclusive, is 21 years.

21	**N**
5	**I/Y**
–2,000	**PMT**
CPT	**PV**

ans. <u>25,642.305</u>

Example 2.8:   You are just dying to buy that new television set, but you have no money. The salesperson notices you reading the price tag — $779, all taxes included — with a hopeless look. She tells you she can make you a deal. If you pay just $38 down and $38 each month thereafter for a total of only 24 payments, you can walk out of the store with the set right now. Your bank will lend you money at 1% per month. If you decide to go into debt to buy the set, should you borrow from the bank or take the store's offer?

Answer: Another annuity, this time an annuity due. The calculator will handle this one in one pass, too.

First, you must set it to calculate an annuity due.

2nd	**BGN**	END appears on display
2nd	**SET**	BGN appears on display
2nd	**QUIT**	BGN remains above the numbers to remind you that it is now calculating any annuity as an annuity due.

779	**PV**
24	**N**
–38	**PMT**
CPT	**I/Y**

ans. <u>1.4222%</u>

You should borrow from the bank, since the interest rate implicit in the store's offer is much higher. Another way to solve this problem is to calculate the size of the payments the bank would require to repay a loan of $779 at 1% over 24 months. These payments would be at month-end, because bank loans are deferred annuities.

24	**N**
–779	**PV**
1	**I/Y**
CPT	**PMT**

ans. <u>$36.67</u>

The payment of $36.67 is lower than the store requires, and it is deferred for one month as well.

■ A NOTE ON ROUNDING

Electronic calculators and computers produce lots of decimal places, but the implied precision is frequently invalid. If you are planning how much you need to save for your retirement in 20 years, rounding the answers to thousands is more reasonable. Even for short-term planning we suggest that rounding to the nearest dollar is the most precise you can be. On the other hand, we would round to the nearest $0.25 when pricing bonds or shares, since that is how they are priced in the market. Mortgage rates and bond yields may need to be calculated to several decimal places, because they have considerable effect on the value of annuities that pay out over many years.

There are no precise rules. Common sense and experience will tell you how much to round or how precise you need to be in personal financial planning.

Constant Growth Annuity

In contrast to an annuity where the periodic payments are the same there are many examples in finance where the payments are not equal. A **constant growth annuity (CGA)** is a stream of payments that grows at a constant rate. For example, suppose Dale currently earns $50,000 per year and he expects that his income will grow at a constant rate of 5% per year until he retires at age 65. Then his lifetime income stream is an example of a constant growth annuity. Although we are not going to show the mathematical derivation, there are formulae for the future value and the present value of a constant growth annuity (CGA).

Let x be the first payment or cash-flow of the CGA, payable at the end of the first year. Let g be the constant growth rate. It can be shown that the future value of the constant growth annuity (FVCGA) is:

$$\text{FVCGA} = x \left\{ \frac{\left[(1+k)^n - (1+g)^n \right]}{(k-g)} \right\}$$

If the first payment is paid at the beginning of the year, we have a constant growth annuity due (CGAD). The future value of a constant growth annuity due (FVCGAD) is simply:

$$\text{FVCGAD} = (1+k)(\text{FVCGA})$$

Example 2.9   Dale, 30, plans to invest 10% of his income every year until he retires at age 65. His current income is $50,000 and it is expected that this will increase at 5% per year.

If the rate of interest on investment is 10% per year, (a) How much money will he have at retirement? (b) If he makes the contributions at the beginning of every year, how much money will he then have?

Answer

(a) His initial investment, x, is equal to 10% of $50,000, or $5,000. Substituting into the above equation for:

$$x = \$5,000$$
$$n = 65 - 30 = 35$$
$$k = .10$$
$$g = .05$$

$$\text{FVCGA} = \$5,000\left\{\frac{\left[(1.10)^{35} - (1.05)^{35}\right]}{(.10 - .05)}\right\}$$

$$= \$2,258,642$$

(b) $\text{FVCGAD} = (1 + k)(\text{FVCGA})$
$$= (1.10)(\$2,258,642) = \$2,484,506$$

There are many applications where it is required to calculate the present value of a constant growth annuity. It can be shown that the present value of a constant growth annuity (PVCGA) is:

$$\text{PVCGA} = x\left\{\frac{1 - \left[\dfrac{1 + g}{1 + k}\right]^{n}}{(k - g)}\right\}$$

If the payments are made at the beginning of every year, the present value of a constant growth annuity due (PVCGAD) is:

$$\text{PVCGAD} = (1 + k)(\text{PVCGA})$$

Example 2.10 Mr. Figo, 65, has just retired. He estimates that his expenses will be $25,000 next year, and that the annual expenses will increase at the rate of 3% per year. He does not expect to live beyond the age of 90. The rate of interest is 6%. Ignoring taxes and inflation, (a) how much money does he need to support his post-retirement expenditures? (b) If the expenses are payable at the beginning of every year, how much money will he need then?

Answer   (a)   Substituting into the formula:

x = $25,000
n = 90 − 65 = 25
k = .06
g = .03

He will need PVCGA

$$= x\left\{\frac{1 - \left[\dfrac{(1.03)}{1.06}\right]^{25}}{(.06 - .03)}\right\} = \$426,794$$

(b)   PVCGAD = (1 + k)(PVCGA)
= (1.06)($426,794)
= $452,401

FACTORS AFFECTING DISCOUNT RATES

Reprinted with permission — The Toronto Star Syndicate. © 1994 GREG HOWARD distributed by King Features Syndicate.

We observe that there are many rates of return prevailing in the market at the same time. Some of them have specific names, others are the yields on different bonds or other investments. We have already said that we obtain our discount rates by looking at the best alternative use for the money. How do we choose which of these many possible discount rates is equivalent to the best available alternative? We can collect the factors that influence these rates into four categories: pure time premium, risk, income tax, and inflation.

Pure Time Premium

The **pure time premium** is the price that we demand for waiting before we consume. Since we let someone else use our money when we invest it, we need some compensation for deferring the pleasure of using it to buy something we can consume. This premium is the rate of return that would theoretically exist if there were no risk of any kind that the rate will change or not be paid, and if there were no inflation and no income taxes. Economists estimate that it is 2–4% per annum.

Risk

The many different discount rates may have different amounts of *risk*. The risk may take the form of a probability that we won't be paid a promised sum. It may be that we know an investment will produce variable returns, which we can't predict in advance. An investment may pay exactly what it promised in dollar terms, but every other competing investment may do better than expected. Investors will bid more for these other investments, and the market price of our investment will fall.

For example, a Canadian government bond carries very little risk of default. However, if we buy a bond paying 10% for $1,000, and all interest rates rise unexpectedly in the market the next day, the value of our bond will decline because we could have waited one day and invested at a higher rate. This **interest rate risk** is hard to avoid in debt investments at fixed rates.

We might decide to invest in the common shares of a small oil company that has very little production and reserves, but is drilling on some promising land. The common shares promise no dividends or maturity payment as bonds do. If the company finds a lot of oil, the share price will triple and we will make a lot of money. If the company finds no oil at all and runs out of money to do more drilling, our share price may drop to only pennies.

Naturally, these risks affect the discount rates we use to value the expected or possible future cash flows. We said earlier to pick the best alternative rate of return. In the case of risky investments, you would try to find the rate of return realized on other similar investments. For example, the oil company would have to offer a high rate of return (which implies a low share price), because of the high probability that you wouldn't get anything at all. Previous share prices on small oil companies would have been priced likewise to yield high returns in the event of success.

We discuss many different aspects of risk in Chapters 14–16. For now, all we wish to say is that different risk is the most important factor leading to different discount rates in the market at the same time. The other factors affect the general level of discount rates on all investments and loans.

Income Tax

We are going to state an important rule of discounting:

> *Use after-tax discount rates for after-tax cash flows. Use before-tax rates for before-tax cash flows.*

Income tax rules apply different rates to different sources of income and allow some expenses to be deducted from taxable income, but not others. The effects are often very large. We buy goods and services using after-tax dollars, but so far we have been doing time value calculations based on the before-tax rates. Insofar as market prices are concerned, this is all right — we discount the before-tax cash flows at the before-tax rates. When we make individual personal decisions, we have to consider individual tax situations. Mechanically, we must make two adjustments. We calculate the cash flows to be discounted in after-tax dollars. We discount these after-tax dollars using an after-tax discount rate. Think back to our rule that we use the best alternative rate available as the discount rate. If all we get is 60% of the dollars from an investment because of taxes, then the rate of return on the investment is only 60% of the pre-tax rate. Therefore, we use the lower after-tax discount rate when considering a choice which is expressed in after-tax dollars.

Let us consider the example of the GIC that costs $905 at the credit union and matures in one year at $1,000. We established earlier that the before-tax rate of return is 10.50%. Now suppose that a potential purchaser has a **marginal tax rate** of 40%. The marginal rate is the rate that applies to the next dollar of income. In this case we mean that the income from the GIC will be taxed at 40%. Since she only receives (100% – 40%) = 60% of the income, the after-tax rate of return *for this person only* is (.6 × 10.5%) = 6.3%.

Let us illustrate the rule by continuing the same example. The holder of the GIC collects ($1,000 – $905) = $95 in interest, but has only 60% of it, or $57, left after-tax. There is no tax on the principal amount of $905, since it is not income but a repayment of the money originally invested. The holder's total after-tax receipt is ($905 + $57) = $962. We already know that the original price is $905. If we discount $962 for one period at 6.3%, we get $904.99, which is the original price with a rounding error. Therefore, we must use the after-tax rate to get the answer that we already know is correct.

We go into more detail on Canada's tax system and the effect it has on personal finance in Chapters 7 and 8. There we will see how different sorts of investments and other incomes are taxed, and how to evaluate decisions concerning income tax planning.

Inflation

We are going to state another important rule of discounting:

> *Use nominal discount rates for nominal cash flows and real discount rates for real cash flows.*

Let us explain what this rule means:

Money is only a medium of exchange. We acquire money and manage it to use it to buy goods and services that we need or want.[8] **Inflation** is a general rise in the prices of all goods and services. If there is inflation present in an economy — and there has been inflation in the Canadian economy every year since 1939 — we want to measure our success in personal financial management by how much we are able to consume in physical terms, not by how many dollars we have.

For example, you want to buy a new car in three years' time. The model you like costs $15,000 today, including taxes. You don't want to borrow to buy it in three years, so you must save the entire price. You have $10,000 now, in short-term investments yielding 5% p.a. How much do you have to save each year to reach your goal of buying the car?

You might say that you would calculate how much the $10,000 will accumulate to in three years, then find the three-year annuity at 5% that will make up the difference. There is a practical problem here, because the car won't cost $15,000 in three years; it will cost more if there is any inflation.

Dollars are somewhat elastic measures of value — they don't stay constant. If we want to buy something in the future, we will buy it with dollars in the future, not dollars today. We still remember when a loaf of bread cost $0.25 and a quart (not a litre!) of milk cost $0.24. Does that mean that somehow life is impossibly expensive today? Not really. When those prices prevailed, our parents' total income was well under $10,000 p.a., which would put them in poverty today in Canada. The problem is that for financial planning we have to adjust the *purchasing power* of the dollars so that we are planning for a level of consumption rather than a fixed amount of money.

There are two ways to do this. One is to inflate every dollar measure for every year of the plan by the rate of inflation expected to occur. Then, the goal is measured in **current dollars** of the future year, and all the dollar amounts in the interim are measured in the current dollars when they occur. The calculations can be very messy, although with a personal computer and a spreadsheet program they are feasible.

The alternative is to measure everything in **constant dollars**. That is, we discount all future amounts back to today's dollars (or some other fixed time point) and express all our planning as if we were doing it in today's dollars. This method generally assumes that all amounts inflate at the same rate.

---

[8] We recognize that this is a simplifying assumption. Money also fulfills symbolic functions in our society beyond the consumption it permits, and it is a key mechanism in the attainment and perpetuation of power relationships. Nonetheless, we will stick to the traditional financial interpretation in this textbook.

The advantage of using current dollars is that we are getting the values that we expect will occur. Depending on how income taxes are levied, this may be more accurate, as long as our forecast is accurate.

The advantage of using constant dollars is that we can understand and relate to amounts expressed in today's dollars. As we update our plan in future years, we can adjust the amounts by the inflation rate so that they will then be in current dollars of each future period when we are in that period of time. Constant dollars are easier to work with, since they allow us to use annuities and we can avoid having large and messy spreadsheets.

Just as we calculated discount rates to allow for taxes, we must find the appropriate discount rates for inflated and uninflated amounts. We call the discount rate for inflated or current dollars the **nominal rate**, and the dollars that we are discounting are **nominal dollars**. They are expressed in the purchasing power of the period in which they occur, not any other.

We call the discount rate for uninflated or constant dollars the **real rate**, and the dollars that we are discounting **real dollars**. It may seem an odd contradiction in terminology, but real dollars don't exist. They are a fictional creation that allows us to keep money and what it buys constant. Thus, if we express a future amount in real dollars, what we are saying is that if we want to buy something in the future, it would cost us that real dollar amount if we were buying it today. If inflation is zero, then the real and nominal discount rates, and the real and nominal dollars, are equal.

There is a simple relationship between real and nominal dollars, and real and nominal discount rates. The nominal rate is simply the real rate compounded at the rate of inflation. This is exactly what inflation does to the cost of goods and services over time as well. Every year the general price level rises by the rate of inflation, and over time that rate compounds on today's prices. For example, we said that we remembered bread at $0.25. Today a comparable loaf might cost $2.19. Over a 48-year compounding horizon, that implies an inflation rate of 4.6%. If we had been planning in 1957 how we would afford to buy bread in 2010, we would have had to save enough to buy it at $0.25, compounded at a real rate, or enough to buy it at $2.19, compounded at a nominal rate. Thus, we have an inflation premium in the nominal discount rate, and it will be higher than the real rate. Letting k_{nom} be the nominal rate, k_r be the real rate, and i be the rate of inflation, the relationship can be expressed as:

$$1 + k_{nom} = (1 + k_r)(1 + i)$$

For example, suppose the inflation rate is 2% and the real rate of interest is 3%. Then:

$$k_{nom} = (1 + .03)(1 + .02) - 1$$
$$= .0506 \text{ or } 5.06\%$$

This equation is called the Fisher equation, after the economist who developed it.[9] Let's return to our problem of saving to buy a car to see how all this fits together.

Let us assume that inflation is 2% p.a. In three years the car will cost $15,918 ($15,000 \times 1.02^3$). In three years the $10,000 grows to $11,576. The shortfall you must save to make up is $4,342. At 5%, the annual savings required to accumulate this amount is $1,377. Let us analyze what we have done. We have converted the cost of the car from today's dollars into dollars of three years hence when we want to buy it. Then we compounded our current savings into the amount we would have in three years' time. Finally, we calculated the amount we would have to save annually, expressed in future dollars. If all the rates stay constant and we save exactly $1,377 per annum, we will have enough to buy the car in three years.

The one problem with the nominal approach in this example is that we expressed the savings amount in year 3 dollars, but we will be saving it in years 1, 2, and 3. It will be harder to save it in year 1, because our income will be somewhat less in dollar terms, and relatively easier to save in year 3.

If we do the same problem in real dollars, we get a different savings number, and a different interpretation. First, we need to calculate the real rate of return, given that we know the nominal rate. We rearrange the Fisher equation to get:

$$
\begin{aligned}
k_r &= \frac{1 + k_{nom}}{1 + i} - 1 \\
&= \frac{1 + .05}{1 + .02} - 1 \\
&= .0294 \text{ or } 2.94\%
\end{aligned}
$$

Now we don't have to express the cost of the car in any new dollars, because we are working in constant dollars. The present savings of $10,000 will compound at the real rate of 2.94% to yield $10,908 in constant dollars. The constant dollar amount you need to save is thus $4,092. The PV of the savings annuity, in constant dollars at 2.94%, is $1,325. If you are trying to reach the goal of buying the car, you could now ask yourself: Did I save $1,325 last year? Could I have saved that much if I wanted the car badly enough?

We don't save in real dollars, though; we save in nominal dollars each year. The solution in nominal dollars, however, is also a constant number since it is an annuity. It would work, but a more feasible plan is to save an increasing number of

---

[9] This relationship assumes that we know future cash flows for certain, but it is a reasonable approximation for the level of accuracy that we can hope for in personal financial planning.

dollars every year to reach the final total of $4,342. We can calculate what the value in nominal dollars is each year by inflating the real dollar figure each year as we check our plan. Look at the following timeline to see what will happen:

	Real $				Compounds to
	Save	1,325	1,325	1,325	4,092
Time	0	1	2	3	
		1,352	1,379	1,406	4,345
	Nominal $				Compounds to

The lower half of the timeline is the value of $1,325 compounded by the inflation rate of 2%. This is the amount you would have to save in each year's dollars. The first year's saving is compounded for one year because it occurs at the end of the year (using annuity deferred). If we now compound each of these savings amounts by the nominal rate of 5%, the sum is $4,345, which is the same as we got previously (with a rounding error) when we did everything in nominal terms. Thus we can see that the two approaches are equivalent.

In this simple example it wouldn't matter much which one you used, since the numbers aren't much different. If you were planning to retire in 20 years, and expected to live for many years after retirement, inflation would make a big difference. The most important lesson from this section is that you must allow for the effect of inflation. Whether you do it by keeping everything in real dollars and updating as you go or whether you do it by creating a messy spreadsheet in nominal dollars for each of the years in the future is not so important. We will tend to do a lot of our planning in real dollars in this book because it is easier to present that way.

SUMMARY

This chapter teaches you how to compare monetary amounts received at different times — the fundamental arithmetic of personal finance. The basic relationship between the present value (PV) and future value (FV) of cash flows received at time t in the future, at a discount rate of k, is

$$FV = PV(1 + k)^t$$

If we have a series of equal payments at equally spaced intervals, we can calculate the PV and FV using annuity formulas.

A discount rate is the opportunity cost of spending your money now instead of investing it in the best available investment. You determine how much a future series of cash flows is worth to you today by discounting them at the rate that is the best alternative. Expressed differently, the discount rate is the rate of return that you expect to earn on an investment.

Comparing discount rates that are charged for different periods requires a convention. We express all discount rates as annual rates, using the effective annual rate method if the rate is applied for some period other than a year.

Discount rates are affected by the pure time premium, risk, income tax, and inflation. The pure time premium is the price we demand for delaying consumption by investing money instead of spending it. Risk means the possibility of not getting what we expected. The riskier the returns on an investment, the higher the average or expected rate must be to persuade us to invest.

Income tax reduces the return that we actually receive. Furthermore, the form of the investment return — interest, dividends, capital gains, rental income — is taxed in different ways. We discount after-tax returns using discount rates adjusted for income taxes to make them comparable with one another.

Inflation reduces the consumption value of future dollars, and therefore we use inflation-adjusted discount rates to discount inflated future dollars. We can also adjust the future dollars to be in real or constant dollars and use real discount rates.

MULTIPLE-CHOICE REVIEW QUESTIONS

1. Which of the following cannot be used as a discount rate?

   (a) The nominal rate of interest
   (b) The real rate of interest
   (c) The after-tax nominal rate of interest
   (d) The after-tax real rate of interest
   (e) All of the above can be used as a discount rate, depending on the situation

2. Mr. Lazrak wants to invest $1,000 for one year. Which of the following bank accounts offers the best deal?

   (a) 7.00% interest with annual compounding
   (b) 6.85% interest with semi-annual compounding
   (c) 6.75% interest with quarterly compounding
   (d) 6.55% interest with monthly compounding
   (e) 6.45% interest with daily compounding

3. Janet Jopper owes her friend some money. She is given the following alternatives of payment. If the current rate of interest, 6%, is used as the discount rate, which of the following alternatives of payment is the best for her?

(a) Pay $9,750 now

(b) $2,000 per year for 5 years, each payable at the end of the year

(c) $1,950 per year for 5 years, each payable at the beginning of the year

(d) $1,800 per year for 6 years, each payable at the end of the year

(e) $2,000 at the end of year 1, $5,000 at the end of year 2, $3,000 at the end of year 3, and $1,200 at the end of year 4

4. If the rate of interest (the discount rate) increases, which of the following statements is false?

(a) The future value of an investment will increase.

(b) The present value of an annuity will decrease.

(c) The present value of an annuity due will increase.

(d) The present value of an uneven stream of cash flow will decrease.

(e) All the above statements are false.

5. If the nominal rate of interest is positive, theoretically which of the following cannot be negative?

(a) The before-tax real rate of interest

(b) The after-tax real rate of interest

(c) The rate of return on a stock

(d) The after-tax nominal rate of interest

(e) All of the above can theoretically be negative.

PROBLEMS

1. Jane has $10,000 to invest. She has three options at the local bank: (i) an investment account that pays 5% p.a., compounded monthly; (ii) a guaranteed investment certificate (GIC) that pays 5.25% p.a., compounded quarterly; and (iii) a term deposit that pays 5.35% p.a., compounded semi-annually. Which account is better for Jane? How much money will she have after five years?

2. The historical rates of return on the Jurkowski mutual fund for the last five years are 11%, 12%, 25%, –13%, and 7%. The rate of inflation was 3% per year.

(a) What is the geometric mean nominal rate of return?

(b) What is the geometric mean real rate of return?

(c) What is the arithmetic mean real rate of return?

3. You have won an "income-for-life" lottery ticket. It will pay you $20,000 per year for as long as you live. Alternatively, the prize will pay a lump sum of $500,000 now. You have average health and expect to live at most 40 more

years. If you can invest your money at 4% p.a., which alternative will you choose?

4. You place $20,000 in a savings account paying annual interest of 6%, compounded quarterly, for three years and then move it into another savings account that promises to pay 9%, compounded monthly. What is your balance at the end of six years?

5. Randy buys a boat for $30,000, pays $5,000 down, and agrees to pay the balance over the next five years in equal monthly payments. If the rate of interest is 12% annually, what is the monthly payment?

6. If Niru were offered $1,079.50 10 years from now in return for an investment of $500 today, what annual rate of return would she earn?

7. The historical rates of return on the emerging market mutual fund for the last five years are 10%, 6%, 23%, –15%, and 11%. Vincent's marginal tax rate on investment is 30%. Since he traded frequently, he had to pay taxes on the mutual fund every year. The rate of inflation was 3% per year. Calculate the following:

   (a) The geometric mean after-tax rate of return
   (b) The geometric mean after-tax real rate of return

8. Jimmy Wallingford, 30, earns $40,000 (before tax) this coming year, and he plans to spend $25,000. He expects both his income and spending will increase at the rate of inflation, which is expected to be 2% per year. He plans to put his savings every year in a bank to earn 5% interest. Assuming that his average tax rate is 25% and his marginal tax rate is 30% every year, how much money will he have after 35 years?

9. Stephen Conally has agreed to buy a computer from the local electronic store. The price of the computer is $2,000, but the manager has agreed to accept Stephen's old computer for a trade-in value of $300. The balance is to be financed by the bank at a rate of 1% per month and repayable in 30 equal monthly payments. Calculate the following:

   (a) The monthly payment if payable at the end of each month
   (b) The monthly payment if payable at the beginning of each month
   (c) The effective annual rate (EAR) that the bank is charging for this loan

10. Theresa Pau has just inherited $15,000. She plans to invest the money for the next 10 years. The bank manager advises her two options of investing the money with the bank:

(i) Invest the money in a four-year GIC earning 5% with semi-annual compounding and then at maturity roll the money to a six-year GIC earning 6% with monthly compounding,

(ii) Invest the money in an escalating-interest account, which increases the interest rate by 0.5% every year. The interest rate for the first year is 3.5%, with annual compounding.

Which option is better for Theresa? Present your calculation.

11. You have just won a contest. The prize is a perpetuity that promises to pay $10,000 annually. If the interest rate is 8%, what is the value of your prize? Assume there is a provision in the contest agreement that allows for the payment to increase to compensate for inflationary pressures. If the inflation rate is expected to average 3% annually, what is the value of the prize?

12. The following parts of the question are not related.

(a) You have the opportunity to buy a term deposit for $1,000, which will pay no interest during its 10-year life and have a value of $3,106 at maturity. What rate of return does this term deposit pay?

(b) Son-Nan Chu wants to borrow $20,000 and agrees to repay this sum in equal quarterly payments over 10 years. If the cost of borrowing is 12%, what is the quarterly payment?

(c) In 10 years you are planning on retiring and buying a house in Florida. The house you are thinking about costs $100,000 and is expected to increase in value each year at a rate of 5%. Assuming you can earn 10% annually on your investments, how much must you invest at the end of each year in order to buy your house when you retire?

(d) After reviewing the various personal loan rates available to you, you find you can borrow from a finance company at 11.5%, compounded weekly, or from a bank at 12.5%, compounded monthly. Which option is most attractive?

13. You are comparing a perpetuity with annual payments of $5,000 with a 20-year annuity having the same payments. The market rate of interest for these instruments is 7%. How much more is the perpetuity worth?

14. You have $9,500 which you plan to invest for a term of five years. The following choices are available:

(i) You can buy a five-year GIC at the current interest rate of 10% p.a., interest payable annually.

(ii) You can buy a five-year Miron Company bond with face value of $10,000 that pays $375 interest semi-annually.

43

(iii) Your neighbour, Ronald, who owns a small manufacturing company, urges you to loan him the money. He says he will pay you an increasing stream of interest as follows:

Year 1	$ 200
Year 2	$ 400
Year 3	$ 800
Year 4	$1,600
Year 5	$2,500

At the end of the fifth year, you will get back your $9,500.

(a) Which investment will you choose?
(b) Are there any factors other than the rate of return that should affect your decision?

15. The following prices on two stocks were observed over the last five years.

Time	Stock A	Stock B
0	$11	$18
1	12	15
2	10	16
3	13	14
4	15	13
5	16	18

Stock A paid no dividend during the five years. Stock B paid a dividend of $1 per share per year in the first three years and $1.15 per share per year in the last two years. Calculate the following:

(a) The rate of return for each stock for each of the five years
(b) The arithmetic mean for both stocks
(c) The geometric mean for both stocks

16. A recent newspaper talks article about building your retirement nest egg. The author assumes that prices, annual savings, and retirement income will all rise by 3% per year and that savings will earn 6% in an RRSP. You can read the article but you can answer the following questions without reading that article.

(a) If you are 10 years from retirement, how much money in today's dollars (i.e., real dollars) do you need as your retirement nest egg if you need $10,000 (real dollars or today's dollars) per year for 15 years? For 20 years? For 25 years? (Hint: If you are discounting real dollars, use the real rate of interest.)
(b) How much money must you save per year in each of the above?

(c) David, aged 30, wants to retire early at age 55 and needs $1,000,000 at that time. How much must he save to reach his goal?

17. Jack and Jill Moore have just inherited a substantial amount of money and they want to put aside enough of it in a special investment account earmarked for their three children's university education. Their children, David, Joe, and Janet, are expected to start university in 4 years, 5 years, and 8 years, respectively. The Moores' plan to support each child for four years of university. Each child needs $12,000 per year in tuition fees, books, room and board, and other sundry expenses. Attending the local university and commuting from home will cut that to $5,000 per year. Assume payments are made at the start of each school year. If the expected rate of return on investment is 10% and the expected rate of inflation is 3%, how much must they set aside now,

   (a) if all three children go to out-of-town universities?
   (b) if David goes out of town and Joe and Janet attend the local university?
   (c) if all three children stay home and attend the local university?

18. You are celebrating your 35th birthday today and want to start saving for your retirement at age 60. You want to withdraw $10,000 from your retirement fund on each birthday for 20 years following your retirement. The first withdrawal will be on your 61st birthday. You plan to invest your money in mutual funds paying 11% per year. You want to make equal investments on each birthday into mutual funds for your retirement fund.

   (a) If you start making these investments on your 36th birthday and continue to do so until your 60th birthday, what amount must you invest annually in order to make the desired withdrawals at retirement?

   (b) Assume you have just won a lottery. Rather than making equal annual investments, you have decided to make one lump-sum payment on your 36th birthday to meet your retirement goal. What amount do you have to invest?

   (c) Suppose your employer will contribute $125 to the mutual fund account every year as part of the firm's profit-sharing plan. Additionally, you expect a $12,000 distribution from a family trust fund on your 50th birthday, which you will also put into the mutual fund account. What amount must you invest annually now to be able to make the desired withdrawals at retirement?

19. Professor Kelly Thomson has just finished helping her two children pay for their university education. Susan, 22, and Randy, 25, have jobs and have left home. Kelly would like to help them a bit more, perhaps with their first home or some other expense in a few years, but she needs to plan some

savings. She wants to be fair to each one, and she decides to give each one the same amount of money at age 30. She starts with $10,000 in savings now, which she allocates to an account for Randy, since he reaches age 30 first. She plans to give Randy $25,000. She earns 5% on the savings before tax, and her marginal tax rate is 40%. The inflation rate is 2%.

(a) How much will she need to save each year to have $25,000 to give to Randy?

(b) If she is to be fair to Susan, how much should she give Susan when she reaches 30?

(c) How much should she save per year, starting now, to reach the amount in (b) for Susan?

(d) Kelly's mortgage will be paid off in five years. Until then she can only put a total of $3,000 p.a. into the "kid fund". After that she can allocate as much as $20,000 p.a. How much will she have to save each year after the mortgage is repaid to reach her goal for Susan?

20. Xiaofei Li is only 30 years old, but he believes in planning ahead. His salary as a curator at the Financial Derivatives Museum is $70,000 p.a. He expects raises of 3% p.a. for the next five years. Then the director of the museum will retire and Xiaofei will get his job, with a pay raise of 30%. Thereafter he expects pay raises of 3% p.a. until he retires. He will save 5% of his salary for the first five years. He will save 7% of his salary for the next 15 years, until his house mortgage is paid off. Then he can save 20% of his salary each year. He saves in an RRSP and there is no tax on the 4% interest he earns on his savings. All savings are at the end of the year.

(a) How much will he have saved at age 55?

(b) If he retires at 60, he will need to have saved $800,000 for a comfortable retirement. How much more does he need to save each year from age 55, in addition to the 20% of his salary already given, to retire at 60, assuming the additional savings is an ordinary annuity, not a growth annuity?

21. Your daughter wants to go to college. She has three years of high school left, and then she would attend college for four years. She thinks she can save $2,000 in today's dollars from her summer jobs each year, both while she is in high school, and while she is in college. Tuition fees are presently $2,500 p.a.; and living costs (she will attend a college in another city), $9,000 p.a. These costs are inflating at 5% p.a. You can earn 6% after-tax on your savings. She pays no tax and can earn 10% on her savings. How much will you have to deposit today (time 0, earning 6%) to be able to make up her shortfall in

each of her four years of college? To simplify the question, assume that she receives all her earnings at the end of years one through six. She starts college at the end of year three and must pay all the fees and costs at that time, so she pays everything at the end of years three through six.

22. Mary Labatia graduated from York University's School of Administrative Studies with her B.A.S. degree in accounting six months ago. She lives with her parents, who charge her no rent or food costs. She has landed a good job as an accountant for a hotel chain and takes home $3,000 per month after taxes and other deductions. She expects her take-home pay will rise 3% per year for the next few years. She has to start paying off her student loan of $20,000. The interest rate is 4% p.a., compounded monthly, and the amortization period is five years. She wants to buy a car and will have to finance the entire $15,000 purchase price at 4% p.a., compounded monthly, with a term of three years. She pays $700 per month for the things her parents don't pay, like transportation, clothes, and entertainment. This cost will rise at 2% p.a. At the end of next year, she will travel to England for her brother's wedding at a total extra cost of $6,000 for clothes, travel, holiday, and gifts. At the end of three years, her vacation entitlement rises to three weeks and she plans a European cruise costing $10,000. She will invest savings at a rate of 3% EAR, taxable at a marginal rate of 30%.

(a) What discount rate should Mary use for her savings if she makes the monthly payments on her two loans exactly as scheduled?

(b) How much will Mary have saved at the end of three years?

(c) What is Mary's correct discount rate? That is, what is the opportunity cost of her money?

(d) What does the answer to part (c) tell you that she should be doing with her financial management to be most efficient with her money, while not sacrificing any consumption?

APPENDIX 2.1: SAMPLE PROBLEMS SOLVED WITH A SOFTWARE†

Problem: If you deposit $5,000 in an RRSP account at a guaranteed annual rate of 7%, how much will you have when you retire 10 years from today?

Answer: Log into PlanPlus for Students and select the "Present & Future Values Calculator" from the drop-down menu list of calculators.

Type	Single Deposit
Frequency	Annual
Number of Payments	10
Interest Per Year	7%
Present Value	5000

Press the Calculate button beside the Future Value field to calculate the future value. The future value is $9,835.76.

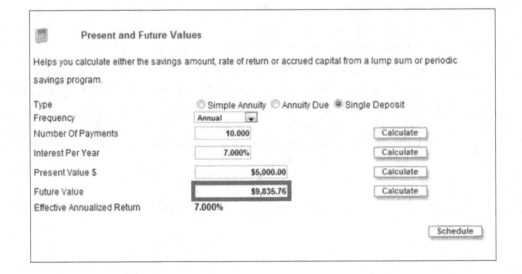

† The software we use here is *PlanPlus for Students*, a free online financial planning software offered by PlanPlus Inc. To obtain access, visit PlanPlus website: <www.planplus.com>,

Problem: Your fairy godmother appears at the bedside when you are born, and promises to deposit in an account paying 5% interest per annum $2,000 p.a., on each birthday from your first to twenty-first, inclusive. What is the present value of her gift on the day you were born?

Answer: Select the "Present & Future Values Calculator" from the drop-down menu list of calculators.

Type	Simple Annuity
Periodic Payment	2000
Frequency	Annual
Number of Payments	21
Interest Per Year	5%

Click on the Calculate button beside the Future Value field to calculate the present value. The Present Value of $25,642.31 will be displayed.

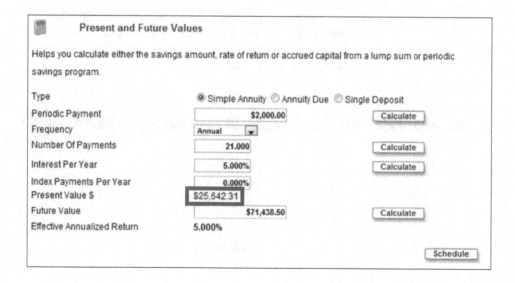

Present and Future Values

Helps you calculate either the savings amount, rate of return or accrued capital from a lump sum or periodic savings program.

Type	⦿ Simple Annuity ◯ Annuity Due ◯ Single Deposit	
Periodic Payment	$2,000.00	Calculate
Frequency	Annual ▾	
Number Of Payments	21.000	Calculate
Interest Per Year	5.000%	Calculate
Index Payments Per Year	0.000%	
Present Value $	$25,642.31	
Future Value	$71,438.50	Calculate
Effective Annualized Return	5.000%	

Schedule

Problem: You are just dying to buy that new television set, but you have no money. The salesperson notices you are reading the price tag — $779, all taxes included — with a hopeless look. She tells you she can make you a deal. If you pay just $38 down and $38 each month thereafter for a total of only 24 payments, you can walk out of the store with the set right now. Your bank will lend you the money at 1% per month. If you decide to go into debt to buy the set, should you borrow from the bank or take the store's offer?

Answer: Select the "Loan Calculator" from the drop-down menu list of calculators. The Loan Calculations window will open.

Amount	779
Existing Interest Rate	1%
Compounding	Monthly
Amortization	24

As a consumer type loan, the interest is compounded monthly. Click on the Calculate button beside the payment and the payment will be calculated. The Payment is $32.80; the bank loan is the better option.

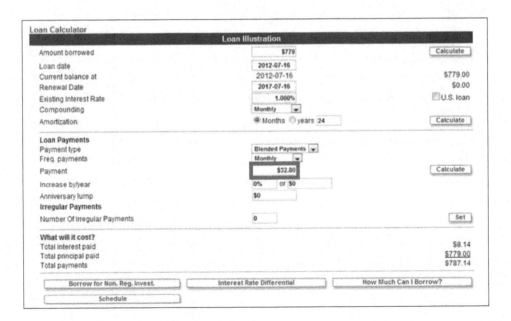

CHAPTER 3

Setting Goals and the Financial Planning Process

John Ross is an ambitious 25-year-old who wants to be a millionaire by the time he is 40. He has $20,000 to start with and estimates he can save $5,000 annually. What rate of return must he earn to reach his goal? Does this goal seem realistic? See "The Financial Planning Process".

LEARNING OBJECTIVES

> ➢ *To distinguish between a financial desire and a financial goal.*
> ➢ *To learn the process of setting goals.*
> ➢ *To learn the process of financial planning to achieve goals.*

There is a lesson to be learned from the old saying, "Knowing your destination is half the journey." The lesson is particularly important in the area of personal finance because many people do not have a clear idea of where they want to go or what they want to achieve in their financial affairs. Some may feel that the idea of setting precise financial goals is rigid and uncreative; others may think it is easier to "go with the flow" and assume all monetary matters will work out in the end. However, managing personal finances without well-defined goals is like driving a car without knowing where you want to go: You will never "arrive".

A crucial component to the success of your financial affairs is establishing well-defined goals that reflect what is important to you. Whether they realize it or not, most people have financial desires — to be rich, to be financially independent, to retire early and comfortably, to buy a better house, etc. However, it is unlikely that these desires will be achieved because they are too vague and it is very difficult to formulate plans and take action to reach vague goals that are not well-defined.

DESIRES AND GOALS

There is some confusion about what a financial goal is and how it differs from a desire. Indeed, the key to setting financial goals successfully is to understand the difference between goals and desires. When individuals are asked to write down their financial goals, they very often come up with a list of desires. The following is just a sample:

I want:
- to be rich
- to be financially independent
- to gain financial security
- to retire early and comfortably
- to send the children to university
- to move to a bigger and better home

None of the above items is a goal. They are all too vague and there are no deadlines for their completion. As such the likelihood of achieving them is small. A **financial goal** must possess two attributes: First, the goal's outcome can be measured precisely in dollars; second, there is a deadline for its completion. Thus, the

Reprinted with permission — The Toronto Star Syndicate. © 1994 GREG HOWARD distributed by King Features Syndicate.

statement "I want to be rich" expresses a financial desire, while the statement "I want to have $1 million in ten years' time" expresses a clear financial goal.

The following are some examples of financial goals:

I want:
- to have $1 million in 10 years' time
- to buy a house in 5 years' time that will cost $200,000
- to retire at the age of 55 with $700,000 cash in addition to my house, which will be totally paid off
- to send the two children, now aged nine and ten, to university, which will cost $20,000 per year
- to save 10% of my earnings every month and put the money in a good stock mutual fund
- to cut the family's entertainment spending by $100 per month, starting this month
- to buy a car next year that will cost $18,000

Note that each of the above items has the two attributes of a financial goal: (i) it is expressed and measured in dollars, and (ii) a completion time is set.

How to Set Financial Goals

Now that you know what a financial goal is and how it differs from a desire, how do you set it down and develop it? Is there any magic process? How many goals should you set?

The best way to start is by brainstorming. Write down all your desires and goals in your financial affairs. At this stage, don't separate the goals from the desires; just put down what you think is important. Include everything you can think of without assessing the reasonableness of it at the moment. Your goals should include both short-term ones, such as a special vacation or a new piece of furniture next year, and long-term goals, such as buying a house in five years' time. You should look at every aspect of your financial affairs and at all your desires.

Now you have a list of goals and desires. The next step is to examine each item carefully and convert every desire into a financial goal. This may be difficult for some items, such as the desire to become rich or financially independent. You have to do some deep thinking to convert that desire into a specific goal, such as having $1 million in 10 years' time. At the end of this step you will end up with a list of goals only. Each goal should be expressed in dollar amounts and with a time for completion.

The Fundamental Financial Goals

Most of the financial goals that families set can be translated into the goal of achieving a specific amount of money by a certain date. For example, a goal of early retirement implies accumulation of enough savings — including pensions — to support the desired level of consumption after retirement. As we shall see in Chapter 17 (**Retirement Planning**), the goal for retirement is the present value of the desired level of consumption from the date of retirement to the expected date of death. Similarly, all expenditure goals — buying a car next year, switching to a bigger home in five years, sending the children to university, etc. — can be translated into the fundamental goal of accumulating a specific amount of money by a specific date.

THE FINANCIAL PLANNING PROCESS

If goal-setting is half the journey to success in personal financial management, then the other half lies in devising a plan to achieve the goal, following through by taking action, and monitoring your progress until you reach the destination. Do you know why the majority of people never achieve their goals? First, they fail to plan. A worthwhile goal cannot be accomplished in one step. You need an action plan that takes a goal and breaks it into a series of sub-goals. By following the sub-goals, you know where you are heading day by day. Second, even if people *do* plan, they do not take action. The best plan in the world will not help you if you do not follow through with action. We shall now examine the important concept of the financial planning process.

The **financial planning process** is the system of setting goals, devising action plans, and monitoring progress. It is a dynamic process that requires continuous changing and monitoring. The process has four main steps:

1. Goal Setting
2. Action Plan
3. Take Action
4. Feedback (Monitoring Progress)

The first step, **goal setting**, is essentially what we have discussed so far. We will illustrate the financial planning process by an example. John Ross (JR) is a 25-year-old who wants to be financially independent. He sets a goal of having $1 million by the time he reaches 40, 15 years hence. Note that this is a specific financial goal with a time for its completion. Thus, JR has completed step one in the financial planning process.

To reach a financial goal, individuals normally have to do two things: First, they invest the money in the right investment — one that can generate sufficient return so that the goal can be achieved. JR has $20,000 now, and he estimates that he can save $5,000 each year in the future. What must he do to achieve his financial goal? If the rate of return is too low, the goal cannot be achieved. What is the minimum rate of return on investment that must be earned to reach his goal? Let k be this minimum rate of return. If he invests the $20,000 to earn $k\%$ per year, the compound value of the investment after 15 years will be $20,000 $(1 + k)^{15}$. Also, if he invests the $5,000 that he will save every year for 15 years, the compound value of this investment — it is an annuity of $5,000 per year for 15 years — will be $5,000 $[(1 + k)^{15} - 1]/k$. Thus, the total future value of his wealth in 15 years' time is $20,000 $(1 + k)^{15}$ + $5,000 $[(1 + k)^{15} - 1]/k$. Since his goal is for this amount to be equal to $1 million, we have the following equation:

$$\$20,000\,(1 + k)^{15} + \$5,000\left[\frac{(1 + k)^{15} - 1}{k}\right]$$
$$= \$1,000,000$$

Solving the equation by trial and error, k is equal to 23.92%, or 24% after rounding. Therefore, JR must find an investment that is expected to generate a return of 24% in order to reach his financial goal. To summarize, the first two steps of JR's financial planning process are as follows:

Step 1 Goal setting:
> To have $1 million after 15 years.

Step 2 Action plan:
> To invest his current wealth of $20,000, and $5,000 every year for 15 years in an investment that has an expected rate of return of 24% per annum.

The third step means JR has to take action according to the **action plan** — i.e., he must find an investment that has an expected rate of return of 24%. At this step, there are three possible cases. First, JR finds such an investment and is happy with the risk involved. In this case he simply invests his money according to the action plan. Second, JR cannot find an investment that can generate such a high return. The second case quite commonly occurs when a goal is set that calls for a very high rate of return. That is why the goal of making $1 million in a year from an investment of $10,000 is unrealistic: There is simply no investment vehicle in the world — except maybe the casino! — that can generate the required rate of return of 10,000%. In this case, JR must either revise his financial goal (Step 1) or revise his action plan (Step 2) or both. (More on this later.) Third, JR finds some investments that are expected to generate the required rate of return of 24%, but he finds all of them incur more risk than he likes. He is uncomfortable with the prospect of placing his money in these investments. This case is an example of how an individual's risk preference affects his financial goals and plans. Although theoretically his goal is achievable, JR's risk attitude prevents him from taking action. The third case is, therefore, similar to the second case, and JR must either revise his financial goal (Step 1) or revise his action plan (Step 2) or both.

In addition to risk preference, individuals' value standards and ethical attitudes sometimes prevent them from acting according to the action plan. For example, some people refuse to invest in companies that are known polluters, even though the rate of return is satisfactory.

When the goals become unattainable, there are two things that you can do. First, re-examine your goal and revise it, if necessary. Second, re-examine the action plan to see if changes can be made so that the goal becomes achievable.

Formal Model for Analysis

We can model the financial planning process in a concise mathematical form. The mathematics should not intimidate anyone, as we use it simply to express what we have already said in words. We will use this model to show how everything in the rest of the book fits together in the process of meeting financial goals. Recall the basic equation from Chapter 1:

Financial goal (at time n)
= Existing savings + Investment income for n years on existing savings
  + (Earnings – Consumption each year)
  + Investment income on the annual savings, n.

Let us model the plan using the following symbols to represent the elements of personal financial planning. The subscripts represent time: t is any particular future year; n is the year the goal is to be met; and 0 is now, the starting point of the plan. Thus, if you plan to retire in 10 years, $n = 10$, and t runs from 1 to 10.

W_n The financial goal. This is the amount of money you are trying to accumulate for some purpose by a particular year. It might be enough savings to retire on at age 65, or perhaps the down payment on a house in five years' time.

W_0 The amount of money you have today that can be dedicated to the future goal.

k The rate of return that you earn on savings. It is expressed as $1 + k$ because you have both the original amount invested and the earnings.

E_t The money you earn in year t, other than investment income.

C_t The money you consume or spend in year t, other than that used to purchase investments.

$$W_n = W_0(1 + k)^n + \sum_{t=1}^{n}(E_t - C_t)(1 + k)^{n-t} \tag{1}$$

To reiterate, the left-hand side of the equation is the financial goal of the plan. The first term on the right hand side is the initial savings at the start of the plan, compounded at the rate of return, and the second term is the sum of the annual savings $(E_t - C_t)$ as it is invested and compounds. Note that the compounding period for the annual savings is $n - t$, allowing for the shorter and shorter period of compounding as you approach the time of the goal. For example, if you have a 10-year horizon, the money you save in year 4 will earn investment income for six years $(10 - 4)$.

Most financial planning issues relates to some part of this equation. Chapter 2, **Time Value of Money**, covers the basic arithmetic of finance that allows us to compare amounts of money received or paid at different times. This chapter, **Setting Goals and the Financial Planning Process**, discusses how to find a W_n that you can expect to achieve with your current and future savings. Chapter 4, **Measuring and Controlling Personal Finances**, shows you how to determine your present financial position (W_0) and plan for future saving $(E_t - C_t)$. Chapter 6, **The Life Cycle and Financial Intermediation**, puts personal finance into the context of the family's stage in the life cycle and its relationship to financial institutions. This context determines different needs as n changes. Chapters 7 and 8, **Personal Income Tax** and **Income Tax Planning**, provide a basic introduction to this extremely complex topic, which plays a major role in determining both k and $(E_t - C_t)$. Chapter 9, **Risk Management**, is the theoretical basis for insurance, and is thus the way you determine how certain you are that each of the specific elements of a financial plan will turn out as intended. Chapters 10 and 11, **Life, Health, and Disability Insurance** and **Property, Home, and Automobile Insurance**, are the principal means of ensuring that W_0 and E_t don't go up in smoke (sometimes, literally!). Chapter 12, **Credit and Debt Management**, deals with times in the life cycle when $(E_t - C_t)$ is negative and the family must borrow money. Chapters 13–16 deal with investing money to earn k in a wide variety of ways, including the personal residence, stocks, bonds, and bank accounts.

Chapters 17 and 18 take us back to square one as we try to determine how much we need to live in retirement and how much our current savings pattern will provide. Thus, our goal of wealth available for retirement must equal the present value of all the consumption during retirement. If n is the age at retirement, d is the expected age of death and we assume that all payments or consumption expenditures occur at year-end, the previous planning equation becomes:

$$W_n = \sum_{n+1}^{d} \frac{C_t}{(1 + k)^{t-n}}$$

Once we determine the desired standard of living and what it entails in wealth at retirement, we can return to the first equation and try to see if this goal is feasible. Essentially, the first steps in retirement planning are another application of the tools learned in Chapters 2–4.

We can use this financial planning model to analyze JR's options.

W_n = 1,000,000,
n = 15,
W_0 = 20,000,
$E_t - C_t$ = 5,000

so that we have

$$\$1,000,000 = \$20,000(1 + k)^{15} + \$5,000\left[\frac{(1 + k)^{15} - 1}{k}\right], \text{ or}$$

on a BA Π Plus

–1,000,000	**FV**	
20,000	**PV**	
5,000	**PMT**	
15	**N**	
CPT	**I/Y**	ans. <u>23.92</u>

He must earn 23.92%.[1]

Suppose JR has decided not to make the investment because he feels it is too risky. What can he do? He can choose any of the following actions:

1. He can change his goal, W_n.
2. He can change the amount of initial investment, W_0.
3. He can change (e.g., increase) the amount of annual investment, $E_t - C_t$.
4. He can change the investment horizon, n.
5. He can choose a different investment that has a different rate of return, k.
6. He can choose any combination of the above.

---

[1] In case you have forgotten the time value formulas, the factor $(1 + k)^{15}$ is simply the future value factor, and $[(1 + k)^{15} - 1]/k$ is the future value factor of an annuity.

To illustrate, suppose JR changes his goal to $500,000, i.e., $W_n = 500,000$. Then, the rate of return required to achieve this goal is:

−500,000	**FV**
20,000	**PV**
5,000	**PMT**
15	**N**
CPT	**I/Y** ans. <u>17.17%</u>

An investment with an expected return of 17% is less risky than one with a return of 24%.

Goals should be reviewed periodically. If you find that the goals set in the past are no longer important to you and that there are other more important needs, you should change the goals to reflect that change. Goal setting and financial planning is a dynamic process that requires necessary changes to adjust to the ever-changing economic circumstances and to the changes in needs of the individual as he/she goes through the different stages of the life cycle.

Suppose JR does not want to change his goal (i.e., he still wants $1 million in 15 years). Suppose he cannot find any additional money to increase the initial investment (i.e., W_0 remains at $20,000), but he estimates that he can save $10,000 per year. Then his required rate of return becomes 19.71%.

Priority or Ranking of Goals

You may now have a lengthy list of financial goals. Most can be combined into a few key ones, which would include two or three big savings/net worth/asset accumulation goals. There should be a good balance between short-term and long-term goals; and you have to estimate the cost of each. For a short-term goal of saving, or an asset purchase, the cost of the goal is simply the intended saving or the price of the asset. For a long-term goal, you can use the formal model of analysis and equation (1) to estimate the cost of the goal. Depending on your action plan, the cost of the goal may be one lump-sum investment right now, or a series of future investments, or a combination of the two. For example, the cost of the goal of accumulating x in 10 years could be in the form of investing y now and z per year for a number of years. Every goal calls for the sacrifice of either current or future consumption, so it is unrealistic to expect yourself to be able to accept all goals. You will have to set priorities, rank all your goals, and accept only the most important ones.

THE PROFESSIONAL FINANCIAL PLANNING PROCESS

The four-step process we introduced earlier is designed for the family working through its own finances. The professional planner needs a more specific and detailed model, and we present here the six-step model used by Certified Financial

Planners around the world, and reprinted here with permission of Financial Planners Standards Council.[2] This section is written from the point of view of a person who hires a financial planner, but it also makes very clear how the financial planner should proceed.

Financial planning is a comprehensive, iterative process. The following steps should guide your planner. Be familiar with them. They'll help you get the most out of the process. And remember, it's this big-picture approach that sets financial planners apart from all other financial advisors who may have been trained to focus only on one aspect of your finances. [...]

Establish the client–planner engagement

Your planner should:

- Explain issues and concepts related to the overall financial planning process that are appropriate to you.
- Explain the services he or she will provide and the process of planning and documentation.
- Clarify your responsibilities as a client.
- Clarify his or her responsibilities as your planner. This should include a discussion about how and by whom he or she will be compensated.

You and your planner should:

- Discuss the scope of the client/planner engagement.
- Agree on how decisions will be made.

Gather client data; determine your goals and expectations

Your planner should:

- Obtain information about your financial resources and obligations through interviews or questionnaires.
- Gather all the necessary documents before giving you the advice you need.

You and your planner should:

- Define your personal and financial goals, needs and priorities.
- Investigate your values, preferences, financial outlook and desired results as they relate to your financial goals, needs and priorities.

---

[2] Reproduced from FPSC website: <https://www.fpsc.ca/financial-planning-process>. Published by Financial Planners Standards Council (FPSC), reproduced by permission.

Clarify your present financial status; identify any problem areas and opportunities

Your planner should:

- Analyze your information to assess your current situation (cash flow, net worth, tax projections, etc.).
- Identify any problem areas or opportunities with respect to your:
  - Capital needs
  - Risk management needs and coverage
  - Investments
  - Taxation
  - Retirement planning
  - Employee benefits
  - Estate planning
  - Special needs (i.e., adult dependent needs, education needs, etc.)

Develop and present the financial plan

Your planner should:

- Develop and prepare a financial plan tailored to meet your goals and objectives, values, and risk tolerance, while providing projections and recommendations.
- Present the plan to you.
- Establish an appropriate review cycle.

You and your planner should:

- Work together to ensure that the plan meets your goals and objectives.

Implement the financial plan

Your planner should:

- Assist you in implementing the recommendations discussed if you want. This may involve coordinating contacts with other professionals such as investment funds sales representatives, accountants, insurance agents and lawyers.

Monitor the financial plan

You and your planner should:

- Agree on who will monitor and evaluate whether your plan is helping you progress toward your goals.

If your planner is in charge of the process, your planner should:

- Perodically contact you to review the progress of the plan and make adjustments to the recommendations required to help you achieve your goals. This review should include:

- ○ A review and evaluation of the impact of changing tax laws and economic circumstances.
- ○ A review of your life circumstances and an adjustment of the recommendations if needed as those circumstances change through life events such as birth, illness, marriage, retirement, etc.

SUMMARY

This chapter introduces and examines goal setting and the financial planning process. It is important to know the difference between desires and goals. Most goals in personal finance can be expressed in terms of the fundamental financial goal of achieving a specific amount on a certain date. We have examined the financial planning process and its four stages. We have shown how to use a simple mathematical model to analyze different aspects of goal setting and action planning. Finally, we present the Certified Financial Planner's six-step professional financial planning model, particularly for students who may wish to choose financial planning as a career.

MULTIPLE-CHOICE REVIEW QUESTIONS

1. Which of the following is not a goal, as defined in this chapter?

   (a) Dave wants to have $500,000 on June 30, 2014.
   (b) Jill wants to save and invest 10% of her annual income every year, from now until she retires at 65.
   (c) Jeff wants to buy his son a car when he graduates at the end of the year.
   (d) Chris wants to cut his expenses by 10% per month.
   (e) All of the above are goals.

2. Jason inherited $80,000 when his father passed away recently. He wants to invest the money so that he can buy a house in five years, and the expected down payment required is $100,000. What is the rate of return that he must earn to reach his goal?

   (a) 10%
   (b) 4.56%
   (c) 13.25%
   (d) 15.78%
   (e) None of the above

3. David Siu, 50, wants to have $550,000 in 15 years. He plans to save and invest an equal amount of money at the end of every year for the next 15 years in order to reach his goal. If the rate of interest is 10%, what is the amount he must save every year?

   (a) $79,542
   (b) $19,042
   (c) $17,311
   (d) $72,311
   (e) None of the above

4. Barbara Bowens, 65, is planning to retire soon, but she wonders if she has enough money to support her retirement. Since her parents and her siblings all died before they reached age 80, she does not expect to live beyond the age of 85. With the help of a personal financial planner, she estimates that her post-retirement lifestyle will cost $30,000 in today's dollars, per year, payable at the start of each year. If the real rate of interest is 3%, what is the minimum amount of money that she needs today in order to support her retirement?

   (a) $459,714
   (b) $358,138
   (c) $446,342
   (d) $830,295
   (e) None of the above

5. Sho-Lan, 35, plans to invest 10% of her income every year until her retirement at age 65. Her current annual income is $30,000, and this is expected to increase at the rate of 3% per year. If the rate of interest that she can earn on her investment is 8%, how much money will she have at retirement? Assume that she invests her money at the end of every year.

   (a) $905,639
   (b) $458,132
   (c) $494,774
   (d) $339,850
   (e) None of the above

DISCUSSION QUESTIONS

1. Explain the significance of the following entries:

   financial goal / financial planning process: goal setting — action plan — taking action — feedback, monitor progress / goal versus desire / priority or ranking of goals / required rate of return on investment / risk preference

2. What are the two attributes of a financial goal?

3. Explain the four steps of the financial planning process.

4. Write down as many things as you can think of that would give you the most joy out of the financial aspects of your life. These may include wishes, desires, dreams, and goals. Separate the items into desires and goals. Change every desire into a goal. Rank your goals in the order of importance to you. Devise an action plan for each of the top three goals.

PROBLEMS

1. Woody Williams, 35, set a retirement goal of having $1,500,000 by the time he retires in 30 years. He plans to achieve this by saving $5,000 per year, which he will invest in term deposits, expected to generate an average return of 10% in the next 30 years.

   (a) Will he achieve his goal?
   (b) If not, what can he do in order to reach his goal? List all the possible alternatives of action.
   (c) For each of the alternatives that you have listed in (b), perform the appropriate mathematical analysis and present the **action plan**.

2. You would like to have $50,000 in 15 years. To accumulate this amount, you plan to deposit each year an equal sum in the bank, which will earn 7%, compounded annually. Your first payment will be made at the end of the year.

   Required
   (a) How much must you deposit annually to accumulate this amount?
   (b) If you decide to make a lump-sum deposit today instead of the annual deposits, how large should this lump-sum deposit be? (Assume you can earn 7% on this deposit.)
   (c) At the end of five years, you will receive $10,000 and deposit this in the bank towards your goal of $50,000 at the end of 15 years. In addition to this deposit, how much must you deposit in equal annual deposits in order to reach your goal? (Assume you can earn 7% on this deposit.)

3. Assume a world without inflation. Janice Lewisberg, 38, plans to retire at age 68. Her life expectancy is age 90. She wants to live a retirement lifestyle that will cost $35,000 per year, payable at the beginning of each year. She now has $20,000 in her investment account and plans to invest an equal amount annually for her retirement. The rate of interest that she expects to earn is 6%.

(a) What is her retirement goal, i.e., the amount that she will need at retirement?

(b) What is the annual investment that she must make in order to reach her goal?

(c) If she dies at age 85, how much money will she leave for her estate?

(d) Repeat the calculation of (a), (b), and (c) if the rate of interest is 8%.

4. Mr. Goldman, 36, has just received an inheritance of $250,000. He wants to retire in four years' time, with $500,000. He has no other liquid assets, and cannot save anything more. Calculate the rate of return he needs in order to achieve his retirement goal.

5. Assume a world without inflation. Mr. Littlewood, 35, plans to retire at age 60. His life expectancy is age 87. He wants to live a retirement lifestyle that will cost $30,000 in the first year of retirement, payable at the beginning of the year. Subsequent retirement expenses will grow at a rate of 3% p.a., payable at the beginning of each year. He now has $20,000 in his investment account and plans to invest an equal amount annually for his retirement. The rate of interest that he expects to earn is 5%.

(a) What is the amount that he will need at retirement?

(b) What is the annual investment that he must make in order to reach his goal in (a)?

6. Jonathan Letters has just inherited $10,000 and has decided to invest the money towards his long-term goal of wealth accumulation. Also, he was inspired by the concept of "pay yourself first" that he learned recently. He intends to put 10% of his salary at the end of each month into this investment plan. He is currently earning $36,000 annually, but expects his salary will increase at the rate of 0.5% per month. His financial advisor recommended a mutual fund with an expected rate of return of 10% p.a. Assume monthly compounding:

(a) What is the effective annual rate (EAR) of the mutual fund?

(b) How much money will he have after 10 years?

(c) Will he achieve his goal of $1 million after 15 years?

(d) If he wants to have $2 million after 25 years, how much must he invest per month?

7. Jonathan Ho, 30, recently graduated from university as a mature student. He has landed a job at the local bank that will pay him $45,000 per year. He expects pay raises of 4% per year for the next five years. Then, he will be promoted to the next level with a 25% pay raise. Thereafter, he expects pay raises of 3% per year until he retires at age 65. He will save 5% of his salary

for the first 5 years, and then he will save 10% of his salary for the next 15 years, and then 20% of his salary until retirement. Assume that all savings are at the end of the year and that he can earn 6% interest on his savings.

(a) How much money will he have at age 55?

(b) Suppose he wants to retire early, at 60, with $1,000,000. Will he achieve this goal? If not, what additional amount must he save each year, from age 55, in addition to the 20% of his salary already given, to reach his goal, assuming that the additional savings is an ordinary annuity, not a growth annuity?

8. (a) Assume that your company pension plan offers to pay a lump sum of $200,000 on your 65th birthday, or an amount of $X at the end of each of the 15 years after your 65th birthday. Assuming an annual interest rate of 8%, what is the amount of the annuity that would make you indifferent between the two alternatives on a present value basis?

(b) Suppose you join the company pension plan at age 30. You now have $10,000, which you will invest in mutual funds to earn 10% compounded monthly. You will also pay $1,200 into the pension fund at the end of each year in order to have a total balance of $600,000 at age 65. Assuming that your individual contribution will be matched by the employer and that the pension plan funds will earn an annual interest rate of 8%, will you reach your goal?

CHAPTER 4

Measuring and Controlling Personal Finances

How much does a family save in a year? Appearances can be deceiving, because some cash outflows create family wealth in the long run. Follow the example of Harold and Donalda Woodhaven in this chapter to learn how to estimate true savings. Tables 4.10 and 4.11 provide details of the process.

LEARNING OBJECTIVES

> ➢ *To prepare a family balance sheet that shows the resources and debts, and how much the family is worth in financial terms.*
>
> ➢ *To prepare a family income statement that shows where the money came from and where it went during the year.*
>
> ➢ *To prepare a budget for the next period of time that incorporates the family's objectives.*
>
> ➢ *To develop control mechanisms so that the family meets its budget and continues to move towards its objectives.*
>
> ➢ *To explain the concept of human capital and how to value it.*

This chapter shows you how to do the accounting work that is essential in personal financial management. You can do very little planning unless you know the resources available, where they come from, and where they are spent. Many families get into financial troubles because they do not pay attention to the basic "housekeeping" of personal finance. Managers of financial institutions will tell you that they see this problem with their professional and small business customers all the time, even when these people earn substantial incomes and should have no difficulties in making ends meet.

You will recall that we cast the basic financial planning model in terms of your wealth today and the wealth you will accumulate in the future by saving. By the time you finish this chapter, you will know how to pull together the figures so that you have a large part of the raw material for doing personal financial management.

ACCOUNTING AND PERSONAL FINANCE

You will notice that this chapter is similar to the financial accounting used by businesses. The similarity is deliberate. As we are using it here, planning and controlling your personal finances is nothing more than keeping track of how well you are doing, and families and businesses both need to do that. If you have previously studied accounting, you should find this chapter easy to understand, though this prior experience is not necessary. Family finances are not as complicated as those of most businesses, and there are some significant differences.

First, the only reason you prepare personal financial statements is for managing the family finances. No one outside the family will use them, except to help you with your planning. Lenders will make their decisions based on some specific amounts, such as total debts and value of the house, but they won't use the entire statements. There is no such thing as generally accepted accounting principles for personal financial statements. Therefore, you prepare them in the way that works for you. We provide a detailed guide, not a set of inviolable rules.

Second, the articulation that is necessary for a business balance sheet and income statement isn't critical in personal finance. **Articulation** means that the income statement items all link directly to the balance sheet, and the net worth amount (or retained earnings on a business balance sheet) is exactly the sum of all the previous incomes minus dividends paid. For example, if a business asset increases in value, then eventually the value is recorded as part of income, at which time it also increases retained earnings and the asset on the balance sheet. If your house increases in value we could record the increase on the balance sheet and in net worth without going to the trouble of recording it as income. Since you will live in the house for a long time, the value increases aren't something you can control, plan for, or consume.

Third, we will tend to deal in cash rather than accrual income. For example, your investment in a university degree creates valuable human capital that increases your future earnings. A business might capitalize and amortize such an asset, but we treat it as an expense for personal planning.[1]

HOW MUCH IS THE FAMILY WORTH?

The family **balance sheet** or **statement of net worth** is a photograph of the family's financial standing at a point in time. It summarizes the major assets and liabilities, with the balancing figure being the net worth. The balance sheet is essential for two reasons.

First, it provides a benchmark or measure of progress in meeting the family's goals. The type of assets you have acquired relative to your goals and your net worth are the most relevant items. You may have stated one of your goals as some level of net worth at the end of the year. If you are trying to save for retirement, a comparison of this year's balance sheet with last year's will tell you how far you have progressed.

Second, the listing and valuation of assets shows what you have to manage. In particular, it will provide a listing for determining how much property insurance to carry (see Chapter 11).

The arithmetic is quite simple, but there are tricky questions:

1. Who is a member of the family?
2. Which items should be included?
3. How do we value the assets and liabilities?

---

[1] Though you should see the section on human capital later in the chapter.

Defining the Family

We define a family as any group of people (including a single person) who share their wealth, revenues, and expenses. By sharing we mean that they pool them, and make communal decisions about their use and management. Some members might have resources that they do not share, but the primary resources needed to live are held in common. Usually they occupy a common residence, but not always, or not at all times. This definition is broad enough to include the traditional married couple with children, same-sex couples, single parents, and common-law relationships. The family can be the nuclear family or the extended family.

The problems occur when we look at the edges. A grown child who is staying at home while searching for a job is sharing finances, but not for long (the parents hope!). Dependent children in joint custody of separated parents are part of both families since they live in both homes and the finances are shared. Some of the planning will have to be done as if the parents were still together.

Most assets are held legally by a single individual or a couple, but for most planning purposes we ignore the strict ownership since we want to look at the joint planning decisions.

What Assets Do We Include?

The short answer is to include all assets. You must aggregate them into general categories and not try to list everything in detail. Your financial planning will not benefit from a detailed inventory of every tea towel and book you own. The most important assets are the valuable ones, and especially the ones that relate to something you can control or plan into the future.

We group assets into three categories. **Financial assets** provide income or are part of what you will consume in retirement. These are the most important for planning purposes, because they are the resources that determine progress toward financial goals. Aside from insurance and the principal residence, most personal financial management is directed towards these assets. **Personal use assets** are the ones you use in everyday life — the house, car, clothing, etc. One of your personal goals is to have the appropriate (for your family) accumulation of personal use assets. They don't yield income, they provide consumption. **Luxury assets** are also for personal use, but they are very marginal to the family's needs. This categorization depends on what the family considers necessary. Many assets that Canadian families consider basic are luxuries for most families in less-developed countries. A major difference between luxury and personal use assets is that luxury assets are of high value if liquidated. Your kitchenware and used furniture will not bring much money, and will have to be replaced soon if you are to live any kind of comfortable existence.

Table 4.1 provides a checklist of the personal assets, but it is not meant to be exhaustive.

| TABLE 4.1 | | |
| A Checklist of Personal Assets | | |
Financial Assets	**Personal Use Assets**	**Luxury Assets**
Cash on hand	Principal residence	Jewellery
Deposits in financial institutions	Car(s)	Vacation property
Retirement savings plans	Furniture	Valuable collections
Tax refunds expected	Clothing	
Cash value of pensions	Household supplies	
Shares	Kitchenware, dishes	
Bonds	Maintenance equipment	
Mutual funds	Sporting equipment	
Options, futures, commodities	TVs, stereos, VCRs	
Precious metals, gemstones		
Real estate		
Direct business investment		

The amount of detail you include depends on the use of the statements. If you are calculating insurance coverage required, or you want to estimate your change in total wealth during a period, you will need all the detail we have discussed. For most planning, you need only the financial assets, the liabilities, major luxury assets you could sell, and perhaps the principal residence. These are the items you manage in providing future consumption. We concentrate on these items in most of our examples in the other chapters.

What Liabilities Do We Include?

You include any amount that any member of the family owes to someone outside the family. Table 4.2 contains a convenient checklist, divided into two categories.

Current liabilities are due within one month. **Long-term liabilities** are due later than one month, and often are payable monthly for many years. The current liabilities include the current month's portion of any long-term liabilities. This distinction is similar to that employed in business accounting, except that businesses treat anything due within one year as current. Most businesses operate on annual cycles. Households operate on a financial cycle determined by how often they are paid, which may be weekly, bi-weekly, or monthly. While the choice of one month is arbitrary, it coincides reasonably with the cycle within which bills have to be paid, and hence is useful for decision-making. The distinction becomes most important earlier in the life cycle, when meeting the monthly bills is a close

TABLE 4.2 A Checklist of Personal Liabilities	
Current	**Long-term**
Credit card(s)	Consumer loans
Telephone	Mortgage on home
Electricity	Other mortgages
Natural gas, oil	Investment loans
Repair services	Student loans
Rent	Pledges
Property taxes, water	Amounts owed on leases
Income taxes	
Insurance premiums	
Current portion of long-term loans	

call. By calling debts due within one month current, we draw attention to the risk of having to liquidate investments in order to pay them if the current income is insufficient.

Valuation of Assets and Liabilities

Valuation of assets and liabilities depends on what you want the information for. This issue is highly contentious in corporate accounting, but we will try to make it fairly simple for personal finance. There are several possible valuation rules. None of them is ideal for every purpose.

Market value is what someone else would pay for the asset in a fair, arm's length, unhurried transaction. **Historic cost** is the original price. **Depreciated cost** is the historic cost minus an allowance for wear and obsolescence. Historic and depreciated cost are the principal measures used in corporate accounting. **Replacement cost** is the price to replace the asset in new condition. Replacement cost is close to market value for assets for which there is a ready market, like financial assets, homes, and cars. The differences are due to depreciation, if any, and transactions costs. Personal use assets like clothing have little market value relative to their replacement cost.

Financial Assets

Value them at market, always. We hold financial assets for the purpose of their income or cash value, and thus they are a means to consumption. The historic cost is irrelevant for planning (except for calculating taxes), since what we want to know is how much we can consume by cashing them in. Transactions costs to liquidate them will range from 0.1% to 5% of the market value. It is rarely worth the trouble to estimate the transaction costs item by item, so we suggest deducting 2% if you want to be very precise, or just ignoring it, which is what we will do in our examples.

One particular aspect you can't ignore is accumulated income taxes. You will learn more about the details in Chapters 7 and 8. For now, let us say that the major tax issues for asset valuation are capital gains and sheltered retirement savings. The asset values must be recorded net of the tax payable in these cases, if the amount is material.

Personal Use Assets

The valuation rule depends on the circumstances. The value of many personal use assets is irrelevant to financial planning, except for insurance purposes. Your future consumption depends on your future earnings from labour and investment, and not on selling the personal use assets. Therefore, if you value them at replacement cost and hence increase your net worth on the balance sheet, it is misleading. You can't consume the net worth increase, because you are already consuming it by using the personal assets. On the other hand, their ownership is an important part of your financial position. A family spends more early in the life cycle to build up the fundamental assets. A family near retirement has a stock of these assets, and so it is better off financially, even if it never intends to sell any of them.

Another factor is the future plans of the family, especially when approaching retirement. If the family plans to dispose of some of the personal use assets and use the money generated as part of the retirement fund, then these assets should be valued at market less cost of disposition.

We follow these general rules, though there are always exceptions:

1. Value the house and cars at market value. If you are planning to sell them and use part or all of the proceeds for something other than buying another house or car (retirement fund, purchase of a business, for example), value them at market less all costs associated with the sale.

2. Value all other personal use assets at replacement cost. Value any assets you are planning to sell and not replace, at market less all costs associated with the sale.

Don't bother with detailed valuations of every asset. Aggregate all the ordinary household assets into one estimate, with house and car(s) separated.

Luxury Assets

Value them the same as personal use assets other than the house and car. The difference between replacement cost and market is much larger for luxury assets in general.

Liabilities

Value all liabilities at the current value that you owe. This is not the same as market value, since if interest rates have changed, a loan might be worth more or less than the balance owing. For example, you would have to check the amortization schedule or calculate the balance owing on a mortgage as shown in Chapter 13, since the present value will be less than the initial loan.

Estimating the Financial Standing — A Detailed Example

You are a financial planner advising this family. You may learn more from this example if you do the suggested exercises at each step without looking at the following material.

Donalda and Harold Woodhaven ("Call us Donnie and Harry — everyone does") have no children. They readily describe their financial position to you. Harry, 30, is a recycling supervisor in the City of Toronto's waste management department. Donnie, 31, is a bookkeeper for a processing plant. Two years ago they bought a modest house for $360,000, with a down payment of $50,000. They are very pleased that they bought when they did, as real estate prices have soared in Toronto since then. They have $500 in a chequing account, $500 in a savings account and $25,000 in RRSPs. Donnie has some mutual fund units whose current market value is $30,000. They guess that their clothes would cost $8,000 in total to replace and that the rest of their household effects would cost $20,000 to replace. Donnie drives a new car that costs $18,000, including taxes. Harry drives an older compact that is in good condition, and would sell for about $2,000.

They have outstanding balances on three credit cards: Visa ($20,000 @ 18% interest); Master Card ($12,000 @ 16% interest; and a department store charge card ($4,000 @ 24% interest). Last year, they paid about $1,075 per month on these cards. On top of the credit cards, there is still a car loan with an outstanding balance of $5,500 @ 6% interest, and monthly payments of $450.

Problem:	Take on your role as advisor now.
	Before you can answer their questions, you will need to make sense of their financial position. Start by preparing a balance sheet. Do you think there are omissions in the information they have given you? What questions would you ask? Take time now to sketch a preliminary balance sheet, and then write down your questions.
Answer:	You could have asked any number of questions about missing assets and liabilities and valuation. You should have asked, for example, if they have any luxury assets and if there is a car loan outstanding on Donnie's new

car. You will want a current market value for the house and the present value of the mortgage.

Let us suppose that they have no luxury assets. Given the rapid rise in Toronto real estate prices, they guess that the house is worth $430,000 now. As of December 31, 2011, the outstanding balance on their mortgage is $296,000. They could sell Donnie's car for $15,000.

Now prepare the balance sheet. Turn to page 76 for the answer.[2]

What Is Net Worth?

Can the family spend its net worth? The Woodhavens seem to be pretty well off, with a net worth of $193,500. Look again at the balance sheet. They have a total of $1,000 in cash, and that is what they can spend. If they sell the other assets to provide cash to spend, they lose the income, or the retirement income, or the use of the asset, whichever they sell. The house has gained $70,000 in value, but they still need a place to live. In the short run, therefore, net worth isn't something you can spend. It is simply the excess of your assets over your debts.

In the long run, net worth converts to cash as the family starts selling its assets. A family could sell a large house and buy a smaller one at retirement age, and sell some of the household assets. The members of the family stop contributing to pension plans and convert them into annuities to support everyday consumption.

One thing to remember is that most personal use and luxury assets depreciate over time. Maintaining and/or replacing them requires that you continue to spend part of your income. If you use all of your income for current consumption without maintaining the fundamental asset base, you will be worse off in the long run, because you will have to replace the assets using current income. When you add inflation to the equation, you must increase your net worth in nominal dollar terms in order to maintain the same level of well-being.

Keeping Track of Assets

Every family needs to keep track of its assets and liabilities in a way that makes identification of them easy in the event of death or incapacity of one or more adult members. The required information includes identifying numbers, names, addresses, and physical location of documents or assets. This list will also help with insurance claims.

---

[2] Table 4.3 uses the more customary corporate format of assets and liabilities shown separately. Software such as PlanPlus may use a different format, but the principles are the same.

TABLE 4.3
The Woodhaven Family Balance Sheet, December 31, 2011

Financial Assets:		Liabilities:	
Cash	$ 1,000	Credit cards	$ 36,000
Mutual funds	30,000	Car loan	5,500
RRSPs	25,000	Mortgage	296,000
	56,000		337,500
Personal Use:			
Clothing	8,000		
Household	20,000		
Cars	17,000		
House	430,000		
	475,000	**Net worth** (Assets − Liabilities)	193,500
Total Assets	$ 531,000		$ 531,000

The family should keep a copy of this list, and update it regularly. The family lawyer and the executors of the will or other family members or friends should also have copies. Thus, if anything tragic happens, at least someone will know where to find the relevant documents to handle the estate. Table 4.4 lists common items the family should record. The level of detail for household items and personal effects depends on their value and the needs of the insurance company.

HUMAN CAPITAL

Human capital, in financial terms, is the earning power that a person possesses. A doctor has more human capital than a carpenter, because she has spent many years to learn difficult skills that society rewards well. Even though human capital is very valuable, we don't put it on the balance sheet. Consider two people at age 18.

One becomes a carpenter, learning on the job and getting progressively higher wages. The wage level peaks in less than 10 years, and after that the carpenter's income rises in real terms only by inflation or overtime work. Today, at age 35, the carpenter is earning $40,000 p.a.

The other person studies for many years, becoming a doctor. At age 28 she starts earning a reasonable income. By age 35, that income is $90,000 p.a.

At age 30, the doctor probably still has a negative net worth on the balance sheet as far as tangible assets are concerned. She has student loans and loans to set up a practice. At the same age, the carpenter has substantial net worth from 12 years of earning and saving. The carpenter's family balance sheet might look

TABLE 4.4
Listing Assets and Documents

- Houses, including vacation home
- Cars: serial numbers, licence plates
- Household items and personal effects
- All financial institution accounts: bank, trust, credit union, broker
- Insurance policies: held directly, through employer, on credit card
- Investment assets held directly: real estate, securities
- Safe deposit box and location of key
- Last four years' income tax returns
- Pension plans: employer(s)', including previous employers
- Registered Retirement Savings Plans
- Private business investments
- Social Insurance Numbers, Health Card numbers of family members
- Drivers' licences
- Credit cards
- Lawyer's name and address
- Executor(s) name(s) and address(es)
- Trustee(s) name(s) and address(es)
- Insurance agent

like the Woodhavens'. The balance sheets do not tell the whole story, because in the future the doctor's human capital will produce a higher income. At some point the doctor's financial net worth will exceed the carpenter's.

Why don't we correct the balance sheet by adding an estimate for human capital? The practical reason is that the estimation is very difficult and may be seriously wrong. We keep the family's human capital in mind when making decisions, though. For example, lenders extend a lot more credit to a young professional with few tangible assets than to a construction labourer with the same net worth. The difference is that the human capital provides a form of security.

There are three important personal finance decisions related to human capital. The first is the decision to acquire it. Higher material wealth is closely linked to higher levels of education. The person with grade 10 education and no other training rarely has the same material success as someone with a trade. In turn the university-educated professional enjoys even higher income, on average. In addition, higher levels of education provide non-financial satisfaction due to the achievement, status, and generally more pleasant working conditions that attach to occupations requiring education. The second decision is to protect human capital. Higher levels of human capital require more life and disability insurance, because there is more to lose. The third decision is to maintain the human capital. Like any other asset, it depreciates over time. Perhaps there was a time when a person could acquire some trade or profession and then practise it for life without further formal study. That time has passed forever. Now, you must engage in lifetime education if your skills are to stay current. More people are finding that they must plan for possibly several occupations and employers during their working life.

This lifetime education, and flexibility to change work, is not necessarily formal. There are many ways to learn, including self-study, research, experimentation, formal courses and practical experience. What is critical is to realize that education in the broadest sense must continue throughout the working life, and money and effort spent on it is not a luxury, but a basic expenditure to maintain or improve the existing human capital and the income it commands.

To give you some idea of what different occupations earn, on average, we display some Statistics Canada data in Table 4.5. You can see that the median real income in Canada has risen only a little bit between 2000 and 2005. We will not be able to track these numbers by occupation in the future because the Harper Conservative government cancelled the long-form census, removing all kinds of data used by countless organizations in their planning. You will also see from the table that the spread between low-income and high-income occupations continues to widen. Doctors, lawyers, and dentists continue to enjoy incomes rising much faster than the inflation rate, while barbers, retail clerks, farmers, and workers in hospitality fall further behind.

THE FAMILY INCOME STATEMENT

The balance sheet shows the family's position today. The income statement shows how it got to today's position from last year's. We want an income statement so that we can see *how* we are moving towards our goals. It provides the basis for the **budget** that is the plan for next year.

We don't advise you to be too precise about the income statement. We call it income because that is the commonly recognized term, but actually it is a **cash flow statement**, since in personal finance we don't do much accrual accounting. That is, we record income and expenditure when they are received and paid, not when they are earned. A business would capitalize a car and then depreciate its value over several years. We will record it as a cash flow in the year purchased. This makes for lumpy results, and sometimes negative cash flows, but that is appropriate. Businesses have much more flexibility to raise capital to cover the uneven cash flows. Families should recognize them directly in their planning, since they will have to either save up money in advance or reduce consumption after a major purchase.

Basic Format

We summarize the basic format in Table 4.6. Income is net of income tax and other withholdings (Canada Pension Plan, Employment Insurance premiums,

TABLE 4.5
Employment Income by Occupation in Canada
in Constant 2005 dollars

Title	Median Annaul Earnings	
	2000	2005
All occupations	40,443	41,401
Management	54,630	57,285
Financial managers	67,079	70,587
Financial auditors and accountants	50,471	53,983
Sales, marketing, advertising managers	62,920	68,137
Managers in retail trade, food, accommodation services	33,646	33,979
Managers in public administration	68,542	79,925
Securities agents, investment dealers and brokers	53,016	52,719
Loan officers	40,297	40,769
Secretaries	33,407	32,505
Clerical supervisors	44,800	45,715
Clerical workers	33,742	35,028
Professionals in natural and applied sciences	62,804	65,601
Civil, mechanical, electrical and chemical engineers	68,041	72,693
Technical occupations natural and applies sciences	49,347	50,092
Family physicians	116,069	124,688
Specialist physicians	134,890	164,551
Dentists	103,148	106,578
Pharmacists	67,207	84,765
Registered nurses	53,771	60,122
Lawyers and Québec notaries	84,120	96,527
Social workers	47,431	52,046
University professors	82,839	86,230
College and other vocational instructors	58,343	59,103
Elementary and secondary school teachers	56,258	58,309
Professional occupations in art and culture	44,823	44,010
Cashiers	19,054	17,758
Retail salespersons and sales clerks	28,077	27,225
Occupations in travel and accommodation	33,656	31,946
Chefs and cooks	22,512	21,684
Hairstylists and barbers	20,199	16,956
Police officers, non-commissioned	67,661	75,482
Security guards	28,040	27,712
Child care and home support	22,182	21,980
Construction trades, all	37,914	35,639
Plumbers	44,834	44,412
Electricians	47,620	46,974
Mechanics	44,849	45,942
Truck drivers	40,443	41,100
Farmers and farm managers	19,429	15,062
Machine operators in manufacturing	35,971	37,981
Assemblers in manufacturing	36,046	37,565

Source: Statistics Canada (2006). Employment Income Statistics (4) in Constant (2005) Dollars, Work Activity in the Reference Year (3), Occupation — National Occupational Classification for Statistics 2006 (720A) and Sex (3) for the Population 15 Years and Over With Employment Income of Canada, Provinces, Territories, Census Metropolitan Areas and Census Agglomerations, 2000 and 2005 — 20% Sample Data. <http://www12.statcan.gc.ca/census-recensement/2006/dp-pd/tbt/Rp-eng.cfm?LANG=E&APATH=3&DETAIL=0&DIM=0&FL=A&FREE=0&GC=0&GID=0&GK=0&GRP=1&PID=96282&PRID=0&PTYPE=88971,97154&S=0&SHOWALL=0&SUB=0&Temporal=2006&THEME=81&VID=0&VNAMEE=&VNAMEF=>

TABLE 4.6
The Personal Income Statement

+	All sources of income, net of withholdings
−	Taxes not paid at source
+	Tax refunds
=	Net revenue
−	Expenses
=	Net income
−	Non-discretionary expenditures
=	Discretionary cash flow
−	Discretionary expenditures
=	NET CASH FLOW

insurance paid by the employee but administered through the payroll),[3] and net of income tax paid or refunded on the income tax return. Self-employed persons should also deduct contributions to the Québec or Canada Pension plan, since they will have to make contributions directly to cover both their personal and employer portion.[4]

Expenditures are any outlay of cash. **Expenses** are recurring expenditures made for everyday living. Defining which is which is a matter for the family. We do it because we want to control spending using a budget. **Non-discretionary expenditures** are ones over which the family has no immediate control — usually repayments of debt principal. **Discretionary expenditures** are ones the family chooses, usually purchases of major assets or very large charitable donations.

The **net cash flow** that is the bottom line will add to cash reserves or be invested in income-producing instruments. It is the savings left after consumption and debt repayment.

Revenues

Revenue is not too hard to calculate, as you can see from Table 4.7. We do not include unrealized capital gains or windfall gains (like lotteries and inheritances) in the income statement. These do increase the value of the assets and the equity on a balance sheet, but we already said that perfect articulation of the statements is not necessary. We don't include unrealized capital gains because

---

[3] This amount is often called take-home pay.
[4] We will return to the issue of non-discretionary savings later, since such savings do create an asset for the family.

TABLE 4.7
Family Revenues

Take-home pay from employment: Deduct everything withheld by employer — taxes, employment insurance premiums, pension contributions, etc.

Self-employed net income: business, professional, commission, farming, fishing

Unemployment insurance benefits

Welfare

Alimony and separation allowance

Child support

Old Age Security

CPP or Québec Pension Plan

Other pensions

Investment income:
• cash dividends (actual, not grossed-up value)
• net capital gains
• rental income
• interest income
• other investment income

Deduct: Income tax payments made directly (i.e., not deducted by employer)

Add: Income tax refunds due to overpayments

---

the income statement deals with cash flow. The chief reason to prepare an income statement is to lay the groundwork for a budget. Windfall gains are unusual and completely unpredictable, so there is no way that you can budget for them.

Expenses and Expenditures

Collecting all the expenses is quite difficult if you haven't kept detailed records. Most people don't. Table 4.8 shows a summary of the expenses a family normally incurs. If you get bank statements with all the cheques returned, and keep copies of your credit card statements, that will include a lot of the outlays. Missing will be all the cash purchases. While you can figure out how much cash you spent by going backwards — how much went into the bank accounts, and how much is there now — this doesn't help much in controlling or planning, since you need to identify what you spent the money on. You may have to guess a lot. Food, health, hygiene, and entertainment are the biggest areas for cash

TABLE 4.8 Expenses and Expenditures	
Shelter	Principal residence: interest, utilities, taxes, maintenance, insurance, condominium fees; or rent, utilities not included in rent
Health and hygiene	Personal and household cleaning materials, dry cleaning, laundry, drugs, toiletries
Alcohol and tobacco	
Food	Show meals bought at work separately if material
Clothing	Separately for each member of the family
Entertainment	Movies, plays, cable fees, dining out, books, records, subscriptions, membership fees, sports clothing and equipment, babysitting, children's allowances, toys
Transportation	Car(s): loan interest, gasoline, maintenance, licence, insurance Car rentals Taxis Public transportation Bicycle maintenance
Daycare	
Insurance	Not included elsewhere
Gifts and donations	
Financial and professional	Union dues, memberships, bank service charges, tuition fees
Vacations	
Vacation property	Show separately from principal residence

expenditures. If you don't use credit and/or debit cards, you will have even more unidentified items.

One way to collect the information is to keep very careful records for a couple of months. You can reasonably extrapolate the cash items to the full year, and use the actual amounts from the other payment records for the full year. An important consideration is how much use you will make of detailed expense records. If you won't change your spending habits by knowing how much you spend in particular categories, then keeping track of them is a waste of time. You do need to know how much you spend and earn in a year in order to see how much you are saving and to plot progress toward your goals, but further detail may not be useful.

Table 4.8 summarizes a categorization scheme for expenses. The family must determine its own categories.[5] Any of the items included in the main categories might be so important that it needs to be followed separately. For example, a family with four children actively engaged in a variety of competitive sports might want to record expenses for sports equipment, clothing, and fees as a separate category.

As a matter of convenience, some expenses inevitably end up lumped into the wrong category. For example, some health and hygiene items are bought at the supermarket, but it is rarely worth the trouble to allocate the bills to each category, and so you include them with food.

Expenditures are a matter of definition for each family. We distinguish between expenditures and expenses, because the latter are "used up" within the year, or at least fairly quickly. However, we call clothing and house repairs expenses, even though they do last for a long time, because they recur so regularly. A business might capitalize such expenditures and depreciate or amortize them over many years, but such a procedure is unnecessary for a family.

Two particular purchases will cause some planning problems no matter how we handle them. Most families purchase cars every few years. About half of Canadian families own their own home. Each car purchase, and the initial home purchase, will produce a very strange income statement if they are deducted as expenditures in arriving at net cash flow. The net cash flow will be a very large negative, and the money comes not out of current revenues, but from cash saved in previous years and/or money borrowed. As we have already noted, a business would capitalize such expenditures. Families are not formed to make profits; therefore, their balance sheets and income statements do not have to be linked as carefully.

Our suggestion is that a family record the purchase of cars and houses, including vacation homes, on the balance sheet, without putting them on the cash flow or income statement. Maintenance on either asset, short of full additions to a house, would be expenses. Since cars need to be replaced every few years, the wise family plans for this large expenditure, a subject we discuss further under budgeting.

Expenditures we record in two categories on the cash flow statements: discretionary and non-discretionary. The non-discretionary expenditures are primarily debt repayments. You can split blended payments (which most personal debts require) into the principal and interest portions, with the interest portion as an expense and the principal repayment as an expenditure. Blended payments include interest and principal repayments in an annuity that retires a loan over a specified period (see Chapter 13). This method is necessary in calculating true savings. A

---

[5] Personal finance software packages have a variety of categorization schemes.

simpler way is to record the entire payment as a non-discretionary expenditure, which is all you need for budgeting and control. We used this simple method in Table 4.9.

The discretionary expenditures are items like furniture, home computers, cameras, etc. The family has the greatest opportunity to change its spending habits in this category, because these expenditures are relatively large and not essential. Of course, expenses like entertainment and vacations are also discretionary, and it is the family's choice of what to call expenditures or expenses, and what is discretionary.

The Woodhaven Example Continued

Donnie and Harry also provide some estimates of their expenses in 2011. You already know that they paid about $1,850 per month on the mortgage. Their other shelter expenses included: taxes, $2,500; utilities, $1,800; insurance, $251; and main-tenance, $200. Hygiene cost $2,400; food, $10,000; clothing $5,600 for the two of them; entertainment, $6,500; gifts, $1,000; donations, $600; financial, $400; and a trip to the Caribbean, $5,000. They haven't saved much in the last two years, with the mortgage and car payments. Oh, yes, their cars cost $4,800 in gasoline and maintenance last year, in addition to the payments of $450 on Donnie's car. They also got tax refunds of $1,350. You already know their combined take-home pay is $7,100 per month.

Donnie inherited the mutual fund a few years ago when her aunt died. Although it does not pay dividends, they would really like to keep it, but they are willing to sell if it helps their financial situation. Both work for small companies near their home and they have a combined take-home pay of $85,200. They do not have any pension plans or other benefits. They plan to have children in the next few years.

They spend freely, and live from one paycheque to another. They find it very difficult to keep up with the monthly mortgage payment of $1,850. They find saving money hard. They can borrow money at 6% interest for investment purposes.

Problem:	Take your role as advisor again.
	Start to put together an income statement for them. You should find some problems, and ask them some questions. Try to see for yourself what you might ask them before you read on to the answers.
Answer:	The most important problem is that the cash flow their numbers yield is clearly wrong. They said they haven't saved much in the last two years, since they bought the

house, and yet their surplus cash flow is about $5,000 on the basis of this statement.[6]

This is not unusual, since most people underestimate how much money they spend. As advisor, you would ask them to consider a list of potential expenses, such as Table 4.8, and try to get the numbers closer. They could also try to get at the net cash flow by calculating how much their bank account and investments have changed since December 31, 2010.

You should ask them about insurance on the cars, which is required by law but is not mentioned in their figures. They have indicated no asset purchases, no alcohol or tobacco, no spending on taxis and public transit. Food, health, and hygiene also look a bit low, and since there are so many individual purchases made in these categories, it is easy to miss a lot.

After some more thought and checking, they added $1,800 in car insurance, another $1,000 in food, $500 in entertainment, furniture purchases of $1,000, and a compact disc player for $300 to the total. They don't smoke, alcohol was included in entertainment, and they guess they spent about $200 on taxis and buses last year. Based on this information, you should now complete their income statement. Try it before you turn to Table 4.9 on the next page.

HOW MUCH DID YOU SAVE?

Donnie and Harry seem to have saved $199, if their income statement is now correct. Appearances are deceiving, however, and they have saved a good deal more than that. The net cash flow is the amount of discretionary saving — the amount that they can control. However, they have been forced to save by repaying the principal on the mortgage, and by contributions to pension plans. As well, the employers have to contribute to pension plans, too. The money in the employer pension plan will be earning a return, as will any money in RRSPs and other investments. To the extent that these investment returns are unrealized (i.e., not included in income), they are also savings. If you estimate your total savings, as shown in Table 4.10, you may be pleasantly surprised.

---

[6] Try for yourself and see.

TABLE 4.9
Woodhaven Family Income Statement, 2011

Take-home pay		$ 85,200
Tax refunds		1,350
Net Revenue		86,550
Expenses:		
Shelter	4,751*	
Food	11,000	
Health and hygiene	2,400	
Clothing	5,600	
Entertainment, including alcohol	7,000	
Transportation	6,800	
Gifts	1,000	
Donations	600	
Financial and professional	400	
Vacations	5,000	
Total Expenses		44,551
NET INCOME		41,999
Non-discretionary Expenditures:		
Credit card minimum payments	12,900	
Mortgage payments	22,200	
Car loan payments	5,400	40,500
DISCRETIONARY CASH FLOW		1,499
Discretionary Expenditures:		
Furniture	1,000	
Compact disc player	300	1,300
NET CASH FLOW		$ 199

* This amount excludes mortgage payments.

You have to search for some of this information, but you can find it, or make reasonable estimates. The sum of the year's pay stubs or the T4 (which is the employer's report of the employee's earnings for tax purposes) will provide most of it. Let us consider the Woodhavens again. Harry and the employer each contributed $1,600 to the CPP. Donnie earned less than Harry and she and the employer contributed $850 each. They lost $500 in the mutual fund last year. The Woodhavens' savings for 2011 are shown in Table 4.11. Note that the repayment of the car loan is not counted as a saving, but the house mortgage repayment is. The car will have to be replaced within a few years, but the house, if kept in good

TABLE 4.10
How Much Did You Save?

	Canada/Québec Pension Plan: employer and employee portions
+	Employer pension: employee's contributions + interest
+	Employer pension: employer's contributions + interest, if vested
+	Mortgage principal repayments
+	Deferred profit sharing plan contributions and interest
+	Unrealized capital gains on investments
+	Net cash flow

TABLE 4.11
The Woodhavens' Savings in 2011

Canada Pension Plan	$ 4,900
Mutual fund loss	−500
Mortgage principal repaid*	6,362
Net cash flow	199
	$ 10,961

* From their mortgage statement.

repair, could last a lifetime. To look at it another way, if a person saves up money to buy a car and takes no loan, that person still has nothing saved once the car wears out. Therefore, borrowing to buy the car and repaying the loan does not create savings.

USING PERSONAL FINANCIAL STATEMENTS

The personal financial statements are generally useful as tools in further financial planning, rather than in their own right. For example, the income statement provides the basis for budgeting next year's spending. The balance sheet provides some information for risk management. Both statements are part of the process of setting goals. We will discuss all of these uses and others in future chapters and sections.

These financial statements do allow us to make a few statements about the Woodhavens:

1. They don't seem to have enough cash on hand for prudent management.

2. When Harry's car needs replacing, they will have trouble finding the money to buy another one, and they can't cover all their debts now.

3. They will have to budget for reduced spending next year. The most likely targets appear to be entertainment and discretionary expenditures.

4. Aside from the problem of too much debt, they seem to be in pretty good shape. They have bought a house, are paying down the mortgage, and have good jobs.

There are popular guidelines (also called tips, rules of thumb, or recommendations) that are widely used by financial planners. These guidelines are applicable to the average family but not all families. One should not be too rigid in their applications, and should make adjustments to allow for differences among families and individuals.

We will cover debt and credit management in depth in Chapter 12. We note that a family that experiences difficulties in its personal finance usually has problems with debt management; therefore, we shall introduce here four popular guidelines for personal debt management. Once we have prepared the financial statement for a family, it is straightforward to apply these four guidelines.

Guidelines (Tips or Recommendations) in Personal Debt Management

1. Consumer debt should not exceed 20% of take-home pay.

   A family should avoid borrowing for consumption. There are two disadvantages of a consumer loan when compared to in investment loan. First, the interest rate charged on consumer loan (e.g., credit card balances) is typically much higher than that of an investment loan. Second, the interest expense on a consumer loan is not tax deductible. Therefore, if a family has to borrow at all, they should borrow to invest rather than to consume.

2. The family should pay down or pay off consumer debt as soon as possible.

   But where does the family find money to do so? This may come from selling investments, if appropriate. Or, more often, this requires changes in spending and saving habits. Changes require commitment and discipline.

3. "Convert" consumer loan into investment loan. It is better to borrow for investment, not for consumption. If a family has liquid investments and consumer debt, the family can sell the investment, pay off or pay down the consumer debt, then borrow the same amount and invest in a similar investment.

4. On any new borrowing, check if there is negative cash flow and ensure the family can service the debt.

   Suppose a family borrows $10,000 at 5% interest to invest in a mutual fund that does not pay dividends. The family has to pay the bank at least $500 interest per year, but the investment brings in no income. This is called a negative cash flow situation. We must ensure that the family has income from other sources to service the debt.

Application to the Woodhaven Family
Let us apply the four guidelines to the Woodhaven Family.

1. We note that their consumer debt of $41,500 (credit card balances of $36,000 and car loan of $5,500) exceed 20% of their take-home pay (20% × $85,200) or $17,040. According to this guideline, this family has too much consumer debt.

2. The family should pay down or pay off consumer debt as soon as possible.

   But, where does the family find money to do so? The Woodhaven Family can sell $30,000 of their mutual fund to pay off the credit card balance, resulting in substantial savings in interest payments. See next point.

3. "Convert" consumer loan to investment loan.

   The Woodhaven family has $30,000 of mutual fund, and $36,000 of credit card balance. They can sell $30,000 of the mutual fund, use the proceeds to retire $30,000 of credit card balance, and then borrow $30,000 to invest in a similar mutual fund. By doing so, they will have "converted" a consumer debt to an investment loan. The credit card balances charge high interest rate. An investment loan to buy mutual fund charges much lower interest, say 5%. In addition, the interest expense on the investment loan is tax deductible.

   There are two benefits of this "conversion". First, they save on interest expense. They will pay off the credit cards in descending order of interest rates, i.e., $4,000 of department store charge card at 24%, $20,000 of Visa card that charges 18% interest, and $6,000 of Master Card that charges 16% interest. Total interest savings will be ($4,000 × .24) + ($20,000 × .18) + ($6,000 × .16) = $5,520 per year. The interest on the $30,000 investment loan at 5% is equal to (.05 × $30,000) or $1,500. In addition, the interest expense is tax deductible. If their marginal tax rate is 30%, they will save ($1,500 × .30) or $450 in taxes. Total savings will be $5,520 – $1,500 + $450 = $4,470 per year.

4. Check negative cash flow and payment for it.

   If the mutual fund they purchase does not pay dividend, the investment loan will have a negative cash flow of $1,500 per year. This is relieved by a tax saving of $450. But they have paid off $30,000 of credit card balances with a substantial savings in interest expense. The savings is more than enough to pay for the negative cash flow of the investment loan.

Other Personal Financial Planning Guidelines

We will now mention some other popular personal financial planning guidelines:

1. Save 10% of take-home pay (or set similar monthly savings goal). Here, the saving refers to the net cash savings in the income statement, not the theoretical savings of Table 4.11.

2. Pay Yourself First. Analyze expenditure and cuts later.

   Many people do not have the discipline to save money. They need a system of forced saving. Pay Yourself First is such a system. Each time you are paid, you write a cheque to yourself, and deposit your cheque before you pay anyone else. You will then be forced to cut expenses because the money is already gone! Your bank or credit union can set up an automatic withdrawal from your periodic pay, and transfer it to whatever you set up — an RRSP, a loan repayment, or a tax-free savings account (TFSA), for example.

3. Set up an emergency fund equal to three to six months of take-home pay. The fund is used to pay for any unanticipated or urgent expenditures. People who rely on commissions, which are uneven or seasonal, will also find such an emergency fund useful. A TFSA is a useful place to keep such funds.

4. Set short-term goal(s), with deadlines of three years or less.

5. Set long-term goal(s), with deadlines of three years or more.

Application to the Woodhaven Family

1. They should save ($85,200 × .10) or $8,520 per year. Last year, they saved only $199, which means they should save a lot more.

2. They will write a cheque to themselves every month before paying anyone else. Deposit the cheque in an investment account, and let the money accumulate for long-term investment later. Make a commitment not to touch the money. The cheque will be about $8,520 ÷ 12 or $710 per month.

3. They have only $1,000 cash, which is too low. Aim for at least three months' take-home pay, which is equal to $21,300. Leave the money in a liquid interest-bearing account to cover emergencies or unevenness of cash flow.

4. Set short-term goal, such as cutting expenses, and set deadlines for the goals. See Chapter 3 for examples of goals.

5. Set long-term goals, such as retirement goals. See Chapter 3 for examples.

BUDGETING

Reprinted with permission — The Toronto Star Syndicate. © 1994 GREG HOWARD distributed by King Features Syndicate.

The **family budget** is a projection of revenues, expenses, and expenditures for a future period. It takes the same form as the income statement. The time frame may be for a week, a pay period, a month, or a year. Budgets for more than one year are not useful, except in highly summarized form, e.g., estimates of net cash flow and total savings for several years.

A family prepares a budget for several reasons: controlling spending, checking short-term liquidity, and short- and long-term planning.

1. **Controlling spending**. A budget provides a benchmark against which to compare actual and planned spending. This works only if the family keeps careful track of its actual spending by category, compares it to the budget, and adjusts spending, all on a regular basis.

2. **Checking liquidity**. **Liquidity** relates to the ability of a family to pay its current and near-future bills without borrowing money. As we have seen, the Woodhaven family is quite illiquid, since it does not have enough money and income from the next month to pay all of the bills. When a family is illiquid, it should be preparing budgets for short periods — even weekly — in order to monitor the situation and control spending. For example, if the Woodhavens had seen this problem coming, they might have deferred the purchase of the compact disc player.

3. **Planning**. In the short run, the budget focuses attention on the family's goals, since many of them relate to accumulation of money. If the family wants to take a special holiday next year, it must plan where the money will come from. In the longer run, the net cash flow and the total savings become the planning variables for house purchases and, ultimately, for retirement. A family estimates how much it needs for long-run goals, then plans how much it must save each year to accumulate the required amount. The time value of

money calculations equate the dollars over time. This long-run planning is necessarily more imperfect, since so much will change, but without it the family is unlikely to meet its goals.

The budgeting process is trial and error. The family uses its previous year's income statement (if it has one) as the starting point. The expected revenues are usually easily determined. The expenses are more difficult, and discretionary expenditures are a matter of which goals the family wants to achieve first. After the first run, the budget often fails to balance. That is, the results don't give the desired net cash flows, total savings, and expenditures that are aimed to meet both the short-run and long-run goals. This process is also discussed in Chapter 3, where we show you how to set goals and monitor progress. The hard part is cutting expenses and expenditures, but it must be done. After some revisions, the budget meets the goals, or the goals must be changed to match what is feasible.

If you want to see the expenditure pattern of the "average" Canadian household, take a look at Table 4.12.

Practical Control

The textbook method to control budgets sounds easy. The family divides the annual budget into sub-periods, say monthly. Each month the results are compared with the budget. Some differences may have been unavoidable, or perhaps the family came in under the budget due to luck or good management. Maybe some expenses were deferred, but must be made in a later month. Once the differences are understood, the family decides how to change its behaviour, if necessary. Every member then implements these changes into his or her spending behaviour.

The reality is quite different. The previous paragraph refers to the way businesses control budgets.[7] A family that can follow that process and make it work probably doesn't need to put much effort into budgeting. There are also personal money management software packages like Quicken and Microsoft Money that provide detailed accounting, budgeting, cheque writing, etc., for families. In our experience, not many people have the time and patience for such detailed record-keeping. The process of comparing actual and budgeted results is useful, but more practical controls are necessary for families who are having troubles meeting their goals.

One solution is an **envelope system**. Every paycheque is divided into the budget sections it has to cover. Once the section's money is exhausted, spending on it has to stop. The envelopes may be actual envelopes of money, or separate bank accounts. There are many variations on this system.

---

[7] Businesses have their own human problems with budgets, but the framework is at least honoured in theory.

TABLE 4.12
Average Household Expenditure, Canada, 2001 and 2009

Item	2001 $	2001 %	2009 $	2009 %
Food	6,438	11.1	7,262	10.2
Shelter	10,984	19.0	14,095	19.8
Household operation	2,619	4.5	3,428	4.8
Household furnishings and equipment	1,655	2.9	1,896	2.7
Clothing	2,398	4.2	2,841	4.0
Transportation	7,596	13.2	9,753	13.7
Health care	1,420	2.5	2,004	2.8
Personal care	960	1.7	1,200	1.7
Recreation	3,453	6.0	3,843	5.4
Reading materials and other printed matter	276	0.5	232	0.3
Education	898	1.6	1,238	1.7
Tobacco products and alcoholic beverages	1,313	2.3	1,506	2.1
Miscellaneous	865	1.5	1,180	1.7
Games of chance (net)	267	0.5	255	0.4
TOTAL CURRENT CONSUMPTION	41,140	71.2	50,733	71.3
Personal income taxes	12,218	21.2	14,399	20.2
Personal insurance payments and pension contributions	3,125	5.4	4,269	6.0
Gifts of money and contributions	1,259	2.2	1,715	2.4
TOTAL EXPENDITURE	57,744	100.0	71,116	100.0

Note: Average household size is 2.56 persons in 2001 and 2.5 persons in 2006.

Source: Statistics Canada. *Table 203-0001 — Survey of household spending (SHS), household spending, summary-level categories, by province, territory and selected metropolitan areas, annual*, CANSIM (database): <www5.statcan.gc.ca/cansim/a01?lang= eng>.

For example, a family might use a chequing account for deposits and regular living expenses — food, clothing, etc. When every paycheque is deposited, the budgeted amounts are left in the account. The rest is distributed into savings accounts, cash held in the home, an RRSP, and a mutual fund. One account might be to save for a new car, another for major furniture purchases and home repairs. The mutual fund and the RRSP deposits are meeting the goal of saving for retirement.

Many personal financial planners recommend "pay yourself first" as a means of achieving savings goals. Set a target of how much you are going to save from each paycheque, and then take that amount out first and deposit it outside the spending accounts. The popular advice is a target of 10% of take-home pay. The difference between this and the budgeting as we have described it so far is that saving, or net cash flow, is not allowed to become a residual, but rather is predetermined. The family is obliged to curtail its spending to balance a budget that yields the target saving.

If the family cannot control its spending without help, many employers and financial institutions have enforced savings plans. The employer deducts money from the paycheque and puts it into Canada Savings Bonds, for example, or the institution puts part of each deposit into an RRSP automatically. In the worst case, a family can sign over its affairs to a financial counsellor who will take in all the deposits and allow the family only enough money to pay living expenses. The counsellor takes charge of paying off debts and accumulating savings. This latter alternative is both humiliating and expensive (the counsellor must be paid), but sometimes it is the only way to avoid ruin.

Credit cards are very helpful in managing personal finances for those who can control their use. They provide a record of spending for budget purposes, and free credit for a period of time. However, the uncontrolled spender can destroy any budget created by using too much credit. One way to avoid this might be to have several cards, each with very low limits. Financial institutions may not co-operate with this plan to the extent needed to be effective. A better control is to use the credit card for only certain types of purchases. If the family is unable to control its spending on credit cards to match the budget, then it should cancel the credit cards and operate with cash and cheques only. **Debit cards**, which charge the bank account immediately, would be helpful to avoid carrying too much cash.

An important issue in the budgeting process is the right to privacy. We believe that every member of the family should have some amount of money, however small, that he can spend freely, without accounting for how it was spent. Children should have a small allowance to start their understanding of money, and they should be able to spend it on anything that they would ordinarily be allowed to buy. They will learn to deal with budget constraints much more effectively if they have some of their own money to spend wisely or foolishly.

Each adult should have some "walking around" money as well. It might go on treats or a frivolous item of clothing you don't really need. What this freedom does is make the restrictions of a budget less irksome.

LIVE GREENER, LIVE CHEAPER, WORK HAPPIER, SPEND HAPPIER

We have talked about how you manage your money in an unemotional way as if only the amount of money you have, earn, spend, and save matters to your welfare. Personal finance textbooks are concerned primarily with those topics, but we want to emphasize that money alone is not the key to happiness.

In the following sections we will discuss three important aspects of personal finance that don't usually appear in a finance textbook: reducing our impact on the ecosystem, how we earn our living, and how we spend our money.

Live Greener, Live Cheaper

The human race is a small part of an immeasurably rich and complex ecosystem on the planet. Our unique contribution to this ecosystem includes the greatest destruction that any species has ever wrought on its own home. If we want those who come after us to enjoy happy lives, we need to reduce the level of our impact. Many of the actions we need to take require collective purpose, but some of them are also at the family level. Furthermore, some of the most worthwhile reductions in our ecological footprint will also save us a lot of money.

Robinson et al. investigated the financial impact of an average middle-class Canadian family of four reducing its ecological footprint significantly while still living a middle-class life.[8] They found that a moderate reduction, starting with the two parents at age 30 and ending at age 60, could save about $392,000 in after-tax real dollars of 2001 accumulated at age 60. An amount of this size would allow the parents to retire several years earlier than otherwise. Two areas of spending reduction and ecological impact reduction produced most of the result: transportation and housing.

The transportation reductions came from going from two cars to one car, and using public transit, bicycles, and shoe leather to make up the difference. The saving was estimated to be $7,262. The housing reduction was achieved by living in a 1,500 square foot house instead of a 2,000 square foot house. The extra cost of construction was not included as a saving since the family could expect it to behave like an investment and eventually sell the larger house for a higher price. Savings in taxes and utilities are significant, and the net annual saving was estimated to be $2,040.

Switching to some organic food costs a bit more. Switching to organic cotton costs an extra $1,000 per year at the time, but this cost has reduced greatly since 2001. The authors note that the usual methods of growing cotton with chemicals are among the worst contributors to pollution and resource depletion of all agricultural products. In 2001 you could hardly find any store that would clean your garments without using perchloroethylene, and the added cost was substantial, but non-perchloroethylene dry cleaning has become much cheaper and easier in 2012.

After all the effects were summed, the net annual saving was $8,231. This is in real dollars of 2001, and furthermore it is after-tax since consumption savings are

---

[8] Chris Robinson, Shuhao Chen, and Jennifer Qiu (2002), "Live Greener, Live Cheaper", paper presented at the Academy of Financial Services Conference, San Antonio.

not taxable. It is also a riskless annuity. A reasonable discount rate for this number is 3%, which in 30 years yields the family a future value of $392,000. Given that the costs of organic clothing and non-perchloroethylene cleaning have declined and given 10 years of inflation, it would be reasonable to project a future value of $.5 million in 2012 dollars in 30 years.

Work Happier

Our next suggestion may not make you more money, and it is simple common sense. You should try to work to earn a living doing something you like doing. We think that has two aspects. First, you spend a lot of your life at work, and happiness is hard to achieve if you are unhappy for 40 hours a week. Second, you are far more likely to be successful and earn more money if you like what you are doing.

Spend Happier

Dunn et al. summarize a large body of recent research on what makes people happy when they spend money.[9] This research is a great deal more sophisticated than "retail therapy". This research considers what we call discretionary spending rather than necessities — you don't meet these principles by not buying any food. They arrive at eight principles for gaining more happiness from your spending:

- Buy experiences rather than things.

- Spend money on others rather than on yourself.

- Buy many smaller things rather than one large thing. The accumulation of many smaller pleasures like your daily fancy coffee is worth more than the pleasure of one big new piece of expensive furniture.

- Delay consumption because anticipation increases enjoyment when you get it. If you consider our discussion of reasonable spending controls and debt limits, delaying buying something until you can pay for it will also help your financial health directly.

- Don't buy so much insurance against unhappiness. They are not talking about life, health, and car insurance, but warranties against product breakage and failure. We would argue that such insurance is usually very unfairly priced. They say that when people do experience an uncovered loss on a product, they don't suffer enough unhappiness to have made the insurance worth the price.

---

[9] Elizabeth Dunn, Daniel Gilbert, and Timothy Wilson, "If money doesn't make you happy, then you probably aren't spending it right", *Journal of Consumer Psychology* (2011) 21(2), 115–25.

- Think about all the effects from your purchase, not just the obvious ones that are the reason for buying. For example, cottages are lovely to spend at, but you have to spend a lot to maintain them, as well as time and money to travel to them in heavy weekend traffic, and you donate a lot of blood to mosquitoes when you are there.

- When you do comparison shopping, think carefully about the attributes that are presented to you and be sure that those are the attributes that matter to you. Two equal-sized chocolate bars may be priced differently, but perhaps it is the type of chocolate that really matters to you.

- Don't look at the picture, read the ratings. We are more likely to make good decisions on consumption by learning what others thought about the item. The modern explosion of consumers rating virtually everything via websites does indeed make for happier spending.

SUMMARY

In this chapter you have learned how to prepare three family statements: balance sheet, income statement, and budget. The balance sheet shows the assets, liabilities, and net worth of the family at a point in time. The income statement shows the net revenues, expenses, and expenditures for the past year. The final figure is the net cash flow, which is also the family's discretionary saving for the year. As well, you learned how to calculate the family's total savings, including all the pension contributions.

The family budget projects the next period's income statement. It provides the basis for controlling spending and meeting the family's goals. Different families will use it in a variety of ways. We also provided some suggestions for how to spend your money more ecologically, and how to spend happier.

These statements are tools for financial planning rather than ends in themselves. We will use them in our subsequent work in this book.

MULTIPLE-CHOICE REVIEW QUESTIONS

1. In the statement of net worth, which of the following statements is true?

   (a) Financial assets are valued at fair market value.
   (b) The family home is valued at replacement cost.
   (c) Net worth is the assets that the family can spend.
   (d) Liabilities are recorded at historical cost.
   (e) None of the above.

2. Which of the following are discretionary expenses?

   (a) Gifts and donations
   (b) Mortgage payments
   (c) Car loan repayments
   (d) Furniture purchase
   (e) (a) and (d)

3. Which of the following statements concerning human capital is false?

   (a) Human capital depreciates over time.
   (b) Human capital is the earning power that a person possesses.
   (c) A doctor normally has higher human capital that an unskilled labourer.
   (d) Human capital is normally easy to estimate.
   (e) All of the above.

4. Which of the following is normally not classified as personal use assets?

   (a) Car(s)
   (b) Valuable jewellery
   (c) Clothing
   (d) Electronic equipments such as TVs and VCRs
   (e) Furniture

5. Which of the following is not a good reason for preparing a family budget?

   (a) Paying yourself first
   (b) Controlling spending
   (c) Checking liquidity
   (d) Planning
   (e) None of the above

DISCUSSION QUESTIONS

1. Explain the significance of the following entries:

   articulation / balance sheet / budget / cash flow statement / defining the family / discretionary expenditure / envelope system / expenditures / expenses / human capital / liquidity / net cash flow / net worth / non-discretionary expenditures

2. **Personal Project 1**
   Prepare a complete balance sheet for your family. Explain what valuation rules you used for each group of assets and liabilities, and why. Note any shortcuts or guesses you used to make this a manageable task, without losing too much information.

3. **Personal Project 2**
   Prepare a complete income statement for your family. Why did you choose the particular set of categories? Verify that your estimates are reasonable by comparing the net cash flow with the increase or decrease in financial assets.

4. **Personal Project 3**
   Calculate the total saving for your family for last year.

5. **Personal Project 4**
   Use the answers to the first three questions to assess whether there are any issues raised by the financial statements. Does it look as if your family is saving enough money for retirement (without getting too detailed)? Is the family sufficiently liquid?

6. **Personal Project 5**
   Prepare a budget for your family for a one-year period. Explain how you arrived at the amount in each category.

7. The savings control mechanism of "pay yourself first" means that you deduct 10% of every paycheque (that is, 10% of pay after deductions) and put it into savings. The rest goes towards meeting all expenses and expenditures. This simple measure ignores both the family life cycle stage and the enforced savings in the routine expenses and deductions. Critically evaluate the validity of the 10% rule with respect to the following situations:

   (a) A couple with three children under 10 years old. The husband is a dock worker currently receiving unemployment compensation. The wife works as a waitress and brings home $300 per week.
   (b) A single male, aged 30, who works as a stockbroker.
   (c) A couple in their 50s, whose children have left home. He is a self-employed lawyer and she has her own consulting business. They have enjoyed a very good lifestyle for many years, including paying for all the education expenses for their children at private schools and universities. Neither of them has a pension plan, and their savings are quite modest.

8. We say in this chapter that you should ignore individual ownership of specific assets because you are planning for the family. Identify some aspects of financial planning, or some situations in which the individual ownership of assets is relevant.

PROBLEMS

1. It's New Year's Day, 2012, and Vincent and Anne Crago have decided to be more careful with their money. Lately, they seem to go from paycheque to

paycheque. They want to look seriously at their financial situation and put themselves on a budget. "At the rate we're saving, we'll be 90 before we can retire!" says Anne.

They have two children: Jenny, 4, and Ross, 18 months. They are planning to have another child in a year or so, but they would like to buy a larger home first. With the way real estate prices fluctuate, they are worried that they won't be able to afford to move.

The Cragos have come to you for advice and have provided you with the following information:

(i)   Vincent is a production manager in a small manufacturing firm. His salary is $54,000. His net bi-weekly pay after payroll deductions is $1,371.37. Anne has a part-time job as a legal secretary and makes about $250 a week after deductions. Her gross salary is $15,700. The children stay in a home daycare in the neighbourhood while Anne is working, at a cost of $65 per week.

(ii)   They have a chequing account that is used to pay all their household bills and from which they draw their pocket money. The balance in the account at the end of December is $407.27. Their savings account has a balance of $4,123, and pays interest of approximately 5% p.a. on the minimum monthly balance.

(iii)   Vincent always buys a Canada Savings Bond for $1,000 through his employer's payroll savings plan. When he receives the fully paid bond in November he cashes it and the proceeds pay for all their additional expenditures during the holiday season.

(iv)   Vincent gets a performance and salary review on the anniversary of his employment. He thinks he will get a 2% increase this year.

(v)   Monthly mortgage payments on their $85,000 mortgage are $998.90. Monthly life insurance premiums for Vincent are $173. As of December 31, the policy had a cash surrender value of $2,133.

(vi)   Monthly car loan payments are $273. Licence fees of $90 are due in October and March.

(vii)   Anne belongs to a fitness and social club. She pays annual dues of $650 on October 1. The club requires a minimum food and bar expenditure of $50 per quarter. Their payment cycle is March, June, September, and December.

(viii) As one of the beneficiaries of her great-aunt's estate, Anne expects to get about $20,000 by the end of August.

(ix)   Their average utility bills are as follows:
$100 for gas, monthly
$ 80 for telephone, monthly (includes long distance)
$100 for hydro, bi-monthly (February, April, etc.)
$ 25 for water, per month, billed March, June and November
$ 25 for cable TV per month, billed quarterly (January, April, etc.)

(x)   Vincent has a car valued at $13,000 with a $6,000 loan outstanding (originally taken out for a four-year term). Anne's car is three years old and fully paid, with an estimated value of $10,000. Gasoline and parking cost $50 a week for both of them together, and repairs cost $1,350 last year. Vincent's car is still quite new, but Anne's is starting to show signs of age. For example, radiator problems (warranty expired) cost them an unexpected $465.

(xi)   Insurance premiums are paid annually for the house and vehicles. House insurance will be $600 in May, car insurance on both cars totals $1,500 in October.

(xii)   They spend about $150 per week on food, drugs, and toiletries and about $10 per week on alcohol. Vincent figures he spends about $220 per month for lunches and coffee at work. They think they go through $50 a week on miscellaneous expenditures.

(xiii) They have a $400 subscription for season's tickets to the symphony (paid in June). Before the concerts they treat themselves to dinner, which costs about $100 for two. There are concerts in November, January, February, and May. The children go a play group on Saturdays, which costs $150 every term. The term starts in September, January, and May.

(xiv)   Semi-annual dental check-ups for the two of them cost $100–120 in June and December.

(xv)   Anne has a balance of $755 owing on her Visa card and Vincent owes $250 on his charge card. They do not always pay the full balances owing, but they try.

(xvi)   There are other costs that must be covered — clothes, gifts, miscellaneous household utensils, etc. Vincent says, "Thank goodness for credit cards. If there is anything left, I try to save some, but it never seems that there is anything left at the end of the month. We have tried budgets before, but it is impossible to stick to them. I guess you could say that I am a little skeptical that a budget will work for us."

(xvii) Vincent owns listed company shares worth $10,000 that paid $750 in dividends last year. He has $3,500 in Canada Savings Bonds (in addition to the payroll savings one that they just used up over Christmas), paying interest of $315 p.a., and RRSPs holding $15,000. Anne has $3,500 in her RRSPs and $5,000 in CSBs. Anne's interest income is $350 p.a.

(xviii) Household contents would cost about $40,000 to replace, according to the insurance agent. They feel that they could get about $250,000 for their house, before real estate commissions, legal fees, and moving expenses. This year's property taxes will increase 2% over last year's taxes of $2,354. They are due in equal instalments in February, March, April, June, July, and August.

Required:

(a) Prepare a balance sheet and income statement for last year for the Cragos. Assume that they had no taxes owing or refunded.
(b) Prepare a monthly cash budget for the period of January to December, this year. State clearly any assumptions you make.
(c) Comment on the Cragos' current situation with regard to their cash budget and make recommendations on what they should do with respect to their current spending and saving habits. Discuss all issues that you feel are relevant to the Cragos' financial situation. How realistic is their desire to buy a larger house?

2. The most recent balance sheet of Sharon and Huckle is as follows:

Assets		Liabilities and Net Worth	
Cash	$ 1,000	Credit card balances	
Stock mutual funds		Department store card	$ 5,000
(expected rate of return 12%)	15,000	(21% interest)	
House	300,000	Visa Card (18% interest)	9,000
Car (personal use)	15,000	Master Card (16% interest)	6,000
		Car loan (10% interest)	5,000
		Mortgage on home	180,000
		Net Worth	???

Both of them work and their take-home pay is $40,000. Currently, they are not saving any money (other than the "mandatory" savings such as CPP contributions). They can borrow money for investment purpose at 5% interest.

Required:

(a) What is their net worth?
(b) As their financial advisor, describe briefly four recommendations with respect to managing their debt, and three other personal financial planning recommendations to the family.
(c) They have heard that there will be some savings if they "convert" all their credit card debt into an investment loan. Calculate (i) the amount of interest savings annually and (ii) the amount of tax savings if their marginal tax rate is 30% and their average tax rate is 20%.

3. Jack and Natalie Novak, aged 32 and 30 respectively, are living in a house they bought last year. They have only one child, Martin, aged 3, but they plan to have another child in two or three years. They have become a little concerned about their finances lately.

Jack is an engineer for a large auto parts manufacturer and Natalie is a legal secretary. Jack's gross salary is $65,000 per year, but after all deductions he takes home $3,700 per month. Natalie gets $31,000 per year and nets about $1,950 per month. Jack's eight-year-old Volvo has been giving him lots of costly troubles in the last year, so he has asked the bank about a car loan. Also, the Novaks are interested in getting a personal line of credit as they sometimes experience cash-flow problems. They have been asked by the bank to supply a personal balance sheet and an income and expenditure statement. They have asked you to prepare these for them. They have provided you with a list of financial information as follows:

Cash on hand	$ 175
Bank account balance	950
Term deposit	5,000
Canada Savings Bond	1,800
Home	250,000
Home mortgage balance	180,000
Jack's car (8 years old)	3,000
Natalie's car (1 year old)	15,000
Car loan on Natalie's car	12,500
Monthly mortgage payment	1,292
Monthly car-loan payment	403
Bills outstanding:	
Telephone	35
Hydro	95
Visa (minimum due $83)	2,816
Master Card (minimum due $10)	150
Insurance (cars)	2,220
Estimated monthly expenditures:	
Groceries	800
Gas and auto expenses	180
Daycare/nursery	600
Utilities	350
Newspaper and magazines	50
Alcohol and cigarettes	100
Entertainment	300
Clothes	200
Miscellaneous	200
Personal assets	20,000
Jack's RRSP (in term deposits)	3,000
Natalie's RRSP (in a stock mutual fund)	6,000

Jack comments further, "Before we bought the house last year we had no money problems. By the way, I have forgotten the property tax of about $1,800 and the home insurance premium of $450. Last year, I spent over $700 on landscaping. We really enjoy the home and the neighbours are nice, but it is costing us a lot more than we thought. I borrowed $25,000 from my father for the down payment. He is kind enough to charge me no interest, but I hope to pay him back as soon as possible, like several thousand dollars a year. Fortunately, I have a nice job and the benefits are good — medical and drug plan, pension plan, life and disability insurance ... You name it, I have it! Natalie does not get any of those things, but my medical plans cover the whole family. Last year, we got tax refunds of $500 and $250, which we spent on a one-week vacation.

We usually take a vacation once a year. How much does it cost? Well, it depends on where we go ... about $2,000, I would say."

Required:

(a) Using the information provided, prepare a statement of net worth and a statement of income and expenditures for the Novaks.

(b) Based on the statements you prepared, discuss and comment on their financial situation.

(c) If their income increases by 5%, their total expenses by 4%, and their total assets (excluding personal assets and the cars) by 6%, what will be their net worth one year from now?

CHAPTER 5

Family Law

Laura's husband Eustace works all the time at his successful business, and she is lonely. The children from their marriage of 35 years have grown up and left home. Eustace has refused to try marriage counselling with her. She has heard that if she leaves him she can only get alimony if he has been unfaithful or cruel, and he hasn't. She has no assets of her own and she is afraid she couldn't support herself because she has never worked outside the home. Eustace is 60 and Laura is 57. What would you advise her?

This chapter is based entirely on our understanding of the various cases and statutes relating to family law. The application of law may vary according to the circumstances and the province in which you reside. Our intention is to help you understand the important issues and the possible financial planning choices and consequences. We are not lawyers, and we cannot guarantee that what we say can be applied to the facts of any particular case. You or your client must consult a lawyer with respect to any legal problem that you encounter.

LEARNING OBJECTIVES

> ➤ *To understand the financial implications of the following:*
>   ➤ *A separation agreement*
>   ➤ *Spousal and child support*
>   ➤ *Property rights under the Family Law Acts*
>   ➤ *Divorce*
>   ➤ *Methods of dispute resolution in marriage breakdown*

INTRODUCTION

Family law is the entire body of statutes, regulations, and precedents[1] that govern relations between spouses and between parents and minor children. It covers marriage, annulment, separation, divorce, custody and care of children, property rights within the family, and aspects of the taxation of the family's income. The relevant statutes include the federal *Divorce Act*, the provincial *Family Law Acts*, the federal and provincial *Income Tax Acts*, and all the regulations attached to them. Most experts in family law do not include the *Income Tax Acts* in this list, but in practice income taxation is quite important, particularly now when the definitions of marriage and spousal couple are so contentious and hotly debated. Sadly, most of the writing on family law concerns the breakup of families, and this chapter is no exception.

Nothing that we write in this chapter can replace competent legal advice. We are providing you with a basic understanding and the knowledge to ask questions and handle the painful situations better, but you or your clients will still need a lawyer. If you are a financial planner, this understanding is essential for you to work effectively with your clients and their lawyers to make the best financial plans related to family law issues.

One basic distinction to understand is the difference between separation and divorce. A **separation agreement** is a contract between spouses in which they agree to live separate lives and set various conditions. Contract law governs separation agreements, and the spouses have a great deal of freedom in determining the arrangements.[2] When we speak loosely of a "legal separation", we mean a separation agreement that has been prepared and signed, and contains the necessary characteristics to be a binding contract. Separated spouses are still married.

---

[1] Precedents are decisions reached in cases that went to trial and that are relevant to the issue under consideration. This body of law is also called case law.

[2] The most important limitation concerns the welfare of minor children, which has to meet external standards.

A **divorce** is granted by a court upon application by a petitioner. The *Divorce Act* governs all divorces in Canada, and a divorce does end a marriage.

One of the complications in this subject is the split in jurisdictions between the provinces and the federal government. The *Divorce Act* is a federal statute that governs all divorces across Canada. It grants to the court the power to make orders on all subjects relating to marriage dissolution except one — division of family property. That power rests in provincial jurisdiction, and every province has its own *Family Law Act* (FLA) or equivalent. The FLAs also deal with many of the other aspects of marriage breakdown, but a couple can end a marriage only with a divorce or annulment. In this text, we follow the Ontario FLA. The principles are similar in other provinces, but they also differ in ways that can be very important in some situations.

Throughout this chapter we will refer to **married couples** or marriage, which will mean two persons who completed a ceremony of marriage that is recognized by Canadian law. A **spousal couple** means any two persons, same sex or opposite sex, who are living in a conjugal relationship, regardless of whether they are married.

WHAT IS A FAMILY?

For financial planning purposes, a **family** is any grouping of persons whose affairs are so closely related that they plan their personal financial affairs together. A single person is a family, as is any spousal couple, regardless of gender and marriage status. We make no distinction between same-sex and opposite-sex couples, though in some situations the law makes distinctions. Dependent children are part of the family of the parent(s) with whom they live or upon whom they depend. The most common families are single persons and spousal couples, with or without children. Sometimes children stay in the home long after an age at which we would consider them independent, but whether they are part of the family for financial planning purposes is not always evident. Some families comprise several generations and related persons outside the spousal/child relationship: grandparents, aunts, uncles, etc. Some families consist of different groupings of people who are not closely related and are not spousal couples, but who live and plan their financial affairs together.

Some laws define spousal couples much more narrowly, and families are not usually defined to include anyone other than spouses and dependent children. On December 9, 2004, the Supreme Court of Canada issued a decision agreeing that the federal government was within its powers to allow same-sex marriages, on the basis that not to do so would violate the constitutional rights of gays and lesbians. Subsequent federal and provincial legislation gives marriage of same-sex and opposite-sex couples identical legal status.

Under the *Divorce Act*, the definition is narrow. A spousal couple is only a family if they are legally married.[3] If a marriage does not exist, then you cannot terminate it under the *Divorce Act*, and thus none of the legal provisions it allows are available.

The federal *Income Tax Act* recognizes a much wider category of spouse: any spousal couple who have cohabited for at least one year, or who are married, or who have cohabited for less than one year but the union has produced a child. Their dependent children are also specifically recognized as part of the family, and the age of dependence may extend as late as the end of a post-secondary degree. Same-sex couples are spouses. Other dependent relatives may qualify as part of a family if they are totally dependent on a taxpayer, thus allowing some tax relief for extra expenses.

The *Family Law Act* is a bit narrower. With respect to support obligations only, couples who have cohabited continuously for at least three years, or who are in a relationship of some permanence and have one or more children, including adopted children, are spousal couples. With respect to support obligations only, this definition includes same-sex couples. Each spouse so-defined has an obligation to support him or herself and her/his partner to the extent that he/she is able to do so. These spouses also have an obligation to support their dependent children.

With respect to other matters, however, the *Family Law Act* defines a spouse as a person who is married. Thus, married same-sex couples will also be covered under the provisions of the Act. The one omission lies in property rights. Only married spouses can claim property rights under the *Family Law Act* on breakdown of a marriage. Unmarried spouses, whom we would treat as families for financial planning and income tax purposes, are not the same under the *Family Law Act*. The *Succession Law Act* allows an unmarried spouse to claim against the estate of a deceased partner as if they had been married.

MARRIAGE AND DOMESTIC CONTRACTS

The two partners in a married couple obtain certain rights and assume certain obligations under law, as already noted. The unmarried partners of a spousal relationship acquire fewer rights and obligations, though in some respects they are treated no differently. Married couples may write and sign legally binding domestic contracts during the period of the relationship, with any provisions regarding the following during the relationship, upon breakdown of the relationship or upon death of one or both parties:

---

[3] See Malcolm Kronby, *Canadian Family Law*, 8th ed. (Toronto: Stoddart, 2001), Ch. 2, for a detailed discussion of what constitutes a "valid and subsisting marriage".

1. Ownership of property or division of it, particularly upon relationship breakdown.
2. Support.
3. The right to direct education and moral training of their children, but not custody.
4. Any other matter in settlement of their affairs.

In Ontario, Newfoundland, P.E.I., and the Yukon, an unmarried spousal couple can create a **cohabitation agreement** with any of the same provisions. If they subsequently marry, the agreement continues as a valid domestic contract until they revoke it formally.

A third class of domestic contract is a separation agreement.

A domestic contract is generally accepted by the courts as valid and enforceable even where the provisions do not follow the *Family Law Act*. We want to allow families to arrange their own affairs and be able to rely on those provisions. Nonetheless, courts will set aside or vary some provisions in domestic contracts that were prepared properly and would otherwise be binding:

1. A domestic contract cannot usually limit spousal rights to possession of the matrimonial home.

2. Support obligations in the contract may be set aside if the lack of support causes "unconscionable circumstances",[4] if the person losing support is dependent on public welfare, or if the person giving support defaults on an order.

3. Someone did not fully disclose assets, liabilities, or sources of income.

4. One party was unable to understand the provisions of the agreement.

5. The agreement was obtained through fraud or threats.

6. The court may decide that the contract does not provide for the best interests of the children of the relationship.

All this said, courts generally accept domestic contracts and a party who wishes to challenge one will have to provide evidence that there is something very wrong with the contract before a judge will set it aside or vary the terms.

---

[4] Legalese for "really rotten and unfair", e.g., the person who is denied support lacks the necessities of life while the other former partner is wealthy.

ENDING A RELATIONSHIP

As in previous sections, the rules governing the end of a relationship may depend on whether the couple is married or not. Most of what follows concerns termination of a spousal relationship by separation and divorce rather than death.

Separation

The first step in ending a relationship is for the couple to stop living together. A separation agreement is the contract in which they determine how this happens with respect to property division, support of each other and dependent children, custody of children, right to visits with children, possession of the matrimonial home, and, less frequently, other matters like maintenance of life insurance or specific payments contingent on unforeseen future needs.

A separation agreement is also a domestic contract, and is bound by the same rules as marriage and cohabitation agreements except that child custody may form part of the agreement. You do not need to be married to create a separation agreement, but there is one crucial difference between married and unmarried couples. The provisions of the *Family Law Act* do not apply with respect to division of property and so an unmarried spouse cannot enforce any division of property under the law. The *Divorce Act* does not cover division of property, though it can deal with any other aspect of the dissolution of a marriage.

One of the two most important and often contentious parts of the process of creating a separation agreement is the **financial disclosure** by both parties. Each province has its own set of forms. They ask for a great deal of detail, but the fundamental requirement is a balance sheet including considerable information about major assets, an income statement, and a budget for each individual. Chapter 4 of this text covers most of what you need to know to do this, though there are specific details that must follow the provincial laws precisely. Failure to meet the disclosure requirement can invalidate a separation agreement and even lead to serious penalties. Kronby provides the example of the Ontario forms required.[5]

Custody and access to children is the other most contentious issue in separations. One family law expert advised us that if a couple can resolve this issue, everything else is relatively easy. Since this is a personal finance textbook, we will happily skip this topic except for the financial issues involved, to be discussed in a later section.

Support obligations for children are not quite as contentious as they once were, due to guidelines now in place. We discuss all forms of support and division of property in separate sections.

---

[5] Malcolm Kronby, *Canadian Family Law*, 8th ed. (Toronto: Stoddart, 2001), pp. 168–82.

Separation agreements require a large quantity of other details, too numerous to relate here. Michael Cochrane provides an example of the sort of provisions that a separation agreement may include.[6]

Divorce

Fiction creates the most dramatic situations out of divorce laws, which some jurisdictions make it very difficult to achieve even today. In 1986 the federal *Divorce Act* set three **grounds for divorce**:

1. Intentional separation for one year because of marital difficulties.
2. Adultery.
3. Husband or wife subjects the other to intolerable physical or mental cruelty.

Most divorces are granted on the basis of a one-year separation. A divorce starts with a petition by one party to a court asking that the marriage be dissolved. If the respondent agrees with the petitioner and does not contest the divorce, it is granted quickly and easily, and the lawyers don't get too rich. In fact, the parties need not attend the actual court hearing of the petition except in Newfoundland and Québec (this latter only if there are dependent children of the marriage). Contested divorces are not common, and when they do occur can cost the couple a lot of money in legal fees.

The problems in divorce arise when the couple has not satisfactorily worked out the details of living apart through a separation agreement. The *Divorce Act* gives the court no authority over division of property, but it can change or set aside provisions in a separation agreement regarding other matters, particularly the support of dependent children. If a court decides that the support provisions are not in the best interests of the children, it may change them.

SUPPORT

Dependent Children

Every parent has an obligation to provide support for unmarried dependent children who are under the age of 18 or who are in full-time attendance at an educational institution, according to need. This obligation does not extend to a child at least 16 years of age who is no longer under parental control. Children with disabilities may require support for their lifetime, and a court can order this. Separation agreements often contain clauses that require one parent to continue to provide support for children who are older than 18 but continue to live at home

---

[6] Michael Cochrane, *Surviving Your Divorce*, 3rd ed. (Etobicoke: John Wiley, 2002), pp. 268–87.

and attend an educational institution full time, without necessarily specifying need. Such a provision is enforceable, like any other in a separation agreement.

The word "child" under the *Family Law Act* means:

> ...a person whom a parent has demonstrated a settled intention to treat as a child of his or her family, except under an arrangement where the child is placed for valuable consideration in a foster home by a person having lawful custody. (*Family Law Act*, R.S.O. 1990, c. F.3, s. 1.(1))

Thus, a person who marries or cohabits with someone with dependent children from a previous relationship will have a support obligation to the children if they continue to live with the new spousal couple or receive support from them. In addition, under a separate rule, a person who is the natural parent of a dependent child but is not living with that child may nonetheless be ordered to provide support.

Almost every day we can read in the newspaper of some court case in which a separated parent is requesting huge sums for child support from the other parent, who is very wealthy. Most support cases do not involve the rich, however, and the *Divorce Act* now provides guidelines, which provincial *Family Law Acts* follow closely or even exactly. As a result, the issue of how much child support to pay has become much less contentious. The parents may agree that more support is needed and build that into their separation agreement, but the court is unlikely to allow less except when special circumstances prevent a non-custodial spouse from being able to contribute the required amount. For example, the non-custodial spouse might be disabled and have much greater living expenses than normal. There are also many contingent provisions that may be built into separation agreements, such as provision for additional educational expenses if they are subsequently needed. The guidelines vary by province, although not by much. We have not included them in the textbook for reasons of space, but the most recent guidelines, along with all kinds of information on how to apply them, are to be found at the Department of Justice Canada website.[7]

The guidelines contain specific amounts calculated for the number of children and the income of the spouse who is contributing the support, up to an income of $150,000 per annum. For income above that level, the court has discretion to either apply the guidelines pro rata or determine an appropriate amount, having regard for the needs of the dependent child. The application of the guidelines without variation means the amount per month payable at $150,000, plus a fixed percentage per month times the annual earnings in excess of $150,000. In the *Divorce Act* this fixed percentage over $150,000 is 0.74% for one child, 1.26% for two children,

---

[7] Go to the federal Department of Justice website, <www.canada.justice.gc.ca>, select "Programs and Initiatives", then the "Child Support" link.

1.54% for three children, and 1.84% for four children. The monthly amounts payable for the first $150,000 are $1,263, $2,012, $2,611, and $3,102, respectively. These amounts are not the same in each province. For example, if a father in British Columbia earning $250,000 p.a. had to provide support for two dependent children, the guideline method would yield $2,104 per month for two children, plus 1.26% × $100,000, for a total per month of $3,364. The differences between the provinces are not very large. The parent who is paying has to file financial statements every year since the child support payments are dependent on his or her income.

Under the *Income Tax Act*, child support is not taxable in the hands of the recipient (who is normally the custodial spouse), nor can the spouse who is paying support deduct it for income tax purposes. This was not always the case prior to 1997, and some support agreements attract different treatments. This brings up the issue of tax efficiency. Since the support is normally paid by the taxpayer with the higher income, there is a tax disadvantage to the payment of a periodic amount. The payment of a lump sum is more efficient because the income from it will be taxed in the hands of the lower tax bracket taxpayer, who will also be taking the various tax credits associated with a dependent child. Courts do not like this form of payment and so it is rather difficult to arrange it unless strong safeguards exist to ensure the child receives the benefit of the lump sum over time. The lump-sum arrangement becomes particularly tax-effective if paid directly to the child (which is only possible for a child of 18 or older) because it would normally be while the child is in full-time attendance at school, and therefore likely to pay no tax on the income from the lump sum.

Spouse

The old term of **alimony** does not exist except for decisions made prior to the current *Family Law Acts* and the *Divorce Act*, and carried forward as support orders. Alimony under the old laws was an allowance a man paid to his former wife for her living costs, but he had to pay it only if he had been guilty of adultery, cruelty, or desertion. The modern concept of **spousal support** means that in the event of a marriage breakdown, each spouse has an obligation to assist the other spouse financially to the extent that support is needed and can be afforded.

Unfortunately, these are very broad provisions, and court decisions vary widely both within and across jurisdictions. Spousal support can be ordered under both the *Divorce Act* and the provincial FLAs, which makes it even more difficult to lay down specific principles. The *Divorce Act* principles do generally apply throughout the field, including to unmarried spouses under the FLAs, however. The *Divorce Act* recognizes four objectives of spousal support:

(a) recognize any economic advantages or disadvantages to the spouses arising from the marriage or its breakdown;

(b) apportion between the spouses any financial consequences arising from the care of any child of the marriage over and above any obligation for the support of any child of the marriage;

(c) relieve any economic hardship of the spouses arising from the breakdown of the marriage; and

(d) in so far as practicable, promote the economic self-sufficiency of each spouse within a reasonable period of time. (*Divorce Act*, R.S.C. 1985, c. 3 (2nd Supp.), s. 15.2(6))

While this short section alone could provide the material for many books, we will make just a few comments. Most spousal support awards go to wives, though there are an increasing number flowing from wives to husbands. Under the FLAs, the couple need not be married, but they cannot use the *Divorce Act* to affect any decision reached under the FLA, nor any separation agreement. A common observation is that female spouses who take custody of children typically end up poorer than the fathers, because of the lost opportunities for advancement in the work place. The spousal support provisions are an attempt to correct that, but it is quite difficult to achieve. At the same time, spouses have an obligation to provide for themselves, and support orders or agreements should contain provisions to encourage them to retrain or otherwise make themselves employable in the long run. This is easier to achieve the younger the spouse and shorter the time out of the work force.

Michael Cochrane ventures into this minefield with some general principles, which we summarize here:

• Spouse's ability to pay. A spouse should not expect to maintain the same standard of living as before if the payer would be impoverished.

• A spouse should not be required to take any possible job in order to support his or her own needs. The job should be reasonable considering the skills and ability of the recipient spouse.

• Spousal support is not intended to equalize the incomes of the two spouses.

• The need for spousal support should be determined after division of property. The income the spouse can generate from the property will form part of the calculation of how much spousal support is required, if any.

• The prudent investment of the assets from division of property will be included in the calculations. The spouse is not required to be an expert investor, but must use the assets to reduce dependency.

• The spouse's employment qualifications will be considered.

• Spousal support may be denied where both spouses worked throughout the marriage and after breakdown and the sale of the matrimonial home generates additional funds for investment, even if the marriage was lengthy.[8]

Rogerson and Thompson have developed a set of guidelines for spousal support that are somewhat similar to those for child support. The spousal support guidelines are not enshrined in law, however, and are to provide guidance, not an entitlement.[9]

Spousal support paid according to a legally binding agreement (which usually means a court has approved the agreement) is taxable in the hands of the recipient and tax-deductible for the payer. Since it is common that the payer is in the higher tax bracket, the tax-efficient method is a regular support payment rather than a lump-sum settlement. Unfortunately, the record of unpaid support is quite extensive and the ability or even willingness of courts and governments to enforce it quite weak. As a result, an inefficient lump-sum payment may be the safest way for a spouse to secure his or her entitlement. It is not completely tax-inefficient, since the income earned on the lump sum is taxed at the lower marginal rate.

Now you can give Laura part of the advice she needs in her troubled relationship with Eustace. First, she is going to need to consult a lawyer. If she decides to leave Eustace to live on her own, he will have a support obligation towards her. Alimony and the law attached to it no longer exist or apply to them. She is already 57 and has never worked outside the home, so the prospect of her being able to earn her own living now is slight. Eustace has a successful business, and so his ability to pay support is not in question. You have probably realized by now that there is also an issue about the assets in the marriage, but let's leave that until we discuss division of property.

Parents

32. Every child who is not a minor has an obligation to provide support, in accordance with need, for his or her parent who has cared for or provided support for the child, to the extent that the child is capable of doing so. (*Family Law Act*, R.S.O. 1990, c. F-3)

For baby boomers, you could call this the family law sandwich!

---

[8] Michael Cochrane, *Surviving Your Divorce*, 3rd ed. (Etobicoke: John Wiley, 2002), pp. 129–30.
[9] Carol Rogerson and Rollie Thompson, Spousal Support Advisory Guidelines, Presented to Family, Children and Youth Section, Department of Justice Canada, July 2008. Available online: <www.justice.gc.ca/eng/pi/fcy-fea/spo-epo/g-ld/spag/pdf/SSAG_eng.pdf>.

For income tax purposes, a child who is supporting a dependent adult may deduct some of the expenses. Any gift made by a child to a parent to help support the parent is not taxable or tax-deductible.

DIVISION OF PROPERTY

Upon breakdown of a marriage, the actual ownership of any property in the marriage is largely irrelevant, because a division is required and applies to all property unless explicitly excluded. Division of property occurs only through domestic contracts and the FLAs. The *Divorce Act* contains no rules regarding such division, though the effect of it may be considered regarding support orders. Only married couples can claim division of property under the rules of the FLAs. Unmarried couples whom we would consider to be spousal couples for financial planning purposes, and who are considered equivalent to married under the *Income Tax Act*, have no rights under the FLAs. More about that later, but for now we are discussing property division upon breakdown of marriages only.

The way we go about property division is to value all of the property that each party owns or that is owned jointly. Once again, this is a balance sheet exercise as in Chapter 4, and the valuation is market value minus costs of realization (including selling costs and taxes) and minus debts. Everything must be put on the table initially. Leaving out any property at this point can invalidate a separation agreement. Then, subject to a variety of rules, the value of the property that was acquired during the marriage is divided between the two spouses. The ownership of property itself need not be transferred. All that is required is payment of an amount of money or transfer of property that meets the requirements of the division.

Under the FLAs, in general, the principle is that the property acquired during the marriage is to be divided "fairly". The initial presumption is that a fair division is an equal division, barring some special circumstances. In some provinces, unequal division is allowed only when not to do so would be grossly unfair or unconscionable. In others, unequal division is allowed whenever the result would otherwise be merely unfair. For example, suppose one spouse built a successful business and raised the children, while the other spouse spent the entire marriage hanging out in cafés and bars. It would seem unfair under any rules to give the barfly any significant share of the business the other spouse created in the event of a marriage breakdown. Now suppose that we replace the non-working spouse in this example with a spouse who contributed little help in housekeeping or raising the children, but did work throughout the marriage and contributed to the financial costs of maintaining the household, though to a lesser degree. Should the spouse who created the business keep the entire value of it in a marriage breakdown? It seems unlikely that an equal division could be called unconscionable, but it would seem unfair.

Leaving aside the difficult judgments about fairness, there are some general rules that determine which property (or its value, more strictly speaking) is excluded from the division of property. You must not rely literally on this list because the rules do vary materially between the provinces, and this is a particular area where legal advice is always required. The general exclusions are as follows:

1. Property excluded explicitly in a marriage contract.
2. Property owned by one spouse in advance of the marriage.
3. A gift, inheritance, or proceeds of a court award or settlement for damages suffered personally.
4. Personal items like clothing and sporting goods.
5. Proceeds from a life insurance policy.
6. Family heirlooms and antiques.
7. Property acquired after the date of separation.

You are now in a position to offer some more advice to Laura about the financial effects of a decision to end her marriage to Eustace. She is entitled to an equal share of the property accumulated during the marriage. Certain assets may be excluded from the division, but since their marriage is of such long duration, it seems almost certain that there will be substantial division owing to her. You may also realize that it will be a significant problem for Eustace if most of the value of the family assets is tied up in the business because paying her a fair share may require sale of the business.

The Matrimonial Home

The matrimonial home is a special asset, particularly if there are children of the relationship who will continue to live with one parent. All provinces have rules that prevent either spouse from selling the matrimonial home or taking a mortgage on it without the permission of the other spouse.

If there are no children, then couples often agree to sell the home and the net proceeds become part of the property to be divided. They may also agree to count the home as part of the division at market value without selling it. If there are children, the usual arrangement is that the spouse with custody, or with whom the children spend more time in the case of joint custody, continues to occupy the house and the couple retains ownership as joint tenants of the home for some period of time. After that period of time the property is sold and the value divided as already agreed.

If one spouse brought a house into the marriage and the couple subsequently lives in it on a full-time basis, it becomes the matrimonial home. It is then subject to equal division of property. If the spouse who owns the home coming into the marriage wishes to protect that interest like any other property brought into the marriage, the couple must create and sign a valid marriage contract specifying that.

Possession/occupation of the matrimonial home does not necessarily equal ownership. Some provinces allow either spouse to ask for an order giving him or her exclusive possession. Other provinces do not grant this right. However, in either case, if one spouse is in sole possession of the home and there are children, it is likely that spouse will have custody of the children. On the other hand, the spouse granted custody has a very strong case to retain possession of the home. The spouse who has neither custody nor possession of the matrimonial home will automatically be liable for child support, and can also be required to help with the costs of maintaining the home until final disposition of the issues in the marriage breakdown or sale of the home.

An important power that spouses have during the process of a marriage breakdown is to request that a court prohibit a spouse from dealing with some or all of his or her property until further order of the court. This preserves assets intact in the jurisdiction of the court so that they will be available for satisfaction of any judgment.

Unmarried Spouses

Unmarried spouses are out of luck when it comes to property division upon breakdown of the relationship. Perhaps we should say that one spouse is out of luck, and the other one is lucky. Ownership of the property determines how it is divided and there is no equalization unless the couple has executed a valid domestic contract, either a co-habitation agreement or a separation agreement, that provides otherwise. Don't confuse this with support because the FLAs specifically provide a support obligation.

This omission seems quite unfair and has led to some obvious injustice in the past. If one spouse of an unmarried couple dies, the survivor can claim survivor benefits as if married, but if the marriage breaks down, no similar right exists. Claims in common law have succeeded on one basis — **constructive trust**. Suppose an unmarried couple contributes jointly over a long period of time to some significant endeavour, like the development of a valuable business that is legally owned by only one of them. If the relationship breaks down, the one who did not have ownership may claim that the entire pattern of behaviour of the couple established an implicit ownership interest in the business as a constructive trust. The claim for a fair share of the value created is then a valid claim to be determined on the facts of the case, and the FLA does not apply.

Example 5.1: Paul and Mary were separated on January 30, 2010, and they were legally divorced recently, on January 31, 2012. They were legally married on January 30, 2001. At point of marriage, Paul owns a condominium valued at $150,000 and a bond portfolio valued at $100,000, while Mary owns a mutual fund valued at $150,000. They lived in the condominium during the marriage. The condominium was valued at $200,000 on January 30, 2010, and $220,000 on January 31, 2012. In 2003, Mary inherited a rental property from her father when he died. The rental property's value has steadily increased as follows: $200,000 in 2003 at her father's death, $280,000 on January 30, 2010, and $320,000 on January 31, 2012. There was no change in value in Paul's bond portfolio, but Mary's mutual fund was valued at $190,000 on January 30, 2010, and $180,000 on January 31, 2012. Neither Paul nor Mary had any debt when they separated. How much does Paul owe Mary and how much does Mary owe Paul?

Answer: The following is a summary of their assets at different points in time:

		Married Jan. 2001	**2003**	**Separated Jan. 2010**	**Divorced Jan. 2012**
Paul	Condo	150,000		200,000	220,000
	Bond	100,000		100,000	
Mary	Fund	150,000		190,000	180,000
	Property		200,000	280,000	320,000

1. The condominium is a matrimonial home, and Mary is entitled to half. Therefore, Paul owes Mary (1/2 × $200,000) = $100,000. Note that the relevant values of all assets are as of the date of separation.

2. The general rule of thumb is that an increase in asset value during the marriage is part of family assets and should be shared equally. However, there is no increase in the value of the bond portfolio, so Paul does not have to share his bond portfolio with Mary.

3. Mary's stock portfolio has increased in value, and the increase should be equally shared. Therefore, Mary owes Paul [1/2 × ($190,000 – $150,000)] = $20,000.

4. If the inherited property has been kept separate from other assets, then Mary does not owe Paul anything on it, since inheritances are excluded from asset division. She should keep proper documentation.

> If the rental property value is commingled with other assets, then she will owe Paul [1/2 × ($280,000 – $200,000) =] $40,000.

> The date of divorce is irrelevant. Division of family property is done on values at the date of separation.

SETTLING YOUR DIFFERENCES

Any lawyer who has the client's best interest at heart will suggest a variety of ways of resolving the various issues that arise when a spousal relationship ends. The costs of the different methods vary widely, and can deplete the assets to a surprising extent.

The normal and most common course of events finds the spouses each hiring a lawyer and negotiating a separation agreement. As we have already seen, some things in this agreement are already limited, such as child support and disposition of the matrimonial home. Eventually the two spouses reach agreement on the terms of the agreement, they sign it, and it takes effect. This brief paragraph summarizes a lot of things than can happen, which you can read more about in Cochrane (2002, Ch. 9).

What if they cannot agree following this method? Going to a court to litigate a settlement is very expensive, time-consuming and hard on everyone involved, particularly children. Only the lawyers get rich, and even they would rather you settled out of court.

One method to try is mediation. A **mediator** is an independent third party who works with couples to help them find different ways to resolve disputed issues. Each person still has a lawyer for advice on the law. The best mediators have specific training in mediation. Lawyers, social workers, and psychologists are usually well-equipped to develop the skills necessary to mediate.

Both parties must agree to the mediation and must have fairly equal negotiating positions. For example, if one party is well-educated and the other party is not, they are not on an equal footing. You could use mediation when you reach an impasse in negotiations, or you could agree to mediation right at the start of the process. Mediators' fees may be less than lawyers' fees on an hourly basis, but the serious savings occur elsewhere. As soon as you start on the court litigation route, the lawyer will run up some very serious bills for preparation of the case, getting the court date, appearing in court, and sometimes having to wait while other cases are finished in the court or the opposing counsel is held up in another case, etc. Lawyers generally bill by six-minute intervals, and they do not leave any work time unbilled.

If mediation does not work, you are left where you started it or perhaps with some further agreement, but not a complete settlement. Mediators cannot impose anything on you; they try to help you find ways to learn more about your differences and how to overcome them.

Another option that is usually faster and may be cheaper than going to court is hiring an **arbitrator** who will decide the case in private. Arbitrators who hear cases that would otherwise be in a court are usually lawyers or retired judges with expertise in the sort of matters referred to them. The problems of clogged courts and unavoidable delays in the system don't affect arbitration when you are paying the arbitrator. He or she will hear the case and subsequently render a decision, usually much faster than the public courts. However, you will still be paying the lawyers to represent you, and you will have to pay the arbitrator's fee of several hundred dollars per hour.

Cochrane (2002) suggests **collaborative family law** to settle disputes. The lawyers and their clients agree to a binding commitment that they will negotiate a settlement without resorting to litigation in a court. As long as they are negotiating, neither side can turn to the courts. If the negotiations do not succeed, the clients can still turn to the courts. The lawyers agree that they will not represent the clients in a subsequent court action. Thus, the lawyers have every incentive to help the clients settle since they have no further income possible. The clients naturally want to settle if they agree to such a process; furthermore, if they have to engage new lawyers, the cost will be much greater for them to become familiar with what has already happened. Thus everyone has a reason to deal honestly and respectfully, and the hope is that this leads to a fair and fast agreement. The one risk is that the parties may not have assessed the likelihood of reaching agreement accurately, and this process may prove to be an expensive delay to an inevitable court appearance.

None of these alternative methods of dispute resolution is meant to be therapy, marriage counselling, infallible, or really cheap. They may, however, save money, perhaps a great deal. If they succeed, both parties will probably get a better agreement and feel better about it. If there are children and any sort of joint custody or visitation rights, both parties will feel more comfortable in the continued relationship they must have with each other to care for their children if the marriage breakdown is handled in a non-adversarial way.

NOT SETTLING YOUR DIFFERENCES

Make no mistake about it, differences between two spouses over a breakdown of the relationship do get settled — they just cost more money and misery if you have to go to court and fight about them. Every honest lawyer will urge you to avoid the court if you can. Indeed, lawyers have an obligation to inform their clients of alternatives and to attempt to resolve disputes by negotiation before resorting to litigation in a court.

Unfortunately, many cases still end up in the courts. As financial planners we don't have much more to say about courts and marriage breakdowns, except the following:

- Going to court will cost more money.

- Everyone will get hurt.

- Therefore, don't go to court unless you and/or your children need something very important that you cannot get without doing so. Think about this decision very carefully, and try to distance yourself from your very natural feelings of anger and sadness when you get professional advice on what is best for you and your children.

DISCUSSION QUESTIONS

1. Explain the significance of the following entries:

   alimony / arbitrator / child support / cohabitation agreement / collaborative family law / dependent children / division of property: matrimonial home — constructive trust / divorce / family / grounds for divorce / married couples / mediator / separation agreement: financial disclosure — custody and access to children / spousal couple / spousal support

2. Professor Carol Rogerson of the University of Toronto Law School and Professor Rollie Thompson of Dalhousie Law School released a draft of proposed Spousal Support Guidelines in January 2005. Summarize in one page how you think such guidelines should be designed. Compare your ideas with the proposal.

3. Was the decision in 1997 to make all child support payments non-taxable to the recipient and non-deductible for the payer a good idea from a financial planning point of view?

4. Should indexation be mandatory in all support orders and agreements? Does it matter in the case of child support that follows the Child Support Guidelines in the *Divorce Act*?

PROBLEMS

1. Work out the child support payable under the applicable guidelines in the following situations:

   (a) Three children under the age of 16 in British Columbia, parent who is to pay support earns $50,900 per annum.

   (b) Four children under the age of 12 in Ontario, parent who is to pay earns $70,000 per annum.

   (c) One child aged 10 living with her mother; one aged 14 at a boarding school who attends a summer camp when not at school; and one aged 17 living in a shared apartment in the same city and attending school full time. The father and mother have not spoken to each other, nor to the two older children, in two years. They all live in Ontario and the father earns $170,000 per annum. How much child support must he pay?

2. Jeremy and Alan are a same-sex couple who are confronting the realities of changing legal status. They have been living together for many years and are not married, though it is now legal in their province. Is there any personal financial advantage to them to get married?

3. Sergey and Yulia were married in Russia before Sergey emigrated to Canada. They have lived in Canada for seven years now, own a house with a mortgage, and have jobs with pension plans. Sergey was a Russian citizen but Yulia was born in Canada of Canadian parents. Sergey is threatening to return to Russia where it will be almost impossible for Yulia to enforce any orders from a Canadian court. Leaving aside any custody rights, laws about kidnapping, etc., which are beyond the scope of this book, does Yulia have any rights regarding personal finance matters in this situation?

4. Tony and Anne separated recently and will divorce at the end of the year. They were married on January 10, 2000. They lived in the condominium Tony inherited in 1999 when his father died. Other than the condominium and some basic personal used items, they did not have anything at the point of marriage. Tony has a good job and was able to support Anne to go to school full time and build up an investment portfolio of stocks and bonds (market value is $200,000 on date of separation). Tony found out that Anne had won $4 million in a lottery ticket last year but she kept it a secret from him. She has spent some of the money so that there is only $3 million left. The current market value of the condominium is $300,000.

   How are their assets to be divided under Ontario law?

CHAPTER 6

The Life Cycle and Financial Intermediation

Sam and Jaime each earn $45,000 annually and both are 35 years old. Do they have the same financial planning needs? Not at all, because Sam is single while Jaime is married with two young children. Learn how to use the concept of "family life cycle" to identify the most important financial planning issues for each of them.

LEARNING OBJECTIVES

This chapter places personal finance in a theoretical context in institutions and the family life cycle, and the specific objectives are as follows:

> ➤ *To gain an understanding of the concept of the family life cycle and how it can be used to diagnose the most significant requirements of a family at different stages in the life cycle.*

> ➤ *To explain the idea of financial intermediation and the role of financial institutions. Personal finance is a practical application of the concept of financial intermediation.*

THE FINANCIAL LIFE CYCLE

People have a limited life expectancy, and during their lives they go through stages of differing financial positions and earning power. We call the lifetime pattern of these stages the **financial life cycle**. Franco Modigliani and Richard Brumberg developed a formal model of it.[1] Zvi Bodie, Jonathan Treussard, and Paul Willen expand the application of the financial life cycle hypothesis to financial planning issues.[2]

Early in your life you are totally dependent on your family for financial support, and your parents do the financial planning for the family unit that includes you. We don't consider this part of the cycle from your point of view, though we note that you are making a critical investment in your human capital during this dependent stage, and your human capital is the principal determinant of your future earnings when you are independent.

When you become independent, you have to find a way to earn enough money to at least match your consumption. Let us repeat the basic equation from Chapter 3, which provides a model of a financial goal, W_n:

$$W_n = W_0(1 + k)^n + \sum_{t=1}^{n}(E_t - C_t)(1 + k)^{n-t}$$

Early in the life cycle, your consumption is likely to exceed your income at least some of the time. Perhaps you are following a course of study that will

---

[1] Franco Modigliani and Richard Brumberg, "Utility Analysis and the Consumption Function: An Interpretation of Cross-Section Data", in Kenneth F. Kurihara, (ed.), *Post-Keynesian Economics* (New Brunswick, NJ: Rutgers University Press, 1954), pp. 388–436.
[2] Zvi Bodie, Jonathan Treussard, and Paul Willen, "The Theory of Life Cycle Saving and Investing", Public Policy and Discussion Papers, Federal Reserve Bank of Boston, 07-3 <www.bos.frb.org/economic/ppdp/2007/ppdp0703.htm>.

raise your future earnings, even though it necessitates taking a student loan now. We consider the use of a house and other durable, long-lasting goods as consumption of their value over a period of time, rather than as consumption of the whole price in the year of purchase. You buy the durables because you want to enjoy their value over many periods, and this means you try to maximize your satisfaction over a long time frame, not for a short time only. During this early stage you are likely to have a lot of debt.

As you proceed through the life cycle, you start to earn more than you consume: $E_t - C_t > 0$. As your children grow, so likely does your earning power until it peaks in middle age. As the children become independent and you pay your debts off, you find yourself with surplus income, or savings. The rate of savings increases every year, and of course the total balance of savings increases. Eventually, you reach retirement, and then your earning power becomes very low or zero. You start to consume the accumulated savings balance, and the savings rate is negative. If you plan perfectly, you spend your last dollar the day you die![3]

The essence of personal financial planning is arranging to meet the differences in earnings and consumption through borrowing and saving as appropriate. To some extent you plan your entire life rather than each individual step, in order to make the most of the resources you have now or may have in the future. Buying a house is a good example of the trade-offs. Most families buy their first house long before they have the money to pay for it. They borrow in the form of a mortgage, and repay the mortgage over a period of five to twenty-five years. The interest on the mortgage, plus the principal repayments, poses a heavy burden for most families, and also a significant risk if they suffer even temporary financial reverses like job loss or disability. On the other hand, as the mortgage principal declines, their earnings rise; when the mortgage is paid off, the children (if any) will be at or close to the stage of independence. Now the family is in a good position to save for retirement because the housing costs are quite low and will remain so, while the current saving rate is high and rising. Their pension contributions, the high savings from the time the mortgage is paid off until retirement, and the house itself provide the means for a comfortable retirement.

The original idea of the financial life cycle of a person has led to many important thoughts in economics and finance. As a practical matter, we don't do our financial planning alone, however; we do it in family units. The field of marketing has developed the notion of the family life cycle, based on the pioneering work of William Wells and George Gubar.[4] We turn to this concept in the next section.

---

[3] Assuming that you don't want to leave an estate for your children, if any.

[4] William D. Wells and George Gubar, "Life Cycle Concept in Marketing Research", *Journal of Marketing Research* 3 (November, 1966): 355–63.

Reprinted with permission — The Toronto Star Syndicate. © 1994 GREG HOWARD distributed by King Features Syndicate.

THE FAMILY LIFE CYCLE

Compare two individual males, each aged 35, each earning $45,000 per annum as mail carriers. The financial life cycle hypothesis would tend to treat them as identical. Now we tell you that Sam is single with no romantic attachments. Jaime is married with two children, aged 10 and 7. His wife, Sonia, is working part-time as a waitress, earning $15,000 p.a. Sonia's mother also lives with them and does a lot of the child rearing. Even without any further information, we know that Sam and Jaime have different financial planning needs. For example, Sam and Jaime both need disability insurance, but Sam has no evident need for life insurance — he has no dependants. If he chooses to, Sam can do some discretionary saving and think about how to invest it. Jaime and his wife will be on a tight budget while the children are dependent on them, and will have to make up their retirement savings faster when they are older.

We can group families into different categories in the family life cycle by looking at age and other factors. Marketers have found this way of identifying people very useful for market segmentation in consumer products. John Lansing and James Morgan find a relationship between a person's financial position and his or her stage in the family life cycle.[5] Claire Matthews finds that differences in family life cycle and the consequent differences in complexity of banking relationships are related to the perception of switching costs in banking choices.[6] Barry Mayhew and Neil Murphy and Ronald Rogers find that the family life cycle is more useful than age as a variable for identifying and analyzing demand for con-

---

[5] J.B. Lansing and J.N. Morgan, "Consumer finances over the life cycle", in L.H. Clark (ed.), *Consumer behaviour: The dynamics of consumer reaction* (New York: New York University Press, 1955), pp. 36–51.

[6] Claire Matthews, "The Family Life Cycle and Banking Relationships", paper presented at the Academy of Financial Services Conference, Anaheim, California, October 9–10, 2009.

TABLE 6.1
Family Life Cycle Categories

Category	Description
1	Younger, single
2	Younger couple, no children
3	Couple, dependent children
4	Single, dependent children
5	Older couple, children independent or nearly so
6	Older, single
7	Couple, retired
8	Single, retired

sumer financial services.[7] At the same time, the family life cycle captures the effect of the income patterns in the financial life cycle, even though they are more directly related to age.

A Modern Family Life Cycle Segmentation

We introduce the family life cycle to ease our task of diagnosing a family's personal finance requirements. The initial diagnosis based on this basic information is always subject to revision as the specific circumstances of a family become clearer, but it does help to put us on the right track.

No single scheme of family life cycle groupings is perfect, because there are always some families that don't fit into any category. Furthermore, the growing number of marriage breakdowns, changing demographics (an aging society in North America), and reduced family sizes have altered the picture that prevailed when William Wells and George Gubar developed their grouping pattern in the 1960s. Patrick E. Murphy and William A. Staples propose a different segmentation that allows for single parents, for example.[8]

Our categories, shown in Table 6.1, are a hybrid of those proposed by William Wells and George Gubar, and by Gilles Bernier and Chris Robinson.[9]

---

[7] Barry Mayhew, "Relationship banking and the life cycle concept", *Canadian Banker* May–June (1987): 26–9; Neil Murphy and Rogers Ronald, "Life Cycle and the Adoption of Consumer Financial Innovation: Empirical Study of the Adoption Process", *Journal of Bank Research* Spring (1986): 3–8.

[8] Patrick E. Murphy and William A. Staples, "A Modernized Family Life Cycle", *Journal of Consumer Research* 6 (June 1979): 12–22.

[9] Gilles Bernier and Chris Robinson, *Personal Financial Management*, 2nd ed. (mimeo) (Montreal: Institute of Canadian Bankers, 1987).

DIAGNOSING PERSONAL FINANCE NEEDS WITH THE FAMILY LIFE CYCLE

Now we can do a rough diagnosis of the most important issues by matching the stage in the life cycle against the different elements in the book. This matching isn't perfect. The family unit may not fit in a category, or might be right on the boundary between two categories. The level of income, the expected future income and the level of liquid wealth may render a specific element more or less important than it would be for most families at a given stage in the life cycle. Nonetheless, Table 6.2 provides a good first diagnosis.

For example, consider the average single parent, life cycle stage 4. Money is tight, and so budgeting and debt management are very important. Income tax may be important if there are special considerations relating to a separation agreement, and there are the complexities of taking advantage of provisions of the income tax rules relating to child deductions. The single parent typically has little free cash for investing and can do little about retirement planning. Risk management is perhaps

TABLE 6.2
Significance of Personal Finance Issues by Stage in Life Cycle

Family Life Cycle	Budgeting	Income Tax	Risk Management	Debt Management	Investment	Retirement Planning
1. Younger, single	H	L	L	M	L	L
2. Younger couple, no children	H	M	M	M	M	L
3. Couple, dependent children	H	M	H	H	L	L
4. Single, dependent children	H	M	H	H	L	L
5. Older couple, children independent or nearly so	M	H	M	M	H	M
6. Older, single	L	H	L	L	H	H
7. Couple, retired	L	M	M	L	M	H
8. Single, retired	L	M	L	L	M	H

Notes: **L** — low; **M** — medium; **H** — high. The stages correspond to the categories in Table 6.1.

the most critical issue, because there may be no backup at all if the single parent becomes disabled or dies.

Let us recall where we started, with an individual or family optimizing lifetime consumption and saving. How do we accomplish this desirable situation of being able to trade off money now for money at some other time? We turn to that question in the next section.

FINANCIAL INTERMEDIATION

Financial intermediation is the process of transferring money from surplus economic units to economic units that have a productive use for the money. Intermediation takes place between sectors, and over time. Surplus units in one period may need more money for productive investments in another period. The surplus unit collects a rent on the money that economists call interest in a general sense, although it might be in another legal form, such as dividends. The financial intermediary collects a fee for effecting the transfer.

For example, you might imagine the house purchase discussed previously being intermediated this way. Jim and Tammy buy a house when they are both 25 years old. They advertise in the paper for someone to lend them the 70% of the purchase price. Ruth and Isaac are 50, and their savings are increasing at a good rate as they start planning for retirement. They lend the money to Jim and Tammy. For the next 20 years Jim and Tammy pay interest and repay the loan principal. Ruth and Isaac invest their subsequent savings into mutual funds (described in Chapter 16), retire at age 60, and finance their consumption with the mortgage payments. By the time Ruth and Isaac reach age 75, they need to start selling the mutual funds units. To whom do they sell them? Jim and Tammy, of course. They are now 50 and have savings to invest. Thus, at different stages the same family is borrower and lender.

The financial intermediation system in Canada rarely functions like the example, because we could not maintain our sophisticated economy if it did. Imagine how difficult it would be for the couples to find the right match. They would need to have the same amount in mind, and the same time frame. Ruth and Isaac would have to be able to enforce the collection of the debt if necessary, and would have to know how to write the loan contract so it would be enforceable. People would spend much more of their productive time on financial transactions, and would be able to achieve fewer objectives.

Financial institutions have emerged to act as intermediaries between all the different families and organizations that have money to invest or need money to consume. The financial institutions collect deposits or money for investment, risk pooling or transactions from all the families and organizations, and repackage this money in the amounts and forms that different units need. Deficit units get money in return for paying interest that goes to the surplus units (with a cut for the intermediary). They have specialized employees to handle all the technical details. As to matching terms, a financial institution needs to make sure that the total pot of money it owes is less than the amount it holds or is owed and that the cash flow in and out is reasonably balanced at any point in time.[10]

You can see that the financial institutions play a very valuable role in our society. Without them, our ability to save up for a rainy day would be very constrained. Money wouldn't necessarily move to the most productive uses, and thus we would all suffer from a weaker economy. A lot of the actions in your financial plans will require financial institutions for implementation.

CANADIAN FINANCIAL INSTITUTIONS

As you might imagine, the literature on this subject is enormous. We will content ourselves in this book with brief descriptions of the major kinds of institutions and the personal finance products/services they offer. A recent trend in finance is for institutions to seek the right to provide a wider range of products than previously allowed. The regulatory stance in Canada has been for specific types of products to be reserved for one group of companies, leading to the term "**four pillars**". The four pillars are banks, trust companies, life insurance companies, and investment dealers. Separate statutes and regulatory bodies have developed for each of these groups. The reasoning is that conflict of interest and incompetent advisors are less likely that way. Canada has decided to reduce this separation a great deal, and both the Canadian and the provincial governments have been and are continuing to allow more cross-ownership and the offering of most products in most institutions. The protection for consumers is to be provided by rules governing the products and services, not just the institutions.

During the 1970s and 1980s the different types of institutions had consolidated by buying rival firms in the same segment of the industry. This trend was particularly strong among investment dealers and trust companies, where many of the companies were too small to realize economies of scale. In the 1990s the large banks have responded to the loosening of regulations by purchasing the merged investment dealers and trust companies, to the point where they control almost the whole of those two formerly separate business segments. In some cases they started their own trust companies and investment dealers. In addition, they have launched their own mutual funds and promoted them aggressively, and they have arrangements to sell both life and general insurance, though they are still restricted in these areas.

---

[10] The details of the balancing function are too complicated to discuss in this book, not least because the amounts that will flow in or out at any time cannot be known for sure in advance.

The following description of the different financial institutions that provide intermediation services is coloured by the fact the big six banks now dominate financial services in Canada. Only the life insurance companies are large enough to compete head-on, and the banks have a substantial advantage in size, geographical coverage, and breadth of products and services.

Chartered Banks

The *Tyrannosaurus rex* of financial institutions, everyone recognizes the traditional symbol of Canadian capitalism — the large national bank with branches across the country. Canada has two classes of banks: **Schedule A** and **Schedule B**.

The Schedule A banks are Canadian controlled, and most of them offer a wide range of products and services to the retail customer through an extensive branch network. That range of services includes virtually any transaction service, all investment services, trust management, consumer and residential mortgage loans, and a limited amount of insurance.[11] The Schedule A banks operate the payments clearing system that transfers cheques, deposits, and other transactions among all the banks and other financial institutions. **The Bank of Canada**, which is controlled by the federal government, regulates the money supply and provides temporary liquidity support to the banks.

The Schedule B banks are much smaller, and much more numerous, but most of them have no retail branches at all. Their business is concentrated either in the corporate and commercial sectors, or occasionally in a particular ethnic community. A few of these banks do offer some retail services, but, in general, when we refer to banks in this book, we will mean Schedule A Banks. Banks are regulated federally under *The Bank Act*. They must have a formal federal charter granted by Parliament.

Trust Companies

Trust companies' original business was to manage estate and special trust funds and to act as executors. Over time, they moved into services provided by banks. Now, only a few small trust companies exist independently of the banks.

---

[11] The insurance area is changing too quickly and is too complicated to provide details. Until quite recently, banks could not sell insurance directly, but had found ways to offer it indirectly. For example, they offer life and disability insurance on their customers' loan balances, and life and automobile insurance for rented cars through their credit cards. They are entering the retail insurance markets directly now, but it is too early to predict how complete their coverage will b, and what it will do to competition in the market.

Caisses Populaires and Credit Unions[12]

These are mutual associations owned by their own customers. To belong to one you buy a share or open a special account that is treated as share capital. Some or all of the interest paid on accounts will be legally a dividend. The common factor of the membership in a caisse populaire or credit union may be the community in which it is located, the employer, the ethnic or religious group, or some fraternal order. They are distinguished from other financial institutions by the collective, social nature of their formation and governance. Their early success sprang from the need of people left out of the mainstream of financial power to have financial services responsive to their situation. Thus, even today there is a strong flavour of social responsibility and community ownership that is not present in other institutions.

The caisses populaires and credit unions vary in size but are much smaller than the trust companies and banks and offer a more limited menu of services. The basic transactions services, term deposits, credit cards, RRSPs, and consumer and mortgage loans make up most of their business. They are regulated provincially. All the credit unions in a province also belong to a co-operative "central" that handles cheque clearing with the chartered banks and provides liquidity support in much the same way that the Bank of Canada does for the banks.

Mortgage and Loan Companies

Mortgage and loan companies, including finance companies, provide consumer and residential mortgage loans, and take deposits from the public. They do not provide any other services. Their deposits are not insured by either the Canada Deposit Insurance Corporation (CDIC) or an industry-sponsored co-operative. The retail depositor has to be wary, since they are generally quite risky, but may appear to be the same as trust companies.

Investment Dealers

Investment dealers provide primarily investment services. Their main retail service is acting as an agent to buy and sell securities — shares, bonds, and other more exotic instruments. They also provide access to other institutions' term deposits and offer self-managed RRSPs. They will manage your money and make investments using their own judgment if you wish, usually based on some general instructions you give them.[13] They make margin loans to their customers

---

[12] They offer virtually the same menu of services in French and English regions, respectively, although the origins are different. Alphonse Desjardins founded the first caisse in 1900 in Levis, Québec. The first credit union started in 1932 in Nova Scotia, and the movement has since spread to the rest of English Canada, with its strongest representation in the West.

[13] For example, a customer might specify that he wants the money invested in Canadian common shares of sound industrial companies, with the dealer to decide which shares to buy within that group.

for security purchases. The name of the loan comes from the fact that these loans are limited to a specified percentage or margin of the value of the securities that the dealer is holding in trust for the customer.

The large securities dealers act on both sides of the intermediation, either as agents or holding securities in inventory for resale. They advise companies and governments on when and how to issue securities to raise capital and carry out the decisions. They trade on their own accounts.

When the banks bought up virtually all of the large investment dealers, they changed this sector permanently. From a personal finance point of view, most investors who own securities directly (instead of through a mutual fund) now buy and sell them through a bank or a bank-owned dealer.

"Discount" brokers are capturing a growing share of the market for family direct investments in securities. Discount brokers provide no advice to the client and limited services other than executing transactions, but they also charge lower fees than "full service" brokers who provide advice. Every bank has a discount brokerage operation, and almost all the independent firms have disappeared from this market, too. The discount brokers operate in two mediums: telephone and Internet. A telephone discount broker speaks with the client and takes the order over the phone. The client can make an Internet trade without any personal interaction at all after the initial account opening meeting. Internet trades carry the lowest fees, but both forms of discount fees are far lower than full-service brokerage fees, which average a bit more than 1% of the value of a transaction.

The remaining small investment dealers are specialists, or niche players. Some deal only with institutions. Those who serve retail clients specialize in higher risk areas like junior mining and oil companies or high technology start-up companies.

Life Insurance Companies

The principal business of life insurance companies is offering life, health, and disability insurance for individuals, the subject of Chapter 10. However, the premiums paid up front accumulate very rapidly while the payouts occur later and so life insurers have huge pools of money to invest. They invest most of their money in the corporate-commercial sector, but many companies offer residential mortgages as well. In addition, they offer a variety of RRSPs, Registered Retirement Income Funds (RRIFs), and annuities. These retirement investments are discussed more fully in Chapters 17 and 18. The life companies are competing vigorously with the mutual fund companies and banks for the retirement investment market.

General Insurance Companies

They are also called property, casualty, and liability companies, describing the types of insurance they provide for individuals and companies. General insurance is the subject of Chapter 11. Like life insurers, they have a large pool of investable funds, but until recently have not been able to participate in other areas of financial services. They now have the right to offer residential mortgages but are not yet major participants in this market.

Mutual Fund Companies

The term "mutual fund" applies to both the company that offers it and the product itself. A mutual fund is a pool of securities held by a company. The company sells units or shares in the fund to individuals. Each unit gives the owner a proportionate share of all the securities in the fund, and is thus just another way of investing in securities. A fuller description of mutual funds can be found in Chapter 16. Many independent mutual fund companies exist to offer this service (and no other service). However, all of the previously described institutions, except general insurers, also sell mutual fund units. Some have their own mutual funds, others act as agents to sell mutual fund units of the independent mutual fund companies, and some do both. The mutual fund companies themselves sell their fund units in one of two ways but not both. Either they sell directly to the public, or they sell through agents paid on commission.

SUMMARY

Unlike corporations, people have limited lives, and so their patterns of financial activity follow a reasonably predictable life cycle. Early in life, a person develops earning power, borrows money, and saves little. Later in life, after he or she has purchased the major durable assets and paid off much of the loans, the individual starts to accumulate savings for retirement. Income tends to peak in middle age, usually before retirement. The retiree consumes the savings built up.

We gain further insight into the cycle when we look at family units rather than individuals. The formation of couples and the birth of children affect the amount of saving and the sort of durable purchases. Marketing has developed the family life cycle and has defined categories that are useful to predict consumption behaviour of families. We present our own set of categories, and show in Table 6.2 how personal financial needs are related to the stage of the family life cycle.

The theoretical economic relationship behind the life cycle is the financial intermediation process. Early in the life cycle, families tend to consume more than they earn or can draw from savings, while later in the cycle the relationship is reversed. A complex and varied group of financial institutions exists in Canada to serve these changing intermediation needs. These institutions are specialized to some extent, but most of them are moving into different fields so that the differences between are less clear than they were even a few years ago, and the largest banks are starting to dominate the entire field.

MULTIPLE-CHOICE REVIEW QUESTIONS

1. Which of the following statements concerning mutual funds is true?

   (a) It refers to a pool of securities held by a company that offers it to the public to invest.
   (b) It refers to a pool of securities held by two or more related persons.
   (c) It refers to a portfolio of stocks that a financial institution holds as investments.
   (d) Mutual funds are not sold by insurance companies.
   (e) None of the above.

2. For a retired couple, which of the following elements of personal finance is of high priority?

   (a) Budgeting
   (b) Tax planning
   (c) Debt management
   (d) Retirement planning
   (e) Risk management

3. For a couple with dependent children, which of the following is normally not of high priority?

   (a) Budgeting
   (b) Investment
   (c) Risk management
   (d) Debt management
   (e) All of the above are of high priority.

4. Canadian financial institutions include which of the following?

   (a) Chartered banks
   (b) Trust companies
   (c) Life insurance companies
   (d) Mutual fund companies
   (e) All of the above

5. A typical life insurance company does not offer which of the following products?

   (a) Health insurance
   (b) Disability insurance
   (c) Mortgage financing
   (d) Mutual funds
   (e) Auto insurance

DISCUSSION QUESTIONS

1. Explain the significance of the following entries:

   diagnosing personal finance needs / family life cycle / financial life cycle / financial institutions / financial intermediation / four pillars

2. Which stage in the family life cycle are you in? What general categories of personal financial planning should concern you most now?

3. Discuss the appropriateness of the categorization scheme in Table 6.1. Can you think of any family situations not covered by the categories? What sort of changes would you suggest in these categories?

4. Demography is the study of the vital statistics of a population — births, deaths, age structure, etc. The demographics of a given population affect the economy in critical and long-lasting ways. Once a particular trend is established in the population, it is largely irreversible. For example, the low birth rate of the 1930s and early 1940s plus the huge baby boom that followed that period have created a population in Canada that has a large number of middle-aged people (the baby boomers) who will form a large group of retired people in the next 20–40 years. At the same time, changes in health care and diet have led to much longer life expectancy for all ages. Our total population profile is thus showing rising proportions of older people in the future, with a large bulge of people aged 30–45 right now.

   (a) The above description of the demographic pattern of the Canadian population is very sketchy. Do some library research using Statistics Canada materials and anything else you can find to develop a more complete pattern. Try to include the effect of immigration and the multi-ethnic character of Canada's urban population in your research.
   (b) What effect do you think the demographics of the Canadian population will have on personal financial needs?
   (c) If you were the head of a financial institution, what long-run strategy would you consider to meet the changing demographic patterns?

5. Discuss the following statement in both practical and ethical terms:

   Men make most of the significant financial decisions in Canadian households. A financial institution should develop a personal financial counselling service targeted exclusively at men in order to increase its share of the retail financial services market.

6. List the financial institutions you patronize and the services you get from each one.

7. Following up on Question 6, find a retail branch or agent of each of the following financial institutions: life insurance company, Schedule A bank, credit union or caisse populaire, investment dealer. Obtain information about *all* of the retail services offered by each institution. Organize this information into a chart, with the columns being the four institutions; and the rows, the different services. This chart will show both the extent of the overlap and the extent of the unique services offered by different institutions. In the information you collect, try to include the fees for each service.

8. Financial supermarkets, which are more or less closely linked groups of different financial services and/or institutions in one location to serve consumers with "one-step financial shopping", have developed to some extent in the United States though they have not been as successful as expected. The idea is well-known in Canada, but few institutions have tried it. Considering both the personal finance aspects and the broader issues of how organizations compete:

   (a) What are the strengths and weaknesses of organizing financial services into a financial supermarket instead of independent companies and professional advisors?

   (b) Why has the model for financial services become one of bank takeovers and consolidation in Canada?

   (c) You can organize a financial supermarket in more than one way. Suggest two different organizational structures for a financial supermarket and what advantages or disadvantages the different structures would have in competing in the retail financial services market.

CHAPTER 7

Personal Income Tax

Mr. Jay owns shares that pay him a dividend of $100 during the year. Does it matter which company paid the dividend? Ms. Kay receives no dividends on her shares but sells them for a gain of $100 during the year. Do they have the same amounts left after tax? Learn about the taxation of investment income in this chapter.

The authors thank Joanne Magee for her exhaustive review of this chapter.

LEARNING OBJECTIVES

> ➢ *To provide you with a basic understanding of the structure of personal income taxation in Canada.*
>
> ➢ *To explain and illustrate the differences in taxation of different forms of investment income.*
>
> ➢ *To understand and calculate marginal tax rates and after-tax discount rates.*

In this chapter we describe the general structure of income taxation in Canada, with some particularly important specific provisions spelled out in detail. We show you how to calculate marginal tax rates and after-tax discount rates, the essential tools for financial planning.

We caution you that your understanding of income taxation will be very general indeed after you master Chapters 7 and 8. The *Income Tax Act* is a statute of Parliament, and as such you must apply it literally — by the letter of the law — including the various Regulations attached to it. Since it is a very long and complicated Act, complete mastery of it requires years of study and practice. Each province also has an income taxation statute. Except for Québec, the provinces base their taxation on the federal rules and forms, but there are differences, which are inconsistent between provinces. Most of the topics in this book are governed by fairly basic principles of finance, so you can understand and implement practically anything you will require after this course from a finance point of view. The specific application of the law to any given situation depends on the facts, and you may require expert advice for any tax planning you undertake.

Furthermore, the *Income Tax Act* and Regulations change frequently since different parts of them are affected by every federal government budget, as well as many other pieces of legislation. The Act itself is administered by the Canada Revenue Agency (CRA),[1] which has built up a large number of procedures that are not recorded in the Act to carry out the law. Many of these procedures are documented in Interpretation Bulletins, Information Circulars, and rulings on specific cases. Many years of court decisions on assessments made by the CRA and disputed by companies and individual taxpayers add to the complexity since these decisions are used as precedents in deciding future disputes. The same comments apply to the provincial statutes, although the complications are fewer.

We can deal with the most important considerations that will affect the majority of people in their income tax planning. We discuss the strategic aspects of planning in Chapter 8. You should view Chapter 7 as a necessary evil. It is quite

---

[1] The CRA's website is <www.cra-arc.gc.ca>.

TABLE 7.1
Basic Format of Personal Income Taxation in
Canada and Most Other Coutnries

	Income
–	Allowable Deductions
=	Taxable Income
×	Income Tax Rate
=	Income Tax Payable before Credits
–	Tax Credits
=	Send cheque to government

technical and picky, but without it you can't understand Chapter 8, nor can you implement tax strategies. The concepts of a marginal tax rate and an after-tax discount rate are very important in later chapters as well.

GENERAL CONCEPTS OF INCOME TAXATION

Canadian income taxation is based on **self-assessment**. Table 7.1 shows the basic format of personal income taxation in Canada and most other countries. With a few exceptions, every resident — limited corporations, trusts, or individuals — is required to complete an income tax return on **prescribed forms**. Someone else may prepare the return, but the resident is legally responsible for it. The final entry on the form shows whether the taxpayer owes money to the government or is owed money, and how much.

The fundamental rules are the same for companies and individuals, although in practice they may seem rather different and the forms are quite different. The tax scheme for individuals in Canada is outlined in Table 7.2.

The Canadian system for individuals is **progressive**. This means that higher levels of taxable income are taxed at higher rates. The lower rate applies to all income up to a specified level, then all income above that level is taxed at the higher level. We can calculate both **marginal** and **average tax rates**. The average tax rate is simply the total tax payable divided by total income. The marginal federal rates are shown later in Table 7.3.

The marginal tax rate is the rate that applies to one more dollar of income. If you are currently in the highest category or **tax bracket** and you are deciding whether to invest your money in a term deposit, the marginal after-tax rate of return you receive will be (1 – marginal tax rate) × (interest rate). Under a

---

TABLE 7.2
Basic Outline of Personal Income Taxation Keyed to T1 Form

Page 1 of the T1 is identifying information.

1. Add all sources of income (pg. 2 of T1)
   -   Deductions (pg. 3 of T1)
   =   Taxable Income (carried forward to Schedule 1 and Form 428)

2. Add all personal tax credits (pg. 1 of Schedule 1) = P
   Tax credit is 15%, or .15P

   Add all charitable donations = D
   Tax credit for D is 15% on first $200, 29% on the rest
   =   .15 × MINIMUM (D, 200) + MAXIMUM [0, (.29 × (D − 200))]

   Total non-refundable tax credits (Schedule 1, pg. 1)
   =   .15P + .15 × MINIMUM (D, 200) + MAXIMUM [0, (.29 × (D − 200))]

3. Federal Tax (Schedule 1, pg. 2)
   [Calculation: Tax the first x dollars of Taxable Income (T1, pg. 3, carried forward to Schedule 1, pg. 2) at the lowest rate, then the next x dollars at the next higher rate, and so on.]
   +   Split income; minimum tax carried forward
   −   Non-refundable tax credits (Schedule 1, pg. 1, carried forward to pg. 2)
   −   Dividend tax credit
   =   Basic Federal Tax

   +/− Other charges/credits
   =   Net Federal Tax, carried forward to T1, pg. 4, line 420

4. Provincial Tax (Form 428, pg. 2)
   [Calculation is similiar to Federal Tax.]
   −   Provincial tax credits (including dividend tax credit)
   +   Provincial surtax (rate and method differ by province)
   +/− Other charges/credits
   =   Provincial Tax, carried forward to T1, pg. 4, line 428

5. Federal Tax + Provincial Tax (= line 435)
   −   Tax withheld at source
   −   Tax paid by instalments
   −/+ Various other credits/charges
   =   Tax owing/Tax refundable (if negative) (pg. 4 of T1)

progressive system, the average rate will be equal to or less than the marginal rate. If addition or subtraction of an amount of income would put you into a different tax bracket, then you have to use the two different rates pro rata on the amount of income to which each one applies. We discuss the issue of after-tax discount rates in detail in a later section.

The tax payable on taxable income in the different tax brackets is added up, and then **tax credits** are deducted to arrive at Basic Federal Tax. You calculate provincial taxable income and tax by bracket in the same way, and you then deduct provincial tax credits to arrive at provincial tax. In most situations, federal and provincial taxable income are identical. There may also be **surtaxes** payable. Surtaxes are taxes based on the tax; they are temporary (or so governments claim) and usually apply most heavily on upper tax brackets. Although they have a somewhat different legal form, their financial effect is identical to an increase in the basic tax rate, as far as financial decisions are concerned.

Finally, the taxpayer may have paid instalments or had tax withheld at source. Employers and certain institutions dealing in investments are required to withhold part of the amounts they pay out and remit them to the government on account of the taxpayer's ultimate income tax liability. These amounts are deducted from the tax payable for the year to arrive at a final balance.

Let us turn to the details of completing an income tax return to make your understanding more concrete. If you have completed your own income tax return for several years already, you will find that the next section of the chapter requires only a quick skim.

COMPLETING AN INCOME TAX RETURN

The personal Income Tax Return is the T1 GENERAL. The T1 return is slightly different for each province,[2] and it changes somewhat every year. We recommend that you have on hand a copy of the most recent T1 package in paper or in electronic format and read this section while following along on it. Otherwise, you are unlikely to understand much of the discussion. If you filed a T1 last year, that would be suitable. The T1 package, which includes two copies of the return and schedules and a detailed line-by-line guide to completing it, is available in post offices from about February to early May every year. During the rest of the year, you will have to obtain one from the nearest CRA office (check your phone directory), or download it from the CRA's website (see footnote 1), or use a software package.

First, some basic detail. The T1 General is four pages long and all the lines that have numbers entering into the calculations are numbered. The CRA employees enter each form into a computer format using these numbered lines, and

---

[2] Québec uses its own forms for provincial tax and we do not discuss it further in this book as the differences are beyond our scope. For the most part, the principles are the same as for other provinces, and the effects on financial decisions are the same. The Québec tax rates are also progressive, and you use the marginal tax rate for incremental decisions, just as in every other province.

the program then verifies all calculations. The line numbers are the link to the extensive Guide that accompanies the Return. For most people, all the knowledge they require to complete their returns is in the Guide.

On the front page the taxpayer enters some basic personal information. A taxpayer who filed the previous year will receive a T1 package in the mail in January, with two personalized labels to attach to the Return. Individuals must file their personal returns based on calendar years. For most individuals, the deadline to file the return (postmark date) is April 30 of the year following the calendar year. Taxpayers who have business income (and their spouses) get an extended deadline: Their returns are due June 15, although they must still pay any balance owing by April 30. An increasingly popular option is to file electronically on Netfile. The CRA can then capture the numbers without retyping them, process the return faster, and send refunds sooner.

Total Income

The first section of entries accumulates all forms of income: employment, investment, business, etc. All of page 2 is devoted to it. Note that several lines have both a gross and a net amount. The self-employment sources of income allow the taxpayer to deduct expenses from the gross revenue to the extent that the expenses were incurred to earn it. The unincorporated taxpayer will file an income statement and balance sheet to document this part of the return. If the taxpayer incorporated the business, then the business will have to file its own corporate income tax returns. The taxpayer-owner's income on the personal return will be salary, dividends, interest, and/or commissions paid to him/her by the corporation.

We will discuss the taxation of investment income: dividends (line 120), interest (line 121), and taxable capital gains (line 127) in separate sections later in this chapter.

Taxable Income

The sum of the incomes is totalled on line 150 and transferred to page 3. The next two blocks of entries are various deductions from total income to arrive at net income and then taxable income. The *Income Tax Act* specifies specific items that are deductible and the limits on deductibility. For example, contributions to Registered Pension Plans (employer–sponsored plans) and Registered Retirement Savings Plans are deducted from total income within specified limits. The contributions will be taxed later, along with accrued income, as the taxpayer receives them as part of a pension or lump-sum withdrawal. The taxable income remaining after all the deductions is on line 260 and is transferred to Schedule 1.

Tax Credits

Page 1 of Schedule 1 contains the calculation of federal **non-refundable tax credits**. These tax credits are deductions from taxes otherwise payable, with a limit that tax payable cannot be reduced below zero. The items listed on page 1 include some basic allowances for the taxpayer and dependants (these credits in effect ensure that low-income taxpayers pay no tax), employment insurance and Canada Pension Plan or Québec Pension Plan premiums, educational expenses, medical expenses, and charitable donations. The total is multiplied by 15% (29% for charitable donations totalling in excess of $200) to get the total non-refundable tax credit and carried forward to page 2 of Schedule 1. The non-refundable provincial tax credits are calculated in the same manner on Form 428. In addition, some provinces use the tax return to deliver other rebate/refund/tax credit programs. We do not discuss them in this book.

Federal Tax

Page 1 of Schedule 1 contains the calculation of federal tax before deduction of tax credits at progressive rates. At one time there were 10 federal tax brackets, which led to some messy calculations and numerous tax planning opportunities. Now there are only four brackets, but the government has suggested that it may reduce the number of brackets even more. You may wonder why everyone is complaining about high taxes, given these seemingly low rates in Table 7.3. The answer is that we haven't dealt with surtaxes and provincial taxes. Hold on......

Continuing with the mechanics of the return, we see that on Part 2 of Schedule 1 we deduct a variety of items from the federal income tax calculated on page 1. The commonly encountered ones are the non-refundable tax credits that we have already mentioned, political donation tax credits, and the dividend tax credit, whose intricacies we will discuss later in the chapter. The net of the tax payable and the tax credits is transferred back to page 4 of the T1 Return (line 420).

The next two lines are important, but they have nothing to do with the *Income Tax Act*. The Income Tax Return is used as a mechanism for making end of year

TABLE 7.3				
2011 and 2012 Rates of Federal Income Tax				
		Tax Brackets		
Tax Rates			**2011**	**2012**
15%	on the first		$41,544	$42,707
22%	on the next		$41,544	$42,707
26%	on the next		$45,712	$46,992
29%	on the amount over		$128,800	$132,406

corrections to social service collections like CPP, EI, and OAS. The next line is the provincial tax, and now we have to make another detour. Turn to the provincial return, Form 428. The province or territory appears at the top of the page. Line 421 charges the taxpayer for CPP contributions on self-employed income, and line 422 is the repayment of social benefits. Chapter 17 gives more information on these items.

Provincial Tax

This return will differ from province to province and we will not discuss all the differences in this book. The most important factor is the *effective* provincial rate. The provinces also use a "tax-on-income" system under which they base their taxes on provincial taxable income and have their own provincial tax credits. The rules for calculating income and tax credits are similar and sometimes identical to the federal method, but each province has its own rates and brackets. The provincial taxes, when calculated, are transferred to line 428 on the Return. Table 7.4 displays the effective 2011 and 2012 rates and surtaxes for the provinces and territories.

Balance Owing or Refund

In line 435 you total the federal and provincial taxes plus the other social service collections to arrive at the total payable for the year. The last block of numbers adds up the credits. The largest one for most people is the income tax already deducted at source and paid in instalments, but there are other credits. Deduct the credits from the total payable for the year. If the number is positive, you owe money and must pay by April 30; if the number is negative, you will receive a refund.

Everything Else

If you have been following along in your T1 General Return, you will have realized by now that we have only sketched in the outline. There are a host of subsidiary schedules and forms, only some of which are included with your return. For example, if you want to claim daycare expenses, you will have to get Form T778 plus instructions from your district office of the CRA. If you want to claim moving expenses (allowable, within certain limits, if you move in order to start a new job), you need a pamphlet called *Are You Moving?* and you must complete Form T1-M included in it, and so on. There can be a lot of "and so ons" in some returns, but it is beyond the scope of this book to cover them all.

What we have done is lay out the basic structure. You gain more familiarity with the details through practice — doing your own return or the problems in this chapter. For most of the important personal financial planning work, this basic structure covers the material things that will affect your decisions.

PlanPlus will calculate personal income tax, though it does not print a tax return. There are many personal tax software packages that will calculate the taxes

TABLE 7.4
2011 and 2012 Provincial Tax Rates

	%	Tax Rates and Brackets	2011	2012	%	Surtax Rates and Thresholds 2011	2012
Alberta	10.00	All income (flat tax)					
British Columbia	5.06	on the first	$36,146	$37,013			
	7.70	+ on the next	$36,147	$37,015			
	10.50	+ on the next	$10,708	$10,965			
	12.29	+ on the next	$17,786	$18,212			
	14.70	+ on the amount over	$100,787	$103,205			
Manitoba	10.80	on the first	$31,000	$31,000			
	12.75	+ on the next	$36,000	$36,000			
	17.40	+ on the amount over	$67,000	$67,000			
New Brunswick	9.10	on the first	$37,150	$38,190			
	12.10	+ on the next	$37,150	$38,190			
	12.40	+ on the next	$46,496	$47,798			
	14.30	+ on the amount over	$120,796	$124,178			
Newfoundland & Labrador	7.70	on the first	$31,904	$32,983			
	12.50	+ on the next	$31,903	$32,982			
	13.30	+ on the amount over	$63,807	$65,785			
Northwest Territories	5.90	on the first	$37,626	$38,679			
	8.60	+ on the next	$37,627	$38,681			
	12.20	+ on the next	$47,092	$48,411			
	14.05	+ on the amount over	$122,345	$125,771			
Nova Scotia	8.79	on the first	$29,590	$29,590			
	14.95	+ on the next	$29,590	$29,590			
	16.67	+ on the next	$33,820	$33,820			
	17.50	+ on the next	$57,000	$57,000			
	21.00	+ on the amount over	$150,000	$150,000			
Nunavut	4.00	on the first	$39,612	$40,721			
	7.00	+ on the next	$39,612	$40,721			
	9.00	+ on the next	$49,576	$50,964			
	11.50	+ on the amount over	$128,800	$132,406			
Ontario*	5.05	on the first	$37,774	$39,020	20.0	$4,078	$4,213
	9.15	+ on the next	$37,776	$39,023	56.0	$5,219	$5,392
	11.16	+ on the amount over	$75,550	$78,043			
	12.16	+ on the amount over		$500,000			
P.E.I.	9.80	on the first	$31,984	$31,984	10.0	$12,500	$12,500
	13.80	+ on the next	$31,985	$31,985			
	16.70	+ on the amount over	$63,969	$63,969			
Saskatchewan	11.00	on the first	$40,919	$42,065			
	13.00	+ on the next	$75,992	$78,120			
	15.00	+ on the amount over	$116,911	$120,185			
Yukon	7.04	on the first	$41,544	$42,707	5.0	$6,000	$6,000
	9.68	+ on the next	$41,544	$42,707			
	11.44	+ on the next	$45,712	$46,992			
	12.76	+ on the amount over	$128,800	$132,406			

* The Ontario surtax is 20% on Ontario tax that falls between the two tax amounts, plus 56% on Ontario tax that is in excess of the higher tax amount. Tax rate on taxable income over $500,000 will increase to 13.16% in 2013.

and print both the return and the schedules. We caution you that their main benefit is to avoid mistakes in the routine calculations and do them faster. If you provide the wrong data or fail to recognize specific tax-planning opportunities, the software will rarely be able to do it for you.

Who Is a Spouse?

While this might seem to be a silly question, the answer has changed over the years, as far as the *Income Tax Act* is concerned. Traditionally, persons who are legally married are spouses under the *Income Tax Act*. A couple who have separated, but not divorced, may elect not to be treated as spouses but may also be treated as such. Having a spouse brings up a host of issues both in the mundane business of completing a tax return and in tax planning, as you will see in Chapter 8. A spousal couple may claim only one personal residence between them for exemption from capital gains tax, for example. Certain tax credits and deductions apply only to a spouse, and some of them are optional, others mandatory. Transfers of assets between spouses are deemed not to occur at arm's length and hence have different rules for tax purposes, including rules attributing income to a spouse who provided an income-earning asset, regardless of who owns it legally. A spouse may contribute to a spousal RRSP. And so on.

A spouse includes any spousal couple, same sex or opposite sex, who have cohabited for one year, or who are married, or who have cohabited less than one year but have a child from the union, including one adopted child. See Chapter 5.

INVESTMENT INCOME

Not all investment income is created equal in the eyes of the *Income Tax Act*. The treatment of different forms of investment income affects planning materially for most people since you must invest your savings if you are to have enough money to retire.

Expenses incurred to earn investment income are deductible from income generally, though there are some restrictions. The most significant of these expenses are interest on investment loans and fees paid for money management by third parties.

Dividends

A limited company must pay income tax on its earnings. A dividend is a distribution to shareholders of some portion of the corporation's earnings after the corporation has paid tax on them.[3] The dividend on preferred shares is specified by

---

[3] Dividends may also include a repayment of capital, but that portion is not a dividend for income tax rules and is not included in taxable income.

the terms of the issue, while the dividend on common shares is at the discretion of the board of directors. The personal taxation situation is the same in most circumstances. When shareholders receive dividends from the company, they must pay income tax on the dividends. This is double taxation, and in order to neutralize its effect, approximately, the *Income Tax Act* includes the **dividend tax credit**. The mechanics sound deceptively simple: For example, in 2011, any dividend received from a Canadian company[4] is **grossed up** by 41% (that is, multiplied by 1.41) and the grossed-up amount, called the **taxable amount**, is included in income. The recipient deducts from federal tax payable a dividend tax credit equal to 23.17% of the actual dividend paid or 16.44% of the grossed-up amount. If you receive a dividend of $100, the gross-up is $41, and the grossed-up amount that is reported on the tax return is $141. The dividend tax credit can be calculated in two identical ways:

$$\$100 \times .2317 = \$141 \times .1644 = \$23.17$$

Each province has a dividend tax credit as well, but the rates vary. The total effect is to tax dividends paid by Canadian corporations less than an equivalent amount of interest. Table 7.6 includes the gross-up, the federal dividend tax credit, and the provincial dividend tax credit rates as a per cent of the dividend paid for 2009–2012.

The marginal tax rate is the total tax payable divided by the original cash amount of the dividend. Be careful to deduct taxes from the cash amount and not the taxable amount. The taxable amount is just a fiction used in the tax rules. See Table 7.5 for an example, using 2011 rates.

This seemingly simple calculation leads to a great number of financial issues because lower tax bracket investors benefit more from the dividend tax credit than do the top bracket investors. We will see more of this issue in later sections and in Chapter 8.

Capital Gains and Losses

If you buy an asset either for the income it generates or for personal use and subsequently sell it for more or less than you paid for it, the difference may be a **capital gain** or **capital loss**. A capital gain occurs when you sell a capital item for more than the sum of its original price and all the transaction costs of buying and selling it. A capital loss occurs when the selling price is less than the purchase and transaction costs. Capital transactions are taxed differently than income items, and so the first step is to distinguish between the two. It might sound trivial, but in fact defining what is a capital item and what is an income item raises difficult issues that lead to many disputes between the CRA and taxpayers.

---

[4] The dividend tax credit does not apply to dividends paid by foreign corporations to Canadian investors. These dividends are taxed at the same rate as ordinary income.

TABLE 7.5
Dividend Tax Credit Example

Problem: Seamus O'Flaherty lives in Newfoundland and earns taxable income of $55,000 p.a. in 2011. He receives a dividend of $100 from a Canadian company and interest income of $100 from a bond. How much income tax does he pay on each amount and what is the marginal tax rate?

Answer:

	Dividend	Interest
Cash received	$100.00	$100.00
Taxable amount	$141.00	$100.00
Federal tax @ 22%	$ 31.02	$ 22.00
– Federal dividend tax credit @ 23.17%	(23.17)	
Basic federal tax	$ 7.85	$ 22.00
Provincial tax @ 12.50%	$ 17.63	$ 12.50
– Provincial dividend tax credit @ 15.51%	(15.51)	
Provincial tax	$ 2.12	$ 12.50
Total tax payable	$ 9.97	$ 34.50
Marginal tax rate	9.97%	34.5%

What Is a Capital Item?

Imagine you own a peach orchard. You sell the peaches from it every year. Your annual income from this business is the revenue minus the expenses incurred to earn it, including an allowance for depreciation. This income enters into your taxable income and is taxed in the same way as employment income.

Now you sell the peach orchard to another farmer for a price that is equal to the present value of the future net cash flows it will generate. The capital gain on the sale of the orchard is taxed differently because the orchard is a capital item — one that involves earning capacity in its own right. The general principle that used to be invoked was that income tax applied only to periodic earnings from labour and/or capital, not to the sale of the source of the income. Therefore, capital gains used to be untaxed (at least, until 1972).

Today, most capital gains are taxed but at a lower rate than ordinary income. Some capital gains are still tax-free. As a result, taxpayers have a strong incentive to declare any profits on investment as capital gains rather than as interest or ordinary income, and sometimes prefer to declare them as capital gains instead of dividends also.

TABLE 7.6
Dividend Gross-up, Federal Dividend Tax Credit (DTC$_f$),
and Provincial Dividend Tax Credit (DTC$_p$)
as a % of Actual Dividends Paid for Eligible Dividends

	2009	2010	2011	2012+
Gross-up (G)	45.00	44.00	41.00	38.00
Federal (DTC$_f$)	27.50	25.88	23.17	20.73
Alberta	14.50	14.40	14.10	13.80
British Columbia	15.95	15.60	14.53	13.80
Manitoba	15.95	15.84	15.51	11.04
New Brunswick	17.40	17.28	16.92	16.56
Newfoundland & Labrador	14.14	15.84	15.51	15.18
Northwest Territories	16.68	16.30	16.22	15.87
Nova Scotia	12.83	12.74	12.48	12.21
Nunavut	9.00	8.80	8.20	7.60
Ontario	10.73	9.22	9.02	8.83
Prince Edward Island	15.23	15.12	14.81	14.49
Saskatchewan	15.95	15.84	15.51	15.18
Yukon	15.95	15.60	21.26	20.81

Capital Gains

Capital gains, except of those that are tax-free, are multiplied by one-half, and this amount is called a **taxable capital gain**. Taxable capital gains are added to income on line 127 of the T1 Return.

Tax-free Gains

The gain on the sale of a family's principal residence, including one-half hectare of land, is not taxable. If part of the residence was used to earn business or rental income, the gain may be partly taxable.

If a capital gain comes from disposition of "qualified farm property" or qualified shares of a small business corporation, a lifetime **capital gains deduction** of $500,000 is available for individuals. Once again, the details are quite complicated.

Capital Gains Reserves

If the proceeds from the sale of an asset are not all received within the year, the taxpayer may claim a reserve on a reasonable portion of the gain, but it must all be included in income in equal annual amounts over the next five years or when the rest of the proceeds are received, whichever comes first.

Capital Losses

If the sale creates a capital loss, one-half of it is an **allowable capital loss**. An allowable capital loss is first used to reduce taxable capital gains in the year it occurs. If there is any unused loss remaining, it may be carried back three years and carried forward forever for use in reducing taxable capital gains in other years. The effect of an amount carried back is that the taxable income and tax owing for that year would be recalculated and a refund sent to the taxpayer in respect of the earlier year. Available allowable capital losses realized prior to 1985 may be deducted from other income to a maximum of $2,000 p.a.

Interest Income

Interest income is taxable at the same rate as all other income, and interest income accrued but not yet received must be included in income.

Return of Capital

If a company or an income trust pays an amount that is deemed a return of capital, it is not taxable. The payment will be clearly identified, and so the recipient doesn't need to know the legal details of how return of capital is distinguished from a taxable dividend in practice. A return of capital is simply repaying to the owner of a share or trust unit part of the money invested rather than a return on it. The tax consequence is that the capital repayment is deducted from the adjusted cost base of the original investment. When the owner sells the investment at some later date, this reduction in the ACB will increase the capital gain or reduce the capital loss.

CALCULATING COMBINED MARGINAL TAX RATES

The concept of "marginal" is very important in economic theory and personal and corporate finance. Marginal revenue, or income, or expense is the amount that is added to or subtracted from the existing cash flow because of a particular decision or event. For example, if you move $10,000 from a bank account paying 2% p.a. to a guaranteed investment certificate (GIC) paying 5% p.a., the marginal income is 3% of $10,000, or $300. The total income for one year from the GIC is $500, but only $300 of that is marginal, or *incremental*, because of this decision.

The marginal tax rate is the rate that applies to the next dollar of income. It is very useful to know when you want to compare two investment opportunities that are taxed differently. The after-tax cash flow is what you receive, and so it is what you must base your decision on. The relevant marginal tax rate is the one that combines provincial and federal taxation, and allows for whatever differences apply to the particular type of income.

The marginal rate is essential for long-term financial planning where we are trying to estimate how much a particular savings plan will accumulate, say for retirement. The savings will compound at the after-tax discount rate if they are not invested in a tax shelter. We need to know the marginal tax rate to calculate the after-tax discount rate.

The way to calculate the marginal tax rate is to model the application of the income tax rules using simple algebra. These models change as tax rules change, so you must modify the models often. If the rates change while the rules applying them are the same, then the models still work but with different values for the variables.

First, we set up some notation:

t_c combined marginal tax rate
t_f marginal federal rate
t_p marginal provincial rate
t_{sp} provincial surtax rate on the marginal provincial tax
DTC_p provincial dividend tax credit as a % of the dividend paid (see Table 7.6)
DTC_f federal dividend tax credit as a % of the dividend paid (see Table 7.6)
G dividend gross-up as a % of the dividend paid (see Table 7.6)

These notation are then used to form the combined marginal tax equations for different types of income.

Interest or Ordinary Income with Surtaxes

$$t_c = t_f + t_p (1 + t_{sp})$$

To calculate t_{sp}, we determine which provincial surtax brackets the taxpayer is in.[5] In Table 7.7, Mr. Dutta is an Ontario taxpayer. As an illustration of how to calculate income tax payable from taxable income using 2011 rates, we will also

---

[5] In the earlier editions, we included a federal surtax rate, t_{sf}. Then the equation was $t_c = t_f (1 + t_{sf}) + t_p (1 + t_{sf})$. We have left t_{sf} out of this edition because the federal government has not used a surtax for many years.

TABLE 7.7
Average and Marginal Tax Rates Example

Problem: What is Mr. Dutta's total tax bill and his average and marginal tax rates for 2011 if he has $80,000 in taxable income, $2,000 in non-refundable federal tax credits, and $770 in non-refundable Ontario tax credits?

Answer:

	Calculations			Tax Payable
Taxable income	$80,000			
Federal tax on first	41,544	(15%, from Table 7.3) is		$ 6,232.00
on next (80,000 – 41,544)	38,456	@ 22% is		8,460.32
				$14,692.32
– Federal non-refundable tax credits				(2,000.00)
Federal tax payable				$12,692.32
Ontario Tax:				
Taxable income	$80,000			
Tax on first	37,774	@ 5.05% is		$ 1,907.59
on next	37,776	@ 9.15% is		3,456.50
on next (80,000 – 75,550)	4,450	@11.16% is		496.62
				$ 5,860.71
– Ontario non-refundable tax credits				(770.00)
				$ 5,090.71
Ontario surtax	.2 × (5,090.71 – 4,078) =			202.54
Ontario tax payable				$ 5,293.25
Total tax payable				$17,985.57
Average tax rate		17,985.57 ÷ 80,000 =		22.48%
Marginal tax rate on ordinary income	22% + (11.16% × 1.20) =			35.39%

calculate the total tax bill for Mr. Dutta. You should follow along using Schedule 1 of the T1 General Return and the Ontario Schedule 428.

Dividends and Capital Gains with Surtaxes

The equations for the dividends and capital gains are changed from the equations without surtaxes in the same way. For a Canadian dividend, the combined marginal rate with surtaxes is as follows:

$$t_c(\text{dividend}) = [(1 + G)t_f - DTC_f] + [(1 + G)t_p - DTC_p](1 + t_{sp})$$

TABLE 7.8
Example of Marginal Tax Rates

Problem: What is Mr. Dutta's 2011 marginal tax rate for interest or ordinary income, dividends, and capital gains in Ontario, using the formulas?

Answer:

Income Type	Taxable Income		
	$55,000	**$80,000**	**$130,000**
Ordinary	31.15%	35.39%	46.41%
Dividends	11.73	18.33	28.20
Capital gains	15.58	19.70	23.20

For a capital gain, the combined marginal rate with surtaxes is as follows:

$$t_c(\text{gain}) = (.5t_f) + .5t_p(1 + t_{sp})$$

Table 7.8 gives the results of using these equations to calculate Mr. Dutta's marginal rate.

AFTER-TAX DISCOUNT RATES

Remember that we defined the discount rate for a decision as the best alternative rate available, all else being equal, including the effect of income taxes. Therefore, we need to use **after-tax discount rates**, since the rates of return we receive are after-tax. To calculate the after-tax discount rate, we call k_b the before-tax rate, k_t the after-tax discount rate, and t_c the combined marginal tax rate. Then, for ordinary or interest income:

$$k_t = k_b (1 - t_c)$$

We can demonstrate that this formula is precisely correct with a simple example. There can be only one price for a security on the market. Suppose the competitive rate for one-year treasury bills is 6%. Recall that a treasury bill is a pure discount instrument. It sells at issue at a discount priced to yield 6%, and by convention it matures at an even value. Suppose we have a $10,000 T-bill, and our marginal tax rate is 49.78%.

We know that the market is competitive, so the 6% rate is exactly the rate that makes the future payment equal to the price we pay today. What must that price be? Today's price is the $10,000 future value discounted one year at 6%, or $9,433.98.

After income tax, we won't get $10,000 because we have to pay income tax on the interest earned. The tax paid is:

$$.4978 \ (10,000 - 9,433.98) \ = \ \$281.76$$

This makes the after-tax receipt $(10,000 - 281.76) = \$9,718.24$. The present value of this amount today is still $9,433.98, because that is the price on the market. If we discount $9,718.24 at 6%, we will get a much lower value. Now discount it at the after-tax marginal rate, $(1 - .4978) \times 6\% = 3.0132\%$. The answer is $9,433.98. Conclusion: You must use after-tax discount rates to discount after-tax cash flows.

Note that if you are discounting cash flows from a bond that is partly taxed as a capital gain or loss at maturity and partly as interest or a share with capital gains/losses and dividends, the discount rate is different for the different types of cash flow.

INDEXATION

Inflation can increase the real dollar value of income taxes through a subtle mechanism called "bracket creep". Over time, as your income increases with inflation, you move into a higher tax bracket. You aren't earning any more in real dollars, but your average tax rate increases. Two different numbers in the system can cause this hidden increase in taxes. If the brackets themselves are fixed, then the cut-off points are declining in real terms. Therefore, your real dollar income may stay fixed, but in nominal dollars it increases until it moves you into the next income bracket at a higher marginal tax rate. In addition, if tax credits like the personal amount for each taxpayer do not increase at the inflation rate, their value also declines in real terms even if you don't move into a higher tax bracket.

Indexation — adjusting the credits, deductions, and brackets for inflation each year — is the correct method to neutralize the effect, assuming the government doesn't use bracket creep as an easy way to collect more tax. Canada started indexing the brackets and some deductions in the 1970s, but stopped doing so in the early 1990s. Most of the personal deductions became tax credits at the same time.

The federal budget of February 28, 2000, restored indexation to the tax brackets and to most of the credits. Credits based on actual expenditures do not require indexation, e.g., Canada Pension Plan premiums and charitable donations. Since the federal surtax was removed for 2001, the effective tax rate has dropped at the federal level for all taxpayers.

The provinces may also index their brackets and tax credits, and most of them are doing so, as you can see in Table 7.4. Nova Scotia is not indexing, which means its effective rates continue to rise slightly with inflation. Alberta has a flat tax. The other provinces have chosen to implement their own indexation based on provincial inflation rates, and so their brackets are now drifting slightly away from the federal brackets. Newfoundland and Labrador did not start indexing until after the other provinces did.

The restoration of indexation makes the use of real dollars and real discount rates more accurate in after-tax terms than it has been. Without indexation, the tax amounts rise more rapidly than a real dollar calculation shows.

KEEPING UP-TO-DATE

How do you know what is happening in tax if the field changes so quickly? If your needs are very complex, or you aren't sure how complex they are, then you will have to hire professional help if you can afford it. If you can't afford it, the odds are very high that the amount at stake in your tax problems is modest.

You should be able to complete your return yourself and do most of the tax planning. The Guide accompanying the T1 General Return is quite helpful and clearly written. There are also guides for many of the special forms required in the various circumstances. The CRA also publishes pamphlets on some areas of income tax that many people have questions about. You can call your district office or visit it in person to get free assistance with your tax affairs. You should use this source for basic information, not for rulings on complicated situations. Most of the CRA's material is available online at <www.cra-arc.gc.ca>.

If you want to learn a lot about taxation, the universities and community colleges have a variety of courses. You can get current textbooks and updates from legal publishers like Carswell and CCH. The largest public accounting firms and the provincial associations of CGAs and CAs publish fairly detailed booklets on tax planning every year. You can get these booklets free with a phone call in most cases. The largest public accounting firms also have detailed tax information on their websites. One way to find these websites is to go to the Canadian Tax Foundation website at <www.ctf.ca> and click on "Links".

SUMMARY

Rather than summarize, we repeat three important lessons:

1. Income taxes affect personal financial decisions. We give you the basic outline of the effects in the chapter, and we cover most issues you will encounter.

2. Income taxation is very complicated, and we have left out a huge number of rules that will trip you up if you try to do sophisticated tax planning using only this book as a guide.

3. You must use marginal tax rates and after-tax discount rates in financial planning whenever the cash flows are affected by income taxes.

MULTIPLE-CHOICE REVIEW QUESTIONS

1. Which of the following statements is false?

   (a) The average tax rate is total taxes payable divided by total income.
   (b) The marginal tax rate is the tax rate on the next dollar of income.
   (c) The average tax rate is lower than or equal to the marginal tax rate.
   (d) Both the average tax rate and the marginal tax rate depend on the individual's taxable income.
   (e) All of the above are true.

2. David, a resident of Manitoba in 2011, has taxable income of $50,000. His average tax rate is _____.

   (a) 27.72%
   (b) 31.80%
   (c) 36.00%
   (d) 34.75%
   (e) none of the above

3. Jane, a resident of British Columbia, has taxable income of $60,000. Her marginal tax rate on dividend income in 2011 is _____.

   (a) 31.15%
   (b) 15.89%
   (c) 14.07%
   (d) 31.17%
   (e) none of the above

4. Frances, a resident of Ontario, has taxable income of $120,000. Her marginal tax rate on realized capital gain income in 2011 is _____.

   (a) 32.27%
   (b) 23.20%
   (c) 21.20%
   (d) 46.41%
   (e) none of the above

5. Which of the following items should not affect taxable income when you file the tax return?

    (a) Proceeds from the sale of your home
    (b) $50 received from your brother for mowing his lawn
    (c) The capital gain on the stocks that you are holding
    (d) (a) and (c)
    (e) (b) and (c)

DISCUSSION QUESTIONS

1. Explain the significance of the following entries:

    after-tax discount rate / allowable capital loss / capital gains deduction / capital gains reserve / combined marginal tax rate / dividend tax credit / federal tax / grossed-up dividend / indexation / investment income / provincial tax / surtax / taxable capital gain / taxable dividend / taxable income / tax brackets / tax credits / tax rates: marginal and average / T1 General Income Tax Return / T1 Special Income Tax Return / total income

2. A popular idea among conservative tax reformers is the flat income tax. The basic notion is to remove most of the deductions and tax credits, and eliminate the progressive tax brackets. These steps would simplify the tax calculations greatly, and end many complicated income tax dodges that add nothing to real economic activity. The flat tax would be at a relatively low rate, say 20%, because of all the deductions that are removed. What do you think of this proposal?

3. Under the federal budget of February 28, 2000, the level of income for each tax bracket and some of the personal deductions and credits are indexed for inflation. That is, they increase each year by the inflation rate.

    (a) Why is this necessary? What would happen if they weren't indexed?
    (b) What will happen without tax indexation if inflation continues at 1% for the next 10 years to a pensioner with fixed taxable income of $28,000 that is itself indexed to inflation?

PROBLEMS

1. Rita Songbird has taxable income of $85,000 in 2011 in Peggy's Cove, Nova Scotia. She has $1,800 of federal and $600 of provincial non-refundable tax credits. Calculate the following:

    (a) The total amount of income tax she has to pay for 2011
    (b) Her average tax rate

    (c) Her marginal tax rate on interest
    (d) Her marginal tax rate on eligible dividends
    (e) Her marginal tax rate on realized capital gains
    (f) The additional income tax she will pay if her employer gives her a $15,000 bonus on December 31, 2011

2. Andre Gagnon bought 100 shares of BCE for $30 per share and paid a commission of $33 on the transaction. In 2011 he sold the shares for $32 and paid a commission of $29.95. He received dividends of $2.10 during the year. He lives in Cornwall, Ontario. Calculate the following:

    (a) The adjusted cost base per share
    (b) The capital gain
    (c) The taxable capital gain
    (d) The taxable dividend
    (e) The tax on the capital gain and the 2011 dividends if he has taxable income from other sources of $112,000

3. Paul Gross has net income for tax purposes of $68,000 from his acting work in 2011. In addition to this he received interest of $2,000; royalties of $25,000 from *Passchendaele*; a dividend of $200; and capital gains, net of costs, of $30,000. He lives in Grande Prairie, Alberta. He has $3,000 in federal and $900 in provincial non-refundable tax credits.

    (a) What is his taxable income for 2011?
    (b) How much income tax does he pay?

4. You are a taxpayer with a marginal tax rate of 44% (all surtaxes included) for interest income. You are considering buying a 5% bond for $950. It matures in five years and pays interest semi-annually.

    (a) What is the yield-to-maturity? What is the effective annual rate?
    (b) What is your expected after-tax EAR?

5. Linda Resch is an investment dealer in Brockville, Ontario. She has identified two low-risk investments that are appropriate for clients who want secure earnings. One is a guaranteed preferred share to be issued tomorrow by a Canadian company. The price is $25 and it pays a quarterly dividend of $0.25. It will be redeemed at par in 10 years by the company. The payment of dividends and the redemption payment are guaranteed by a large bank. The other investment is a 10-year Canada bond to be issued at par tomorrow, with a yield-to-maturity of 5.4%. It pays a semi-annual coupon. She has two customers for whom the risk level of these investments seems appropriate:

(a) Peter Poor has a taxable income of $25,000. Which of the two securities is better for him?

(b) Wendy Wealthy has a taxable income of $150,000. Which of the two securities is better for her?

6. Mary James, a self-employed interior designer in P.E.I., has earned $45,000 in consulting fees. She also received $2,000 interest income. If she has $1,800 and $925 in non-refundable federal and provincial tax credits, respectively, what is her total income tax bill for the year?

7. For each part of this problem, non-refundable federal tax credits are $2,400 and non-refundable provincial tax credits are $698.

(a) Nick Orlando earns $70,000 p.a. at Alcan in Hamilton, Ontario. He recently received a dividend of $4,500 from Bell Canada. How much tax does he have to pay on the dividend?

(b) How much tax does he pay on the dividend if his salary is $50,000?

(c) How much tax does he pay on the dividend if his salary is $90,000?

8. Syed has a federal marginal tax rate of 29% and a provincial rate of 11.16%, with no surtax. He is considering buying a one-year treasury bill paying 5%. Calculate his expected after-tax rate of return.

9. Rose Slovens is moving to a province on the east coast and she worries that the move may affect the taxes she pays next year. More specifically, she wants to find out how much tax she has to pay on her investments. Her friend told her that at her income bracket, she has to pay the following tax rates:

- Marginal federal tax rate = 29%
- Marginal provincial tax rate = 12%
- Marginal provincial surtax rate = 20%
- Provincial dividend tax credit rate = 9%

There will be no federal surtax.

She wants to invest her savings of $20,000 for one year, at the end of which she will use the money for a vacation. She is considering the following alternatives:

(i) A bank term deposit that pays 6% interest, compounded annually

(ii) A stock that pays 8% dividends but no capital gains

(iii) A stock mutual fund that does not pay any dividends but is expected to grow at a rate of 11%

For each of the three investments, calculate the future value of the investment after paying all relevant taxes.

163

10. Mr. Kotewall has recently moved from Ontario to New Brunswick. He wants to know how the move will affect his marginal tax rates and taxes payable. Since he is earning a very high income from employment, he is at the highest income tax bracket.

    (a) Calculate his marginal tax rates for 2011 and 2012, assuming no change in rates from those currently known, on
        (i) interest income
        (ii) dividend income
        (iii) capital gains

    (b) He is expected to get $1,000 of interest on a personal loan that he lent to a friend, $2,000 dividend income from the Royal Bank shares he holds, and is planning to sell some stocks to realize a capital gain of $4,000. Calculate the total amount of taxes that he will have to pay on these.

11. Jean Alphonse Chrétien owns 100 units of the Gomery Royalty Income Trust (GRIT), a very profitable operation that sells labelled golf balls in Québec. In 2011 GRIT distributed $.50 in return of capital, $1.00 in dividends, $.20 in capital gains, and $.30 in interest to each unitholder. Each unit is worth $20. Jean Alphonse received $62,000 in taxable income from other sources during 2011.

    (a) What was the before-tax yield on the GRIT units?

    (b) What was Jean Alphonse's after-tax yield if he lives in
        (i) St. John, New Brunswick?
        (ii) Truro, Nova Scotia?

CHAPTER 8

Income Tax Planning

▶ Rose Vino owns a winery and several vineyards, while her husband, Andre, is disabled and has only a small investment income. See Example 8.2 for a method they can use to split income and reduce income tax.

▶ Sarah Goldberg plans to start an MBA part-time, and take a one-year leave of absence from her job to finish the degree in full-time study. She will finance the leave with the sale of stock she owns that has a capital gain of $20,000. How much can she save by timing the disposition of her stock correctly? See Example 8.5.

The authors thank Joanne Magee for her many contributions to this chapter.

LEARNING OBJECTIVES

> ➤ *To explain the four fundamental tax minimization strategies: income deferral, income splitting, income spreading, and tax shelters.*

> ➤ *To illustrate these strategies with the specific techniques commonly available at the present time in Canada.*

> ➤ *To provide basic information on two important income tax planning topics: medical expenses and disabled persons and post-secondary education.*

Now that you understand the general structure of income taxation in Canada, we consider how you can legally minimize the amount of income tax you pay. The same warnings apply. The *Income Tax Act* is a complex statute of Parliament, and it changes frequently. The specific details of any situation may require more specialized knowledge than we provide in this book.

We establish the fundamental principles and provide examples of how to apply them in situations that will cover most of the tax minimization opportunities available to you. The principles hold true even when the Act changes because they arise from three basic aspects of the nature of income taxation in Canada and most other countries:

1. The tax rates are progressive and the rate for each higher bracket applies only to the additional or marginal income.

2. Governments try to achieve several objectives at once with taxation laws: raise revenue; promote social equity; encourage/discourage certain financial actions; and manage economic trends.

3. Tax deferral often saves money because of the time value of money.

An important consideration in income tax planning is the definition of spouse and family. You should read Chapter 5 before going further in this chapter.

INCOME DEFERRAL

The general principle involved in **income deferral** is that if you can't use the income for consumption purposes, you shouldn't have to pay tax on it until you can use it. If you can invest the tax-deferred income at a rate of return that is untaxed, then you get a second advantage with faster compounding.

Registered Pension Plans

A **Registered Pension Plan (RPP)** is established by an employer to defer income payable to employees to provide retirement income for them. Such a plan may have payments made into it by either or both the employer and the employee, depending on the terms of the plan. The contributions are deposited with a plan trustee who invests them. When the employee retires, he receives a pension from the plan. We discuss pension plans in more detail in the retirement planning chapters, but the key tax aspect is that the contributions to the plan are not taxed as income in the employee's hands at the time they are put into the plan.[1] The employee pays tax on the pension as it is received. Thus, the employee's pension contributions are deductible from taxable income and accumulate at the before-tax rate of return. The employer's contributions are not included in the employee's income until they are paid out of the plan in retirement, and these contributions also accumulate at the before-tax rate of return.

The contributions are fixed by the terms of employment. Occasionally, the plan may be retroactively amended to allow for higher contributions for past service, or to allow employees to join the plan who were not previously in it, and to gain credit for past service. If such an amendment allows a person to make **past service contributions**, they are almost always worth doing. In effect, you get a tax deduction now for buying more pension income.

Registered Retirement Savings Plan

A **Registered Retirement Savings Plan (RRSP)** is a do-it-yourself pension plan. The taxpayer contributes part of her income to a trusteed fund. The contribution is deducted from income for tax purposes in the year it is paid into the fund, and income on it accumulates tax-free. When the taxpayer withdraws it for spending purposes, the entire amount, principal and accrued earnings, is taxable.[2] The amount you can contribute in a year is the lesser of 18% of your earned income in the preceding year and a specified total dollar limit,[3] plus any unused contribution allowance from previous years, starting in 1991. If you have an employer pension plan, the RRSP contribution limit is reduced according to a complex formula. We discuss RRSPs in much more detail in Chapter 17. You can read and understand the RRSP section of Chapter 17, together with Chapter 8, without having to read any of the intervening chapters first.

The RRSP is primarily for use as retirement savings, but it can be used legally to defer income tax in shorter horizons, too. If you know that you will want

---

[1] The employer can deduct its own contributions for income tax purposes when they are paid.

[2] In both RRSPs and RPPs, the differential treatments of capital gains and dividends paid by Canadian companies do not apply. All withdrawals are treated as ordinary income.

[3] See Table 17.5 in Chapter 17.

more cash than you will earn in some future year, you could contribute to an RRSP for the intervening years and allow the income to accumulate at the before-tax rate. You will have to pay tax when you withdraw the money, but the increased earnings rate while it was sheltered will leave you with more money. The one thing to be careful about is that the extra income in the later year could push you into a higher tax bracket. A taxpayer in the highest bracket needn't worry about this situation; otherwise, some careful calculation is required. If you make the withdrawal in a year of low income, like a year when you return to school or take a maternity leave, you may even benefit from a lower marginal tax return on the withdrawal than the tax rate you saved when you contributed. If tax brackets change during the intervening years, you may lose out even if you made the correct decision originally.

Example 8.1: Sarah Goldberg likes her job with the credit union, but she feels that she must finish her university degree in order to move into management. She has started the courses this year at the Atkinson School of Administrative Studies in Toronto North University, and in three years she plans to take a year off in order to finish it, going from September of year 4 to August of year 5. Her tax bracket is 26% now and would stay at that rate in the two years during which she is in school full time. Suppose she can save $3,000 p.a. for each of the next three years. She could do this either by depositing it into an RRSP and paying the tax in year 5, or she could invest it outside an RRSP and pay the tax each year. In the fourth year she starts school and uses that year's savings to carry her to December. In January of the fifth year she cashes in the first three year's savings, including any accrued earnings. The timeline looks like this, assuming each deposit of savings is made at year end:

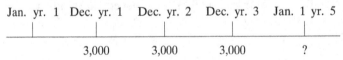

Jan. yr. 1	Dec. yr. 1	Dec. yr. 2	Dec. yr. 3	Jan. 1 yr. 5
	3,000	3,000	3,000	?

She can withdraw on January 1, year 5, the accumulated value of a three-year annuity of $3,000 p.a., compounded for one more year. Withdrawing the entire amount from an RRSP in year 5 wouldn't change her tax bracket. In either case, she will choose a safe credit union rate of 6% p.a. An important point that you should note concerns how you get the tax deduction for your RRSP.

You can file a form with the CRA declaring your RRSP contribution during the year, and get your employer to reduce the tax withheld from your regular pay by the amount attributable to the RRSP deduction. Thus, you can use your RRSP deduction to generate more cash to make another RRSP contribution. The limit of this process is (cash saved)/(1 − tax rate). That is, if Sarah reduces her consumption by $3,000 to put into an RRSP, she can actually generate $3,000/.74 = $4,054 in tax-sheltered savings.[4] How much more will she have to spend in year 5 if she uses an RRSP?

Answer: The RRSP is worth:

PMT	$4,054
N	3
I/Y	6
FV	$12,906
FV yr. 5	$12,906 × 1.06 = $13,680
After-tax	$13,680 × .74 = $10,123

The unsheltered amount is worth:

PMT	$3,000
N	3
I/Y	4.44
FV	$9,406
FV yr. 5	$9,406 × 1.044 = $9,820

The RRSP saving method accumulates to $303 more. The higher the tax bracket and the longer the period, the larger the value of the tax deferral.

Other Uses of an RRSP

You may withdraw money from an RRSP for two uses other than retirement without having to pay tax on the withdrawals, provided you pay them back as required. In each case you cannot make a deposit to the RRSP less than 90 days prior to the withdrawal.

The **Lifelong Learning Plan (LLP)** allows you to withdraw up to $10,000 in a year for education expenses for you or your spouse, and up to $20,000 in total.

---

[4] To implement this, she may have to take out a loan ($1,053) at the end of February and repay it when she receives the tax refund.

The year after you finish being a student, you must start repaying the "loan" from your RRSP by depositing at least one-tenth of the amount withdrawn each year. You pay no interest on the "loan" and the repayments do not affect your contribution limit. Even if you have no contribution room, you must make the repayments. Failure to make the repayments on time causes them to be added back to your taxable income each year that they fall due.

The **Home Buyers Plan (HBP)** allows you to withdraw up to $25,000 to help buy the family's first home. You have to start repaying the amount withdrawn to your RRSP the second year after the withdrawal, in equal instalments of one-fifteenth until it is all repaid.

Capital Gains Deferral

No tax is payable on capital gains until they are realized. A portfolio of shares can increase in value at the before-tax rate of return if the return consists of capital gains instead of dividends. Thus, you should invest in assets that will realize more of their rate of return from capital gains because you can defer paying tax on the returns until you cash them in; and when you do, you will pay tax only on one-half of the gain (under the current rules).

This strategy makes two strong assumptions. First, you do not require the dividend or interest income from the portfolio for current consumption. This assumption should hold for people who are saving for future retirement.

The second assumption is that you can continue to hold the identical portfolio. In reality, you may expose yourself to a lot of risk if you do so. Some of the companies will do very well and become a larger part of the portfolio while others will decline in value. The well-diversified portfolio you started with may not stay that way. See Chapter 14 for more on the importance of diversification.

You may also want to change your investment position because you think that the securities that have gained the most are not going to perform as well in the future. If you sell them, the capital gains will be realized. In some cases, you will have no choice about disposition — another company may take over one of yours and pay cash for the shares.

These considerations do not eliminate the deferral benefit of capital gains; they simply reduce it.

INCOME SPLITTING

If different members of the family have different marginal tax rates, it would be nice to allocate income from the higher tax brackets to the lower ones. Legal allocation of income in this fashion is called **income splitting**, and it is possible in limited circumstances. Most of the techniques involve investment income in some way.

Between Spouses

The simplest method is for the spouse with the higher income to pay all the living expenses. The lower income spouse does all the saving and accumulates investment assets, whose income is taxed at a lower marginal rate.

Gifts between spouses are presumed to occur at their adjusted cost base (ACB). If the gift is an income-earning asset, then the income is **attributed** to the spouse who gave the gift. In other words, you can't split income simply by giving investments to the lower income spouse. The gift could be given at fair market value, with the spouse paying for it. Now, this doesn't help much since if the spouse had the money, she could buy the asset on the open market anyway. However, the selling spouse can take payment in the form of a loan bearing interest at market rates. As long as the investment asset transferred earns more than the market interest rate (e.g., a portfolio of common shares would do so, on average), then some income is split. This is not a very efficient way to split income, however, and is quite risky. If the investment asset loses money, the income split works in reverse because the lower income spouse will have even less income.

Income attribution does not apply to the compounding of earnings. The income earned on a gift is attributed back to the spouse who gave it every year. However, the income on that income in the second year is not attributed. Thus, a high-income spouse could give a bond to the low-income spouse. The low-income spouse deposits each coupon amount in a separate account. The coupons will be taxed in the high-income spouse's hands, but the earnings on the separate account will be taxed in the low-income spouse's hands. This method requires a fairly substantial amount of assets and a lengthy time period for significant effects.

Example 8.2: Rose Vino owns and manages a winery and several vineyards. Her husband, Andres Vino, is disabled and has only a small investment income. Rose's marginal tax rate is 50%; Andres's rate is 26%. Rose "lends" him a warehouse with a fixed rental income of $15,000 p.a. for 10 years. She has enough surplus income to pay the tax annually on the attributed income without receiving the $15,000. He deposits the earnings into a money market fund earning 5% p.a. At the end of 10 years he gives the warehouse back and continues to earn in his own name the interest at 5% on the accumulated money market fund. How much does he earn in the 11th year if all payments are assumed to occur at year end?

Answer:

PMT	$15,000
N	10
I/Y	5% × (1 − .26) = 3.7%
FV	$177,606

Next year he earns 5% × $177,606 = $8,880 before tax, or $6,571 after tax. Note that Rose has paid $7,500 tax every year on the $15,000 earnings. Only the earnings on the saved earnings are taxed at Andres's lower rate.

One useful device that both splits and defers income tax is the **spousal RRSP.** A taxpayer may contribute to an RRSP for his spouse but claim the tax deduction. If the contributing spouse will be in a higher tax bracket at retirement, then the ultimate tax payable on the RRSP withdrawals will be lower. This technique is especially important in a family where one spouse has spent most or all of the potential earning years working in the household, and consequently has no pension. The limit on how much can be contributed is determined by the contributing spouse's income and RPP entitlements, just as for a regular RRSP. The total contributed to a taxpayer's own RRSP and a spousal RRSP must fall within that limit — there is no "double deduction" by establishing a spousal RRSP. The spouse may not withdraw contributions until after two years have elapsed without triggering attribution of the income back to the contributing spouse.

The spousal RRSP has become much less important because of a significant recent change in taxation of pensions. A spousal couple may opt every year to split their *eligible pension income* between them, up to 50%, for income tax purposes only. Eligible pension income is generally the total of the following amounts received by the pensioner in the year (these amounts also qualify for the pension income amount):

- The taxable part of life annuity payments from a superannuation or pension fund or plan

- If they are received as a result of the death of a spouse or common-law partner, or if the pensioner is 65 years of age or older at the end of the year:
  - annuity and registered retirement income fund (including life income fund) payments
  - Registered Retirement Savings Plan (RRSP) annuity payments

Canada Pension Plan, Old Age Security, and Guaranteed Income Supplement amounts are *not* eligible pension income.

They would each sign a declaration, filed with the tax returns, and then report the fraction of pension income thus divided as if it were received by each of them. This sounds confusing. Look at Example 8.3:

Example 8.3 Al and Amanda Charters are each 60 years of age and retired. Al received employer pension payments of $50,000 in 2011. Amanda received no pension income, but she did withdraw $4,000 from an RRSP. They live in Beardmore, Ontario. They decide to split their eligible pension income 50% each. What effect does this have on their taxable income and on their marginal tax brackets if they have no other income?

Answer

The $4,000 payment from the RRSP is not eligible pension income. Al can elect to split $23,000 of his $50,000 pension because the employer pension payments qualify for pension income splitting. Therefore, Al's taxable income becomes $27,000 ($50,000 – $23,000), and Amanda's taxable income becomes $27,000 ($4,000 + $27,000). Before pension splitting, only Al is eligible for the pension credit (a $2,000 federal credit at 15% and a $1,259[5] Ontario credit at 5.05%); after pension splitting, both he and Amanda are eligible for the pension credit. But there are also marginal rate savings.

Al's marginal tax rate before pension splitting is based on $50,000 taxable income. A person's marginal tax rate is not affected by tax credits. He lives in Ontario, so we have to check whether he is subject to Ontario surtax.

2011 Ontario basic tax before splitting
= .0505 × ($37,774) + .0915 × ($50,000 – $37,774)
= $3,026.27

Al pays no Ontario surtax even without splitting pension income.

Amanda's marginal tax rate doesn't change; $27,000 is in the same federal and provincial tax bracket as $4,000. Al's marginal rate changes twice because the federal and provincial brackets are different, and the break-point for each one falls between $50,000 and $27,000. How much income tax do they save as a couple? You add together the tax savings/losses from the bracket changes and the value of the added pension tax credit. The bracket changes value is the product of the difference between the bracket rates and the amount of income that shifted from one bracket to another. The provincial and federal bracket break-points are different, and so you must calculate it separately for the bracket effect. If one of the spouses is pushed into a higher tax

---

[5] The Ontario credit is indexed but the federal credit is not. The Ontario credit is $1,259 for 2011 and $1,300 for 2012.

bracket, the sign of the bracket change will be negative, signaling that the effect is a loss, not a gain. The saving due to the added pension tax credit is also calculated separately for federal and provincial tax because the amount allowable for a tax credit and the tax credit rates differ. For Al and Amanda, the total effect is calculated as follows:

Federal tax saving for Al:
$(.22 - .15) \times (\$50,000 - \$41,544)$ $= \$\ 591.92$

Provincial tax saving for Al:
$(.0915 - .0505) \times (\$50,000 - \$37,774)$ $= \$\ 501.27$

Bracket change for Amanda $= \$\quad\ 0$

Federal pension credit for Amanda:
$.15 \times (\$2,000)$ $= \$\ 300.00$

Provincial pension credit for Amanda:
$.0505 \times (\$1,259)$ $= \$\quad 63.58$

Total saving $= \$1,456.77$

Although it does not affect this example, there are other possible complications. The additional income assigned to the spouse may affect clawback of OAS; and so, if one member of the spousal couple is not subject to clawback and the other one is, assigning pension income to the spouse not subject to clawback will also save 15% of the amount that escapes clawback in the lower income spouse's hands.

Between Other Family Members

Income splitting between other family members is usually from parents to children, although others, such as dependent parents, may benefit from it, too. There is no analogue to the spousal RRSP with other persons.

The higher-income person should pay all the living expenses. This may be particularly evident when a dependent child receives inheritances or gifts from other relatives. These amounts should be invested and the parents pay expenses as long as their marginal tax rates are higher.[6]

---

[6] The principle of giving children some responsibility for their affairs may well take precedence over tax minimization at some age. The parents may well decide that the child should start to pay for his or her own entertainment, for example. Saving taxes is not the only important issue in family life!

The income attribution rule does not apply to children aged 18 and older.[7] In the case of younger children (minors), the income attribution rule does not apply to capital gains on a gift from a parent, although interest, dividends, and other income are attributed. Thus a parent can give a minor child a significant income with a gift of publicly traded common shares whose future return is mostly capital gains, and pay little or no tax on attribution.[8]

Estate Freezes

This complex technique freezes the value of a property in the hands of the original owner, who places it in the estate freeze. All further appreciation in value accrues to the heir. This technique is useful for family businesses or large investment portfolios — hundreds of thousands of dollars. Depending on how it is structured, the freeze can allow the original owner to retain control of the asset during his lifetime, or receive some income from it. The control aspect is important if the asset is the family business which the original owner continues to manage. Relatively few families need estate freezes, and expert guidance is required to establish one. We discuss estate planning in a bit more detail in Chapter 18.

Single Parent Families and Marriage Breakdowns

The single parent family is becoming a common situation with the increasing rate of marriage breakdowns. The sharing of deductions and costs between two separated or divorced parents can involve significant income tax consequences, and we will cover only two here.

One simple tax-saving device is for the parent who supports the children to claim one of them as equivalent-to-married, which is explained in Schedule 6 of the General Tax Guide. Certain other dependants may also qualify for this tax credit.

---

[7] The attribution rules apply to loans to older children, but the rules are beyond the scope of this book.

[8] Over the years, certain tax planning arrangements have allowed taxpayers running small businesses to split substantial amounts of income with their minor children. To stop this form of income-splitting, starting in 2000, minor children must pay tax at the top rate on dividend and business income derived from such sources. No tax credits except for the dividend tax credit and the foreign tax credit are allowed. (That is, no basic credit or tuition or education credits can be claimed to offset this so-called "kiddie tax".) The "kiddie tax" only applies to certain types of income derived from a parent's business or corporation. It does not apply to other types of income, including the following:

  i. Dividends and shareholder benefits relating to publicly owned shares that are not owned through a private corporation
  ii. Income received by minors who have no Canadian resident parent
  iii. Income from property inherited by a minor from a deceased parent
  iv. Income from property inherited from persons other than a parent if the minor is a full-time student at a post-secondary institution or is eligible for the disability credit
  v. Interest income, employment income, and capital gains

Since only one married or equivalent-to-married credit may be claimed in a year, you should check to see which arrangement of dependants is most beneficial.

An important planning consideration is how to structure the settlement under a separation agreement. A basic rule in the Act governs how separation payments are taxed. Payments may be deducted by the payer and reported as income by the recipient if they meet all of these conditions:

1. When the payments were made, the spouses were living apart and continued to do so for the rest of the year.
2. The payments were made under a decree, court order, judgment, or written agreement.
3. The payments were made for the maintenance of the recipient.
4. The payments were an allowance to be paid periodically.
5. The payments were made to the spouse or former spouse, who has discretion over how they are spent.

An exception applies to child support payments made pursuant to an agreement or court order made or changed after April 30, 1997, which are not deductible by the payor or taxable to the recipient.[9]

The separating couple can minimize income taxes by arranging that the spouse making the payments does so as an allowance for spousal support if she is in the higher tax bracket, and as an allowance for child support or a lump-sum payment if she is in the lower income tax bracket.[10] The correct choice reduces taxes more for the payer than it increases taxes for the recipient, and thus the two will have more after-tax income to share. The only weakness with this form of income splitting is the risk that the payer will not make all the periodic payments, and hence a lump sum is better for the recipient even if it is less tax efficient. Nonetheless, the tax benefits can be considerable.

> *Example 8.4:* Gertrude and Claudius are separating. Claudius gets the castle, and Gertrude will also pay him some money. She offers to pay him $35,000 in a lump sum now, or to invest $50,000 in Canada Savings Bonds at 6% p.a. and pay him an annuity (spousal support) at the end of each of the next five years. His best alternative riskless

---

[9] Child support payments made pursuant to older court orders or agreements can be treated in this manner provided that the payer and recipient make a joint election for the treatment to apply. Otherwise, they are treated in the same way as spousal support — taxable in the hands of the recipient; tax-deductible by the spouse paying them.

[10] This useful technique may be eroded by new guidelines that specify the appropriate amounts for child support and spousal support. The child support guidelines are now fully in force across Canada; the spousal support guidelines are at the stage of consideration of the detailed rules to see if they are suitable.

investment is also CSBs at 6%. Her tax rate is 42% and his is 26%. They think the tax rates will stay the same for each of them for the next five years. Claudius trusts Gertrude to pay the annuity. Which way should they do it?

Answer: First, calculate the annuity payment:

PV	$50,000
I/Y	6
N	5
PMT	$11,870

Next, calculate their after-tax discount rates:

Claudius: 6% (1 − .26) = 4.44%
Gertrude: 6% (1 − .42) = 3.48%

Next, calculate their after-tax payments:

Claudius receives: $11,870 (1 − .26) = $8,784
Gertrude pays: $11,870 (1 − .42) = $6,885

Now we can calculate what the after-tax payments are worth:

	Claudius	*Gertrude*
PMT	$ 8,784	$ 6,885
I/Y	4.44%	3.48%
N	5	5
PV	$38,626	$31,104

Thus, they should structure it in annual payments. The after-tax cost to Gertrude is less than the $35,000 lump sum, while Claudius gets more than $35,000 after-tax.

Note that Claudius is assumed to have received spousal support in the above example. If the payment had been child support, Claudius would pay no tax on the $11,870 payment and Gertrude would get no deduction. What would the answer be then?

INCOME SPREADING

A taxpayer who has highly variable income may want to **spread income** over several years to reduce the marginal tax rate. This method of tax reduction does not have many applications because the difference between the second and third brackets is now quite small, and the top bracket kicks in at a fairly modest income level.

Furthermore, most people earn relatively even streams of employment income, and thus spreading income has no effect on their marginal rates.

A few people — professional athletes and entertainers, commissioned salespersons, professionals with irregular large contracts — may benefit from deferred compensation arrangements. These require carefully structured contracts.

Anyone with substantial accrued capital gains should be careful to realize them over several years rather than all at once to avoid a higher tax bracket. Taxpayers in this situation are most often in the top bracket anyway, and income spreading is of no value (though deferring the realization of the capital gains is still worthwhile).

One income spreading situation that many people can use occurs when a taxpayer will be earning much less income for one or two years than in the years before and after. A person might take a long maternity or paternity leave or an unpaid leave of absence, return to university, or have a long period of involuntary unemployment or underemployment. In this situation, a person can withdraw part or all of the money in an RRSP for consumption and pay tax immediately, but at a lower marginal rate than the original deduction provided. This does compromise retirement savings, but it is sometimes the cheapest way of bridging a period of low income. Some people use their RRSPs deliberately for this purpose.

Example 8.5: Sarah Goldberg, from Example 8.1, now has a degree and a middle-management job, but needs an MBA to move into senior management. She plans exactly the same pattern of saving and school time as in Example 8.1, but now her salary is higher. She is in the 42% tax bracket, and would drop to the 26% bracket in years 4 and 5. How much more can she save using an RRSP compared with not using it?

Answer: The annual payment, taking advantage of the tax deduction, is now

$$\frac{\$3,000}{(1 - .42)} = \$5,172$$

The RRSP is worth:

PMT	$ 5,172
N	3
I/Y	6
FV	$16,466
FV yr. 5	$16,466 × 1.06 = $17,454
After-tax	$17,454 × .74 = $12,916

The unsheltered amount is worth:

PMT	$3,000
N	3
I/Y	3.48
FV	$9,317
FV yr. 5	$9,317 × 1.044 = $9,727

The difference is now $3,189, which illustrates how much income spreading can save in the right situation.

TAX SHELTERS

In some situations a taxpayer can arrange affairs so that **tax shelters** allow a lower or zero rate of tax, without any deferral or other sacrifice required. Many shelters are transitory because they relate to government attempts to affect the economy in some way.

Tax-Free Savings Account (TFSA)

The federal government created the *tax-free savings account (TFSA)*, which took effect starting January 1, 2009. It allows savings to accumulate tax free without creating any complications in later taxes and social assistance payment qualifications, but it is a useful planning tool for almost everyone. We discuss complications TFSA helps to address in Chapters 17 and 18.

The TFSA allows a person (the beneficiary) to contribute up to $5,000 annually to a registered TFSA account in a financial institution. The contribution is not tax-deductible, and income in the account is not taxable at any time. The beneficiary of the account may withdraw any amount from the account at any time, and the withdrawal is not taxable and is not added to income for tax purposes. Amounts withdrawn and/or earned in the TFSA do not affect eligibility for social assistance programs.

The unused contribution for each year accumulates and can be used in any future year to make larger contributions. The one minor complication is that withdrawals may also be replaced in the account, but not until the next calendar year. See Example 8.6.

Example 8.6   Femida contributed $3,000 to a TFSA in 2009, the first year that TFSAs were introduced. She contributed nothing in 2010. In 2011 she contributed $2,000 in January and then withdrew $1,000 in May. What is her contribution limit for the rest of 2011 and for 2012?

Answer	Limit for 2009	$	5,000
	– Contributed in 2009		3,000
	Carried forward to 2010	$	2,000
	Contribution room added in 2010		5,000
	Total contribution room for 2010	$	7,000
	– Contribution in 2010		0
	Carried forward to 2011	$	7,000
	Contribution room added in 2011		5,000
	Total contribution room for 2011	$	12,000
	– Contribution in 2011		2,000
	Carried forward to 2012	$	10,000
	Contribution room added in 2012		5,000
	Total contribution room for 2012	$	15,000
	+ Withdrawal in 2011		1,000
	= Total contribution room for 2012	$	16,000

Capital Gains

Capital gains have been a common shelter, with the rules varying considerably over the years. Until 1972, capital gains were tax-free.[11] The taxable portion has been various amounts at different times since 1972 — the inclusion rate is currently 50%. During the period 1985 to February 22, 1994, an individual taxpayer could claim a lifetime exemption for a maximum of $100,000 in capital gains. A lifetime exemption for a maximum of $500,000 in capital gains on sale of a family farm or "qualifying" small business still exists (the details are too complicated for us to cover).

For most people who don't own farms or small businesses, the untaxed one-half of a capital gain still represents a considerable potential for tax saving and is one reason why investment in risky securities with growth potential is so popular.

The principal residence of a family is exempt from any capital gains tax (except for the portion of the gain assigned to a part of the house that has been a rental property). Given the long-run trend of property values to increase, this is a powerful incentive for a family to buy a home as early as possible and bend its savings efforts towards paying off the mortgage. Even if the capital gain doesn't materialize, the family has a place to live. Another benefit may be income splitting. If the couple sells the home at retirement and moves into a smaller home or an apartment, the capital gain can be split between the partners to provide income for both, without income attribution, even if one spouse paid most of the cost of buying the home.

---

[11] There are transitional rules that allow a taxpayer to claim part of the capital gain as tax-free on assets owned prior to 1972 and sold subsequently.

Dividends vs. Interest Income

If you want to receive a relatively steady stream of income from investment assets, then securities paying dividends or interest are preferred. The tax treatment is different, and so the question arises as to which one you should choose, assuming risk and maturity are the same. You compare them using the after-tax cash flows (see Chapter 7). Depending on the relative pricing and your tax bracket, you may prefer either dividends or interest, and your preferences may change over time. The price you pay on the market will reflect some equilibrium average of all the market participants, but your own marginal tax may be different and so you may be able to pay less tax by your choice of investment.

Example 8.7:   Dwayne Webb is in a tax bracket of 50.74% for interest income and 34.26% for dividend income. Cesa Sarmazian is in a tax bracket of 26.86% for interest income and 7.24% for dividends. Both have $1,000 to invest, and the choice is between a bond and a preferred share of equal risk, maturing in 10 years. The bond pays interest of $100 annually; the preferred share pays a dividend of $77 annually. Which investment should each person choose?

Answer: Dwayne should choose the preferred share.

$$\text{Preferred return after-tax} = (1 - .3426) \times \$77$$
$$= \$50.62 \text{ or } \underline{5.062\%}$$

$$\text{Interest return after-tax} = (1 - .5074) \times \$100$$
$$= \$49.26 \text{ or } \underline{4.926\%}$$

Cesa should choose the bond.

$$\text{Preferred return after-tax} = (1 - .0724) \times \$77$$
$$= \$71.43 \text{ or } \underline{7.143\%}$$

$$\text{Interest return after-tax} = (1 - .2686) \times \$100$$
$$= \$73.14 \text{ or } \underline{7.314\%}$$

Specialized Tax Shelters

A specialized tax shelter is an investment that allows the investor to recover a significant portion of the initial investment very quickly through income tax reductions, regardless of the subsequent earnings on the investment. Many writers use the term *tax shelter* only to refer to this kind of shelter rather than to all shelters as we have done.

These investments have five characteristics in common, regardless of their stated terms:

1. They are granted the tax shelter status because the government wants to encourage investment in that part of the economy.
2. They are exceedingly risky, which is why investment incentives are required.
3. The promoters are well aware of the advantage of the tax shelter and price the investment to take taxes into account.
4. The tax shelters come and go as government objectives change.
5. These specialized tax shelters are very susceptible to fraud.

Our general advice is to avoid them altogether. The high risk of the investment plus the risk of fraud makes them dubious investments. A CRA registration number does not mean that the CRA has approved a particular shelter, and an investor may face large tax bills later. We have not met anyone who prospered from tax shelters. In some cases, the investment money never reaches the productive operation but is wholly consumed by the organizers, the promoters, the lawyers, and the accountants.

If you are still determined to invest in these sort of shelters, you should only do so if you are in the top tax bracket and expect to stay there during the period when deductions are available. It is worth even more if your tax bracket will be lower when the investment starts to generate cash flow. Self-employed professionals nearing retirement fit this tax profile, if they are willing to take the risk.

Tax shelter deals usually involve either **flow-through securities** or limited partnerships. These two structures are advantageous because they allow the individual investor to claim tax shelter deductions while limiting his or her liability to the amount invested. The business giving up these deductions does so in return for capital (and because it is in an early stage of development and has no taxable income against which to apply them).

Another form of tax relief for investing involves government tax credits as a proportion of the amount invested in specified sectors, usually small business. Both the provincial and federal governments have been involved in this activity at various times.

MEDICAL AND DISABILITY TAX ISSUES[12]

This topic becomes increasingly important now that the baby boom generation is reaching retirement and more and more people are coping with a disability and significant medical expenses. Advances in medicine have also increased the life expectancy of people with severe disabilities and that too creates a much longer timeline of additional expenses. Income tax law provides tax relief for unusually

---

[12] The authors thank Victoria Zaremba and Meredith Perren for their valuable comments on this section.

large medical expenses that universal medical health care and private health care plans do not cover. We warn you that this area of taxation is quite complex and we do not provide all the details. You need to do more research and/or consult a professional tax expert if you are doing anything more than a simple claim for excess medical expenses. If you wish to learn more, start with CRA's Web page for individuals at <www.cra-arc.gc.ca/tx/ndvdls/menu-eng.html> and search under D for Disability and M for Medical Expenses.

The tax relief provided falls into five categories, all of which are related but need to be determined separately. A person who qualifies for relief of one sort does not automatically qualify for other kinds of relief, even when the terminology used seems to be similar. The first four are government tax relief in which the tax collector gives up some revenue permanently. The fifth involves government grants, income deferral, and income splitting all in one package. Here are the five categories:

- Medical expense tax credit
- Disability tax credit (DTC)
- Dependant claims for individuals dependent by reason of mental or physical infirmity
- Disability supports deduction
- Registered Disability Savings Plan (RDSP)

Medical Expense Tax Credit

A taxpayer who incurs unreimbursed medical expenses may claim a tax credit for them if the expense is included in a long and complicated list of eligible expenses (e.g., wheelchair, prescription drugs, travel). Eligible medical expenses include expenses of the taxpayer, his or her spouse, and children under the age of 18 at the end of the year.

The amount that is available for the tax credit is calculated as follows:

Eligible medical expenses
-    lesser of a fixed amount indexed annually and 3% of the taxpayer's net income
=   amount available for tax credit
×   lowest marginal tax rate
=   medical expense non-refundable tax credit

The fixed amount referred to in the formula is $2,052 for 2011 ($2,109 in 2012), and it is indexed each year by the same percentage as is used for other indexed amounts like the personal tax credit. The current lowest marginal tax rate at the federal level is 15% and it varies from province to province. A taxpayer can also claim the medical expenses of another dependant (e.g., an adult child or parent), but it is a separate claim and the formula uses the dependant's income rather than the taxpayer's income.

This medical expense tax credit is non-refundable and if the total of all non-refundable tax credits exceeds the tax otherwise owing, the taxpayer does not receive a refund for the difference. Low-income working individuals may also be eligible for a refundable medical expense supplement, which is a refundable credit for medical expenses.

Disability Tax Credit (DTC)

A person who has a significant disability qualifies for a disability tax credit each year this disability exists. A doctor must generally certify that the disability is the result of one or more "severe and prolonged impairments in physical or mental functions", and it must be serious enough to prevent the person from performing at least one of the basic actions of normal living — feeding oneself, dressing, etc. A blind person also qualifies for the DTC. Note that a person may be receiving disability insurance payments but not qualify for the DTC because disability insurance depends on the inability to work, which is a less difficult standard to meet.

The disability tax credit is calculated like other non-refundable tax credits. A specified amount is multiplied by the lowest marginal federal and provincial tax rates to provide the credit amount. The specified federal amount in 2011 is $7,341 and $7,546 in 2012. The specified amount is indexed each year. Each province specifies its own amount for provincial tax.

The DTC is transferable in certain circumstances. A supporting individual (e.g., a spouse or parent) may claim the DTC. A DTC supplement may be claimed for a child under 18.

Qualifying for the DTC credit is also important as it allows a taxpayer to be a beneficiary of a Registered Disability Savings Plan (discussed below) and may qualify the taxpayer and/or his family for enhanced deductions, credits, and benefits and eligible medical expenses. See <www.cra-arc.gc.ca/tx/ndvdls/sgmnts/dsblts/ddctns/menu-eng.html> for some examples but read carefully: Some of the examples have a less severe test than the DTC does. For example, there are rules that require dependants to be "dependent by a mental or physical infirmity" (see heading immediately below), and there is a Disability Supports Deduction that requires a disability (or "impairment") but does not require it to be severe (see Disability Supports Deduction below).

Individuals Dependent by Reason of Mental or Physical Infirmity

The normal rule is that a taxpayer can only make a dependant credit claim for a child who is under 18 years of age and/or a low-income spouse but exceptions are made for certain other individuals who are "dependent by reason of mental or physical infirmity" and have low income (e.g., an older child or a parent). Alternate claims are available for these other dependants: equivalent to spouse, an infirm dependant. In addition, starting in 2012, an extra non-income tested "Family Caregiver Credit" claim is being allowed for any dependant (child under 18, spouse, other) who is dependent by reason of mental or physical infirmity. The specified federal amount for 2012 is $2,000. The specified amount is indexed every year. Note that while a person who qualifies for the DTC may be "dependent by reason of mental or physical infirmity", it is not always the case. For example, a disabled person may be working and self-supporting and the infirmity that results in the dependence may not be the type of "serious and prolonged impairment" that the DTC requires.

Disability Supports Deduction

A disabled person may claim attendant care expenses and other disability support costs if they are incurred in order to attend school or earn income. This claim is distinct from the DTC in that it does not require such severe disability (or impairment), and it is only allowable when used to support education or work. In addition, it is a deduction from net income, not an amount used to calculate a non-refundable tax credit.

Registered Disability Savings Plan (RDSP)[13]

A **Registered Disability Savings Plan** (RDSP) is a tax-assisted savings vehicle designed to allow a person who is eligible for the DTC, and others who wish to contribute to the welfare of this person, to help save for his or her retirement. As well as being eligible for the DTC, the beneficiary of an RDSP must be under the age of 60 while contributions are being made and be a Canadian resident with a social insurance number.

As discussed earlier, RDSPs combine government grants, income deferral, and income splitting all in one package. There is no tax deduction for contributions because taxpayers eligible for the DTC are unlikely to be high-income earners needing tax relief. As well, taxpayers eligible for the DTC may not have the money to contribute to the plan. Thus, the appropriate help is to allow others to make non-deductible contributions, to allow tax to be deferred on the income earned on the savings, and to supplement the amount contributed, providing some government money directly with more money provided to plans for low-income taxpayers than high-income taxpayers. The result is something more akin to an RESP than an RRSP.

---

[13] For further inforation, see <www.cra-arc.gc.ca/tx/ndvdls/tpcs/rdsp-reei/menu-eng.html>.

The RDSP accumulates money in four ways:

- One or more persons make contributions to the plan.
- The government contributes money in the form of a **Canada Disability Savings Bond** (CDSB, described more fully later).
- The government contributes money in the form of a **Canada Disability Savings Grant** (CDSG, described more fully later).
- Income is earned on the investments in the plan.

Contributions to the plan are made with after-tax dollars and the income earned inside the RDSP is not taxed while it stays in the plan. There is no annual limit on contributions, but there is a lifetime limit of $200,000 per beneficiary. The plan must be started and all contributions made by the end of the year in which the beneficiary turns 59. There can be more than one contributor, and there can be more than one beneficiary of a plan, but no beneficiary can have more than one plan. Anyone may contribute to an RDSP.

Beginning July 2011, the proceeds from a deceased individual's RRSP, RRIF, and RPP can be rolled over into the RDSP of a financially dependent child or grandchild. Unused CDSB and CDSG entitlement can be carried forward for up to 10 years, but no more than $10,500 in total for CDSG and $11,000 for CDSB will be paid in respect of an individual in any one year. The carry forward period starts in 2008.

Canada Disability Savings Bond[14]

The federal government provides additional financial support for lower income families supporting a disabled dependant. The RDSP must be open for a beneficiary to receive a CDSB but no contribution is required:

- The CDSB will be paid until the end of the year (December 31) the beneficiary turns 49 years old.

- The maximum CDSB is $1,000 per year and $20,000 for an individual's lifetime.

- The CDSB is income-tested. It is reduced for family income in the previous year above $24,183 and completely eliminated when family income exceeds $41,544. These limits apply to 2011 contributions (the limits are $24,863 and $42,707, respectively, for 2012) and are indexed annually. If the beneficiary is a minor, the income test is based on family net income. Upon reaching the age of 18, the income test is based on the beneficiary's net income and that of the spouse's, if applicable.

- Unused CDSB entitlements can be carried forward 10 years.

---

[14] Except for the 2011 limits in the fourth point, others can be found <www.cra-arc.gc.ca/tx/ndvdls/tpcs/rdsp-reei/cdsg-eng.html>.

	TABLE 8.1 Canada Disability Savings Grants		
Beneficiary's Family Income	**Contribution**	**Grant**	**Maximum**
2011 $83,088 or less 2012 $85,144 or less	On the first $500	$3 for each $1 contributed	$1,500
2011 $83,088 or less 2012 $85,144 or less	On the next $1,000	$2 for each $1 contributed	$2,000
2011 Over $83,088 2012 Over $85,144	On the first $1,000	$1 for each $1 contributed	$1,000

Canada Disability Savings Grant[15]

The CDSG provides partial federal government matching of contributions to an RDSP for lower and moderate income Canadians.

- The RDSP must be open and a contribution must be made for the beneficiary to be eligible for a CDSG.

- The CDSG may be paid until the end of the year (December 31) the beneficiary turns 49 years old.

- The federal government will pay a maximum CDSG of $3,500 per year. The lifetime maximum total grant is $70,000.

- The CDSG is income tested. Government matching is reduced when annual family income is more than $83,088 (2011 limit). The limit is indexed every year (e.g., for 2012, it is $85,144). If the beneficiary is a minor, the income test is based on family net income. Upon reaching the age of 18, the income test is based on the beneficiay's net income and on the spouse's, if applicable.

- Unused CDSG entitlements can be carried forward 10 years.

Table 8.1 shows how the grant formula works.

---

[15] Ibid.

Withdrawals

Withdrawals must begin by the end of the year in which an individual turns 60 until either the plan is terminated or the beneficiary dies. Withdrawals may start earlier than age 60 but are subject to an annual maximum amount based on life expectancy of the beneficiary and the fair market value of the plan. These maximums allow beneficiaries with shortened life expectancies to have access to amounts accumulated in the plan. The income withdrawn does not affect eligibility for most social benefits.

There are two types of withdrawals: Lifetime Disability Assistance Payments (LDAPs) and Disability Assistance Payments (DAPs). There is no restriction on what the LDAPs and DAPs can be used for. They do not have to be used for disability-related expenses.

LDAPs are regular annual payments. Once these payments have commenced they must continue until either the plan is terminated or the beneficiary dies. Payments may begin at any age; however they must begin by the end of the year in which the beneficiary turns 60. There is a maximum allowable amount that can be withdrawn on an annual basis.

DAPs are lump-sum withdrawals. These withdrawals may be requested by the beneficiary once he or she turns 27 years of age. Restrictions apply to DAPs. The total of CDSGs and CDSBs must be greater than all plan holder contributions at the beginning of the calendar year.

Currently, all CDSGs and CDSBs held in the RDSP for fewer than 10 years must be repaid to the government if any RDSP withdrawals are made. The purpose of this 10-year repayment rule is to ensure that the CDSGs and CDSBs are used for long-term savings, but it has been considered harsh in certain circumstance. Accordingly, two exemptions are available. The first exemption is for RDSP beneficiaries with life expectancies of five years or less, with medical certification. A second exemption was proposed in the 2012 budget for small withdrawals after 2013. In such cases, the 10-year repayment rule will be a "proportionate": $3 of CDSG/CDSB repaid for every $1 withdrawn (rather than 100%). However, a large withdrawal or the closing or de-registering of a RDSP will still trigger the full 10-year CDSG and CDSB repayment.

Currently, if the beneficiary of the RDSP is no longer eligible for the DTC, the RDSP is de-registered. After 2013, an RDSP may remain open for four years after the first full year that a beneficiary loses his or her DTC qualification. To take advantage of this rule, the plan holder must make an election in prescribed form on or before December 31 of the year following the first full calendar year for which the beneficiary is eligible.

Earnings generated in the plan and CDSG and CDSB are added to taxable income when they are paid to the beneficiary. The portion of payments attributed to RDSP contributions are not taxable income.

A Warning About This Section

The entire topic of tax, medical expenses, and disability relief is more complicated and contains more detailed treatments than we can possibly include in a general personal finance textbook. You need to be aware of the material we present here, but in most situations you will need expert help.

POST-SECONDARY EDUCATION AND INCOME TAX ISSUES

Primary and secondary education is free in Canada, but post-secondary education is not. The cost of post-secondary tuition and books has risen faster than inflation in the past 20 years. At the same time, well-paid summer jobs are less plentiful, and many more students from less wealthy families now go to college and university. The result is rapidly rising student debt levels. The various forms of assistance are available only to students registered in qualifying institutions for courses lasting specified lengths of time (three weeks is the minimum, but there are many special circumstances). The qualified institutions include Canadian and many foreign universities, community colleges, and various post-secondary institutions certified by the government to provide education or training. The student should verify before enrolling that an institution is so qualified if the tax assistance is needed.[16]

Students can get tax and/or government and/or institution-specific assistance in five ways:

- Scholarships, bursaries, student loans, and employer subsidies are available.
- Interest on student loans (but only student loans) is tax-deductible.
- The cost of tuition fees to approved institutions and textbooks and some other supplies gives rise to non-refundable tax credits.
- A student can be the beneficiary of a **Registered Educational Savings Plan** (RESP), which also incorporates a federal government matching grant.
- If the family can manage additional savings and thinks they are needed, there are tax-efficient ways to do so.

We do not discuss the first source in detail. Every institution has a large number of forms of direct student assistance. Some employers will pay tuition fees and sometimes other expenses for part-time students taking approved courses. Student loans from governments are a major source of support, but they leave graduates with a debt burden to start their working life.

---

[16] A useful reference for many tax issues affecting post-secondary students is <www.cra-arc.gc.ca/E/pub/tg/p105/>.

Student loans do not require interest and principal repayments until the recipient has graduated or ceased attending. In a relatively recent development, the graduate may include interest paid on a student loan from a government program in the calculation of non-refundable tax credits. Interest paid may be carried forward up to five years, which is helpful if the graduate has little or no taxable income in the first years after graduation. Only interest on student loans from the government programs may be claimed in this way. Interest on credit cards, line of credit, or any other loan is not claimable. The interest amount claim may not be transferred to any other person.

There are a number of other tax creditable claims available for cost of text-books, tuition fees, and time spent in full-time and part-time education. The tuition must be at least $100 per course. The education amount is $400 for each month in full-time enrollment and $120 for each month in part-time study. The textbook amount is $65 for each month in full-time enrollment and $20 for each month in part-time study.

The student must use these non-refundable tax credits first to reduce his or her taxable income to zero. If there are excess amounts remaining, the student may transfer them to a parent or grandparent, or to a spouse, or to a spouse's parent.

The overall effect of all these non-refundable tax credits is to ensure that full-time students will normally pay no income tax. Even a well-paid summer job plus part-time work during the year will rarely produce more income than the total non-refundable tax credits will offset. For the undergraduate student who goes from high school directly to post-secondary education, there are no important additional planning opportunities, although recognizing that earned income will be untaxed is useful for planning.[17] A student who is returning to school full-time at any time other than January 1 should plan for these additional credits to create a tax refund on income tax paid on income prior to the return to student status.

Registered Educational Savings Plan (RESP)[18]

An RESP is a trusteed savings plan whose sole purpose is to provide tax and government assistance in saving for post-secondary education for one or more students who are under the age of 18 when the plan is opened. The subscribers, usually the parents or grandparents of the child or children, make contributions to the plan. They receive no tax deduction or credit for the contributions. The institution holding the plan invests the money and no tax is paid on the income as it accumulates.

---

[17] CRA rules will often require employers to withhold income tax on the work that students do even though the student will not owe any tax at year-end. Students must file tax returns to recover these overpaid income taxes.

[18] A useful source of information is <www.cra-arc.gc.ca/tx/ndvdls/tpcs/resp-reee/menu-eng.html>.

When they were first created, RESPS had annual contribution limits. Since 2007, there is only a total limit on all contributions of $50,000 for a beneficiary, in all plans combined. This limit applies to each beneficiary separately. A plan may name more than one beneficiary, and the limit is $50,000 for each beneficiary. The income of the contributor does not limit the contribution. Another way to put it is that up to $50,000 per beneficiary may be tax-sheltered in RESPs. What happens if the contributors are careless and the total contributions exceed $50,000? Each subscriber for that beneficiary is liable to pay a 1% per-month tax on his or her share of the excess contribution that is not withdrawn by the end of the month. The tax is payable within 90 days of the end of the year in which there is an excess contribution. An excess contribution exists until it is withdrawn.

No contributions are allowed after the 31st year of the plan's existence, and it must be completed by the 35th anniversary of its establishment.

Canada Education Savings Grant (CESG)

Human Resources and Skills Development Canada (HRSDC) administers both the CESG and the Canada Learning Bond (CLB) that we describe subsequently.

HRSDC pays into the RESP a basic grant of 20% of the value of the contributions in a year, up to a maximum in one year of $500 and a lifetime maximum of $7,200 for each beneficiary until the end of the calendar year in which the beneficiary turns 17. If there is grant room carried over from previous years, the maximum grant is $1,000 per beneficiary. To make this clearer, suppose a contributor did not contribute in 2010 but put $10,000 into an RESP in 2011. The maximum grant for 2011 is $1,000 (including $500 grant room carried forward from 2010). In fact, this contribution "earns" $2,000. HRSDC would pay another $500 basic CESG in 2012 as well as 2013, even without any further contribution.

An additional CESG is payable at the rate of either 10% of the first $500 contributed, or 20% of the first $500 contributed each year in respect of each beneficiary. The additional CESG depends on the net income of the family of the child's primary caregiver. The 20% rate applies when the family has net income less than $41,545 in 2011. The 10% rate applies when the family has net income between $41,544 and $83,088 in 2011. These thresholds are indexed to inflation each year. If the net income of the family exceeds $83,088, HRSDC pays no additional CESG. (Table 8.2, including 2012 figures, shows how the grant works.)

Canada Learning Bond (CLB)

A family that is eligible for the **National Child Benefit** (NCB) supplement[19] may also receive additional assistance in saving for education for children born on or after January 1, 2004. The family must open an RESP, but no contribution is

---

[19] We do not discuss the NCB and the associated tax credits in this textbook. The HRSDC also manages the NCB. For more information, see <www.nationalchildbenefit.ca/eng/home.shtml>.

TABLE 8.2 Canada Education Savings Grants				
	CESG on annual RESP contribution			
Net Family Income	first $500	$501 to $2,500	Maximum yearly CESG	Lifetime maximum CESG
2011 $41,544 or less 2012 $42,707 or less	40% = $200	20% = $400	$600	
2011 $41,545–$83,088 2012 $42,707–$85,414	30% = $150	20% = $400	$550	$7,200
2011 Over $83,088 2012 Over $85,144	20% = $100	20% = $400	$500	

required. In the first year, the CLB provides $500 contribution to the RESP plus $25 to help meet the cost of opening the RESP. For subsequent years, but not later than the year the child turns 15, an additional CLB of $100 may be paid each year that the family is eligible for the NCB. The lifetime limit of the CLB is $2,000 per child.

Payments from an RESP

Educational assistance payments (EAPs) are paid from the accumulated income, the CESG and the CLB. They are added to the recipient's taxable income in the year paid. The promoter will pay them only if the student is enrolled in either a **qualifying educational program** or a **specified education program**. A qualifying program is full-time, and a specified one is part-time with the student to be at least 16 years of age. If it is the first time the student is attending, the maximum EAP is $5,000 for the qualifying program in the first 13 weeks and $2,500 for the specified program in the first year. Since the student will have low income, the marginal tax rate is very low or zero. The contributors would have had much higher marginal tax rates when they contributed. An RESP is thus both an income deferral and income splitting instrument.

Accumulated Income Payments (AIPs) are paid from the accumulated income to the plan's contributors. The promoter pays the income to the contributors only when it becomes virtually certain that the beneficiary will not use the money for post-secondary education. These payments are taxable income to the contributors in the year paid, except that they may be partially or wholly offset by making a contribution to the contributors' RRSPs if they have contribution room available. Regular income tax applies, but there is also an additional 12% tax in Québec and 20% in the rest of Canada. This additional tax is intended to make it less beneficial for a taxpayer to set up an RESP for a child solely to use it to defer tax on the adult's income.

The plan's promoter may pay out any part of the original contributions at any time. Usually these payments are to the beneficiary. If the beneficiary is not going to enter post-secondary education, the promoter may repay the contributions to the contributor(s) or to the beneficiary. These payments are not taxable income because there was no tax deduction or tax credit for them when they were paid into the plan.

If the plan is terminated or any one of several rules violated, the plan will have to repay the CESG and CLB, plus accrued earnings, to the government. This will usually occur only if the beneficiary is clearly unable or unwilling to attend post-secondary schools.

SUMMARY

There are four fundamental tax minimization strategies (and sometimes combinations of them):

1. **Income deferral**, bringing income into taxable income at a future date and so deferring the payment of income tax until later. This is beneficial because the present value of the future tax payment is less than if it were paid at once.

2. **Income splitting**, allocating income to family members with lower marginal tax rates to reduce the total family tax bill.

3. **Income spreading**, shifting income from years of higher marginal tax rates to years of lower marginal tax rates.

4. **Income sheltering**, reducing tax paid on income (usually investment income) because of some special characteristic.

The major accounting firms and associations all provide helpful tax guides that you can get at no charge. We found the following to be useful and clearly written:

Strategic Personal Tax Planning, Certified General Accountants Association of Ontario, revised annually.
Personal Tax Strategy, PricewaterhouseCoopers LLP, revised annually.
Personal Tax Planner Guide, Canadian Institute of Chartered Accountants, revised annually.

These firms and associations also provide tax information on their websites. The Canadian Tax Foundation provides very useful material as well as links to other websites. The address is <www.ctf.ca>. Click on "LINKS" for links to other sites.

MULTIPLE-CHOICE REVIEW QUESTIONS

1. Which of the following does not provide an opportunity for tax deferral?

   (a) Registered Pension Plan
   (b) Registered Retirement Savings Plan
   (c) Registered Education Savings Plan
   (d) Capital gains on one's home
   (e) None of the above

2. Income splitting refers to the legal allocation of income from a person with higher tax brackets to a related person of lower tax brackets. Which of the following does not provide an opportunity for income splitting?

   (a) Spousal RRSP
   (b) Registered Educational Savings Plan (RESP)
   (c) Gift of a government bond from one spouse to another
   (d) Gift of a dividend-paying stock to a 20-year-old daughter
   (e) All of the above

3. _____ is not a tax minimization strategy.

   (a) Income deferral
   (b) Income splitting
   (c) Income spreading
   (d) Income sheltering
   (e) None of the above

The following information pertains to questions 4 and 5.

Emily Dickens' marginal tax rate is 40%. She plans to put $10,000 per year into her RRSP, investing the money in term deposits earning 6% interest.

4. She plans to retire after 30 years. If her marginal tax rate remains at 40% and if she withdraws her RRSP in one lump sum, after taxes she will have _____.

   (a) $790,582
   (b) $57,435
   (c) $137,648
   (d) $474,349
   (e) none of the above

5. If she invests her money outside her RRSP for the next 30 years, how much money will she have after taxes?

    (a) $474,349
    (b) $314,883
    (c) $524,806
    (d) $790,582
    (e) None of the above

DISCUSSION QUESTIONS

1. Explain each of the following terms:

    income attribution / income deferral / income splitting / income spreading / Registered Educational Savings Plan (RESP) / Registered Pension Plan (RPP) / Registered Retirement Savings Plan (RRSP) / spousal RRSP / tax shelters

2. What is the dividing line between ethical and unethical behaviour in tax minimization?

PROBLEMS

1. Can you suggest an additional tax minimization strategy for Rose and Andres in Example 8.2?

2. Inmoo Kwan works as a shift supervisor in a factory in Summerside, P.E.I., for a salary of $40,000 p.a. He wants to take a one-year manufacturing technology program that will improve his future income and job-security prospects substantially. His employer has agreed to give him a one-year unpaid leave from his job, starting either immediately on January 1 or on July 1 following. From an income tax point of view, which date should he choose if

    (a) he will finance his studies by cashing $30,000 of Canada Savings Bonds?
    (b) he will finance his studies by withdrawing money from his RRSP?

3. Elizabeth and Anita are living with their two children from their previous marriages in a large four-bedroom apartment. Elizabeth (42 years old) is a lawyer, earning about $120,000 p.a. Anita (41 years old) used to be a free-lance secretary and housepainter, but she has worked in the home for several years. Neither of them has a pension plan. The children are aged 13 and 10.

    On the breakdown of their marriages, each one of them negotiated lump-sum settlements from their husbands in lieu of child support payments (Elizabeth, $60,000; Anita $150,000). Anita has used the interest income and a part of the principal to pay a reasonable share of the household expenses. The largest single expense is the apartment, at $2,000 per month. They have been quite modest in their lifestyle. As a result, Elizabeth has been able to save quite a bit, and she now has $140,000 in term deposits at the bank. Anita has $130,000 in certificates at a trust company. They earn about 6% on their money. They have $2,000 in a joint chequing account.

Although they have always been careful with money and make saving a priority, they are starting to worry about retirement and also how to help the children if they want to go to college or university. Without setting a specific dollar target, suggest how they can make the most of their savings under two different assumptions:

(a) They are a spousal couple (see Chapter 5).
(b) They are not a spousal couple and do not plan to live together after the children are independent.

4. Alas, Maggie and Pierre have separated after 10 years of marriage and three children. Maggie is a successful actress with a large income. Pierre is an unemployed former politician. He is taking custody of the children and will stay home with them for the next six years. As a fair settlement to split up their tangible assets at the date of separation, he gets the marital home. However, since he will have no income, Maggie will have to pay him an additional amount to help support him until he returns to work after six years. The problem at hand is whether a lump sum or a periodic annuity is better, and how to equate the two.

You are the advisor. You expect Maggie to have a marginal tax rate of 48% throughout the six years, and Pierre to have a marginal rate of 26%. The *Income Tax Act* makes spousal support under a separation agreement taxable for the recipient and tax deductible for the payer. Lump-sum payments and child-support payments are not taxable for the recipient nor tax deductible for the payer. You observe that the current EAR on six-year Canada bonds is 7%. To simplify matters, assume that any lump sum is paid today, and that the first payment of any series of annual payments occurs one year from today.

(a) What are their after-tax discount rates?
(b) Maggie offers $65,000. What before-tax annual payment stream of spousal support payments for six years is equivalent to the lump sum from her point of view?
(c) Pierre asks for a lump sum of $80,000. What before-tax annual payment stream for six years is equivalent to the lump sum for him?
(d) "You rotten free-loader," yells Maggie. "I don't have anything more than $65,000, and I don't have the house either. Why don't you go back to that Liona Whatsername, she's got lots of money." Pierre's reply was altered in Hansard. After you cool them down, how do you advise them so that they both do better financially on this part of the separation agreement? Explain how your advice works in general for any separation.

(e) Now, to make the problem more interesting, assume that expected inflation is 3% p.a. Pierre wants the payment indexed to the rate of inflation. That is, the payment at the end of this year will be $1.03x$, the payment at the end of two years will be 1.03^2x, and so on. They agree on a payment of $21,000 in real dollars for the first year, which means the first payment at year-end will be $21,630. The marginal tax rates are unchanged. The 7% bond rate is unchanged (i.e., it is nominal). What is the expected present value of the after-tax cost to Maggie? What is the expected present value of the after-tax receipt to Pierre? You can't do this with annuities, you must do it year by year (see next part). That is, you discount the inflated (nominal dollar) amounts each year by the nominal rates.

(f) Redo part (e) by treating the $21,000 amount as a real dollar annuity and discounting by the real after-tax discount rate.

5. Do Example 8.4 over, assuming the payments are child-support payments.

6. Victoria Zaremba and Basil Kalymon have been living together for four years in Mississauga, Ontario. Basil has been selling real estate for six years and Victoria finished her pharmacy degree a few months ago. Victoria likes everything about her new job with a large pharmaceutical company and plans to stay long term. She gets a good salary and benefits, including a pension plan and long-term disability insurance. Basil has no benefits from his employer, but he ordinarily earns over $100,000 p.a. In the year just past he had an unexpectedly large extra commission of $100,000, which he has just received and put into a savings account at the bank. Today is January 15, 2012, and here is their balance sheet:

Assets		Liabilities	
Chequing account	$ 500	Credit cards current	$ 5,500
Savings account	100,000	Overdue credit cards	10,000
Car	10,000	Student loans	10,000
Personal	15,000	Line of credit	40,000
	$125,500	Net Worth	60,000
			$125,500

They live in an apartment now. Until recently they have been living from paycheque to paycheque, but now that Victoria is working they plan to save. They would like to buy a house in a few years.

(a) How should they use the $100,000 in the savings account to minimize income tax, and why?

(b) How should they manage their savings in the future?

7. Lawrence Kryzanowski has a diversified portfolio of securities with a market value of $70,000 and an ACB (adjusted cost base) of $50,000. He expects an average compound growth rate of the value of the portfolio to be 8% p.a. Every purchase or sale costs .2% of the market value. His marginal tax rate is 40% now and in the future. He could sell the portfolio now, pay tax, and reinvest the remainder, or he could hold it without selling until he retires in 14 years. In either case he will sell everything at the end of 14 years.

(a) How much more money will he have in 14 years, after tax, if he chooses to hold everything until then instead of selling now and reinvesting?

(b) In practice, he probably wouldn't sell everything when he retires. Why not? What part of the question is invalid if he sells everything in one year? How can he avoid the problem?

CHAPTER 9

Risk Management

Everyone should have plenty of life insurance. Is that true? How do you assess the risks facing the family and plan for them? Learn about "the law of large numbers", "moral hazard", "self-insurance", and how to apply the life cycle concept to managing a family's financial risks.

LEARNING OBJECTIVES

> ➤ *To develop the concept and practice of a five-stage personal risk-management process: identify, evaluate, control, finance, and monitor.*
>
> ➤ *To explain the theoretical role of insurance in financing personal risks.*

When families think about the financial risks they face, they turn immediately to insurance to protect themselves. In this chapter we postpone the visit to the insurance agent in order to develop a conceptual model of personal risk management. Insurance plays a critical role in the process, but it is not the only factor, nor is it the first thing you should consider.

We discuss financial risk only in this book. There are tragedies worse than losing money — who could put a price on losing an only child? — but we leave them for others more qualified to offer advice.

The risk management process we describe is equally useful in business management, which is where it developed. Although we won't discuss business risk issues much, the applications will be quite evident.

DEFINING RISK

We all have an intuitive understanding of risk — the possibility of losing something valuable. We can divide risk up into two types to understand them better.

Speculative risk involves loss and gain, but in uncertain amounts. You buy a lottery ticket, and you have a very small chance of winning a lot of money and a big chance of losing the dollar you paid for it. You buy common shares in a company with uncertain future dividends and capital gains prospects. You leave your secure job and start your own business. Each of these actions may make more money for you, or it may cost you money. In this formal definition, *speculative* does not mean gambling on something in the way that the term is used in common language.[1] A speculative risk has a probability of winning and a probability of losing. Speculative risks are generally those that you choose to accept rather than those that you encounter simply because of your circumstances. All investments, for example, are speculative risks, though some are riskier than others.

We defer consideration of speculative risk to the investments and retirement chapters. The same basic risk management principles apply, but their application is more appropriate in the context of those chapters.

---

[1] Gambling is, however, entirely a speculative risk since you may win or lose.

Pure risk involves the possibility of loss only. Early death, disability, and theft of your car are all pure risks. Generally, pure risks are ones that happen to us without us having made a conscious choice to seek them out.

THE RISK MANAGEMENT PROCESS

Step 1: Identifying the Risks

This is perhaps the most important step, though it seems easy. Many people avoid this step because they believe "It won't happen to me." Others fail to recognize which risks are the most serious. Regrettably, many people buy the wrong insurance, or the wrong amount, because they listen to skilled salespeople before they assess their own needs. Some of the risks are related to the life-cycle stages, and must be reviewed as the family situation changes. We can group them into three general categories: personal, or life and health; property; and liability to other persons for our actions that affect them. We expand on these three categories in Table 9.1.

A table like this cannot capture all the possible risks, but it is a useful guide. The life cycle stages for health and disability risks show those risks that are most likely to be important, but others are possible. For example, a retired single could have both dependent parents and dependent children. We added a category of child to this table because the disability of a child may be a serious financial problem for the parents. The death of a child is not, however, because the child is not contributing significant income to the family.

Most Canadians think the risk of liability means third-party liability insurance on a car (mandatory in all Canadian jurisdictions). That is, if you cause harm to another person with your car, you may be found liable for the other person's losses. These losses might be very large, e.g., present value of lifetime earnings if you kill someone.

Other liabilities could be just as material. You are required to ensure that your property does not pose a danger to a reasonable person. If George Clooney comes to call, breaks his leg by falling over a loose step, and can't act again, you are in big trouble. You could be in even bigger trouble if Kirsten Dunst were the injured party because she is younger and therefore has more years of future earnings.

The rule governing these sort of liabilities is the common law applying to **torts** — legal wrongs or injuries one person causes another. Common law is the part of the law determined by court decisions over a long period of time rather than by statute. The court will not find you responsible for someone else's losses as long as you take reasonable care. For example, if a hurricane blows a healthy tree from your property onto someone's car, you wouldn't be responsible. If you knowingly left a dying and weakened tree on your property and it fell on a car in a light breeze, you probably would be found liable for the damage to the car.

TABLE 9.1 Significant Personal Risks		
	Risk	**Possible Losses**
Life and Health		
Stage in Life Cycle:†		
All stages	Disability	Extra expenses, family duties
1–6	Disability	Income (limited time or permanent)
2–5	Death	Income
2–5, 7	Death	Extra expenses, family duties
Child	Disability	Extra expenses
Property		
Source of Risk:		
Rental residence	Damage or destruction	Cost of finding other accommodation, including hotel bills
Owned residence	Damage or destruction	Repair or replacement, cost of temporary accommodation
Automobile	Theft, damage or destruction	Repair or replacement, cost of temporary replacement rental
Other Assets	Theft, damage or destruction	Repair or replacement, additional expenses while waiting
Liability		
Source of Risk:		
Unincorporated business	Liability to second, third party	Amount lost by other parties, legal costs
Property	Liability to third party	Amount lost by third party, legal costs

† As shown in Chapter 6, Table 6.1, stages are 1, single; 2, childless couple; 3, 4, families with children; 5, older couple; 6, older single; 7, 8, couple, single retired.

Limited companies are also liable for their actions (or inaction), but the limited liability means that the investors are not responsible beyond the amount of money paid for the investment.[2] Unincorporated businesses and professionals are

---

[2] Both legislatures and courts are imposing increasingly broad and significant personal liabilities on directors of companies and other organizations. This is a specialized topic beyond the scope of this book. If you are a director of any legally constituted organization — company, charity, government agency, etc., you should get expert legal advice on your responsibilities.

	TABLE 9.2 Evaluation of Risks		
		Probability of Occurrence	
		High	**Low**
Size of Loss	**Large**	Insupportable	Insupportable
	Small	Supportable	Immaterial

personally liable without limit for all losses they cause. These losses may be to their customers and creditors (second party, or contractual liability) or to a third party. This unlimited liability is the most important reason why most small businesses incorporate since otherwise the owners put not only their direct investment at risk, but also virtually everything else they own.

Once you have identified the risks, you need to evaluate them.

Step 2: Evaluating the Risks

We did some preliminary evaluation of the risks in the previous step by listing only those that could be important. Now we evaluate them using two criteria: (i) the size of the potential loss, and (ii) the frequency or probability of occurrence. Which risks you wish to avoid and which you can live with is a personal decision, but Table 9.2 gives some guidance. The basic rule is that a risk is insupportable if it materially affects the family's standard of living.

The normal family cannot run the risk of very large losses even if the probability is quite low, if it can avoid them somehow. The death of one of the parents in a family with young, dependent children is such a loss. While the occurrence is not common, the lost income and family duties constitute a huge and potentially unmanageable financial loss.[3] On the other hand, small losses are not a big problem even if relatively frequent.

We haven't defined "large" and "small" in terms of the size of the losses. This depends on the family's resources. Theft of a car costing $15,000 to replace is a loss some families can afford; others cannot. It is quite small compared with the

---

[3] This loss is quite severe even for a homemaker spouse since the work done by him or her must be replaced. If the other spouse is to continue to be the breadwinner for the family, paid help (daycare, cleaning person, occasional babysitters) is usually necessary. Even so, the surviving spouse will have a substantially greater workload to carry.

potential loss if you are negligent and cause an automobile accident. Thus, if we were advising you on your car insurance policy, we would say, first, take all the liability insurance you need. Then, assess how much you can afford to pay for any other problem with the car. Perhaps you have very little reserve cash and need to be insured almost totally. Perhaps you can afford to write off the car and so you take nothing but the third-party liability coverage.

Probability of occurrence is not precisely defined, either. None of the events subject to risk management occur frequently — they would be part of ordinary life if they did so. Your chance of dying in an airline crash is probably even less than the proverbial one in a million. By contrast, if you drive a car 10 kilometres to work every day, you have something like a one in three chance of an accident serious enough to at least cause material property damage during your working life. Even so, a one-third probability over a 30-year period is not a high probability on a daily basis.

Once you have decided which risks are insupportable, you must consider how to control them, if possible.

Step 3: Controlling the Risks

One method is **avoidance**. For example, you can avoid the risk of injury in a dangerous sport by not engaging in it. You can avoid the risk of air crashes by taking the train. Avoidance applies to actions where we have some choice in what we do.

A second method for controlling some risks is **separation**. Parents who travel on different airplanes will not be killed in the same accident, leaving the children without support. Spouses who work for the same company increase the severity of the risk of job loss since both might lose their employment at the same time. This method only applies in a few situations for families because much of their life is spent together. It tends to be more useful for large organizations.

Prevention or **reduction of frequency** is the most widely applicable method. We reduce the risk of disability or premature death with good nutrition, regular exercise, and preventive medicines. We protect property with smoke detectors, bolt locks, and preventive maintenance. We reduce the likelihood of being sued for negligence by driving carefully and incorporating the family business.[4]

The size and probability of the loss will dictate the amount of time and money you will spend to control it. Another factor is the availability of a means of financing it. If there is no way to finance a risk, then you will do more to control it. If financing is readily available, then you may discard all precautions if that is the cheaper way to deal with it.

---

[4] The children's lemonade stand need not be incorporated, though you may wish to reduce risk by ensuring that they serve lemonade without adding anything from the liquor cabinet!

Step 4: Financing the Risks

For families, **financing a risk** means finding someone to share it with through insurance. We detour from the applications for a short explanation of the principles of insurance.

Basic Principles of Insurance

Insurance is based on the **law of large numbers**. If the occurrences of some particular event are independent of each other, then in a large population the probability of their occurring can be represented by the average observed frequency. The population can share the risk of an event involving an insupportable loss to a family by pooling its funds. Every family contributes an amount equal to the probability of the occurrence times the value of the loss. The specific families who suffer losses receive compensation from the pool and the ones who suffered no loss are poorer only by their contribution to the pool. *Ex ante* (before the fact), we don't know which families will suffer the losses. Every family finances its risk by paying the premium, which is a certain cost but supportable.

This pooling or insurance works only under some conditions. We have already said the occurrences must be independent. If they are related in some way, then the probability is not stable since the existence of some occurrences increases the probability of more of them. For example, private insurers do not insure against job loss because it is not an independent occurrence. If a factory closes down in an area, other jobs are more likely to disappear, too. The most dramatic example of this is the recent shutdown of much of Canada's East Coast fishery. The loss of some fishing jobs signals the loss of more since all are dependent on the same fish stocks. Then the fish-packing plants close, and all the small retail and service businesses in the fishing communities are threatened because their customers have no work.

For some of these dependent conditions that are uninsurable, the government provides what it calls insurance. In the example, it is Employment Insurance (EI) benefits. EI is not insurance, because some people have virtually no chance of losing their jobs and would never choose to pay EI premiums if they had a choice. Instead, our society agrees that it has to share risk in a very general sense and allows the government to tax and redistribute wealth through a variety of welfare mechanisms. EI premiums are a tax, and EI is a form of welfare.

As a practical matter, the insurer must be able to establish the time, the place, the cause, and the amount of the loss. In some cases, less than perfect determination of some of these factors is acceptable. The time and place an illness first occurred may be uncertain. The cause of a car accident may be uncertain. The amount must be determinable; otherwise, compensation is impossible.

Widespread catastrophes like war and earthquakes are not generally insurable because no insurer is large enough to spread the risks. Risks subject to **moral hazard** are not insurable. Moral hazard occurs when the loss is due to deliberate actions or choices of the insured. For example, no one will insure you against the risk of personal bankruptcy because such insurance would give you a terrific incentive to gamble on the lottery. If you win, you are rich; if you lose, the insurer pays off.

One myth we wish to dispel is **self-insurance**. It is not insurance at all; it is a decision not to finance a risk. If the decision is rational, then the family has judged that the loss is not great enough to materially affect its standard of living. Alternatively, a family may have money to cover only more pressing needs and be forced to gamble on risks that it can neither afford to insure nor to incur. Once again, this is the absence of insurance, not a special kind of insurance called self-insurance.[5]

Mechanics of Insurance

In our society, insurance companies pool the risks and write contracts with many individuals and organizations. Since they have expenses in doing this work and shareholders who want profits, they charge more than the average value of the losses. They handle this intermediation of risk more efficiently than we can as individuals, so we are prepared to pay the extra cost.

An important part of their expenses lies in the determination of the premiums to be charged. Their staff use vast quantities of statistics on the occurrence of certain events in order to develop **actuarial tables** that show probabilities of occurrences for every possible combination of age, sex, occupation, etc.

For example, there are **mortality tables** that show the probability that a Canadian will die within the next year, for each age up to 110+ (see Appendix B). The detailed tables show the same statistic separately for men and women, smokers and non-smokers, male smokers, male non-smokers, males working in coal mines who smoke, males working in coal mines who don't smoke, and so on. The life insurance company can use these tables to calculate the probability of death for an applicant during the next year. It then adds an amount for its expenses, and offers the policy, priced at $x per $1,000 of principal amount.

The insurance business has become segmented into life and health insurance, discussed in Chapter 10; and property, casualty, and liability insurance, discussed in Chapter 11.

Step 5: Monitoring the Risk Profile

You don't manage your risk once and then forget about it for 20 years. The material risks will change as you move through the life cycle, both because of the

---

[5] Some organizations are so large that they do not carry certain types of insurance because their operations and employees are numerous enough to allow the law of large numbers to apply without pooling risks with others. For them, self-insurance is an acceptable way of avoiding paying administration costs to insurance companies.

risks you have and your financial ability to support them. You needn't spend much time on revision since all you have to do is reconsider Tables 9.1 and 9.2 with your basic work already done.

When would you be most likely to revise your estimation of your risk situation? Changes in the life cycle — marriage, birth of a child, marriage breakup, children becoming independent, retirement, death of a spouse — are the most likely triggers. When one of these occurs, you should go through the risk management process again.

Even without such obvious changes, occasional reflection is useful. Some people review their insurance coverage annually. As we have shown, risk management is more than insurance, but an annual review of both together is a good idea. Perhaps as you sit reviewing your insurance over a cigarette and your third brandy of the evening, you will remember your last medical checkup, and consider other methods of reducing your risk of heart attacks!

SUMMARY

Risk management is a lifelong process that involves five steps: identification, evaluation, control, financing, and monitoring. The important risks you face will change over the life cycle. You should evaluate risks based on both the possible losses and the probability of occurrence. You can manage risk with control techniques, or you can finance it using insurance. You must review your risk profile regularly and particularly when you change stages in the life cycle.

MULTIPLE-CHOICE REVIEW QUESTIONS

1. In the evaluation of risk, an insupportable risk is a risk that _____.

    (a) may result in a potential loss that the insured person cannot afford
    (b) no insurance company will insure
    (c) the insurance premium is very high
    (d) one cannot provide evidence to make an insurance claim
    (e) none of the above

2. _____ is a method to control risk.

    (a) Self-insurance
    (b) Avoidance
    (c) Separation
    (d) (a) and (b)
    (e) (b) and (c)

3. _____ involves potential gain and loss, but in uncertain amounts.

    (a) Pure risk
    (b) Insurance risk
    (c) Speculative risk
    (d) Supportable risk
    (e) Insupportable risk

4. It is recommended that people should monitor their risk profile periodically because _____.

    (a) an insupportable risk may become supportable
    (b) a supportable risk may become insupportable
    (c) they may want to increase self-insurance
    (d) they may need more insurance coverage
    (e) all of the above

5. _____ is based on _____.

    (a) Insurance / the law of large numbers
    (b) The result of the evaluation of risk / the person's education level
    (c) Whether to buy insurance or not / the person's wealth
    (d) (a) and (b)
    (e) None of the above

DISCUSSION QUESTIONS

1. Explain the significance of the following entries:

   insurance: actuarial tables — law of large numbers — moral hazard — self-insurance / pure risk / risk management process: identify — evaluate — control — finance — monitor / speculative risk

2. Draw up a risk profile for your family, and evaluate the risks.

3. List the control measures and insurance you have for the answer to Question 2. Are you satisfied with your risk management? Can you do anything about it?

4. Discuss the appropriateness of the categorization scheme in Table 9.1. Can you think of any family situations not covered by the categories? What sort of changes would you suggest in these categories?

PROBLEMS

1. Identify and evaluate the most likely material risks for these families:

    (a) Reed Chalmers is a 62-year-old professor of alchemy at York University, where he has been employed for 30 years. He will retire shortly with a comfortable pension. His wife, Florimel, is 50. She has stayed at home with the children, now independent, for almost all her adult life. She does not plan to work outside the home in the future.

(b) Schmendrick the Magician is an itinerant performer in circuses and local fairs. His wife, Molly Grue, works the sideshows or cooks. They are both 35 years old, have no children, and have no assets to speak of.

(c) Brian M. is the former prime minister of a medium-sized country. He is in his fifties, with a wife a fair bit younger and three dependent children. He has a pension that is inadequate for the family's accustomed standard of living, and no full-time job.

(d) Salvatore Cuchimel is the former police chief of a small city in a small country where the government changes frequently. He is on a forced leave of absence at the age of 55 because of his heavy drinking and excess weight. He has no savings, a small house, and the expectation of modest pension granted by the national government's justice minister. If and when he returns to work he will receive back pay for his leave period and several years of unclaimed holidays, in addition to his generous regular salary. His wife is dead, but he has a physically handicapped child who will be dependent on him for life.

2. Eustace Wingtip, 44 years old, is a world-famous poet, renowned for his books of Spenserian sonnets. Last year he earned $2,400. Fortunately, he is not married, has no children, and is the only child of Sam and Samantha Wingtip, who made millions selling cut-rate men's shoes. His parents dote on him and have provided moderate income supplements for many years. They will not provide a large lump sum for him to spend. He is their sole heir (they are in their late 70s). Eustace lives with his cat, his typewriter, and thousands of books in a luxurious apartment in downtown Vancouver. What are his significant risks requiring insurance? Give specific reasons for your answer.

3. George has been courting Russian women over the Internet. He has been separated for several years and he wishes to remarry. He visited several of them this year in Russia and he and Sophia hit it off at once. Now he is trying to arrange a visa for Sophia to visit Canada when they will get married and start making arrangements for her to get permission to immigrate to Toronto. The Russian government will create no obstacles but she will have to meet Canadian rules to immigrate. Being married to a Canadian citizen is not a sufficient condition for entry to Canada, though it helps a lot. George is currently an underemployed engineer whose job is part-time and will not last, and since he is 51, jobs are hard to find. He owns a small condo with a substantial mortgage and has no significant financial assets. He pays monthly child support for one child, age 15. Sophia is a university graduate 15 years

younger than him, and she works as a computer technician in St. Petersburg. She is divorced and has no children. Identify and evaluate George's risks and suggest ways to deal with them. This problem requires some general knowledge of Canada's immigration rules, but if you don't know, assume what you think is reasonable. Do not include plutonium, the KGB, or James Bond in your solution.

CHAPTER 10

Life, Health, and Disability Insurance

Max Brownlie, 35, earns $30,000 per year and expects his income to increase at the rate of inflation every year. His wife also depends on his income. He intends to retire at 65. Is there a simple way to estimate the amount of life insurance he needs now? See Example 10.1.

LEARNING OBJECTIVES

> ➢ *To determine the amount of life insurance coverage that a family needs by (a) the income approach and (b) the expense approach.*
>
> ➢ *To explain the most common insurance policies sold in the market, including term life, whole life, universal life, and endowment policies.*
>
> ➢ *To describe a method that can be used to compare different life insurance policies.*
>
> ➢ *To explain the major features of a typical disability insurance policy.*

Risk management is a very important component in personal financial management. Many families are exposed to risks that are insupportable. In this chapter, you will learn how to deal with two of those insupportable risks. First, you will learn how to use life insurance to finance the risk of loss of income due to the premature death of a family member. Second, you will learn how to use disability insurance to finance the risk of loss of income due to the disability of a family member.

LIFE INSURANCE

Life insurance is a means of financing the risk of the premature and untimely death of a family member. Most people cannot afford the risk of very large losses that materially affect the family's standard of living. The loss of income due to the unanticipated death of a family member is an **insupportable risk** for most families. The most common way to finance such risk is, as we have discussed in Chapter 9, to find other people to share it — through insurance. A relatively small premium is exchanged for the insurance company's promise to pay a potentially large amount, which will ensure that income will be provided to financial dependants of the insured in the event that the insured dies. Before we proceed, we must introduce some basic terms:

Insured: The person upon whose death the death benefit (or the face value) of the insurance policy will be paid.

Beneficiary: The person(s) who receives the death benefit or face value of the policy upon the death of the insured.

Death Benefit or Face Value: The dollar amount that will be paid to the beneficiary if the insured dies.

Premium: The dollar amount that must be paid to the insurance company. The premium may be payable in one lump sum or periodically — monthly, quarterly, semi-annually, or annually.

Owner: The person who pays the premiums. The owner can be the insured, his or her employer, the beneficiary, or other third parties. If you buy life insurance for your son, you are the *owner* and your son is the *insured*.

Policy Term: The period during which the insurance is in force. The term can range from one year to an entire lifetime.

Rate: The cost of each unit of insurance. A rate of $2.50 per $100 unit means that the premium for $10,000 of insurance is equal to ($2.50 × 100) or $250.

Insurability: The qualification for the insured to be insurable. There are certain requirements that the insured may have to meet before an insurance policy can be bought; for example, the insured may have to pass a medical examination.

Guaranteed Insurability: A provision that allows the insured to buy additional life insurance at certain specified future dates without proof of insurability — e.g., without undergoing a new medical examination.

Do You Need Life Insurance?

We have already provided a framework for you to analyze and answer this question in Chapter 9. Basically, you simply evaluate the risk of your premature and untimely death and ask whether it is supportable or insupportable. The basic purpose of life insurance is to ensure that your financial dependants will be provided for financially in the event of your unanticipated death. Therefore, if you do not have financial dependants, you do not need life insurance. Still, you should not skip this chapter because it is important for you to know about life insurance for at least two reasons. First, your situation will change much sooner than you think. When you move to the next stages of the life cycle — getting married, having children, and so on — you will probably need life insurance because you will then have financial dependants. Second, there are plenty of employment opportunities in the financial planning and the insurance industries, where a good knowledge of life insurance is very important.

Who needs life insurance? An individual who has financial dependants who will suffer financially (in the sense of a material fall in the standard of living) will need life insurance. Here it is important to understand the difference between "financial dependants" and "dependants". Let us take a family of four as an example. Suppose the father is the only breadwinner and the mother is a full-time homemaker.

The loss of a daughter is an enormous emotional loss to the father, but the father does not need life insurance protection against the daughter's death because he is not financially dependent on her; however, the reverse is not true. The death of the father is not only an emotional loss to the daughter but also a big financial loss because she relies on him financially. In this example, the father should buy insurance to protect the family in the event of his death.

Does the family need insurance on the life of the wife who is a full-time homemaker? Although she does not earn a salary in explicit monetary terms, she certainly provides valuable services that would cost money to replace. Furthermore, the odds are good that she will work outside the home later in the family life cycle when the children are able to look after themselves. Her earnings later in the life cycle will be important in building a retirement income for the couple. Therefore, it is reasonable to consider life insurance coverage based on the value of the services she performs — child care, cooking, cleaning, etc. — and the possible future income.

The ultimate test of whether a family needs life insurance is whether the standard of living of the remainder of the family will fall materially in the event of the death of one family member. Does a very wealthy businessman with a full-time housewife and four young children need life insurance? The answer is no because the standard of living of the wife and the children is not expected to fall.[1] On the other hand, a childless couple, both working and each earning a good salary, may need life insurance coverage if the standard of living of the remaining spouse is expected to fall substantially.

Three Important Questions in Life Insurance

There are three important questions in life insurance that everyone should answer:

1. Do you need life insurance? Who needs life insurance?
2. How much life insurance do you need? How can people estimate the appropriate amount of insurance they should buy?
3. What kinds of life insurance are sold in the market? What kind of life insurance should you buy?

We have already analyzed and answered the first question. To say it again, one needs life insurance if one has financial dependants and if the standard of living of these dependants is expected to fall as a result of one's premature and unanticipated death. We will now turn to the next two questions.

---

[1] Many wealthy people buy a large insurance policy for the purpose of paying taxes in the event of death, but this is tax planning rather than life insurance planning.

How Much Life Insurance Does a Family Need?

Many people buy too much or too little life insurance without knowing it. In fact, they do not know how to determine the right amount of life insurance. Very often, they bought their current life insurance policies as a result of chance — for example, policies are often sold to purchasers who succumb to aggressive salesmen calling at the right time and the right place. Other people may have bought their life insurance policies because they seemed to be good deals — for example, an employee says to himself, "My employer pays 70% of the premium, so how can I go wrong? Why should I buy only $30,000 just because my annual salary is only $30,000?"; or "My employer will pay 70% of the premium on a policy amount equal to my annual salary. Anything above that, I have to pay the full premium myself. But — do I need more insurance than the equivalent of my total annual salary?"

There are many methods in the life insurance literature to calculate one's required life insurance face value. We will describe two approaches: the income approach and the expense approach. Both are very popular methods used to estimate the amount of life insurance coverage that a family needs.

The Income Approach

The **income approach** estimates the face value of the life insurance (i.e., the amount that the individual needs to buy) by calculating the present value of the insured's expected future income. From a conceptual viewpoint, this is, theoretically, the correct method. The present value of the insured's expected future income is conceptually the insured's **human capital**. Even though human capital cannot be traded in the market like other assets, it has a theoretical value. Life insurance can be viewed as an insurance policy that is protection against the loss of an asset — in this case, the insured's human capital. From this viewpoint, the theoretically correct face-value amount to insure is the value of the insured's human capital, which is simply the present value of the insured's expected lifetime income.

There are three issues that must be dealt with:

1. What is the present discount rate of the insured's expected future income?

2. How do we handle inflation? The insured's income may appear to rise every year but, after accounting for inflation, there may not be any increase at all.

3. The income stream of an individual is very uncertain and, hence, fraught with risk: Income over one's lifetime may go up or down; indeed, it may become zero if and when the person is unemployed.

The first two issues can be easily handled by looking at real income (i.e., income after it is adjusted for inflation) and using the real rate of interest. Let us illustrate this with an example.

Example 10.1: Max Brownlie, 35, is currently earning $30,000 per year. He expects his income will increase at the rate of inflation, which is expected to be 5% every year. He intends to retire at the age of 65, 30 years from now. We want to use the income approach to estimate the face-value amount of the life insurance that Max should buy.

The easiest way to handle inflation is to deal with "real numbers" — real income and real interest rates. Although Max Brownlie's income increases in nominal terms, in real terms, after accounting for inflation, his income remains constant at $30,000 per year for the next 30 years. We can discount this annuity of $30,000 per year for 30 years at the real rate of interest. The **real rate of interest** is usually measured by the nominal rate of interest minus the expected rate of inflation. In Canada, the real rate of interest has been between 2% to 4% in the last four decades. Let us assume that the real rate of interest for the next 30 years will be 3%. The present value of Max's lifetime income is equal to the present value of a 30-year annuity of $30,000 per year. Using a discount rate of 3%, the present value of the annuity is equal to:

$$\$30,000 \times \left[\frac{1}{.03} - \frac{1}{.03(1.03)^{30}} \right] \text{ or } \$588,000 \text{ after rounding.}$$

The Basic Benchmark of the Income Approach

We will call the case in the above example the basic benchmark. Thus the basic benchmark is simply the present value of the insured's lifetime earnings assuming *no growth* in real earnings and using the real rate of interest as the discount rate. It is simple to calculate and to apply. It will take you only two minutes to calculate the basic benchmark for anybody, including yourself. You simply find the present value of an annuity of your current salary. The length of the annuity will be the expected number of working years and the discount rate will be the real rate of interest, say 3%. This basic benchmark will be the amount of life insurance coverage that you should buy, using the income approach. In the above example, Mr. Brownlie should buy about $588,000 of coverage.

Usual Adjustments to the Basic Benchmark

The actual situation of an individual usually differs from the basic benchmark and the individual may want to make adjustments for those differences. The lifetime earning stream is risky and individuals may want to use a higher discount rate than the real rate of interest. Also, for many workers there is usually growth in their real income streams.

The Income Tax Issue

The basic benchmark assumes that the beneficiary pays income tax on the receipts at the same rate as the insured paid on the original income. The income we used to calculate the benchmark was before-tax, and we used a before-tax discount rate. If the beneficiary now pays tax at the same rate on the amounts withdrawn from the proceeds of the policy, then doing everything before tax is correct. By replicating the lump-sum amount that yields the income annuity before tax, we place the beneficiary in the same financial position after-tax as if the insured were still living.

The beneficiary will pay tax at a lower rate in most situations, however. The face amount of a life insurance policy is not taxable income for the beneficiary because the premiums are not tax deductible.[2] The interest earned on the face amount after it is paid out is taxable like any other interest. Thus, the payments the beneficiary lives on for the years after the insured's death are partly taxable interest and partly non-taxable return of principal (just as the blended principal and interest repayments would be for a bank or trust company). Therefore, the principal amount required to replace the insured's income is less than the amount calculated by the basic benchmark method.

We can illustrate this effect with the Max Brownlie example again. Max would have included the entire $30,000 in his calculation of taxable income. His beneficiary will not include the $588,000 lump sum in income, but will declare the interest on it each year. Suppose the beneficiary lives for 50 years more and uses the $588,000 to buy an annuity. The annual payment, in real dollars, using a 3% real rate of interest, would be $22,853. The payments the beneficiary will receive over the 50 years total $50 \times $22,853 = $1,142,650. The beneficiary thus receives ($1,142,650 − $588,000) = $554,650 of taxable interest. To simplify matters, assume away the usual declining balance factor of higher interest payments in the early years. The beneficiary receives on average $554,650 ÷ 50 = $11,093 of income that has to be reported for tax purposes. This amount will attract a lot less tax than the $30,000 p.a. that Max was receiving. If the death benefit provides most of the beneficiary's future income, the income taxes will be very low or zero.

Rule-of-Thumb Adjustment

It is possible to account for all these factors by making the appropriate adjustments in the formula that is used to calculate the present value of the individual's lifetime earning stream; however, the insurance industry has come up with the following rule of thumb. Rather than insuring 100% replacement of the insured's

---

[2] The principal exception is the company that insures a key executive and deducts the life insurance premiums for income tax purposes. The company will have to pay income tax on the policy's face value if the insured dies.

income, families may want to insure only 70% to 80% of the insured's future income. Returning to our example, Max Brownlie may want to insure only 75% of his basic benchmark ($588,000), or $441,000.

The Expense Approach

The **expense approach** is another popular method to estimate the amount of life insurance coverage that a family needs. The idea of the expense approach is as follows. A life insurance face-value amount that the family needs is the amount that will provide enough funds to pay those expected expenses of the beneficiaries that are not covered by government transfer income or other income. If the insured dies, the life insurance death benefit is invested and used as the expenses occur. As we said earlier, the primary objective of life insurance should be to provide income to the dependants so that they can maintain the same standard of living as before. Nevertheless, some people use insurance to provide an increased inheritance or much improved lifestyle to the beneficiaries that is in excess of their needs. This latter approach would leave the family much better off financially in the event of the insured's death. We do not think families should want this; and it would certainly make insurance companies nervous! What we will suggest then is a simple method for determining the life insurance need for the objective of providing the same standard of living to the surviving family members.

The difference between the income approach and the expense approach is that the former calculates the present value of the insured's future income, while the latter calculates the present value of the beneficiaries' future expenses. The implementation of the expense approach is, therefore, very similar to that of the income approach. First, one has to estimate the beneficiaries' expected lifetime expenses and income from all sources. The difference of expenses and income is the "income shortfall" to be financed by the life insurance. As with the income approach, one can handle inflation here by simply using real dollars. One therefore simply estimates the expected expenses in current dollars and then discounts that estimate by using the real rate of interest, say 3%. Example 10.2 illustrates this concept.

Example 10.2: Billy Stieger, 35, is a mining engineer earning $60,000 per year. His wife Nellie, also 35, works part-time as a secretary in an insurance company, earning $20,000 per year. The current family expenditure is $45,000; but if one of them dies, it is expected that the family expenses will fall to $35,000 per year. They expect their income and expenses will increase at the rate of inflation. They want to buy enough life insurance so that in the event of premature death, the surviving spouse will not suffer from a drop in the standard of living.

(a) What is the annual income shortfall if Billy or Nellie dies?

(b) Using the real rate of interest of 3% as the discount rate, what is the amount of life insurance under the Expense Approach that the Stieger family needs?

Answer:

(a) The easiest way to deal with inflation is to use real dollars to measure income and expenditure. If Billy dies, Nellie will still earn $20,000 in real dollars per year until she retires at, say, 65, and the family expenses will be $35,000 in real dollars per year. Therefore, there will be an annual income shortfall of ($35,000 – $20,000) or $15,000 in real dollars per year until age 65. If Nellie dies, Billy's income of $60,000 is more than enough to cover his expected expenses of $35,000, so the annual income shortfall is zero.

(b) The Expense Approach assumes that the purpose of buying life insurance is that in the event of premature death, the surviving family does not suffer from a fall in the standard of living. The amount of life insurance coverage for Billy is the present value of $15,000 real dollars per year for (65 – 35) or 30 years. This is equal to:

$$\$15,000 \times \left[\frac{1}{(.03)} - \frac{1}{.03(1.03)^{30}} \right] \text{ or } \$294,007$$

If Nellie dies, there is no income shortfall, so the amount of life insurance coverage for Nellie is zero.

Note that we calculated the present value of the shortfall up to the point of retirement in our example. The implicit assumption here is that after retirement there will be no income shortfall (because the family will have enough savings, pension income, and government transfer payments to cover expenses). If there is expected income shortfall post-retirement, we can simply extend the present value calculation to include the post-retirement income shortfall.

The Basic Benchmark of the Expense Approach

We will call the amount in the above example the basic benchmark. Thus, the basic benchmark is simply the present value of the insured's expected income *shortfall* from now until retirement. If there is no income shortfall, there is no need to buy life insurance under the expense approach. Thus, a very wealthy person does not need life insurance under this approach because there is no income shortfall if he dies; the surviving family will have enough wealth to support the same standard of living.

In general, the income shortfall may vary from year to year. For example, if a family has children, there will be relatively big income shortfalls in the early years when the children are dependent, but the income shortfall will decrease or even disappear once the children become independent. Theoretically, an individual can be as detailed as he or she wants in the estimation of the annual income shortfall, but such detail is not often done in practice.

An Approximate Benchmark

In practice, many insurance advisors and financial planners adopt an approximate method to estimate the amount of life insurance under the expense approach. This is done by dividing the average annual income shortfall by the discount rate, and then multiplying the answer by an adjustment factor of 70% to 80%, say 75%. In Example 10.2, the amount of life insurance that Billy should buy for himself is [($15,000) ÷ (.03)](.75), which is equal to $375,000.

How do people estimate the beneficiaries' expenses? Many people do not have a good idea about their current expenses: They never seem to know where the money goes. To ask these people to forecast their beneficiaries' future expenses is asking for the impossible. It is much easier for them to use the income approach because these people at least know how much they earn.

You have already learned how to prepare a statement of net worth (or balance sheet), a statement of income and expenditure, and a budget. You already have substantially more knowledge of personal finance than most people. It should therefore not be difficult for you to implement the expense approach, which is a more complete method than the income approach, for calculating the amount of life insurance that your family needs.

If you have not done so already, prepare your family's statement of net worth, its statement of income and expenditure, and its budget. To estimate your beneficiaries' future expenses in the event of your death, the best place to start is your latest statement of income and expenditure.

Examine each item on the statement of income and expenditure carefully. It may be helpful to compare each item with that of your budget. Now change each amount to the expected and desired level of expenditure, assuming that you have died. Some expenses will decrease — e.g., there is one less mouth to feed; there is no need for a second car; there will be less eating out; and so on. Other expenses would increase — e.g., education and child-care expenditures will increase as the children grow older. There may be liabilities that fall due shortly after your death — e.g., mortgage on your home that is not life-insured, tax liabilities, and so on.

After making adjustments and changes for every item on your statement of income and expenditure, you will have a good idea of how much your beneficiaries will need in the event of your death. We shall now introduce a more detail method for determining the amount of life insurance coverage that your beneficiaries need. There are six steps in our approach:

Step 1   Draw up the (projected) balance sheet of the individual at death. This must include the income taxes that will be payable with respect to the year of death. With certain exceptions, a taxpayer is deemed to dispose of all assets at death, and consequently capital gains may be realized.

Step 2   Determine the capital and the assets available that can be invested to generate an annual income for the dependants. Only the liquid and the surplus assets, at liquidation value, should be included. For example, the family home should not be included because the dependants will still be living there. Estimate the annual income that can be generated from this capital and these assets.

Step 3   Add to the above (i) all government payments, such as the survivor benefits from the Canada Pension Plan, Worker's Compensation, etc., and (ii) the spouse's income. Don't forget that even if the spouse is a full-time homemaker now, she can work, especially when the children grow older.

Step 4   Estimate the expenses required for the dependants to live comfortably, preferably at the standard of living currently enjoyed. This is the most important step (and we have already described how one can estimate the beneficiaries' expected expenses).

Step 5   Subtract the amount in Step 3 from that of Step 4 to get the required income shortfall. This is the amount that must be generated from the life insurance face value.

Step 6   Calculate the capital (the life insurance face value) needed to generate the supplemental income in Step 5.

Table 10.1 is a guide and a summary of this process.

Table 10.1 oversimplifies the problem in another important way. The implication is that the required expenses will continue as is until the death of the beneficiary. This is not true. The family expenses may change in the future — for example, as the children grow older, their clothing and food will cost more. When the children are no longer dependent on the surviving parent, expenses decrease a lot, and they may decrease even further when the survivor retires. The largest changes will correspond to changes in the family life cycle stage.

TABLE 10.1
Calculation of the Amount of Life Insurance Needed

1. **Personal Balance Sheet** (after death)

   Assets:

Individual life insurance	$ _____
Group life insurance	_____
CPP death benefits	_____
Cash	_____
Bank accounts	_____
Cash value of pension plans	_____
RRSPs	_____
Investments (stocks, bonds)	_____
Other redundant, saleable assets	
TOTAL ASSETS (A)	$ _____

   Liabilities:

Funeral expenses	_____
Immediate expenses after death	_____
Consumer debt, income taxes	_____
Mortgages; other non-life-insured loans	_____
Contingency fund	_____
TOTAL LIABILITIES (B)	$ _____

2. **Available Capital (C) = (A) – (B)** ..... $ _____

3. **Annual Revenue:**

Income generated by capital (C) $_____ invested at ___% yields	_____
Plus: Spouse's income	_____
Spouse's CPP pension	_____
Children's CPP pension	_____
Spouse's share of employer pension	_____
Other income	_____
Minus: Income taxes	_____
Total = Available Annual Income (D)	$ _____

4. **Expected expenses that the dependants will incur during the period of dependence (E)**

5. **Income shortfall (D) – (E) = (F)**

6. **An annual income of (F) _____ after taxes, at an interest rate of ___, requires a capital of (G)**

(G) is the required amount of life insurance. Leaving aside taxes, (G) is the present value of the annuity of amount (F), using the real rate of interest, say 3%, as the discount rate. As in the income method, taxes are quite tricky since part of the payout will be tax-free, and part will be taxable. The expense method, however, underestimates the amount required since the expenses must be paid in after-tax dollars.

Table 10.1 will still give a reasonable estimate of the insurance needed using rough lifetime averages for the numbers. You can do it more accurately by re-estimating it for each different stage and then discounting the net value for each block of years. You will require a timeline to keep track of all the values.

The Human Capital Approach

A slightly different approach incorporates features of both income and expense methods of estimating required life insurance. In Chapter 4 we discussed the importance of human capital. Life insurance shares the financial risk of your human capital on the dimension of how long you live. Valuing your human capital is thus another way to estimate how much life insurance you need. This method starts with the income approach, but then adjusts it for the unpaid income aspects of shared household duties and the expenses that would not be incurred once the person dies. It is therefore a more accurate estimate than the plain income method but requires more work.

The human capital method should yield a higher value than the expense method if both are done carefully. Managing the risk of your human capital is not exactly the same thing as providing for the expected expenses of your dependants in the event of your premature death. The value of the difference between the two estimates is the **expected bequest** left to the next generation. The expense method includes only the expenses of the dependent children until they reach the age of independence and earn their own living, and the expenses of the surviving spouse until his/her death. Many families will accumulate assets during their working life (i.e., save from their income) that are worth more than the amount needed to support them during their expected period of retirement. Some of these assets are pensions that will cease when both spouses are dead, but some assets will pass to the next generation. An insurance policy that covers only the expected net expenses of this generation should not generate money that will also provide a bequest, on average. Of course, if both spouses die relatively earlier than expected, then the insurance may end up providing much more to the next generation than expected. Conversely, if they live longer than expected, the bequest may shrink or even disappear.

THE PRINCIPAL TYPES OF LIFE INSURANCE

There are many different kinds of life insurance that are sold in the market, and new products are being developed every day. There are term life, whole life, endowment, universal life, group life, single premium, level premium, increasing premium, participating, non-participating, and decreasing term policies, to name just a few. Nevertheless, we can classify all these into two types:

1. Term life policies, which are pure life insurance policies without savings/investment features.
2. Insurance policies that have savings/investment features. Whole life and universal life policies are examples of this second type.

Term Life Insurance

Term insurance is plain life insurance without a savings component. Term insurance pays the face value to the beneficiaries if the insured dies before the expiry date (i.e., within the term). If the insured does not die, the beneficiaries and the insured collect nothing.

There are different kinds of term insurance and we shall mention the most common ones. A **participating term policy** is one on which the insurance company will pay back to the insured each year an amount of money called **dividends**. A **non-participating term policy** means the policy pays no dividends back to the insured. Normally, the premium on a participating policy is higher than the premium on a non-participating policy. Dividends are derived from the investment that the insurance company makes out of the higher premiums the participating policy holders pay. Dividends can be viewed as a partial return of the premium. **Net premium**, defined as the premium minus dividend, is the true annual cost of a participating policy.

If the face value of the policy stays the same throughout the term of the insurance contract, the insurance is called **level term insurance**. If the face value declines as the policy approaches expiry, the insurance is called **decreasing term insurance**. Decreasing term policies are very useful for mortgage borrowers since the principal of the mortgage declines over time.

Term insurance, in other words, is pure insurance with no frills. It offers protection of the face amount of the policy and nothing more. If the insured wishes to terminate the policy, she gets nothing back from the insurance company. The word "term" in a term policy is misleading: Many people think that a term policy is "not permanent" or "non-renewable". This is not true. Generally, as long as the policyholder pays premiums on time, the policy is automatically renewed each year without additional proof of **insurability** — for example, no follow-up medical examination is required. *Term* means the number of years the policy is automatically renewed. One-year, 10-year, 20-year and Terms to Age 100 are common policies offered.

The Pure Premium

To understand the difference between term insurance and insurance with an investment feature, it is important to know how insurance companies calculate premiums. If they charge premiums to the policyholders so that the present value of the revenues received by the insurance company is exactly equal to the expected present value of the benefits paid to the beneficiaries (i.e., the insurance company does not make a profit), then the premium charged is called the **pure premium**. Of course, the premium that one must pay is higher than the pure premium because the insurance companies have to pay administrative and other costs; also, they have to make a reasonable profit. In other words, the insurance premium that one pays is equal to the pure premium plus the insurance company's service costs and profit.

The pure premium depends on the likelihood of the insured dying during the insurance coverage period. How can one find out one's likelihood of dying? The historical death rates for many defined groups of people have been observed and reported in mortality tables. Mortality tables report the historical death rates of various groups of people according to specific characteristics, such as age, smoking addiction, sex, occupation, and so on. Insurance companies can use these mortality tables to predict the number of deaths and the expected payout to the beneficiaries of the group of insured persons in a particular category.

Appendices B1 and B2 contain standard Canadian mortality tables for females and males, respectively. These tables follow a hypothetical group or cohort of 100,000 persons from birth to death and report the actual number of deaths each year for that year. To see how to read the table, turn to Appendix B1 and look at the first line. It says that during the first year of life, Canadian females have a .476% chance (or probability = .00476) of dying. The next line shows the probability of living from age one to two, given that the person has already survived to age one. The cohort at the start of the year is reduced to 99,524 (due to the 476 predicted deaths in the first year of life). The mortality during year 2 is 29 girls, or .029% of 99,524.

> **Example 10.3:** Let us illustrate how the premium of annual term insurance would be calculated. Suppose a male aged 35 wants to buy $200,000 of term insurance for a year. The mortality rate of this specific group of people — 35-year-old males — is .108% (see Appendix B2).

In that case, the life insurance company expects to pay to the beneficiaries on average an amount of:

$$\$200,000 \times .00108 = \$216$$

Thus, the insured must pay $216. This premium, paid by every other person in his category, is just enough, when pooled over a large number of policies, to pay the death benefits that the insurance company expects to have to pay during the year. As we discussed in the risk management chapter, the law of large numbers implies that the actual occurrence of deaths in a large group approaches very closely to the average or expected number of deaths.

Premiums are paid at the beginning of the year, but benefits are paid throughout the year. The insurance payout must be discounted for this period. Let us assume that all benefits are paid at year end. If the appropriate discount rate is 5%, the pure premium that must be charged is equal to ($216 ÷ 1.05) or $205.71. Finally, service costs (including profits) will be added to the pure premium. If servicing costs are $35, then the final premium is equal to ($205.71 + $35.00) or $240.71.

From the above analysis, we see that the premium on a term insurance policy will increase with the insured's age because the probability of death increases with age. Term policies are best suited for the person who wants lower life insurance premiums in the early years of the policy in order to have more money to spend or invest. Term policies are also suitable for the person who will not need life insurance in the later years of life when the premiums become very high. For example, some people feel no need for life insurance when the children are grown up and are financially independent.

We often buy life insurance for many years at once, not just one year at a time, and we need for that the conditional probability that a person will live to age y, given that he is already x years old.

> **Example 10.4:** What is the probability of a 35-year-old woman surviving to age 65?
>
> **Answer:** At age 35 there are 98,695 women surviving out of the original 100,000. At age 65 there are 90,899. The probability of survival, given that the woman has already reached 35, is: 90,899 ÷ 98,695 = 92.1%.

Suppose we want to apply conditional probability to an insurance premium for more than one year. How would the insurance company calculate the level pure premium for a $200,000 policy?

Each year a number of the cohort die and the insurance company pays the full face value of life insurance policies to the beneficiaries. The rest of the insured get no cash payment. The next year, only those still surviving could be eligible for a payout in the event of their death. Therefore, the probability of receiving such a payment in the second year is slightly less because there is a possibility that you died during the previous year. Thus, we can calculate the probability of the death of an individual for each year for a specified number of future years, conditional each year on having survived to that year.

We need this probability to calculate the present value of the expected future payouts. We will not derive it formally, but use the following notation:

M the face amount of the insurance policy, i.e., the death benefit

$_xP_i$ the probability that an individual aged x will survive i more years

Q_{x+i} the probability that an individual aged $(x + i)$ will die during the next year
k the discount rate
T the term of the insurance policy

$$\text{Net Single Premium (NSP)} = M \sum_{i=0}^{T-1} \frac{_xP_i \times Q_{x+i}}{(1 + k)^{i+1}}$$

The final step is to use the same interest rate and term of the policy to convert the net single premium (NSP) into an annuity of net annual premium (NAP), as follows:

$$\text{Net Annual Premium (NAP)} = \text{NSP} \div \sum_{i=0}^{T-1} \frac{_xP_i}{(1 + k)^i}$$

> **Example 10.5:** A 35-year-old single mother requires a $1 million life insurance policy on herself, in favour of her son. When she reaches 40, she will no longer need it because he will receive a trust fund. She wants to pay a level premium. The appropriate interest rate is 7%. What is the pure level premium (no costs, no saving component)?

We can use the two equations for NSP and NAP and the mortality table in Appendix B1 to answer this question. More specifically, $x = 35$, $M = \$1,000,000$, $T = 5$ and $k = .07$, so we have:

$$\text{NSP} = \$1 \text{ million} \times \sum_{i=0}^{4} \frac{_{35}P_i \times Q_{35+i}}{(1.07)^{i+1}}$$

$$= \$1 \text{ million} \times \left[\frac{_{35}P_0 \times Q_{35}}{1.07} + \frac{_{35}P_1 \times Q_{36}}{1.07^2} + \frac{_{35}P_2 \times Q_{37}}{1.07^3} \right.$$
$$\left. + \frac{_{35}P_3 \times Q_{38}}{1.07^4} + \frac{_{35}P_4 \times Q_{39}}{1.07^5} \right]$$

$$= \$1 \text{ million} \times \left[\frac{(1)(.00047)}{1.07} + \frac{(98649/98695)(.00049)}{1.07^2} + \frac{(98600/98695)(.00071)}{1.07^3} \right.$$
$$\left. + \frac{(98530/98695)(0.00058)}{1.07^4} + \frac{(98473/98695)(.00074)}{1.07^5} \right]$$

$$= \$1 \text{ million} \times [.00044 + .00043 + .00058 + .00044 + .00053]$$
$$= \$1 \text{ million} \times (.00242)$$
$$= \$2,420$$

Then to convert it to an annual level premium, we can use the equation for NAP:

$$NAP = NSP \div \sum_{i=0}^{4} \frac{_{35}P_i}{(1.07)^i}$$

$$= \$2,420 \div \left[\frac{1}{1.07^0} + \frac{(98649/98695)}{1.07^1} + \frac{(98600/98695)}{1.07^2} + \frac{(98530/98695)}{1.07^3} + \frac{(98473/98695)}{1.07^4} \right]$$

$$= \$2,420 \div [1 + .93414 + .87260 + .81493 + .76118]$$

$$= \$2,420 \div 4.38285$$

$$= \$552.15$$

Note that the NAP calculation is based on an annuity due because insurance premiums are paid at the start of the period.

Term Life Insurance Premiums

Numerous factors affect the actual premium the insured pays to the insurance company:

• Age
• Gender
• Specific health conditions
• Cost of selling and administering the policy
• The ability of potential insured persons to choose policies beneficial to them
• Duration of the policy

The older the insured, the higher the probability of death during the next year. Men die earlier than women on average. Smokers die earlier on average. These are the most common factors that insurance companies price in their general quotations. A person who takes a medical examination that reveals some specific health risk — heart condition, diabetes, etc. — may be able to get life insurance, but the premium will be much higher.

Individual policies cost more to sell and to administer than group policies. Life insurance agents receive substantial commissions for every policy they sell, whereas large group policies are sold directly by the company for a much lower cost relative to the value of the premiums. Also, the size of the policy matters because it takes the same time to administer a single policy, regardless of size. Therefore, all non-group term life insurance quotations apply to a policy of the specified size. The quotation always includes an implicit fixed **policy fee** and a variable premium that depends on the risk factors.

A person who takes out a policy that expires at the end of one year will get a relatively cheap premium because the company has only one year of risk to assume. If the person wants to renew the policy, he or she must take another medical examination. A person who takes out a 10-year policy may become a serious risk after the first year, but the company cannot rescind the policy. Therefore, a 10-year policy will carry a higher annual premium than a series of one-year policies for someone who is healthy at each annual renewal date because the company cannot avoid the higher risks that some of the 10-year policyholders will pose after the initial purchase of the policy. Ten and 20-year term policies ordinarily have a pre-determined fixed premium rate per year or month.

Group term insurance is usually renewable every year but without further medical testing required. Group term insurance has the advantage of cheaper administrative costs but the disadvantage of what we call **adverse selection**. Adverse selection occurs wherever something is priced to reflect an average quality. The item which is above average quality commands the same price as the item of poor quality. In this case, people who are healthy know they are healthy, but they still pay the same average life insurance premium. The ones who aren't healthy pay an average premium that is too low.

The people who are healthy can always leave the group and buy cheaper insurance as they age and the general rates rise. People in the group who are unhealthy will stay in the group and take advantage of the right to renew their insurance every year without a medical examination. As a result, as the ages rise in a group, the death rate is likely to rise faster than in the general population since those who are least healthy have the greatest incentive to stay insured within the group. Insurance companies must price to compensate for this adverse selection. Group policies are usually priced at a rising rate by age, rather than a fixed rate, because the actual term itself is not fixed.

We could say a great deal more about pricing of insurance policies, but the subject is too large for us to continue. Table 10.2 shows comparative life insurance premiums for level term insurance for 10- and 20-year terms. This type of policy is for long-run coverage. The insured takes out the policy at the age shown, and pays the same premium, in nominal dollars, for the term agreed. At the end of the term, if he or she wants to renew the insurance, a new policy, a new medical examination, and a new rate schedule are all required. The particular prices shown are quotations by a variety of companies and are the lowest available in each category. These quotations will change over time.

Group life insurance premiums vary greatly between groups. Such policies have annual terms but with an option for the insured to renew each year. Each group may have a different mortality table, and there will be different features between the policies set up for the groups. The premium is usually per unit of insurance,

TABLE 10.2
Term Life Insurance Premium Quotations
Annual Premium for $250,000 of Level Term Insurance

These premiums are for 10- and 20-year terms. The premium is the same for each year of the term, starting at the age indicated.

	Non-smoker							
	Average Health				Excellent Health			
	Male		Female		Male		Female	
Age	10-Year	20-Year	10-Year	20-Year	10-Year	20-Year	10-Year	20-Year
25–29	185.00	250.00	115.00	195.00	170.00	222.50	102.50	180.00
30–34	185.00	267.50	132.50	217.50	172.50	235.00	115.00	200.00
35–39	205.00	305.00	162.50	257.50	180.00	277.50	145.00	237.50
40–44	270.00	422.50	207.50	317.50	225.00	355.00	192.50	292.50
45–49	382.50	625.00	280.00	445.00	305.00	507.50	242.50	395.00
50–54	537.50	1,010.00	392.50	697.50	445.00	792.50	330.00	550.00
55–59	785.00	1,667.50	602.50	1,035.00	642.50	1,222.50	475.00	745.00
60–64	1,352.50	2,800.00	957.50	1,912.50	987.50	2,075.00	725.00	1,400.00

	Smoker							
	Average Health				Excellent Health			
	Male		Female		Male		Female	
Age	10-Year	20-Year	10-Year	20-Year	10-Year	20-Year	10-Year	20-Year
25–29	282.50	397.50	165.00	252.50	235.00	340.00	132.50	255.00
30–34	302.50	455.00	197.50	347.50	265.00	367.50	170.00	300.00
35–39	332.50	645.00	252.50	485.00	297.50	495.00	230.00	397.50
40–44	495.00	975.00	365.00	665.00	382.50	742.50	332.50	570.00
45–49	807.50	1,590.00	517.50	905.00	590.00	1,170.00	460.00	770.00
50–54	1,387.50	2,512.50	802.50	1,362.50	1,120.00	2,052.50	695.00	1,117.50
55–59	2,055.00	3,785.00	1,177.50	2,120.00	1,847.50	3,132.50	1,007.50	1,770.00
60–64	3,120.00	5,730.00	1,935.00	3,195.00	2,905.00	4,597.50	1,650.00	2,710.00

Note:
The term "average health" describes someone who does not have an increased risk of death due to a medical/lifestyle condition.

The term "excellent health" describes someone who has much better than "average" health.

Source: Compulife Software Inc. (<www.compulife.ca>.) The quotations are from different companies. Each quotation is the lowest available in that category at the time of writing. These quotations will change over time.

with no difference between smaller and large policies. The premium schedule may change at the option of the insurance company at any annual renewal date. This is different from non-group term policies, other than annual ones. If the insurance is automatic for every member of the group, then there is no medical examination required. For example, many employers provide some amount of life insurance to every employee as long as he or she is employed. This insurance is usually **convertible insurance**, which means that on leaving the employer, the employee can convert the insurance to a non-group policy, provided he or she can pass a medical examination.

If the members of the group have the option to take the insurance or not, then they will have to pass a medical examination when they take the insurance. Once passed, no further medical examination is necessary except for an increase in the face amount of the policy. Commonly, members of the group and their spouses are eligible to apply for coverage. Table 10.3 shows the premiums for a specific group whose members take the insurance at their option, the Institute of Chartered Accountants of Ontario.

Life Insurance with Savings/Investment Features

Are there life insurance policies whose premium does not increase with the insured's age? The answer is yes. There is a type of life insurance policy where premiums are constant, or even decreasing, each year, even though the probability of dying increases with age. Example 10.5 shows how this apparently contradictory situation can occur. The insurance company sets the premium at a level that is higher than the expected mortality costs in the early years of a policy, and lower than the expected mortality costs in the later years of the policy. In other words, the policyholder is "overpaying" in the early years and "underpaying" in the later years of the policy. The overpayment in the early years is invested and accumulated by the insurance company as a **cash surrender value** or, as it is frequently and more simply called, the **cash value**. If you cancel the policy, the cash value will be returned to you. Thus, the cash value is really your investment that is being kept by the insurance company for the purpose of keeping future premiums at the same or at an even lower level than they are currently. An insurance policy of this kind is actually a combination of term insurance and an investment account. There are many examples of this type of policy. We will mention the most common ones:

Whole Life Insurance This is a policy that pays the face amount to the beneficiaries when the insured dies. The face amount is paid without any restrictions because the policy remains in force for the life of the insured. The premium is constant throughout the insured's lifetime. This is called the **level premium**. When the insured cancels the policy, he or she gets back the cash surrender value, which is really the savings component of the policy.

TABLE 10.3
Group Term Life Insurance Premium Quotations
Monthly Premium for $25,000 of Term Insurance
Institute of Chartered Accountants of Ontario

These premiums are for annual terms but are renewable every year without further medical examinations. The premium schedule may be changed at any renewal date.

	Non-smoker		Smoker	
	Male	Female	Male	Female
Under 30	$ 1.10	$ 0.70	$ 2.75	$ 1.50
30–34	1.35	0.90	3.00	2.00
35–39	1.60	1.15	3.75	2.80
40–44	2.40	1.60	5.80	4.10
45–49	4.00	2.50	9.40	5.90
50–54	6.10	4.00	15.00	8.75
55–59	9.90	6.75	23.00	13.15
60–64	14.75	10.00	35/00	20.40
65–69	18.75	12.50	58.50	32.50
70–74	37.50	25.00	94.25	57.50
75–79	92.25	65.00	158.50	95.00
80–84	158.50	108.50	233.50	150.00

Note: Maximum coverage is $1.25 million for the member and for the spouse. There are some other special features of the policy not included in this table. Rates over age 64 apply to renewal of existing coverage only. The Manulife Insurance Company provides the policy. Rates as of August 24, 2011.

Endowment Life Policy This is a form of insurance that will pay the face amount to the beneficiaries if the insured dies. However, unlike other insurance policies, it will also pay the face amount to the insured — the amount paid is called the endowment — if the insured lives to a certain age. How is this possible? Recall that the insurance is actually a combination of two things: a pure term insurance and a savings account. The premium of an endowment policy is set in such a way that the savings component will be invested to reach the endowment value at a specific date.

Universal Life Insurance A universal life insurance policy is a combination of a term insurance and a side investment fund. The policyholder pays a premium, which the insurance company separates explicitly into an insurance component and an investment component. First, the insurance company deducts from the premium an amount for the insurance coverage plus costs plus a profit margin; the remainder becomes an investment on which the policyholder earns interest. As long as the policyholder maintains the insurance portion of the premium every year, the insurance policy is in force. The money accumulated in the investment portion of the policy can be used to pay the minimum premium required to maintain the insurance portion of the contract. This makes universal life insurance policies very flexible. After some money has been saved up in the investment fund, the policyholder can make whatever premium payment he wants — lower premium payments or even skip premium payments for a while. The insurance company prepares a report periodically that shows how much of the premium goes to pay the pure insurance premium, administrative costs, and other costs, and how much goes to the side investment fund.

Term Policy vs. Non-Term Policy

Although there are numerous different kinds of insurance policies in the market, there are only two major types. First, there are the term policies. These are the pure insurance policies without a savings/investment component. The premiums on such policies are based on the way pure premiums are calculated, as we have discussed earlier. Since the most important factor affecting the premium rate is the mortality rate of the insured, the premium rate of a term insurance policy will always increase as the insured gets older.

The second type of life insurance are the **non-term insurance policies**. These are insurance policies that have a pure insurance component and a savings/investment component. Except for the term life insurance, all the insurance products that we have described — whole life, endowment policy, universal life, and so on — are insurance policies with an insurance component and a savings component. The policyholder pays a higher premium than that of a comparable term insurance in the early years of the policy because part of the premium goes into a "savings account". The money in the savings account will be used to reduce the future premiums or will be returned to the policyholder if he or she cancels the policy. This concept is depicted in Figure 10.1. The amount of money that the policyholder gets back when the policy is cancelled is called the cash value or the cash surrender value. Thus, the cash surrender value is actually the amount of money accumulated in the "savings account" at the point of cancellation of the policy.

Which is better: term life insurance or non-term life insurance such as whole life and universal life? Many financial experts advise that you should buy term life insurance for protection and "invest the difference" between term and whole life premiums rather than buying whole life insurance. The argument rests on the belief that whole life (and other non-term policies) insurance is more costly, and the purpose of insurance is risk management.

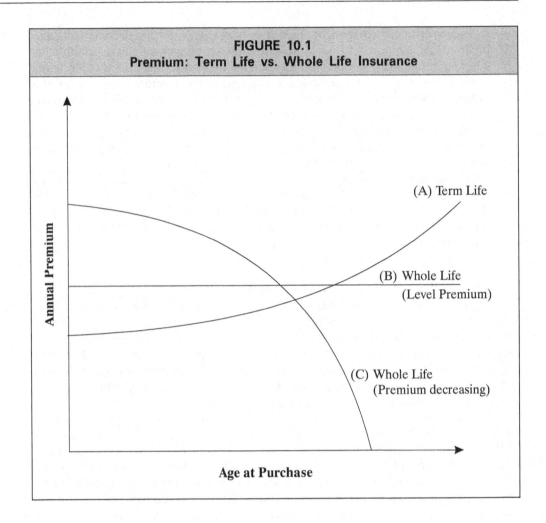

FIGURE 10.1
Premium: Term Life vs. Whole Life Insurance

Risk Management

Recall that the need for life insurance is higher during the stages of the life cycle when the family will have the greatest demands on its financial resources: dependent children, mortgage, incomes below the peak level, perhaps one spouse staying home with the children. The risk management need is to cover the loss due to the premature death of one of the parents. Most families will have only a limited amount of money that they can afford to put into life insurance. Term policies cost far less than non-term because they require only the pure premium plus costs. A family that takes on extra risk by putting its limited dollars into a non-term policy is very unwise.

On the other hand, a family may have sufficient resources that it can put some money into enforced savings at the same time as it buys life insurance. The universal policies, with their flexible savings amount, could be worthwhile. This brings us to the other considerations in the comparison.

Who Is the More Effective Investor?

First, can you invest the difference to earn a higher return than the life insurance company? Empirical studies in the past find that the rate of return on whole life is inferior to that available on comparable savings instruments. In other words, there is evidence that you would earn a higher return by putting the monetary "difference" in a chartered bank savings account than by putting it in whole life insurance. But why is that the case? We think this is due, to a large extent, to the high commission fees that insurance companies pay to agents. In general, the insurance companies pay a much higher commission fee to agents for selling whole life than they do for selling individual term life. Since the commission is a percentage on the total premium that you pay, this means that you pay a commission for saving money with an insurance company. Banks do not charge you a commission for putting your money into a savings account!

Do You Need Someone to Make You Save?

Do you have the self-discipline to invest the difference between term and whole life premiums? If you do not, many insurance agents would suggest that you may be better off buying a whole life policy that will force you to save. But automatic savings plans offered by chartered banks, trust companies, and brokerage firms will do the same job. The benefits of using whole life policies to force you to save are not obvious.

Are There Benefits of Whole-life Insurance over Term-life Insurance?

There are two advantages of whole-life insurance over term-life insurance. The first benefit is tax deferral. If you save and invest the difference in premium in a bank or investment account, the investment income is taxable annually; in other words, you must pay taxes annually. If you save and invest your money in a whole-life insurance policy, the investment income is tax deferred, which means you do not have to pay taxes until the time you cancel the policy and receive the cash surrender value.

The second benefit lies in the certainty of the premium. In a whole life insurance policy, the premium is guaranteed at the time you purchase the policy; it will not change in the future. In the case of a term life insurance policy, the premium is not guaranteed and is subject to change in the future at the time of renewal.

The above discussion is just a qualitative comparison of the two types of life insurance policies: term life, which has no savings components, and non-term life, which does have such a component. The qualitative comparison does not lead to a clear conclusion of which is better. We will next describe a quantitative method to shed more light on this issue.

Buy Term and Invest the Difference

This is a quantitative method to compare term and non-term life policies. Although we will use a numerical example that compares a term policy versus a whole life policy, the method can be used to compare any two policies that provide the same death benefit. As we have seen, the question of whether term or non-term life policies are better depends on whether you would be better off buying a term policy and investing the difference of the whole life premium and the term premium. This method assumes the mortality tables do not change during the time period of the comparison.

Take a whole life policy and a term life policy, both of which are similar in all respects including their face value. For each year of the policy term, write down the premium for each policy.[3] Then, calculate the difference between the whole life premium and the term life premium — this is the amount that you invest each year. Assume that you will invest this difference in premiums every year at the after-tax rate of interest and accumulate an investment fund with these investments. Since the term policy and the whole life policy are identical in all other respects, the comparison of the two now boils down to comparing the amount accumulated in the investment fund and the cash surrender value or the cash value of the whole life policy. We will illustrate this with an example.

Example 10.6:   Consider the quotes from a life insurance company for a term insurance policy and a whole life policy for a 35-year-old male who wants insurance coverage from now until the age of 54, after which he does not need the coverage because the children will be independent. The premiums for each policy are shown in Table 10.4.

      Let us assume that the individual can invest money to earn an after-tax interest rate of 4%. Is the term policy better or is the whole life policy better? The analysis and calculation is shown in Table 10.5.

Let us analyze the results. If the person purchases the term policy and invests the difference, he would have an investment fund of $16,097, which is already after

---

[3]   For a participating policy, you should use the net premium, i.e., subtract the expected dividends from the premium paid.

	Whole Life		Term
Age	Net Premiums	Cash Value	Net Premiums
35	$1,316	$ 0	$163
36	1,165	0	166
37	1,127	500	169
38	1,085	1,500	176
39	1,043	2,600	185
40	994	3,740	196
41	945	4,880	214
42	896	6,020	231
43	847	7,160	249
44	798	8,300	265
45	736	9,500	288
46	672	10,700	310
47	609	11,900	336
48	546	13,100	369
49	482	14,300	406
50	407	15,480	432
51	332	16,660	461
52	257	17,840	494
53	182	19,020	535
54	103	20,200	574

TABLE 10.4
Comparing Term and Whole Life (Face Value of $100,000)

taxes. If he buys the whole life policy, he will receive $20,200 when he cancels the policy at 54. So, in our example, the whole life policy is better than the term policy. But there is one more thing to consider. Under the current tax law, the cash value is taxable. Cash value is the difference between the cash surrender value and the adjusted cost base (the premiums paid less dividends received). In our example, the adjusted cost base is the total sum of all the net premiums, i.e., column (2) in Table 10.5, and this is equal to $14,542. Thus, the amount $20,200 – $14,542 or $5,658 is taxable. Assuming the individual's tax rate at 54 is 40%, the amount of taxes paid is $2,263. So, after taxes, he ends up with $20,200 – $2,263 or $17,937. This is still better than the $16,097 in the investment fund under the "buy term and invest the difference" policy.

The example in Tables 10.4 and 10.5 shows the whole life policy in the best light because it assumes that the policyholder has to invest the difference in a

TABLE 10.5
Calculating the Difference between Term and Whole Life

(1)	(2)	(3)	(4)	(5)		
Age	Whole Life NP	Term Life NP	(2) − (3)	Balance in Investment Fund at A-T Rate of 4%		
35	$1,316	$163	$1,153		1,153 × 1.04 =	1,199
36	1,165	166	999	(999 +	1,199) × 1.04 =	2,286
37	1,127	169	958	(958 +	2,286) × 1.04 =	3,374
38	1,085	176	909	(909 +	3,374) × 1.04 =	4,454
39	1,043	185	858	(858 +	4,454) × 1.04 =	5,524
40	994	196	798	(798 +	5,524) × 1.04 =	6,575
41	945	214	731	(731 +	6,575) × 1.04 =	7,598
42	896	231	665	(665 +	7,598) × 1.04 =	8,594
43	847	249	598	(598 +	8,594) × 1.04 =	9,560
44	798	265	533	(533 +	9,560) × 1.04 =	10,497
45	736	288	448	(448 +	10,497) × 1.04 =	11,383
46	672	310	362	(362 +	11,383) × 1.04 =	12,214
47	609	336	273	(273 +	12,214) × 1.04 =	12,986
48	546	369	177	(177 +	12,986) × 1.04 =	13,690
49	482	406	76	(76 +	13,690) × 1.04 =	14,317
50	407	432	−25	(−25 +	14,317) × 1.04 =	14,864
51	332	461	−129	(14,864 −	129) × 1.04 =	15,324
52	257	495	−238	(15,324 −	238) × 1.04 =	15,689
53	182	535	−353	(15,689 −	353) × 1.04 =	15,949
54	103	574	−471	(15,949 −	471) × 1.04 =	16,097

taxable account, not a tax-deferred one. If a policyholder has exhausted all other tax-deferral mechanisms, which means primarily an RRSP, and has no mortgage to pay down, then Table 10.5 gives the right answer. If the policyholder still has RRSP contribution room left, which is the case for most Canadians, then he or she can invest the difference with an RRSP contribution that will generate a tax refund and will accumulate untaxed as long as it is inside the RRSP. Using the same numbers as in the example, a 4% return after-tax is equal to a 6.7% (4% ÷ (1 − .4)) pre-tax return. Column 5 in Table 10.5 accumulates at 6.7% instead of 4%, for 20 years. If we assume that the tax refund lags the contributions by one year, and invest the tax refund outside the RRSP at an after-tax rate of 4%, we have two funds accumulating for the "buy term and invest the difference". When the term life premiums exceed the whole life premiums from age 50–54, he pays the difference by withdrawing money from the pool of invested tax refunds, and the RRSP simply continues to accumulate without further contributions. At age 54 he has $26,094 in the RRSP and $5,379 in the tax refund account. If he withdraws all the RRSP funds and pays tax at 40%, he has $15,657 left. The tax refund account is already after-tax, and so he has a total of $21,087, which is well ahead of the $17,937 in the insurance cash fund, after taxes are paid. See Problem 11 for more practice.

This is only an example to illustrate the mechanics of the "buy term and invest the difference" approach. It can be used to compare any two insurance policies.

Secondary Policy Provisions

We have described the most important elements in a life insurance contract — face value or death benefit, premium, cash surrender value, term policy, whole life policy, dividends, insurability, and so on. If you read a typical insurance policy, you may find a lot more terminology: the secondary policy provisions that spell out the details of the policy. We will describe briefly the more common of these clauses. Note that these are by no means standard clauses; they may be present or absent in your insurance policy.

Waiver of Premium. By this provision, premiums will not have to be paid although the policy will remain in force if the insured becomes totally disabled before a specified age, usually 65.

Guaranteed Insurability. This is a provision that allows the policyholder the right to buy additional life insurance in the future without providing evidence of insurability — e.g., without passing a medical examination.

Smoker/Non-smoker Provision. You pay lower premiums if you are certified as being a non-smoker. Table 10.2 shows how large the reduction is.

Reinstatement Time Limit. This is the maximum length of time before a lapsed policy can be reinstated without proof of insurability. For example, if one becomes unemployed and cannot make premium payments, the insurance policy becomes lapsed. This provision allows for the reinstatement of the policy within time limits.

Suicide Time Limit. Believe it or not, many insurance policies pay the death benefit even when the insured commits suicide. The suicide time limit is the number of years that must pass from the date of purchase before the policy will pay death benefits in the event that the insured makes a successful attempt on his own life.

Loan Provisions. Many life policies allow the policyholder to borrow money, usually up to the cash surrender value of the policy. The loan provisions state the conditions under which the loan will be made (e.g., the interest rate charged, the amount of the loan, and so on).

239

Settlement Options. These refer to the options available to the beneficiaries for receiving the death benefits. Two common options are to receive the benefits in one lump sum and to receive the benefits periodically, e.g., in monthly payments, with the balance being invested in the insurance company.

Convertibility. This is a provision that allows the holder of a term policy to convert it to a whole life policy under the specified terms and time limits.

Accidental Death Benefits. This provision means that the face amount paid to the beneficiaries will be increased (usually by two or three times) to the stated amount if the insured dies from an accident (e.g., car accident), rather than if the insured dies in some other way.

Grace Period. This is the short period of time (usually 30 days) after a premium due date has been missed that the insurance policy is still in force.

Life Insurance from the Canada Pension Plan

Chapter 17 contains more information on the Canada Pension Plan (CPP), which is primarily intended as a retirement plan. The CPP also provides life insurance benefits to the survivors of people who have made enough contributions to the CPP. The benefits take three forms. The estate receives an automatic lump-sum death benefit worth a maximum of $2,500. This benefit has not been indexed in the past. The spouse of the deceased contributor receives a survivor pension up until the survivor's age 65. The amount of this pension depends on the amount that the deceased spouse had contributed to the CPP. At age 65, the surviving spouse receives the same survivor pension as any spouse surviving the death of a pensioner under the CPP, which is 60% of the pension that the spouse would have received. The maximum pension after age 65 that one person can receive is the maximum CPP for a single person. Thus, the survivor pension benefit is capped to the amount needed to bring the survivor up to the maximum for one person. These spousal survivor benefits are indexed to the CPI in the same fashion that CPP retirement pensions are indexed.

The dependent children of a deceased contributor also receive indexed survivor benefits. Once the children are qualified, the benefit is automatically at the maximum of $218.50, regardless of the amount the deceased had contributed to CPP. This survivor pension is paid to the children's caregiver (who is usually their surviving parent) to age 18. If they remain full-time in school, they can apply to receive the pension themselves up to age 25. Table 10.6 gives the current maximum and average amounts for CPP death and disability benefits.

Spouse is defined to include a person who was married to the decedent or a person who was a common-law spouse at the time of death. Same-sex and opposite-sex couples qualify equally.

TABLE 10.6
Canada Pension Plan Monthly Death and Disability Benefits 2011–2012

Recipient	Maximum		Average	
	2011	2012	2011	2012
Death Benefits				
Surviving spouse under 65	$ 529.09	$ 543.82	$ 370.26	$ 378.91
Surviving spouse 65+	$ 576.00	$ 592.00	$ 302.07	$ 309.11
Surviving child to 18 or 25	$ 218.50	$ 224.62	$ 218.50	$ 224.62
Lump sum to estate	$2,500.00	$2,500.00	$2,266.26	$2,279.96
Disability Benefits				
Disabled contributor	$1,153.37	$1,185.50	$ 822.32	$ 843.27
Dependent child to 18 or 25	$ 218.50	$ 224.62	$ 218.50	$ 224.62

HEALTH INSURANCE

This is often called medical insurance. In Canada, most basic medical procedures are provided for under the various provincial health-care plans. It is therefore not necessary for most Canadians to carry additional coverage for medical expenses; however, if you want to supplement this basic level of health care, private insurance coverage can be purchased from many insurance companies such as Blue Cross. The typical additional coverage includes semi-private or private rooms for hospital stays, prescription drugs, eyeglasses, dental care, and medical services from practitioners other than medical doctors and hospitals (e.g., physiotherapists, certified psychologists).

Health-care costs outside Canada, especially in the United States, can be very high and may not be fully covered by provincial health-care plans. A Canadian can purchase additional protection for health-care costs incurred outside Canada from many private insurance companies at quite reasonable rates. Some credit cards provide out-of-Canada health-care coverage for limited periods of time.

CRITICAL ILLNESS INSURANCE

Critical illness insurance is a relatively new insurance product in Canada. It provides a single lump-sum tax-free payment to the insured person when he or she has been diagnosed with a critical illness. The insured person has total discretion over how the lump sum is used — it is not restricted only to expenses related to the critical illness. Typically, the insurance company requires the insured person to survive 30 days following the diagnosis of the critical illness. If one does not survive the 30-day period, most plans will return only the premium to the beneficiary.

What kind of illness is covered in a critical illness insurance policy? As usual, there is no such thing as a standard policy. Different insurance companies define critical illness differently, so you have to read the fine print. Most policies cover heart attack, stroke, and life-threatening cancer. Other illness that may be covered are angioplasty, Alzheimer's disease, aortic surgery, benign brain tumour, blindness, bypass surgery, coma, cancer, coronary artery disease requiring surgery, deafness, heart attack, heart valve replacement, kidney failure, loss of limbs, loss of speech, major organ transplant recipient or on waiting list, motor neutron disease or Lou Gehrig's disease, multiple sclerosis, occupational HIV infection, paralysis, Parkinson's disease, severe burns, and stroke. A cheaper policy may be so because it does not cover as many illness as a more expensive policy.

Does one need critical illness insurance? If yes, how much does one need? The theory of critical illness insurance is quite similar to that of life insurance, except that it is the critical illness, not death, that triggers the benefits. Many of our discussions on life insurance also apply to critical illness insurance. The main purpose of buying critical illness insurance is to provide the same standard of living to the family in the event the insured person suffers from a critical illness. With minor modifications, either the income approach or the expense approach can be used to estimate the amount of critical illness insurance that one should buy.

The following table shows the recent quotes of monthly premium obtained from four insurance companies for three hypothetical candidates. The insurance companies are Manulife, Maritime, Empire, and Pitch (not in the same order shown on the table). The quotes are based on the following assumptions: All are non-smokers in relatively good health; the policy face value is $200,000; the policy is a 10-year term policy that is renewable. The three candidates are a 27-year-old female, a 42-year-old female, and a 53-year-old male. Note that the difference in monthly premium may be partly due to the slight difference in what is covered as critical illness.

Candidate	Company A	Company B	Company C	Company D
Female, 27	$ 41.13	$ 44.91	$ 50.22	$ 42.12
Female, 42	$104.31	$100.53	$102.78	$ 97.20
Male, 53	$269.01	$249.93	$254.34	$243.73

DISABILITY INSURANCE

Disability insurance protects the insured and the insured's family against the risk of serious illness or accident that would render the insured incapable, to a greater or lesser extent, of self-care or of full employment.

The risk of disability cannot be totally avoided. It depends to a large degree on one's lifestyle and one's occupation. Studies have found the probability of a significant period of disability is much higher than the probability of death at any age up to the normal age for retirement. Also, studies have found that more than half of the disabilities experienced at any age exceed one year in duration. Not many families have enough savings to support the loss of income for a full year or more. The evidence suggests that most families need disability insurance even more than they need life insurance because the cost of total disability of a breadwinner is greater to the family than death since additional expenses may be incurred to take care of the disabled person.

How much disability insurance coverage do you need? Theoretically, the income approach or the expense approach, both of which were described earlier, can be used. As a practical matter, insurance companies and many financial experts recommend coverage for 60% to 80% of one's current gross income. For example, if your annual income is $40,000, you would buy a disability insurance that will pay you $24,000 to $32,000 per year in the event of disability. The amount that you receive from the insurance company is not taxable because the premium that you pay is not tax deductible. The amount you will get is therefore not too much below the amount of your current after-tax income. Of course, if the disability involves substantial additional expenses, you and your family will still be worse off.

Like any insurance policy, the terms and conditions of a disability policy are very important. The following should help you to determine whether the policy is suitable for you:

1. Definition of **Total Disability**.
   The definition is not standardized, and it varies from one insurance company to another. Ideally, it should include the loss of speech, sight, hearing, the complete loss of the use of both hands or feet, or one hand or foot. Read this very carefully in your contract.

2. **Waiting Period** or **Elimination Period**.
   This is the period from the start of the disability to the time when the benefits begin under the policy. The shorter the waiting period, the higher the premium you pay. For that reason, if you can afford some self-insurance, you can ask for a longer waiting period.

3. **Length of the Contract** or the **Term**.
   It should be non-cancellable and renewable at the insured's option up to the age of 65.

4. **Period of Benefits**.
   This is the length of time over which the benefits may be payable. The longer the period, the higher the premium.

5. **Period of Deemed Total Disability**.
   This is the length of time after which the disability is deemed to have permanently prevented the insured from returning to normal work. Under this

provision, a disabled person who recovers after a prolonged period is not cut off when she cannot realistically resume her previous occupation.

6. **Waiver of Premium**.

This is a provision that allows for the cancellation of all premiums if the insured is disabled before age 65. Every disability insurance policy should contain this clause.

7. Definition of **Partial Disability**.

This provision covers the question of whether or not you will be paid benefits if you are unable to carry on your normal occupation but can carry on another occupation that is paid at a lower rate.

8. **Exclusions**.

This term refers to things not covered by the policy. Usually, insurance does not cover acts of war, a state of war, or a normal pregnancy. What you should be careful about is that some policies cover disability only from accidents and not disability due to a prolonged illness. Read your policy very carefully on all the exclusions.

Many people have access to group disability insurance plans through their employers. Since the employers usually pay part or all of the premium, you should take it. Be aware, however, that the policy does not necessarily provide you with adequate coverage. Study your employer's group disability insurance contract — benefit periods, waiting periods, causes of disability, definition of disability, and amount of coverage. You may have to buy additional disability insurance from an outside insurance company.

Disability Insurance Premiums

Disability insurance premiums vary widely, even for persons of the same age and gender, because of the different features a policy can have. Group disability insurance is quite a bit cheaper than an individual policy, but the provisions and premiums of group policies also vary greatly. Table 10.7 provides premiums for one group, but you should realize that this table applies only to that group with that specific set of features in the policy.

Disability Insurance from the Canada Pension Plan

The Canada Pension Plan (CPP) disability benefit is available to people who have made enough contributions to the CPP and whose disability prevents them from working at any job on a regular basis. The disability must be long-lasting or likely to result in premature death. People who qualify for disability benefits from other programs may not qualify for the CPP disability benefit. The qualifications are fairly stringent. Notice that the disability is not just for own occupation but

TABLE 10.7
Group Disability Insurance Premiums
Institute of Chartered Accountants of Ontario

Each unit is $100 of monthly income. Maximum coverage is lesser of (i) $8,000 per month or (ii) 50% of earned income reduced by other disability insurance other than CPP and reduced by income continued by the employer or partnership. Other key features:

- Total disability — unable to do normal duties of regular occupation
- Indexed to inflation, up to 8% p.a.
- No coverage for disabilities from self-inflicted injury, active participation in a criminal offence, insurrection or war
- Partial payments available for partial disability

| | Monthly Premium Per Unit* | | | |
| | Waiting Period in Days | | | |
Age	30	90	180	365
Male				
Under 40	$0.85	$0.65	$0.60	$0.50
40–49	1.50	1.25	1.15	1.00
50–64	3.25	2.65	2.50	2.00
65–69	3.75	3.00	2.75	2.50
Female				
Under 40	1.00	0.85	0.75	0.65
40–49	1.65	1.40	1.25	1.10
50–64	2.90	2.35	2.25	1.75
65–69	3.25	2.60	2.50	2.25

* Rates as of August 24, 2011.

for any occupation. Furthermore, it has to be quite prolonged and severe to trigger a disability pension. The waiting time is usually more than three months after application, though it may be shorter if the disability is expected to cause death very soon.

There are two types of benefits payable. The disabled contributor receives a disability pension to age 65, after which time the pension becomes whatever he or she has earned as a regular retirement pension. The dependent children of the disabled contributor receive the same pension as they would have if the contributor had died. The pension is paid to their caregiver up to age 18, and to them if they apply for it and qualify by continuing in full-time education, up to age 25.

There is no pension payable to the spouse of a disabled contributor.

The current payment amounts are shown in Table 10.6 earlier.

Other Government-Controlled Employment and Disability Insurance Plans

The federal Employment Insurance (EI) program provides a form of medium-term disability insurance and maternity/paternity benefits as well as the more commonly known protection against job loss. Every person who is employed more than a specified minimum number of hours per week must contribute 1.78% of gross pay, up to an annual maximum for 2011 of $786.76. This translates into contributions on earnings up to the annual average insurable wage, which is set at $44,200 for 2011. The employer contributes 1.4 times the employee's payment, to a maximum of $1,101.46 for the year.

The conditions under which an unemployed person can claim EI benefits are complicated, and we will not go into such detail. The basic payment is 55% of the lost earnings up to a maximum employment insurance payment of $468 per week. Once again, this is based on the average insurable wage of $44,200. The usual limit is 45 weeks of benefits. There is usually a two-week period before the benefits start — a sort of deductible.

Someone who is disabled can also claim employment insurance, again for a limit of 35 weeks. If the claim is for illness, the limit is 15 weeks. The weekly dollar limits are the same as for unemployment benefits, but the two-week waiting period may be waived. This is a valuable form of disability insurance for someone who may have nothing else immediately available, but it covers a limited amount and time period. To some extent, the EI disability benefit and the CPP disability benefit are complementary since the CPP disability benefit takes much longer to start but continues to age 65 if the person remains seriously disabled.

EI benefits are also available for maternity and paternity. The mother or surrogate mother may claim up to 15 weeks of maternity leave, and both parents can claim up to 35 weeks of parental leave, which may be shared between them in any combination desired. That is, one parent could take 35 weeks of EI benefits; and the other, none; or each could take 17.5 weeks or any other combination. The same elimination period of two weeks applies, and the same benefit limits.

Worker's Compensation is another significant form of disability insurance that the provincial governments mandate. The details vary by province and we provide only a general outline. The employer is assessed an insurance rate based on the claims experience of the company and the industry, and the provincial agency uses the money to fund the insurance plan. Only injuries or illness that are directly related to the workplace are eligible for compensation. The compensation is typically a percentage of take-home pay, which is approximately the gross pay minus estimates of income tax, Canada Pension Plan premiums, and Employment Insurance premiums that the employer would have deducted. For example, British Columbia pays 90% of this net pay for the first 10 weeks, then shifts to a more detailed schedule. Ontario pays 85% of net pay. The disability pension continues until the disabled person is able to return to work or reaches age 65. There is also a ceiling on the total payment, based on some value like the provincial average industrial wage. For example, in 2011 the maximum in Ontario was 85% of 175% of the average industrial wage of $79,600. The maximum disability pension from this calculation is $67,660 p.a.

Worker's Compensation may also cover many other costs, such as additional attendant fees for individuals who are unable to care for themselves, cost of attending legal hearings, lost retirement contributions, and cost of physical therapy.

Worker's Compensation is more generous than the CPP, EI, and many employer-sponsored long-term disability plans. Far fewer people qualify, however, because the majority of long-term disability occurs due to sickness or accident outside the workplace.

LONG-TERM CARE INSURANCE

Long-term care insurance is a new insurance product that is now appearing in the Canadian market, although only some life insurance companies will provide it. The insured pays either a lump sum, or a continuing premium, in return for insurance that pays some or all of the costs of long-term care, either in a long-term care facility or in the person's home. Canadian medicare pays the basic costs of these services, with variations by province. The cost of a standard nursing home accommodation, which is typically four beds to a room, is paid by the government. The government pays various agencies, or runs them directly, to provide in-home assistance like weekly baths, hot lunches, respite care to allow a family member free time, physiotherapy, housecleaning, and shopping. There is a limit to the amount of in-home care that these agencies provide, and there are sometimes long waiting lists. Serious illnesses and disabilities cannot necessarily be handled with the available in-home support. A family caregiver usually has other responsibilities or is an ageing spouse who is unable to continue giving the care needed.

The basic situations that will trigger eligibility for payments under long-term care insurance, admission to a long-term care facility supported by government funding, and many other forms of support are as follows:

- Substantial human assistance to perform at least two of the six activities of daily living (bathing, dressing, feeding, toileting, transferring from a bed or chair, and continence)

- Continual supervision to protect themselves from threats to health and safety due to deteriorated mental abilities (for example, as a result of Alzheimer's disease or senile dementia)

This risk increases rapidly with age. We are living longer on average than previous generations, but we are doing so partly at the cost of suffering more frequent disabilities for longer periods at the end of the life cycle. Long-term care insurance is, in effect, a form of insurance against living too long and becoming seriously disabled in combination with the long life. There are three types of insurance plans that companies offer now:

- Income plan: Once you are eligible to claim, you receive a predetermined weekly benefit. You are free to use the benefits for whatever long-term care services you wish.
- Reimbursement plan: Once you are eligible to claim, you must submit proof that you received services that are covered under the plan. Eligible expenses are reimbursed up to a predetermined daily maximum.
- Indemnity plan: Once you are eligible to claim, you receive a predetermined daily benefit if you prove you received a covered service.

Each of these plans would provide coverage for both in-home and institutional care costs that are above those provided by the government health insurance. For example, if you need a nursing home with round-the-clock medical and support service, the co-payment in Ontario in 2012 was $2,274.86 per month for a private room.[4] Co-payment is the amount the resident must pay, with the government covering the rest of the cost. A nursing home is one example of the costs that a long-term care insurance policy may cover, depending on the specific contract.

We cannot provide a table of premiums for long-term care as we did for term insurance because the contracts have so many different features and because the cost rises also with age. What we provide, in Table 10.8, is a sample of rates that a major life insurance company quoted in 2007 to provide an idea of what long-term care insurance premiums are. We do not identify the company because these examples are solely for educational purposes and are not actual rates offered to any one person. To get a quotation, you have to work with the company or an agent, provide a lot of personal information, and make many decisions about the specific coverage.

---

[4] See Ontario Ministry of Health and Long-Term Care website: <www.health.gov.on.ca/en/news/bulletin/2012/hb_20120530_1.aspx>.

TABLE 10.8
Sample Rates for Long-term Care Insurance Plan

With the purchase of a long-term care insurance plan that has
- lifetime payment of premiums
- $500/week benefit
- 250 weeks of benefit duration
- 90-day waiting period
- no inflation protection, no "return of premium on death"

The following people will pay the corresponding amount

• 40-year-old male	$37.89/month
• 35-year-old female	$38.16/month
• 55-year-old male	$74.16/month
• 60-year-old female	$141.35/month

HOW SAFE IS YOUR INSURANCE COVERAGE?

Assuris (formerly CompCorp) provides partial insurance of policies of its members in the event of a company's insolvency and inability to meet its policy liabilities. Virtually all life and health insurance companies belong to Assuris. The rules include a number of complicating features. Group insurance and joint policies can be particularly tricky. We provide only the basic outline in this book — you should contact Assuris directly at 1-866-878-1225.

Assuris provides protection to policyholders of its member companies with life insurance, health insurance, disability, money accumulation, or annuity policies that promise to pay either a fixed or a minimum amount of money to a person at some point in time, or on the person's death to the beneficiary.

The policies are defined in four categories and then grouped into classes with specified coverage limits. The coverage applies to each company; so, if you hold policies with different companies, you are covered to the limit for each company. The four categories are individual, individual registered (e.g., an RRSP), group, and group registered (e.g., pension plan). If you have three individual life insurance policies with a single company, the coverage limit applies to the three policies together. If you have an individual life insurance policy and a group life insurance policy with the same company, each policy receives coverage to the limit for that category.

Protection Benefits

- Monthly income: $2,000 per month
  - Payout annuities
  - Disability income insurance
  - Long-term care insurance
  - Payments from RRIFs

- Death benefit: $200,000 total
  - Life insurance

- Health expenses: $60,000 per insured person
  (may include family members)
  - Travel insurance
  - Extended health care
  - Dental insurance
  - Critical illness insurance

If the total benefits exceed the above amounts, Assuris covers 85% of the promised benefits but never less than these amounts.

Savings Benefits

- Cash value: $60,000 total or 85% of promised value, whichever is higher
  - CSV from whole life and universal life
  - Guaranteed values for segregated fund policies
  - TFSA in a segregated fund

- Accumulated values: $100,000 total
  - Accumulation annuities
  - Side funds of universal life policies
  - Premium or dividend deposit accounts attached to life policies
  - RRSPs, RRIFs
  - TFSA in an accumulated annuity

If the total benefits exceed the above amounts, Assuris does not cover the excess.

Other Rules

The limits apply to the combined total amount payable under all policies in the same class with the same insurer covering the same *person*. What do the rules mean by "person?"

- Death benefit — the person whose life is insured
- Monthly income — the annuitant or disabled person

- Health expense — the person incurring the expense
- Cash value and accumulated value for individual policies — the policy owner (There is no cash value in group insurance plans.)
- Accumulated value for group policies: defined contribution plan — plan participant; defined benefit plan — the plan sponsor

Only Canadian policies are covered. The policy must be in Canadian funds. The policyholder must have been a Canadian resident when the policy was issued, or now be a Canadian resident, with the policy shown on the insurer's Canadian books. The policy must not be covered by any other compensation arrangement. (There are no such other arrangements at present in Canada.)

Finally, we repeat that there are complications that can arise in various circumstances that we have not covered.

Example 10.7: Colonel Mustard has a life insurance policy for $300,000 with Itsadogs Life Insurance Co. He also has a disability income policy that pays out 60% of his annual income if he becomes seriously disabled and unable to work. His wife has a life insurance policy for $225,000 with the same company. His wife also has her spousal RRSP (i.e., the Colonel made all the contributions, but she is the owner) with Itsadogs Life, invested in a $120,000 guaranteed account of the company. Finally, they have a group health plan with Itsadogs through the Colonel's employer, which covers them and their three children. The Colonel earns $60,000 p.a. If Itsadogs Life goes bankrupt tomorrow, and the trustee-in-bankruptcy pays out 50% on claims, how much are they covered for?

	At risk	Coverage	Trustee pays	Assuris pays
Colonel death benefit	$300,000	$255,000	$150,000	.85(300,000) – 150,000
Wife death benefit	225,000	200,000[1]	112,500	200,000 – 112,500
Disability pension	3,000/mo.	2,550	1,500	.85(3,000) – 1,500
RRSP	120,000	100,000	60,000	100,000 – 60,000
Health benefit	unknown	60,000	½ of claims	½ of claims to $60,000

---

[1] Her coverage is $200,000 because .85 × $225,000 = $191,500 (i.e., < $200,000).

SUMMARY

This chapter introduces and explains two important topics in insurance: life insurance and disability insurance. Life insurance is a very useful method to protect a family from the risk of loss of income due to the premature and unanticipated death of a family member. We examine four important questions: (i) Who should buy life insurance? (ii) How much life insurance coverage does a family need? (iii) What type of insurance should an individual buy? (iv) Is term insurance better than whole life insurance? Several analytical tools have been introduced: the income approach and the expense approach to determine insurance needs, and the "buy term and invest the difference" approach to compare different insurance policies. Many common terminologies of the insurance industry have been described and used.

Disability insurance is the method used to protect a family from the loss of income when a breadwinner becomes disabled. Past studies have indicated that many families need disability insurance even more than they need life insurance. The important terminologies found in a typical disability contract have been intro-duced. After studying this chapter, the reader should have a firm foundation of knowledge to analyze and make decisions on different life insurance and disability insurance policies.

MULTIPLE-CHOICE REVIEW QUESTIONS

1. The premium on a term life insurance policy is _____ the premium of a whole life insurance policy.

    (a) higher than
    (b) lower than
    (c) equal to
    (d) lower than or equal to
    (e) none of the above

2. Under the income approach, a very wealthy person will _____ need to buy life insurance.

    (a) never
    (b) always
    (c) definitely
    (d) sometimes
    (e) none of the above

3. Which of the following is not an advantage of whole life over term life?

    (a) Premiums are guaranteed at the time of purchase.
    (b) The savings portion of the premiums can grow tax deferred.
    (c) You are not required to take a medical exam if you want to increase your coverage.
    (d) You are forced to save money.
    (e) None of the above.

4. The deductible in a disability insurance policy is called _____.

    (a) the waiting period
    (b) the elimination period
    (c) the medical expenses that the insured person must pay
    (d) (a) and (b)
    (e) none of the above

5. When one cancels a whole-life insurance policy, one normally gets a lump-sum cash payment from the insurance company. This payment is called _____.

    (a) the cash surrender value
    (b) a bequest
    (c) a cash bonus
    (d) the residual investment
    (e) none of the above

DISCUSSION QUESTIONS

1. Define or describe each of the following terms:

    "buy term and invest the difference" method / cash value or cash surrender value / death rate / decreasing term policy / dependants versus financial dependants / disability insurance: exclusions — period of benefits — period of deemed total disability / endowment policy / expense approach / group insurance / human capital approach / income approach: basic benchmark / insupportable risk / life insurance: insured — beneficiary — death benefit or face value — premium — owner — policy term — rate — insurability — guaranteed insurability — smoker/non-smoker provision — reinstatement time limit — suicide time limit — loan provisions — settlement options — convertibility — accidental death benefits — grace period / level premium policy / level term insurance / net single premium (NSP) / non-participating policy / participating policy: dividends / pure premium: mortality rate / real rate of interest / term insurance / whole life insurance / universal life insurance

    For the next two projects, if you are a young student you may not have these insurance needs/policies. Use your parents or another older family member instead.

2. **Personal Project 1**
    (a) Do you need life insurance?
    (b) Using (i) the income approach and (ii) the expense approach, determine the amount of life insurance coverage that you need.

3. **Personal Project 2**

   Get a copy of the group disability insurance policy from your employer.
   (a) Go through each clause in the policy. Do you understand each one? Discuss any questions in class or with your instructor.
   (b) Do you have sufficient disability insurance coverage? If yes, why? If not, why not?

PROBLEMS

1. What is the probability of the following?
   (a) A 50-year-old man living to age 56
   (b) A 30-year-old woman living to age 34

2. Calculate the pure premium for a man buying a one-year policy at age 48, assuming payout at year-end and an interest rate of 8%.

3. Calculate the pure level premium for a woman buying a policy at age 35 that will mature at age 65. The interest rate is 8%. [The calculations will be very time consuming unless you use a computer spreadsheet.]

4. Using the information and the premium quotes in Table 10.4, suppose an individual needs coverage until age 50. Which policy is better, assuming that the individual can invest his or her money at the following after-tax rates of return:
   (a) 3%
   (b) 6%
   (c) 10%

5. Assume you work for TTW Company and you have disability insurance of 75% of your annual salary of $50,000 with CCC Insurance Inc. You have a life insurance policy of 3.6 times your salary with CCC Insurance Inc. paid by the employer. You also have insurance policies of $85,000 in your name, $50,000 in your spouse's name, and $15,000 each in your three children's names with CCC Insurance Inc. TTW's health and dental plans, with a lifetime payout of $100,000 for each member of the insured's family, is also with CCC Insurance Inc. You have $100,000 in RRSPs and $40,000 in mutual funds with CCC Insurance Ltd.

   Required:
   If the insurance company becomes bankrupt, how secure is your insurance coverage and your investments?

6. Your friend Laura Lobo, 32, owns $200,000 of whole life insurance at a cost of $1.70 (per thousand of coverage) per year. The policy can be cancelled, and the cash surrender value is $1,500. Laura would like to get more coverage without increasing her premium by switching to a term insurance. Using Table 10.2, how much insurance can she buy for the same premium? What other factors should she consider before she makes the switch?

7. Mary Qi, 29, earns an annual after-tax income of $70,000 per year. If she died, her company insurance and government benefits would pay her husband and children $15,000 per year. Her husband, Tony, 31, works part-time and earns a net income of $20,000 per year. Since Tony does all the housework, if he died, the family would need an additional $12,000 a year to cover the homemaking services that he currently provides for the family. The family wants to buy enough life insurance so that in the event of premature death, the remaining family members will not suffer any income loss. How much life insurance does the family need? Using the premium quotation in Table 10.2, how much does the life insurance cost?

8. Walter and Maria McKay are 30 and 29, respectively. They have children aged six and three. Walter works for the City of Regina in maintenance. He earns $31,000 p.a. and takes home $25,000. He has long-term disability insurance covering 75% of his income (and it will be tax-free). He has life insurance coverage for two times his salary through an employer group plan. He has good medical coverage with the employer. They have adequate insurance on the house and car.

   Maria works part-time in a local submarine shop and earns $4,000 p.a. She is paid less than the minimum wage and does not report the income for tax purposes. The employer does not claim it as an expense. She spends most of her time working in the home.

   If Walter dies, Maria and the children get Canada Pension Plan (CPP) survivor benefits, all indexed to inflation:

Lump sum to Maria	$3,000
Pension to Maria until age 65	$300/month
Pension to Maria age 65 to death	$250/month
Pension to each child to age 18	$110/month

   Maria hasn't worked legally and so gets no CPP pension on her own account, nor would Walter get any survivor benefits. Maria would get Walter's pension value (to be rolled into an RRSP to avoid immediate taxation). Each one would get Old Age Security (OAS) at age 65. The present rate of OAS is $4,799, and it is indexed to inflation.

They currently save only a few hundred dollars a year, what with mortgage payments, children's clothing, etc. If either one dies, the family would save about $2,000 p.a. in food and other expenses but would have extra child-care expenses for about seven years.

Maria has little education or training for work outside the home.

The mortgage on the house will be paid off in 15 years at the current interest rate of 9% p.a. Maria and Walter don't plan to finance the children's education beyond high school because they will need to save for their own retirement.

Maria and Walter McKay
Family Balance Sheet

Assets

Cash and bank accounts	$ 2,000
Walter's RRSP	3,000
Walter's pension plan	21,000
Family car (depreciated cost)	5,000
Home (market value)	80,000
Household effects (replacement cost)	15,000
Clothing	10,000
	$136,000

Liabilities and Equity

Credit cards	$ 300
Car loan	700
Mortgage on home	55,000
	56,000
Family equity	80,000
	$136,000

Required:
What do you think Walter and Maria should do about life and disability insurance? Using the premium quotation in Table 10.2, calculate the premium for the life insurance you recommend. Do you think it is feasible?

9. Anthony Howard, 30, is currently earning $35,000 per year. He plans to retire at age 65. He expects that his salary will increase at the rate of 5% per year for the first 10 years, 4% per year for the next 10 years, and then 3% per year until he retires. If the appropriate discount rate is 6%, calculate the amount of life insurance he should buy using the income approach.

10. Jeffrey and Sophia, 35 and 30, respectively, live a comfortable lifestyle with their one-year-old daughter in a suburban home in Markham, Ontario. Jeffrey

earns $100,000 per year working for an insurance company, and his average tax rate is 30%. Sophia works only one day per week, earning $12,000 per year, and does not have to pay taxes. They do a lot of household chores for the baby and the home, and if one of them dies, it would cost $5,000 and $10,000 to hire someone to do what Jeffrey and Sophia are doing, respectively. Like most young families, they live on a tight budget and have to spend all their income every month. If one of them dies, family expenses would fall by about 25%. Jeffrey has a group life insurance policy that will pay his wife a lump sum of $150,000 in the event of his death, which can be used to buy an annuity at the real rate of interest of 3%. Assuming that their income will increase at the rate of inflation, what is the amount of life insurance that the family should buy, using the expense approach?

11. Table 10.5 shows how to calculate the benefit of "buy term and invest the difference", assuming that the policyholder has no tax deferral opportunities left and so the difference has to be invested in a taxable account. The text also explains how to compare whole life and term life when the premium difference can be invested in an RRSP, and gives the net effect after 20 years. Create a table that matches the text description of how to invest the difference in an RRSP, and show that the end result is a total of $21,036 after-tax for the term insurance choice.

CHAPTER 11

Property, Home, and Automobile Insurance

Property, home, and automobile insurance policies are full of complicated provisions and rules that vary among companies and policies sold by the same company. Other rules are standard in the industry. A family must be careful or it could suffer unexpected losses. For example, the Doyles suffer $30,000 fire damage to a house valued at $100,000 (not including land), but their insurance policy is for $70,000. The insurance company probably will pay only $26,250 of the loss. See Example 11.1.

LEARNING OBJECTIVES

> ➤ *To describe the basic principles and terminology in property insurance.*

> ➤ *To explain the concepts and terms of home insurance. We shall pay particular attention to the characteristics and policy provisions that you will find in a typical home insurance policy.*

> ➤ *To introduce and describe automobile insurance. We shall introduce and explain the terminology, the coverage available, and the provisions of an automobile insurance policy.*

In this chapter, we describe the basic concepts, characteristics, and policy provisions of property insurance. In particular, we examine home insurance and automobile insurance — the two major areas in which the average Canadian family is exposed to potentially large and catastrophic losses. We shall show that the concepts and theories that you learned in Chapters 9 and 10 can be applied to property, home, and automobile insurance.

At the end of this chapter, you will be ready to make intelligent decisions about home insurance and automobile insurance.

PROPERTY INSURANCE

People face a vast amount of *pure risk*[1] as a result of owning or using properties — home, automobile, furniture, clothing, etc. The most important risk is damage or destruction. If you own a home, it is exposed to the risks of damage by fire, lightning, explosions, windstorms, riots, vandalism, etc. If you own a car, it is subject to the risk of damage due to theft, collisions, and so on; in addition, you are exposed to the risk of bodily injury to yourself, to your passengers, and to other third parties. Indeed, if you examine a typical home insurance policy or an automobile insurance policy, you will see a list of most of the risks to which you may be exposed; some of these may be familiar to you while others may not be.

Property insurance insures your physical properties — your home, clothing, furniture, appliances, jewellery, and so on — against damage or destruction. For the average Canadian family, the most important property insurance is home and automobile insurance. They will be described separately in this chapter.

---

[1] Recall that a pure risk is one that involves the possibility of loss only.

The theories and concepts of risk and insurance that you learned in Chapters 9 and 10 apply to property insurance. You will find a basic principle being applied over and over again in every type of insurance: One buys insurance to insure for large and catastrophic expenses but not for small ones. In other words, one transfers most of the risk to an insurance company in return for paying a premium. The required premium depends on both the statistical probability of the loss (or the expenses) and the expected amount of the loss (which may not be the same as the insured face value since property is rarely totally destroyed).

HOME INSURANCE

Home insurance protects the family against the risk of loss, damage, or destruction of the home, its related outbuildings (e.g., a garage), and its contents (e.g., clothing, furniture, appliances); it also covers liability to third parties for injuries suffered on the property. There are two important questions that you must ask before buying a home insurance policy: (i) What are the risks that are covered? (ii) How much home insurance do I need?

The following is a list of typical risks of damage or destruction that are covered by a home insurance policy:

- Fire, lightning
- Falling objects
- Riots
- Windstorm, hail
- Explosion
- Vandalism
- Theft and break-in
- Glass breakage, window breakage
- Freezing
- Water, flood
- Weight of ice, snow, sleet
- Collapse of building
- Smoke
- Aircraft or other vehicles
- Faulty electrical wiring

There is no such thing as a "standard" home package; the above list is by no means complete. You should read your home insurance policy carefully to find out what is covered and what is not. Obviously, the more risks covered by the policy, the higher the premium will be.

How Much Home Insurance Do You Need?

Contents of the Home

A home insurance policy typically covers damage or destruction to the contents of your home — clothes, furniture, appliances, and so on. There are two ways to estimate the amount of coverage required. One way is to estimate the value of the contents as some per cent (usually around 20%) of the value of the structure (which is the home excluding the land). For example, for a home valued at $100,000, one would buy $20,000 insurance coverage (20% of $100,000) for the contents. The second way to estimate the insurance coverage for the contents is to list and value every item. This approach is recommended by many insurance companies and agents, who have forms to help their clients to list everything. It is recommended that a copy of this list be kept in a safety deposit box or other location away from the insured property.

How Do You Value the Home Contents?

There are two forms of home insurance that you can buy: One form covers the depreciated value of the damaged or lost item, and the second form covers replacement value.

The **depreciated value** of an item is the value of replacement or repair for the item to the condition it was in when lost or damaged. For example, if the lost item was a three-year-old, 28-inch colour television, the depreciated value is the cost of buying a three-year-old, 28-inch colour television of the same quality — and *not* the cost of a brand-new television.

The standard insurance policy pays the depreciated value. This is usually calculated by subtracting from the price of a new item an allowance for depreciation based on the age of the item that is to be insured.

The **replacement value** of a damaged or lost item is the cost of buying a new item of the same quality. In the above example, the insured would receive the cost of a brand-new, 28-inch colour television of the same quality as the lost one.

In general, the depreciated value is less than the replacement value, so most people would probably prefer a replacement value policy. Of course, the policy for replacement value requires a higher premium.

You should be aware of how payments for damaged or lost items are made under a **replacement cost policy**. The lost or destroyed items must be replaced with new ones of comparable quality. If the insured chooses not to replace, the claim will be settled at the depreciated value only. In the case of damaged items, repairs must be made to return the items back to the best possible condition. Again, if one chooses not to make the repair, one will be paid the depreciated value only.

Replacement Value of a Home

The replacement value of a home for insurance purposes is not its current **market value**. The method to estimate the **fair market value** of a home will be described in Chapter 13, where we talk about buying one's own home. For insurance purposes, however, the fair market value of the home should not be used because it includes the value of the land and foundation. In most cases, the land and foundation of a home cannot be destroyed by typical disasters. Therefore, what you want to insure is the replacement value of your home's structure. This is what it would cost to replace the **home's structure** (defined as everything except the land and foundation) if the home were totally destroyed. In Chapter 13, we will describe a method called the **cost approach of valuation**, which is a method to determine the replacement cost of the home's structure. In general, it is quite difficult and complicated for one to estimate the replacement value of a home's structure. It is more practical to pay for an appraisal of the home, indicating to the appraiser that the appraisal is for the purpose of buying home insurance. Such an appraisal will give you a professional estimate of both the depreciated value and the replacement value of the home's structure.

Some insurance companies automatically set the amount of the home insurance equal to the amount of the mortgage on the house. Very often, the banks or the loan companies require this insurance amount to be in place before they will grant you a mortgage. While insurance set at the amount of the existing mortgage protects the lender's interest, it is not intended to cover the owner's interest in the structure.

The 80% Rule

Most insurance companies will not pay the full loss on partial damage unless the insured has bought insurance to cover at least 80% of the home's replacement value. If the insured buys insurance coverage for less than that, the insurance company will only make payments proportional to the percentage of required minimum coverage taken. This practice is called the **80% Rule**; the best way to illustrate this rule is by a numerical example.

Example 11.1: John and Mary Doyle own a house whose current replacement value (not including the value of the land) is $100,000. They bought a home insurance coverage equal to $70,000. Their home suffered a fire loss equal to $30,000. How much will the insurance company pay?

The Doyles have coverage for only ($70,000 ÷ $100,000) or 70% of the replacement value of their home; this is below the required minimum coverage of 80%. Therefore, because the Doyles have not met the 80% Rule, the insurance company will pay only [$30,000 × ($70,000 ÷ $80,000)] or $26,250.

The next example shows that because replacement value increases over time it is advisable to check your policy periodically to ensure that you have the minimum required coverage.

Example 11.2: Jonathan and Janice Carter bought a house five years ago that had a replacement value of $150,000. They bought insurance coverage for $125,000 but they have not increased the coverage since the time of the original purchase. Because of inflation and other factors, their home has a current replacement value of $180,000. Their house suffers fire damage of $10,000. How much of this $10,000 will be reimbursed by the insurance company?

The required minimum coverage is 80% of current replacement value — in this case, 80% of current replacement value is ($180,000 × .80) or $144,000. Their current insurance coverage is only $125,000, which is below the minimum required coverage. Therefore, the insurance company will pay only [$10,000 × ($125,000 ÷ $144,000)] or $8,681.

Note that, in the example, the Carters had 83.33% coverage ($125,000 ÷ $150,000) when they bought the home five years ago; at the time of purchase, then, the 80% Rule was satisfied. This example illustrates the importance of reviewing your insurance policy periodically to see if you have adequate coverage. The inflation protection that we will describe later is a very useful feature in your policy.

Finally, it is extremely important that you know exactly how replacement value, or replacement cost, is defined in the policy. This term is not standardized. In some insurance policies, it refers to the structure's value without the foundation; in other policies, it refers to the structure and the foundation.

Inflation Protection Provision

Inflation and the increasing dollar value of the replacement costs of homes are very important considerations in your home insurance policy. If your policy does not take inflation into account, then the real value of your coverage will decline over time. Also, as we saw in Example 11.2, your policy may fail to meet the 80% Rule in the future.

Many insurance companies offer an **inflation protection provision** that automatically increases the coverage amount each year in accordance with the increase in some inflation index such as the Consumer Price Index (CPI). Naturally, you have to pay an additional premium for this provision.

If you live in an area of the country where housing costs are expected to rise faster than the average rate of inflation (as represented by the CPI), then even the inflation protection provision may not provide adequate coverage. Most insurance companies, for additional premiums, provide additional coverage in excess of that provided by the inflation protection provision.

Deductibles

A **deductible** is the part of a claim that you must pay first before the insurance company will pay anything. For example, suppose you have a $2,000 insurable loss from your home due to theft and there is a deductible of $500 in your home insurance policy. In this case, you pay the first $500 on the loss and the insurance company pays the rest, or $1,500.

The higher the amount of the deductible, the lower the premium that you have to pay. There are three reasons why premiums will be lower if deductibles are higher. First, since you share part of the damages or loss, the insurance company does not have to pay as much on the claims. Second, the insured will try harder to avoid the damages, losses, and accidents against which he is insuring valuable property if there is a significantly large deductible. Finally, there is a fixed cost of administration for settling any claim that is largely independent of the size of the claim. The insurance company would rather avoid numerous small claims, and will charge a high premium on policies with low deductibles to encourage customers to deal with their own smaller losses.

"Higher Deductible, Lower Premium" vs. "Lower Deductible, Higher Premium"

Is there any theory that will tell you the optimal amount of deductible that is the best for you? In theory, the answer is yes; but for practical purposes, the answer is no. If individuals know their utility function for money, then theoretically they can calculate the optimal amount of deductible that is the best. However, in practice, nobody knows their utility function, which means it is impossible to determine the "right" amount of deductibles.[2]

Rigorous theory aside, high deductible policies (and, hence, lower premiums) make more economic sense than low deductible policies. Let us recall that the basic principle of buying insurance is to insure against large rather than small losses. Your insurance dollars should first be spent to insure against losses that would be insupportable to you and your family. By buying a policy with a large deductible, you are spending your insurance money to cover large losses, reducing the premium cost per dollar of insurance and can therefore afford a higher total coverage.

---

[2] A utility function is a mathematical representation of an individual's risk–return preferences. In the case of an insurance deductible, for every combination of deductible (or potential loss) and premium, a utility function would indicate how much each is valued by that person.

Example 11.3:   Suppose Mr. Wolfgang can afford only $500 annually on home insurance. Suppose he has two choices: (i) he can buy $50,000 of coverage provided that he takes a $100 deductible; and (ii) he can buy $100,000 of coverage provided that he takes a $300 deductible. Economic logic suggests that he should take the higher deductible policy of $300 because it would provide more protection against catastrophic losses.

Rule of Thumb

Although it cannot be proven rigorously, many financial experts recommend a deductible equal to 3% of your net worth. For example, if one's net worth is $50,000, one should seek an insurance policy with a deductible equal to $1,500.

The incentive aspect of a high deductible policy should be emphasized once more. If there is a high deductible, one would try much harder to avoid or reduce the risk. The homeowners will, for example, put in smoke detectors, buy more fire extinguishers, install a security system, regularly check the electrical and gas appliances for leaks, and so on, to avoid or reduce the risks. They have a higher incentive to do so if there is a larger deductible in the home insurance policy.

Another incentive relates to loss of personal property away from the house, a common peril covered in home insurance policies. A homeowner with a $500 deductible will be quite careful to lock up a bicycle away from home since he will pay most or all of the cost if it is stolen.

Third Party Liability Insurance

Apart from the home's structure and contents, a typical home policy also covers **liabilities to third parties**. This insurance coverage protects you from the liability to other people for injuries suffered on your property or by anything attached or related to your property. You are required to ensure that your property does not pose a danger to a reasonable person; however, your responsibility as a homeowner is not well defined. For example, would you be liable if someone, falling on your driveway and breaking his leg, claimed that his accident was caused by your fault in not clearing the driveway sufficiently of snow accumulated during the previous week's heavy snowstorm (even though you had used the snow-blower to clean it twice)?

There are many "grey" areas in **third party liability** that make it almost impossible to determine how much **liability insurance** one should buy, especially in view of the changing court decisions in recent years. There are some factors that you should consider: the nature of any non-household activities carried out in your home; whether or not there are any domestic servants; whether or not there is a swimming pool; whether or not there are any dogs or other pets; and anything else that you can think of that might increase your risk exposure to third party liability.

Once again, the basic principle that one should insure for potentially catastrophic losses applies here. Homeowner's liability insurance is still fairly cheap because claims against homeowner policies are quite infrequent. Many insurance agents advise the average family to carry $1,000,000, which does not cost a lot more than $500,000 in coverage.

Types of Home Insurance

The home insurance market has developed to the extent that it can provide a policy tailored to almost any need. Clauses and provisions with the appropriate premiums can be added or deleted from a policy to suit a family's particular need. Nevertheless, we can classify all home insurance policies into three types: (i) comprehensive home insurance; (ii) fire insurance; and (iii) tenant's insurance (also called the renter's insurance).

The most common type is the **comprehensive home policy**, which covers the three major sources of risk: the home structure, its contents, and third party liability. It covers all the risks listed earlier. Other provisions are usually added to suit the insured's specific needs. The following is a list of additional provisions that can be added to a comprehensive policy at the insured's option:

- Damaged property removal
- Removal of debris
- Trees, shrubs, and plants — usually covered up to a certain maximum, e.g., a maximum of $200 per tree or a maximum aggregate value of 5% of the home insurance
- Fire department surcharges — up to a specified maximum amount
- Expensive jewellery, furs, and other valuable personal properties
- Earthquake
- Temporary repairs to prevent further damage to the property

Fire Insurance

This is a no-frills insurance policy that provides the most basic protection: mainly fire, lightning, smoke damage, as well as other specifically listed perils. It usually excludes the risks of theft, window breakage, goods in transit, and third party liability. This policy is only advisable for families who have separate liability coverage and little risk of theft.

Tenant's Insurance or Renter's Insurance

Tenant's or **renter's insurance** covers the contents in the home, excluding the home structure. If you rent an apartment or a house and it burns down, the landlord loses the apartment or the house, but you lose your possessions. The landlord is not liable to reimburse you for the loss of your possessions; you therefore need a tenant's insurance package. Your tenant's insurance policy should include third party liability coverage. If someone is hurt in your apartment and has sustained significant injury, you may be liable for substantial expenses; you therefore need a liability protection provision in your policy.

AUTOMOBILE INSURANCE

Automobile insurance covers a number of risks, the damages from which are potentially very large. First, there is the risk of injury or death of the owner and his or her passengers. Second, there is the risk of damage, destruction, or theft of the car. Third, and most important, there is the potential liability to others (third parties) for injury, death, or damage to their cars or property. This third party liability — injury to others caused by you and your car — is the largest potential claim on you. Liability insurance is the means to finance this potentially devastating risk. Furthermore, the probability of a car accident in which significant losses are incurred is much higher than the probability of major damage to your home.

Most provinces require that the registered car owners carry liability insurance and a few additional coverages; however, the minimum amount of insurance required by the provincial legislatures is usually not the optimum amount of insurance. The concepts and theories that you have learned should be used to assess the amount of auto insurance that you need. Again, the basic principle is this: Insure large losses and pay for small expenses yourself.

Types of Automobile Insurance

Liability Insurance (Auto)

Liability insurance of an automobile covers the injury, death, and damage to the property of other persons (third party). There are two components to this coverage: bodily injury coverage and property damage coverage.

Bodily injury coverage covers the injury or death of other people (e.g., people in your car, people in other cars, pedestrians) resulting from the accident that you caused. The car owner's policy covers the car owner and persons using the car with the car owner's permission. If you drive someone's car with permission and have an accident in which you cause bodily injury to other people, the liability claim will be settled under the bodily injury coverage of the owner's auto policy. If the car owner is uninsured, then your own policy will cover you.

Property damage coverage covers the damage your car causes to someone else's property in the event you were the cause of the accident. For example, if you ran the red light and hit another car, you were clearly at fault (that is to say, you were the cause of the accident). If $5,000 of damage resulted from the accident, the bill less the *deductible* will be paid by the property damage coverage of your auto insurance policy.

How Much Liability Insurance Do You Need?

Liability to others is an insupportable risk to most people. It could instantly wipe out your wealth and your future if you were the cause of a severe injury or death to another person in an accident. Admittedly, the probability of such a serious injury happening is very small, especially if you are a careful driver; nevertheless, because this is a potentially catastrophic loss, you should buy enough liability insurance.

But how much is enough? First, there is a minimum coverage for bodily injury liability required by each province. If your net worth is small (and you have to determine what is small), there is no financial need for you to buy more coverage than the minimum amount required by the law. Ethically, you might prefer to carry more insurance. If you do cause serious harm or death through careless driving, you might be found liable for a very large amount — even a sum equal to the expected lifetime earnings of the person injured. If your net worth is large enough that you don't want to lose it, it is advisable to purchase a lot more than the minimum liability insurance (which includes bodily injury liability). The common amount for prudent car owners in Canada is now $2 million. It is conceivable that you could be found liable for a greater amount, but such cases are quite rare. Since major losses are infrequent, insurance companies do not charge a lot for the higher liability coverage.[3]

Other Auto Insurance Coverages

Collision Coverage

This coverage pays for damage to your car from an accident in which you are at fault. (Recall that if the other driver is at fault, the damage will be paid by his insurance policy under the property damage coverage already described.)

The **collision coverage** normally pays only the *depreciated value* of the car. For example, your 15-year-old car, worth $200, is damaged in an accident in which you are at fault. If it would cost $3,000 to repair the car, the insurance company will pay you only $200 minus the deductible. Therefore, you should periodically reduce your collision coverage to reflect the car's current value. Considering the purpose of risk management is to eliminate or finance insupportable risks, you should probably drop collision coverage altogether on older cars. Collision coverage is quite expensive because of the large number of relatively small claims that insurance companies have to settle.

---

[3] Car accidents are common, but serious personal injury or death, coupled with demonstrable negligence by the other driver, are infrequent. Hence, the losses spread over a large population are quite small.

Comprehensive Coverage

The **comprehensive coverage** pays for the damage to your car resulting from "non-accidents" — theft, vandalism, fire, etc. This coverage pays only the *depreciated* value of the car; for this reason, you should periodically reduce this coverage to reflect the decrease in the value of the car.

Medical Payment Coverage or Medical Insurance (Auto)

This coverage pays for the medical costs for you and your passengers as a result of an accident in which you are at fault.

Uninsured Motorists Coverage

This provision covers you and your family for bodily injury caused by another driver who is either uninsured or does not have enough insurance. **Uninsured motorists coverage** also covers you and your family members in the case of injuries caused by a hit-and-run driver. Usually only bodily injury is covered and not the damage to the car.

No-fault Insurance

No-fault insurance allows you to collect insurance payments from your own insurance company even if the accident is someone else's fault. Some provinces (e.g., Ontario) have imposed laws that require insurers to offer no-fault insurance. The idea is that if fault did not have to be proved in accidents, legal costs would be saved and car insurance premiums would be lowered. As a result of recent legislation, some provinces even require the insured to give up his or her right to sue, thereby reducing legal fees even more and lowering premiums further. Nevertheless, there are counter-arguments insisting that no-fault insurance will not lower premiums: First, no-fault insurance gives many drivers less incentive to be careful; second, insurance companies have less incentive to penalize drivers who have frequent accidents because they will not always pay for the accidents caused by the persons they insure.

Deductibles in Car Insurance

As in home insurance, taking a bigger deductible will lower your premiums. Deductibles are available with the collision coverage and the comprehensive coverage parts of your car insurance policy. If you follow the basic principle of buying insurance only, then you should increase the amount of deductible and use the savings in premiums to buy more coverage for the potentially big losses; for example, you should use the savings to buy more coverage for bodily injury and uninsured-motorists insurance.

Rental Car Insurance

If you rent a car, you should be aware of the insurance coverage since you face the same risks as if you owned the car. In Canada, and most other jurisdictions, the rental fee will automatically include liability insurance. You should make sure of this, however, and find out the amount covered. In our experience in Canada, it is usually $1 million.

All other perils are at your risk, unless you specifically request coverage, have coverage through your insurance policy on your own car,[4] or have coverage on a premium credit card. You can opt to pay an extra fee for extra insurance and also for some life insurance. This extra insurance is quite expensive. Since you should have planned your life insurance coverage according to the principles in Chapter 10, you should not need the life insurance offered by the car rental agency (and it, too, is quite expensive).

SUMMARY

In this chapter we examine property insurance, which protects your properties such as clothing, furniture, car, and home against the risk of damage or destruction. In particular, we introduce and discuss two important property insurances: home insurance and automobile insurance. Most of the concepts and theories that we have discussed in Chapter 9 and Chapter 10 can be applied to property insurance as well. For example, the basic principle that you buy insurance for large and catastrophic losses only has been applied to both home insurance and automobile insurance.

Home insurance protects your home and its contents against the risk of damage and destruction, and protects you against third party liability. A home and its contents can be covered either by a depreciated value policy or a replacement value policy. Some important characteristics of home insurance — deductibles, inflation protection provision, and so on, have been introduced and described. If you rent an apartment or a house, you should buy a renter's insurance policy to protect your possessions.

Automobile insurance provides the protection in three major areas: (i) liabilities to third parties; (ii) the injury or death of the owner and the passengers; and (iii) the damage, destruction, or theft of the automobile. A typical auto insurance policy has the following coverages: bodily injury coverage, property damage coverage, collision, comprehensive, medical payments coverage, and uninsured motorists coverage. The concept of a no-fault insurance policy has also been discussed.

---

[4] Many automobile insurance policies now contain a special rider that extends collision and theft coverage to cars rented by the family that buys the policy.

MULTIPLE-CHOICE REVIEW QUESTIONS

1. Other things being held constant, _____ the deductible in a car insurance policy will _____ the premium.

   (a) decreasing; not change
   (b) increasing; decrease
   (c) decreasing; decrease
   (d) both (a) and (b)
   (e) both (b) and (c)

2. Collision coverage in auto insurance covers _____.

   (a) damage to your own car
   (b) the replacement value of the car
   (c) the depreciated value of the car
   (d) both (a) and (c)
   (e) none of the above

3. Liability insurance in an auto policy covers _____.

   (a) injury to pedestrians from an accident that you cause
   (b) death to other people in your car
   (c) damage to other people's property that you cause
   (d) (a) and (b)
   (e) (a), (b), and (c)

4. The 80% Rule of home insurance says that _____.

   (a) the insurance company will pay only 80% of the damage to your home
   (b) you must buy insurance to cover at least 80% of the home's replacement value
   (c) the insurance company will pay for your full loss about 80% of the time
   (d) your policy value must be at least 80% of the value of your home in order for you to get full payment for the loss
   (e) none of the above

5. Which of the following statements is true for no-fault auto insurance?

   (a) You can collect payment from your insurance company only if you are not at fault.
   (b) You can collect payment from your insurance company even if another person is at fault.
   (c) You can collect payment from another person's insurance company if the other person is at fault.
   (d) Your insurance premium will not go up even if you are at fault in an accident.
   (e) None of the above.

DISCUSSION QUESTIONS

1. Explain or describe the following key words and terms:

    automobile insurance: liability insurance (auto) — bodily injury coverage — property damage coverage — collision coverage — comprehensive coverage — medical payment coverage / comprehensive home policy / fire insurance policy / home insurance: home's structure — home's contents — 80% Rule or required minimum coverage — inflation protection provision / liability insurance (home) / no-fault insurance / property insurance: deductible — depreciated value — replacement value or cost / renter's insurance / tenant's insurance / third party liability / uninsured-motorist coverage

2. If you have a limited budget for property insurance, which would you prefer: a "higher deductible and lower premium" policy or a "lower deductible and higher premium" policy? Why?

3. What are the three basic components of a comprehensive home policy?

4. "No-fault insurance was introduced in Ontario because it was expected that premiums would drop very significantly."

    (a) What are the reasons to expect a drop in the premium?
    (b) Are there any reasons to believe that premiums may increase rather than decrease?

5. What is the basic principle in insurance that has been applied many times in this chapter?

6. What are the major components of a car insurance policy?

PROBLEMS

1. **Personal Project 1**
    Get a copy of an actual home insurance policy — yours, your parents', or a friend's. Read the policy from the beginning to the end.

    (a) Describe the coverages of the policy in terms of the home, its contents, and liability insurance. Be as specific as possible; for example, does "home structure" include the foundation?
    (b) Jot down all the new terms that were not discussed in this chapter. Find the definitions of these terms in the insurance policy.
    (c) If this is your home policy, assess whether it has the right coverage for you.

2. **Personal Project 2**

    Get a copy of an actual automobile insurance policy. Read the policy carefully from the beginning to the end.

    (a) What are the coverage limits and the deductibles (if any) for each major coverage component — bodily injury coverage, property damage coverage, collision, etc.

    (b) Find out the premium for each of the items in (a).

    (c) If this is your car insurance, assess whether it has the right coverage for you.

    (d) How do you know whether the insurer is charging you too much?

3. What is the 80% rule? Mr. J.J. Thompson owns a home with a current replacement cost of $210,000. He has insurance coverage for a replacement value of $100,000. If he suffered fire damage of $10,000, and if the deductible is $500, how much of the loss will the insurer pay?

4. Jan and Gordon Branton bought a house 15 years ago for $150,000. They then bought a home insurance policy to provide coverage for $130,000 replacement value. There is an inflation protection provision in the policy so that the amount of insurance coverage automatically increases every year at the rate of inflation. The current replacement value of the house is $340,000. The average rate of inflation of the last 15 years has been 4% per year. The deductible is $500. Recently, their home suffered a fire damage, resulting in a loss of $100,000.

    How much of the loss will the insurance company pay?

CHAPTER 12

Credit and Debt Management

▶ Mwangi Ndegwa offers great deals on used cars and easy financing. Can you calculate how much the payments will be? See Example 12.2.

▶ Dr. Anderson earns $250,000 annually as a surgeon, and the family has finished paying off the house mortgage. If they are willing to take some additional risk, they can use debt to increase their savings without reducing their current consumption. See Example 12.4.

LEARNING OBJECTIVES

> ➤ *To discuss ways of assessing your debt capacity.*
>
> ➤ *To suggest ways of efficient credit management.*
>
> ➤ *To discuss the common forms of consumer financing, especially the use of credit cards.*
>
> ➤ *To explain the difference between consumer credit and investment loans.*

Most problems in a family's financial affairs arise from the improper use of credit and debt. In order to manage your personal finances successfully and to achieve your financial goals, you must be able to manage debt effectively. We hope that this chapter will make you a better borrower.

In general, the most important debt commitment that one makes during one's life is the mortgage that is used to buy a home. This is a very important topic but we feel it is more natural to postpone it until Chapter 13 when we talk about investing in a home. Right now, it suffcient to say that most of the concepts discussed in this chapter apply to a home mortgage.

DEBT CAPACITY

Why Use Credit?

You may have heard of stories about families ruining their lives by living beyond their means on credit. In fact, many books on personal finance recommend to those people who have overextended themselves in debt to first of all destroy all their credit cards. In the nineties, the word **debt** was perhaps the ugliest four-letter word in finance. Why in the world then would anyone use consumer credit? Isn't credit the reason for most financial problems? For many people, the question is easily answered. There is no cash available, so credit must be used if the product is to be purchased. When you borrow, the lender is giving you a credit, or trust, against your future earnings. You get to use the credit to buy something now. Without credit, you have to wait until you have saved enough money to pay cash, and you must postpone the use and enjoyment of the product. In the early stages of your life cycle, income is typically below consumption needs, whereas in later years, it normally rises above those needs. Borrowing allows the income stream to match the desired consumption stream. By using credit prudently and creatively, you can acquire assets sooner and in larger amounts then you otherwise might. Therefore, if credit is properly used, it can serve a very valuable function.

Reprinted with permission — The Toronto Star Syndicate. © 1994 GREG HOWARD distributed by King Features Syndicate.

Many people, however, overuse their credit. The problem of overindebtedness or borrowing too much initially starts out harmlessly when people borrow an amount that they can handle easily. Then they begin to borrow more and more until they become overindebted and, as a consequence, fall into despair and crisis. We are less concerned about people who become overindebted through circumstances beyond their control, such as unanticipated loss of employment or reduction of income. We are more concerned about people who become overindebted through careless and impulsive use of credit. To ensure that you don't fall into this trap, it is important for you to gain the proper knowledge of debt management. There is a right way and a wrong way to use consumer credits, such as a credit card. The right way is to take full advantage of the many attractive features that the credit card provides — such as the free-loan grace period, detailed record keeping, no need to carry quantities of cash, etc. The wrong way is to build up a large debt balance and pay over 18% non-tax-deductible interest.

Debt Capacity

If overindebtedness is the biggest potential problem in the use of debt, then the natural questions to ask would be:

- How much debt can an individual take?
- Is there an optimal level of debt that an individual can take?
- What are the factors that affect this optimal level of debt?
- How can someone manage his or her credit and debt effectively?

These are interrelated questions. Before we can answer any of these questions, we must first introduce the important concept of **debt capacity**. A borrower's debt capacity is defined as the amount of debt that he or she can reasonably expect to be able to repay under the terms of the loan agreements, given current and expected future financial situations — assets, liabilities, cash flows, income, expenditures, etc. Normally, the borrower's obligation is to make future payments (interest and principal) to the lender, so debt capacity does not look only at what the borrower has today but also at what the borrower will have in the future. The most important determinant of someone's debt capacity is therefore that person's expected future net cash flow, or more specifically, his or her ability to generate sufficient cash flow, after living expenses and required capital outlays, to pay the interest and principal of all loans to maturity. The lender is interested in both the borrower's short-run and long-run ability to pay interest and principal.

Liquidity and Solvency

Liquidity is the ability of a family to meet its debt service payments in the short run. **Solvency** is the long-run ability of the family to pay its debts. A young dentist who has just started a new practice may have good long-run expectations but may not be able to meet next month's interest payment — that is, the dentist may have liquidity problems. On the other hand, a factory worker who will be retiring next year may have no problem in meeting month-to-month interest payments but may have some difficulty in paying off the loan when it comes due.

Assets vs. Cash Flow

The lender is concerned about both the liquidity and solvency of the borrower. The borrower has two sources of cash to pay off the loan: net cash flow and asset sales. For example, you can pay off your loan from your employment income or out of the proceeds of the sale of the antique furniture that you inherited recently. Thus, the most important factors that affect your debt capacity are your expected net assets or net worth and your expected net cash flow each year. Other things being equal, the higher the expected net assets and net cash flow, the higher the debt capacity.

Risk

If the future was known with certainty, determining liquidity, solvency, future cash flows, and future asset values would be trivial. Since the future is uncertain, we have to assess how risky the future cash flows and future asset values are. We will discuss risk in a theoretical context later in the chapters on investment. For now, we will think of risk as how likely the cash flow is to fail to provide for all **debt service charges**. In this sense, risk comes from the variability of cash flow from one period to another, and it is during the time when cash flow is low that the individual would have problems meeting his or her debt obligations.

The variability of the cash flow (the risk) can come from many sources. The biggest variation comes from the changes in earning streams. The following are some causes that can affect changes in earnings:

- Loss of employment
- Pay cut
- Death of a breadwinner
- Disability or poor health
- Failure of a small business
- Withdrawal from work for pregnancy

Asset values can and usually do change over time. Depreciable assets like furniture, cars, and household appliances normally decrease in value over time. Investment assets like houses, stocks, bonds, and mutual funds generally appreciate in value in the long run, but in the short run they can go up or down. As before, this variation in asset values causes the risk to a person's ability to service debt obligations. The following are some examples that can cause the decrease in asset values:

- Depreciation due to wear and tear
- Negative changes in the economy
- Increases in interest rates
- Disasters such as fire, burglary, or termite infestation
- Closing of a major factory in a small town
- Obsolescence of one's professional skills (this leads to a decrease in the value of one's human capital)

Finally, we will point out that a lot of the variability in cash flows and asset valuation can be reduced to manageable levels with appropriate insurance. For example, you can buy insurance to cover the risks due to death or disability and the risk of loss to property value due to fire. The risk of job loss may be partially covered by employment insurance compensation if you are an employee.

How Much Debt Can You Afford?

We have seen that there are three characteristics of a family's assets and cash flow — liquidity, solvency, and risk — that affect the borrower's debt capacity. In practice, however, since these characteristics are difficult to assess and measure precisely, there is no rigorous theory that determines a precise value of debt capacity, nor is there any method to determine a family's "optimal" level of consumer debt. To a large extent, the amount of debt that a family can assume depends on the spending objective and the family's risk tolerance. It is conceivable that a family with gross earnings of $50,000 would assume a larger amount of debt than a family with twice that amount of gross income ($100,000) because the two families have different spending habits and risk preferences (i.e., comfort zones of debt levels). If a family assesses its financial situation according to the three characteristics — liquidity, solvency, and risk — it should be able to come up with a comfort zone of debt for the family.

The most useful tool for assessing debt capacity is a budget of income and expenditure. The technique of preparing a family budget has been discussed in Chapter 4. When you do a budget for the entire period of the loan, the budgeting process will cover both the liquidity and the solvency aspects of your debt. You simply add the proposed debt payments to the expenses in the budget and see if it still balances. Don't forget to include all the additional expenses or revenues caused by whatever the borrowed money is spent on. For example, if the borrowed money is spent on buying a new car, you must include in your budget the additional expenses of running the car. If your budget shows surpluses in every month of the entire loan period, you can afford the loan.

Debt Service Ratios

Most people obtain their consumer credit and debt from the conventional sources — banks, credit cards, department store charge cards, finance companies, etc. It is important to know how these institutions make decisions in their consumer lending practices. A commonly used quick-scoring method for loan applications is the debt-service ratio. The two popular debt service ratios are the **Gross Debt Service ratio** (GDS ratio) and the **Total Debt Service ratio** (TDS ratio). They are defined as follows:

$$GDS = \frac{\text{annual mortgage payments} + \text{property taxes}}{\text{gross family income}}$$

$$TDS = \frac{\text{mortgage payments} + \text{property taxes} + \text{other debt payments}}{\text{gross family income}}$$

See Example 12.1 for an illustration.

Example 12.1: Mr. and Mrs. Smith have an annual gross income of $80,000. There is a first mortgage on their house and the monthly mortgage payment is $1,800. Last year they paid $2,400 in property taxes. Their other debt obligations include a car loan (monthly payment is $210) and a credit card balance (monthly payment is about $150). They have no other debt outstanding.

$$GDS \text{ ratio} = \frac{(\$1,800 \times 12) + \$2,400}{\$80,000} = 30\%$$

$$TDS \text{ ratio} = \frac{(\$1,800 \times 12) + \$2,400 + (\$210 \times 12) + (\$150 \times 12)}{\$80,000} = 35.4\%$$

The two benchmarks most often cited are Gross Debt Service (GDS) ratio of not over 30% and Total Debt Service (TDS) ratio of not over 40%. The GDS and TDS ratios of the Smith family in the example are within those limits.[1]

These ratios and benchmarks are developed by statistically analyzing a large number of previous credit files for which the payment histories are known. They may be useful for financial institutions that require a quick-scoring method to process a large number of loan applications. They make a good rule of thumb for families in the average income brackets, say $40,000 to $60,000. However, for the purpose of assessing your debt capacity, the budgeting process is still superior to these ratios for the following reasons. First, ratios do not allow for risk. A physician and a salesman may have the same expected gross income but the doctor's income is probably much more stable and can therefore support a higher level of debt. Second, these ratios are based on gross income and therefore do not allow for the effect of taxes. After-tax income will be significantly higher with two workers each earning $20,000 than with one earning $40,000. Third, these benchmarks are normally applicable for average incomes only. At the low end, a family of four with an income of $15,000 cannot possibly afford to pay 40% of the family income in debt servicing. At the high end, a four-member family with a $200,000 gross income can afford to spend more than 40% of the family income on debt servicing because most living costs do not rise proportionately with income. Finally, ratios do not give information about the short-run liquidity and long-run solvency that a budget would give.

In spite of these disadvantages, debt service ratios are easy to calculate and financial institutions use them. Therefore, if you want to assess your debt capacity, it is advisable to prepare a budget for the entire loan period and, in addition to that, to calculate these ratios to see if they are within the current benchmarks. At least they would give you an indication of how much you can borrow from a conventional financial institution.

Matching Assets and Debts

There is a rule of thumb in corporation finance that can be applied easily to personal finance. This rule, sometimes called the **matching principle in finance**, suggests that one should match the expected economic life of an asset to the term of maturity of the financing. Assets with long expected economic lives (e.g., real estate) should be financed by long-term debt. For example, if the expected economic life of an asset is 20 years, it should be financed by a loan that matures in 20 years. This is what the banks do with people's term deposits; when banks lend money, they match the term of the loan with the expected economic life of the

---

[1] In recent years, Canadian financial institutions have been approving some mortgage loans with much higher GDS and TDS ratios.

asset. For groceries and perishables that are consumed right away (i.e., their economic life is close to zero), you should pay cash. It does not make sense to use credit card loans to buy groceries or other perishables. Of course, if you always pay off the credit card balance in full, you are using the credit card for convenience and that is a different matter. If you must borrow to buy a car, the term of the loan ideally should be four to six years, which is the average economic life of a car. How about your home? The expected economic life of a home is 25 years or much longer. Therefore, it makes sense to pay off the loan in 25 years — technically, this is called amortizing the loan in 25 years.

CONSUMER CREDIT

When people borrow money to purchase consumer goods or services, they are making use of **consumer credit** financing of one form or another. Examples of consumer credit financing are personal loans, auto loans, credit cards, and home equity loans. Borrowing money to invest, a topic which we will discuss later, does not fall under consumer credit. We restrict the meaning of consumer credit finance to the case where an individual borrows money to purchase consumer assets or services. Thus, borrowing money to acquire a washing machine or furniture or to take a vacation in Europe is consumer credit, while borrowing money to invest in a stock mutual fund is an investment loan. The differences between a consumer loan and an investment loan are substantial, so we will discuss the two topics separately in this chapter.

Consumer Loans and Time Value

In order to budget for them, we need to know how to handle the time value calculations. A consumer loan is almost invariably repayable in equal monthly instalments of blended principal and interest. Thus, it is compounded and payable monthly. The loan rate may be quoted as an APR or as an EAR, depending on the applicable legislation, but increasingly the EAR is the norm.[2] Example 12.2 illustrates the application of the time value mechanics to a consumer loan.

Example 12.2: Mwangi Ndegwa offers the best price in town on used cars. Even better, you can pay in 36 easy, low, low monthly instalments, at an effective annual interest rate of only 11.22%.

---

[2] The APR (annual percentage rate) does not allow for the monthly compounding, while the EAR (effective annual rate) does. See Chapter 2 if you need to review time value of money.

(a) What is the monthly rate Mwangi charges?

(b) If you buy a used Bentley for $70,000 and finance the whole purchase price, what is your monthly payment?

(c) How much do you still owe after 24 months of payments?

(d) Suppose you could deduct the interest expense on the first year as an expense on your tax return because you were using the car for business travel exclusively. How much interest expense would you report?

Answer:

(a) You reverse the compounding process to find the 12th root of 1.1122: $[(1.1122) \mathbf{y^x} .08333] - 1 = .89\%$

(b)

PV	=	70,000
I/Y	=	.89%
N	=	36
PMT	=	$2,281.12

(c) You now owe 12 months of payments of $2,281.12, at .89%. The PV of this loan = $25,853.52.

(d) The quickest way to find the interest for a specific time period during a loan is to calculate the amount of principal owing on the loan at the start and end of that period. The difference is the amount of principal repaid. Now add up the total payments during that period. Subtract the principal from the total payments and you get the interest you paid.

PV of loan with 24 months to go = $49,099.20.

Total payments = 12 × $2,281.12 = $27,373.44.

Amount of principal repaid
= $70,000 – $49,099.20 = $20,900.80.

Amount of interest paid
= $27,373.44 – $20,900.80 = $6,472.64.

Personal Credit Management

Personal debt plays an important role in your personal financial affairs. It is important that you learn some crucial techniques in personal credit management and start to build positive credit habits as soon as possible. The following are the critical areas in which you have to gain knowledge in order to be successful in managing your debt and credit:

1. How do you get credit?
2. How do you build up and maintain positive credit habits?
3. How do you maintain a good credit record?
4. How do you spend the money that you have to borrow?

How Do You Get Credit?

There are many sources of consumer credit. You can get credit from banks, trust companies, credit unions, finance companies, department stores, oil and gas companies, to name a few. Usually the lenders target their loans towards specific risk classes of borrowers. Banks, trust companies, and credit unions normally specialize in lower risk loans. Finance companies and loan companies that are tied to specific sellers (such as department stores like The Bay or Canadian Tire, or automobile manufacturers like General Motors and Ford) normally specialize in slightly higher credit risk loans. On the other end of the scale you would find small finance companies, pawnshops, or even loan sharks who specialize in very high credit risk and, hence, high-interest-rate loans.

As a borrower you want to pay as low an interest rate as possible on a loan. Whether you will be successful in getting the best deal depends on how you present yourself to the lender. The lender generally requires you to fill out an application form for credit or for a loan; and she assesses you on the basis of the information given on that form as well as on the basis of your credit history.

Credit Scoring

Lenders use a predetermined scoring system to make credit decisions. Points are added or deducted for various characteristics elicited by the application form. The typical questions that are asked cover your age, marital status, annual income, number of years in your current job, whether you rent or own your home, age of your cars, your bank accounts, amount of existing debt, type and amount of investment you own, whether you have declared bankruptcy before, and general credit references. Each characteristic will be given a score based on some credit standard. If you score high enough, you will get the credit or the loan.

Lenders view an individual's character as a key factor in deciding whether to grant the loan. Therefore, it is important that you tell the truth. Deceit is not only costly in the short term (you do not get the credit) but in the long term as well (future chances of getting credit are jeopardized). Evidence of deception will remain in your file and become part of your credit history for a long, long time.

Your Credit File

Whether they know it or not, most consumers have credit files in the local credit bureau, which is a credit reporting agency. If you have applied for or used any form of credit before, you can be sure that there is a credit file on you. Do you have a phone? If you do, we are almost certain that there is a credit file on you.

Lenders routinely make a credit check on anyone who applies for a credit card, a loan, a mortgage, or any form of financing; and the local credit bureau is the first place the lender will check. There are many credit reporting agencies; they provide different kinds of credit information to members for a fee. It is easy to find out all the local credit reporting agencies in your city. Simply look under the credit reporting agencies section in the Yellow Pages of your local telephone directory: Every major city in Canada has a credit bureau.

Credit reporting agencies do not evaluate your credit file. Their job is to record all relevant information in your file and make the information available to credit bureau members — a group that includes banks, mortgage companies, trust companies, insurance companies and other lenders and issuers of credit.

If there is one single factor that affects your future borrowing, it is your credit report. An unfavourable credit report will almost certainly jeopardize your future credit and loan applications. Therefore, if you suspect, for whatever reason, that there is incorrect or negative information in your credit file, you owe it to yourself to correct the mistake as soon as possible. By law, you can ask any credit bureau to give you a complete, accurate copy of your file. You can request reverification by the credit bureau if information is incorrect and you have the right to ask that missing data be added to your file. You also have the right to know exactly why you were refused credit. These are just a few examples of the rights that you have with respect to your credit file. Indeed, all provinces, except Alberta and New Brunswick, have legislation to protect your right to know what is in your credit file and which lenders have requested information about your credit-worthiness.

ALLOWABLE RATE OF INTEREST

The maximum allowable rate of interest for a lender to charge is regulated in Canada in the Criminal Code, s. 347. This placement of provisions against "usury" — the charging of unreasonably high interest rates — means that a lender who charges too much may be charged with a criminal offence, and the penalty can include a jail sentence. Such charges are rare, and as we will see in the section on alternative credit markets, they are not presently enforced.

In "Criminal Rate of Interest", s. 347(2) of the Criminal Code, two definitions are important:

"criminal rate" means an effective annual rate of interest calculated in accordance with generally accepted actuarial practices and principles that exceeds sixty per cent on the credit advanced under an agreement or arrangement;

"interest" means the aggregate of all charges and expenses, whether in the form of a fee, fine, penalty, commission or other similar charge or expense or in any other form, paid or payable for the advancing of credit under an agreement or arrangement, by or on behalf of the person to whom the credit is or is to be advanced, irrespective of the person to whom any such charges and expenses are or are to be paid or payable, but does not include any repayment of credit advanced or any insurance charge, official fee, overdraft charge, required deposit balance or, in the case of a mortgage transaction, any amount required to be paid on account of property taxes;

The definition of interest is very broad and includes all the different fees that might be charged. A recent court decision held that the fixed fees or service charges levied by a natural gas utility on people who paid their bills late were interest charges under the Act, and therefore could not exceed 60% on an annual basis even though the fees were quite small in dollar terms and reasonable with respect to the collection costs the utility faced in collecting late accounts.

The criminal rate of 60% is supposed to be an effective annual rate, though that is not explicitly defined in the Code. We are not lawyers, but it seems that EAR as defined in this textbook fits the Code definition. For mainstream lending, this is not an issue since rates never approach 60% in ordinary loan contracts. It is an issue in the alternative credit markets we discuss later in the chapter.

COMMON TYPES OF CREDIT AND LOANS

Open Account Credit and Credit Cards

The most common type of credit is the open account credit. It is a form of credit extended to the consumer in advance of any transactions. Typically, a bank, a lender, a retail outlet, or a utility company agrees to let the consumer buy up to a specified amount on open account. The consumer's obligation is to make payments in accordance with the specified terms. Many people often maintain a variety of open accounts. For example, nearly everybody uses one-month charge accounts to pay their phone bills, utility bills, retail purchases, etc. In addition, many people have one or more bank credit cards, such as Mastercard or Visa. In general, using open account credit is a good idea if you pay the full amount of the account balance before the due date. You do not have to pay any interest charges. In essence, you are getting a free loan from the bank or the issuer. However, open account credit cards generally charge a very high rate of interest on balances that are not paid in full on the due date. In fact, you will find that they are the most expensive kind of debt. You should avoid using credit card financing as much as possible.

What Kinds of Credit Cards Are Best?

There are hundreds of credit cards on the market and new ones are introduced almost daily. Very often the same bank or institution offers several types of credit cards. How do you decide which card is best for you?

The features of a credit card can be divided into four major categories:

1. The annual fee
2. The **grace period** or the **free loan period**
3. The interest rate charged on the unpaid balance and how it is calculated
4. The additional features, such as free life insurance, air mileage entitlement, cash machine linkage, amount of credit available, and so on

How important each of these factors is to you depends on how you use the credit card.

The annual fee is simply a fixed flat fee paid each year.[3] Other things being the same, you would choose the card that charges the lowest annual fee. However, other things are seldom the same: The cards that charge higher annual fees usually provide you with more and better features, such as a higher credit limit (e.g., in the case of gold cards), longer grace periods, and so on. Your choice then depends on whether you can take advantage of these additional features.

If you use credit cards for convenience only — that is, you always take advantage of grace periods and always pay off the previous balance by the due date — you will prefer a card with a low fee, a high interest rate, and a long grace period. You would not mind the high interest rate because interest charges are never incurred. In contrast, if you always carry a loan balance and seldom pay the previous month's balance in full, you would prefer a card with a high annual fee and a low interest rate — of course, the trade-off depends on your average outstanding balance.

Cost and Benefit Analysis

You can use the old common-sense cost and benefit analysis to choose the best credit card for yourself. Go through the list of features that the credit card provides. Delete all the features that are irrelevant to you. For example, if you are always able to pay the balance in full by the due date, the interest charges would

---

[3] Some cards offer a second card, usually for a spouse, without an additional fee; others charge a supplementary fee.

be irrelevant. If you do not drive, a car collision waiver insurance on rental cars would be irrelevant. On the other hand, the annual fee affects you because every user must pay the fee.

Now, you are left with a list of features that are relevant to you. The next step is to price each item according to your expected usage. For example, suppose you expect an average balance of $2,000 every month. That is, every month you spend $2,000 on the card, and pay it off at the end of the grace period. If the opportunity cost of your money is 10% per annum and the grace period is one month, you can price this benefit at $2,000 × 10% or $200 per year. As another example, suppose the credit card provides you with free car collision insurance on rental cars. Each year you expect to rent a car for two weeks on average and the car collision insurance premium that the car rental company will charge is $12 per day; then, the benefit of having free car collision insurance from your credit card can be priced at $12 × 14 or $168. Thus, every relevant feature of the credit card that affects you could be priced according to your expected usage. The net benefit is then equal to the total of all the benefits less the total of all costs. Similarly, you can perform the same cost and benefit analysis on each and every credit card in which you are interested. The best card for you is the one that gives you the maximum net benefit. See Problem 4 at the end of the chapter.

Other Kinds of Credit or Consumer Loans

Interest charges on credit card balances are very high, making them an expensive form of financing. There are other forms of personal credit available. These are often a much better deal because they offer a higher credit limit and at a lower interest rate.

Unsecured Personal Credit Line

You can apply for a personal line of credit at your bank. A **line of credit** is the maximum amount that you can owe at any point in time. Interest will be charged only on the amount that you have actually borrowed. Normally, these credit lines are set up so that interest charged on the amount borrowed is a function of the prime rate, such as the prime rate plus 3%. Repayment is set up on a monthly instalment basis, and the loan is normally repaid in two to five years. The advantage of a personal credit line is that it provides a higher credit limit at a lower rate of interest than credit card financing. Thus, if you have a credit card balance that you cannot pay off in one or two months' time, it is usually cheaper for you to arrange a personal credit line to pay off the credit card balance.

Home Equity Credit Line

If you own a home, the equity on your home can be used as collateral to secure a line of credit. This is called a **home equity credit line**. There are two major advantages of using a home equity line of credit. First, the lender will charge a much lower rate of interest than that charged on other personal loans. If you own your home free and clear of debt and mortgages, you can get a home equity line of credit at a rate of interest that is very close to the current rate of interest on first mortgages. Second, you can borrow a lot more by taking out a home equity credit line than you can draw on from an unsecured credit line. In general, the amount you can borrow is a fraction (which could go as high as 90%) of your equity in your home.

The majority of banks and financial institutions set their maximum credit lines at 75% of the market value of the home. Example 12.3 illustrates the typical situation.

Example 12.3: A couple bought a home for $100,000 15 years ago. The home is now worth $200,000. They still have not paid off the mortgage on the house. Let us say the amount of the mortgage still outstanding is $50,000. This means that the couple has built up $200,000 – $50,000 = $150,000 of equity in their home. Suppose now they want to use the home equity as collateral to secure a home equity line of credit. What is the maximum amount of home equity loan that they can get from a bank?

Assuming that the bank will lend up to 75% of the market value of the home, they can expect to borrow (75% × $200,000) less the $50,000 of the first mortgage, or a maximum of $100,000. This does not mean that they can automatically borrow up to this maximum amount. The bank will assess them on their ability to service the debt, using the debt-service ratios or the scoring systems that we have discussed before.

Overdraft Protection

An overdraft protection is a kind of unsecured line of credit. Normally you apply for overdraft protection on your chequing account. You fill out an application form, which will be evaluated by the bank according to some credit scoring system. If your application is approved, you can overdraw your chequing account up to a predetermined point. Funds advanced from an overdraft protection line carry a very high rate of interest, usually not much lower than that of a credit card advance. Therefore, an overdraft should be used only as an emergency source of funds. Any funds advanced should be repaid as quickly as possible. Some people use it for the convenience of not having to monitor the chequing account balance every time they write a cheque.

Secured Personal Line of Credit

Credit card loans, overdraft protection advances and credit lines are expensive sources of consumer credit. This is so because these loans are risky from the lenders' viewpoint; and the lenders charge a relatively high rate of interest to compensate for the risk they are taking. If the borrower owns assets and is willing to use them to secure the loan, this will reduce the lender's risk and the lender will charge a lower rate of interest on the loan. This is the concept of a secured loan or a collateral loan. The asset used to secure the loan is called **collateral**. In the event of the borrower defaulting, the lender has the right to sell the collateral to get back his or her money.

Not every personal asset is suitable for collateral, however. Lenders want reasonably high-valued assets that they can seize and sell easily. They are not interested in your personal belongings (clothing, kitchen utensils, etc.), your stamp collection, or your bicycle. They want security against cars and investment assets (shares, bonds) if they can get it. A company selling furniture is relatively comfortable lending you the money to buy it, since it can resell the furniture if it has to repossess it. Banks will lend you money to buy furniture only if they think the probability of default is very low, since for them seizing the furniture is often more trouble than it is worth.

ALTERNATIVE CREDIT MARKETS

There are also some high cost sources of borrowing that are not part of the mainstream financial system.

Payday Loans

A payday lender offers small loans, usually from $100–$500 for short periods, one day to at most 31 days. The borrower has to have a bank account, identification, and good evidence of steady employment with the amount of net pay shown (usually the pay stub from the previous period's pay). The lender will advance up to a certain percentage of the next net pay, with the repayment date being the date of the paycheque or direct deposit. The borrower writes a post-dated cheque to the lender for the amount of the principal plus interest. The percentage allowed varies among the lenders; common values are 30–50% of the net pay. Most loans are for 7–14 days, and the average in the industry is 12 days. Payday lenders operate small storefront offices in high traffic areas with very long opening hours, seven days a week.

The payday loan customer usually cannot access other forms of small, short-term credit — credit card loans and bank account overdrafts. Often, the customer has such a bad credit rating that they are not available. Some customers are intimidated by banks, dislike the privacy invasion of a credit check, or welcome the form of control enforced by a loan that must be paid back in full by the next payday. By contrast, credit cards require only a small fraction of the outstanding balance to be repaid, which allows a borrower to run up a large debt quite quickly.

The customer pays a high price for the service, because even a small loan still requires time to process. Fees are charged in several different ways. The most common form is a straight percentage of the principal, regardless of the time to maturity. In Canada, this rate ranges from 15–35% of the principal, though 20–25% is most often seen. This leads to astonishingly high EARs. For example, a loan at 25% of the principal for 12 days yields an EAR of 88,550%, and that is not a misprint.

The maximum permissible rate of interest in Canada under s. 347 of the Criminal Code is 60% per annum. In 2007, the federal government amended s. 347 to allow payday lenders to charge higher rates, provided a province enacted legislation to regulate payday lending. The revision to s. 347 defined payday loans as no more than $1,500 and no longer than 31 days, secured only by a promise to repay based on income in the next period. Most provinces passed legislation to regulate payday lending. Quebec had already set a 36% p.a. interest cap, which closed down all payday lenders. Elsewhere the rate cap is always stated as a percentage of the principal amount, not as an annual interest rate. In Manitoba, it is 17% on the first $500, 15% on the next $500, and 6% on the last $500. Ontario imposed a limit of 21%; British Columbia, Alberta, and Saskatchewan, 23%; PEI and New Brunswick, 24%; and Nova Scotia, 25%. Nunavut and Newfoundland and Labrador have not passed legislation. Only Manitoba investigated the appropriate rates through independent expert research, and consequently the other provinces set rates that are too high by using research provided by the payday lenders themselves. Most of the payday lenders raised their rates when the provinces set the caps. In the United States, thirteen states have banned payday lending. Most of the other states have rate caps of 15%, and the major U.S. payday lending companies are thriving under those lower fees.

Another service in the alternative financial sector is cheque cashing with immediate payout. Banks will not allow access to money from most cheques for five days. In August 2012, new federal regulations required all banks to reduce the hold period on cheques from five to four business days. A bank must allow a depositor to cash the first $100 of a cheque written on a Canadian bank immediately. These two rules may also reduce the number of Canadians depending on payday lenders and cheque cashers.

Pawnbrokers

The ancient symbol of the three golden balls of the pawnbroker has disappeared from our streets, but pawnbrokers are still with us. A pawnbroker lends money on the security of a valuable asset placed in "pawn", which means the pawnbroker keeps it until the borrower repays the principal and interest, plus any storage charges. Pawnbrokers are regulated only by municipalities in most provinces, which has led to an uneven landscape of rules.

Detailed information about pawnbroking practices is hard to find. The rate of interest is generally much lower than it is for payday loans, perhaps because the transaction is so simple. The pawnbroker takes the article, offers the amount he is willing to lend, and records identifying information about the borrower.[4] The pawnbroker gives the borrower a pawn ticket that identifies the item(s) pawned. The borrower usually has one year to redeem the pawn, after which time the pawnbroker may sell the item to regain the money. Pawnbrokers are skilled at valuing the objects they take in pawn and they never offer a very high percentage of the value as a loan, so they face almost no default risk. The pawnbroker then sells all unredeemed pawned items in a normal retail fashion, and keeps all the proceeds. Modern pawnbrokers also buy for resale items like the ones they take in pawn, and so they have become popular places to shop for jewellery, high-value electronics, cameras, watches, and musical instruments.

The rate of interest often quoted is 60%, but the compounding frequency varies. The pawnbroker may also charge a fixed fee for each pawn ticket and a fee for storage of the pawned item, though these amounts are usually quite small. Ontario does regulate pawnbrokers and the maximum rates:

> In addition to the profit on the sum lent, being interest thereon at not more than the lawful rate, a pawnbroker is entitled to make the following charges:
> 1. For a pawnticket, not more than 20 cents.
> 2. For storage of a pledge, not more than 10 cents per month per cubic foot or part thereof of storage space taken up by the pledge.
> 3. For a copy of a pawnticket and printed form of affidavit, not more than 20 cents. (*Pawnbrokers Act*, R.S.O. 1990, c. P.6, s. 28)

The interesting part of this schedule of charges is the interest rate, which is effectively the rate under s. 347 of the Criminal Code, or 60% per annum. We are not aware of any survey of how pawnbrokers implement this charge, but we have seen it done as 5% per month, without compounding. If a borrower redeems a pawn exactly one year after borrowing the money, he would then pay 60% exactly. However, if he redeemed it in a shorter time, he would still pay 5% for each month, which is an effective annual rate higher than 60%. In any case, the cost of borrowing from a pawnbroker is much lower than from a payday lender, provided the borrower redeems the item pawned.

---

[4] This is the part that is regulated most carefully because pawnbrokers are obvious outlets for stolen goods, and they must keep lists that the police can use to trace the identity of persons who may be thieves.

INVESTMENT LOANS — BORROWING MONEY TO INVEST

There are two kinds of assets that we can buy with borrowed money: assets for consumption purposes and assets for investment purposes. Up to this point, we have been talking about consumer credit financing, which refers to borrowing money to acquire assets for consumption purposes. In general, consumption assets depreciate in value over time.

You can also borrow money to acquire investment assets. These are assets that in general increase in value over time, and they usually generate cash flow in the future. Examples of investment assets are stocks, bonds, term deposits, mutual funds, real estate, options, and futures. There are significant differences between consumer debt and investment debt. You must understand the distinction between them before you can manage your personal debt successfully.

First, the use of consumer loans will normally decrease your net worth over time, whereas the use of investment debt will normally increase your net worth. Consumer goods — cars, appliances, groceries, clothes, furniture — depreciate in value over time while the debt obligation remains unchanged. Since net worth is the difference between assets and liabilities it is obvious that the use of consumer loans to acquire consumption goods will decrease your net worth. In contrast, investments — stocks, real estate, mutual funds — generally appreciate in value over time, while the face value of the debt obligation remains constant; therefore, you can expect your net worth to increase over time. Of course, **financial leverage** — that is to say, using borrowed money to acquire investments — is risky. We will discuss the risk of financial leverage when we talk about investments. But, to draw conclusions from the above brief analysis, it is clear that you should pay cash for consumption and use debt to acquire investments if you are going to borrow at all.

There is a second reason for doing this. If you borrow money to invest, the interest expense is tax deductible — you will pay less income tax, whereas if you borrow money to consume (or purchase consumer goods), the interest expenses are not tax deductible. Suppose you can borrow at a 10% rate of interest and your marginal tax bracket is 50%. If you use the borrowed money to buy consumer goods, the interest expense is not tax deductible and the cost of borrowing is 10%. If you use the borrowed money to acquire investments such as stocks or mutual funds, the interest expense is tax deductible and the cost of borrowing is 5%. In addition, lenders usually charge a higher interest rate on consumer loans than on investment loans.[5]

---

[5] The risk pawnbrokers take is quite low, and since the investment asset is supposed to generate income, the loan is self-liquidating — it produces the cash flow to pay the lender.

It is advisable for you to adopt the following good habits of debt management:

1. Whenever is possible, pay cash for consumption and borrow money for investments.

2. If you have investment assets and consumer debt, convert the consumer debt into investment debt. (For example, you can sell your investment, pay off the consumer debt, then borrow again to acquire the investment.)

Why Borrow Money to Invest?

There are three main reasons for people to borrow money to invest:

1. Although there is financial risk involved, if it is done prudently and properly, borrowing money to invest in good investments will result in the growth of the family's net worth.

2. Borrowing is a way to magnify the after-tax investment return in order to reach specific financial goals.

3. If it is done correctly, borrowing is a good way for high-income earners to create their own tax shelters, thereby reducing or deferring taxes.

We have already discussed the first reason for borrowing money to invest. To reiterate the main point, if the investment increases in value faster than the debt obligation, the family's net worth will increase in the long run. For example, if you borrow money at a 10% interest rate and the money is invested to earn an expected rate of return of 15%, your net worth will increase over time. Of course, there is financial risk involved because the rate of return is uncertain. Although over the long term, you expect to earn 15% on your investment, the rate of return in some years will be low. If the rate of return is lower than the rate of interest of 10%, there is insufficient cash from the investment for you to pay the interest. Therefore, you may need other sources of income to make interest payments during the lean years when return on your investment is low.

Borrowing to Reach Specific Financial Goals

Borrowing could be a powerful way to magnify the rate of return on investment so that you can reach specific financial goals. In Chapter 3, on goal setting, we saw that to reach certain specific financial goals may require the individual to earn a very high rate of return. For example, if your goal is to have $1 million in 20 years' time and you want to achieve this goal by investing your initial wealth of $10,000, then you must earn a rate of return of 25.89%. (By now, you should be able to calculate this. If you can't, you should review Chapter 2.) Suppose you cannot find any investment that has such a high rate of return and the closest investment you can find is a mutual fund that has a very good track record but the expected rate of return is only 20%. However, this is not good enough because you need a return of 26% to reach your financial goal.

If you are willing to take more risk, there is a way for you to reach your goal, and that is by borrowing money. Suppose you can borrow money from a bank at the rate of interest of 10%. (Usually, it is quite easy to arrange such a line of credit if the mutual funds acquired are used as collateral to secure the credit.) You borrow just enough money to reach your required rate of return, 26%. How much do you have to borrow?

Suppose for each dollar of your own money (your equity) you will borrow $x from the bank at 10% interest. The ratio $x/$1 or x is called the **debt-to-equity ratio**. That is, if you borrow $0.40 for every $1 you have already, your debt-to-equity ratio is .4, or 40%. This is exactly the same concept as a debt-to-equity ratio in corporate finance. There is a debt-to-equity ratio at which you can reach your financial goal, which requires you to earn 26%. How do you calculate this debt-to-equity ratio, x?

For each dollar of your money, you borrow x dollars and you invest the $(1 + x)$ dollars into the mutual fund, which is expected to earn a 20% return. At the end of the year, the expected value of your investment is $(1 + x)(.20)$, from which you must pay interest equal to $(x)(.10)$. Your rate of return on equity is therefore $[(1 + x)(.20) - x(.10)] \div 1$ and you want this return to be 26%. Therefore, you can set up the equation:

$$\left[\frac{(1 + x)(.20) - x(.10)}{1}\right] = .26$$

Solving the equation, $x = .6$. This means that at the debt-to-equity ratio of .6 — borrow 60 cents for each dollar of your equity — the expected rate of return on your investment is 26% and you can reach your financial goal.

We can generalize the above analysis.

Let r = the required rate of return in order to reach the individual's financial goal;

k = the expected rate of return on the investment opportunity, e.g., mutual fund;

i = the rate of interest charged on borrowed funds;

x = the debt-to-equity ratio required to magnify the rate of return on investment to reach the required rate of return, r.

Generalizing our analysis, we have the equation:

$$(1 + x)k - xi = r \tag{1}$$
$$(1 + x)(.20) - x(.10) = .26$$
$$x = .6$$

To get a feel of how borrowing can magnify a given rate of return on investment to any high required rate of return, you can put some reasonable numbers into equation (1) and examine the results. We want to emphasize that financial risk increases with the amount of borrowing (see Chapter 16). Indeed, many personal and corporate bankruptcies are the direct result of overindebtedness. Nevertheless, it should be clear that borrowing is a powerful tool to help people to reach certain specific financial goals. See Example 12.4 for an illustration.

Borrowing Money to Create Tax Shelters

Borrowing money to invest can be a very useful strategy for some people, especially high-income earners, in setting up their own tax shelters. Recall that a good tax shelter must first of all be a good investment. Regardless of how much tax you can save or defer, if the money is invested in bad investments, you will end up losing money. Many people make the mistake of looking only at the tax aspect of tax shelters — how much money that would otherwise be taxed away can be saved or deferred — and they forget about the investment aspects of tax shelters. Tax considerations aside, there remains the question of whether or not a particular tax shelter is a good investment, and whether or not it is too risky.[6]

The idea of using borrowed money to create your own tax shelter is actually very simple. It is based on two facts:

1. Interest expense on money borrowed for investment purposes is tax deductible: You can deduct the interest against your other sources of income and so save taxes.

2. Capital gains from investments are taxed at a lower rate than other income; and, more important, capital gains are not taxed until you sell the investment so that taxes can be deferred by holding on to the investment.

If you borrow money and put it into investments that have a good potential of growth, you save current taxes because the interest expense is tax deductible, and the capital gains on the investments are not taxed until you sell. Ideally, you will be in a lower tax bracket when you sell the investment.

We show how to borrow to reach a financial goal with an example.

Example 12.4: Dr. Anderson is a surgeon who has a well-established practice in downtown Toronto. Mrs. Anderson is a full-time homemaker and they have a six-year-old child,

---

[6] The CRA challenges some complicated tax shelters, adding to their risk. Even if you successfully defend your position, the cost in legal fees and your time may exceed the tax savings.

Janet. They have just paid off the mortgage on their house and are debt-free. Here is a summary of the Andersons' financial situation from the most recent information that they provide:

Net professional income	$250,000
Taxes paid last year	$100,000
Consumption	$ 90,000
Savings (including RRSP contribution)	$ 60,000

Dr. Anderson wants to invest his money to achieve two objectives: long-term growth of net worth and tax savings. Currently, he puts his savings in several growth mutual funds. The funds pay very little in the way of dividends, but over the long term they are expected to generate an average rate of return of 16% in the form of capital gains.

Let us analyze Dr. Anderson's current investment program. To make things simple, assume that he will save and invest $40,000 per year into a basket of several mutual funds. The mutual funds do not pay dividends but their expected rate of growth is 16%. The value of his portfolio in 10 years' time is equal to $40,000 × $[(1.16^{10} - 1) \div .16]$ = $852,859.

The values of his portfolio in 15, 20, and 25 years are $2.06 million, $4.62 million, and $9.97 million, respectively. As long as he does not sell the investments, there are no taxes payable. Although the above values seem attractive or even enviable for many people, Dr. Anderson is not happy with the amount of taxes that he pays every year, and he wonders if he can do better. "It would be nice if I could cut taxes by 40%, or $40,000," he complains. Let us assume that his goal is to cut taxes by $40,000. If he can create an investment loss of $80,000 by borrowing money, then at his marginal tax rate of 50%, the loss would save him $40,000 in taxes. How can he create an investment loss of $80,000? We will give you two minutes to suggest an answer.

Yes, your answer is right! Dr. Anderson should go to the bank and get an investment loan. Using the mutual funds that he will be buying as collateral, and with the healthy cash flow from his professional practice, it would not be difficult for him to get an investment loan to buy the mutual funds. Some banks are more conservative and may require Dr. Anderson to provide additional collateral, such as his home.

Suppose that he can get an investment loan at the rate of interest of 10%. If his goal is to generate an investment loss of $80,000, he must borrow $80,000 ÷ .10 or $800,000 so that the interest expense is $80,000. Since the mutual funds do not pay dividends, that will give him a loss of $80,000, as follows:

Investment income	$ 0
Interest expense ($800,000 × .10)	80,000
Investment loss	($80,000)

If he borrows $800,000 now and invests the money in the basket of mutual funds that is expected to generate a 16% return, the value of his portfolio in 10 years will be:

$$[(\$800,000 \times 1.16^{10}) - \$800,000] \text{ or } \$2.73 \text{ million}$$

This is substantially higher than the value of his portfolio if he does not borrow ($852,859). Of course, when he sells the investment he has to pay capital gains taxes. Still, the difference is significant. Here is a summary of the values of his portfolio in 10 years, after liquidation, payment of tax, and repayment of the loan (round to the nearest $10,000):

Program I:

FVA	$40,000 (16%, 10 yr)	=	$ 850,000
ACB	10 × $40,000	=	400,000
Capital gain		=	$ 450,000
Tax on 50% of gain at 50%	= .25 × $450,000	=	$ 110,000
Net after tax	= $850,000 – $110,000	=	$ 740,000

Program II (tax shelter):

FV	$800,000 (16%, 10 yr)	=	$3,530,000
ACB		=	800,000
Capital gain		=	$2,730,000
Tax on 50% of gain at 50%	= .25 × $2,730,000	=	$ 680,000
Net	= $3,530,000 – $680,000	=	$2,050,000
	– $800,000 (repay loan principal)		

Value of Portfolio

Number of Years After Start	Program I (millions)	Program II (tax shelter) (millions)
10	$ 0.74	$ 2.05
15	1.70	4.96
20	3.67	11.08
25	7.73	23.92
30	16.21	50.91

Suppose you don't do as well as we showed in the example. As you can see from Appendix D, a rate of return of 16% is much higher than the long-run average return on equity. Suppose that you earned only 10% in the mutual funds, which equals the cost of borrowing. Using the same mechanics, Program I is worth $1.92 million after tax at 20 years. Program II is worth $3.43 million after tax at 20 years. If you were going to invest anyway and you can cover the interest expenses in the interim, borrowing to invest pays off even if you only realize the same rate of return as you pay in interest because you get the tax deduction now and pay tax on the income later.

Caution!   Borrowing money to invest is risky and is not for everyone. We used the above example only for the purpose of describing the use of financial leverage to create a tax shelter. Its suitability depends on each family's financial situation (e.g., cash flow, net worth) and risk preference. Indeed, in the example, we cannot say Program II (the tax shelter) is better than Program I. Certainly, the expected portfolio values under Program II are much higher than those under Program I, but the risk is also higher. The return on the mutual fund is not certain and interest rates may increase in the future (which makes servicing the debt more difficult). If you are considering the use of borrowed money to invest, we advise you to check your cash-flow situation before and after the borrowing. To illustrate, let us look at Dr. Anderson again. The family's cash flow before and after setting up the tax shelter is as follows:

	Before	*After*
	(Setting up Tax Shelter)	
Net professional income	$250,000	$250,000
Taxes	$100,000	$ 60,000
Consumption	$ 90,000	$ 90,000
Annual contribution to mutual funds	$ 40,000	0
Interest expense	0	$ 80,000
Other savings (RRSP, etc.)	$ 20,000	$ 20,000

As you can see, the Andersons do not have to sacrifice any consumption to support the tax shelter investment. They are simply channelling tax savings to support an investment program that will increase their net worth faster.

SUMMARY

In this chapter we have discussed personal debt management. There are two kinds of personal debt: consumer debt, or credit, and investment debt. They are different concepts and call for different methods of management. Normally, you are advised to use cash to buy consumption goods and to borrow money to invest if you borrow at all. There are three main reasons for this: First, interest charges on consumer loans are much higher than those on investment loans; second, interest expenses on consumer loans are not tax deductible whereas interest expenses on investment loans are tax deductible; third, borrowing money to acquire consumption goods will normally decrease net worth while borrowing money to invest will normally increase net worth.

It is important that one does not overextend oneself. We recommend that you evaluate your debt capacity, liquidity, and solvency in order to arrive at a comfort zone of debt. How much you should borrow to a large extent depends on how much the banks and other financial institutions will lend to you. Understanding the scoring systems and the debt service ratios that the lenders use is therefore very helpful.

There are many sources and types of consumer loans and credit, including credit card loans, unsecured personal credit line, overdraft protection, secured personal credit line, and home equity credit line. In order for you to get a loan easily, it is important that you maintain a good credit history. We recommend a cost and benefit analysis if you want to evaluate the numerous credit cards that are available.

There are three main reasons why people want to borrow money to invest: (i) borrowing to invest normally leads to an increase in net worth; (ii) borrowing to invest is a powerful tool for people to use in reaching certain specific goals; and (iii) borrowing to invest is a useful method for creating tax shelters for some people.

MULTIPLE-CHOICE REVIEW QUESTIONS

1. The amount of loan that a bank is willing to lend an individual depends on which of the following reasons?

    (a) The person's employment income
    (b) The value of collateral available
    (c) The amount of other debt outstanding
    (d) (a) and (b)
    (e) (a), (b), and (c)

2. On which of the following loans will the bank charge the highest rate of interest?

    (a) Home equity credit line
    (b) Investment loan
    (c) Home mortgage
    (d) Unsecured credit line
    (e) Uncertain

3. Which of the following statements concerning investment loans is true?
   (a) The interest expense on the loan is not tax deductible.
   (b) The rate of interest charged on an investment loan is lower than that of a consumer loan.
   (c) Investment loan does not depend on the borrower's income.
   (d) (b) and (c).
   (e) None of the above.

4. Mr. Harris has $2,000. He wants to borrow another $1,000 from the bank at 5% interest so that he can invest $3,000 in a mutual fund that has an expected rate of return of 11%. What is the expected rate of return on investment?
   (a) 11%
   (b) 6%
   (c) 14%
   (d) 8%
   (e) None of the above

5. Eddie and Cecelia have an annual gross income of $55,000. Their monthly mortgage payment is $1,150. If their GDS ratio is 0.28, what is the annual property tax on their condominium?
   (a) $1,450
   (b) $1,500
   (c) $1,600
   (d) $1,800
   (e) None of the above

DISCUSSION QUESTIONS

1. Explain or describe the following key words and terms:

   collateral or secured credit line / consumer credit and debt / credit bureau / credit file / credit scoring system / debt capacity / debt service ratios: gross debt service ratio — total debt service ratio / free loan or grace period / home equity credit line / investment loan: financial risk — rate of return required to reach a financial goal — debt-to-equity ratio — financial leverage — tax shelter / line of credit / liquidity / matching assets and debts — matching principle in finance / pawnbroker loan / payday loan / solvency / unsecured credit line

2. **Personal Project 1**
   Go to several banks or financial institutions and get information about the credit cards that they offer. Take any two credit cards you like, e.g., Visa and MasterCard, or Visa and Visa Gold.

(a) Put down all the features that each card offers, including grace period, interest rate, etc.

(b) Based on your expected usage, delete all the features that are irrelevant.

(c) Price all the remaining items that are relevant to you.

(d) Use the cost and benefit analysis to examine which card is better for you.

3. **Personal Project 2**
Find the addresses and phone numbers of all the local credit bureaus in your city. (The Yellow Pages in the phone book is a good place to start.) Request a copy of your own credit file. Record what you had to go through (e.g., what forms have you filled out?) before the credit bureau gives you a copy of your credit file. Examine your credit file. Are there any missing data or incorrect pieces of information? What is your right, as provided by the provincial legislation, if there are incorrect or missing data in your file?

PROBLEMS

1. Refer to Dr. Anderson and his family in Example 12.4 in the chapter.

(a) Using the usual benchmark for GDS ratio and TDS ratio, what is the maximum amount of cash flow that the Andersons can apply to service debt?

(b) If the rate of interest is (i) 8%; (ii) 10%; (iii) 12%, and if he can get a loan that requires him to pay interest only, what is the maximum amount of the loan that he can get?

(c) How would your answer to (b) change if the bank requires Dr. Anderson to amortize the loan in 10 years?

2. (a) *Goal Setting*
Mr. Johnston wants to have $1 million when he retires in 25 years. He plans to achieve this goal by saving and investing $3,000 per year at the end of each and every year for 25 years. What is the required rate of return that he must earn in order to reach his goal?

(b) *Investment Loan*
He wants to invest his annual savings of $3,000 in a mutual fund. The expected rate of return on the fund is 14%. He can borrow from the bank at an interest rate of 8%, provided that he uses the mutual fund as collateral. What is the debt-to-equity ratio that Mr. Johnston must maintain in order to reach his goal in (a)?

3. Friendly Freddie always has his customers' best interests at heart. They want to know exactly what they have to pay without any tricky financial

calculations. Friendly Freddie charges 24% p.a. on consumer loans. To make it easy for his customers, he divides the interest and principal into 12 equal monthly amounts. Thus, on a $1,000 loan you pay $103.33 monthly [(.24 ÷ 12) × 1000)] + (1000 ÷ 12)], and just as easy as anything you've paid off the whole loan.

(a) What would your loan payment be if it were calculated in the usual way for consumer loans at 24%, compounded monthly?
(b) What is the effective annual rate of Freddie's loan?

4. Wayne and Joan are comparing two credit cards, the basic Master Card versus the Visa Gold card. The relevant features of the two cards are as follows:

	VISA Gold	Basic Master Card
Grace period	20 days	25 days
Rebate on every purchase (paid at year-end)	0.5%	none
Card fee at beginning of year	$120	$15
Monthly interest rate on overdue balance	1.8%	1.5%
Collision damage waiver on rental cars	yes	no

Their average month-end balance on the credit card is $3,000 which they will pay off on the last day of the grace period. Every year they will take a seven-day holiday, rent a car, and drive around various parts of the country. The car rental agencies normally charge $14 per day to insure them against collision damages. The current interest rate they can earn on a bank account is 3%.
Which credit card should they choose?

5. The due date for the balance of $2,000 on your credit card is tomorrow and you have only enough money to survive the next six months without paying this debt. In six months you will have enough money to pay off the debt. The credit card company charges 18% p.a., compounded monthly. Kneecap Finance offers a better rate, 16%, compounded weekly (assumes 52 weeks in a year).

(a) Should you borrow $2,000 from Kneecap to pay the credit card bill? Assume there are 26 weeks in six months.
(b) Suppose you were earning enough money each week during the next six months that you could repay a loan in the usual form of blended payments (principal and interest). How much would you pay each week if you borrowed $2,000 for six months from Kneecap?
(c) In reality, there is a bit of a problem comparing the two alternatives by assuming there are 26 weeks in six months. You can do it mechanically, but do credit card companies all charge interest on part months?

6. Marge Ciccone has applied to you, the assistant manager at her trust company, for a three-year loan to buy a car. She wants $7,000 at the current rate
of 1% per month. She and her husband, Lou, have four children, aged 6–13,
with the youngest about to start grade 1 in a few days. Lou earns $32,000 a
year as an accountant for a factory. He is in the fourth year of the certified
management accountants' (CMA) program, and expects to finish in less than
two years.

    Marge wants the car so that she can start working outside the home
again, after being out of the labour force for almost 10 years. She can work
as a commission salesperson for a small food processing company that is just
starting to expand its lines. Up to now, it had concentrated on restaurants and
caterers; now it wants to sell to small speciality food retailers in the Montreal
area. Marge has worked in the food business as both a food store clerk and a
sausage stuffer, and she feels she understands the business well enough to sell
successfully. She speaks French, Italian, and English fluently.

    She talked to the two salesmen who currently handle the restaurant
clientele, and discovered they make "about $35–40,000" before automobile
expenses, which they must pay themselves. She would sell to the proposed
new target market, so she wouldn't be in competition with them. They warned
her that it would take at least a few months to make any reasonable level of
sales, and several years to build up a good clientele with repeat business. She
cannot work a full day for at least two or three years because she still wants
to be home when the children aren't in school. She figures that gives her
about five hours on the road, compared with their eight hours, but she can do
some of the paperwork and telephoning from home.

    Marge and Lou own their own house in a pleasant suburb of Montreal.
The mortgage payments of $748 per month run for four years to renewal, and
the mortgage has 10 years after that. They pay property tax of about $1,200
p.a. and $180 per month on another car loan that has two years to run. Lou's
take-home pay is $25,000. They put $1,000 into an RRSP for Lou in 1994
(in several instalments), the first such deposit they have made. They keep
$1,000 in a savings account for contingencies, and they have saved up another
$3,500, which Marge plans to use for the rest of the $10,500 purchase price
of the car.

    (a) What advice would you give her?
    (b) Will you grant the loan?

7. Annette earns a gross income of $45,000 p.a. She owns a condominium
in North Vancouver, valued at $218,000. She still has a mortgage on it, with
11 years of monthly payments of $650. The annual property taxes are $3,000
and the condominium fee is $250 per month. She has no other debts, and

$10,000 invested in a mutual fund. Recently, she has been longing to buy a car that costs $28,000. The current interest rate is 8.5% for a four-year term.

(a) If she has to meet the standard bank lending tests, can she finance the entire purchase price of the car?

(b) How much is the minimum down payment she should make?

8. Marlene Walter and Bruno Dietrich are getting married, but they don't have enough money to buy furniture for their modest flat in Toronto. Bad Girl Furniture offers this choice:

• Pay $2,700 cash now for $3,000 retail value of furniture. No credit cards allowed.

or

• Pay no money down except for a $25 fee for a credit check and no payments for six months. Then pay $3,000 over two-and-a-half years in monthly instalments of $121.99.

Since Marlene and Bruno have no extra cash, they have to borrow the $2,700 for plan A. Smiling Herb Karajan will lend it to them at an annual rate (APR) of 14%, compounded and payable monthly over three years.

Neither loan may be repaid or transferred before maturity without a prohibitive penalty. Which deal should they take?

9. Paycheque Co. Ltd. offers payday loans for a flat fee of 10% of the principal, for up to 20 days. Yumi Co. Ltd. offers payday loans for a fee of $9.00 per loan, plus 8% of the principal, plus 58% effective annual rate of interest.

If you want to borrow $500 for 16 days from one of the two companies, which one would you choose? Show your calculations on the following:

(a) Calculate the cost in dollars that each company will charge.

(b) Calculate the EAR that each company will charge.

CHAPTER 13

Buying a Home and Mortgage Financing

▶ Mr. Wong has bought a house and taken on a 30-year mortgage of $100,000 at 7%. Learn how to calculate his monthly payments in Example 13.2.

▶ Jack and Jill want to live in a condominium costing $150,000 for the next three years. Should they rent or buy? See Example 13.9.

▶ A real estate agent tells Mr. and Mrs. Perren that the house they have been living in for 40 years is now worth over $2 million. How can they find out the value of their house without actually putting it for sale?

LEARNING OBJECTIVES

> ➢ *To introduce the most common form of mortgage financing and go through the calculation of the major costs.*
> ➢ *To discuss how large a house a person can afford.*
> ➢ *To evaluate home ownership as an investment.*
> ➢ *To introduce methods for valuing a house.*
> ➢ *To introduce a framework for making the rent versus buy decision.*

For most people, expenditures on housing — whether as a homeowner or as a tenant — take the largest bite of the family's monthly income. Decisions concerning housing represent some of the biggest financial decisions that people have to make in their financial affairs. For example, the family must decide whether to own or to rent, where to live, the size and the type of the dwelling to choose, how to finance a home purchase, and so on. Many people also want to know whether buying a house is a good investment.

Since very few people are fortunate enough to be able to come up with one lump sum of cash to buy a home, most people must deal with a mortgage. Financing a home and mortgages have become a complex and confusing task for many people since so many types of financing and mortgages have been developed in recent years. It is important for a homeowner or potential home buyer to have the basic knowledge of how a standard mortgage works.

MORTGAGE FINANCING

For most people, buying a home is such a big financial commitment that they must borrow money to finance the purchase. **Mortgage financing** is the traditional way of borrowing money to purchase a home; however, many people do not understand the basic terminology of a mortgage contract. Most do not know how the monthly mortgage payments are calculated and simply assume the numbers given by the lenders are correct. Although most lenders — the banks, trust companies, insurance companies, credit unions, and most private lenders — are trustworthy and will not cheat the borrowers on the mortgage payments, the individual is still better off and can make much better decisions if he or she has more knowledge about mortgage financing and the calculation of the monthly mortgage payments. This is especially true because there are so many different types of mortgages to choose from.

In this section, we will first introduce some basic concepts and terminology. The mathematics of mortgages will be described so that at the end of this section you will have enough knowledge to make the right decision about mortgage financing. You will know the relationship between the key variables: the monthly payment, the rate of interest, the term, the amortization period, and so on.

Home Mortgages

To many people, a **home mortgage** is a real estate loan with equal monthly payments. They know that the monthly payments may increase or decrease according to changes in interest rates but they do not know precisely how the monthly payments are calculated. Most people also know that they must keep paying the lender each month for 15 to 30 years, after which they will own the house "free and clear". In the interim, if they do not keep up with the monthly payments, they may lose their homes. The above description is essentially correct. However, this is not what a mortgage actually is. We will now describe more precisely how a mortgage works.

Mortgage

A **mortgage** is defined as the transfer of an interest in property to a creditor as security for payment of a debt with a **right of redemption** by the borrower upon repayment of the debt. In other words, if you get a mortgage from a bank to purchase a home, the title of ownership of the home is actually conveyed to the bank and what you have is a right to reclaim clear title to the home upon full repayment of the debt. This right to reclaim title from the lender is called the **equity of redemption**. Thus, a mortgage is not in fact a loan *per se*, but rather, it is the security for a loan (see Example 13.1). Nevertheless, we will use the term "mortgage" in its more widely acceptable form of use for the rest of this chapter.

> *Example 13.1:* John and Janet Coulson have bought a house from Paul Evans for $200,000. The Coulsons paid Mr. Evans $80,000 cash and assumed his first mortgage of $120,000. The mortgagee, the Bank of Nova Scotia, had approved the latter transaction — that is to say, the bank had allowed the Coulsons to assume the mortgage.
>
> Mr. and Mrs. Coulson, like many home buyers, believed that they had acquired a new home, including the title to the home. In fact, the bank has title and what had transferred between the Coulsons and Mr. Evans was the possession and use of the home and the equity of redemption.

The two parties to a mortgage transaction are called the mortgager and the mortgagee. The **mortgager** is the person who gives the security to obtain the loan — in other words, the mortgager is the homeowner. The mortgager receives funds and maintains possession (but not the legal title) of the property. The **mortgagee** is the lender who receives the title to the property until the debt is fully repaid.

There can be only one legal mortgage with respect to any particular piece of property because title can be conveyed only once. The mortgage where the conveyance of title is involved is commonly called the **first mortgage**.

Second Mortgage

If there can be only one legal mortgage for a particular property (since title of a property can be conveyed only once), then what security do second and third mortgages have? From the foregoing discussion it should be clear that when one mortgages one's home, a right known as the equity of redemption — the right to reclaim the title to the home upon full repayment of the loan — is retained by the mortgager. Clearly then, this right is an asset that has value of itself and may be used as security for another loan. Therefore, the act of making a second mortgage consists of using the equity of redemption as security or collateral for a loan. In fact, the **second mortgage** conveys the right to a further equity of redemption which can again be mortgaged — and if this further equity of redemption is mortgaged, the resulting mortgage is called a **third mortgage**. There can be successive mortgages of equities of redemption following the first mortgage and the borrower retains at all times an equity of redemption in the *last* mortgage given. In a red-hot real estate boom, it is not uncommon to hear of borrowers with fourth and fifth mortgages on their properties!

Some Basic Concepts and Terminology

Principal This is the amount of money that is being borrowed.

Interest Interest is the price paid by the borrower to the lender for the use of the lender's money.

Amortization This is the gradual retirement of a debt by means of partial payments of the principal at regular intervals.

Amortization period This is the time period required to retire completely a debt through scheduled repayments of principal.

Blended payments This is the method of repayment of a debt where the periodic repayments are constant and each payment includes interest and repayment of part of the principal.

Term This is the actual length of time for which the money is loaned at a particular rate of interest. The most common terms for home mortgages are 6 months, 1 year, 2 years, 3 years, 4 years, and 5 years.

Maturity date The final date in the *term* of the mortgage is called the maturity date.

Conventional mortgage This term is used to describe a first mortgage granted by an institutional lender, such as a bank, mortgage, loan, or trust company, where the amount of the loan does not exceed 75% of the appraised lending value of the property.

High ratio mortgage A mortgage that exceeds 75% of lending value and must be insured, via a *National Housing Act* loan or a private insurer. The insurance is paid by the borrower in favour of the lender to protect the lender against default.

Default This is failure to meet the obligations imposed by the debt (an example is failure on the part of the mortgager to make monthly payments).

Foreclosure Remedial court action taken by a mortgagee, when default occurs on a mortgage, to cause forfeiture of the equity of redemption of the mortgager.

Power of sale The right of a mortgagee, such as a bank, to force a sale of the property should default occur.

Mortgage Financing Mathematics

Mortgage financing is another application of time value calculations. If you mastered Chapter 2, then this section should be easy for you. There are *five important elements* in a mortgage:

1. The *principal*
2. The *term*
3. The *rate of Interest* and the compounding frequency
4. The *period* of payment, usually a month
5. The *amortization period*

They are stated in the mortgage contract between the *mortgager* and the *mortgagee*. Once they are known, you can carry out the following calculations to make the right decisions about mortgage financing.

Example 13.2: Mr. Wong has just bought a house. He obtained a three-year first mortgage of $100,000 from the Bank of Montreal at an interest rate of 7% p.a., compounded semi-annually. The loan is to be amortized over 25 years by blended monthly payments. What is the amount of each monthly payment?

The *five elements* in this mortgage are as follows:

1.   The *principal* = $100,000.
2.   The *term* = 3 years.

3. The *rate of interest* = 7% p.a., semi-annual compounding. This is equivalent to a monthly compounding rate of 0.575%. We explain why in the next section.
4. The *period* of payment = a month.
5. The *amortization period* = 25 years or 300 months.

Answer: The monthly payment is $700.41.
             Here is how you get the answer from your calculator:

100,000	**PV**
300	**N**
.575	**I/Y**
CPT PMT	answer = $-$700.41

We will now go through the mathematics and the theory that provide the above calculation.

Canadian Home Mortgage Rates

In Canada, mortgage rates are stated as an annual rate with semi-annual compounding but the loan is normally repaid by monthly payments.[1] Thus, the **compounding period** (six months) is different from the **repayment period** (one month). How can we translate the stated rate — such as 7% p.a., semi-annual compounding — to an effective monthly rate with monthly compounding?

■ THE STATED RATE AND THE EQUIVALENT MONTHLY
   COMPOUNDING RATE

Let k = the stated annual rate, with semi-annual compounding
     m = the equivalent monthly compounding rate

Because of the semi-annual compounding, the effective annual rate of interest is equivalent to:

$$\left[1 + \frac{k}{2}\right]^2$$

Since we want the equivalent monthly rate to compound to this effective annual rate, we can set up the following equation:

---

[1] By law, residential mortgages may not be compounded more frequently than semi-annually.

$$(1 + m)^{12} = \left[1 + \frac{k}{2}\right]^2 \qquad\qquad (1)$$

$$or \ (1 + m)^6 = \left[1 + \frac{k}{2}\right]$$

In Example 13.2, $k = 7\%$, so from equation (1),

$$(1 + m)^{12} = \left[1 + \frac{k}{2}\right]^2$$

$$(1 + m)^6 = 1.035$$

$$m = .00575 \ \text{or} \ .575\%$$

On a BA II Plus calculator,

$$1.035 \ \mathbf{y^x} \ .16667 = 1.00575$$

Then

$$1.00575 - 1 = 0.00575 \ \text{or} \ .575\%.$$

How to Calculate the Monthly Mortgage Payment

If you recall the basic concepts in Chapter 2, the answer is based on the simple logic: "The mortgage payments should be such that the present value of the stream of mortgage payments, when discounted by the appropriate interest rate, equals the amount of the loan (i.e., the principal)." Now go back to Example 13.2 again, the *principal* = \$100,000, the **equivalent monthly compounding rate** = .00575, the number of months = 25 × 12 or 300 months. Let \$x = the monthly mortgage payment. The present value of an annuity of \$x for 300 months at the discount rate of .00575 is equal to:

$$x\left[\frac{1}{.00575} - \frac{1}{.00575 \times 1.00575^{300}}\right]$$

Since this is equal to the amount of the loan of \$100,000, we can set up the equation:

$$x\left[\frac{1}{.00575} - \frac{1}{.00575 \times 1.00575^{300}}\right] = 100,000$$

$$x = 700.41$$

This is the theory behind the programs in your calculator and in PlanPlus; it is important that you understand the theory before you use the programs.

How to Calculate the Outstanding Principal at Any Future Point in Time

The **outstanding principal**, or the **outstanding balance** of the loan, is equal to the present value of the remaining stream of mortgage payments, discounted at the equivalent monthly compounding rate. Let us continue with the above example. What is the outstanding balance of the loan after two years?

After two years, Mr. Wong would have paid 24 monthly payments so that there will be (300 − 24) or 276 monthly payments remaining. The outstanding balance is the present value of an annuity of 276 monthly payments of $700.41 each. Using the equivalent monthly compounding rate of .00575 as the discount rate, this is equal to:

$$\$700.41 \times \left[\frac{1}{.00575} - \frac{1}{.00575 \times 1.00575^{276}} \right]$$

$$= \$96,782 \text{ after rounding}$$

Only if you understand the theory are you entitled to use your calculator. The procedure is:

276	**N**
−700.41	**PMT**
.575	**I/Y**
CPT PV	answer = $96,782

Change in Mortgage Rate

The rate of interest is guaranteed and fixed only for the term of the mortgage. Thus, the rate of 7% p.a. in Example 13.2 is fixed for three years only. At the end of the three-year term, the mortgage has to be renewed or refinanced at the rate of interest that applies at that time. Since the future rate may rise or fall, the future mortgage payment may rise or fall accordingly. How do you calculate the new monthly payment? The procedure is illustrated in Example 13.3.

> **Example 13.3:** To continue with Example 13.2, suppose at the end of three years the rate of interest for a three-year term has increased to 9% p.a., semi-annual compounding. What is the new mortgage payment?

After three years, the remaining number of monthly payments is equal to (300 − 36) or 264 months. The outstanding balance of the loan is equal to:[2]

---

[2] The outstanding balance is equal to the present value of an annuity of 264 monthly payments of $700.41 each, at the discount rate of .00575.

$$\$700.41 \times \left[\frac{1}{.00575} - \frac{1}{.00575 \times 1.00575^{264}} \right]$$

$$= \$94,999$$

Next, we have to calculate the new equivalent monthly rate, by using equation (1), that is,

$$(1 + m)^{12} = \left[1 + \frac{.09}{2} \right]^2$$

$$m = .00736$$

Finally, let y be equal to the new monthly payment. The present value of an annuity of 264 months of $\$y$ is equal to:

$$y \times \left[\frac{1}{.00736} - \frac{1}{.00736 \times 1.00736^{264}} \right]$$

and we want this to equal $\$94,999$. We therefore have:

$$y \times \left[\frac{1}{.00736} - \frac{1}{.00736 \times 1.00736^{264}} \right]$$

$$y = 817.09$$

Make sure that you understand the theory before you use the calculator to find the answer, which is as follows:

264	**N**
.736	**I/Y**
94,999	**PV**
CPT PMT	answer = <u>−$817.09</u>

Therefore, as a result of the increase in the interest rate from 7% to 9%, the monthly mortgage payment would increase from $700.41 to $817.09.

Problem: In Example 13.2, if the three-year mortgage rate falls to 5% after three years, what is the new monthly mortgage payment?

Answer: $591.26

Summary of Mortgage Financing Mathematics

There are *five elements* in a mortgage: the principal, the interest, the term, the period of payment (a month, a week, and so on), and the amortization period. All these can be easily found out from the mortgage contract.

Based on these five elements, we can calculate the following:

1. The equivalent monthly compounding rate
2. The periodic mortgage payment
3. The outstanding balance of the principal at any point in time
4. The new mortgage payment when there is a change in the rate of interest or in the amortization period. Such changes usually occur at the end of the term of the mortgage

HOW MUCH HOME CAN YOU AFFORD?

Minimum Down Payment and Other Rules

A financial institution may not lend more than 95% of the appraised value of the property for a residential mortgage loan or, conversely, a borrower must provide a down payment of at least 5%. If the down payment is 5–20%, the mortgage is high risk and the financial institution must require the borrower to qualify for mortgage insurance. The cost of the mortgage insurance is added to the mortgage payments, and it can be very expensive. Canada Mortgage and Housing Corp. (CMHC), which is a federal Crown Corporation, provides much of the mortgage insurance in Canada and charges a premium ranging from 0.5% to 7% of the value of the mortgage. Premiums are higher for smaller down payments and higher for self-employed borrowers with no independent verification of their income.

Recent federal government changes taking effect in July 2012 will also slow down growth of mortgage financing, because consumer debt was rising to such high levels that many experts felt a Canadian debt crisis was developing. The maximum permitted amortization period for an insured loan drops to 25 years, and the limit on refinancing a loan falls to 80% of the loan, down from 85%. The maximum gross debt service ratio (GDS) is fixed at 39% and the maximum total debt service ratio (TDS) is fixed at 44% for all loans. Loans on homes with a purchase price higher than $1 million cannot be insured. You will recall that in Chapter 12 we said the standard benchmarks are 30% for GDS and 40% for TDS. Although these are the commonly quoted values, Canadian and American financial institutions have gone far beyond them in recent years when making mortgage loans. We said in Chapter 12 that GDS and TDS limits are rough rules of thumb that are not always accurate, but prudent financial planning requires some limits on borrowing. Accordingly, we usually adhere to the long-established GDS and TDS limits in this chapter's examples. CHMC uses a lower limit than the banks seem to have followed in recent years — its stated GDS limit for insuring a mortgage is 32%.

Using Debt Ratios to Calculate How Much You Can Afford

Since very few people can afford to pay cash for a home, how much home one can afford depends on how much mortgage financing one can obtain. The *traditional* (or *conventional*) sources of mortgage financing are provided by financial institutions, such as banks and trust companies. The GDS rule says that your monthly mortgage payment plus property taxes must be less than a certain percentage of your monthly gross income. Based on this, the lender will calculate the maximum amount that you can borrow, subject to other criteria if applicable. Example 13.4 illustrates the calculations, using a limit of 30% for GDS.

Example 13.4: Brenda and Bobby Black both work for the federal government. Their jobs are stable and last year they earned a combined household gross income of $75,000. They are very careful with their personal finances and have no debt. They want to buy a house and wonder how much they can borrow based on their income. They have saved $80,000, which they are willing to use as a down payment. The current home mortgage rate for a three-year term mortgage is 8% p.a. The houses that they have been looking at require about $3,000 in annual property taxes.

Based on a GDS ratio of 30%, the amount of principal, interest, and property tax payment that the Blacks can afford is equal to (30% × $75,000) = $22,500/year or $1,875/month. Since property taxes amount to $3,000/year or $250/month, the maximum amount of principal and interest that lenders would allow is equal to ($1,875 − 250) or $1,625/month.

The equivalent monthly compounding rate, m, is calculated from equation (1), as follows:

$$(1 + m)^{12} = \left[1 + \frac{.08}{2}\right]^2$$

$$m = .00656 \text{ or } .656\%$$

Assuming a 25-year amortization period, the maximum amount of mortgage that the Blacks can get is equal to the present value of an annuity of 300 months of $1,625 each, using .656% as the discount rate. This is equal to:

$$\$1,625 \times \left[\frac{1}{.00656} - \frac{1}{.00656 \times 1.00656^{300}}\right]$$

= $213,000 rounded to the nearest thousand.

If you want to use your calculator, the sequence is:

300	**N**
.656	**I/Y**
−1625	**PMT**
CPT PV	answer = $213,000 (rounded to the nearest thousand)

The amount of housing that they can afford = $80,000 + $213,000 = $293,000, or about $300,000.

Saving Up for a Down Payment

For young families in the early stages of their life cycle, it is unlikely that they have enough money for the minimum down payment. If they want to buy a home in the future, their short-term financial goal should be to save up money for the down payment of the house. The above analysis should give you some idea of how to set this financial goal. To summarize, this is what you have to do:

1. Estimate the amount of mortgage that you can get, based on your expected gross income, the current GDS ratio (say 30%) or TDS ratio (say 40%), and the current mortgage rate.[3]

2. This amount of mortgage is approximately equal to 75% of the value of the house; for this reason, you can find the amount of housing you can theoretically afford.

3. The minimum down payment is equal to 25% of the value of the house obtained above.

4. You set up a deadline for acquiring this minimum down payment.

See Example 13.5 for an illustration.

Example 13.5: Suppose the Blacks in Example 13.4 have no down payment. They want to save up enough money for the minimum down payment in five years' time. Based on their current income and the current mortgage rate, what is the amount that they must have for the minimum down payment in five years time?

---

[3] If you can forecast the future mortgage rate, that is what you should use. Empirical studies have, however, found that forecasting future interest rates is very difficult. Many economists think the current rate is the best estimate for the future rate.

First, as shown in Example 13.4, they can borrow about $213,000 from the bank. Second, as this is about 75% of the value of the house, the theoretical home value that the Blacks can afford is equal to ($213,000 ÷ .75) or $284,000. Third, the minimum down payment is equal to 25% of $284,000, which is $71,000. Finally, their financial goal would be to have $71,000 in five years' time. You may recall from Chapter 4 that this is a financial goal because the amount is precise ($71,000) and there is a deadline (five years for its completion).[4]

Balancing the Budget

The rules we have presented on how much mortgage you can afford have been constraints imposed by outside lenders. These are rough approximations of the true limit, which is how much money you can afford in your budget. For most families, these rules are a reasonable guideline. However, suppose a family enjoys being able to travel to Europe every summer and ski at Whistler every winter. The members eat at the best restaurants and stay in four-star hotels. Their budget may not support even 30% GDS. Conversely, we know many families that carry 50% GDS and manage to pay off the home by being very thrifty.

What it comes down to is a choice of goals. If owning your own home is the first priority, then you may have to give up some other goals, at least temporarily. Bankers tell us that they are more likely to find well-off families getting into debt troubles because they couldn't cut their luxury spending than they are to find modest income families who took on too much.

The mechanical solution to this problem is in Chapter 4. In addition to the tests presented in this chapter, the prospective home buyer needs to balance the budget. All the costs of home ownership — mortgage, utilities, taxes, repairs and maintenance, and insurance — must be factored in. The cost of renting (including utilities, if they are separate from rent) are deducted. One issue to watch out for is inflation. On average, the cost of renting rises over time. The mortgage amount is fixed, and hence it is in nominal dollars already. Thus, the budgeting exercise, if done in nominal dollars, will include the inflation hedge of buying over renting.

Other Sources of Financing and Mortgages

So far we have described the conventional mortgages, which are the major sources of first mortgages provided by banks and other financial institutions.

If one wants to borrow more than what is allowed by the constraints of the GDS ratio or the 75% value criterion, one has to look for other sources of financing. These are usually provided by private lenders who do not use the stringent

---

[4] The next thing the Blacks should do is to set up an action plan, take action, and so on, to reach their goal. In other words, they should follow the Personal Financial Process described in Chapter 3 in order to reach their goal.

criteria of the banks. In return for the higher risk, these lenders normally require a higher rate of interest. The more common sources of financing are higher mortgages — second mortgage, third mortgage, and so on. Another very popular source is a vendor-take-back (VTB) mortgage.

A **vendor-take-back (VTB) mortgage** is a mortgage that the seller of a home has taken from the purchaser as part payment of the purchase price for that property. This is sometimes called **seller financing**, since in essence the seller acts as the lender to the buyer. The seller offers a mortgage (or a loan) to the buyer, usually a short-term loan, at a below-market interest rate. Thus, instead of receiving in a lump sum the sales price of the home, the seller receives monthly mortgage payments from the buyer over a specified period of time. A high-ratio first mortgage can be covered with mortgage insurance, providing yet another alternative for those who cannot raise a 25% down payment.

> *Example 13.6:* Lynn Buyer wants to buy a home from Jill Vendor for the price of $80,000. Since Lynn Buyer has $10,000 for a down payment, she cannot get a first mortgage of $70,000 from any financial institution. (Why?)

Since Jill Vendor really wants to sell her house, she accepts a VTB mortgage of $70,000 for a three-year term and 7% interest and amortization period of 25 years. The monthly payment is $490.29 (you should check this!), and since this is within Lynn Buyer's budget, the transaction is closed.

As this example shows, using non-conventional sources of financing allows a buyer to acquire a more expensive home than that which a conventional lender would normally allow.

Summary: How Much Home Can You Afford?

How much home one can afford depends to a large extent on how much mortgage money one can get from the banks or loan or trust companies. This in turn depends on the usual qualifying rules — GDS, TDS, etc. — that these institutions have used. The major factors affecting the lender's decision are the family's income, the value of the home, the current mortgage rate, and the institution's credit criteria. Also, it depends on how much money the buyer has for the down payment. We have gone through the basic analysis of how to estimate the value of the home that you can afford. The estimate is nothing more than a benchmark. You can buy a more expensive home than the benchmark by using non-conventional sources of financing — but this is usually more risky. On the other hand, you are free to buy a smaller home than the benchmark. In fact, you can even choose not to buy a home. We shall discuss the rent versus buy decision later in this chapter.

VALUATION OF A HOME

For most people, buying a home is the biggest investment in their lives. Until recently, most people believed that houses were the best investments an individual could buy; indeed, real estate was a good investment during the boom of the 1970s and the early part of the 1980s when house prices skyrocketed in many parts of Canada, especially in large cities like Toronto and Vancouver. In the "go-go" years of the real estate market, some went so far as to think that a person was financially ignorant not to own a home. Many so-called financial experts advised people to buy the biggest possible home that they could afford — which meant borrowing up to a family's debt capacity. Realtors would say that the best time to buy a house was always "NOW": Prices of houses would keep on climbing.

The collapse of the real estate market in the late 1980s and the early 1990s in most of Canada[5] reminds us of something that the shrewd investors have always known — that investing in a home, just like investing in any other type of investment, is a risky business. There is always a possibility of losing money. The value of a house, like almost any investment, can rise, fall, or remain constant over time.

The House as an Investment

There are two important characteristics of any investment: (i) the *return on investment* and (ii) the *risk*. Investing in one's home certainly has these characteristics, too.

There are two sources of return from a home. First, there is the potential capital gain. If you buy a home today for $100,000 and sell it in five years for $150,000, then you will have earned a capital gain of $50,000. Under current Canadian tax law, the capital gain on your home — formally, it is called your **principal residence** — is tax exempt. Second, if you invest in a home, you save on the rental expenses you would otherwise have to pay. This is called the **imputed rental income** of your home. Under the current tax law, the imputed rental income is also tax exempt; therefore, by investing in a home, you expect to earn an after-tax rate of return on your investment, which is composed of the total imputed rental income plus the total expected capital gain.

Example 13.7: Ronald and Catherine Allan are the proud owners of a three-bedroom detached house, which they bought recently for $200,000. To rent a similar house in the same neighbourhood would cost about $1,500 per month, exclusive of utilities. On the other hand, if the Allans

---

[5] In the same period, the real estate market suffered major setbacks in the United States and Japan as well.

were renting such a home, they would not have to pay the property taxes and maintenance of $2,400 per annum ($200 a month). Furthermore, historical data show that the prices of homes in that neighbourhood have been increasing at about 3% per year. What is the expected rate of return on the Allans's investment?

The expected rate of return

= the return from the imputed rental income
   + the expected capital gain

$$= \left[\frac{(\$1,500 - \$200) \times 12}{\$200,000} \right] + 3\%$$

$$= 7.8\% + 3\%$$

$$= 10.8\%$$

Since the imputed rental income and the capital gain income are both tax exempt, the 10.8% is the after-tax rate of return on investment.

Is this a good investment for the Allans? The answer depends on two things: (i) How risky is the home? What is the historical price variation of home prices in that neighbourhood? (We will discuss the nature of risk in greater depth in the next chapter.) (ii) Can the Allans earn an after-tax rate of return of 10.8% on investments of similar risk as their home? If they cannot, then the home is a good investment.

Although the return from a home investment is tax-exempt, the expenses are not tax-deductible. The usual expenses associated with home ownership are interest on mortgages, insurance, property taxes, utilities, and maintenance. A landlord renting the property to you can deduct these expenses, however. Part of this tax shield is reflected in the level of rents, so there are also implicit tax advantages to renting.

Non-financial Aspect of Home Ownership

A home is not just an investment. It is one of the few investments that has both utilitarian and enjoyment value: In short, it is a place to live that provides its owner with a very real and personal pride of ownership. And even though a similar home in the same neighbourhood can conceivably be rented more cheaply, renting a property does not give a person the same unquantifiable pride of ownership as does owning a home. Consequently, it may very well be the case that it is partly for this reason that studies have found that most people prefer home ownership to renting shelter; it may very well be that the superior performance of real estate over other investments in the 1970s and the first half of the 1980s does not constitute the entire reason for this finding. Home ownership also offers security of tenure, and the right to decorate as you please. These subjective values may not have measurable market values by themselves, but they do affect house prices.

HOW DO YOU VALUE A HOUSE?

The market value of most investments, such as stocks and bonds, is readily observable. You can find out the latest price of a stock by calling a stockbroker. In contrast to that, the price of a home is not observable. The market value of a home must be estimated, and the process of estimating a home's value is called **appraisal**. If the market value of a home is not observable, what do people mean when they use the term "market value"?

Market Value

The **market value** of a home is defined as the highest price that a willing buyer will pay if the house is offered for sale in the open market, allowing a reasonable time to find a willing buyer with neither the buyer nor the seller acting under necessity, compulsion, or any peculiar circumstances.

The above definition suggests that one can find good deals (or undervalued properties) if the seller is under financial pressure or distress. For example, one may find good buys if there is a power of sale, loss of employment, or a marriage breakup.

Valuation Approaches

There are two common methods for valuing a home: the direct market comparison approach and the cost approach. We will describe each method and use a numerical example to illustrate how each method works.

The **direct market comparison (DMC) approach** is a method of valuing properties by comparing the prices at which similar properties have been sold. Because no two homes are exactly the same, one must make adjustments to the various differences that exist among the properties.

Major Factors That Affect House Value

You have probably heard about the three major factors that affect home value: location, location, location. Clearly, when you buy a house, you are also "buying" the surrounding neighbourhood: the quality of the schools, the crime rate, the neatness of adjacent yards, the quality of the air, and so on.

The following is a list of other factors that affect house values:

- Lot size
- Building size
- Number of rooms
- Number of baths
- Type of construction (e.g., all brick, brick veneer, aluminum siding, etc.)
- Number of garages
- Number of fireplaces

- Family or recreation room
- Deck
- Recent sale prices of homes in the area
- Other factors

To apply the direct market comparison approach to value a home, you must first locate a number of properties that are as similar as possible to the **subject property** (i.e., the home that is to be appraised) and have recently been sold in the local market. Detailed information for each sale can be acquired from the city, county, township, registry, or land title offices, and the local real estate board. The best way to illustrate the direct market comparison approach is by an example.

The following information has been gathered by David Hudson, who wants to appraise a house that he intends to buy (the subject property). He has also collected information on four comparable homes that have been sold in the last year.

The subject property is a three-year-old, all-brick home located on a 45′ × 110′ lot in a good residential subdivision. The house size is 2240 square feet (s. f.); it has a finished recreation room, one four-piece bathroom, and no garage. There is a fireplace in the living room, which is estimated to add $3,000 to the value of the house. The information about the four comparable sales is summarized as follows:

Sale 1: Sold six months ago for $167,400. All features are similar to the subject property except the following: house size = 2120 s.f.; lot size = 40′ × 100′; it has one four-piece bathroom and one two-piece bathroom, and a single-car, attached garage, which is expected to add $3,000 to the sale price.

Sale 2: Sold recently for $189,000; it has no fireplace or recreation room; lot size = 50′ × 110′; house size = 2340 s.f.; the property has a heat pump, which is expected to add $2,000 more to the house's value; other things are similar to subject property.

Sale 3: Sold 12 months ago for $165,000; lot size = 55′ × 105′; it has a recreation room but no fireplace; it has a single garage; it is on a corner lot and corner lot properties sell for about $3,000 less than similar houses; other features are similar to subject property.

Sale 4: Sold last week for $192,000; it is on a ravine lot, which is quantifiably superior to the subject property by about $4,000; lot size = 45′ by 110′; it has one four-piece and one two-piece washroom; there is no recreation room or garage but there is a walkout basement, which is expected to add $2,000 to value; other features are similar to the subject property.

TABLE 13.1
Summary of Relevant Information

	Subject Property	Sale 1	Sale 2	Sale 3	Sale 4
Sale Price	N/A	167.4M	189.0M	165.M	192.0M
Sale Time	now	6 mon.	recent	1 yr.	recent
Location	address	similar	similar	corner	ravine
Lot Size	45' × 110'	40' × 100'	50' × 110'	55' × 105'	45' × 110'
House Size	2240 s.f.	2120 s.f.	2340 s.f.	same	same
Washrooms	1	1 1/2	1	1	1 1/2
Garage	0	1	1	1	0
Fireplace	1	1	0	0	1
Rec. Room	1	1	0	1	0
Extras	—	—	Heat Pump	—	Walk-out bsmt.

An analysis of the real estate market indicates that a two-piece washroom adds $1,500 to value; recreation rooms, $2,000. As such, sales prices have risen gradually and evenly by 10% over the last year. Lots in the area sell for $500/front foot, and the depth of the lot does not add much value. The present construction cost for this type of dwelling is $40/s.f.

Summary of Data

It is useful to summarize the relevant information in a table, such as Table 13.1. The table is very useful because it shows clearly how each comparable sale differs from the subject property. We have to make an adjustment for every difference.

The Adjustment Process

Adjustments are made for each of the differences between the comparable sale and the subject property. The idea is to adjust the comparable properties so that they become as similar as possible to the subject property. Let us illustrate this by comparing the subject property to Sale 1. First, Sale 1 was sold six months ago, at a time when there was an increase of 5% in selling prices; therefore, we have to add a time adjustment to its sale price. The time adjustment is equal to ($167,400 × .05) or $8,370. This is an "add" adjustment because if the house were to be sold today it would be sold for a 5% higher price. Second, the Sale 1 property has a smaller lot size (40' × 100') than that of the subject property (45' × 100'). We have to "add" a lot size adjustment to Sale 1 to bring it to the same as the subject property. Since lots sell for $500/front foot, we "add" ($500 × 5) or $2,500 to Sale 1. The third difference is in the home size — the subject property has 2240 s.f. versus Sale 1's house size of 2120 s.f. Since construction cost is $40/s.f., the home size adjustment is [(2,240 – 2,120) × $40] or $4,800. We have to add this to Sale 1 to bring it to the same home size as the subject property. The fourth difference is in the number of washrooms — subject property (one four-piece) versus Sale 1 (one four-piece and one two-piece). We have to "subtract" a two-piece washroom from Sale 1, or $1,500, to make it similar to the subject property. The result of all the adjustments as shown in Table 13.2.

> *Exercise:*　　Make the necessary adjustments to each of the comparable properties — Sale 2, Sale 3, and Sale 4 — and check your answer in Table 13.2.

Reconciliation — the Final Step

If you look at the bottom line of Table 13.2, you will see four different adjusted sale prices: Each one is an indicated value of the market value of the subject property. The process of reducing this series of value indications to a final estimate of value is called **reconciliation**.

In order to reconcile the adjusted sale prices, you should do the following:

- Check all calculations.
- Discard sales that require extreme adjustments.
- Choose the sales with the highest degree of comparability with the subject property.
- Make the final value estimate.

In our example, Sale 1 and Sale 3 are not recent sales and therefore cannot be considered as ideal comparables. Of the remaining two, Sale 4 requires the least number of adjustments. Thus, the indicated value of the subject property is $187,000 (to the nearest thousand). The direct market comparison approach can be used only if there are sales of comparable homes in the recent past and the data about those sales are available. Sometimes there are homes that are quite unique in their features — e.g., a newly built "monster" home with unique structures — for which there are few, if any, comparable sales data available. In this case, the cost approach can be used to value the home.

The idea behind the cost approach is that at any point in time, home values cannot rise above their reproduction cost. The cost approach involves four basic steps:

1. Estimate the value of the land.
2. Estimate the cost of reproducing the existing home as though it were new.
3. Estimate the accrued depreciation suffered by the home from all causes — such as wear and tear, obsolescence, and so on.

TABLE 13.2
Adjustments for Direct Market Comparison

	Sale 1	Sale 2	Sale 3	Sale 4
Sale Price	167,400	189,000	165,000	192,000
Time	+ 8,370		+ 16,500	
Location			+ 3,000	− 4,000
Lot Size	+ 2,500	− 2,500	− 5,000	
Home Size	+ 4,800	− 4,000		
Washrooms	− 1,500			− 1,500
Garage	− 3,000	− 3,000	− 3,000	
Fireplace		+ 3,000	+ 3,000	
Rec. Room		+ 2,000		+ 2,000
Extras		− 2,000		− 2,000
Total adjustments	+ 11,170	− 6,500	+ 14,500	− 5,500
Adjusted Sale Price	178,570	182,500	179,500	186,500

4. Add the value of the land (Step 1) and the value of the reproduction cost (Step 2), then subtract all accrued depreciation (Step 3) to arrive at an estimate of the market value of the home.

Before we proceed, it is important to distinguish between reproduction cost and replacement cost.

Reproduction Cost — This is the cost of exactly reproducing the subject property using identical or highly similar materials at current costs.

Replacement Cost — This is the cost of replacing the subject property with a new structure of the same size and utility using current technology, materials, and equipment instead of trying to reproduce it detail by detail.

In the cost approach, it is the reproduction cost that we are using in Step 2. We will now use an example to illustrate the cost approach.

Example 13.8: You are asked to estimate the market value of a bungalow (using the cost approach). You find that the present construction cost per square foot (s.f.) for this type and quality of structure[6] is $54.94. After measuring the bungalow very carefully, you estimate that its area is approximately 1250 s.f. The lot size is 55′ × 105′ and lots in the area sell for $350/front foot. Your personal inspection of the house reveals the need for interior and exterior painting, which will cost $1,450 and $1,960, respectively. A window is damaged and the estimated replacement cost is $420. The flooring is broadloom and you notice that about 700 s.f. is worn out. The cost of replacing it with similar quality broadloom is $2.50/s.f. There are no other indications of depreciation that you can find.

Since there have been no transactions — buying or selling of similar types of homes — in the last two years, you cannot use the direct market comparison approach to estimate the home's value; consequently, you have decided to use the cost approach:

Step 1   Estimation of land value
= $350 × 55 = $19,250

Step 2   Estimation of reproduction cost
= ($54.94 × 1250) = $68,675

Step 3   Estimation of all accrued depreciation:

Interior painting	$1,450
Exterior painting	1,960
Replacing window	420
New broadloom ($2.5 × 700)	1,750
Total accrued depreciation	$5,580

Step 4   Market value by the cost approach
= land value + reproduction cost – accrued depreciation
= $19,250 + $68,675 – $5,580
= $82,345

SHOULD YOU BUY OR RENT?

You can either rent or buy a home. Is there a theoretical framework whereby one can analyze this buy versus rent decision? The answer is yes. It turns out to be a very simple cash-flow analysis of the two alternatives. You list all the cash flows required under home ownership and also all the cash flows required under renting and compare the two. We shall illustrate by an example.

Example 13.9:   Jack and Jill are considering buying a $150,000 two-bedroom condominium and living in it for three years. They have saved up $48,000 to be used for a down payment and for covering closing costs (estimated to be about $3,000). They will take out a first mortgage at an interest rate of 8% p.a., to be amortized over 25 years. Apart from the monthly mortgage payments, there are other home ownership costs, which are estimated as follows:

Property taxes	$2,400/year
Insurance premium	360/year
Condominium maintenance fee	3,600/year

Alternatively, they can rent the condominium at $1,200/month. If they rent, they do not have to pay property taxes, insurance, and condominium fees — the landlord will pay. They can invest money to earn an after-tax rate of return of 5%. They expect that rent will increase at a rate of 4% per year; likewise, the same rate of increase is expected for property taxes, insurance premiums, and condominium maintenance fees. Should they buy or rent?

Assume that the value of the condominium will appreciate at 4% per annum. There is also an initial one-time cost of home ownership: the down payment of $45,000 plus the closing cost of $3,000 = $48,000.

If they choose to rent and not buy, they can invest the $48,000 to earn 5% after-tax return. After three years, the compound value of the $48,000 will be ($48,000 × 1.05^3) = $55,566.

Their annual home ownership costs are summarized in Table 13.3.

The last row in Table 13.3 represents the money available for investment every year if they choose to rent instead of buy. At an after-tax rate of return of 5%, this stream of investment will become:

$$\$1,576.49 \times 1.05^2 + (\$1,254.89 \times 1.05) + \$920.43$$
$$= \$3,976.14$$

The total amount of money that they will have at the end of three years if they choose to rent instead of buy = $55,566 + $3,976.14 = $59,542.

If they buy the condo unit, the value of the condo after three years = ($150,000 × 1.04^3) = $168,730.

The amount of the mortgage outstanding after three years = $100,438. (You should be able to check this by now!)

The amount of home equity that they will have = $168,730 – $100,438 = $68,292.

329

TABLE 13.3 Jack and Jill's Annual Home Ownership Cost			
Annual Cost	Year 1	Year 2	Year 3
Mortgage Payment*	$ 9,616.49	$ 9,616.49	$ 9,616.49
Property Taxes	2,400.00	2,496.00	2,595.84
Insurance	360.00	374.40	389.38
Condo Fees	3,600.00	3,744.00	3,893.76
Gross Home-ownership Costs	$15,976.49	$16,230.89	$16,495.47
Rent	(14,400.00)	(14,976.00)	(15,575.04)
Net Home-ownership Costs	$ 1,576.49	$ 1,254.89	$ 920.43

* Principal = $105,000; interest = 8%; amortization = 25 years.

Their equity under the "buy" is therefore greater than their equity under "rent" ($68,292 versus $59,542). Thus, in this example, Jack and Jill are better off buying than renting.

The above example is used to explain the framework to analyze buy versus rent. Clearly, it is not always true that buy is better than rent. Indeed, we want you to show in the following exercise that renting is better than buying.

Exercise: Assuming all the information of Example 13.9 holds except that the value of the condominium increases at the rate of 2% per year and that Jack and Jill can rent the condominium unit for $1,000/month. Should they rent or buy?

Answer: They should rent.

OTHER ISSUES IN BUYING A HOME

How Do I Know It Isn't a Lemon?

You don't. You have to do your homework, but there are no guarantees. Questions such as the suitability of the location, the number and type of rooms, etc., are personal matters that you should judge for your own family interests.

What you may not be capable of judging are more technical matters, such as the soundness of construction. Perhaps you have a good friend or relative who is knowledgeable and will look over a prospective house with you. If you have found a house that suits all your other needs and all you are worried about is if it really is what it appears, most urban areas have firms of consulting engineers or home-assessment experts. The sorts of things these assessors do is look for signs of structural damage or flaws, e.g., termites, concealed fire damage, crumbling foundations, leaks, rotted beams. One of them will examine the house in some detail and write a report on good or bad items for a fee of $200–$500. If you are concerned about someone else buying the house while you wait for the report, you can make an offer conditional on an acceptable assessment.

Another way to protect against specific problems is to include a warranty in the offer to purchase the home. The **warranty** says that the purchase is conditional on certain conditions being met. For example, the seller might warrant the house against containing any asbestos insulation (which is very messy to check for, and both expensive and hazardous to remove). If it subsequently proves to have asbestos, the buyer has legal recourse against the seller for the cost to remove it and any other expenses. Sellers are rarely willing to accept many warranties, however.

If you can't afford the cost of an assessor and have no relatives or friends who can help, you may wish to learn more about how to assess a house. There are books written on the subject, but we will confine our discussion to personal finance, and leave you to pursue this at your local library.

Lawyers and More Lawyers

You don't need a lawyer to handle the purchase or sale of a house, but we would advise that you hire one. Real estate transactions are bread and butter for most lawyers, and they know all the pitfalls. The most important job they perform is the **title search**. They check the land records to ensure that the seller owns the property and that there are no undisclosed debts or restrictions on it. In most cases they guarantee the validity of the transfer of the property so that if you later discover some further debts or liens, or a defect in the title, and you lose money, they will reimburse you. You can also buy title insurance, which is used to give assurance of a clear title.

In addition, lawyers will help you file the various legal documents required, and will advise you on things like land-transfer taxes or other taxes exacted by the provincial government.

As there is quite a bit of competition for legal business these days, you should shop around a bit to get a reasonable fee. Some lawyers will quote fixed fees for standard real estate transactions. The fee will still be several hundred dollars.

If you are determined to do the legal work yourself, be prepared to spend some time reading, and then some time going to various offices. Any business bookstore carries one or more books that contain detailed instructions and appropriate forms to enable you to do the legal work yourself. Personally, we prefer to hire lawyers.

SUMMARY

This chapter covers one of the biggest commitments in many people's financial affairs — buying a home and taking out a mortgage. The most common type of mortgage is the conventional mortgage loaned by the banks, loan, and trust companies. These institutions use credit standards such as GDS or TDS ratios to qualify potential borrowers. The usual rule of thumb is that they will lend up to 75% of the home's value and up to 30% of the borrower's GDS ratio. There are five important elements in a mortgage: the principal, interest, term, payment period, and amortization period. These elements can be found easily from the mortgage contract. Based on these five elements, we can carry out all the mathematics on mortgage financing. We can calculate the equivalent monthly compounding rate, the monthly mortgage payments, the outstanding principal, and so on. We can also examine the effect of changes in the interest rate and the amortization period on the monthly payments.

How much home you can afford depends on (i) how much money you have that can be used as down payment and (ii) how much you can borrow. If you do not have enough down payment, you should set that as one of your financial goals. You are free to buy a smaller home than you can afford. You can even choose to rent instead of buy. A framework to analyze the rent versus buy decision has been discussed.

The market value of a home is not observable. The process of estimating the market value of a home is called appraisal. Two methods of valuing a home have been described — the direct market comparison approach and the cost approach.

Finally, a home is not just an investment. It is also an asset that you can enjoy. It provides the pride of ownership and other utilities. A home generates a rate of return on investment in two ways: There is the imputed rental income and the potential capital gain. Both are tax-exempt income. On the other hand, interest expenses on the home mortgages are not tax deductible. Investing in a home, just like any other investment, is a *risky* business. There is no guarantee of a positive return on investment.

MULTIPLE-CHOICE REVIEW QUESTIONS

1. The monthly payment on a mortgage does not depend on _____.

   (a) the principal
   (b) the rate of interest
   (c) the frequency of compounding
   (d) the amortization period
   (e) the term

2. If the borrower defaults on the mortgage payments, which of the following rights does the lender have?

   (a) Equity of redemption
   (b) Power of sale
   (c) Foreclosure
   (d) (a) and (b)
   (e) (b) and (c)

3. In the direct market comparison approach, you do not have to make adjustment for which of the following factors?

   (a) Location
   (b) Lot size
   (c) Historical cost
   (d) Building size
   (e) None of the above

4. Calculate the monthly payment on the following mortgage:
   Principal = $150,000
   Interest rate = 6%, compounded semi-annually
   Amortization period = 20 years

   (a) $966.45
   (b) $959.71
   (c) $1,068.28
   (d) $1,074.65
   (e) None of the above

5. Canadian chartered banks do not normally deal with _____.

   (a) residential first mortgages
   (b) high-ratio mortgages
   (c) vendor-take-back mortgages
   (d) open mortgages
   (e) none of the above

DISCUSSION QUESTIONS

1. Define or explain each of the following terms:

   amortization / amortization period / appraisal / blended payments / compounding period vs. repayment period / comparable sales / conventional mortgage / direct market comparison approach / equity of redemption / five elements of a mortgage / foreclosure / home mortgage: first mortgage — second mortgage — third mortgage / power of sale / imputed rental income / market value of a home / minimum down payment / mortgage / mortgagee / mortgager / principal residence / reconciliation / right of redemption / seller financing / subject property / vendor-take-back (VTB) mortgage

2. What is used as security in (i) a first mortgage, (ii) a second mortgage, and (iii) a third mortgage?

3. Describe how each of the following would affect one's blended monthly mortgage payments:

    (a) An increase in the mortgage rate of interest
    (b) A decrease in the amortization period
    (c) An increase in the length of the term without a change in interest rates

PROBLEMS

1. The current mortgage rates on three-year and five-year mortgages are 8% and 8.5%, respectively. Both rates are semi-annual compounding rates.

    (a) Calculate the equivalent monthly compounding rates.
    (b) If you borrow $150,000, amortized over 25 years, what is the monthly payment under each alternative?
    (c) What will be the outstanding balance of the mortgage at the maturity date if you:
        (i) borrow the three-year term?
        (ii) borrow the five-year term?
    (d) What are the advantages and disadvantages of a three-year term (at a lower rate) versus a five-year term (at a higher rate)?

2. A bank quotes a rate of 7.75% for a three-year residential mortgage of $100,000, with a 25-year amortization period.

    (a) What is the effective annual rate?
    (b) How much are the monthly payments?
    (c) How much will you owe at the end of one year? At the end of three years?
    (d) How much interest will you pay during the second year of the mortgage?

3. Joe and Maria Vincente recently bought their dream home. They financed it with a two-year mortgage loan from the Royal Bank of Newfoundland for $170,000. The nominal rate of interest on the loan is 8.75%, compounded semi-annually. They chose a 25-year amortization period.

    (a) Calculate the monthly blended payment.
    (b) Calculate the balance of the loan outstanding at the end of two years.

(c) If they renew the mortgage at the end of two years at a new rate of interest of 11% p.a., what will be the new monthly payment, given an amortization period of 23 years?

4. You have a five-year mortgage on your house with two years remaining on it with the Tottery Dominion Bank (TD). The quoted interest rate is 11.25%, the principal amount when you took out the mortgage was $90,000 and the amortization period was 25 years.

(a) How much are your monthly payments?
(b) How much principal do you owe now?
(c) Collapsible Trustco (CT) offers to pay you $300 to switch your mortgage to it. You would get a five-year mortgage with a 22-year amortization at 8.25%. TD would charge you a three-month interest penalty (i.e., the next three months of interest you would have paid on its mortgage) and $100 in legal fees to cancel its mortgage. Should you make the switch?
(d) In case you didn't notice it, you had to make a critical assumption to answer part (c). What was it? [**Hint**: Think about why we specified CT's mortgage to have a 22-year amortization instead of the more usual 25 years. It was one step in making the question easier.]

5. Tony and Betty have just signed a contract to buy a house for $300,000. They will put a down payment of $80,000 and take over the current first mortgage, which is a five-year mortgage borrowed by the vendor three years ago from the Royal Bank, with initial principal of $200,000 at 6% interest and 25 years amortization. The vendor has agreed to lend them a second mortgage for the remaining balance of the purchase price for a two-year term at 8% interest and 15 years amortization.

(a) What is the monthly payment on the first mortgage?
(b) What is the current outstanding balance on the first mortgage?
(c) What is the amount of the second mortgage that they must borrow?
(d) What is the monthly payment on the second mortgage?
(e) At the end of two years, how much do they owe (i) the Royal Bank, and (ii) the vendor?
(f) After two years, the mortgages in (e) will be due. If they refinance the outstanding balances of these mortgages by a five-year conventional mortgage, at 7% interest and 23 years amortization, what will be the monthly payment on the new mortgage?
(g) If the property tax on the house is $5,000 per year, what is the minimum family income that they must earn in order to qualify for the conventional mortgage in (f)?

6. Mr. Brian Turner has recently inherited $200,000. Since he does not own a home, he is contemplating buying one in the $200,000 price range. The property tax on the house is about $2,400/year. To rent a house of the same quality in the same neighbourhood costs $1,300/month plus utilities. If he does not buy a house, he plans to invest the money in a term deposit yielding about 5% p.a. His marginal tax rate is 40%. Do you think a home is a good investment for Mr. Turner? Why?

7. Robert and June Campbell have a combined income of $80,000. They always wanted to own their home some day and have saved up $50,000. The property tax of the kind of homes they are interested in is about $3,000/year. Below are the recent mortgage rates for different terms quoted by the Royal Bank:

Term	Rate % (Semi-annual compounding)
1 year	7.00
2 years	7.50
3 years	8.00
4 years	8.25
5 years	8.50

(a) Using a GDS ratio of 30%, calculate the amount of first mortgage they can get under each term (five answers).
(b) Now impose the 75%-appraised value rule. Can they get the loan in (a)?

8. Noemi graduated last year from York University with an MBA and is currently working for an environmental consulting firm. Her salary is $44,000, she has savings of $16,000, and she has no debts. She wants to buy a condominium in downtown Toronto, but the cheapest she can find is $120,000 with property taxes of $2,200 p.a. and condominium fees of $200 per month. The banks rejected her application for a first mortgage, and so she has decided to save her money and buy a similar condominium in three years time. She estimates the rate of inflation of real estate prices will be 3% p.a., and she can earn 6% by investing her savings in treasury bills. She will also have to pay about $3,000 in legal and moving costs in three years time when she buys the condo.

(a) Why did the banks reject her mortgage application?
(b) How much does she need to save each year to qualify for the first mortgage in three years?

9. Lillian Thong and Garsen Yap have been married for several years, and have good jobs with a joint income of over $85,000 p.a. They are each 28 years old, and wish to buy a house in Toronto by the time they are 30. The house they want would cost about $250,000 in current dollars, plus $5,000 for moving

and legal expenses. Taxes and utilities would cost $3,000 p.a. They live now in a two-bedroom apartment renting at $900/month with heat, light, water, and taxes included. They are presently saving about $6,000 p.a. They have no children, but plan to have children in their early thirties. Their balance sheet follows:

Lillian Thong and Garsen Yap
Family Balance Sheet

Cash and bank accounts	$ 500
Investments	85,000
RRSPs	0
Company pension plans:	
Lillian	18,000
Garsen	15,000
Two cars (replacement cost)	30,000
Personal stuff	20,000
Liabilities	
Credit cards	3,000
Car loans	8,000

Assume that inflation is expected to be 2% p.a. for the next five years. The investment portfolio is shown at market value.

Required:
What advice would you give them about planning for their house purchase? You are responsible for estimating their tax bracket. Five-year mortgage rates are currently 8.25%. See also Problem 5 in Chapter 14.

10. Gilles and Lisette are planning to buy a new house in Outremont. They have seen their dream house, which is offered at $300,000. Taxes are currently $3,000 p.a. on this house. Their current home on the south shore is fully paid, and they have received an offer to purchase for $120,000, which leaves $110,000 after paying the realtor and legal fees. They are planning to use this for the down payment, and they will cover other costs from their savings. The residential mortgage rate for a five-year term is 7.9%. Their combined gross income is $65,000 p.a. and they will be paying off a student loan for the next six years, at a rate of $229 per month.

(a) How much will their monthly mortgage payment be if they take a five-year term, amortized over 25 years?
(b) Will they qualify for a first mortgage of $190,000 under normal bank lending practices?
(c) If they do get a mortgage, what will be the outstanding balance after four years?

(d) At the end of five years, they can change the terms of the mortgage. Suppose that the interest rate is 7% in five years, and they change to bi-weekly payments of $700. How long would it take them to retire the mortgage?

(e) Suppose that at the end of three years after the initial mortgage, interest rates are 6.5% for a two-year mortgage. For a penalty payment equal to the next month's interest added to the principal, Gilles and Lisette can switch to this rate for the two years remaining in the term of the mortgage, while continuing to make the same monthly payment. Thus, they would pay off the principal faster for two years until the renewal date. At that time, the terms would again be open, and the bank would adjust the interest rate to the market rate. Should they make the switch?

11. Mr. Maxi has hired you to sell his house and the direct market comparison method seems to be the best way to establish a price for Mr. Maxi's house. You have compiled the following information:

Features	Mr. Maxi's House	Sale 1	Sale 2	Sale 3
Selling Price	N/A	$220,000	$200,000	$250,000
Time of Sale		recent	3 months	recent
Lot Size	50' × 110'	50' × 110'	48' × 110'	55' × 110'
House Size	2400 s.f.	2300 s.f.	2200 s.f.	2500 s.f.
Air Conditioning	no	yes	yes	yes
Fireplace	yes	yes	no	yes
Finished Rec. Rm.	no	no	yes	yes

Additional information:

 (i) House prices increased by 2% per month starting three months ago.
 (ii) Each foot of frontage on the lot costs $2,000.
(iii) Each 100 square foot of space costs $1,000.
 (iv) Air conditioning costs $1,000.
 (v) Fireplace costs $5,000.
 (vi) Finished recreation room costs $10,000.

Required:
Estimate the selling price of Mr. Maxi's house.

12. John and Lara are considering buying a house now that their combined gross income is $72,000. They have no debts and no savings to use for a down payment. Their goal is to buy a house in five years, financed with a first mortgage and no second mortgage. Currently, taxes are $300 per month on houses in the neighbourhood and price range they want. The legal fees, moving costs, and other costs are $4,000 in today's dollars. The inflation rate is

4% p.a., and they expect their salaries to rise by 5% p.a. This question could be done in either real or nominal dollars — explain which you are using and how to interpret the required savings figure in part (b).

(a) What is the maximum they can afford to pay for a house and still qualify for the first mortgage, assuming they have saved enough for a 25% down payment?

(b) How much do they have to save each year to make the down payment?

13. You are asked to estimate the market value of a 2800 s.f. two-storey house. You find that present construction cost per square foot for this type and quality of structure is $78. The lot size is 46′ × 110′, and the lots in the area sell for $870 per front foot.

The personal inspection of the property reveals that a storm door is damaged beyond repair and estimated replacement cost is $350 installed. A window in the living room is damaged and it will cost $900 to replace it.

The house also needs exterior and interior painting, which will cost about $4,600. About 200 square metres of broadloom is worn to the point of requiring immediate replacement. The cost to replace it with similar quality broadloom is $39/square metre. No other depreciation is evident.

14. Jonathan and Yuko have a combined gross income of $90,000. They have saved up $80,000 for purchasing their home. They want to buy their dream home, which is offered at $280,000. Property taxes on the house are about $4,000 per year. They are still paying off a car loan and a student loan at the rate of $444 per month and $295 per month, respectively. They want to borrow a conventional mortgage from the local bank, and the current residential mortgage rate for a five-year term is 7.2%, with an initial amortization period of 25 years. Legal fees, real estate commission, and other expenses are estimated to cost $6,000.

Required:

(a) What is the amount of the first mortgage?
(b) What is the monthly mortgage payment?
(c) Will they qualify for the first mortgage in (a) under normal bank lending requirements? Show your calculations.
(d) Assuming they qualify for the first mortgage, what will be the outstanding balance after five years?
(e) Suppose at the end of five years, the mortgage interest rate falls to 6.5%.
   (i) What will be the new monthly payment?
   (ii) If they switch to monthly payment of $1,500, how long would it take them to retire the mortgage?

(iii) If they switch to bi-weekly payments of $700 per period, how long would it take them to retire the mortgage?

15. Angela and Peter work for the Town of Michelina. Each has a gross salary of $40,000 per year, and this amount is expected to increase by 2.5% annually. Below is a statement of their assets and liabilities.

Assets

Cash (earning 0.25% annually)	$ 6,000
GICs (earning 1.5% annually)	5,000
CSBs (earning 2.75% annually)	7,000
Automobiles	32,000
Current residence (cost)	230,000

Liabilities

Credit cards (18% annual rate; 3% minimum payment on balance)	$ 10,000
Car loans ($500 per month, three years left)	15,000
Current property taxes (per year)	2,400

Mortgage (a mortgage loan of $165,000 was contracted two years ago)
Amortization period, 25 years
Three years left on the 7.0% five-year mortgage term

Angela and Peter want to purchase a new house costing $320,000. They may qualify for a blended 5.75% three-year mortgage with an amortization period of 20 years. Property taxes on the new residence are $3,600 per year. They think they can sell their current residence for $247,900 and incur legal, real estate, and land transfer fees totalling $7,500. They hope that the net proceeds from the sale of their current residence will be applied as a desired down payment of $80,000 on their new house. If the net proceeds are less than $80,000, then they will use some of their cash savings to ensure that their down payment is $80,000.

(a) Will they have the $80,000 down payment needed from the sale of the current residence?
(b) What is the monthly mortgage payment on the new house, assuming they have the $80,000 down payment? Will they qualify for the new mortgage loan?
(c) Suppose Angela and Peter have a provision in their new mortgage agreement that allows them to renew their mortgage in three years at the current rate for five years by making a payment of $20,000 three years from today and $25,000 eight years from today. If the monthly

mortgage payment remains the same, how long will it take them to pay off the new mortgage?

(d) Angela is considering a second alternative. She thinks that, instead of buying a new house, they should apply for a $55,000 home equity loan on which the interest rate will be 4% and the minimum monthly payment will be twice the interest payment. They will use the $55,000 to purchase a condominium on which there will be a conventional mortgage. Would they quality for the home equity loan? Ignoring legal and real estate fees, what is the maximum purchase price for the condominium?

16. Cecilia and Matt finally find a house, which they really love. The asking price is $250,000 and last year's property tax bill was $2,340. They offer to purchase the house for $240,000, providing that they can arrange adequate financing. They have saved $45,000 for a down payment. Matt's gross annual salary is $42,000 while Cecilia's part-time salary is $18,000 annually. They have $25,000 in mutual funds, which they are willing to liquidate so that they have their required down payment. Their current debts include a car loan, which costs $360 monthly and an RRSP loan, which costs $340 a month. Matt and Cecilia do not like interest rate volatility and are considering a five-year mortgage with a fixed rate of 7.15% to be amortized over 25 years. Also, they have the option of making a repayment of $15,000 at the end of year 5 and at the end of year 10.

(a) Will Cecilia and Matt be eligible for a conventional mortgage if their purchase offer is accepted by the vendor?

(b) Assuming that they have the required down payment, will they qualify for a mortgage loan?

(c) What is the monthly payment if they qualify for a mortgage loan?

(d) How much interest will they pay over 25 years, assuming that interest rates remain the same and they make no repayments?

(e) Compare the difference in total interest, and the effect on the time to repay the mortgage, if Cecilia and Matt make a repayment of $15,000 after five years?

(f) How long will they take to repay the mortgage if they make a repayment of $15,000 at the end of year 5 and another repayment of $15,000 at the end of year 10?

17. You are working for Justway.com and have an annual salary of $50,000. You make a monthly payment of $250 on your credit cards and have $20,000 in mutual funds earning about 9.8% annually. You want to buy a house in four years for about $200,000 with annual property taxes of $1,800. You decide that you will save $300 a month, which you will invest in mutual funds earning 9.8% annually. You estimate that the inflation rate will

average about 2.5% annually over the next four years. Your combined tax rate is 35%. You will have to pay about $6,000 in legal and related fees when you purchase your house in four years.

(a) Will you have enough funds to qualify for a conventional mortgage and pay legal and related fees in four years?

(b) Instead of saving $300 a month, you want to apply that amount towards a four-year loan you are considering. The interest rate on the loan is 6.25% annually. You will invest the loan in a dividend fund that offers to pay 12% compounded monthly. What is the maximum loan you qualify for?

(c) With the loan obtained in part (c), will you reach your goal of having enough funds to cover the down payment and legal and related fees?

(d) If you cannot reach your goal in part (a) of having enough funds to meet the down payment and legal and related fees, what is the leverage ratio necessary to achieve your goal?

(e) Suppose it is four years later and you are renting a house similar to the one you are thinking of purchasing. The monthly rent is $1,400. Is the house a good investment?

CHAPTER 14

Principles of Investment

How should an investor measure the *risk* and *return* of different investments? How should a family trade off higher returns for higher risk? Why is it always important to *diversify*? What are implications of an *efficient market* for personal investing? Learn these essential principles of investment management in this chapter.

LEARNING OBJECTIVES

➢ *To discuss the first basic principle in investment: the risk–return trade-off. The basic concepts of return, risk, and risk aversion will be described.*

➢ *To discuss the second basic principle in investment: "One should diversify." The various aspects of diversification — diversification over time, portfolio diversification, international diversification, and asset allocation diversification will be discussed.*

➢ *To discuss the third basic principle in investment: the efficient market hypothesis. We shall answer some frequently asked questions such as:*
  ➤ *Is it possible to make a killing in the stock market by picking the right stocks?*
  ➤ *Is it possible to time the market (i.e., buy at the bottom and sell at the top)?*
  ➤ *Can one benefit from looking at charts?*
  ➤ *Is there any way to "beat" the market?*
  ➤ *Is it possible for one to get rich from the stock market?*

Investing is a very important part of personal finance. When people think of personal finance, they immediately think of investing. Of course, you now know that investing — although it is very important — is, nevertheless, just one of the components of personal finance. Most of us have some kind of investments at any point in time. If you have some money in a savings account, you have an investment.

There have been two major developments in the investment world in the last three decades. First, there has been an enormous expansion in scholarly knowledge about investments. Hundreds of research studies about investing have been done both in the business and academic world. As a result, we can fairly say we now know a great deal more about investment than we did 40 years ago. The second development is the enormous explosion of investment products available, even for the small investor. As a result, even the experts find it difficult to keep up with all of the new investments that come to the market every day.

This is the first of three chapters about investing. This chapter describes the fundamentals of investing and discusses the three most important concepts and findings of over 40 years of research. We will call these the **three basic principles of investment**. These principles and the concepts therein are the basic knowledge that you should have before you venture out into the investment world. The next chapter introduces and describes the different types of investments available in the Canadian market. Finally, in Chapter 16 we introduce and discuss mutual funds, which provide the most efficient means for small investors to implement their investment programs.

At the end of this chapter, you will have a firm foundation of knowledge about investment. This knowledge is a summary of a substantial part of over 40 years' research in investments. You will then be ready to go to Chapter 15 to examine the different types of investments available in Canada.

Investing and Saving

First, investing and saving are two different concepts. **Saving** is simply the money that you did not spend; it is money left over after your consumption. Thus, the money that you take from under a pillow and put into a safe or safe-deposit box is *savings*.

What is investing, then? **Investing** means using the savings that you have and "making it work" — putting it in investments to earn a rate of return. Normally, saving money by itself will not be enough to achieve your financial goals. As we have seen in Chapter 3, in goal setting, in order to reach your financial goal normally you have to earn a minimum rate of return. The only way to earn the required rate of return is by putting money into the right investment that is expected to generate the required rate of return. Thus, you invest because you want to reach your financial goals.

BASIC CHARACTERISTICS OF AN INVESTMENT

All investment — stocks, bonds, real estate, term deposits, gold, and so on — have some basic characteristics that affect your investment decisions. The following are the more important characteristics:

1. Return
2. Risk
3. Liquidity
4. Marketability
5. Term (short term, long term)
6. Management
7. Tax considerations
8. Divisibility

While all these characteristics affect an investor's investment decision, the first two — return and risk — are the most important.

Return on Investment

There are two ways that an investment can earn a return for you: an income return and a capital gain return. The **income return** is the periodic cash flow that the investor receives. For example, if you have a rental apartment, the periodic rental income (net of all expenses) is the income return. If you own a bond, the interest income that you receive is the income return. In the case of a stock, the dividend income is the income return. A **capital gain return** of an investment is generated when you sell it for a price higher than what you paid for it. For example, if you sell a stock for $20 and you bought it for $15, the capital gain return is ($20 – $15) or $5. The **total return** is defined as the income return plus the capital gain return.

Rate of Return

In order to compare returns of different investments, it is more useful to define return in terms of a rate, as follows. The **rate of return** (r) or **holding period return** (*HPR*) is defined as follows:

$$r \ (or \ \text{HPR}) = \frac{P_1 - P_0 + D}{P_0} \tag{1}$$

where P_0 = the price at the beginning of the holding period
  P_1 = the price at the end of the holding period
  D = the income return (interest or dividend) during the holding period

Example 14.1 John bought a stock at the beginning of the year for $20. At the end of the year he sold it for $25. During the year he received total dividend income of $1. The rate of return ($r$) or the holding period return (*HPR*) is equal to [($25 – $20 + $1) ÷ $20] or 30%.

Note that for a bank account or a Canada Savings Bond (because there is no capital gain) the rate of return is simply the rate of interest.

Expected Return E(r) vs. Realized Return

The **realized rate of return** is the rate of return that has actually occurred in a past period. If we look at any historical period — such as the year January 1, 1991, to December 31, 1991, or the period from February 15, 1990, to March 31, 1990 — all the prices and the income are known with certainty, so we simply calculate the rate of return actually earned during that period, using equation (1). The realized rate of return can be positive, zero, or negative.

The **expected rate of return** is the return that is expected to happen in the future. It is what we are expecting to earn for buying and holding the investment. More precisely, the expected rate of return, *E(r)*, is defined as follows:

$$E(r) = \frac{E(P_1) - P_0 + E(D)}{P_0} \qquad (2)$$

where P_0 = the price today, or the beginning of the period; and
$E(D)$ = the expected income during the period.

Example 14.2: Tony received a call today from his stockbroker, who recommended a stock currently selling for $10. The stockbroker said his company's research department had just published a very favourable forecast on the stock. According to the report, the stock price is expected to rise to $20 after one year. Last year the stock paid a dividend of $1. It is not expected that the company will increase its dividend in the near future. Based on the stockbroker's information, what is the expected rate of return?

Assuming Tony forms his expectation according to the broker's research report, then he would expect the stock price, *E(P₁)*, to be $20; and he would expect to receive dividends, *E(D)*, of $1. Hence, the expected rate of return, using equation (2) is as follows:

$$E(r) = \frac{E(P_1) - P_0 + E(D_1)}{P_0}$$

$$= \frac{(20 - 10 + 1)}{10}$$

$$= 110\%$$

Note that in the above example, the rate of return is not guaranteed because the future price and dividends are uncertain. The actual rate of return may turn out to be higher or lower than 110% — this is what risk is about.

INVESTMENT RISKS

What do people mean when they say an investment is *risky*? To some people, this simply means the probability of losing their invested money. In other words, risk means the probability of a negative rate of return on investment: the higher the probability of a negative rate of return, the higher the risk of the investment. This, however, is only one type of risk.

TABLE 14.1 Annual Return Series 1957–2010		
Investments	**Arithmetic Mean (%)**	**Standard Deviation (%)**
Treasury Bills	6.39	3.84
Long-term Canada Bonds	7.87	7.99
S&P/TSX Composite	10.74	17.03
S&P 500 (U.S. Stocks)	10.58	15.91
International Stocks (1970–2010)	10.35	16.43
For a benchmark, look at inflation:		
Inflation (CPI)	3.98	3.15

Suppose the rate of return on a stock was 6% during a period when the rate of return on a term deposit was 8%. Even though the rate of return on the stock was not negative, it was still a "loss" because you could have earned a higher return of 8% in a term deposit. You would not have put your money in the stock if you had known for sure that the return would be 6%. This suggests a more precise definition and measure of risk.

Risk is the uncertainty about the rate of return that you will earn from an investment. One way to measure risk is the **variability** in an investment's rate of return. Investments with more variability in their rate of return are riskier than investments with less variability because the larger the variability, the higher the probability of getting a rate of return lower than the expected rate of return.

A more formal treatment is to look at the rate of return, r, defined in equation (1), as a random variable. At the time you make the investment, only P_0 is known; P_1 and D are future values and, as such, are uncertain. Because P_1 and D are random variables, r is also a random variable. The expected value of the random variable r is the expected rate of return, $E(r)$. The most commonly used measure of the variability (or the spread) of a random variable is the *standard deviation*.[1] In the investment literature, one of the popular measures of risk is the standard deviation of the rate of return.

Table 14.1 shows the arithmetic average nominal rate of return and standard deviation of some major Canadian investments. The last column is the standard deviation, based on historical data from 1957 to 2010, of the different investments. Using the standard deviation as a measure of risk, we see that stocks are the

---

[1] We assume that the reader knows the basic statistical concepts of expected value (or mean) and standard deviation. See next section for formulas.

TABLE 14.2						
Range in Which 68% of the Investment Returns Would Fall						
Investments	**Expected Range**					
Treasury Bills	6.39%	±	3.84%	=	2.55% to 10.23%	
Long-term Cda Bonds	7.87%	±	7.99%	=	−0.12% to 15.86%	
S&P/TSX Composite	10.74%	±	17.03%	=	−6.29% to 27.77%	
S&P 500	10.58%	±	15.91%	=	−5.33% to 26.49%	
International Stocks	10.35%	±	16.43%	=	−6.08% to 26.78%	

riskiest, long-term bonds are less risky and, as expected, government treasury bills are the least risky.

To further elaborate on why the standard deviation is a measure of risk, let us assume that the rates of return are normally distributed for all five investments: treasury bills, long-term bonds, common stocks, small company stocks, and international stocks. From basic statistics, 68% of the investment's returns over the period will fall between the mean minus the standard deviation and the mean plus the standard deviation. Table 14.2 shows the ranges for the five investments. Note that the bigger the standard deviation, the bigger the range (or spread) and the bigger the variability in the investment's rate of return. In other words, the bigger the standard deviation, the greater the risk of the investment.

Another Measure of Risk: Beta

In the academic investment literature, there is another measure of risk of an investment. This measure of risk is called **beta**. It measures the co-movement of the stock's return with the stock market's return. Beta measures the risk of the investment relative to the risk of the market. The higher the value of beta, the more sensitive the stock is to moves in the market. Beta is defined in such a way that the stock market has a beta of 1. Here, the stock market is usually represented by a market index; the S&P/TSX Composite Index is an example. If a stock has a beta of .5, this means its risk is only half that of the S&P/TSX Composite. If the stock has a beta of 2, this means its risk is two times that of the S&P/TSX Composite.

Total Risk

The idea of using the standard deviation[2] of an investment's rate of return is a fundamental concept in academic investment literature. The **total risk** of an

---

[2] Some people use the variance, which is simply the square of the standard deviation.

investment is defined as the standard deviation of its rate of return. Thus, the total risk measures the total variability or volatility of an investment. Since investment decisions are based on future returns, much care must go into estimating the expected returns and the expected risk statistics (i.e., standard deviation, or beta) for all the investments under consideration. This is the security analyst's job. There are books that describe explicitly the techniques and the procedures that security analysts use to estimate risk and return statistics;[3] it is beyond the scope of this book to go into these estimation techniques in depth.

For most investments, there are two ways to formulate a probability distribution (including the expected value and the standard deviation) of the possible rates of return. First, an **objective probability distribution** is formed by measuring objective historical data. For example, one can estimate the mean and the standard deviation of the rate of return on a stock (such as the common stock of the Bank of Montreal) by using five years of monthly data. In other words, one calculates the actual rate of return for each month of an historical five-year period and then uses basic statistical formulas to calculate the mean and the standard deviation. One then uses this historical probability distribution as an approximation for the future probability distribution. This approach is useful only if the investment's rate of return probability distribution is stationary — in other words, if it does not change — over time. Fortunately, empirical studies have found that most firms' probability distributions of rates of return and the statistics describing them (e.g., the mean and the standard deviation) do not seem to change very much over time. Thus, using objective probability distribution is very popular, at least as a first approximation.

The second method for estimating an investment's probability distribution is to forecast the future in some way. A **subjective probability distribution** is formed by writing down one's perception of all the possible rates of return of the investment and then assigning probabilities to them. Table 14.3 is an example of a subjective probability distribution of the rate of return on an investment.

Recall from basic statistics that the expected rate of return, $E(r)$ (i.e., the expected value), and the standard deviation, $S.D.$, are given by equations (1) and (2):

$$E(r) = \sum_i P_i\, r_i \tag{1}$$

$$S.D. = \left[\sum_i P_i\, [r_i - E(r)]^2 \right]^{1/2} \tag{2}$$

---

[3] For example, J.C. Francis and E. Kirzner, *Investments Analysis and Management*, First Canadian Edition (Toronto: McGraw-Hill Ryerson, 1988).

TABLE 14.3	
Example of a Subjective Probability Distribution	
Outcome (possible rate of return), r_i	Subjective probability of the outcome, p_i
.35	.10
.25	.15
.15	.20
.10	.30
−.05	.15
−.20	.10
	1.00

The expected rate of return of the investment in Table 14.3 is:

$$= (.35 \times .10) + (.25 \times .15) + (.15 \times .20) + (.10 \times .30) - (.05 \times .15) - (.20 \times .10)$$
$$= .105 \text{ or } 10.5\%$$

The standard deviation (*S.D.*) on the rate of return, using equation (2), is:

$$= \left\{ \begin{array}{l} [.10 \times (.35 - .105)^2] + [.15 \times (.25 - .105)^2] \\ + [.20 \times (.15 - .105)^2] + [.30 \times (.10 - .105)^2] \\ + [.15 \times (-.05 - .105)^2] + [.1 \times (-.20 - .105)^2] \end{array} \right\}^{1/2}$$

$$= (.0225)^{\frac{1}{2}}$$
$$= .150 \text{ or } 15\%$$

Most financial and scientific calculators have functions that will calculate mean and standard deviation for you. To get them to calculate expected values using probabilities, you may need to trick the calculator by multiplying the probabilities by 100 and calling them frequencies. The mean and standard deviation of a distribution of 10 outcomes at 35%, 15 outcomes at 25%, etc., are the same as for a distribution of 10% chance of 35% return, 15% chance of 25% return, etc. The exact keys and steps vary by calculator.

The Risk-free Asset

There are investments whose rates of return are guaranteed. In other words, the rate of return is equal to a certain guaranteed rate of return with a probability of one. For this type of investment, there is no variability in the rate, and the standard deviation is zero. Such an investment is called a **risk-free asset**. The best example of a risk-free asset is a short-term government **treasury bill** or **T-bill**. This is a short-term note issued by the government. T-bills are sold in the money market and are priced in such a way that if you hold them until maturity, the rate of return is guaranteed.

If you invest your money in T-bills, the so-called risk-free asset, is your investment really risk-free? The answer is no. First, it depends on inflation. Although T-bills guarantee a nominal rate of return on your investment, they do not guarantee the purchasing power of your money — that would depend on the rate of inflation during the holding period. This is called **inflation risk**. Second, if your investment horizon is longer than the maturity period of the T-bill, which usually has short maturities of 60 days, 90 days, 120 days, and so on, up to one year, then you have to reinvest your money into another T-bill when the first one matures. The rate of return on the future T-bill is uncertain. It could be higher or lower than the current rate. This is called **reinvestment risk**.

Other Risk Factors

This section introduces some other investment risk factors. The variability of an investment's rate of return is not the only source of risk, even though it is a very important one. As we have discussed, even putting money in the risk-free asset is not necessarily risk-free!

Default Risk

Default risk is the risk of losing part or all of the future cash flow that the investor expects to get when making the investment initially. For example, when one buys a corporate bond, one expects to receive the promised interest income periodically and the principal when the bond matures. The company may become bankrupt or run into financial difficulty and therefore be unable to make payments. In this latter case, we say the company has defaulted on its obligation. Other default risks are systematically related to the economy, which affect almost all companies. Some default risks are caused by factors that are unique to the afflicted company, such as losing a lawsuit.

Interest Rate Risk

This is the risk that is caused by the changes in the level of market interest rates, which affect the values of all assets. In general, asset values will rise when interest rates fall and they will fall when interest rates rise.

Liquidity Risk

This is the risk of not being able to cash in your investment in time of need. For example, it may take a long time to sell investments like real estate.

Reinvestment Risk

This is the risk associated with the uncertainty of not knowing at what rates of return your money can be reinvested in the future. Suppose you have a term deposit that will mature next month. Since you do not need the money, you plan to reinvest it then; however, you won't know the rate of return on your reinvestment for another month.

Inflation Risk

This is the risk that the return on your investment will not keep up with inflation. Investments that are expected to keep pace with inflation are called **inflation hedges**. Normally, short-term financial investments like short-term T-bills or money market funds have little inflation risk because their rates will change fast enough to reflect the changing inflation rates.

RISK AND RETURN TRADE-OFF

Risk Aversion

People do not like risk. Given two investments that are identical in every respect except for risk, people will choose the investment with the lower risk. This behaviour is called **risk aversion**.[4] This does not mean that people will not take risk. Risk aversion implies only that people require higher returns for taking greater risks.

Return: An Increasing Function of Risk

Assuming that all investors are risk-averse, investments will be priced in the marketplace to reflect this behaviour. In order to induce investors to take risk, some incentive will be given in the form of a higher return. Given two investments, one riskier than the other, they will be priced in the marketplace so that the rate of return on the riskier investment will be higher than that of the less risky one. Over 40 years of research, effort has been devoted to establishing this fact rigorously. We will call this the **first fundamental principle in investment**: The expected rate of return on an investment is an increasing function of its risk. The higher the risk of an investment, the higher the expected rate of return. Thus, risk and rate of return go hand in hand. If you want a higher rate of return on your investment, you will have to accept a greater exposure to risk.

---

[4] People who choose the riskier of the two investments are said to be **risk-loving**. People who are indifferent between the safer investment and the riskier one are said to be **risk-neutral**. From casual observation, very few people are risk-loving or risk-neutral.

Dominance

Given two investments, A and B, if A is always preferred to B for all investors, then we say A *dominates* B. We will provide two examples. First, suppose A and B have the same expected rate of return but B is riskier than A. Then A is always preferred to B by all investors. As a second example, suppose A and B have the same level of risk but A has a higher expected return than B. Then A is always preferred to B by all investors.

We cannot, however, rank all investments by the **dominance** concept. Suppose there are two investments, C and D, and that C is riskier than D but C has a higher expected return. In this case, we cannot make any statement about which dominates which. In the last 40 years, much research effort has been devoted to comparing investments with different risks and returns, and we have now some well-known theories and economic models that measure the **risk–return trade-off**.[5] These theories are quite popular in the academic world and some professional investment managers use them. However, using these theories requires a great deal of data, time, and effort. Unless you have a huge multi-million-dollar investment portfolio to manage, these theories will not be very useful to you.

As a practical matter, it is more important for you to remember that there are two important attributes of any investment — risk and return — and they go hand in hand. High returns are generally associated with high risks; this being the case, the next time you get a cold call from a stockbroker who recommends a stock that he says will double in a week, the word *risk* should immediately come to your mind. One of the biggest mistakes you can make in the world of investment is to fall for stockbrokers' phone pitches. It is this mistake that causes the investor to end up with a substantial portion of his or her net worth invested in a very risky proposition. We summarize the risk–return trade-off in Figure 14.1. To reiterate, in the field of investments, there is a positive relationship between risk and return. The more risk you take, the higher the return that you should expect to get from the investment.

DIVERSIFICATION

Is it possible for individuals to lower their investment risk exposure without sacrificing their expected return on investment? The answer is yes — through the strategy of diversification. **Diversification** means putting one's money into a broad basket of

---

[5] The Capital Asset Pricing Model (CAPM) and the Arbitrage Pricing Theory (APT) are two well-known examples. While they can be used to price any investment, empirical studies found that they are more accurate when used to compare portfolios.

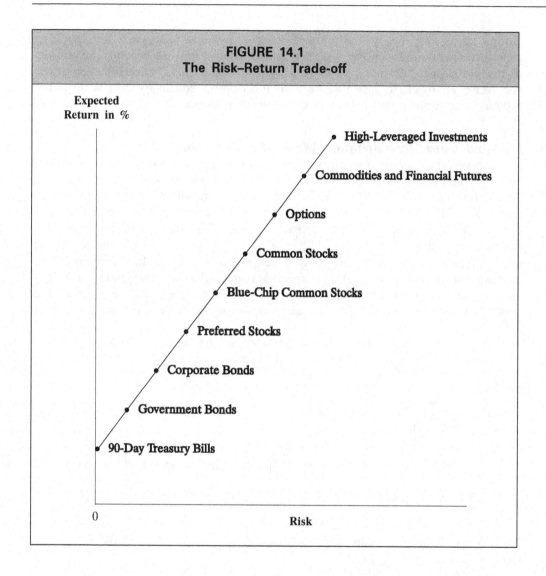

FIGURE 14.1
The Risk–Return Trade-off

Expected
Return in %

- High-Leveraged Investments
- Commodities and Financial Futures
- Options
- Common Stocks
- Blue-Chip Common Stocks
- Preferred Stocks
- Corporate Bonds
- Government Bonds
- 90-Day Treasury Bills

0
Risk

different investments. As we will explain later, for diversification to work, the investments chosen must not be perfectly correlated: This means that the stock prices of the investments chosen do not always move in the same direction (up or down) at the same time.

Diversification is such an important concept in investment that we will call it the **second basic principle of investment**. This principle simply says that you should avoid putting all of your investment in one kind or type — i.e., you should avoid putting all of your money into a single stock or a single bond issue. By spreading your investment funds among several different issues, you are proving the wisdom of the old saying, "Do not put all your eggs in one basket." Diversification is the risk-averse approach to investing because it involves reducing your risk exposure without necessarily sacrificing expected return on investment.

How Does Diversification Work? An Example

Suppose there are two investments, X and Y. Suppose your expectation of their rates of return are as follows: For half of all the future years, X will give an annual rate of return of 20% and half of the years it will give an annual rate of return of –5%. Y is expected to produce the same pattern: Half of the future years it yields 20%, and half of the future years it yields –5%. Suppose further that when the rate of return on X is 20%, the rate of return on Y is –5% and when the rate of return on X is –5%, the rate of return on Y is 20%. In other words, we suppose that X and Y are *perfectly negatively correlated* — i.e., they move in exactly opposite directions. When X is at its best, Y is at its worst and vice versa. The expected rates of return on X and Y, using equation (1), are respectively as follows:

$$E(r) \text{ of } X = (.5 \times .20) + (.5 \times -.05) = .075$$
$$E(r) \text{ of } Y = (.5 \times -.05) + (.5 \times .20) = .075$$

The standard deviations of the rates of return of X and Y are, respectively, and using equation (2):

$$\text{S.D. of } X = \{[.5 \times (.20 - .075)^2] + [.5 \times (-.05 - .075)^2]\}^{\frac{1}{2}} = .125$$
$$\text{S.D. of } Y = \{[.5 \times (-.05 - .075)^2] + [.5 \times (.20 - .075)^2]\}^{\frac{1}{2}} = .125$$

Thus, X and Y have the same expected rates of return of 7.5% and the same standard deviations (risk) of 12.5%.

Suppose you have $1,000. If you put all the $1,000 in either X or Y, you will expect to earn 7.5% and your risk exposure will be 12.5%. Now, suppose that you diversify, and allocate your $1,000 equally between X and Y — i.e., suppose that you invest $500 in X and $500 in Y. There are two possible outcomes on your investment. First, the rate of return on X is 20% and the rate of return on Y is –5%, then the rate of return on your investment is equal to:

$$\left[\frac{(\$500 \times .20) + (\$500 \times -.05)}{\$1,000}\right] = .075$$

Second, the rate of return on X is –5% and that on Y is 20%, then the rate of return on your investment is equal to:

$$\left[\frac{(\$500 \times -.05) + (\$500 \times .20)}{\$1,000}\right] = .075$$

Therefore, you will earn .075 or 7.5% with certainty.[6] This example shows that you can reduce risk — from 12.5% to zero — without sacrificing return, which stays at 7.5%. This is the benefit of diversification. In fact, you can often increase return and reduce risk.

Portfolio Theory

A **portfolio** is a collection of securities, so it is diversified in more than one asset. For example, you can have a stock portfolio that contains 10 stocks, or you can have a bond portfolio that contains 5 bonds. In the last four decades, economists have built rigorous **portfolio theories** that examine various ways of investing and diversifying efficiently. Such theories can be found in any standard textbook about investment.

The idea behind diversification and portfolio theory, however, is actually very simple. You choose investments that are not highly correlated with each other — that is to say, they do not move at the same time with the same magnitude. When one of the investments in the portfolio experiences a bad year, hopefully there are other investments in the portfolio that are having good years.

From basic statistics, the relationship between the returns on any two investments is expressed by the **correlation coefficient**, which measures the extent to which two sequences of numbers (in this case, the rates of return of two investments) move together. The correlation coefficient can range from –1 to +1. It is usually greater than zero for returns on investments because most investments are affected in the same way by the same economic factors such as interest rates and the rate of inflation. A correlation coefficient of zero means that the two investments are *uncorrelated*. For diversification to work effectively, ideally you should choose investments that are uncorrelated, or better still, *negatively correlated* with each other. Indeed, in our example, the investments X and Y are perfectly negatively correlated and for that reason we are able to derive the maximum reduction in risk — we ended up with a risk-free portfolio of which the standard deviation is zero! In practice, however, returns on assets are almost always positively correlated because to some extent they depend on the same economy. Still, for diversification purposes, you should select assets that have low correlation coefficients with each other.

---

[6] The standard deviation on the rate of return is zero. Why?

Figure 14.2 shows the reduction in **portfolio risk** (measured by the standard deviation of the rate of return of the portfolio) as assets are added to the portfolio. Notice in Figure 14.2 that the risk of the portfolio does not become zero, regardless of how many assets or stocks are added to the portfolio. This means that there is a certain amount of risk that cannot be reduced, no matter what kind of assets, and how many, are added. Thus, even if you hold every asset and every stock in the market, your portfolio is still risky because the entire market and the entire economy are risky. The risk that cannot be diversified away is called market risk, systematic risk, or undiversifiable risk.

How many shares would an equity portfolio require to achieve "enough diversification"? Cleary and Copp (1999) discuss this question and conclude that something like the TSX 60 index would be reasonable.[7] Domian et al. (2007) find that even 100 shares might not be enough in the U.S. market, which is broader than the Canadian market.[8] Another aspect of this question is which specific shares are chosen. An equity portfolio with 60 different oil and gas companies would not be properly diversified. In the language of finance theory, the shares should have as low correlations with each other as possible to get an efficiently diversified portfolio. While the individual investor is unlikely to have the technical skill and software to calculate a matrix of correlation coefficients, a good proxy is to choose companies that are in different businesses.

Three Dimensions of Diversification

There are three important reasons why you want to diversify your investments. First, you diversify to avoid having your money all tied up in one or a few investments that might do very poorly and wipe out your entire wealth.

Second, you diversify because you cannot perfectly predict the "hot" and the "cold" years of each investment category. In this case, the benefit of diversifying over time is that you avoid doing all the transactions in years with big losses so that you do not lose much on the average annual rate of return over a long time period. Third, you diversify globally to reduce the market risk (or systematic risk or undiversifiable risk or country risk) of the portfolio. As noted earlier, general economic conditions affect most investments within a single country, such as Canada. Diversifying across Canadian-based investments will not eliminate or reduce those general market factors — that is why the risk is called **undiversifiable risk** — but investing on an international scale will help. We will call these three reasons and the strategies for dealing with them the **three dimensions of diversification**:

---

[7] Sean Cleary and David Copp, "Diversification with Canadian Stocks: How Much is Enough?" *Canadian Investment Review*, (Fall 1999), 21–25.

[8] Dale L. Domian, David A. Louton, and Marie D. Racine, "Diversification in Portfolios of Individual Stocks: 100 Stocks Are Not Enough", *The Financial Review*, 42 (November 2007), 557–70.

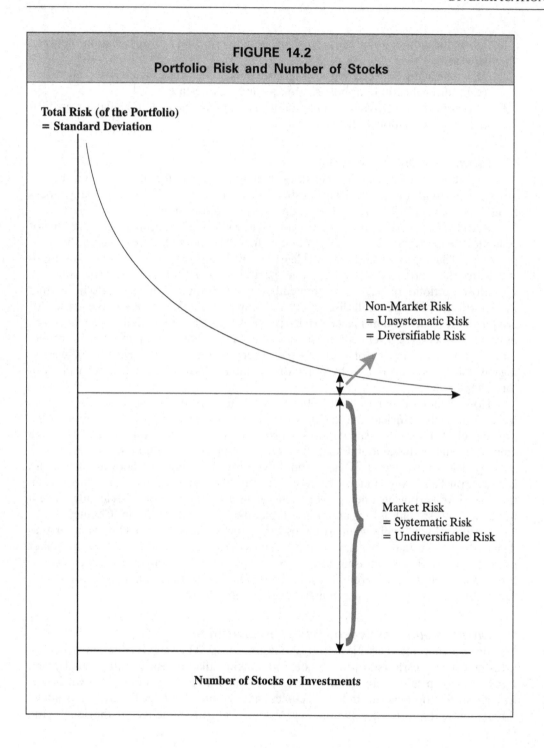

FIGURE 14.2
Portfolio Risk and Number of Stocks

Total Risk (of the Portfolio)
= Standard Deviation

Non-Market Risk
= Unsystematic Risk
= Diversifiable Risk

Market Risk
= Systematic Risk
= Undiversifiable Risk

Number of Stocks or Investments

1. Diversification within each type of investment (e.g., diversification between stocks)
2. Diversification between types of investments, sometimes called asset allocation (e.g., diversification in bonds, stocks, and real estate)
3. Diversification across different countries, sometimes called global diversification or international diversification

Diversification in Stocks

If you want to invest in the stock market, you should allocate your money among a portfolio of stocks. Two questions must be answered: (i) How many stocks should be bought? (ii) How should one choose those stocks?

Recall from earlier discussion (also see Figure 14.2 again) that the major reduction in portfolio risk comes from the first 20 stocks that you include in your portfolio. Thus, you should buy at least 20 different issues. Further addition of stocks to the portfolio will reduce the portfolio's risk but at a slower rate.

Most portfolio managers recommend at least 30 stocks in a portfolio so that the portfolio can be well-diversified, meaning that the **diversifiable risk** (or **unsystematic risk** or **non-market risk**) is almost totally diversified away; however, buying 30 stocks (or even 20) requires a substantial amount of investment capital that is beyond the means of most people. There is another effective way of achieving diversification and that is by purchasing mutual funds, a topic that we will leave for Chapter 16.

How should the set of 20 to 30 stocks be picked? As we shall see later when we introduce the efficient market hypothesis, the answer is surprisingly simple. One way to select a well-diversified portfolio is to randomly select the stocks. Although empirical studies have found that this random selection method works very well, most people think that it is counterintuitive. Another way of choosing the stocks is the "armchair" way: Let professional experts choose them for you. Once again, this may involve buying one or more mutual funds. The matter of selecting mutual funds for investment is an important topic that we will cover in Chapter 16.

Finally, if you really want to choose the stocks yourself, you may want first to divide the stocks into business or industrial groups (e.g., banks, utilities, consumer products, oil and gas, transportation, gold, etc.) and then randomly select two or three stocks within each group. Again, let us emphasize that empirical studies have found that there is little additional benefit from doing this.

Diversification between Types of Investment

Investments are classified into different types. The most common types of investments are cash (short-term safe investments like treasury bills), bonds, and stocks. One can add more to the above list — such as real estate, one's own home, foreign stocks, options, futures, collectibles, and so on — but traditionally the above three represent the most common way of classifying investments. In the long term, the rates of return on stocks are higher than those on bonds, which in turn are higher than treasury bill rates. (Of course, the riskiness of these assets is correlated.) However, over any short period in time, the rates of return may not follow the above order; indeed, there have been many periods in the past where bonds realized a higher return than stocks. If one could predict perfectly what investment type would do best at any point in time, one would invest all one's money in that type of investment and then move money from one investment type to another to maximize return. This is called **market timing**. This investment concept means that investors move their money into the investment type when the value is low, sell when it reaches its highest point, move the proceeds of the sale into another investment type whose value is low, and so on. It is important to remember, however, that this ideal strategy requires perfect prediction of what will do best in any given point in time. Studies have found that such perfect timing is almost impossible.

If one cannot predict what investment type will perform the best at any point in time, a natural approach will be to diversify across asset types — that is, have some of one's money invested in each major investment type at all times. Diversification between different types of investments is called **asset allocation**. Asset allocation works because the major asset types — stocks, bonds and cash — are not perfectly positively correlated. In fact, returns on cash (treasury bills) are often negatively correlated with stocks and bonds; therefore, the concept of portfolio diversification can be applied. You create a portfolio of cash, bonds, and stocks to achieve the desired "risk–return mix". In other words, you choose a portfolio that is expected to generate the rate of return that you want and the risk that is within your comfort zone.[9]

Diversification across Different Countries

As discussed earlier, even if you hold every stock in the Canadian stock market, the **market risk (systematic risk)** will still remain. This is the risk of all the economic conditions within Canada that affect all investments. Broadening your horizons by investing in the investments of other countries will help because their economic conditions are not perfectly correlated with those of Canada. By combining investments of different countries whose patterns of return are different, an international portfolio achieves a less volatile rate of return and hence reduces your risk exposure. This is called **international diversification** or **global diversification**.

---

[9] Computer software, such as PlanPlus, will compute the allocation among cash, stocks, and bonds. You may add other investment types such as foreign stocks. The program requires historical data or information about asset returns, and your acceptable level of risk (or your required rate of return).

Can the Average Person Do It?

The second fundamental principle of investment — diversification — has many implications as to what you should do with your money. First, you should put some money into each of the major types of investments — cash, bonds, stocks, foreign stocks, etc. Second, within each type of investment, you should diversify; as mentioned, where feasible, you should hold about 20 to 30 stocks in the stock portfolio.

Can individuals who are thinking of saving at most a few hundred dollars a month benefit from these recommendations? How can they afford to buy so many stocks? The answer may lie in *mutual funds*. Mutual funds allow a person with modest savings to benefit from all the knowledge and most of the investment products developed in recent years. Indeed, with the proper knowledge of how to use mutual funds, an average person (in terms of wealth) is no more disadvantaged than a wealthy person.

THE EFFICIENT MARKET

The stock market is said to be an **efficient market** if current stock prices always reflect all information (past, current, and future) about the company, the industry, and the general economy. If there is good news or bad news that affects a stock, this information will be immediately incorporated into the stock price. The implication is that for a small investor, there are no bargains available.

Is the market efficient? This is the question that hundreds of research studies have tried to answer in the last 30 or 40 years. Their findings are so important that we will call this the **third fundamental principle of investing**. The efficient market hypothesis says that the financial markets (which include the stock market, the bond market, the option market, and the futures market) are efficient: Stock prices reflect all the relevant information at any point in time.

There are several implications for the investor:

1. Stocks are fairly valued at any point in time. The bad news about this is that there are no undervalued stocks. The good news is that there are no overvalued stocks, either. This means that you will never have to second-guess the fair value of a stock.

2. There is no need for you to spend time on drawing charts, analyzing stocks, learning fancy techniques for picking stocks, or forecasting the turning points of the market because none of these will help you to gain any superior performance on your investment.

3. The best investment strategy is a **buy-and-hold strategy**. You simply buy a stock that fits your desired risk–return mix and hold that stock until the end of your investment horizon. More important, you should not trade actively

because trading will not improve your investment performance. Rather, trading will incur heavy commissions or transaction costs.

4. Do not buy stocks because of news or "hot tips". By the time you know the information everybody in the market also already knows it.

What Should an Investor Do in an Efficient Market?

The efficient market implications do not negate what we have discussed so far. In other words, you should still concentrate on doing the right things:

1. Based on your financial goal and your risk preference, determine your desired risk–return mix. For example, do you prefer a portfolio with $E(r) = .15$ and $S.D. = .20$ or a portfolio with $E(r) = .10$ and $S.D. = .15$?

2. Buy a diversified portfolio of investments to achieve your desired risk–return mix.

3. Diversify along the three dimensions of diversifications — within the type of investment, across different types of investment, and internationally.

4. Reduce the costs of buying and selling investments — for example, by trading less, using a discount broker, adopting a buy-and-hold strategy, etc.

5. Reduce taxes on investment returns — for example, by comparing the after-tax return from different sources of income — interest, dividends, capital gains.

6. Learn how to choose the proper mutual funds, which will be covered in Chapter 16.

Market Inefficiencies

The stock market is not perfectly efficient. A few techniques have been found to select stocks that give above-average returns on investments, even after adjusting for risk. However, these **market inefficiencies** are relatively small and, unless you have a large portfolio, it is quite uneconomical for a small investor to exploit any of them. The potential benefits are normally not enough to justify the time and effort that must be spent to exploit these market inefficiencies.

The best-known ones are the **small firm effect** and the **January effect**. Researchers have discovered that smaller companies listed on stock exchanges tend to have higher than average returns, even after adjusting for their risk. The evidence isn't perfect, however, because the methods of adjusting for risk and the statistical techniques are contentious. Many mutual funds have developed small cap funds. Nonetheless, the average excess returns are not enormously greater and the risk seems to be higher as well.

Researchers have also found that share prices tend to be lower in December and then rise in January. The effect is not large, but the small retail investor who can afford to time purchases might try to do them in late December. The often-cited reason for this is people selling losing holdings at year-end to establish capital losses to set against capital gains. More careful research does not support this as the only cause, so we still don't know why we see this pattern.

THE LONG vs. THE SHORT RUN

One thing we haven't discussed is your time horizon. We all have a limited lifespan, and so we have finite horizons. A company, or a mutual fund with an ever-renewing supply of investors, has infinite horizons and should always look to the long run. The average lifespan of a North American male is over 70 years and a female can expect to live to her late 70s. If you are now 50 years old, you can expect to live to an even greater age, on average, since you have successfully escaped such common killers as childhood diseases, child-bearing, and military service in a war. Therefore, you should look to the long run in your investment decisions now.

In the long run, we have an effect that some authors call **time diversification**. If you hold riskier assets over a long time period, they will almost certainly return more than a less risky portfolio. We are not suggesting an undiversified portfolio within an asset class but, rather, a diversified portfolio concentrated on the riskier classes, such as real estate and equity. The effect is that, over time, the losses from the bad years are more than overcome by the good years, and you should get the higher mean return shown in Table 14.1. A portfolio of bonds cannot offer very high returns over 30 years, but a portfolio of common shares likely will. As long as your holding period is expected to exceed 10 years, the portfolio of risky assets will almost certainly yield you more money at the end than a portfolio of safe assets.

For most people in the early and middle stages of the life cycle, therefore, investment in equities is preferred. If you will have an early need for money you might wish to stick to a low risk, liquid portfolio, but such a situation is not common. We think that a planned purchase of a house or other major asset is the most likely exception. We will deal with the question of time diversification in more detail when we talk about retirement planning.

SUMMARY

In this chapter, we introduce and describe many basic concepts in investment. We summarize the most important findings of over 40 years of research in three fundamental principles of investment:

1. The most important attributes of any investment are its expected return and risk. Return and risk go hand and hand. If you want to earn a higher return, you must take more risk.

2. An investor should diversify according to the three dimensions of diversification:
   (a) Diversify across assets within the same investment type.
   (b) Diversify across different types of investments.
   (c) Diversify internationally.

3. The financial markets, and especially the stock markets, are fairly efficient.

   We explain the importance of these three basic investment principles and how they would affect your investment program. We provide a list of basic instructions on how to invest in an efficient market. Finally, we point out that if you have a long investment horizon (over 10 years), you should concentrate your investments in the riskier asset classes since they will almost always give you a higher return as long as you hold them for a long time period.

MULTIPLE-CHOICE REVIEW QUESTIONS

1. Which of the following can never be negative?

   (a) The real rate of interest
   (b) The realized rate of return on a bond
   (c) The holding period return on a stock
   (d) The standard deviation on the rate of return on a stock
   (e) The correlation coefficient between two stocks

2. If the stock market is efficient, it implies _____.

   (a) one cannot outperform the market consistently
   (b) stocks are fairly valued at any point in time
   (c) the best investment strategy is to buy and hold
   (d) (a) and (b) only
   (e) (a), (b), and (c)

3. The risk and return trade-off implies _____.

   (a) the higher the risk of an investment, the higher the expected return
   (b) the lower the default risk on a bond, the higher the holding period return
   (c) it is impossible to get rich in the stock market
   (d) that one must diversify to reduce risk
   (e) none of the above

   The following information applies to questions 4 and 5.

   Lisa Sadowska purchased 100 shares of AMB Inc. one year ago. She paid $11 per share and, at the time of purchase, she expected the company would pay a dividend of 50 cents per share and that the stock price would increase to $13 after one year. The actual dividend paid was 40 cents per share, and she just sold her stocks for $11.50 per share.

4. The expected rate of return on the stock was _____ .

    (a) 8.18%
    (b) 22.73%
    (c) 18.18%
    (d) 21.82%
    (e) 4.55%

5. The realized rate of return was _____ .

    (a) 8.18%
    (b) 3.48%
    (c) 22.73%
    (d) 20.87%
    (e) 17.27%

DISCUSSION QUESTIONS

1. Define or explain each of the following terms:

    characteristics of an investment / diversification: portfolio — portfolio theory — correlation coefficient — portfolio risk — market (non-market) risk — systematic (unsystematic) risk — diversifiable (undiversifiable) risk / efficient market: market inefficiency — buy-and-hold strategy / inflation hedges / investing / measure of risk: beta — total risk — objective probability distribution — subjective probability distribution / return on investment: rate of return — income return — capital gain return — holding period return / risk factors: default risk — interest rate risk — liquidity risk — inflation risk / risk-free asset / risk–return trade-off: risk aversion — dominance / saving / three dimensions of diversification: mutual fund — asset allocation — global diversification or international diversification / time diversification

2. How do we measure the risk and the return of an investment?

3. Why are investments issued by the government default-risk free?

4. What is the advantage of investing in stocks as compared to investing in bonds?

5. Is investing in a government treasury bill risk free? Discuss.

6. Your stockbroker called you with a "hot tip" and he said the stock would double in one month. How are you going to respond?

7. "The efficient market implies that you can never get rich by playing the stock market." Comment and discuss.

8. Discuss the concept of dominance of one stock over another.

9. How does diversification help investors?

10. How can investors diversify?

PROBLEMS

1. Calculate the expected rate of return and standard deviation of the following stock:

rate of return	probability
−.015	.08
−.010	.12
0	.25
.120	.20
.170	.20
.200	.15

2. Calculate the expected rates of return and the risk of the following investments:

Investment A		Investment B	
rate of return	probability	rate of return	probability
−.10	.05	−.20	.05
−.05	.10	−.10	.10
0	.15	−.05	.10
.08	.30	0	.15
.14	.25	.10	.20
.20	.10	.20	.25
.25	.05	.30	.10
		.40	.05

Can you say anything about dominance?

3. **Personal Project 1**
Assessing your risk–return preference.

(a) Choose one of your financial goals. If you do not have one yet, go back to Chapter 3, follow the suggestions there, and set a financial goal.

(b) Based on your current wealth and expected future savings, what is the required rate of return to achieve this goal?

367

(c) Find out from the newspaper at least three mutual funds that historically have generated your required rate of return in (b). Find out their historical standard deviations.

(d) Assuming that all the returns on the mutual funds are normally distributed, find the probability that you will lose money if you invest in each of the funds.

(e) For each of the three mutual funds, what is the probability that you will earn less than (i) 3%, (ii) 6%, (iii) 10%?

(f) Are the mutual funds' return-risk characteristics within your comfort zone?

4. Nathan, 33, recently won a lottery prize of $26,000. His goal is to retire at age 65, with $3 million in addition to his pensions (the contributions for his pension plans are automatically deducted from his paycheques). He is considering whether to invest his winnings in bonds or stocks.

(a) What rate of return must he earn in order to reach his goal?

(b) How would you advise him to invest the $26,000?

CHAPTER 15

Types of Investments

What a soup of odd names and acronyms the investment business has created — T-bills, GICs, CSBs, S&P/TSX, S&P/TSX 60, strip bond, CDIC, puttable bonds, Dow Jones, S&P 500, etc. These terms have entered into everyday language, but do you know what they mean when choosing among alternative investments? Read on for descriptions of the risk and return characteristics of everything from the humble bank account to the risky call option.

LEARNING OBJECTIVES

➢ *To describe the major investments such as treasury bills, Canada Savings Bonds, government and corporate bonds, preferred shares, common shares, mutual funds, and so on.*

➢ *To describe the characteristics of each investment — risk, return, liquidity, maturity, etc.*

➢ *To introduce very briefly other investments, such as options.*

In the last chapter, we introduced and discussed some fundamental concepts and theories in investment. We emphasized three particular topics that are very important in the investment literature. These three topics are summarized in terms of three fundamental principles in investment:

1. **Risk–return trade-off**
   Every investment has two important characteristics — *return* and *risk*. This principle says that return is a positive function of risk; the higher the risk of the investment, the higher the expected return.

2. **Diversification**
   This principle states that (i) one should allocate one's money among the major types of investments — cash, bonds, and stocks; (ii) one should also diversify within each type of investment (for example, one is well-advised to invest in a portfolio of common stocks rather than to hold one stock only); and (iii) one can benefit from global diversification.

3. **Efficient markets**
   This principle states that financial markets are efficient, by and large. Stocks and bonds are fairly valued at any point in time. One cannot outperform or "beat" the market by picking stocks, by timing the market, or by switching one's investments from one to another. Although some market inefficiencies have been detected, it is very difficult for small investors to exploit these inefficiencies because small investors do not have the time or the financial resources.

In this chapter, we will apply these investment principles to evaluate different kinds of investments. There is no such thing as a perfect investment. Each one has its own characteristics in terms of risk, return, liquidity, maturity, and so on. The investor must choose the investments that fit her economic circumstances (such as wealth, income, age, and stage in the life cycle) and her risk preference.

This chapter is *not* about picking the right stock or about choosing the right time to switch one's investment from one category to another. By virtue of the principle of efficient markets, we have emphasized that a small investor cannot expect to benefit much from such activities. On the other hand, we believe that one should have a good understanding of the characteristics of each type of investment — stocks, bonds, mutual funds, and so on — so that individuals can make the right choice of investment that will achieve their financial goals.

You have already learned that there are many kinds of risk and that technically speaking there is no such thing as a risk-free investment.[1] The major kind of risk that worries most people is *default risk* — the risk of losing part or all of one's investment due to the inability of the issuer to honour the obligations of the security. We shall introduce various types of investments in order of their default risk; in other words, we will first go through investments with little or no default risk and continue by describing investment with increasingly higher default risk. In this chapter, we will describe the three major categories of investments: cash and cash equivalents, bonds, and stocks, with a brief reference to options, futures, and commodities. We will leave mutual funds to Chapter 16.

CASH AND CASH EQUIVALENTS

Federal Government of Canada Securities

The federal government borrows money by selling securities. It borrows money when current revenue from taxes is not sufficient to meet all expenditures. When the government runs a deficit, it funds the deficit by borrowing money through the issuance of government securities. These government securities are considered to have virtually no default risk because the federal government can always get money to pay its debt — by virtue of its legal right to levy taxes on its citizens and resident corporations as well as its ability to create money.

There are three major types of securities sold by the federal government: treasury bills, Canada Savings Bonds, and Government of Canada Bonds. Each has its own investment characteristics — return, risk, liquidity, maturity, and so on. The first two are cash equivalents.

Treasury Bills (T-Bills)

Treasury bills are short-term debt obligations issued normally in denominations ranging from $1,000 to $1 million, and with 91-day, 182-day, and occasionally, one-year terms. They are issued by auction once every week. In the past, T-bills were mainly of interest to large institutional investors such as banks and loan and trust companies, but recently they have become accessible to small investors since many investment dealers have begun buying T-bills in large quantities and then selling

---

[1] Government securities are default risk-free; however, one is still exposed to inflation risk in government securities.

them in small packages to individual investors, making a small profit by paying a slightly lower interest rate than they receive from the government.

T-bills have no default risk; however, if you want to cash them before the maturity date, you may suffer a capital loss or enjoy a capital gain. They are very liquid; you can therefore normally sell them through the same investment dealer from which you bought them.

T-bills do not pay interest; instead, they are bought at a discount from their face value. The **face value** is the amount that the federal government will pay on the maturity date, and is in denominations ranging from $1,000 to $1 million. Buying at a **discount** means that you pay a lower price than the face value. This makes the calculation of the rate of return on a T-bill a little complicated.

Example 15.1: The current market price of a $10,000 treasury bill is $9,500. The bill matures in 181 days. What is the effective annual rate of return?

The holding period is 181 days, and the holding period return (HPR) is equal to:

$$[(\$10,000 - \$9,500) \div \$9,500] = 5.26\%$$

This is the rate of return for a holding period of 181 days. The effective annual rate of return is therefore equal to:

$$[(1.0526)^{365/181} - 1] = [(1.0526)^{2.0166} - 1] = 10.89\%$$

Even though T-bills do not pay interest, the difference between the face value and the initial price paid is considered as interest income for tax purposes. Thus, in Example 15.1, the $500 (which is the difference between the face value of $10,000 and the initial price of $9,500) would be considered as interest income for the investor and would be taxed at the investor's marginal tax rate.

The rate of return on T-bills is usually higher than the rate of inflation. For individuals who pay little or no taxes, or non-profit organizations, T-bills are good hedges against the risk of inflation. For people in higher tax brackets, however, T-bills may not be good inflation hedges as the following example will show.

Example 15.2: Mr. Wong, a relatively well-off retired man, is very worried about the erosion of his wealth by inflation. The expected rate of inflation is 8% for the coming year and Mr. Wong is contemplating buying the T-bill in Example 15.1. If Mr. Wong's marginal tax rate is 53%, is the T-bill a good hedge against inflation?

The before-tax rate of return is 10.89%, which is higher than the expected rate of inflation of 8%. Thus, for people or organizations that pay little or no taxes, the T-bill would be a good inflation hedge; however, that is not the case for Mr. Wong. After paying taxes on interest income at the rate of 53%, the after-tax rate of return on the T-bill is equal to:

$$[10.89\% \times (1 - .53)] = 5.12\%$$

This is lower than the expected rate of inflation of 8%. Mr. Wong would lose 2.88% in terms of the purchasing power of money. This example illustrates that even though T-bills are considered as the "risk-free" investment in the investment literature, T-bills are actually free of default risk only.

Canada Savings Bonds (CSBs)

Canada Savings Bonds (CSBs) are sold once a year with the actual issue date and the maturity date falling on November 1. CSBs offer a fixed rate of interest compounded annually and the interest rates are normally adjusted for later years.

There are two types of CSBs: the regular interest bond and the compound interest bond. The **regular interest bond** pays annual interest either by cheque or by direct deposit into the investor's bank account on November 1 each year. This type is available in denominations of $300, $500, $1,000, $5,000, and $10,000; you must pay cash to purchase them. The **compound interest bond** does not pay annual interest but reinvests the interest payable automatically until maturity or redemption. This type is available in denominations of $100, $300, $500, $1,000, $5,000, and $10,000 and can be purchased by cash, by a monthly instalment plan through banks and other financial institutions, or through payroll savings plans offered by many companies in Canada.

CSBs are sold to Canadian residents and registered in the names of individuals.[2] There is a maximum limit of any one series that an individual is allowed to hold. Ownership of a CSB cannot be transferred or assigned; therefore, CSBs are not traded in the market like other bonds. The only seller is the government and the only legal buyer of bonds already issued is the government.

If the holder of a new CSB issue cashes the bond within a few months — usually the first three months — from the issue date, he normally receives the face value without the payment of interest. After this initial "waiting period", CSBs can be redeemed at any time for the face value plus accrued interest. You can cash the bonds at any bank in Canada on any business day.[3]

---

[2] CSBs can also be held by the estate of a deceased person or a trust for an individual.

[3] Redemption of CSBs should be done on the first business day of a month for maximum interest advantages because the government pays accrued interest as of this date.

A CSB is a very unusual investment. It is free of default risk. It is perfectly liquid and the value of the bond is always equal to the face value. There is no downside risk because when the market interest rate rises, the CSBs are still worth their face value. The prices of all other bonds rise when interest rates fall and vice versa. See next section on bonds. In fact, the government usually adjusts the interest rate on the CSBs upward to prevent high redemptions of the bonds. On the other hand, when the market interest rate falls, the rate on the CSBs remains unchanged until the next November. In addition, the government pays all the commissions for the buying and the selling of the CSBs through financial institutions; for this reason, the individual investor does not have to incur any commission expense. The yields of CSBs are usually slightly lower than that of treasury bills and other government bonds; nevertheless, investors should realize that they hold a valuable option — namely, investors can force the government to redeem the bond at face value at any time they want. The redeemability of CSBs therefore justifies their lower return. Overall, the conservative investor who wants perfect liquidity and zero default risk should find CSBs to be suitable investments. Many financial experts advise a family to set aside an emergency fund equal to three to six months' take-home pay. This emergency fund should be put in a low-risk and liquid investment. CSBs are excellent investments for this particular purpose.

Deposits with Financial Institutions

Deposits with banks and other financial institutions are one of the most popular investments for Canadians. They are easy to understand and, in terms of investment characteristics, they are *safe* (very low risk), *liquid*, and *convenient*, but the rate of return is low. The most common types of deposits are interest-bearing savings and chequing accounts, term deposits, and guaranteed investment certificates.

Bank Accounts

Three basic types of accounts are available at banks, loan and trust companies, and credit unions. They are chequing, chequing-savings, and savings accounts. **Chequing accounts** usually do not pay interest. You are allowed to write cheques on the account and the cheques can be returned to you with a monthly statement. There is a service charge, which is usually a function of how many cheques you write and the amount of money you have in the account. **Savings accounts** do not allow chequing but pay interest to the account holders. The **chequing-savings account** has the attributes of the other two; it allows chequing but pays a lower interest rate than savings accounts. These three accounts are the basic types although financial institutions offer many varieties of accounts, each with slightly different features and charges.

Bank accounts are safe and almost default-risk-free — in terms of relative default risk, they are next in line after treasury bills and CSBs. They are also perfectly liquid. Banks and financial institutions have always honoured investors' withdrawals even though legally they can ask you to wait several days on withdrawals from savings accounts. Bank accounts are also very convenient with the numerous branches that banks have all over the country. In addition, the introduction of **automated teller machines (ATM)**,[4] which offer 24-hour service, has made banking more and more convenient. Indeed, it is expected that in the near future individuals will be able to take care of all their banking needs without ever leaving home. A limited range of such services is already available with some financial institutions.

In return for the safety, liquidity, and convenience for the consumer, bank accounts offer a low rate of interest — lower than CSBs and T-bills, for example. In some ways, the consumer is paying for the convenience and other services by accepting a lower rate of return. Many institutions calculate the interest on savings accounts on the minimum monthly balance and compound it semi-annually. For example, if you have $10,000 in a savings account from the beginning of the month until the 30th day, when you must withdraw $9,999 because of an emergency, the interest for the month will be based on the minimum balance of the month, which is the $1 on the last day of the month. What this means in effect is that you lose interest for the entire month! It is therefore important for you to find out how interest is calculated for each type of account. The retail banking industry has become more competitive, and most financial institutions now offer **daily interest accounts** where interest is calculated daily and compounded semi-annually. If you expect many fluctuations in your savings account balance, these accounts may be more suitable for you.

Term Deposits

In contrast to savings accounts, which have no guaranteed interest rate and no set term, you can deposit your money in **term deposits**, which guarantee a rate of interest for a specified *term*. You give up some liquidity[5] in return for a higher rate of interest, however. The typical terms range from 30 to 364 days and, usually, the longer the term, the higher the rate of interest. Interest is normally paid semi-annually or annually. In some cases, there may be a minimum deposit required, and the amount of the deposit usually affects the rate of interest. In terms of investment characteristics, term deposits are as safe as savings accounts, less liquid than savings accounts, and capable of earning a higher rate of return than savings accounts.

---

[4] An automated teller machine is a terminal that allows you to get cash, make deposits, pay bills, and transfer funds between accounts.

[5] Money is put in for a specified term. If you withdraw before the term, there is usually a penalty.

Guaranteed Investment Certificates (GICs)

GICs are really long-term term deposits. These certificates have terms ranging from one to five years. During the term, the interest rate is guaranteed. In most cases, a minimum deposit will be required. Interest is usually paid semi-annually or annually and some GICs have automatic compounding of interest. GICs are as safe as savings accounts and term deposits. They are less liquid because they have longer terms but you can normally expect a higher interest rate on GICs.

Deposit Insurance

How safe are savings accounts, term deposits, and GICs? Is their default risk equal to zero, just like T-bills and CSBs? What happens to a depositor's money when a trust company goes bankrupt? These questions bring us to the deposit insurance at the federal and provincial levels.

The federal government in 1967 established a Crown corporation, the **Canada Deposit Insurance Corporation (CDIC)**, to provide investors with insurance against any loss on their deposits should a member institution become insolvent or bankrupt. Who are the members of CDIC? Membership in the CDIC is restricted to banks, trust companies, and mortgage loan companies.[6] Thus, not all financial institutions are members of the CDIC. To check the status of an institution in this respect, you should ask a senior officer at the institution or call the CDIC directly at 1–800–267–1999. The CDIC publishes a list of its members, which is available upon request.

The CDIC insures savings and chequing accounts, term deposits, guaranteed investment certificates, debentures, and other obligations issued by member institutions. The maximum coverage is $100,000 for each person in each member institution; this amount applies to the combined total of principal and interest. The deposit insurance does not cover investments in stocks, bonds, mortgages, or mutual funds. Joint accounts and joint deposits are separately insured from the individual's accounts. For example, if you have a term deposit under your own name and a joint savings account with your spouse and another joint account with your sister, the term deposit will be covered up to $100,000 and each joint account will also be covered up to $100,000. If you have more than $100,000 to deposit, you should spread it around so that no more than $100,000 is deposited with any one CDIC-member institution. Are deposits to Registered Retirement Savings Plans (RRSPs) or to Registered Retirement Income Funds (RRIFs) insured? If the monies are invested in a type of deposit that qualifies for deposit insurance, they are insured to the $100,000 maximum. In addition, the deposits are separately insured from any regular deposits or other types of registered plan deposits the person may have in the same member institution.

---

[6] Assuris provides investors with insurance against any loss on deposits, RRSPs, and RRIFs of life and health insurance companies. See Chapter 10.

Example 15.3: Edward Booth has a term deposit in his name for $50,000, a joint savings account with his wife for $25,000, another joint savings account with his son for $10,000, an RRSP account for $45,000 invested in stock mutual funds, and an RRIF account for $20,000 invested in a mortgage mutual fund. All the accounts are with a bank that is a CDIC member. Are Edward's accounts fully covered by CDIC insurance?

Edward's term deposit is covered up to $100,000. Each of the joint accounts are also fully covered, up to $100,000 for each account. The RRSP account is not covered because the money is invested in "unqualified" investments.[7] For the same reason, the RRIF account is not covered. If the monies in the RRSP and the RRIF accounts had been invested in qualified investments — term deposits, GICs, etc. — both accounts would be covered up to $100,000 for each account.

Example 15.4: Leslie Carter is a loyal customer at her local bank branch. In addition to a savings account with a $35,000 balance, she has three term deposits of $20,000 each. She also holds a two-year GIC of $20,000. Are Leslie's investments fully covered?

First, she should check to see if the bank is a CDIC member. Assuming that it is, the insurance coverage is $100,000 for each person in each member institution. Her total investments amount to [$35,000 + (3 × $20,000) + $20,000] or $115,000, which exceeds the $100,000 limit. In addition, the accrued interest will add to the total. Thus, her investments are not fully covered. She is well-advised to put at least $15,000 in another CDIC-member institution.[8]

Credit unions and caisses populaires are regulated provincially and do not participate in the CDIC coverage. They do have their own deposit coverage, which varies by province and is insured by provincial central organizations, and also partly guaranteed by the federal central credit union organization. This deposit coverage does not have the same powerful backing as the CDIC, but it has so far proven successful. It is likely that a really large failure, which would have to involve several credit unions at once, would also attract support from the federal government if the credit union centrals were unable to cover it.

---

[7] The CDIC does not cover investments in stocks, bonds, mortgages, or mutual funds.
[8] As a practical matter, she may be able to transfer some of the deposits to a separate mortgage company that the bank owns, and get full CDIC coverage. Banks have developed this to reduce deposit-switching.

The provincial coverages have varying details surrounding them that are outside the scope of this book. The stated limits cover several different types of accounts, so a customer might have coverage for the limit for a deposit account, a term deposit, a joint account, and a term deposit inside an RRSP, each one covered separately. The limits by province are currently as follows: Alberta, British Columbia, Manitoba, and Saskatchewan — 100% of all deposits; New Brunswick, Newfoundland and Labrador, and Nova Scotia — $250,000 per deposit; Ontario and Québec — $100,000; and Prince Edward Island — $125,000.

BONDS

Bonds are fixed income securities issued by various levels of governments — federal, provincial, and municipal — and corporations. When corporations and governments need long-term financing, they borrow money by selling bonds. When you buy their bonds, you become their creditor and you receive a bond certificate by which the issuer promises that the principal (or face value or par value) will be repaid on the maturity date and that interest will be paid on stated dates. The following important items of information are stated on the bond certificate:

Face Value — This is also called the **principal**, the **par value**, or the **maturity value**. It is the amount that the issuer has promised to pay on the maturity date. It is usually in denominations of $500, $1,000, $10,000, or more.

Maturity Date — This is the date on which the face value will be paid.

Coupon Rate — This is the rate that forms the basis for calculating interest. The annual interest payable is the coupon rate times the face value. For example, if the face value of a bond is $10,000 and its coupon rate is 8% p.a., the annual interest payable is ($10,000 × .08) = $800.00. Interest is normally paid semi-annually on the stated dates. In many bonds, there are **interest coupons** attached to the bond certificate; they can be clipped and cashed on the stated dates.

Coupon Bonds are bonds with a series of interest coupons attached to the bond certificate itself. Printed on the coupon are the value of the interest in dollars, the date when the coupon can be cashed, and the financial institution at which the coupons can be cashed.

Investing in Bonds

Bonds are bought and sold in the bond market through bond brokers. The **bond market** is not a physical place where brokers meet; it is, rather, a communication system where brokers put orders to buy and orders to sell together.

There are some major security firms that act as **investment dealers** (or **bond dealers**) in the bond market. These dealers hold hundreds of millions of dollars of

TABLE 15.1
Example of Bond Quotations

Issuer	Coupon	Maturity	Bid Price	Ask Price	Bid Yield	Ask Yield
Canada	4.00	06/01/2017	112.922	113.962	1.52842	1.34390
Canada	4.25	06/01/2018	115.782	116.842	1.66662	1.50797
Ontario	4.20	06/02/2020	109.834	111.111	2.88338	2.72258
Nova Scotia	4.15	11/25/2019	109.505	110.765	2.80798	2.64034
Bell Canada	5.00	02/15/2017	107.897	110.106	3.32579	2.88356

bonds in inventory and they buy or sell bonds on their own account. On any trading day, the investment dealers will set a price list for the bonds. This price list is called **bond quotations**. There are two prices for any given bond. The **bid price** for a bond is what the dealer will pay to buy the bond; the **ask price** is the price at which the dealer will sell the bond. Table 15.1 shows typical bond quotations that you can find in the fixed income security section of the websites of many investment dealers, such as the TD Waterhouse website.

Let us look at the first row in Table 15.1. This is the quotation of a Canada Government Bond with coupon rate of 4.00% which matures on June 1, 2017. The bond could be sold for $112.922 per $100 of face value or bought for $113.962 per $100 of face value. The **spread**, which is the difference between the *ask price* and the *bid price*, represents the dealer's gross profit margin. Higher spreads are quoted on bonds that are traded infrequently and hence are of poor liquidity. The bond quotations that you find in newspapers normally apply to large lots that may be as high as $250,000; additional spreads or commission may be charged on smaller trades.

Basic Bond Pricing Mathematics and Yields

Accrued Interest

For the sake of convenience, the prices quoted for bonds are all calculated as of the previous interest date. When you buy a bond, you have to pay the ask price plus all interest accrued from the previous interest date to the closing date of the transaction. The following example will illustrate this point.

Example 15.5: Anthony Schilling bought the following Canada Government Bond to settle on June 15:

Face value of the bond: $10,000
Coupon rate: 10%
Interest payable on March 15 and September 15

> How much accrued interest must Mr. Schilling pay
> to the seller?

When September 15 next arrives, Mr. Schilling can clip the interest-coupon and get six months' interest, which is equal to $500. But he will have held the bond for only three months and, therefore, he should not receive six months' interest. Mr. Schilling is obligated to pay for $250 to the seller of the bond, or three months' interest, in addition to the value as if the bond were priced at March 15 (the previous interest date).

Yield to Maturity

The **yield to maturity** is the average rate of return that will be earned on a bond if it is bought now and held until maturity. It is also called the **return to maturity** or the **internal rate of return**. You pay the current price to buy a bond and if you hold it until maturity, you will receive (i) an annuity of interest income and (ii) the face value at maturity. In theory, the current bond price is equal to the present value of the interest-annuity plus the present value of the face value of the bond. This is called the **bond price equation**.

■ BOND PRICE EQUATION

First, we define the following symbols:

P = The current price of the bond
C = The coupon rate, expressed in % p.a.
M = The par value or face value of the bond
n = The number of years to maturity
k = The discount rate

One pays P dollars to buy the bond. If one holds the bond until maturity, one will receive an annuity of interest income of $C(M)$ dollars for n years, plus the face value, M, on the maturity date. The present value of the annuity of interest is equal to $CM(PVIFA)$. The present value of the face value is equal to $M(PVIF)$. Recall that in Chapter 2, *PVIFA* is defined as the present value interest factor for an annuity, and PVIF is the present value interest factor. In other words:

$$PVIF = \frac{1}{(1 + k)^n}$$

$$PVIFA = \frac{1}{k} - \frac{1}{k(1 + k)^n}$$

The bond price equation equates the current bond price to the present value of the annuity of interest and the present value of the face value. It can be written as equation (1) or equation (2):

$$P = CM \, (\text{PVIFA}) + M(\text{PVIF}) \qquad (1)$$

$$P = CM \left[\frac{1}{k} - \frac{1}{k(1 + k)^n} \right] + M \left[\frac{1}{(1 + k)^n} \right] \qquad (2)$$

We can calculate the yield to maturity by solving the bond price equation for the discount rate k, given the bond's price P.

Example 15.6: What is the yield to maturity of the following Canada Government Bond?

Face value = $1,000
Coupon rate = 9.5%, payable semi-annually
Current price = $1,030
Maturity = 20 years

First, note that the bond pays $47.50 in interest every six months for 40 periods. The bond price equation is:

$$\$1,030 = \$47.5 \left[\frac{1}{k} - \frac{1}{k(1 + k)^{40}} \right] + \$1,000 \left[\frac{1}{(1 + k)^{40}} \right]$$

We can solve for k by trial and error, or we can use a calculator. For the BA II Plus,

–1,030	**PV**
40	**N**
47.50	**PMT**
1,000	**FV**
I/Y	Answer = 4.58%

Note that the 4.58% is the rate for the half-year period. The bond's yield to maturity will be quoted in the financial press at an **annual percentage rate (APR)** of $(0.458 \times 2) = 9.16\%$, despite the fact that its effective annual rate is actually $(1.0458)^2 - 1 = 9.37\%$. The latter is the correct annual yield to maturity even though it is not reported in the newspaper.

Current Yield vs. Yield to Maturity

Some financial press reports another yield called the **current yield**. It is the bond's annual coupon payment divided by the bond price. For example, the current yield of the bond in Example 15.6 is equal to $(95 \div 1,030)$ or 9.22%. Clearly, the yield to maturity is not the same as the current yield. The yield to maturity is widely accepted as the measure for the average return on investment if the bond is held to maturity. It can be interpreted as the compound rate of return of one's investment over the life of the bond, under the assumption that all interest coupons can be reinvested at an interest rate equal to the bond's yield to maturity. If this assumption does not hold, the yield to maturity will not be the same as the return over the bond's life.

Investment Risk of Bonds

There are risks associated with investing in bonds. Unlike term deposits or guaranteed investment certificates, the market value of bonds can fluctuate. Even if the bond is issued by the federal government and is therefore free of default risk, the bond's price is guaranteed only at maturity. Before then, the bond's price can go up or down. We will discuss four important risks of bonds: default risk, interest rate risk, reinvestment risk, and option features (such as callable, retractable, extendible features that may make the bond more or less risky to the investor).

1. Default Risk

Default risk refers to the risk that the issuer may not be able to pay part or all of the interest and face value. In the case of bonds issued by the federal government, the default risk is zero. Bonds issued by the provincial and municipal governments are not free of default risk although they are usually considered to be less risky than corporate bonds. The default risk of bonds depends largely on the quality of the assets and cash flows of the issuer. As long as the issuer (company or government) is not in financial difficulty, the bondholders will get their interest and principal as promised.

Assessing the default risk of different bonds is a complicated matter; therefore, there are **bond rating agencies** that specialize in rating the credit risk of different issuers. In Canada, the largest bond rating agencies are Canada Bond Rating Service and Dominion Bond Rating Service. Studies have shown that bond ratings are very reliable and many investors use them as measures of the default risks of bonds. In other words, the **bond ratings** can be used as indicators of the probability of uninterrupted payment of interest and principal repayment. Ratings classify bonds from investment grade to speculative grade and relate one company's ability to meet its debt obligations to those of other companies.

■ DOMINION BOND RATING SERVICE — RATINGS

The following are the bond ratings[9] assigned by the Dominion Bond Rating Service:

---

[9] Canada Bond Rating Service uses different symbols, but the basic idea is the same.

AAA — Highest quality: The protection of principal and interest is of the highest order.

AA   — Superior quality: The protection of principal and interest is high.

A   — Higher medium-grade securities: The protection of principal and interest is substantial but less than AA.

BBB — Medium-grade securities: The protection of principal and interest is adequate but some areas of potential weakness exist.

BB   — Lower medium-grade securities: These are mildly speculative securities; the protection afforded interest and principal is uncertain.

B   — Medium speculative-grade securities: The ability of the company to meet interest and principal obligations on a continuing basis is uncertain.

CCC — Highly speculative securities: These are securities in danger of default of interest or principal.

CC   — Securities in default: This rating is assigned to securities in default of either interest or principal or with other serious problems.

C   — Securities in serious default: These securities are similar to CC securities but they have different liquidation values.

■ HIGH OR LOW

The above rating may also be modified by "high" or "low" to indicate the relative standing within a classification and an improving or declining trend within that classification.

2. Interest Rate Risk

Interest rate risk refers to the volatility or fluctuation of the bond's price due to the fluctuation in interest rates. The coupon interest is fixed for most bonds but the market interest rate can and does change. If, in the course of time, interest rates available on bonds rise, the price of the bond held in your portfolio will fall since the coupon interest it bears is not as attractive as those on other bonds. On the other hand, if interest rates fall, the same bond's price will rise.

If you intend to hold the bond until maturity, then the interest rate risk is irrelevant to you: What matters is the price at maturity, which is known to be par value. Most people, however, may want to sell the bond before maturity and for that reason they face an uncertainty about the bond's price because of possible interest rate changes. Even with zero default risk — as in the case of Canada Government Bonds — bonds could therefore be risky investments. Moreover, the longer the **term to maturity** of the bond, the greater the interest rate risk for the obvious reason that the bondholder is locked into a fixed rate for a longer period of time.

Because most investors are risk-averse, they will pay a little less for "longer" bonds. The relationship between a bond's price and the rate of interest can be analyzed by the bond price equation, as the following example will illustrate.

Example 15.7:   Mr. Lopez has invested in the Canada Government Bond in Example 15.6:

Face value = $1,000
Coupon rate = 9.5%
Maturity = 20 years
Market price = $1,030
Yield to maturity = 9.16%

He has held the bond for one year, during which time the rate of interest in the market has increased substantially. As a result, the required yield to maturity of the bond has increased to 10.04%.

Required:
(a)   What is the bond's price at the end of the year?
(b)   If Mr. Lopez sold the bond, what would be his holding period return (HPR)?

Answers: (a)   After one year, there are 19 years remaining to maturity. The bond's price is equal to the present value of an annuity of 38 interest payments (each = $47.50) plus the present value of the face value of $1,000. The discount rate is equal to (10.04% ÷ 2) = 5.02%. Using a calculator, we get:

47.5	**PMT**
1000	**FV**
38	**N**
5.02	**I/Y**
PV	Answer = –$954.58

The price of the bond has fallen from $1,030 to $954.58 in one year's time.

(b)   Mr. Lopez's holding period return (HPR)
= (95 + 954.58 – 1,030) ÷ (1,030)
= 1.9%

Note that Mr. Lopez has a capital loss of $75.42. Investment in Government of Canada Bonds is not risk-free! We have observed from historical data that there were periods of time when long-term government bonds were more volatile (and hence, more risky) than stocks.

3. Reinvestment Risk

As mentioned before, coupon interest is paid semi-annually or annually to the bondholders and not reinvested in the bond. This means that the bondholder must find somewhere else to invest the interest. Of course, the rate of return on future reinvestments of the coupon interest is uncertain; it could be higher or lower than the current yield on the bond. **Reinvestment risk** refers to the risk of not knowing the interest rate that will be earned on future interest earnings. Other things being the same, the higher the coupon rate of the bond, the higher the reinvestment risk. Thus, a bond that does not pay interest year to year has no reinvestment risk.

■ ZERO-COUPON BOND

A **zero-coupon bond** is a bond that pays no interest — in other words, the coupon rate is zero: It has no reinvestment risk. It is the only long-term investment where the yield to maturity is guaranteed. A zero-coupon bond thus has the advantage of producing a specified amount of money at a specified future date and is therefore a very useful investment vehicle for the goal setting and personal financial planning process that we discussed in Chapter 3. Zero-coupon bonds, nevertheless, do have their disadvantages: The major one is that their market price is very sensitive to interest rates — in other words, they have high interest-rate risk.

■ STRIP BONDS

The Canadian government issues very few zero-coupon bonds; instead, it allows investment dealers to "re-package" regular government bonds and sell them in the form of zero-coupon bonds. For example, a 20-year Government of Canada Bond has 40 semi-annual coupons plus one principal payment; each of these 41 cash flows can be re-packaged and sold as 41 different zero-coupon bonds, with maturities ranging from six months to 20 years. Such a re-packaged zero-coupon bond is called a **strip bond**.

You may want to invest in a zero-coupon bond or a strip bond if (i) you want no reinvestment risk, (ii) you want a guaranteed yield to maturity, or (iii) you want a specific amount of money at a specified future date and you want to achieve this goal without uncertainty.

4. Option Features of Bonds

Many bonds today have certain features in addition to the basic variety that we have described so far. Some of the features are beneficial to the issuer; others are beneficial to the bondholders. Usually, if the issuer has the option to exercise the feature, the feature is beneficial to the issuer; on the other hand, if the bondholder has the option to exercise the feature, then it is beneficial to the bondholders. What follows here is a list of some of the more common option features.

■ CALL PROVISION AND CALLABLE BONDS

A **call provision** allows the issuer the option of buying back the bonds at a specified price before maturity. A bond with a call provision is called a **callable bond**.

■ RETRACTABILITY PROVISION AND RETRACTABLE BONDS

A **retractability provision** provides the bondholder with an option to sell the bond back to the company for a specified price before maturity. A bond with a retractability provision is called a **retractable bond**.

■ EXTENDIBILITY PROVISION AND EXTENDIBLE BONDS

An **extendibility provision** allows the bondholder the option of extending the maturity of the bond for another fixed period of time at a specified interest rate (often the same rate as before). Such a bond is called an **extendible bond**.

■ CONVERSION PROVISION AND CONVERTIBLE BONDS

A **conversion provision** gives the bondholder the option of exchanging the bond for a fixed quantity of stocks of the company. Such a bond is called a **convertible bond**.

STOCKS

Stocks are probably the premier kind of investment: When people think of investments, they usually think of stocks and the stock market. Technically, the common stockholders as a group are the owners of the firm; they have a claim on the net earnings of the company after the claims of the creditors and other claimants have been satisfied. Common stocks are the riskiest of all the investments that a company issues — promissory notes, short-term and long-term debt, bonds, preferred stocks and common stocks — but their expected returns are also the highest. The common stockholders are protected by the **limited liability** provision of the stocks; they are not personally liable for the company's financial obligations. The most that a stockholder can therefore lose is 100% of what he or she has invested in the stock.

Stock Markets

Shares in public companies are traded on what we call **stock markets**. When a company issues new common or preferred shares, it normally does not sell directly to the public; rather, it sells the shares to investment dealers. This is called the **primary market**, where new issues are brought to the market for the first time through investment dealers. After buying the new securities, the investment dealers then sell them to the public through their network of stockbrokers. This process of buying new issues from the company and then selling them to the public is called **underwriting**.

A private company's shares are held by only a few people — usually the executives and/or members of a founding family. The shares are not traded on a stock exchange and are thus very illiquid.

Most of the publicity about the stock markets concerns the **secondary market**, where previously issued stocks are traded. The secondary market includes the stock exchanges and the over-the-counter (OTC) market.

Stock Exchange

A **stock exchange** is a place where members of the exchange buy and sell stocks. A limited number of memberships are available in a stock exchange and these memberships are called **seats**.

Over-the-counter (OTC) Market

The **OTC market** is not a physical place where people trade stocks; rather, it is an informal network among the security firms that allows trading in securities that are not formally listed on a stock exchange. This market operates very much like a bond market.

Stock Quotations

Stock quotations are reported in the financial press or online websites every day. The following is a typical quotation that you can find in the business section of most newspapers and business websites. We look at the Canadian Imperial Bank of Commerce (CIBC) as it was shown in the TD Waterhouse website.

Daily Trading Report for CIBC

52-Wk High	52-Wk Low	High	Low	Last	Volume	Chg	Dividend	Yield	Share Profit	P/E
85.56	67.32	68.80	68.21	68.26	478,415	−.36	3.60	5.2740	6.60	10.3424

Let us explain the information from the stock quotation. The first two numbers are the highest and lowest prices at which the stock has traded in the last 52 weeks; for the CIBC, they are $85.56 and $67.32, respectively. The next four numbers provide information on the trading of the day: From the first trade since opening of the market to the most recent trade (i.e., last trade), the highest price and lowest price per share at which the stock traded were $68.80 and $68.21, respectively. The last trade was at a price of $68.26, which was down .36 of a dollar from the closing price of the previous trading day. The **sales volume**, 478,415 shares, were traded so far during the day. **Dividend** means that the dividend payout to the shareholders over the last year was $3.60 per share on an annual basis. CIBC, which was last sold for $68.26, has a **dividend yield** of (3.60 ÷ 68.26) = .05274 or 5.274%. The **share profit** is the **earnings per share**, which is calculated as the company's net income for the last four quarters divided by the number of shares outstanding. The share profit of the CIBC was $6.60. The last number is the **P/E ratio**, or **price-earnings ratio**, which is defined as the closing price divided by last year's earnings per share. For CIBC, the P/E ratio is equal to (68.26 ÷ 6.60) or 10.3424. The P/E ratio tells you how much you must pay per dollar of earnings that the firm generates for each share. If the dividend yield or the P/E ratio is not reported in the stock quotation, then that means the firm has zero dividends, or zero or negative earnings.

Stockbrokers

You will need a stockbroker (often called an investment advisor) to assist you to buy or sell stocks. There are two kinds of brokers: full-service brokers and discount brokers. A **full-service broker** will execute your buy-and-sell orders and will also provide you with advice or guidance about what to buy and what to sell and when. A **discount broker** will only execute your buy-and-sell orders: He will not give investment advice. Obviously, then, you will pay a higher commission for the full-service broker because part of the commission fee goes to pay for the investment advice that you get from your agent. If you are a knowledgeable investor and know what to buy and sell, you do not need any investment advice. Therefore, you should find a discount broker, particularly as a discount broker's commission can be 70% lower than that of full-service brokers.

Commissions are now negotiable in Canada but that does not mean that they are inexpensive: In fact, the small investor has very little bargaining power and her commissions have gone up since the advent of negotiated commission rates. Typically, commissions have two components — a fixed minimum commission per trade and a variable component based on the value of the trade. The average total commission ranges from 1% to 3% of the value of the trade, buy or sell.

Stock Market Indices

How do you keep track of what the entire stock market is doing? How do you measure the historical performance of the stock market? The answer lies in the use of **stock market indices**.

S&P/TSX Composite Index

The S&P/TSX Composite Index is Canada's best-known stock market indicator.[10] It contains the largest securities, approximately 300, in terms of market value,

---

[10] S&P stands for standard and Poor, and TSX stands for Toronto Stock Exchange.

traded on the Toronto Stock Exchange. It is computed by calculating the total market value of the stocks in the index every day. The percentage increase (or decrease) in the total market value from one day to the next represents the increase (or decrease) in the index. The rate of return of the index is the rate of return that would be earned by an investor who holds a portfolio of all the stocks in the index in proportion to their market value — except that the index does not reflect cash dividends paid out by those stocks. In other words, the S&P/TSX index tracks the capital gains of the stocks.

S&P/TSX 60 Index

This is a 60-stock index composed of 60 of the largest and most frequently traded Canadian companies drawn from a variety of industrial groups.

Other Stock Indices

The TSX also calculates stock indices based on narrow industry groupings such as the Oil and Gas Index, the Gold and Silver Index, the Merchandising Index, and the High Technology Index.

Investing in Stocks

Are stocks good investments? How do stocks compare with other investments, such as bonds, with respect to their return-risk characteristics? Should one include stocks in one's investment portfolio?

Historical Performance of Stocks

Over long periods of time, stocks have consistently paid returns higher than those of bonds. For example, over the period 1954 to 1980, the return on stocks was 10.02% and that for long-term corporate bonds was only 3.93%. This finding confirms the first basic principle in investment: the higher the risk, the higher the return that one can expect to earn. In other words, although stocks are riskier than bonds, there is a higher reward for investing in stocks. A very important feature of stocks is that the longer the holding period, the less fluctuation there is in the rate of return. Researchers have found that the spread between highest and lowest returns shrinks dramatically with longer holding periods. This means that the risk of investing in the stock market decreases as the holding period increases. If you are investing for long-term purposes (such as saving for a comfortable retirement) then you have a long holding period and the stock market can be a rewarding place to be in spite of its short-term volatility.

There is one more important finding: Researchers have found that over long periods of time, stocks have consistently generated returns much higher than inflation. For example, the real rate of return (after inflation) of the S&P/TSX Composite stocks was 3.07% per year during the 20-year period from December 1961 to December 1981; it was 2.92% for the 10-year period from December 1971 to December 1981; and it was 5.23% for the 30-year period from 1981 to 2010. Thus, over the long term, stocks have proven to be good inflation hedges.

Although history may not repeat itself, there are three lessons that we have learned from past performances:

1. Stocks outperformed the other two major categories of investments — cash equivalents and bonds. Nevertheless, stocks are also more risky in the short term.

2. The risk of investing in stocks is substantially reduced if one has long holding periods. In fact, the risk is a decreasing function as the holding period increases. The implication is that long-term investors should include stocks in their portfolios.

3. Over long periods of time, stocks are good hedges against inflation risk.[11]

Investment Risks of Stocks

There are a number of risks involved with stock market investing. The three most important risks associated with "playing the market" are described below.

Price Volatility Risk

This is similar to the default risk of bonds. It is the risk of losing part or all of one's initial investment. As discussed in Chapter 14, there are two measures of this risk — the standard deviation of the rate of return and beta. The former measures the total risk of the stock, whereas the latter measures its systematic risk (or market risk).

One way to reduce the price volatility risk is to diversify. It takes about 15 to 20 stocks to achieve the full benefit of diversification. Another way to reduce this risk is by buying mutual funds, which we will discuss in Chapter 16.

Inflation Risk

This is the risk that the return on investment cannot keep up with the rate of inflation. In the long run, stocks are good hedges against inflation risk, but in the short term, there is substantial inflation risk in stock investments.

Liquidity Risk

This is the risk of not being able to liquidate or cash in one's investment within a short length of time and at a reasonable price. Most stocks are very liquid;

---

[11] We hasten to add that this is not the case in the short term. In fact, researchers have found that there is a short-term negative relationship between stocks and inflation. The reason for this is that interest rates increase as inflation increases; consequently, stock prices tend to fall when interest rates increase. This means that, in the short run, stocks may not be good inflation hedges.

for example, you can sell a large amount of a blue-chip stock within a matter of minutes. On the other hand, there are stocks (usually of smaller companies) that are thinly traded in the market. These stocks will have some liquidation risk.

Selecting Stocks

There are two primary reasons motivating people to spend time and effort in selecting stocks. First, many people believe that there are ways to discover undervalued stocks that would give them an above-average return. Second, one has to choose the stock that has the right risk–return mix. This means choosing the stock that is compatible with one's financial circumstances and risk preferences.

As for the first motivation, by virtue of the third investment principle of efficient markets, finding undervalued securities is very difficult. Although the market is not perfectly efficient, it is very difficult for a small investor to exploit these market inefficiencies. Individuals would likely be disappointed if their objective is to find undervalued stocks. We believe that, by and large, stocks are fairly valued.

Nevertheless, even if every stock is fairly valued in the market, that does not mean that every stock is suitable for any one individual investor. Each stock has its own characteristics in terms of return, risk, liquidity, and so on. It is up to investors to choose stocks that are compatible with their risk preferences and financial circumstances. Go back to Chapter 14 and review how one estimates the expected rate of return and the risk (either the standard deviation or beta) of a stock. Using historical data to estimate an objective probability distribution for the rate of return is usually a good starting point. Full-service brokers normally have all kinds of research reports or forecasts that help individual investors to assess a company's risk and return. There are also investment newsletters and advisory services that forecast the future returns (and risks) of stocks. You can also learn security analysis techniques for the purpose of making your own analyses. Regardless of the method you use, the basic idea is to come up with a reliable measure of a stock's *risk* and *return* so that you can choose stocks that fit your risk–return preference. We will go through this in more detail in Chapter 16 when we discuss choosing a mutual fund.

OTHER INVESTMENTS

Up to this point, you have learned a lot about the traditional types of investments: short-term near-cash investments, bonds, stocks, real estate, international securities, mutual funds, etc. These are the basic investments that should form all or at least a major part of your investment portfolio. There are, however, many other more complicated investment vehicles such as *options* and *futures* that have gained substantial popularity in recent years. We shall describe the major ones in the remainder of this chapter, but before doing so, let us make an important comment. Most of these investments are very sophisticated and carry high risks. You should commit at most a small portion of your portfolio to them and then only if you have learned more about them and can afford to lose everything invested.[12] Do not touch these investments just because of the recommendation of a broker or a so-called financial expert.

Options

An **option** is the right to purchase or sell an asset at a stated price for a specified period of time. A **call option** is the right to buy the asset, and a **put option** is the right to sell it. Every option is written on an asset, which is called the **underlying asset**. An option is always a contract between two parties.

Theoretically, the underlying asset can be anything that the two parties of the contract have agreed upon. The most common underlying assets are stocks and, in this case, the option is called a **stock option**. **Index options** are based on a well-established stock market index, such as the S&P/TSX or the Dow Jones Industrial Average. **Currency options** and **commodity options** are options based on currencies and commodities, respectively.

Exchange-traded Options

Exchange-traded options are options that are traded on an exchange. The best-known ones are stock options that are traded on the Montreal Exchange (MX). Only firms that meet certain quality standards can have their options listed.

For stock options, an option contract generally covers 100 shares of a stock at a fixed price per share — this is called the **exercise price** — within a certain period of time. Stock option prices are quoted in the financial press.

> *Example 15.8:* Mr. Carl Copeland bought a call option of the LMN Co. Ltd. three months ago. He paid a *premium* (which is just another name for the option price) of $2 per option, or $200 for the full contract ($2 × 100 shares). The exercise price of the option is $15 per share. The stock price of the LMN Co. Ltd. has increased from $14 to $21 since the time he bought the option. If he exercises the option now, how much money would he make? What is the rate of return on the investment? Ignore broker's commission.

---

[12] Options and futures can be used for the purpose of hedging. If used as such, they may play an important function in one's investment plan. Again, the first basic principle in investment applies: What is the risk–return trade-off? Are you comfortable with the risk?

He would make ($21 − $15) = $6 per share, minus $2 per share for the cost of the option. This is equal to $4 per share for a total profit of 100 × $4 = $400. The rate of return on investment = $400 ÷ $200 = 200% in three months, which translates into a rate of return of 800% per annum.

Let us warn you once more that options can be very risky. In Example 15.8, suppose the stock price of the LMN Co. Ltd. never increased above the exercise price of $15; then, in nine months' time, Mr. Copeland would have lost $200, or 100% of his investment.

Futures Markets

A **future** is a standardized contract to buy or sell a specific quantity of a commodity on a specified future date at a price agreed upon today. The word "commodity" includes agricultural products (e.g., wheat, corn, coffee, pork bellies, etc.), metals (e.g., gold, copper, silver, nickel, etc.), other natural resources (e.g., lumber, oil, gas, etc.), foreign currencies (e.g., Japanese yen, Deutschmark, British pound, etc.), some financial instruments (e.g., government bonds, treasury bills), and financial futures (e.g., interest rate futures, stock index futures). You can buy and sell commodities in a futures market whether or not you own the particular commodity. In fact, physical deliveries of the commodity are rare because most futures-contract buyers and sellers close out their contracts before the delivery date.

Individual investors are normally speculators in the commodity market because they tend to put down a small margin to buy or sell a large amount of commodities. In other words, one's investment position is always highly leveraged. As a result, even a small price fluctuation can wipe out an investor's entire investment principal. Sometimes one cannot limit one's losses: Unlike the option markets where one can lose at the most 100% of one's principal, in the commodity markets one can lose more than 100% of one's initial principal.[13] The commodity markets are very volatile for the most part, and they are dominated by professional traders who have a lot of knowledge and experience. They make their living in trading and have better information sources than the average investor. Past studies of the performance of the average investor have shown that the odds against the individual are overwhelming. Again, you should not put more than a small portion of your portfolio in the commodity markets.

---

[13] If you do not understand this last sentence, you should take it as proof positive that you are not knowledgeable enough to touch the commodity markets. Do not put any money in the commodity markets until you acquire more knowledge about the risk involved.

SUMMARY

In this chapter, you have learned the three fundamental types of investments — *cash equivalent investments* (such as T-bills and term deposits), *bonds*, and *stocks*. Each has been described in terms of their investment characteristics — risk, return, liquidity, and so on.

Treasury bills and Canada Savings Bonds are investments with zero default risk. They are both very liquid; however, the return is usually quite low. They are good places to park a family's emergency funds.

Next in line in terms of default risk are savings and chequing accounts, term deposits, and guaranteed investment certificates. All are very liquid and the default risk is close to zero. Longer-term GICs usually offer a higher interest rate than T-bills and CSBs. All these investments are generally called cash-equivalent investments. Every family should have some money invested in cash-equivalent investments — at least three to six months' take-home pay as an emergency fund.

The next investment category is bonds. Bonds are issued by the three levels of government as well as by corporations. There are various measures of rate of return — the holding period return (HPR), the yield to maturity, and the current yield. Bonds are risky investments. Even Government of Canada Bonds are not risk-free investments; they are only free of default risk. The major risks associated with bond investments are default risk, interest rate risk, reinvestment risk, and option features (such as call provisions), which make the bonds more or less risky to the bondholders.

The third category of investments is stocks. The stock market performance can be measured by stock market indices such as the S&P/TSX Composite Index. Stocks are riskier investments than bonds, and their risk can be measured by the standard deviation of the rate of return or by their betas. The major reasons for investing in stocks are as follows:

1. Over long periods of time, stocks provide higher returns than cash-equivalent investments and bonds.
2. The risk of investing in stocks is substantially reduced for long holding periods.
3. Over long periods of time, stocks have generated returns that are substantially higher than inflation.

Finally, some complex investments have been described. We introduced the *options markets* and the *futures markets*. These are normally very risky investments, and the markets are dominated by professional traders. You should allocate at the most only a small fraction of your portfolio to these risky investments but only after you learn more about them.

MULTIPLE-CHOICE REVIEW QUESTIONS

1. Dermot wants to invest $4,000 to get a fixed return over a short period of time without any risk. He should consider investing in _____.
   (a) a government bond
   (b) stock mutual funds
   (c) a term deposit at the TD bank
   (d) gold
   (e) none of the above

2. Which of the following investments has positive default risk?
   (a) Canada Saving Bonds
   (b) Treasury bills
   (c) Guaranteed investment certificates
   (d) Canada government bonds
   (e) None of the above

3. Violetta has the following amounts in a trust company that is a member of the CDIC: $5,000 in her chequing account, $45,000 in term deposits, $15,000 in a joint account with a friend, and $30,000 in the trust company's stock mutual fund. If the company fails, which of the following will *not* be covered by CDIC insurance?
   (a) $ 5,000 in her chequing account
   (b) $15,000 in the joint account with a friend
   (c) $45,000 in term deposits
   (d) $30,000 stock mutual fund
   (e) All of the above are covered.

4. A _____ provision provides the bondholder with an option to sell the bond back to the issuing company for a specified price before maturity.
   (a) call
   (b) extendibility
   (c) convertibility
   (d) retractability
   (e) zero coupon

5. Heather plans to invest in a long-term government bond. If she holds the bond until maturity, her return on the bond does not depend on _____.
   (a) the coupon rate
   (b) the term to maturity
   (c) the current price
   (d) the future rate of interest
   (e) none of the above

DISCUSSION QUESTIONS

1. Define or describe all the following terms:

   bond: face value (par value or principal) — coupon rate — maturity date — coupon bonds / bond investment risks: default risk — interest rate risk — reinvestment risk — option features / bond pricing: yield to maturity — return to maturity — internal rate of return — bond price equation / bond quotation: ask price — bid price — spread (of bid and ask) / bond rating agency / bond ratings / bond (types): zero-coupon bonds — strip bonds — callable bonds — extendible bonds — retractable bonds — convertible bonds / Canada Deposit Insurance Corporation (CDIC) / Canada Savings Bond (CSB): regular interest bond — compound interest bond / cash equivalences / commodity market / future / options: stock option — call option — put option — underlying asset — index option — currency option — commodity option — exchange-traded option — exercise price / stock (common): limited liability — primary market — secondary market — underwriting — stock exchange — over-the-counter (OTC) market — seats in a stock exchange / stockbrokers: full-service broker — discount broker — commission (for stock trading) / stock market indices: S&P/ TSX Composite Index — S&P/TSX 60 index / stock investment risks: price volatility risk — inflation risk — liquidity risk / stock quotations: closing price — sales volume — indicated dividends — dividend yield — share profit — earnings per share — price-earnings ratio (P/E) / treasury bills (T-bills): face value — discount — inflation hedge

2. **Personal Project 1**

   Get a copy of the business section of today's newspaper. Examine (i) the bond quotations and (ii) the stock quotations. Go through each column heading and explain in your own words what each term means. Now pick randomly 10 bonds from the bond quotation and 10 stocks from the stock quotation list. Go through the numbers for each bond and each stock. Describe in your own words what information has been conveyed by the market quotations. Verify some of the numbers if possible — e.g., P/E ratio, bond yield, etc.

3. T-bills have zero default risk, and savings accounts are a little more risky. The interest rate of T-bills is often higher than that of savings accounts. Is this inconsistent with the basic principle of risk–return trade-off?

4. Are securities sold by the federal government always default-risk free?

5. Are treasury bills good inflation hedges? How does income tax affect your answer?

6. How safe is one's money in a bank? Describe how the CDIC works. What is the maximum insurance coverage available to an individual depositor?

PROBLEMS

1. The current price of a 91-day T-bill is $9,750. Its face value is $10,000. What is the effective annual rate of return?

2. (a) Find the yield to maturity of the following semi-annual bonds:
    (i) Price = $9,500, coupon = 9.5%, maturity = 20 years, face value = $10,000
    (ii) Price = $10,500, coupon = 10.25%, maturity = 30 years, face value = $10,000
    (iii) Price = $10,000, coupon = 10%, maturity = 10 years, face value = $10,000
   (b) Are these yields to maturity guaranteed? Explain.

3. For each of the bonds in Question 2, if the yield to maturity changes to 11% after one year, calculate (i) the new bond price and (ii) the holding period return during this year.

4. Mr. Wolfe's stockbroker recently sent him a research report on a stock that is currently selling for $25. According to the report, the stock will pay $2 per share of dividends next year and the target stock price after one year is $30. The commission for trading stocks is 1.5% of the stock price, for either buy or sell.

   (a) Calculate the expected rate of return, after all commissions, if Mr. Wolfe buys and holds the stock for one year.
   (b) What is Mr. Wolfe's expected after-tax rate of return if he lives in Ontario and is in the 26% federal tax bracket, the 11.16% Ontario bracket, and the 20% Ontario surtax bracket?

5. (a) A Government of Canada Bond (called a Canada for short) with one year to maturity pays a semi-annual coupon of $65. The current price of the bond is $1,064.56. What is the yield to maturity (YTM)? What is the effective annual rate (EAR)?
   (b) A Canada with 10 years to maturity has a YTM of 7.26% and a semi-annual coupon of $40. What is the current price?
   (c) Interest rates rise in such a way that the required yield (that is, the best alternative rate for this risk and maturity) rises by 1% for all bonds (this is also called a parallel yield shift). What is each bond worth now? Explain the difference in the price changes.

6. Joe and Mary Whitehall have the following accounts/investments at a trust company that is a CDIC member.

In Joe's name:

Savings Account	$ 40,000
Chequing Account	$ 5,000
Term Deposit	$ 75,000
RRSP (in GICs)	$ 35,000

In Mary's name:

Savings Account	$ 5,000
Chequing Account	$ 1,000
GICs	$100,000
RRSP (in mutual funds)	$ 90,000

Joint names:

Savings Account	$ 10,000
Term Deposit	$ 30,000

Discuss the CDIC insurance coverage for the Whitehalls.

7. An 8% Canadian Pacific Railway bond with a quarterly coupon costs $1,172.50 and matures in nine years. What is the yield to maturity? What is the effective annual rate of return (EAR)?

8. Currently the 11% semi-annual bonds of Smith and Daughters have eight years to maturity and are selling at $85.83 ($858.30 per $1,000 of face value).

   (a) Calculate the yield to maturity on the bonds.
   (b) If interest rates do not change, at what price will the bonds sell two years from today?
   (c) Suppose interest rates do change over the next two years. At the end of two years, the bond is priced to yield 12%. What will be the bond's price on that day?
   (d) Given the information in (c), what is the expected before-tax rate of return if the bond is bought today and sold two years from today? State clearly your reinvestment assumptions.
   (e) If your marginal tax rate is 40%, what is the expected after-tax rate of return corresponding to part (d)?

9. Ives and Staicu Ltd. has an outstanding 10% bond issue trading at $1,092.50. It pays interest semi-annually and has seven years to maturity.

   (a) What is the yield to maturity?
   (b) What is the effective annual rate of return?

10. Laura Parker buys for $952.38 a treasury bill that matures in one year at $1,000. She lives in Ontario. She is in the 29% federal income tax bracket and the 56% Ontario surtax bracket. What is her after-tax rate of return on the treasury bill?

11. You are a Prince Edward Island investor in the top tax bracket trying to decide between two investments of equal risk. One is a five-year bond, trading at par, with an 8% coupon, paid semi-annually. The other is a preferred share that will be redeemed at $25 in five years. It pays a dividend of $0.35 every quarter, and is trading at $25. Ignore transactions costs and surtaxes.

   (a) In which security should you invest your money?
   (b) The calculated returns would be different if you included surtaxes, but the decision in part (a) would be the same. Why?
   (c) If the securities were not trading at par, the calculations would be much more complicated. Explain briefly how you would do the calculations for part (a).

12. The following parts are not related.

   (a) A $100,000 181-day T-Bill sells for $97,500. Calculate the holding period return and effective annual rate for this investment.
   (b) Calculate the price of a $1,000 bond that has a coupon rate of 6% and a maturity date of 10 years. The yield to maturity on a similar bond is 7%.
   (c) David Copperfield plans to buy the bond in part (b) today and hold it for one year. If the yield to maturity will increase to 8%, calculate his holding period return.

13. (a) What is the market price of a bond with a coupon rate of 9%, face value of $1,000, term to maturity of 16 years, and yield to maturity of 8%?
   (b) Pauline buys the bond and holds it for one year. If at the end of the year the yield to maturity increases to 9.5%, calculate (i) the new bond price, and (ii) Pauline's holding period return.

CHAPTER 16

Mutual Funds

Mutual funds have become the most popular vehicle for investing savings and so there are thousands to choose from. In this chapter, we answer these questions:

▶ How do you calculate and compare the risk and return of different funds?

▶ How do you read the reports on mutual fund performance and characteristics?

▶ How do you compare different fee structures (see Example 16.1)?

▶ What are the most common type of mutual funds?

▶ What is an ETF (exchange-traded fund)? A hedge fund?

LEARNING OBJECTIVES

> ➢ *To describe the major types of mutual funds.*
>
> ➢ *To discuss the advantages and disadvantages of investing in mutual funds.*
>
> ➢ *To explain how you can compare the fees of different mutual funds.*
>
> ➢ *To explain how you can read the daily, weekly, and monthly mutual fund reports.*
>
> ➢ *To assess the total risk exposure of a portfolio of several mutual funds.*
>
> ➢ *To describe how you should go about buying a mutual fund.*

In Chapter 14 we described the basic concepts in investments. We summarized the major developments in the investment literature in terms of three basic principles in investment. In Chapter 15 we described the three most important types of investments: near-cash investments, bonds, and stocks. In this chapter, we will put everything together and develop an investment strategy that is suitable for most people, especially the average Canadian investor. The investment strategy is built on a firm theoretical foundation; more specifically, it is built on the three fundamental principles of investment. This investment strategy will allow you to allocate your investment money among three basic types of investments — cash, bonds, and stock. If you like, you can easily add other types of investments, such as real estate, your own home, options, foreign stocks, and so on. There is plenty of flexibility in the investment strategy to allow you to choose the proper risk and return mix — at the level you are comfortable with — to reach your financial goals. The things that make our investment strategy possible are mutual funds. We will argue that mutual funds are the best investment choice for most Canadians. Mutual funds provide an opportunity for even small investors with limited financial resources to build an investment plan that satisfies the three fundamental investment principles and, at the same time, allows investors to reach their financial goals.

TYPES OF MUTUAL FUNDS

A **mutual fund** is a financial organization that accepts funds from hundreds and thousands of investors, pools these funds, and invests them in bonds, stocks, real estate, precious metals, or other investments. It issues shares or units to investors in proportion to the funds each investor contributes. Each of the investors owns a fraction of all the investments in the mutual fund.

Conceptually, a mutual fund is not like a stock or a bond; rather, it is a way of investing. Investing in mutual funds provides small investors with an opportunity to hold many different securities, thereby achieving a much higher degree of diversification than they could achieve by investing on their own. While a mutual fund offers investors other benefits, which we will discuss later, we want to stress here that the main contribution of mutual funds is that they provide investors with ready-made diversification at a low cost.

There are many types of mutual funds. They are classified by the way they are organized; for example, closed-end funds and open-end funds. They can also be classified by what they invest in. There are mutual funds that invest in stocks, bonds, gold, real estate, treasury bills, and so on. With stock mutual funds, there are those that invest primarily in conservative stocks and funds that specialize in risky stocks. In fact, there is probably a mutual fund for just about every type of investment. The following is a list of the more common mutual funds.

Open-end Fund

This is a mutual fund that continuously sells its own shares or units to the public. Its investors or shareholders have a continuing right to sell their shares back to the fund itself. This right is called the **right of redemption**. The number of shares or units of the fund changes continuously as shares are being sold and redeemed. Examples: any of the funds in Table 16.1 on page 414.

Closed-end Fund

This is a mutual fund that offers its shares or units to investors at the time the fund is set up; after that, the fund normally will not sell or buy back its shares or units. Proceeds from the initial sale of shares are then invested in a diversified portfolio of investments consistent with the fund's objective. Thus, a closed-end fund's equity base is relatively fixed and seldom changes materially. The shares can be traded among investors in an "after-market"; in fact, the shares or units of most of Canada's closed-end funds trade on the stock exchanges or the over-the-counter market. Example: Canadian World Fund, traded on the TSX.

Exchange-Traded Fund (ETF)

This is a type of open-ended mutual fund that trades as a listed security in the stock exchange. Unlike a close-end fund of which the number of securities is normally fixed, an ETF continuously sells new shares to the market. As long as there is demand, there is no limit to the number of shares that the fund can issue.

Hedge Fund

Historically, hedge funds were set up to reduce risk, such as to hedge against the downside risk of a bear market. Nowadays, a hedge fund is typically an actively managed portfolio that uses advanced techniques, such as leveraging, selling short, trading financial or commodity futures or derivatives, and so on, with the goal of generating higher returns.

RRSP and RRIF Eligible Funds

Because of the investment restriction for RRSPs and RRIFs imposed by Canada Revenue Agency (CRA), not all investments are eligible. An RSP-eligible fund is one that meets the requirement of the CRA.

Treasury Bill Fund

This is a mutual fund that invests exclusively in treasury bills issued by the government of Canada. Example: Green Line Canadian T-Bill Fund.

Money Market Fund

This is a mutual fund that invests in safe, short-term, liquid investments such as treasury bills, term deposits, commercial paper (short-term corporate debt), and short-term bonds. The fund generates a floating rate of return, which rises or falls with the rate of inflation. Money market funds (as well as treasury bill funds) are normally good investments when the rate of inflation is rising. Example: AGF Money Market Fund.

Mortgage Funds

This is a mutual fund that invests primarily in high-quality conventional mortgages (i.e., first mortgages). It may also invest in short-term bonds. It generates a higher rate of return than treasury bill funds and money market funds do, albeit at a slightly higher risk. Example: Green Line Mortgage Fund.

Income Fund or Bond Fund

This is a mutual fund that invests primarily in government bonds, high-quality, high-yielding corporate bonds, some high-yield preferred and common stocks and mortgages. The objective of the fund is to maintain the safety of principal and high income. Examples: CIBC Canadian Bond Fund, Dynamic Income Fund.

Dividend Fund

This is a mutual fund that invests primarily in Canadian preferred and common stocks with high dividend yields. The preferential tax treatment of dividends over interest-bearing investments makes this type of fund highly attractive to some investors. Examples: Prudential Dividend Fund, Royfund Dividend Fund.

Balanced Fund

This is a mutual fund that allocates its money among the three basic types of investments — cash equivalent investments, bonds, and common stocks. In some balanced funds, the portfolio mix remains fairly stable from one period to another and the fund's manager adopts a more or less "buy-and-hold" invest-ment strategy. In other balanced funds, the manager changes the portfolio mix continuously, putting more weight on the investment type that is expected to outperform the other two for the coming period. This strategy of changing the portfolio mix continuously to increase the return on investment is called the **asset allocation** strategy; it is a kind of market-timing strategy. Examples: MacKenzie Industrial Balanced Fund, CIBC Balanced Fund.

Equity Fund or Stock Fund

An equity fund invests primarily in common stocks, although short-term notes and other fixed income securities may be held to maintain liquidity. Because com-mon stock prices are more volatile than those of other fixed income securities, equity funds tend to be more risky than income or balanced funds.

Equity funds have a great range in the degrees of their risk and growth poten-tials. Some are heavily invested in blue-chip, income-producing common stocks and are quite conservative. Examples: Royal Canadian Equity Fund, Green Line Blue Chip Equity Fund.

Other equity funds take a more aggressive investment stance. They invest in companies with higher risk but greater growth potential. These funds are often called **growth funds** and their objective is to achieve above-average growth of capi-tal. Examples: Royal Canadian Growth Fund, Cambridge Growth Fund, Dynamic Canadian Growth Fund.

Index Fund

This is a stock index mutual fund that holds a representative sample of the entire stock market. The objective of the fund is to give the investor the average return yielded by the stock market, no more and no less. Example: Green Line Canadian Index Fund. In recent years, index funds have become quite popular because they have lower management expense ratios (MER) than other non-index funds.

Real Estate Fund

This is a mutual fund that invests primarily in income-producing real estate (such as rental apartment buildings, office buildings, shopping malls, industrial buildings) in order to achieve long-term growth through capital appreciation and reinvestment of income. Examples: Investors Real Property Fund, CIBC Canadian Real Estate Fund.

Specialty Funds

These are mutual funds that concentrate on shares of a group of companies in one industry (e.g., Oil and Gas), in one geographic location (e.g., Japan), or in one segment of the capital market (e.g., Natural Resources). Although there is diversification in their portfolios, these funds tend to be more risky and speculative than most types of common share funds. Examples: AGF Canadian Resources, Saxon Group Small Capitalization Fund, Scotia Bank Precious Metal Fund.

Ethical Mutual Funds

These are funds whose investment decisions are guided by some moral criteria which may vary from fund to fund. One ethical fund may avoid investing in companies that profit from tobacco or armaments, whereas another fund may avoid companies that pollute the environment. Example: Dynamics Green Fund.

International Funds

These are mutual funds that primarily invest in securities of countries other than Canada. Some international funds focus on one single country. In Canada, the most popular single-country funds are the **U.S. Funds** that invest in U.S. securities. Both U.S. bond funds and U.S. equity funds are offered by many mutual fund companies. Examples of other single-country international funds include Investors Group's Japan Growth Fund and Fidelity Investments' Japanese Growth Fund.

Some international mutual funds focus on a certain region of the world, such as Europe, Asia, or South America. Examples: Altamira European Equity Fund, Dynamic Europe Fund, Fidelity Investments' Far East Fund, and Royal Asian Growth Fund.

Some international mutual funds invest in a well-diversified world portfolio. They invest in every major economic region of the world, including North America, Europe, and Asia. They are often called **Global Funds**. Examples: Templeton Growth Fund, MD Growth Fund, AGF Global Fund, Royal International Equity Fund, and CIBC Global Fund.

Finally, there are the international specialty funds that concentrate on a certain narrow sector or on a certain theme. For example, the **emerging market funds** invest primarily in small countries that are expected to grow very fast — e.g., Templeton Emerging Market Fund.

MUTUAL FUND COSTS

Buying mutual funds entails a variety of fees or costs. These fees can be classified into three groups: (i) fees charged when one buys mutual fund shares — these are called the **front-end load** or **front-end fees**, (ii) fees charged when one sells the mutual fund shares — these are called the **back-end fees**, **rear-end fees**, or **redemption fees**, and (iii) management fees charged each year — these are called **annual fees**. Since they are usually reported as a percentage of the fund's total assets, the annual fees are called **management expense ratio** (MER).

No-load Funds

No-load funds are mutual funds that do not charge a front-end fee nor a back-end fee; however, they will still charge annual fees.

Are No-load Funds Cheaper Than Front-load Funds?

In the past, front-load mutual funds charged a very high front-end fee. Sometimes the fee could be as high as 9% of the purchase price. For example, if you purchase $1,000 of a front-end fund that charges a 9% front-end fee, then (9% × $1,000) or $90 would be deducted up front, leaving you with a net investment of only $910.00. Because of this, front-load funds give most people the impression that they are more expensive than no-load funds.

Nevertheless, if a no-load fund charges a higher annual fee or back-end fee than a front-load fund of similar quality, then it is not clear which fund is the cheaper. You should look at the entire fee structure — front-end fees, annual fees, rear-end fees — of each mutual fund, and you should use the analysis employed in Example 16.1 to decide which fund has the lowest set of fees. You may be surprised to find that some so-called no-load funds are actually more expensive than some front-load funds.

Back-end Fees

Many mutual funds charge back-end or redemption fees according to a sliding scale: The longer you hold the fund, the less you will be charged. Because its purpose is to encourage long-term holding, the back-end fee normally is waived after one has held shares in the fund for longer than a specified number of years (usually five). The following is a typical back-end fee structure:

If it is sold in the first year:	5% (of selling price)
If it is sold in the second year:	4%
If it is sold in the third year:	3%
If it is sold in the fourth year:	2%
If it is sold in the fifth year:	1%
If it is sold after the fifth year:	0%

Thus, whether you have to pay a rear-end fee and how much depends on your holding period. Long-term investors normally do not have to pay the rear-end fee.

Example 16.1: (comparing mutual fund fees) ABC Fund and XYZ Fund are two Canadian equity funds of similar quality and past performance. Suppose the ABC Fund has a front-end fee of 8%, an annual fee (MER) of 1.25%, and no rear-end fee, whereas the XYZ Fund has no front-end fee but it does have a rear-end fee of 5% and an annual fee of 2%. If Mr. Stargill's holding period is 10 years, which fund has a lower fee structure?

Suppose the discount rate that Mr. Stargill uses is 10%. We will convert all fees into annual fees and then compare them for the two funds. In other words, we will convert the front-end and the rear-end fee, which are both one-time fees, into annual fees.

Let us first consider the ABC Fund. The 8% front-end fee should be spread out (or, more precisely, amortized) over the 10-year holding period in order to obtain an annual cost. If $x\%$ is the annual "amortized" cost of the front-end fee, we have the following equation:

$$x \times \text{PVIFA} = 8\%$$

$$x \times \left[\frac{1}{.10} - \frac{1}{.10 \times 1.10^{10}} \right] = 8\%$$

$$x = 1.3\%$$

The annual cost of the ABC Fund equals the annual front-end cost plus annual fees plus the annual back-end fee cost, which equals:

$$1.3\% + 1.25\% + 0\%$$

$$= 2.55\%$$

Let us now consider the XYZ Fund. The rear-end fee is a one-time fee and we will spread it over 10 years. If we let y equal the annual cost of the back-end fee, we have the following equation:

$$y \times \text{FVIFA} = 5\%$$

$$y \times \left[\frac{1.10^{10} - 1}{.10} \right] = 5\%$$

$$y = .31\%$$

The annual cost of the XYZ Fund equals the annual front-end cost plus annual fees plus the annual rear-end fee cost, which equals:

$$0\% + 2\% + .31\%$$

$$= 2.31\%$$

Thus, XYZ Fund has a cheaper set of fees than does ABC Fund.

MUTUAL FUND TAXATION

The investment income rules from Chapter 7 apply to the income you earn in a mutual fund. The mutual fund administrator records your share of the interest, Canadian dividends, foreign dividends, net realized capital gains and losses, and net unrealized capital gains and losses. In February you receive T5 information slips reporting your interest, dividends, and realized capital gains for the previous year. You report the income exactly as you would if you had received the amounts directly, and pay tax on them. The mutual fund's management fees are tax deductible.

When you sell the mutual fund units, your share of the unrealized capital gains and losses is realized. The front-end and the back-end load fee reduce the capital gain (or increase the capital loss). Technically speaking, the front-end fee is added to the adjusted cost base, and the back-end fee is deducted from the proceeds on disposition of the mutual fund units.

Thus, all of the tax strategies apply to mutual funds in the same manner as direct investments. For example, if you are saving for retirement a long time in the future and do not need income from the investments now, a growth mutual fund with low dividends is more tax efficient. Most of the return is capital gains, and to the extent that they remain unrealized, the income tax is deferred.

WHY INVEST IN MUTUAL FUNDS?

It has been noted previously that mutual funds are not, conceptually speaking, types of investments like stocks or bonds; rather, they are a way of investing. We shall go on to argue that for the average investor, especially small investors with limited resources, mutual funds are the best way to invest one's money to achieve one's objectives.

Let us examine what a typical investor should do in view of what we have learned so far. First, one should set financial goals and have action plans to reach those goals (see Chapter 3). Second, one should find an investment approach with which one is comfortable and to which one can commit oneself with follow-up action. The investment approach should be based on firm investment principles — the three fundamental principles described in Chapter 14. Finally, one should choose the types of investments that give the desired risk–return mix. The three basic types of investments have been covered in Chapter 15 — cash equivalent investments, bonds, and stocks. Some people may (and usually do) include other investments in addition to the three basic types — for example, one's own home, real estate, precious metals, futures, options, and so on.[1]

---

[1] Every person's investment portfolio also includes human capital — the value of education, occupational training, and experience.

The three fundamental principles in investment speak very strongly for the use of mutual funds in one's investment plan. First, one needs reasonably reliable estimates of the risks and the expected returns of investments before one can make decisions. The historical data of a mutual fund give reliable and objective estimates of the fund's risk and return. Since a mutual fund is normally a diversified portfolio, the risk and return do not shift over time as erratically as that of a single share. In other words, not only is it easier to estimate the risk of a mutual fund than it is to estimate a stock's risk, the estimate made on a mutual fund's risk and return is much more reliable.

Second, the principle of diversification dictates that one should diversify across major investment types (i.e., cash, bonds, and stocks); that one should diversify within each investment type (i.e., hold a stock portfolio instead of just one stock); and that one should diversify across different economies (i.e., hold a global portfolio rather than a portfolio of a single country's issues). Although the benefits to be derived from following the principle of diversification in one's investment decision making are substantial, because the required degree of diversification requires a substantial capital outlay, these benefits are unavailable to a small investor: For example, even one who saves and invests several hundred dollars a month cannot achieve all the objectives of diversification. The average small investor's monthly savings are not enough to buy even a single bond! To make matters worse, average small investors have little time to manage their investments; moreover, a non-professional investor's knowledge about investment is too limited to make good investment decisions. Mutual funds provide the solution to the problem of how to achieve well-selected and well-managed diversification with limited funds, time, and knowledge. The minimum investment required for most mutual funds is quite small: it can go as low as $50. Thus, with several hundred dollars, one can easily buy five or six mutual funds — say, a money market fund, a bond fund, one or two equity funds, a global fund, and a specialty fund — and achieve all the benefits of diversification available. You need not worry about time and knowledge because the mutual fund managers will do all the investing for you.

It is almost impossible for a small investor to achieve better stock selection than a mutual fund manager; it is highly unlikely that a small investor will outperform a professional fund manager even over the short term. The principle of efficient markets supports both of these assertions. Furthermore, even if there are market inefficiencies (empirical studies have detected some), professional fund managers are in a better position than are small investors to exploit these market inefficiencies in order to produce better returns. Professional investors are more knowledgeable than small investors and they have more resources (i.e., time, money, and information) than do small investors.

Advantages of Mutual Fund Investment

To summarize, the following are the chief advantages:

1. Professional Management

Mutual funds are run and managed by professional managers who make all the day-to-day decisions about buying and selling. If you believe that the markets are inefficient and that it is possible to outperform the market (either by timing, picking stocks, or some other technique), the professional manager should stand a much better chance of doing the job well. Even if you believe the market is efficient and that professional managers cannot outperform the average investor, you still benefit from professional management because hired professionals reduce the amount of time and effort that you must devote to investing your money.

2. Broad Diversification

The mutual fund has more dollars with which to purchase a wider range of investments than any one investor can independently provide. A typical fund has a portfolio of over 50 stocks in 15 to 20 industries. By purchasing several mutual funds, a small investor can achieve all the objectives of diversification — to diversify among the major investment types; to diversify within each investment type; and to diversify across different countries.

3. More Reliable Estimates of Risk and Return

Studies have shown that risk measures — whether using standard deviation or beta — are more stable and, hence, more reliable in the case of portfolios than individual stocks. You can use a fund's historical data to come up with objective and reasonably reliable estimates for the fund's return and risk. In contrast, it is much more difficult to assess the risk of your total investment position when you buy your own stocks and investments.

4. Past Performance Record

You can check a fund's past performance record relative to the market or relative to other mutual funds of similar quality and with similar investment objectives. Many newspapers keep track of the performance of mutual funds. These records are reported regularly and are easily available.

5. Record Keeping and Safekeeping

The mutual fund manager keeps the records of all buying and selling of securities and other relevant transactions. You do not have to worry about cashing interest coupons or dividend cheques. You do not have to bother about keeping stock and bond certificates safe. A summary record will be mailed to you before the deadline for filing your tax return.

6. Flexibility of Purchase and Sale

A variety of purchase plans are available, ranging from one-time, lump-sum purchases to regular purchases in small amounts under **automatic contribution plans**.[2] Similarly, various withdrawal plans are available, which are very convenient to retirees who want to cash in a fixed amount every month for consumption.

7. Automatic Reinvestment Plan

You can automatically reinvest your dividends and capital gains. This is a very useful feature because continuous reinvestment and compounding is the key to success in investment.

Disadvantages of Mutual Fund Investment

1. Management Fees

Mutual fund companies charge an annual management fee for managing the investment, operating the fund, administering your account, and safe-keeping your securities. This fee is reported as the management expense ratio (MER) because it is calculated as a percentage of your investment. The MER is around two to three per cent for most actively managed equity funds, and is much lower for passively managed funds such as indexed funds.

2. High Cost for Short-term Investment

Many mutual funds charge a front-end fee or a rear-end fee or both. The fees could be very high for short-term holding periods. For example, how can one justify paying a 9% front-end fee for holding a mutual fund for six months? Mutual funds are therefore more suitable for investors who adopt a long-term, buy-and-hold strategy. Mutual funds are not suitable for investors who have short-term holding periods or who trade frequently. The exceptions are T-bill and money market funds, which are cash equivalents and do not charge as high fees.

3. Vulnerable to Massive Redemption

Financial markets are very sensitive to mass psychology of the market's investors. Investors notoriously move as a crowd and this phenomenon may result in a massive request for redemption. This would force the fund manager to sell stocks and investments at the wrong time in order to meet redemption requests. Thus, your investment could be vulnerable to the mass psychology of the marketplace.[3]

---

[2] You can preauthorize a specific amount to be deducted from your bank account for the purchasing of a mutual fund.

[3] In the early 1990s, due to the decline of the Canadian real-estate market, many real-estate mutual funds experienced massive redemption requests from shareholders who wanted to reduce their exposure

4. Professional Management Is Not Infallible

Although we believe professional management is by and large an advantage for mutual fund investment, there is a counterargument that says there are certain small investors who may have an advantage over large mutual funds. It has been argued that fund managers are subject to tremendous peer pressure because they are constantly being compared to each other. As a result, some tend to emphasize short-term performance rather than long-term results. Also, most mutual funds are very large and they must buy and sell in large quantities so that any significant shift in portfolio holdings necessarily influences market prices; therefore, managers may not always be able to buy at the lowest price or sell at the highest price.

THE AVERAGE INVESTOR'S RESPONSIBILITY

The advantages of mutual funds outweigh the disadvantages and we think mutual funds are the best way for the average investor to invest his money. The investor nevertheless must choose the right mutual funds from the hundreds that are available. How do you choose the right mutual funds? There are several things that you must do and know. First, you must gather information, which means that you must know how to read the daily/weekly market quotations as well as the prospectus of any mutual fund you contemplate purchasing. Second, you must know how to evaluate the risk and the return of each fund that you are considering. Third, you must know how to calculate and evaluate the risk and return of your portfolio, which may be comprised of several mutual funds and other investments. This is important because you have to choose the risk–return mix that is consistent with your financial goal and your risk preference. Fourth, you must monitor your investment results periodically and make adjustments if necessary. These topics will be discussed in the remainder of the chapter.

READING DAILY/WEEKLY MARKET QUOTATIONS

Daily Quotation

Table 16.1 is the typical information found on the Internet or given by the daily financial press; obviously, there may be slight variations among different sources. The mutual funds are grouped under the fund management companies. In Table 16.1, the management companies are AGF Group and CIBC securities. The **daily quotation** reports the following information:

---

to the real-estate market. Some funds were temporarily forced to stop redeeming shares because they ran out of cash and could not sell their illiquid real-estate assets quickly enough to meet the demand for redemption.

TABLE 16.1 Daily Mutual Fund Quotations as of August 31, 2011			
Name	Value ($)	Change	% Change
AGF Group			
American Growth Class	19.17	0.03	0.16
China Focus	17.08	0.34	2.03
Cdn. Traditional Balanced	9.45	0.00	0.00
Cdn. Bond	5.87	−0.04	−0.68
Cdn. Growth Equity	58.25	0.54	0.94
Cdn. Large Cap. Dividend	38.23	0.42	1.11
Europe Equity	10.34	0.18	1.77
Global Equity	16.48	0.18	1.10
CIBC Securities			
Asia Pacific	8.45	0.14	1.62
Cdn. Bond	13.54	−0.10	−0.75
Cdn. Small Cap.	34.44	0.33	0.96
Cdn. Real Estate	20.53	0.05	0.20
Cdn. Resources	25.72	0.13	0.53
Cdn. Equity	23.05	0.30	1.31
Dividend Growth	29.19	0.36	1.25
Monthly Income	12.99	0.04	0.35

Source: Courtesy of Morningstar and PlanPlus Inc.

1. Name of the fund — Usually the name gives some indication of the type of investment in which the fund specializes (e.g., stocks, bonds).

2. Value — The value is the **net asset value per share** or unit last calculated. The net asset value per share is defined as total assets minus current liabilities divided by the number of shares outstanding. Investors buy at this value plus the sales charge, if any, and sell at this value minus redemption fees, if any. The **net asset value per share** (**NAVPS**) is calculated daily for most funds and weekly for some.

3. Change — This column usually gives the change in value since the last calculation, usually the previous day.

4. % Change — The one-day percentage change.

Example 16.2: Let us examine the first fund under the AGF Group in Table 16.1. The name of the fund is the American Growth Class Fund; it is quoted in Canadian dollars. Its last NAVPS was $19.17, which represents an increase of $0.03 or +.16% from the previous report.

Weekly/Monthly Performance Report

A more detailed **performance report** is published weekly or monthly by some financial papers such as *The Globe and Mail* or the *National Post*. Investors desiring more complete and detailed information about funds should consult Internet websites such as <www.globefund.com> and <www.morningstar.ca>. In addition to the typical financial information, many websites provide sophisticated tools of screening or ranking of mutual funds to help the investor to make decisions. Table 16.2 is a compilation of the information by PlanPlus Inc. from Morningstar (a provider of independent investment research in the United States and in major international markets). We will go through the key terms contained in Table 16.2 and later discuss how to use the information to help you with your investment decisions.

Table 16.2 reports the following information for each fund:

1. Fund Name — Listed in alphabetical order.

2. RRSP and RRIF Eligibility — A "Y" indicates that the fund is both RRSP- and RRIF-eligible.

3. Total Net Assets — The total assets minus the current liabilities; indicates the size of the fund as of the date of the survey.

4. Net Asset Value Per Share (NAVPS) — Total net assets (see immediately above) divided by the number of shares outstanding.

5. Management Expense Ratio (MER) — The total operating costs (including annual management fee but excluding front-end and rear-end fees) as a percentage of assets; for example, if the annual operating cost of the fund is $1,500,000 and the total assets of the fund are $100,000,000, then the expense ratio is equal to $(1,500,000 \div 100,000,000) = 1.5\%$.

6. Standard Deviation — The annual variability of the return; this figure provides a measure of volatility and, hence, risk.

7. Simple Rates of Return for one month, six months, and one year — The holding period returns for one month, six months, and one year; the figures represent changes in asset value, including reinvestment of dividends and capital gains and excluding sales or redemption charges during the holding periods, and they are not to be confused with annual rates of return.

8. Annualized Return for three, five, and ten years — Each of these figures measures the average annual change in net asset value per share, assuming all

TABLE 16.2
Mutual Fund Performance Survey† as of June 30, 2012

Fund Name	RRSP/ RRIF	Total Net Assets ($ million)	Net Asset Value per Share (NAVPS) $	MER %	Standard Deviation, % (years)		Simple Rate of Return, % (months)			Annualized Return, % (years)		
					5	10	1	3	12	3	5	10
AGF American Growth Class	N	471.60	20.60	2.99	15.34	14.30	0.15	-2.78	8.71	9.78	-1.10	0.69
AGF China Focus Class	N	166.90	15.92	3.15	25.56	23.42	-1.13	-5.02	-15.30	-5.86	-6.60	7.99
AGF Traditional Balanced	N	407.60	5.74	2.51	10.84	8.77	1.40	-2.39	-1.75	2.25	-0.83	3.61
AGF Cdn. Large Cap. Dividend	Y	2,500.00	8.92	2.26	15.91	N/A	2.88	-1.65	-5.01	2.71	-2.43	N/A
AGF Europe Equity Class	Y	273.40	16.11	3.10	23.75	20.65	1.26	-4.90	-22.36	-12.54	-16.20	-1.43
CIBC Asia Pacific	N	117.90	8.35	3.04	14.56	14.10	2.82	-0.03	-3.68	1.11	-2.14	1.48
CIBC Cdn. Bond	Y	2,300.00	14.10	1.51	3.43	3.46	0.17	2.51	7.50	7.10	6.16	5.41
CIBC Cdn. Equity	Y	314.20	21.66	2.39	17.33	14.42	2.50	-4.60	-7.39	2.91	-4.23	4.60
CIBC Cdn. Real Estate	Y	56.90	25.77	2.96	16.46	13.46	5.70	5.78	20.12	24.92	4.27	10.25
CIBC Dividend Growth	Y	1,000.00	28.89	2.05	13.77	11.17	2.86	-2.43	-2.17	6.55	0.39	7.40
Dynamic Dividend	Y	517.70	11.16	1.58	11.16	9.60	3.90	-0.05	7.25	10.96	1.65	7.87
Dynamic Precious Metals	Y	623.60	7.01	2.73	40.18	36.53	2.19	-12.38	-39.36	6.64	2.81	14.89
Fidelity Cdn. Asset Allocation Sr. A	Y	11,100.00	23.99	2.46	11.30	9.19	1.13	-1.70	-4.87	2.96	0.89	5.90

† Information compiled by PlanPlus Inc. with data from Morningstar.

dividends and realized capital gains are reinvested on the date of distribution or realization, respectively; no sales or redemption charges are figured into these calculations.

Example 16.3: Let us examine the fifth row in Table 16.2. The fund's name is AGF Europe Equity. The total net asset value of the fund is $273.40 million. The net asset value per share is $16.11. The simple rates of return (i.e., the holding period return) are 1.26%, –4.9%, and –22.36% for holding periods of one month, three months, and one year, respectively. The annualized returns are –12.54%, –16.20%, and –1.43% measured over periods of 3, 5, and 10 years, respectively. The standard deviation on the rate of return, measured over the last five years, is 23.75%; and 20.65% over the last ten years. It has an expense ratio of 3.10%.

ASSESSING THE RISK AND RETURN OF A MUTUAL FUND

As mentioned before, the most important characteristics of any investment are its risk and expected return. The **mutual fund performance survey** (Table 16.2) provides historical, and hence objective, estimates of these two characteristics. As a general rule of thumb, many financial experts recommend that one should use historical data of at least 10 years to estimate risk and return because a longer time period provides more reliable estimates of these two characteristics.

In general, the shorter the history of the fund, the poorer the quality and reliability of the estimates for the rate of return and standard deviation. You should bear this in mind when you use the information from the monthly mutual fund performance survey.

The risk of the mutual fund is measured by the standard deviation of the rate of return. Table 16.2 shows a five-year and ten-year standard deviations. The five-year standard deviation should be viewed as a crude measure of the mutual fund's risk.[4] We will continue to use the data from Table 16.2 for the purpose of illustration only; we are not endorsing the accuracy or reliability of the numbers.

Let us use the Fidelity Canadian Asset Allocation Fund — the last row in Table 16.2. The annualized return and the standard deviation are 5.90% and

---

[4] You are advised to focus on funds with longer histories. You can calculate the standard deviation yourself by using at least 10 years of data. You can calculate the standard deviation easily from most business calculators. You can also use the PlanPlus software.

9.19%, respectively, both estimated from 10-year data. How do we interpret these numbers?

Empirical studies have found that the rate of return on a well-diversified portfolio is normally distributed; therefore, we can assume that the rate of return on the Fidelity Canadian Asset Allocation Fund is normally distributed, with an expected rate of return of 5.90% and a standard deviation of 9.19%. We can use the statistical properties of the normal distribution to assess the risk of the mutual fund. For example, we can find the probability of losing money: It is equal to the probability of getting a rate of return less than zero. The point, zero, lies at (5.90% ÷ 9.19%) or 0.64 standard deviation on the left-hand side of the expected value (5.90%), and from a normal distribution table such as Appendix C, the probability of getting a value less than 0.64 standard deviation from the expected value is equal to .2611.[5] In other words, there is a 26% chance that you will earn a negative rate of return (i.e., lose money) in the Fidelity Canadian Asset Allocation Fund in the coming year. Similarly, given any target rate of return (e.g., this could be the minimum rate of return that you require), you can calculate the probability of earning less than that target rate of return. By doing this kind of analysis, you can assess the riskiness of each mutual fund that you are considering.

A simpler, albeit less accurate, way to assess the risk of a mutual fund is as follows. The probability of the rate of return falling within one standard deviation below or above the expected value is equal to 68%, or roughly two out of three times. In other words, in two years out of three, the rate of return on the Fidelity Canadian Asset Allocation Fund will fall between (5.90% – 9.19%) = –3.29% and (5.90% + 9.19%) = 15.09%.

Example 16.4: Using the 10-year annualized return and standard deviation from Table 16.2, the rates of return for the following mutual funds will fall within the indicated lower bounds and upper bounds for two years out of three (i.e., with a probability of 68%).

Name of Fund	Lower Bound	Upper Bound
AGF American Growth	0.69 – 14.30 = –13.61	0.69 + 14.30 = 14.99
AGF China Focus	7.99 – 23.42 = –15.43	7.99 + 23.42 = 31.41
AGF Traditional Balanced	3.61 – 8.77 = –5.16	3.61 + 8.77 = 12.38
AGF Cdn. Large Cap. Dividend	N/A	N/A
AGF Europe Equity	–1.43 – 20.65 = –22.08	–1.43 + 20.65 = 19.22
CIBC Cdn. Bond	5.41 – 3.46 = 1.95	5.41 + 3.46 = 8.87

---

[5] This assumes you have some knowledge about basic statistics and the properties of a normal distribution.

Further Risk Reduction

Even though each mutual fund in Example 16.4 is a well-diversified portfolio and, hence, substantially less risky than a single stock, investing in any one of them still seems to be quite risky; the range for the rate of return is quite large in all cases; and to make things even worse, in one year out of three, the rate of return is expected to fall outside the range, which is already quite wide. Fortunately, there are two more ways to reduce risk substantially: (i) hold the mutual fund for the long term rather than the short term and (ii) hold a basket of mutual funds that are not highly correlated (i.e., low correlation can be had by diversifying the specialization of one's mutual fund holdings across the three main asset types of cash, bonds, and stocks). Let us elaborate on these two topics.

Reducing Risk by Investing for the Long Term

Holding a mutual fund for ten years is substantially less risky than holding it for one year. The reason for this is that there will be some good years and some bad years and the good years tend to cancel the bad years out so that over the 10-year period, the rate of return grows at the expected rate with less variability. In fact, the longer the investment horizon, the less risky the mutual fund will become, assuming the investments it holds remain the same.

Suppose the mutual fund's rate of return is normally distributed with expected value $E(r)$ and standard deviation s. It has been proven that if the mutual fund is held for n years, the annual standard deviation will be reduced to s divided by the square root of n.

Example 16.5: What is the standard deviation of the rate of return of the AGF Traditional Balanced Fund in Table 16.2 if the holding period is (a) one year, (b) two years, (c) five years, (d) 10 years, and (e) 20 years?

Answer: The answers are as follows:
(a) 8.77%
(b) $8.77\% \div \sqrt{2}$ = 6.20%
(c) $8.77\% \div \sqrt{5}$ = 3.92%
(d) $8.77\% \div \sqrt{10}$ = 2.77%
(e) $8.77\% \div \sqrt{20}$ = 1.96%

Thus, longer investing periods make riskier investments more attractive.[6]

---

[6] In practice, we cannot observe the result precisely because the structural assumption that the distribution is stationary (doesn't change over time) is violated.

Reducing Risk by Asset Allocation

Asset Allocation

Asset allocation can be defined as the allocation of one's investment money among the major asset types — non-cash investments, bonds, and stocks. Since these three investment types are not highly correlated, a substantial reduction in risk can be achieved by asset allocation.

Even with a modest amount of investment money, asset allocation can easily be done by buying a money market fund, a bond fund and a stock fund. Many people include other investment types such as real estate, U.S. stocks and bonds, international stocks, and so on. All these can be included by selecting the appropriate mutual funds.

Formal Analysis of Risk Reduction

Two-asset Portfolio

Suppose you have $10,000 and you want to invest part of it (say, 30%) in a T-bill mutual fund and the rest (say, 70%) in a Canadian stock index fund. What is the expected rate of return on your portfolio? What is the risk (the standard deviation of rate of return) of your portfolio?

To answer these questions, we have to introduce some results from the portfolio-investment literature. Suppose there are two mutual funds with expected rates of return $E(r_1)$ and $E(r_2)$, and the standard deviations of their rates of return are s_1 and s_2. Suppose further that the correlation coefficient between the two rates of return is r_{12}. Let x_1 be the fraction of investment money to be invested in the first mutual fund and x_2 be the fraction of investment money to be invested in the second mutual fund. Let $E(r_p)$ be the expected rate of return of the portfolio, and s_p be the standard deviation of the rate of the portfolio's return. The following equations will give the expected rate of return $E(r_p)$ and the risk s_p of the portfolio:

$$E(r_p) = x_1 E(r_1) + x_2 E(r_2) \qquad (1)$$

$$s_p{}^2 = x_1{}^2 s_1{}^2 + x_2{}^2 s_2{}^2 + 2x_1 x_2 r_{12} s_1 s_2 \qquad (2)$$

Example 16.6: Suppose you want to invest 30% of your investment money in a T-bill mutual fund and the rest (i.e., 70%) in a Canadian stock index fund. The following information is given:

Expected rate of return on the T-bill fund,
$E(r_1) = 6\%$

Expected rate of return on the stock index fund,
$E(r_2) = 12\%$

Standard deviation of $r_1 = s_1 = 2\%$

Standard deviation of $r_2 = s_2 = 16\%$

Correlation coefficient between r_1 and $r_2 = r_{12} = .10$

What is the expected rate of return on your portfolio, $E(r_p)$? What is the risk (the standard deviation) of your portfolio?

From equation (1), the expected rate of return on the portfolio is equal to:

$$E(r_p) = (.30 \times .06) + (.70 \times .12) = 10.2\%$$

From equation (2), the standard deviation of the return on the portfolio:

$$s_p = [(.30^2 \times .02^2) + (.70^2 \times .16^2) + (2 \times .3 \times .7 \times .1 \times .02 \times .16)]^{\frac{1}{2}}$$
$$= .1128 \text{ or } 11.28\%$$

Three-asset Portfolio

Suppose you want to invest in three mutual funds; as in the previous case, suppose you will invest a fraction x_1, x_2, and x_3 of your investment money in the first, second, and third fund, respectively. The expected rate of return of your portfolio, $E(r_p)$, and the risk (standard deviation) of your portfolio are given by the equations (3) and (4), respectively:

$$E(r_p) = x_1E(r_1) + x_2E(r_2) + x_3E(r_3) \tag{3}$$

$$s_p^2 = x_1^2 s_1^2 + x_2^2 s_2^2 + x_3^2 s_3^2 + 2x_1 x_2 r_{12} s_1 s_2$$
$$+ 2x_1 x_3 r_{13} s_1 s_3 + 2x_2 x_3 r_{23} s_2 s_3 \tag{4}$$

where r_i = expected rate of return of the ith fund, $i = 1,2,3$
s_i = the standard deviation of the rate of return of the ith fund
r_{ij} = the correlation coefficient between the ith fund and jth fund

Example 16.7: Winnie Dagmer wants to diversify her investment across the traditional three types of investments — cash-equivalent, bonds, and stocks. She has decided to put 20%, 30%, and 50% of her investment money into a money market fund (r_1), a Canadian bond fund (r_2), and a Canadian stock index fund (r_3), respectively. The following information is given:

$$E(r_1) = 7\% \qquad s_1 = 2\%$$
$$E(r_2) = 9\% \qquad s_2 = 11\%$$
$$E(r_3) = 12\% \qquad s_3 = 16\%$$

r_{12} = correlation coefficient between r_1 and r_2 = .20
r_{13} = correlation coefficient between r_1 and r_3 = −.10
r_{23} = correlation coefficient between r_2 and r_3 = .06

What is the expected rate of return on her portfolio, $E(r_p)$? What is the risk (standard deviation) of her portfolio, s_p?

From equation (3), the expected rate of return on her portfolio:

$$E(r_p) = (.20 \times .07) + (.30 \times .09) + (.50 \times .12) = 10.1\%$$

From equation (4), the standard deviation on the rate of return of her portfolio:

$$s_p = \left[\begin{array}{l} (.2^2 \times .02^2) + (.3^2 \times .11^2) + (.5^2 \times .16^2) \\ + (2 \times .2 \times .3 \times .2 \times .02 \times .11) + (2 \times .2 \times .5 \times -.1 \times .02 \times .16) \\ + (2 \times .3 \times .5 \times .06 \times .11 \times .16) \end{array} \right]^{1/2}$$

$$= .007811^{1/2}$$
$$= .088 \text{ or } 8.8\%$$

N-asset Portfolio

The above analysis can be extended to a portfolio of more than three assets (say, N assets). For example, if you invest in six mutual funds, then you hold a six-asset portfolio ($N = 6$). The expected rate of return $E(r_p)$ and the risk s_p of an N-asset portfolio are given by equations (5) and (6), respectively:

$$E(r_p) = x_1 E(r_1) + x_2 E(r_2) + \ldots + x_N E(r_n) \tag{5}$$

$$s_p^{\,2} = \sum_{i=1}^{N} x_i^{\,2} s_i^{\,2} + \sum \sum_{i \neq j}^{N} 2 x_i x_j r_{ij} s_i s_j \tag{6}$$

where x_i = fraction of investment invested in the ith asset
$E(r_i)$ = expected rate of return of the ith asset
s_i = standard deviation of the rate of return r_i
r_{ij} = correlation coefficient between r_i and r_j
N = the number of assets or mutual funds in the portfolio

There are many computer software packages[7] at reasonable prices which will help you with the calculation of equations (5) and (6).

Where to Get Information

The application of the equations (1) to (6) requires some necessary information: the rate of return and the standard deviation of each underlying mutual fund and the correlation coefficients between them. In Examples 16.6 and 16.7 we assumed that these statistics are given. In practice, you have to find these numbers or you must estimate them yourself.

The websites of the mutual fund companies and independent sites like <www.morningstar.ca> and <www.globefund.com> can provide the historical rates of return and the standard deviations of the rates of return of mutual funds for the previous twelve months and for up to the previous 15 years. A major problem is that the correlation coefficients between each pair of funds are not reported. Thus, even if the rates of return and the standard deviations are reliable, you still do not have enough information to use equations (1) to (6) in your analysis.

Fortunately, it is not difficult to estimate these numbers from historical data. As mentioned, financial experts advise investors to invest in funds with a long track record and usually that means 10 or more years. For each of the mutual funds that you are considering, obtain or calculate the annual or monthly rate of return for at least the last 10 years.[8] You can then use any of the many computer software packages or financial calculators on the market to generate the average rates of return, the standard deviations, and the correlation coefficients from the historical data.[9]

Risk of a Leveraged Portfolio

When you borrow money to invest, your portfolio is called a **leveraged portfolio**. In Chapter 12, we discussed the motivation for people to borrow money to invest. Examples of leveraged portfolios include buying stocks on margin,

---

[7] For example, the PlanPlus software.
[8] The websites provide means and standard deviations for up to 15-year periods, but they only provide 10 years of annual return. A 15-year correlation coefficient cannot be calculated.
[9] For example, the PlanPlus software will calculate these statistics from the data you provide.

purchasing your home with a first mortgage, and borrowing money to create a tax shelter. If you borrowed money to invest in mutual funds, your investment would also be a leveraged portfolio.

Leveraging, or borrowing money for investment purposes, is a double-edged sword. On the one hand, it magnifies the expected rate of return on your portfolio; on the other hand, it also magnifies the risk (or the standard deviation of the rate of return) of the portfolio.

Suppose you have W dollars to invest and you borrow B dollars more, agreeing to pay the lender the rate of interest = $i\%$ p.a. You may recall that the ratio $x = B \div W$ is called the **debt-to-equity ratio**. Suppose you invest the $(B + W)$ dollars in an investment, say a mutual fund, that has an expected rate of return, $E(r)$, and standard deviation, s_r. Now you have a leveraged portfolio. It can be shown that the expected rate of return $E(r_p)$ and the standard deviation s_p of the leveraged portfolio are given by the equations (7) and (8):

$$E(r_p) = E(r) + x[E(r) - i] \qquad (7)$$

$$s_p = (1 + x)s_r \qquad (8)$$

Clearly, both the risk s_p and the return $E(r_p)$ are increasing functions of the debt-to-equity ratio x.

Example 16.8: Mr. Bartel has $20,000 to invest. He has an account with a full-service broker who allows him to buy stocks or mutual funds with a 50% margin. This means that he can borrow up to a maximum of $20,000 from the broker and buy a maximum amount of $40,000 worth of stocks or invest $40,000 in a mutual fund. Of course, he is free to borrow less. The broker will charge 10% on any amount borrowed. Mr. Bartel is interested in a mutual fund that has an expected rate of return of 16% and a standard deviation of 25%.

What are the expected rate of return and the standard deviation of the leveraged portfolio if he borrows (i) $5,000; (ii) $10,000; (iii) $15,000; and (iv) $20,000?

Answer: (i) If he borrows $5,000, the debt-to-equity ratio is
$x = 5,000 \div 20,000 = .25$.

From equation (7),
$E(r_p) = .16 + [.25 \times (.16 - .10)] = 17.5\%$

From equation (8),
$s_p = [(1 + .25) \times .25] = 31.25\%$

$$\text{(ii)} \quad x = (10{,}000 \div 20{,}000) = .5$$
$$E(r_p) = .16 + [.5 \times (.16 - .10)] \qquad = 19\%$$
$$s_p = (1 + .5) \times .25 \qquad\qquad = 37.5\%$$

$$\text{(iii)} \quad x = (15{,}000 \div 20{,}000) = .75$$
$$E(r_p) = .16 + [.75 \times (.16 - .10)] \qquad = 20.5\%$$
$$s_p = [(1 + .75) \times .25] \qquad\qquad = 43.75\%$$

$$\text{(iv)} \quad x = (20{,}000 \div 20{,}000) = 1$$
$$E(r_p) = .16 + [1 \times (.16 - .10)] \qquad = 22\%$$
$$s_p = [(1 + 1) \times .25] \qquad\qquad = 50\%$$

Note that both the expected returns and the risks increase with borrowing.

HOW DO YOU SELECT MUTUAL FUNDS?

In spite of the tremendous progress made in knowledge about investments, investing is still an inexact science. There is no foolproof way to select the best mutual funds. Numerous methods to measure the performance of mutual funds have been suggested in investment literature, but academics are still not very satisfied with the existing methods and theories.[10] Although there is no sure-fire method of selecting mutual funds, it is quite easy to be "approximately right". For example, if you are young and saving up for your retirement, you will be "approximately right" regardless of which equity growth fund you happen to choose; by the same token, you will be "approximately wrong" if you put your money in a savings account earning 2% interest. If, however, you are saving to buy a car next year, putting money in that savings account makes more sense than putting your savings in an aggressive equity growth fund. Even better would be a treasury bill maturing at the time you want to buy the car. We shall now describe some guidelines about how to select "approximately right" mutual funds.

1. Diversify across the major asset types: money market, bonds, stocks. You can add real estate, international stocks and bonds, one or two specialty funds such as growth funds, natural resource funds, small company funds, and so on.

2. Decide how to allocate your investment money among the asset types — in other words, decide how much to put in money market funds, bond funds, equity funds, and so on. Your allocation depends on several things. First, it depends on your goals. For example, if one of your goals is to buy some furniture in six months' time, then the money set aside for this purpose

---

[10] For example, even the Capital Asset Pricing Model (CAPM), on which many mutual fund performance measures are based, has become suspect in the minds of many people.

should be put in money market funds. As explained in Chapter 3, your goals dictate the rate of return that you must earn. Second, your investment allocation depends on your risk preference. You have to find your own "comfort zone". With the assistance of computer software packages, it should be easy to perform the risk and return analysis — equations (1) to (8) — explained in this chapter. Try different allocations, create different portfolios, and perform the risk and return analysis.[11] Use the normal distribution table to find out the probability of losing money for each portfolio mix. Can you tolerate the loss? Do you think the expected rate of return can justify the risk that you will take? Only you can determine where your "comfort zone" of risk lies.

3. Make a short list of the mutual funds that are potential candidates for your investment. First, examine the long-term and short-term performances of all the funds on the mutual fund reports, such as Table 16.2. A fund with a solid 10-year record should be the first thing to look for. Ideally, this should come together with a good short-term record. Second, look at the risk (standard deviation) and compare it with those of the other funds on the same table. Clearly, a fund with an above-average long-term rate of return (at least 10 years) and a relatively low standard deviation would be a prime candidate for your short list. At this stage, you are looking for potential candidates and not a firm commitment.

4. Go for funds without front- or rear-end loads. Although sometimes it is worthwhile to pay a low front-end load for truly exceptional performance, normally you will do better with no-load funds. To be avoided as well are funds with high expense ratios: Only a truly superlative past performance can outweigh the disadvantage of a high expense ratio.

5. For the funds in your short list, call or write to the funds to get the sales literature and the prospectus[12] and read them. Always ask for a record of the annual rates of return for as long a time period as possible — the time period examined should be a minimum of 10 years in length. Without these numbers it is impossible to do the kind of quantitative analysis described in this chapter.

6. After obtaining the prospectus and the information about the past record from each fund, read the prospectus carefully and do a quantitative analysis such as

---

[11] At this initial stage, you can use the numbers in Appendix E as the estimates for the rates of return, standard deviations, and correlation coefficients for the major asset types. Later on when you have selected all the mutual funds and decided on the allocation of investment money among the funds, you can do the calculations again.

[12] The **prospectus** is a legal document that describes the securities or mutual funds to be offered for sale to the public.

the risk and return analysis described in this chapter. The objective here is to cut down the short list of the mutual funds that you will buy.

7. When you read the prospectus there are a few things to bear in mind. First, read the **fund's stated objectives** and see if they fit your personal needs: Is the fund's attitude toward the relative importance of income, safety, capital gains, and growth similar to your own attitude towards the relative importance of these investment variables? Second, carefully examine what any given fund invests in: What will it buy and what will it not buy? Have its past purchases been consistent with its stated policy? Third, find out all the charges and fees such as front-end load, annual fees, rear-end fees, deferred sales charges, commission on reinvested income, and other charges: Are you happy with the fee structure? How does it compare with the fee structure of other funds of the same type that are in your short list? Finally, read and analyze each fund's financial results. Normally, the prospectus does not provide you with the recommended 10-year historical record. You may have to make an additional request that this information be sent to you.

8. Buy the funds you like the best. Start a **record-keeping system**. For each fund, put down how much money you invested, the number of shares you bought, and the price at which you purchased them. Arrange to have all the future income and dividends reinvested automatically unless you need this income to live on. In the future, when you receive reports periodically, update your records according to the information contained in these reports.

9. Sit back and relax: Remember that, except for short-term money market funds, investing in mutual funds is a long-term proposition. In other words, do not sell out just because the market falls. Needless to say, however, a caution against premature selling does not mean that you should stick with a loser forever: If, over the course of two or three years, you find your fund's performance is substantially worse than that of other funds of the same type, start searching for another fund to replace it.

10. How safe is your money in the hands of fund management companies? Can fund managers or other people loot the fund? For practical purposes, you need not worry about this because the law requires that all securities are held by a third party custodian, usually a trust company: Even if the mutual fund **management company** goes bankrupt, your investments should be safe because they are segregated from the assets of the management company itself.

HOW ABOUT INDEXING?

An implication of the principle of efficient market is that in the long run, no mutual fund manager can consistently outperform a buy-and-hold strategy of the stock market, represented by a benchmark such as the S&P/TSX Composite. This has motivated the creation of many index funds that attempt to replicate the performance of market indexes. Since indexing is a simple passive investment strategy — basically you buy and hold the basket of stocks that are in the index — typical index funds have substantially lower annual fees (MER) than actively managed equity funds, and they are rarely loaded (front or rear).

For investors who are conscious about lowering costs (both MER and loads), indexing seems to make a lot of sense. We believe indexing should be an important part of an investor's portfolio in that an index fund offers all the advantages of mutual funds that we have discussed but has lower costs. On the other hand, we still believe that actively managed mutual funds can play an important role in your portfolio because of two main reasons. First, the stock market is not perfectly efficient. Empirical studies have found that there are market inefficiencies that fund managers can exploit to generate superior performance. Second, if most investors start to shift their investments into index funds, this will bid up the prices of stocks that are in the index relative to those that are not in the index, which will eventually result in inferior performance of the index funds. The safest strategy is diversification — hold some index funds and some actively managed mutual funds.

Other than investing in index funds, there are two other methods of indexing: index-linked GICs and exchange-traded funds (ETFs).

Index-linked GICs

Index-linked GICs combine the safety of GICs with the upside potential of the stock market because their returns are linked to particular market indexes. For example, there are TSX-linked GICs as well as GICs that are linked to international stock markets. For investors who are concerned about the preservation of their principal and who are uncomfortable with the ups and downs of the market, index-linked GICs should be considered. Most banks provide index-linked GICs and investors should read the detail features of each before investing their money.

Exchange-Traded Funds (ETFs)

An **exchange-traded fund** (**ETF**) is a hybrid — part mutual fund and part stock. It is similar to an index fund in that it is a portfolio of stocks (or bonds) designed to replicate or track the performance of a stock (or bond) market index. ETF is also like a stock in that it is traded in the stock market rather than redeemed. There are ETFs for all major indices, including S&P/TSX Composite, S&P/TSX 60, the Dow Jones Industrial Average, the S&P 500, NASDAQ 100, and EAFE (Europe, Australia, and the Far East). Also, there are ETFs for virtually every industry: financial, industrial, oil and gas, utilities, Internet, biotechnology, pharmaceuticals, technology, real estate, and so on. In the United States, you can find ETFs for a broad range of developed and developing countries. In summary, there is a whole range of ETFs that can provide investors with almost unlimited opportunities to diversification.

Like index funds, most ETFs are passively managed in that the fund managers simply replicate the market indices. They are renowned for their low management fees. If we use the management expense ratio (MER) as the measure of fund cost, Canadian-based ETFs have a range of 0.17% to 0.55% for their MERs. In contrast, actively managed Canadian equity funds have a median MER of 2.7%, and the passively managed Canadian equity index funds have a median MER of 0.95%.

SUMMARY

In this chapter we put the basic theories learned in Chapter 14 and the major types of investments described in Chapter 15 together. We developed an investment strategy whereby even small investors can make investments in all the major investment categories, choose their desired risk–return mix, and reach their financial goals. The investment strategy is to invest through mutual funds. We believe that mutual funds are the best investment choice for most Canadian investors.

A mutual fund accepts funds from hundreds or thousands of investors and uses the funds to make investments. There are many different types of mutual funds. They can be classified by the kinds of investments they make. The major types are Treasury-bill funds, money market funds, mortgage funds, income or bond funds, dividend funds, balanced funds, equity or stock funds, index funds, real estate funds, international funds, and other specialty funds.

The advantages and disadvantages of investing in mutual funds have been discussed. The most important benefits that mutual funds offer are professional management and broad diversification that individual investors cannot otherwise obtain by themselves. The major disadvantage is that there are fees. We described a framework for you to analyze and compare the fee structures of different mutual funds.

Mutual fund quotations are reported daily in newspapers and on websites. More detailed reports are published weekly or monthly. We have described the key terms that appear in these reports, and you should be able to read them without difficulty.

Investing in one mutual fund is still rather risky. Further risk reduction can be achieved by (i) increasing your investment horizon or holding period and (ii) investing in a basket of mutual funds that are not highly correlated with each other. The expected rates of return and the risks of different portfolios can be calculated by the equations (1) to (8) described in this chapter. Using these numbers and the normal distribution table, you can assess the risk level of various portfolios and discover your own risk preference (in terms of a risk "comfort zone").

Investors' responsibility is to allocate their investment money among the major asset types — near-cash, bonds, stocks, real estate, international securities, and so on. The allocation depends on one's financial goals, risk preference, and economic circumstances. There is no foolproof method to determine the "exactly right" allocation and to choose the "exactly right" mutual funds; however, if you follow our guidelines, it is not difficult to be "approximately right" in your investment decisions.

MULTIPLE-CHOICE REVIEW QUESTIONS

1. A(n) _____ is not a mutual fund.

   (a) index fund
   (b) sinking fund
   (c) balanced fund
   (d) equity fund
   (e) bond fund

2. Which of the following is *not* a good reason for investing in mutual funds?

   (a) Diversification
   (b) Professional management
   (c) Record keeping and safe keeping
   (d) Automatic reinvestment of dividends
   (e) None of the above

3. Which of the following is *not* a reason that index funds are better investments than actively managed funds?

   (a) The market is inefficient.
   (b) They have a lower MER.
   (c) Professional management does not add value in an efficient market.
   (d) All of the above.
   (e) None of the above.

4. In general, mutual funds perform _____ when interest rates are _____.

   (a) poorer; low
   (b) better; high
   (c) better; low and falling
   (d) better; rising
   (e) none of the above

5. Which of the following is traded in the stock market?

(a) Closed end mutual funds
(b) Exchange-traded funds
(c) Index funds
(d) Both (a) and (b)
(e) All of the above

DISCUSSION QUESTIONS

1. Describe or explain each of the following entries:

    alternatives to index funds: index-linked GICs — ETFs / leveraged portfolio / mutual fund advantages / mutual fund costs: front-end load or fees — back-end or rear-end fees — redemption fees — annual fees — management expense ratio (MER) / mutual fund types: open-end fund — closed-end fund — RRSP-eligible fund — money market funds — income fund or bond fund — balanced fund — equity fund or stock fund — growth fund — index fund — real estate fund — specialty fund — ethical fund — international fund — emerging market fund — no-load fund — front-load fund / mutual fund information: daily quotation — weekly report — mutual fund performance survey — weekly/monthly performance report / selecting a mutual fund: prospectus — fund's stated objectives — record-keeping system — management company

2. For each of the following statements, say whether you think it is true, false, or uncertain, and explain why. Marks will be given mainly for your explanation.

    (a) There is no risk-free investment in this world.
    (b) Since no-load funds are cheaper than loaded funds, you should never choose a fund with front-end or rear-end loads.
    (c) Since mutual fund managers are full-time professionals with lots of knowledge and experience, they can outperform the small investor nine out of ten times.
    (d) The best investment strategy is to buy an index fund.
    (e) How you allocate your investment money among the different asset classes depends on your financial goals.
    (f) Mutual funds are for long-term investors only. You should not touch mutual funds if your financial goal is short term.
    (g) Buying a bond fund is always less risky than buying a bond.

3. "According to the principle of efficient markets, one mutual fund cannot consistently outperform another one. Therefore, the time and effort spent in selecting mutual funds is wasted." Comment and discuss.

4. Refer to Example 16.1. Why aren't the front-end and back-end loads amortized on a straight-line basis, by dividing by the number of years? The front-end load would be 8% ÷ 10 = .8% p.a. and the back-end load 5% ÷ 10 = .5% p.a.

5. **Personal Project 1**

   Get a copy of the latest Mutual Fund Performance Survey from the library. For each of the fund categories — Canadian equity funds, balanced funds, international equity, and so on, prepare a short list of three mutual funds. Find out the address and telephone number of each fund's sponsor. Write or call for a prospectus and the historical rates of return since the fund's inception. Did you have any difficulty in getting the information? Report to the class or your instructor your experience in getting the required information. Explain how and why you have chosen the funds in your short list.

6. **Personal Project 2**

   State all your financial goals on a piece of paper. What are your action plans to achieve these goals? Write them down as well. Using the numbers in Appendix D as the estimates for the expected rates of return, the standard deviations, and the correlation coefficients of the major asset categories, describe how you would allocate your investment money and your future savings among the major asset categories to achieve your goals. Your answer should include an analysis of your risk preference: e.g., how do you assess your own risk "comfort zone"?

7. **Personal Project 3**

   Choose arbitrarily one bond fund, one Canadian equity fund, and one international fund (if you have done Question 4, you can choose these from your short list) that have at least 10 years of data. Obtain the data necessary to calculate the monthly rates of return for the last 10 years. Use a computer software package (e.g., the PlanPlus program) to generate the average rates of return, the standard deviations, and the correlation coefficients between the three funds. Construct three portfolios from these mutual funds. For each portfolio, calculate the expected rate of return and the standard deviation using equations (3) and (4), respectively.

PROBLEMS

1. The GLE Mutual Fund has a front-end fee of 2%, a rear-end fee of 5%, and an annual fee of 1.75%. Convert this fee structure to a single annual fee using an 8% discount rate and a three-year holding period.

2. Compare the fee structure of the following mutual funds, A and B, which are very similar in terms of quality and past performance.

	Fund A	Fund B
front-load	5%	0%
annual fee	1%	1.5%
rear-load	0%	2.0%

(a) Mr. Fong's holding period is 10 years and his discount rate is 10%. Which fund has the cheaper fee structure?

(b) Mr. Goldberg's holding period is three years and he uses a discount rate of 8%. Which fund has the cheaper fee structure?

(c) In general, are no-load funds always cheaper than front-load funds?

3. The following information about the expected rate of return $E(r_i)$, the standard deviations s_i, and the correlation coefficients r_{ij} of three mutual funds (r_1, r_2 and r_3) are given:

$$E(r_1) = 10\% \qquad s_1 = 12\% \qquad r_{12} = .5$$
$$E(r_2) = 13\% \qquad s_2 = 15\% \qquad r_{23} = .7$$
$$E(r_3) = 18\% \qquad s_3 = 20\% \qquad r_{13} = -.1$$

If x_i = the fraction of initial wealth allocated to the mutual fund r_i, calculate the expected rate of return and the standard deviation of the following portfolios:

(a) $x_1 = .5$ $x_2 = .3$ $x_3 = .2$
(b) $x_1 = .2$ $x_2 = .5$ $x_3 = .3$
(c) $x_1 = .1$ $x_2 = .2$ $x_3 = .7$
(d) $x_1 = .25$ $x_2 = .25$ $x_3 = .5$
(e) $x_1 = .40$ $x_2 = .15$ $x_3 = .45$

4. (a) Assuming that all the portfolios in Problem 3 are normally distributed and using the normal distribution table in Appendix C, calculate the probability of earning a negative rate of return for each of the five portfolios.

(b) If you buy any of the five portfolios on a 50% margin, calculate the standard deviation of each leveraged portfolio.

5. Wally Smally has $100,000 and he wants to have $1 million in 10 years. He wants to invest the money in a stock mutual fund with a rate of return of 20%. He can borrow at the interest rate of 10%.

(a) What is the required rate of return to reach his goal?

(b) What is the debt-equity ratio for reaching his goal?

6. Go to Appendix D. Using the data from years 1973 to 1995 (i.e., 23 years), calculate the following:

(a) The average rate of return and the standard deviation for each asset class.

(b) All the correlation coefficients. You may use a computer software package or a sophisticated calculator to do this question.

7. Mr. Wedgebarry has $50,000 to invest. He picks a portfolio of three mutual funds with different return patterns, and allocates his $50,000 as follows:

Fund	Return (%)	Standard Dev. (%)	Allocation (%)	Correlations
Angmar	7.9	3.6	20	$r_{12} = -0.1$
Gondor	11.9	16.7	45	$r_{13} = -0.2$
Mordor	17.0	29.0	35	$r_{23} = +0.3$

(a) What is the expected rate of return and standard deviation of return of his portfolio?

(b) The statistics he has are based on three-year compound rates of return. Assume that the portfolio returns are normally distributed. What is the probability that he will lose money on his investment during the next year?

8. You are provided the following information on three mutual funds: A, B, and C.

Fund	E(R)	SD	CORRELATIONS A	B	C
A	10%	.14	1	−.25	.30
B	15%	.16	−.25	1	.20
C	20%	.25	.30	.20	1

Mr. Allen approached you for advice and indicated that he has $200,000 to invest and would like to put $50,000 in Fund A, $70,000 in Fund B, and $80,000 in Fund C.

(a) What is the expected return on his portfolio using the above information?

(b) What is the standard deviation of his portfolio using the above information?

(c) If the portfolio is normally distributed, what is the probability that he will:
   (i) lose money in the first year?
   (ii) lose money after five years?
   (iii) earn more than 21% after one year?

(d) A stockbroker has offered Mr. Allen a 50% margin account that charges 5% interest. If Mr. Allen utilizes the full margin available, what is the expected return and standard deviation on the portfolio, assuming that the investor takes full advantage of the margin account?

9. You wish some international diversification in your portfolio and you have narrowed your selection to three funds with similar risk and return histories. Your discount rate for fund costs is 8%. The funds have the following fee schedules:

Fund	Front-load (%)	Back-load (%)	Management Fee (%)
Dune	7	0	2.3
Middle Earth	0	0	4.0
Narnia	0	9	3.3

Which fund would be the best for investment horizons of three, six, and ten years?

CHAPTER 17

Retirement Planning

▶ What is a pension? We explain in the first section of this chapter.

▶ Rose and Sam Wise want to retire when they reach 65, with an after-tax income of $49,000 in today's dollars (i.e., real dollars). They are very unwilling to risk running out of money. What amount of savings do you advise them that they will need when they retire? See Examples 17.3 and 17.4.

▶ Rose and Sam have a shortfall between what their current savings and expected pensions will provide and what they want to have for retirement. How much will they have to save every year if they are 55 years old now? See Example 17.10.

LEARNING OBJECTIVES

> ➤ *To determine the financial resources a family has now that can be used for retirement.*

> ➤ *To set goals for retirement and translate those goals into the financial requirements at retirement date.*

> ➤ *To estimate how much the family must save to meet the retirement goals.*

> ➤ *To explain how to save and invest to provide the estimated financial requirements.*

> ➤ *To explain the nature of government and employer pension plans.*

Retirement planning isn't a separate topic; it is a combination of all the topics we have discussed in the previous chapters. To plan for retirement, you need goals and budgets. You must manage tax, risk, and investment problems, and sometimes even debt. The retirement plan applies to everything we have studied so far. The particularly critical aspect of it is that when the day of retirement dawns, you don't have any chance to correct mistakes. Your earned income has ended, and you must rely on the assets you have built up during your working life.

We consider retirement planning in two steps. This chapter takes you through your working life to the time when you retire. Chapter 18 deals with managing financial affairs at the time of retirement and through the retirement years, and discusses estate planning.

We can summarize retirement planning in three sentences:

- How much have you got now?
- How much will you need at retirement?
- How do you get from here to there?

THE RETIREMENT PLANNING MODEL

Let us model the basic retirement plan as we did earlier in the book, using the following symbols to represent the elements of personal financial planning. The subscripts represent time: t is any particular future year; n is the year of planned retirement; d is the number of years from date of retirement to date of death; and 0 is now, the starting point of the plan. Thus, if you plan to retire in 10 years and expect to die 20 years after that, $n = 10$, $d = 20$, and t runs from one to 10.

W_n The amount of money you are trying to accumulate to provide for retirement.

W_0 The amount of money you have today that can be retained and used to provide retirement consumption. For example, an RRSP is part of W_0, but a savings account that will be used to put a child through university is not.

k The discount rate. It may be different for different periods or different parts of the equation.

E_t The money you earn in year t, other than investment income.

C_t The money you consume or spend in year t, other than that used to purchase investments that will eventually contribute to savings for retirement.

The following equation summarizes the retirement planning problem. The left-hand side is your current savings and expected future savings each year (earnings less consumption) compounding at the rate of return. The middle term is the amount of wealth required at retirement. The right-hand side is the consumption during retirement that you have to fund in order to live at the standard of living you specify:

$$W_0 (1 + k)^n + \sum_{t=1}^{n} (E_t - C_t)(1 + k)^{n-t} = W_n = \sum_{t=n+1}^{d} \frac{C_t}{(1 + k)^{t-n}} \qquad (1)$$

The first steps in retirement planning use the tools learned in Chapters 2–4. Once we determine the desired standard of living and what it entails in wealth at retirement, we juggle saving and consumption in the time left from now until retirement to see how much we must save and whether the goal is feasible. There are many ways to make the equation balance. A family can consume less now in order to save more for retirement, or can decide to consume less in retirement. Investing to reach a higher rate of return will involve more risk. In principle, the adult members could try to increase their earnings, but this option isn't entirely within their control by the time they are making serious plans for retirement. Earlier choices in education and occupation determine most of the earning potential. A homemaker spouse could enter the workforce, but that will entail extra costs, especially if there are children in the family.

What Is a Pension?

A pension is a life annuity financed by a combination of enforced employee periodic savings deducted from employment earnings at source and enforced periodic employer contributions into a trusteed fund. Let us look at each piece of that definition.

A basic life annuity pays a specified sum to annuitants every period for as long as they live and ceases upon the annuitant's death. In Chapter 2 we showed you how to do calculations with term certain annuities that pay a specified periodic amount for a fixed number of periods and then ceased. We can calculate any variable for a term-certain annuity if we have the other variables because all the components are certain. The number of periods a life annuity pays is unknown until the annuitant dies; the value n in the time value calculations is unknown. We treat n as a probabilistic variable distributed according to some mortality table like the ones in Appendices A and B. This property of an uncertain length to the annuity contract makes it an insurance contract, just like a life insurance contract, and only life insurance companies may sell life annuities. We describe the characteristics of different types of life annuities in a later section in this chapter.

The enforced employee savings through payroll deductions and the enforced employer contributions are always specified in a contract or, in some cases, in a law. The contributions by each party are usually equal or very close to equal. All the money goes into a separate fund that is not part of the employer's assets, but is instead governed by a trust that must obey provincial or federal pension legislation. The trustees manage the assets in the fund on behalf of the employees, and each employee is entitled to a pension upon retirement, with the amount determined by the terms of the pension contract. The employee cannot access the money directly until retirement and the employer cannot access it at all except in some very specific cases where the entire plan and the organization are terminated. The employer's contributions are tax deductible for the employer. The employee's contributions are deducted from taxable income, and the pension is taxable. While the funds are still in the trust, all earnings are not taxable. Only the pension paid out is taxable.

For example, the Canada Pension Plan (CPP) and the Québec Pension Plan (QPP) pay a retirement pension that is a life annuity. All Canadians earning labour income must be enrolled in one of them, with minor exceptions, until they retire. The pension contract is set by federal or Québec law. An employer in the CPP pays 4.95% of earnings up to the limit of the Yearly Mean Pensionable Earnings less $3,500, and the employee pays the same amount. Self-employed persons must pay the employer and employee portions on their self-employed income. The Canada Pension Plan Investment Board and the Caisse de Dépôt et de Placements du Québec invest the money for the respective plans.[1]

Old Age Security is not a pension, though it is a life annuity. Annuitants do not make any contributions. The annuity is paid out of general government revenue as a social welfare measure.

Economists view pensions as deferred compensation. The employee cannot spend the money until retirement, but has already earned it. Anyone comparing job offers should always consider whether the employer offers a pension plan other than CPP or QPP. The value of a pension benefit is enormous. The gross wage alone is not a sufficient number for a valid comparison.

---

[1] The CPP and QPP are very similar. These government-mandated plans also provide a significant life insurance and disability insurance benefit to families, which we described in Chapter 10.

We provide this basic description of pension plans at the start of the chapter because you need to know it to understand even the simplest retirement planning. Later sections of the chapter provide much more information about different types of pensions.

Retirement Goal and Basic Examples

As discussed in Chapter 3, the starting point of the retirement planning process is to set a retirement goal, which can be stated as a certain sum of money at the point of retirement. For example, one may want to have $1 million at age 65 when one retires. Equation (1) implies that one way to estimate this goal value is to calculate the present value of one's post-retirement consumption, from the day of retirement until the day of death.

Example 17.1: Marcus Sabatini, 55, is planning to retire in 10 years. With the help of a financial planner, he estimates that he will need $33,000 income per year, in real dollars. To be on the safe side, he wants to use a life expectancy of 90 years in his planning, even though he does not expect to live that long.

(a) If the real rate of interest is 3%, what is the present value of his post-retirement required income (his retirement goal)?

(b) If Marcus has $20,000 now, how much must he save and invest every year in order to reach this goal in (a)?

Answer:

(a) Recall that it is possible to do most personal finance questions, including retirement planning questions, in nominal dollars or real dollars. We will use real dollars and the real rate of interest in this example.

$$\text{His retirement goal} = (\$33,000)\left[\frac{1 - (1.03)^{-25}}{.03}\right]$$

$$= \$574,634 \text{ in real dollars}$$

(b) Let x be the amount that he must invest every year in order to reach his goal. We can set up the following equation to solve for x:

$$(\$20,000)(1.03)^{10} + x\left[\frac{(1.03)^{10} - 1}{.03}\right] = \$574,639$$

$$x = 47,781 \text{ in real dollars}$$

Retirement Goal in Terms of Income Shortfall

Many individuals have income that will automatically start at the point of retirement. These include pension income, CPP, and OAS. Also, there are other sources of income that are available, such as investment income and income from part-time work. If the sum of the income from all sources is insufficient to cover the expected expenses, we call this the **income shortfall**. Conceptually, retirement planning can be viewed in terms of how to finance the expected income shortfall so that the retiree can have the desired lifestyle. Example 17.2 illustrates the concept of the income shortfall and how the retirement goal can be calculated in terms of the income shortfall.

Example 17.2: Rhonda Fernandez, 50, plans to retire in 15 years time. She estimates that she will need, post-retirement, 70% of her current income, or 70% of $35,000. Her employer's human resource department tells her to expect to receive a pension income of $6,500 p.a. in today's dollars. She will also get CPP and OAS at that time, estimated to be $7,300 p.a. in today's dollars. The real rate of interest is 3%. She does not expect to live beyond age 90.

(a) What is the expected income shortfall at retirement?
(b) What is her retirement goal?
(c) If she has no investment now, how much must she save and invest every year to reach her goal?

As before, we will use real dollars and real rate of interest in this example.

Answer:

(a) The expected income shortfall
$$= (\$35,000)(.70) - \$6,500 - \$7,300$$
$$= \$10,700 \text{ real dollars per year}$$

(b) Her retirement goal is the present value of the income shortfall, from point of retirement to day of death.

$$\text{Retirement goal} = (\$10,700)\left[\frac{1 - (1.03)^{-25}}{.03}\right]$$
$$= \$186,321 \text{ in real dollars}$$

(c) Let $\$x$ be the amount she must save and invest at 3% interest.

$$x\left[\frac{(1.03)^{15} - 1}{.03}\right] = \$186,321$$

$$x = \$10,018 \text{ real dollars per year}$$

Retirement planning involves very long time periods, and hence is very uncertain. We use specific numbers and equations in this chapter, but you must understand that the answers are only rough estimates. A person at age 35 should at least think about provision for retirement, but that implies planning for a period of 50 years or more. Many of the assumptions of any financial plan will change. We should not be misled by the apparent precision of the answers that time value calculators and computers can produce.

We need to travel down some side roads for a while before we can use the model, because we need to understand very clearly the principles involved in finding the inputs. Three problem areas stand out: discount rates, life expectancy, and pension plans. We discuss each in turn.

INFLATION, TAXES, AND DISCOUNT RATES

As we have already seen in Chapter 2, taxes and inflation affect discount rates. We explain the complications, then provide some reasonable principles to follow since we need approximate rather than precise solutions. We use the following additional notation:

k_{nom} Nominal discount rate before tax
k_{real} Real discount rate before tax
$k_{nom,AT}$ Nominal discount rate after tax
$k_{real,AT}$ Real discount rate after tax
T Tax rate
i Inflation rate

Inflation

Inflation prevents us from comparing amounts in future years with current amounts because what they will purchase has changed and consumption is what we value, not the actual dollars. We usually think in terms of our cost of living today. We can express everything in today's dollars (constant or real dollars) by discounting the future nominal amounts by the inflation rate. This brings up a crucial rule of discounting:

Discount real dollars using a real discount rate, and discount nominal dollars using a nominal discount rate.

Recall from Chapter 2 that you convert between real and nominal discount rates, using the Fisher relationship, as follows:

$$\frac{1 + k_{nom}}{1 + i} = 1 + k_{real}$$

A common serious mistake in financial planning is the use of nominal discount rates for real cash flows, or real discount rates for nominal cash flows. For example, if you buy a life annuity that pays a fixed amount of $1,000 per month, that is a nominal cash flow, and to value it you would discount the payments at a nominal rate.[2] The OAS is indexed for inflation. That means that every period (quarterly for OAS) the amount paid is multiplied by (1 + inflation rate). Therefore, the specific amount paid at any one time is in real dollars because it will increase in nominal dollars to match inflation. To value this pension, you would discount an annuity of the present amount by the real discount rate.[3]

Since retirement planning covers such long time periods, we should use long-run average inflation rates. At the time of writing this edition, the inflation rate in Canada was running 2–3% p.a. In the 1970s and early 1980s it exceeded 10% in some years. What rate should you use in a retirement plan that could stretch for 50 years? The average inflation rate for 1957–2010 was 4.0%, for example.

Even in real dollars, there is still a positive interest rate, since we have to be compensated for deferring consumption. Estimates of the real risk-free interest rate range from 2–4%. The risky real rate depends on how much risk you assume. Corporate bonds would start at 4% and rise as the creditworthiness of the company declines. A well-diversified Canadian common equity portfolio provided a real geometric mean return of 5.23% for the period 1957–2010, for example.

Income Tax

Discount after-tax dollars using an after-tax discount rate, and discount before-tax dollars using a before-tax discount rate.

Recall from Chapter 7 that the after-tax discount rate is:

$$k_{nom,AT} = k_{nom}(1 - T)$$

where T is the tax rate. Applying these discount rates to retirement planning is complicated, and we will have to be satisfied with a rough approximation. The tax rate applied to the savings portion of equation (1) (the left-hand side) is the *marginal* rate, because the earnings on the savings are on top of the regular earnings of the family. This marginal rate is not easy to calculate, because it depends on whether the saving is invested in a tax-sheltered or unsheltered form.

---

[2] Remember, nominal rates are the rates that we actually observe in the marketplace. Therefore, the rate to discount this annuity would be somewhere around a government bond rate.

[3] Alternatively, you could inflate every year's payment and discount at the nominal rate, but it would be more time-consuming to do so.

Contributions to pension plans and RRSPs are deducted from taxable income and income inside them accumulates tax-free until withdrawn, so the marginal tax rate is zero. Investment earnings on savings outside the sheltered plans are taxable but at different rates for dividends, capital gains, and interest. Investments in a TFSA are not taxed at all. Thus, the marginal tax rate will be some average of the rates on each part of the savings. Furthermore, the tax rate for the first term on the left side, the wealth already accumulated, will probably differ from the tax rate for the future accumulations.

The tax rate applied to the consumption portion of equation (1) (the right-hand side) is the *average* rate because, in retirement, the investment income (including pensions) is the entire income of the family. We cannot calculate the average rate using the formulas in Chapter 7 — the average rate is the total tax divided by the total income. Once again, the source of the income affects the rate because the payments from pensions and RRSPs are fully taxable (since the contributions were tax deductible). The gain on sale of the family home is not taxable. Income from investments outside pension plans and RRSPs is taxable, but the principal amounts are already after-tax and are not taxed when the retiree cashes in the investment for consumption purposes. The tax credits (personal, old age, pension, etc.) further complicate the calculation of the average tax rate.

To get the correct tax rate you prepare a mock tax return for the proposed future situations and calculate the marginal and average rates that arise. A reasonable estimate of the average rate is usually all that you need, given the imprecision of such long-range planning, and Table 17.1 gives the average for a single tax payer for a number of income levels. You can use interpolation to arrive at the approximate tax rate for other situations. Tax rates change over time, but using the current rates is the best we can do.

Income tax is calculated on nominal earnings, not real earnings. This means that you pay tax on the inflation component of your savings, even though you aren't actually any better off. As long as we keep all the values in after-tax nominal dollars, we can use $k_{nom,AT}$ for all cash flows. Sometimes, we can do calculations more easily in real dollars to use the convenience of annuities.

To reflect the taxation of inflation correctly in a real rate, we have to convert a before-tax nominal rate of return into an after-tax real rate by applying the tax factor first, then converting it to real terms:

$$k_{real,AT} = \frac{1 + k_{nom}(1 - T)}{1 + i} - 1$$

For example, suppose you expect to invest in a diversified portfolio of common equity. The long-run average rate of return could be 12%. The long-run average inflation you expect is 4%, and you will be in a 40% marginal tax bracket. The after-tax marginal rate of return is then calculated as follows:

TABLE 17.1
Average Tax Rates for Retirees

Taxable Income	AB	BC	MB	NB	NL	NT	NS	NU	ON	PEI	SK	YT
$ 14,000	0.00	0.00	0.01	0.00	0.00	0.00	0.00	0.00	0.00	0.01	0.00	0.00
16,000	0.00	0.00	0.02	0.01	0.01	0.00	0.01	0.00	0.00	0.02	0.00	0.00
20,000	0.01	0.02	0.04	0.03	0.03	0.01	0.03	0.01	0.02	0.04	0.01	0.01
25,000	0.04	0.05	0.09	0.07	0.07	0.05	0.08	0.04	0.06	0.08	0.06	0.05
30,000	0.08	0.08	0.12	0.10	0.10	0.07	0.10	0.06	0.08	0.11	0.09	0.08
35,000	0.10	0.10	0.14	0.12	0.12	0.09	0.13	0.08	0.10	0.13	0.12	0.10
40,000	0.12	0.11	0.16	0.14	0.14	0.11	0.15	0.10	0.11	0.15	0.13	0.12
45,000	0.14	0.13	0.17	0.16	0.16	0.13	0.17	0.12	0.13	0.17	0.15	0.13
50,000	0.16	0.15	0.19	0.18	0.18	0.15	0.19	0.13	0.15	0.19	0.17	0.15
55,000	0.17	0.16	0.21	0.19	0.19	0.16	0.21	0.15	0.16	0.21	0.19	0.17
60,000	0.19	0.17	0.22	0.20	0.21	0.17	0.22	0.16	0.18	0.22	0.20	0.18
65,000	0.20	0.18	0.23	0.22	0.22	0.18	0.24	0.17	0.19	0.23	0.21	0.19
70,000	0.21	0.19	0.24	0.23	0.23	0.20	0.25	0.18	0.20	0.25	0.23	0.20
75,000	0.23	0.21	0.26	0.25	0.25	0.21	0.27	0.20	0.22	0.27	0.25	0.22
80,000	0.24	0.23	0.28	0.26	0.26	0.23	0.29	0.21	0.24	0.28	0.26	0.24
85,000	0.26	0.24	0.30	0.28	0.28	0.25	0.30	0.23	0.26	0.30	0.28	0.25
90,000	0.27	0.26	0.31	0.29	0.29	0.26	0.32	0.25	0.28	0.31	0.29	0.27
100,000	0.29	0.29	0.34	0.32	0.32	0.29	0.34	0.27	0.31	0.34	0.32	0.29
125,000	0.32	0.32	0.37	0.34	0.35	0.32	0.37	0.30	0.35	0.37	0.34	0.32
150,000	0.33	0.34	0.39	0.36	0.36	0.34	0.39	0.31	0.36	0.39	0.36	0.34
200,000	0.35	0.37	0.40	0.37	0.37	0.36	0.42	0.34	0.39	0.41	0.38	0.36
250,000	0.35	0.38	0.42	0.39	0.38	0.38	0.43	0.35	0.40	0.42	0.39	0.37
350,000	0.36	0.40	0.43	0.40	0.40	0.39	0.45	0.37	0.42	0.44	0.41	0.39
500,000	0.37	0.41	0.44	0.41	0.40	0.40	0.47	0.38	0.43	0.45	0.42	0.40
1,000,000	0.38	0.42	0.45	0.42	0.41	0.42	0.48	0.39	0.45	0.46	0.43	0.41
3,000,000	0.39	0.43	0.46	0.43	0.42	0.43	0.49	0.40	0.46	0.47	0.44	0.42

This table shows the average tax rate for a single retiree in this situation:
• Age 65 or older
• Receives full OAS and enough eligible pension income to get the maximum non-refundable tax credit for pension income
• OAS clawback applied on high income
• Reduction of GIS not included
• None of the taxable income is dividends, capital gains, or return of capital

The previous edition of the textbook provided average rates for both singles and couples because unequal division of income and transfer of tax credits might lead to a lower rate for each member of a couple than for a single person. The introduction of pension income splitting removes this difference in the vast majority of situations, and hence only the average rate for singles is shown for each province and territory other than Québec.

$$\frac{1 + .12(1 - .4)}{1.04} - 1 = 3.1\%$$

The same calculation applies to both the average and the marginal tax rates.

A PRACTICAL APPROACH TO DISCOUNTING RETIREMENT CASH FLOWS

In theory, we could discount post-retirement cash flows before or after-tax, and in real or nominal dollars. In practice, we standardize on one method of discounting to avoid confusion. We are going to convert all our calculations to before-tax dollars, and to real dollars whenever possible. This approach has some advantages and disadvantages:

1. We can relate to real dollars in the context of costs today more easily.

2. We can use annuities instead of a spreadsheet with different nominal figures for every year. When you use software like PlanPlus, this advantage doesn't matter so much.

3. There is no such thing as a truly after-tax annuity. Any lump sum, even if all the tax has been paid up to the date of retirement, will still attract tax on the income earned on it as it is drawn down in retirement. Notionally, we are making the lump sum equal to an annuity in retirement, but the payments are blended principal (tax-free) and interest (taxable). Calculating a blended tax rate is beyond the scope of this book.[4]

4. The disadvantages all relate to income tax. Taxes are levied on nominal income, and if the brackets are not perfectly indexed, then the effective tax rate is understated. Canadian tax brackets, tax credits, and deductions are indexed, but not perfectly. However, capital markets evaluate investments in after-tax dollars, and if the tax system starts to weigh more heavily on nominal income because of inflation, the before-tax rates of return will rise. While we will use real dollars, in practice more precise results may be obtained by using nominal dollars.

Our practical approach works like this. There are four components to value in a retirement plan.

---

[4] The CRA provides prescribed annuities that level out the taxes over the life of the annuity, but we cannot use those calculations when we are notionally annuitizing a mutual fund portfolio.

Consumption Needs in Retirement

We could estimate them in before-tax dollars or after-tax dollars. To convert after-tax dollars to before-tax, use Table 17.1 and the following formula:

$$\text{Before-tax income} = \frac{\text{After-tax income}}{1 - \text{Tax rate}}$$

This process requires trial and error. For example, suppose a person in Manitoba wants $30,000 p.a. after-tax income, or consumption, in retirement. Start with the next higher bracket, $35,000 pre-tax. The average Manitoba tax rate on $35,000 is 14%, from Table 17.1, which yields an after-tax income of $(1 - .14) \times \$35,000 = \$30,100$. In some cases another iteration may be needed to get a more accurate result, but in this case the first trial works.

Pension Plans

Indexed pension plans are already in before-tax real dollars. We subtract them from the required before-tax income. Indexed pensions include CPP, OAS, and some employer pensions. In practice, some plans are fairly well indexed, and most have some degree of indexation. For example, some employer plans have excess interest provisions. At retirement, the retiree receives an annuity calculated at, say, 6% rate of return. If the plan's earnings exceed 6% for a number of years, then the pension is increased slightly. Since a pension fund with a mix of equity and bonds should earn more than 6% nominal in the long run, the pension should keep increasing. Moreover, it will increase more in the long run if inflation is higher because financial markets will adjust to provide higher long-run nominal returns.

Other plans have ad hoc indexation. The employer agrees to increase the payouts to existing and future pensioners from time to time to compensate for erosion in the real value. In practice, most modern plans are at least partly indexed and we will assume the values are in real dollars. In principle, the value of an imperfectly indexed plan should be adjusted, but the calculations are both difficult and imprecise so we do not go into that problem. This is the situation where using financial planning software and nominal dollars may be needed.

Unsheltered Savings

Savings outside pensions, RRSPs, RRIFs, and DPSPs are mostly after-tax. Prior to retirement, they compound at the after-tax marginal rate. After the tax is paid on any income and capital gains, the net amount is in after-tax dollars. The conversion of the lump-sum value at retirement date to before-tax dollars uses the same formula as we used for after-tax income, but the tax rate will be much lower to reflect the fact that only the income on the principal is taxed. This future value, grossed-up to be in before-tax dollars, is then added to W_n.

Sheltered Savings

These amounts are all before-tax. They accumulate at the before-tax rate prior to retirement, and are then added to W_n. There is one exception — the TFSA. The TFSA is defined to be always in after-tax dollars. Investments in a TFSA compound at the pre-tax rate, but at retirement we notionally gross it up to the pre-tax value because that is what we have standardized on.

We will illustrate all these points with numerical examples, but first we must discuss how we determine d, the number of years to discount the cash flows.

LIFE EXPECTANCY

In the model, we assume a known value of d, but the date of death is uncertain or probabilistic. Therefore, we have to make some estimate or approximation, and this estimate creates additional risk. Suppose you outlive the estimated death date and run out of money? Alternatively, suppose you try to provide for a very long life, and have to practically starve yourself and work until age 75, when you really didn't need to? We can't eliminate those risks, but we do have to pick a number in order to plan at all. Let us see what we can learn from the statistical likelihood of death at any age in Canada.

In Chapter 10, you learned how to use the standard mortality tables to calculate the probability of a Canadian male or female dying at a given age from any starting age.[5] Appendix B of the book contains two standard life tables, one each for females and males. If you look at the probabilities of death you see that the likelihood of dying in any given year is very small until quite late ages. For example, a woman who turns 70 has a 1.62% chance of dying within the year. A male who turns 70 has a 3.00% chance of dying within the year.

However, what interests us in this chapter is the cumulative likelihood of surviving to any given age since that is what we have to plan for in retirement. The cumulative probability combines what happens every year until some specified date. This probability is also conditional on the age that is the starting point. If we start considering the future today, then the probability of surviving for 10 years relates to what happens in each of those 10 years. For every year the horizon extends, the probability of dying at or before that horizon increases. The date at the starting point also affects the probability, but in a non-linear fashion. The probability of dying in any one year declines for the first eight years of life, then increases every year thereafter. The life tables stop at 110, because the percentage of Canadians who live beyond 110 is insignificant.

---

[5] If you have forgotten how to do this, review the section of Chapter 10 on calculating the pure premium of a life insurance policy.

	Ages	
TABLE 17.2 Probability of a Person Aged 65 Living to a Given Age		
Probability (%)	**Female**	**Male**
50	87	83
40	89	85
30	91	88
20	93	90
10	96	94

For retirement planning, we want to know how many years of retirement we have to provide income for, the d in equation (1). We can't give a certain answer because the date of death is uncertain, but we can show the probability distribution. Consider a 65-year-old female. If she wants to be virtually certain of having enough retirement income, she must provide for 41 years.[6] She might reasonably say that the chances of living past 100 are negligible, but that still leaves 35 years. What age does she have an 80% chance of reaching? a 70% chance? We can calculate the deciles quite easily, and that is one way to present the risks of outliving your money.

More formally, we want to answer the question, By what age is a woman 50% likely to die, given that she has already reached the age of 65? This is a conditional probability calculation. We note that at age 65, there are 90,899 women remaining of the original 100,000. The 50% percentile is reached when only half that number alive at 65 are still living, or 45,450. Repeating the same calculation for different percentiles yields Table 17.2.

How much risk you want to take of running out of money in retirement is a personal decision. You can guarantee some level of lifetime consumption with a life annuity, a topic we discuss in Chapter 18. For any amount of retirement income required in excess of pensions, regardless of whether you finance it with an annuity or with self-managed investments, you will have to provide for quite a few years. We would suggest that a woman would have to have provided for at least 30 years, and a man for at least 25, to retire at age 65. Even at these values of d, there is still a 30% chance of running out of money if they spend at exactly the planned rate.

---

[6] Absolute certainty presumably requires provision for about 55 years since we understand that the limit of the human body is about 115–120 years, even with modern medicine.

Life expectancy calculations and estimates are a lot more complex in practice than we have shown so far, and Appendices B and C contain fundamental assumptions that bias them in comparison with the information that an insurance company uses in pricing annuities and, hence, should concern us regarding our estimates of how much money you need for retirement.

One issue is the static, historic nature of a life table. If we want to know the probability of surviving one year, then the current table based on recent history is reasonably accurate. For longer periods, we can't use it for very precise calculations because human life expectancy has been rising throughout recent history, and actuaries expect that trend will continue into the future. If an insurance company were to price a life annuity in 2012 using only the most recent life expectancy figures, it would pay out too much, because many years from now its 80-year-old annuitants will be living longer than they would have if they had been that age in 2012. If you were to compare Appendices B and C from this fifth edition of the textbook with the same tables in the fourth edition, you would see longer life expectancies in this edition. The implication for our retirement planning is that we need to allow for a slightly higher probability of living longer than Table 17.2 shows.

A second issue is the average nature of the tables, which incorporate the entire population of Canada. Different segments of the population have quite different life expectancies. On an ethnic basis, the average life expectancy for Aboriginal Canadians is far lower than the average for the country. Each province has slightly different rates. Life expectancy is also strongly positively correlated with education, wealth, and social status.

A third issue is a person's knowledge about his or her health and life expectancy based on genetic history and existing health conditions. If your eight great-grandparents are still alive and going on sky-diving trips, your four grandparents run marathons when they aren't telling you how to properly discipline your children, and your parents work as tree planters in northern British Columbia, you had better plan on saving a lot of money for what is likely to be a long life as a retiree. On the other hand, if you are a diabetic whose parents died from heart attacks in their 60s, a life annuity is probably not a good purchase decision for you. As we learn more and more about the human genome, we may come to the point where we have individual mortality tables.

The individualized knowledge gives rise to adverse selection problems for insurance companies and they price their annuities accordingly. The companies know that purchasers of life annuities have considerably longer life expectancy than the average population, as they have discovered from years of practical experience. If you have bad odds of long life because of family history, you won't buy a life annuity. Furthermore, the people who buy annuities have enough savings at retirement date to pay for an annuity, and, on average, they are the wealthier, better-educated customers, which also biases their life expectancy to be higher than the average. The insurance companies use a special table for pricing life annuities that takes all these factors into consideration.

We now return to the main road, where we apply the results of our analysis of discount rates, inflation, and life expectancy.

HOW MUCH WILL YOU NEED?

Mechanical Calculations

Now we put these different pieces into numerical examples to show how they work.

> *Example 17.3:* Rose and Sam Wise want to retire when they reach 65 (they are the same age). They want an after-tax income of $40,000 in today's dollars. The income will be split equally for income taxes. Assume they will have no pensions. They get an expected before-tax real rate of return of 4% p.a., all from investments in an RRSP. How much will they need to have saved when they retire? They are very unwilling to risk running out of retirement income. They live in Manitoba.

We need to calculate three things (the discount rate is given):

- The length of time to discount the cash flows
- Their average tax rate in retirement and, hence, the before-tax cash flow
- The PV of the annuity of the required cash flow

Rose has a 10% chance of living 31 years, and Sam a 10% chance of living 29 years. We will calculate PVs for 25 and 30 years.

Returning to Table 17.1 and iterating, we find that if they each receive $20,000 and pay an average tax of 4%, they will have a total after-tax income of $38,400. The tax rate on $25,000 each is 9%. Interpolate for a tax rate on $21,000, which would be 5%. Then they receive $2 \times .95 \times \$21,000 = \$39,900$ from a total income of $42,000 before tax, which is close enough.

Taking the PV of the annuity of $42,000 at 4%, we find that to provide for 30 years (25 years) they would have to have accumulated $726,265 ($656,128) in real dollars, by the time they retire.[7]

---

[7] We discount the before-tax real cash flows ($21,000/year) each by the before-tax real rate (4%).

Example 17.4: Now suppose that Rose and Sam Wise expect they will receive $22,000 in pensions at retirement. How much will they need to have saved when they retire to generate a before-tax income of $42,000 in real dollars at 4%?

We deduct the pensions from the expected consumption in real before-tax dollars, because we assume the pensions are indexed to inflation. They need to save enough to provide $42,000 – $22,000 = $20,000 in before-tax income. The PV of $20,000 at 4% for 30 years is $345,841, and for 25 years, $312,442, which gives the range of saving required by retirement, expressed in today's dollars.

How Much Is Enough?

Do you want to travel around the world and stay in the best hotels when you retire? Keep a big house in the city and a cottage at the lake, and two cars? Or do you want a small house with a large garden that provides most of your food? Personal goals determine how much you have to save for retirement. Careful financial planning transforms personal goals into financial goals and shows what you must do to reach them.

How do we know what we need in retirement income? We could use some rules of thumb, such as taking 70% of our current income. The Canadian Life and Health Insurance Association suggests that high-income families could use a lower level of 50%, while lower-income families (below $50,000) should aim for as high as 85%. Such rules do not allow for individual situations. Earlier in the life cycle, all the income might be going towards paying off a mortgage, and only 50% would be necessary once the house is paid. On the other hand, a family with no house will need to save a higher percentage of its income because it won't have the inflation protection of a house. The more accurate approach is to determine your goals in retirement, and then price the desired consumption necessary to achieve those goals. This is not an easy process for most people, especially if retirement is many years away. How do you know what you will want?

The best starting point is current expenditures because they are the best clue to your preferences. Realistically, you can't expect to live better in retirement than before, but you can expect that your expenses will have changed in some or all of the ways outlined in Table 17.3. Of course, not everyone will change in these ways. If your goals include living in the same house, then those expenses won't decline. If you have always taken a homemade lunch to work, then food costs won't decrease as much.

The stage in the life cycle at which you are doing the planning will affect the numbers. For example, a family with young children and a large mortgage will have much higher expenses than it should expect in retirement. A couple nearing retirement, with the mortgage paid and the children gone, will have expenses that are much closer to what should be expected in retirement.

TABLE 17.3
Changes in Expenses after Retirement

Reductions:

- Payroll deductions — EI premiums, health care premiums (in some provinces), CPP, employer pension
- Car expenses — don't drive to work, sell second car
- Food — the older you get, the less you eat
- Meals away from home — no workday lunches
- Clothing and dry cleaning — no business suits and dresses
- House cleaning (maybe!)
- Shelter — move to smaller house or apartment
- Mortgage payments — mortgage is fully repaid
- Disability insurance, life insurance premiums

Increases:

- Health care
- Employer-paid benefits — health plans, dental plans, company car, etc.
- Home maintenance — as you age, you can do less of it yourself
- Recreation — travel, entertainment (more time to enjoy them)

Financial needs are not the only retirement needs that require planning. Retirement involves a significant change in your pattern of life. Most of us will have been working for many years and the behaviour involved is ingrained. Suddenly, no one is telling us to be at work for a large part of our time, and we no longer can define ourselves by our occupation. For some people, retirement is a wrenching blow to their self-image, and they are unable to enjoy it. We do not discuss how to deal with the psychic needs of retirement in this book, but we remind you that they are just as important as financial needs. You should plan what you will do in retirement just as you plan how much money you will need.

Before we deal with the other side of the coin — how much have you got? — we must take another detour to learn about pension plans and RRSPs in more detail.

PENSION PLANS

There are different ways to characterize pension plans. In the next section we explain characteristics that can apply to both government and employer-sponsored plans. In the subsequent sections, we discuss government and employer plans.

Reprinted with permission — The Toronto Star Syndicate. © 1994 GREG HOWARD distributed by King Features Syndicate.

Types of Pension Plans

Defined Benefit and Defined Contribution

A **defined benefit plan** specifies the pension the employee receives upon retirement. There are two common methods:

1. The benefit is a specified number of dollars (per annum, per month, per week) times the number of years of service, to a specified maximum number of years or maximum dollar amount. This type of plan is often part of a labour contract, and the dollar amount is amended every time a new contract is negotiated or is subject to an agreed formula for change (normally, with respect to inflation).

2. The benefit is a specified percentage of the employee's earnings times the number of years of service, to a specified maximum number of years. The "earnings" portion of the calculation may be defined in various ways, but the most common way is as the average of the best five years' earnings.

Defined benefit plans are less risky to employees and more risky to employers since the latter bear the investment risk of the funds invested in the plan. On the other hand, risk has a price, as you learned in Chapters 14–16, and an employer will presumably pay less in other forms of compensation if it provides a defined benefit plan.

A **defined contribution** or **money purchase plan** specifies a per cent of earnings that both the employer and employee contribute to a fund. When employees retire, they get whatever pension (annuity) the accumulated contributions and earnings will buy. A defined contribution plan leaves the investment risk with the employees.

Indexation

A defined benefit plan may be indexed to inflation, usually as measured by the Consumer Price Index. **Indexation** refers to what happens to the payments to the employee after retirement. An indexed plan will increase these payments for inflation every year. An unindexed plan leaves the payment determined at retirement constant.[8] An indexed plan is more desirable from the employee's point of view, but it is very expensive and risky for the employer.

In practice, a plan that is not indexed formally may well keep pace with inflation. Defined contribution plans assume an interest rate below their usual experience when they set the pension amount. Many of them have excess interest provisions that increase the pension payments over time as the pension fund receives returns greater than the discount rate originally assumed in setting the pension amount. In other cases, the company may provide a guaranteed defined benefit that is also less than the amount that the pension is likely to be able to provide. If the returns experienced are larger than needed for the payout level, the company may raise the payouts voluntarily.

Vesting and Portability

The employer's contributions to a plan do not belong to the employee until they are "vested". The vesting period is specified by the plan, and in the past could have been as long as 10 years. Any employee who leaves the employer, voluntarily or involuntarily, prior to vesting, gets no pension. The vesting period has become much shorter in recent years, usually only a year, due to provincial legislation.

Even when the employer's contributions are vested, the employee cannot simply withdraw them at will. Ordinarily, pension plan money is locked in until retirement, or can be transferred only to another locked-in fund.

A problem arises when employees with vested pension credits change employers. If the pension is defined contribution, this presents only a minor inconvenience. The employee can leave the money where it is to accumulate and use it as part of retirement income later. Alternatively, it may be transferred to a locked-in RRSP from which a retirement income can be derived. A few large employers have provisions to transfer pension balances to a new plan.

The problem of portability is much more serious when employees leave a defined benefit plan. The defined benefit will not be indexed for employees who leave, and if the employees are relatively early in their career, the earnings on which the benefit is based will be lower in both real and nominal dollars. Let us illustrate with an example.

---

[8] As previously stated, plans may be amended every year for determining the value of benefits prior to retirement, but this is not the same thing as indexing them for what happens after retirement.

Example 17.5: Miklos Georgas worked for 15 years for Skull and Crossbones Chemical (SCC) in Québec. It has a defined benefit pension paying 2% of best five-year average earnings times years of service, up to a maximum of 70%. In 1978 he left SCC to join a consulting firm, with no pension plan. In 1982 he joined the Ontario government, and retired after another 15 years. The Ontario government pension plan is identical to the SCC plan.

His best five years earnings with SCC averaged $3,000 per month. His best five years earnings at the government averaged $6,000 per month. Thus, his monthly employer pensions are calculated as follows:

SCC:	$3,000 × .02 × 15	=	$ 900
Ontario:	$6,000 × .02 × 15	=	1,800
Total:			$2,700

Suppose he had stayed at SCC for 30 years and retired at the same $6,000 average earnings? His total pension would be $6,000 × .02 × 30 = $3,600 per month.

Governments and private-sector employers are working on this problem of lack of portability of pensions because it is in everyone's interest to have worker mobility. There are no easy solutions, and every worker who is depending on employer plans for part of his retirement income must be aware of this problem when considering changing jobs. In fact, since losing your job would have the same effect, you need to consider that risk with respect to your pension plan when you choose your occupation and employers all through your work life.

Non-contributory Plans

A few employers have pension plans to which employees make no contributions. If the employer really contributes enough to make up for the employee's contributions, then presumably take-home pay is lower than it would be otherwise.

Government Pension Plans

In this section we discuss the universal government plans, not those plans offered by governments to their employees. To determine the exact numbers applying in any situation, a person must consult Human Resources and Skills Development Canada (HRSDC), which has toll-free telephone lines and offices across Canada (listed in the Blue Pages of the telephone directory). We have summarized the maximum amounts available from the different government plans in Table 17.4. These numbers are all indexed for the previous period's changes in inflation (subject to some limitations) and, hence, are subject to changes in addition to any legislative changes. The pensioner, or a representative in case of incapacity, must apply for each of these pensions — they are not automatic.

TABLE 17.4
Maximum Government Pensions — 2011 and 2012

Maximum Monthly Pensions	Details
Canada Pension Plan $960.00 [$986.67]	• For persons retiring at age 65 who contributed at the maximum rate on the MPE for the majority of their career • Actual amount varies according to lifetime profile of contributions, and age of retirement
$2,500 (lump sum) $1,153.37 [$1,185.50]	• Lump-sum death benefit to spouse or estate • Disability benefit prior to age 65
Old Age Security $537.97 [$540.12]	• Every Canadian at age 65, provided they have lived in Canada for a sufficient number of years • Clawback of 15%, starts at net income of $67,668 and is 100% of OAS for net income of $110,123 [2012: Clawback starts at $69,562 and is 100% at $112,772]

Guaranteed Income Supplement
Single: $729.44 [$732.36]
Married to a pensioner:
$483.68 [$485.61]
	• Reduced by 50% of income excluding OAS, GIS, and Spouse's Allowance
	• Maximum income limits:
	  • single — $16,320 [$16,368]
	  • couple both receiving OAS — $21,552 [$21,648]
	  • couple, only one gets OAS — $39,120 [$39,264]
	  • couple, one with OAS, one with Spouses Allowance — $39,120 [$39,264]

OAS + GIS Minimum Income Floor Single: $1,267.41 [$1,272.48] Couple: $2,043.30 [$2,051.46]	• OAS + GIS for a single person/couple with no other income • Retired Canadians aged 65 or over are entitled to this minimum level of income, with some qualifications
Spouse's Allowance $1,021.65 [$1,025.73]	• Person aged 60 to 64 who is a spouse of a person eligible for OAS and GIS • Maximum is equal to OAS + GIS for someone aged 65 and spouse of a pensioner • Net income cutoff: $30,192 [$30,336]

Note: 2012 figures, as of 2012-07-31, are in square brackets. For current rates and other information, <www.servicecanada.gc.ca/eng/isp/oas/oasrates.shtml>.

Canada Pension Plan

In 1966, the federal government started a mandatory contributory defined benefit indexed pension plan for all Canadians. Employees and employers make equal contributions. Self-employed persons must make contributions equal to the sum of the employee and employer contributions. The Canada Pension Plan (CPP) has been very successful for a large sector of the population that previously had insufficient retirement income because of a lack of employer plans. In recent years, the contribution rate has been raised substantially, and the actuaries estimate the plan is now operating on a sustainable basis, which was not true for many years.

The contribution rate was 4.95% × (earnings − $3,500), up to the limit of Maximum Pensionable Earnings, $48,300, in 2011. Both rate and limit have increased to 5.03% and $50,100, respectively, in 2012. Thus, employee and employer each contributes up to $2,217.60 p.a. There are death benefits payable to the spouse and dependent children, explained in more detail in Chapter 10. The details on how to qualify, and how much pension you receive, are quite involved. CPP is an important part of the retirement income package, and we will assume reasonable numbers in our examples in the textbook. Maximum rates appear in Table 17.4. CPP indexation is adjusted annually in January.

Until 1998, the CPP invested entirely in fixed income instruments, usually provincial government bonds. The government formed the Canada Pension Plan Investment Board (CPPIB) to invest in broader financial markets, including equities. The CPPIB operates at arm's length from the federal and provincial governments and is now the largest pension fund in Canada.

The CPP pension is determined for a person starting it on his or her 65th birthday. A pensioner may choose to start it up to five years earlier, but no earlier than his or her 60th birthday. The CPP pays out .6% per month less for each month it is taken early, or 7.2% per year. A person who starts it on the 60th birthday will receive 36% less pension. On the other hand, a person who starts it later than age 65 receives an increase of .6% per month for every month's delay. For pensions started in 2013 and subsequent years, the increase is .7% per month, or 8.4% per year. This increase is also capped at five years, for a maximum increase of 42% for pensions started in 2013. Further delays in taking the pension do not increase the amount paid.

Until recently, a person who started receiving CPP would stop making contributions to the plan. The rules have changed, and now both employee and employer must continue to make contributions to age 65 even if the employee is receiving CPP. Contribution is voluntary for employees between age 65 and 70. However, employers will have to contribute if the employees do. Such contributions may increase the subsequent CPP payments to the pensioner.

Old Age Security

Old Age Security (OAS) is available to Canadian citizens and legal residents of Canada aged 65 or over, who have lived in Canada for at least 10 years since turning 18. Those who met those qualifications at the time they left Canada, but no longer reside here, must have resided for at least 20 years after turning 18. Residence in countries with which Canada has a social security pension agreement may also count towards the 20-year qualifying period. OAS is not dependent on previous employment. OAS indexation is adjusted quarterly. OAS is included in taxable income. Technically, OAS is not a pension because it has no connection to earned income. From a personal finance point of view, it fulfills the same role as a pension in retirement, and we treat it as a pension for planning purposes.

The **spouse's allowance** is an income-tested monthly benefit payable to a 60- to 64-year-old spouse of an OAS pensioner who is also entitled to a GIS. The **widowed spouse's allowance** is an income-tested monthly benefit payable to 60- to 64-year-old widowed spouses of individuals who were eligible for OAS, or would have been had they survived to age 65. Ten years of residence in Canada after age 18 are usually required. A spouse is a legal or common-law spouse.

The government requires repayment of OAS for higher income earners at the rate of 15% of any income above a certain floor. This repayment, colloquially called the "OAS clawback", is included directly on the T1 personal tax return, and so the income threshold specified relates to the same year as the OAS was paid. The current limits are shown in Table 17.4. This clawback has a significant impact on planning for RRSP contributions, as explained in a later section in this chapter.

For example, John Parkinson is 67 and is receiving OAS. His net income for 2011 was $82,000. The amount of OAS that he has to repay is .15 × ($82,000 − $67,668) = $2,149.80. The practice is to reduce the monthly OAS cheque by 1/12th of this amount, or $179.15. Since the reduction has to be estimated based on the previous year's net income, any adjustment will be calculated on the tax return for 2011 and collected or refunded as part of the tax return process, although it is not an income tax but, rather, a repayment to Human Resources and Skills Development Canada (HRSDC).

It is important to note that the eligibility age for OAS is now 65 but will gradually increase to 67 over six years, starting in April 2023. The ages at which the spouse's allowance and the widowed spouse's allowance are provided will also gradually increase from 60–64 (today) to 62–66 (starting in April 2023).

As well, starting in July 2013, Canadians can elect to defer receiving OAS for up to five years past the age of eligibility in exchange for an enhanced monthly benefit of 0.6 percent per month of deferral (or 7.2 percent for a full year of deferral). This deferral election will obviously be useful to higher income-earners who would have otherwise had to repay any OAS they might have received during those five years. This change is discussed in more detail, with an example, in the section Government Pensions in Chapter 18.

Guaranteed Income Supplement

The **Guaranteed Income Supplement (GIS)** is an income-tested monthly pension supplement for OAS pensioners who have little other income. The actual amount received is adjusted every year for changes in the pensioner's financial circumstances and marital status, and the pensioner must re-apply every year. Only OAS recipients who are resident in Canada are eligible, which distinguishes it from OAS, which can be paid to non-residents. GIS is *not* included in taxable income. GIS indexation is adjusted quarterly.

The adjustment of GIS for income is calculated on the previous year's income, excluding OAS and GIS, and it applies to family income. The reduction is 50% of the family income, until GIS reaches 0. The limits are different for a single, a couple both receiving OAS, a couple with one receiving OAS and the other not, and a couple with one receiving OAS and the other receiving spouse's allowance. See Table 17.4 for the current limits. This clawback has a significant impact on planning for RRSP contributions, as explained in a later section in this chapter.

Registered Pension Plans

A **Registered Pension Plan (RPP)** or **employer pension plan** is established by an employer to defer income payable to employees to provide retirement income for them. Such a plan may have payments made into it by either or both the employer and the employee, depending on the terms of the plan. The contributions are deposited with a plan trustee, who invests them. When employees retire, they receive a pension from the plan. Employees pay tax on the pension as it is received. Thus, the pension contributions provide a deduction from taxable income, and also accumulate at the before-tax rate of return.

Most people will have no planning to do with respect to a Registered Pension Plan. The contributions are fixed by the terms of employment. Occasionally, the plan may be retroactively amended to allow for higher contributions for past service, or to allow employees to join the plan who were not previously in it, and to gain credit for past service. If such an amendment allows a person to make **past service contributions**, they are almost always worth doing. In effect, you get a tax deduction for buying more pension income.

Employer plans may be indexed or unindexed, and defined contribution or defined benefit. The specific terms of the plan and the eventual benefits the retiree will receive are entirely a matter of contract, either between the employee and the employer directly or between a union and the employer. There are laws that require the employer to fund a defined benefit plan to meet the expected future liabilities as determined by actuarial consultants. However, if circumstances change, the fund may have **unfunded liabilities**, and the employer will have some time to make up the difference. Employers must also be reasonably current in making their contributions to a defined contribution pension plan. The employee contributions go directly into the fund. In all cases, the money in the pension fund is under the care of an independent trustee. The trustee will retain actuaries to estimate the liabilities, and in the process they will determine the estimated future pension payable to each employee. The employer provides this information to the employees annually, and this amount of expected pension is an important input into retirement planning.

The government places a limit on the amount of income that a person can shelter in tax deferral methods for retirement. After this limit, a person can save more, but there is no tax deferral. This limit takes effect in RRSPs, RPPs, and DPSPs and is supposed to be the same for each one. In practice, this is simple for defined contribution pension plans and RRSPs, but is not possible directly for defined contribution pension plans because the decision variable is the subsequent benefit, and the amount contributed is not necessarily all done in a specific year but may be added to the plan over time in response to funding shortfalls.

The way to determine the limit of the tax deferral shelter for a defined contribution plan is to assume some rate of return and average mortality for pensioners. Then, the government establishes the amount of total retirement saving contribution that can be sheltered in one year. This limit applies directly to the total of employer and employee or independently employed contributions to RRSPs and defined contribution pension plans, combined. Using the rate of return and mortality assumptions, we can work backwards to get the amount of annual benefit that the pensioner is allowed to accumulate in a defined benefit plan. The federal government relies on an estimate from these factors that $9 of contributions is required to get $1 of annual benefit at retirement. The details of how to get to this 9:1 ratio are beyond the scope of this textbook. If we continue working backwards, however, we can see we get the maximum allowed benefit accrual to be equal to the maximum allowed contribution limit for RRSP + defined contribution pension plans by multiplying it by 9. For example, in 2011, the limit for a defined contribution plan was $22,970, which included employer and employee contributions. Thus, the benefit accrual per year of service allowed in a defined benefit plan is $22,970/9 = $2,552.22 This limit could be either the flat rate defined in a labour contract, or the result of the formula of a percentage rate times average earnings.

Table 17.5 shows the limits back to 1991 for RRSPs (the history is sometimes necessary to calculate the amount of unused contribution room carried forward) and back to 2003 for pension plans.

In practice, a person doesn't need to know the pension limits because the employer will not contribute anything in excess of the limit to an RPP on the employee's behalf. The appropriate reduction in the amount a member of an RPP can contribute to an RRSP is reported each year on the T4 as the pension adjustment (PA). The PA affects the amount that the member can contribute to next year's RRSP, as explained later in the chapter. This one-year lag is the reason the limits on RRSP contributions also lag the limit on pension plan contributions by one year in Table 17.5.

TABLE 17.5
Ceiling on Registered Plan Contributions

| Years | Registered Pension Plans (%) | | |
	RRSP	Defined Contribution (DC)	Defined Benefit (Maximum Benefit per Year of Service)
1991	$11,500		
1992	12,500		
1993–1994	13,500		
1995	14,500		
1996–2002	13,500		
2003	14,500	$15,500	$1,722.22
2004	15,500	16,500	1,833.33
2005	16,500	18,000	2,000.00
2006	18,000	19,000	2,111.11
2007	19,000	20,000	2,222.22
2008	20,000	21,000	2,333.33
2009	21,000	22,000	2,444.44
2010	22,000	22,450	2,494.44
2011	22,450	22,970	2,552.22
2012	22,970	23,820	2,646.67
2013	23,820	indexed	1/9 the DC limit

Source: Canada Revenue Agency, <www.cra-arc.gc.ca/tx/rgstrd/papspapar-fefespfer/lmts-eng.html>

The proportion of employed Canadians who work for an employer with a pension plan has declined considerably and now stands at 38%. Although some of those uncovered are self-employed professionals and small business owners with substantial assets, most are workers who have only CPP and OAS to look forward to unless they save for themselves. The declines are primarily in the private sector and coincide with declining industrial union membership. Service industries have grown while industrial firms have declined, and service industries are generally not unionized. In the public sector, pension coverage is quite widespread, currently at 84% of employees. Federal and provincial governments and larger cities, and their agencies, have almost total coverage. At the same time as pension plan coverage has been declining, CRA reports every year that huge amounts of the contribution room available in RRSPs remains unused.

The type of pension plan is changing also. Most public service pensions are defined benefit plans, and many of them are indexed. In the private sector, only a few of the largest, most stable companies still offer DB plans. Many companies that did offer them have converted them to DC plans, or require all new employees to join a DC plan, retaining the DB plan only for those already in it. Indexation is disappearing from private sector plans since it is a very expensive and risky benefit that companies are refusing to offer any longer. In an era of government structural deficits, the continuation of the public sector DB plans, or at least continuation at the same level of benefits, is under siege.

Ten years ago we would not have thought of the risk of a defined benefit pension plan failing to pay the promised benefits, but that risk is now material. Some huge companies in the auto industry, steel, airlines, and Nortel Networks have all had to reduce payments to existing and future pensioners in the last four years in North America. A major cause of the failures was the worldwide stock market crash of 2008. Even plans that were overfunded prior to the crash ended up with unfunded deficits. This risk is not widespread because of the rapid decline in DB plans, and it isn't a risk of anywhere near 100% loss since there are always very large assets left in the plans. Nonetheless, it has become an additional risk in retirement planning. Some countries have pension benefit guarantee agencies mandated by government, but Canada is not well-protected in that area. In any case, the size of the underfunding caused by the 2008 crash is so large that none of these agencies has the assets to cover all the potential shortfalls.

Pension Plans and Human Capital

In Chapter 4 we showed how you can estimate the value of a person's human capital by taking the present value of earnings and employment benefits, plus and minus other adjustments. One of the very important financial decisions a person makes concerns the quality of the pension plan offered by a potential employer. Most RPPs require employers and employees to make equal monetary contributions to the plan. The economic term for pensions is "deferred compensation" because it is money paid for work done, but the employee cannot use the money until retirement. Deferred compensation is a significant part of the total compensation package, but many people forget about it and make decisions between different jobs and careers based on the gross salary.

Example 17.6: William Lim is an experienced statistical analyst. He has two job offers to consider. Milevsky and Salisbury Consulting Mathematicians offers a starting salary of $70,000 and a defined contribution pension plan to which employer and employee each contributes 4% of earnings. Mother Hen Insurance Company offers him a salary of $68,000 and a defined benefit pension plan to which employer and employee presently contribute 8.9%

of salary. All other benefits are equal, and opportunities for higher earnings in the future are the same with either employer. Which job should William take?

Answer: Milevsky and Salisbury contributes 4% of $70,000 = $2,800 annually to the pension plan on his behalf, for a total compensation before other benefits of $72,800. Mother Hen contributes 8.9% of $68,000 = $6,052 annually to the pension plan for a total compensation before other benefits of $74,052. In addition, Mother Hen is taking on all the investment risk and risk of changes in future actuarial calculations that might reduce the benefits, while Milevsky and Salisbury leaves those risks for the employee to face. Mother Hen offers a better total package, even though the gross salary is lower.

The difference is often much greater than shown in Example 17.6, particularly if you are comparing an employer offering a pension plan with another one that does not. Some very well paid occupations — lawyers, doctors, accountants, small business owners, etc. — are often without pension plans. People in this situation must be much more active in saving for retirement to make up for the lack of a pension plan. One rule of thumb that some financial planners use is to deduct 10% of your pay for savings before you spend anything. This sounds sensible, but it completely misses the different needs of different people. Someone with a respectable pension plan who expects to remain in that situation will not need to save much more, if anything, and should concentrate on paying down a mortgage. Additional savings is likely to deprive the family of what it needs immediately, perhaps disability insurance or tutoring for children. On the other hand, a single doctor in private practice needs to target a savings rate of more than 10% in addition to buying a house in order to provide for a decent retirement income.

REGISTERED RETIREMENT SAVINGS PLAN (RRSP)

A **Registered Retirement Savings Plan (RRSP)** is a do-it-yourself pension plan. Taxpayers contribute part of their income to a trusteed fund. The contribution is deducted from income for tax purposes in the year it is paid into the fund, and income on it accumulates tax-free. When taxpayers withdraw it for spending purposes, the entire amount, principal and accrued earnings, is taxable.[9] An RRSP is

---

[9] Note that in both RRSPs and RPPs, the capital gains exemption, the "50% of capital gains" rule, and the dividend tax credit do not apply. Capital gains, dividends, and interest income are treated identically upon withdrawal.

distinguishable from a defined contribution RPP because individuals retain control of how the assets are invested and can withdraw assets before retirement. In the terminology of Chapter 8, an RRSP is an income deferral technique.

Legally, an RRSP is a trust, an arrangement in which certain property is given by a **settlor** to a **trustee**, an independent third party who holds the property on behalf of the **beneficiary** (or beneficiaries), who will receive income and/or capital from the trust. In an RRSP, the settlor is the person who makes the tax-deductible contributions, and we will use the common term — contributor — instead of settlor. The beneficiary is most often the contributor but may also be the spouse if the plan is designated as a **spousal RRSP**.

RRSPs constitute an important part of Canadians' retirement savings, and there are many important complications and opportunities. We will provide the major features in the following sections.

Contribution Limits

The limit that you can contribute to an RRSP and deduct from taxable income is 18% of earned income, minus the pension adjustment (PA) and contributions to a Deferred Profit Sharing Plan (DPSP), up to a legislated maximum amount, plus any unused contribution room carried forward from previous years.[10] Earned income and the adjustments refer to the previous year's figures (e.g., the limit for 2012 is based on 2011 income and pension contributions). This allows contributors to make the full contribution early in the year, if they can, to gain the maximum benefit of compounding income in a tax shelter. In mathematical form, the contribution limit is as follows:

> Min [ceiling, .18(earned income)]
> − PA
> − DPSP deposits
> − past service pension adjustments (PSPAs)
> + reversals of PSAs
> + unused contribution room

Let us consider the terms one at a time. The contribution ceiling is the upper limit before adjustments. Past and present limits are shown in Table 17.5.

---

[10] Inidivudals may contribute up to $2,000 over the limit during their lifetime without penalty, but over-contributions are not tax deductible and are taxed upon withdrawal. The over-contribution accumulates at the before-tax rate, however, and if left in the plan for long enough will overcome the disadvantage of non-deductibility. It is not an important issue especially since most Canadians have trouble finding enough money to contribute to the limit. Over-contributions greater than $2,000 are penalized.

Earned income is the sum of the following:

- Employment income (including taxable benefits)
- Supplementary unemployment benefits
- Alimony and maintenance payments received
- Royalties
- Research grants
- Business and net rental income
- Taxable disability benefits

minus the total of the following:

- Union and professional dues
- Alimony and maintenance payments made

Earned income excludes retirement income sources, investment income, child tax credits, employment insurance, adult training allowances, bursaries, scholarships, and payments from a Registered Educational Savings Plan.

Pension adjustments are calculated by the employer and reported on the next year's T4 slip. They limit the employee in an RPP to about the same amount of tax-deferred saving as someone who has no RPP can achieve at the same income level by using exclusively RRSPs, as explained earlier in the chapter.

A **Deferred Profit Sharing Plan (DPSP)** is a form of retirement saving set up for contributions from the employer only based on the company's net income according to an agreed-upon formula. It enters the calculations for limiting RRSP contribution room because payments into it are tax deductible for the employer and are only taxed in the employee's hands when withdrawn, just as in an RPP.

Example 17.7: Johanna Vision earned $32,000 in wages and $1,000 in overtime in 2011. She earned $125 in interest on her Canada Savings Bonds and received $1,500 in EI benefits while briefly unemployed. She also got a $500 training allowance and won a lottery of $100 during this period. She paid union dues of $400. On her 2011 T4 slip, the employer reported her pension adjustment (PA) of $3,300. She contributed the maximum amount to her RRSP every year since she left school. How much can she contribute to an RRSP for the 2012 year?

Answer: Earned income = $32,000 + $1,000 – $400 = $32,600

.18 × $32,600 = $5,868

Since this is less than $22,970, maximum contribution = $5,868 – $3,300 = $2,568

A person may carry forward **unused contribution room** indefinitely. That is, if you don't have enough money to contribute to the limit in one year, you may make up the lost contribution in the future by contributing more than the limit in those years, up to the amount of the unused contribution. This carry-forward is available only from 1991 onward. Large carry-forwards are not very valuable for two reasons. First, they may reduce the tax bracket if all taken in one year, and thus make the tax saving on the deduction less valuable. Second, the point of an RRSP is to get the money into it as quickly as possible in order to receive the maximum benefit of tax-free earnings accumulation. Nonetheless, families will have periods when they don't have the cash to make all their RRSP contributions.

Example 17.8: Lally Lolly started work as a retail representative for an investment dealer in 2009. She earned $15,000 in commissions. In 2010 she earned $62,000 in commissions, $4,000 in capital gains, and $500 in dividends. She joined a professional association with annual dues of $800. In 2011 she earned $150,000 in commissions, suffered $6,000 capital losses, earned $1,000 in dividends, and paid professional dues of $900. The investment dealer contributed $4,000 to a DPSP on her account. The investment dealer does not offer a pension plan, and Lally made no RRSP contributions because it was her first job and she was paying off student debts, buying furniture, etc. How much can she contribute to an RRSP in February 2012? Should she contribute the maximum?

Answer:

Earned income (2009) $= \$ \ 15,000$
Unused contribution (2009) $= .18 \times \$15,000 = \underline{\$ \quad 2,700}$

Earned income (2010) $= \$62,000 - \$800 = \$ \ 61,200$
Unused contribution (2010) $= .18 \times \$61,200 = \underline{\$ \ 11,016}$

Earned income (2011) $= \$150,000 - 900 = \$149,100$
Unused contribution (2011) $= .18 \times \$149,100 = \underline{\$ \ 26,838}$

Since the 2011 amount exceeds the limit, the limit is $22,450, and the unused contribution $= \$22,450 - \$4,000 = \underline{\$18,450}$.

The maximum contribution possible is $2,700 + $11,016 + $18,450 $= \underline{\$32,166}$.

Assuming we have all the information necessary, this would give her a taxable income after RRSP deductions (ignoring CPP and EI premiums) of:

Commissions		$150,000
+ Taxable dividends	+	1,250
− dues	−	900
− RRSP contribution	−	32,166
Taxable income		$118,184

This income is not in the top tax bracket, and so she should estimate next year's income before deciding. If she will earn a lot of income, putting her in the top tax bracket in 2012, then she could contribute $10,000 less this year and contribute the $10,000 in March to offset top-bracket tax in 2012. If she is not sure she will earn as much in 2012, she should contribute the entire $32,166 in this year.

Spousal Plans

A contributor may make part or all of the annual RRSP contribution to an RRSP specifically designated for his spouse. In the terminology of Chapter 8, this is both an income deferral and an income splitting technique. Then, splitting the income into two streams may lower the marginal tax rate on the family income, and also allows both spouses to claim a deduction for pension income when the RRSP is turned into an annuity or a Registered Retirement Income Fund (RRIF). Common-law spouses and same-sex couples qualify for spousal RRSPs.

The contribution limit applies to the contributor's income, not the recipient's. However, Individuals' contribution limit to RRSPs applies to the combined amount contributed to their own RRSP and a spousal RRSP. You cannot "double up" your contributions by putting money into both.

An obvious tax loophole beckons — contribute to a spousal RRSP for a spouse with no income, who then withdraws it immediately at a lower marginal tax rate. This loophole is illusory. If a taxpayer makes a contribution to a spousal RRSP in the two taxation years prior to any withdrawal, or in the year of the withdrawal, the lesser of the amount withdrawn and the amount contributed by the taxpayer is taxed in the contributor's hands.

The spousal RRSP has become much less important because of the pension splitting rules described in Chapter 8. There are situations where it is still useful, when the higher income spouse may not have pension income, but they are not common.

Investment Restrictions

We discuss investment and saving principles in retirement more generally in a subsequent section. However, the law restricts RRSPs to **eligible investments**. The details are complicated, but in general, the following investments are eligible:

- Savings accounts, term deposits and GICs
- Shares of Canadian companies listed on Canadian exchanges
- Some shares of foreign companies listed on Canadian exchanges, some unlisted and foreign shares
- Federal and provincial bonds, some Canadian corporate bonds, stripped bonds
- Certain types of mortgages, including your own
- Mutual funds investing in eligible investments
- Covered call options, warrants, and rights issued by Canadian companies listed on a stock exchange

Note that you need not contribute cash to an RRSP. A contribution could be any of the above eligible investments, and the contribution will be valued at market price. A taxpayer who transfers an asset into an RRSP is deemed to have disposed of it and must declare any capital gain or loss in that year.

What Happens in Death, Dissolution, or Maturity?

An RRSP must be wound up by December 31 of the year in which the beneficiary turns 71. The beneficiary may terminate it earlier, and it will be terminated involuntarily when the beneficiary dies. There are three ways to terminate an RRSP voluntarily:

1. Buy an annuity, either life or term certain, using part or all of the assets in the RRSP. The annuity payments are taxed when received.

2. Liquidate the assets, withdraw the funds, and pay tax immediately.

3. Transfer the assets to a Registered Retirement Income Fund (RRIF) from which taxable payments will be received until the beneficiary dies or the money runs out. This transfer is not a deemed disposition and no taxable gains or losses are created.

Option 2 is rarely a good idea since it raises the marginal tax rate for the beneficiary and pays tax earlier than needed. Options 1 and 3 are different ways of providing a steady retirement income, which is the government's purpose in creating RRSPs. We discuss them in more detail in Chapter 18.

If the beneficiary dies, the RRSP is considered to be terminated in the year of death and is included in income, except under these circumstances:

1. The spouse of the beneficiary is named as the beneficiary in the event of death. A spouse may elect a tax-free rollover of the RRSP into his or her

TABLE 17.6 Withholding Taxes on RRSP Withdrawals		
	Withholding Tax (%)	
Amount withdrawn	Québec residents	Others
Up to $5,000	21	10
$5,001–$15,000	26	20
Over $15,000	31	30

own RRSP. This is a tax deferral strategy. If the spouse is over age 71, the rollover would be to an RRIF.

2. A dependent child or grandchild was named as the beneficiary in the event of death. The child will pay tax, but may elect to buy an annuity whose term is no longer than 18 years minus the child's age. This is an income-spreading technique, and is only useful if the RRSP is large enough to put the child into a high tax bracket if it is received all in one year. An important consideration is the possible loss of provincial family benefits if the child's income becomes too high.

RRSPs are part of the family property, and if spouses end their marriage, a court may order the transfer of assets from an RRSP in one spouse's name to the other spouse's RRSP. Such a transfer occurs tax-free.

Withdrawals from a fund other than the tax-free rollovers or conversion to an annuity are taxable, and are subject to a **withholding tax.** A withholding tax is one that is deducted by a financial institution from some amount it is paying to a person or company, and that is then submitted directly to the taxing authority. The withholding tax is credited to the account of the person who received the balance of the payment. When that person files a tax return for the year in which the withholding occurred, the amount withheld is treated as an instalment payment, so the taxpayer is not penalized. Table 17.6 shows the present withholding tax rates.

Self-Administered RRSPs

Beneficiaries may allow the trustee to make the detailed investment decisions, or may make them themselves. Financial institutions offer plans that invest in pooled portfolios of bonds, shares, and/or treasury bills, according to your preferred allocation. The specific selection of the securities is left to the institution. Alternatively, the beneficiary can have a **self-administered plan**, and choose which securities to buy and sell inside the plan, just like a regular account with an investment dealer. The trustee will require an annual fee in addition to transactions costs and investment management fees. This trustee fee is not tax deductible, although it used to be.

HOW MUCH HAVE YOU GOT?

We discuss how to prepare and use a family balance sheet in Chapter 4, and it provides the basis for this aspect of retirement planning. The net liquid assets that can be maintained and invested as part of the eventual retirement income are the W_0 of the planning equation. Net worth is an essential figure to balance the balance sheet, but it is not the same as W_0, except by coincidence. Net worth relates to all the assets, not just to those that will provide retirement income.

Table 17.7 lists the sources of retirement income. Technically, the current pension fund balances are part of current wealth — that is, they are part of "How much have you got?" We incorporate pensions into the plan in a convenient way by deducting the payments from the required annual consumption in real dollars.

The items on the right-hand side of Table 17.7 are left to be valued today. These amounts and savings from future earnings, together with compounded

| TABLE 17.7 |
| Sources of Retirement Income |

Pensions	Non-Pension Savings
• Old Age Security (OAS) • Guaranteed Income Supplement (GIS) • Canada Pension Plan (CPP) • Employer's Registered Pension Plan (RPP)	• Registered Retirement Savings Plan (RRSP) • Deferred Profit Sharing Plan (DPSP) • House (if you trade down) • Vacation property (if you will sell) • Tax shelters • Reverse mortgage • Unsheltered savings • Locked-in funds • TFSA

income on them, are what the family will have available to cover any shortfall from required income minus pensions.

> *Example 17.9:* Let us return to Rose and Sam Wise, from Example 17.4. Both Rose and Sam are 55 years old. In addition to the pensions noted earlier, they have $50,000 in an RRSP invested in Government of Canada bonds, and $10,000 outside their RRSP in a Canadian equity mutual fund. They now own a modest home worth $110,000 in Saint John, New Brunswick. There is a mortgage of $25,000 outstanding on the home that they expect to have paid off before they retire. They also have $15,000 in a separate bank account to help their youngest son pay for university. How much do they have now for retirement, in addition to their pensions?

Since they need to live somewhere and the house they own is modest, they cannot downsize it to provide an extra income stream for retirement. The mortgage is to be paid from saved income prior to retirement, so it is not deducted. The money for the youngest son is already committed. While a balance sheet would show a net worth of $120,000, for retirement planning calculations they have $50,000 in before-tax dollars and $10,000 in after-tax dollars in addition to their pensions.

HOW TO GET FROM HERE TO THERE

In this section we complete the time value mechanics of calculating W_n and discuss the tax and investment aspects of saving for retirement.

Today, the family has W_0 and it expects to receive various pensions in retirement. Will W_0 compound to a large enough amount to cover any shortfall in consumption provided by the pensions? If not, how much more must the family save? Once again, we illustrate the method with an example:

> *Example 17.10:* Rose and Sam Wise will have a shortfall of $345,841 from pensions alone (see Example 17.4). Will their current savings (see Example 17.9) be enough to cover it if they retire in 10 years? If not, how much will they have to deposit in an RRSP each year for the next 10 years in real dollars? Assume their marginal tax rate now is 20% on equity earnings and 30% on other earnings. T-bills earn 2.5%; equity, 6.1%.

We calculate the FV of their current retirement savings in real before-tax dollars, assuming that they maintain the same investment policies.

1. $50,000 in an RRSP. It compounds before-tax at a real T-bill rate of 2.5%, for 10 years, to yield. $64,004

2. $10,000 in an equity mutual fund. It compounds after-tax at a real after-tax equity rate of $.061 \times (1 - .20) = 4.9\%$, for a value of $16,134. To be consistent with the rest of our calculations we need this amount in before-tax dollars. Since the tax is already partly paid and their tax rate in retirement is quite low, the difference is not great. Their average tax rate in retirement is about 4%, so let us guess at a 5% gross-up.

   Then: $16,134 ÷ (1 – .05) =   <u>16,983</u>

   Total value of current savings compounded to retirement date $80,987

Therefore, they are $345,841 – $80,987 = $264,854 short.

If they save and invest in equity in an RRSP at the before-tax real rate of 6.1%, they need to save $20,000 more p.a. in real dollars.[11] Since deposits in an RRSP reduce taxes, they reduce consumption by a lesser amount. Specifically, the tax reduction is (T × contribution), so the net amount they must save to make the RRSP contribution is $20,000 × (1 – .30) = $14,000 p.a.

You should recognize two things they can do to reduce the shortfall. The initial investment in the RRSP can be converted to equity at a higher expected return, but it will then be more risky. The equity mutual fund can be put into the RRSP as a contribution if there is contribution room. The tax reduction for the RRSP contribution will be much greater than any tax on a capital gain.

MARGINAL TAX RATES, GIS, AND OAS

When we defined marginal and average tax rates in Chapter 7, we did not discuss certain retirement issues explicitly. A low-income person or family over the age of 65 that earns above a certain level of income loses GIS in the next year at the rate of 50% of the extra income earned in the previous year, until the GIS is completely eliminated. A person who earns above a certain level of income over age 65 has to repay the OAS at a rate of 15% of the excess income, until the OAS is completely recovered by the government.

These two effects are not income taxes in a strictly legal sense, but they are income taxes in their economic effect. A person who falls into one of those two groups loses a certain amount of income to the government, and the amount is determined by net income. The GIS recovery is not done through the income tax return system, and the definition of net income excludes OAS and GIS. The OAS recovery is done through the income tax return. The essential effect is

---

[11] This example assumes they have sufficient contribution room in their RRSPs.

that a person or family age 65 and over that falls into the specific brackets pays a marginal tax rate much higher than the rate that you would calculate using the tax tables in Chapter 7.

For the low income family that gets a reduction in GIS the next year, the true marginal rate is 50% plus whatever marginal rate is shown by the income tax calculation. The marginal income tax rate of GIS recipients is always low, and frequently zero, but when we include the lost GIS, the marginal rate is higher than that formally charged in any province for any person who earns much higher income at any age. Although we do not deal with welfare payments in this textbook, the same effect holds for welfare payments that are dependent on the family's income.

The true marginal tax rate for a retiree who has to repay OAS is 15% plus the marginal rate calculated in Chapter 7. Table 17.1, using 2011 tax rates, also includes the effect of OAS clawback, which affects OAS recipients in the $68,000–$110,000 income range in 2011. Pension income splitting makes this even more complicated because clawback is determined after splitting. A couple could reduce their income tax in retirement by splitting pension income, which could also reduce the OAS they receive because of clawback. Each situation must be calculated.

> *Example 17.11:* Andy and Leanne are age 65, receive full OAS, and have net income before pension splitting of $90,000 and $60,000, respectively. They live in Gull Lake, Saskatchewan. What happens if they choose to split pension income so that each has $75,000 of net income? Check the marginal rates for the brackets for Saskatchewan and Canada. The federal 2012 brackets are 22% for income from $42,207 to $85,414; 26% for income over that. The relevant Saskatchewan bracket is 13% (for income from $42,065 to $120,185). They stay in the same provincial bracket before and after pension splitting. Andy will reduce his marginal bracket from 26% to 22%. OAS clawback starts at $69,652 in 2012. Andy's income will always be in the clawback range, but Leanne's will not enter the clawback range until part of the way into the income added by pension splitting.

Effect of the Pension Income Splitting

Leanne's income tax increases:	$(.22 + .13) \times (\$75,000 - \$60,000)$	$5,250
Andy's income tax decreases:	$(.22 + .13) \times (\$85,414 - \$75,000)$	– 3,645
	$(.26 + .13) \times (\$90,000 - \$85,414)$	– 1,789
Leanne's OAS clawback costs:	$.15 \times (\$75,000 - \$69,562)$	816
Andy's OAS clawback decreases:	$.15 \times (\$90,000 - \$75,000)$	– 2,250
Net tax and clawback, negative is a saving:		– $1,618

In this particular case they saved a small amount on income tax and a larger amount on OAS clawback.

The repayment of OAS and the loss of eligibility for GIS at certain income levels complicate retirement planning considerably. The problem is how much a person should contribute to an RRSP. If the subsequent withdrawals during retirement from the RRSP cause GIS eligibility loss or OAS clawback, then the contributions are very likely to be a bad idea. The exact details of how you should plan become very case specific, depending on the provincial tax rates, the federal bracket, the length of time to retirement, the age of retirement, marital status and division of income between spouses, and the rate of return earned on savings. The time to retirement is the most difficult variable to deal with because it increases the uncertainty about whether a person's retirement income will fall within the clawback range.

We can provide some general principles for individuals and families to incorporate the GIS reduction or OAS clawback into their pre-retirement and post-retirement planning:

- Individuals or couples with each person expecting to receive more than the OAS clawback endpoint ($112,772 p.a. in 2012) in retirement income can ignore everything in this section because they will be sure to lose all their OAS anyway. Only a small number of Canadians belong to this fortunate group.

- A family should not contribute to an RRSP if the members expect to be in one of the following categories when retired, where income is defined as any income received over the age of 65 other than OAS, GIS, and spouse's allowance:
    - A single person receiving income below the OAS income limit ($16,368 in 2012)
    - A couple, each one receiving OAS, and family income less than the OAS income limit ($21,648 in 2012)
    - A couple, only one receiving OAS, and family income less than the OAS income limit ($39,264 in 2012)
    - A couple, one receiving OAS, the spouse aged 61–64 receiving spouse's allowance, and family income less than the OAS income limit ($30,336 in 2012)

RRSP contributions in these situations will trigger GIS repayment as well as income tax when they are withdrawn, and hence the RRSP actually costs them money since the tax reduction when deposited will have been far less. Indeed, families in these categories probably shouldn't be trying to save at all pre-retirement since they are almost certainly not earning much more than they will receive in retirement from the government plans. A significant part of the Canadian population falls into this low retirement income category.

- A person who will fall into the OAS clawback category almost certainly should not save any more in RRSPs in the last few years before retirement. A substantial length of time might allow the tax-free compounding to overcome the drawback of the higher tax rate. A couple with one member in or even above the OAS clawback region, and the other clearly below it should save with spousal RRSPs in the lower income spouse's name.

- Any couple or single that might fall into the clawback categories should concentrate on repaying all debt instead of RRSP contributions. As retirement date draws nearer, it is easier to predict the amount of retirement income, and then RRSP catch-up contributions are still possible.

- A single who plans to retire before age 65 or a couple who both plan to retire prior to age 65 can still use RRSP contributions profitably, even if they will fall into the clawback/GIS reduction category after age 65. To do this, they would cash in the RRSPs as the bridge income for the years prior to age 65 since OAS doesn't start until then. The same strategy could also work if the only other pension income will be CPP. This can be deferred until age 70, and so a single or couple could bridge the gap by cashing RRSPs without triggering loss of GIS or OAS, with some care.

- Individuals over 65 with expected income that will very likely fall between the GIS reduction and OAS clawback regions should continue to use RRSPs as savings vehicles, regardless of marital status. These regions are a moving target because of indexing, but for 2012 rates this would be couples who expect retirement income over $35,000, with neither one receiving more than $67,000. A lot of Canadians fit in this category.

A lot of the problems for the low income families are cured by the TFSA. It does not affect GIS and OAS because it is not taxable when withdrawn. A family that is unsure if it will be caught in any of the preceding categories can always use a TFSA. Few families who are likely to get GIS are also likely to have more than $5,000 to save each year per adult.

INCOME TAX IMPLICATIONS

Chapter 8 pointed out four main tax strategies: deferral, spreading, splitting, and shelters. All four apply with respect to retirement saving. The basic principle is to save. using up all tax assistance opportunities first. Once you have exhausted all the tax strategies, save in unsheltered form. The three main savings vehicles are employer pension plans, RRSPs, and the family home.

An employer pension plan defers income tax until it is paid out in retirement. The employee makes few decisions. One important one is the purchase of past service credits. When a company that has not had a plan institutes one, or a company amends an existing plan, there may be an opportunity for the employee to "buy more pension". By paying some money into the plan now, some past years of service that were not credited are added into the calculation of the final pension. The employer usually contributes as well for these past service periods, so the employee should almost always take advantage of it, even ahead of RRSP contributions.

RRSPs allow both deferral and splitting (through a spousal RRSP) of income. To a small degree, they may allow some income spreading for a self-employed person with irregular income. The carry-forward rules are helpful in this regard.

The family home provides a tax shelter. Neither the implicit income nor the capital gain on a home are taxable. By contrast, a renter must pay tax on investment income (the alternative place for the funds that could have been used to buy a home), then pay rent from after-tax income.

The family home also provides a tax-splitting mechanism. If a couple buys a home, with both contributing to the down payment, and one has significantly lower retirement income than the other, the ultimate capital gain on disposal can be split equally to provide retirement income. This is a bit of a grey area, since technically they should contribute equally to all payments. However, the interest portion is a debt that the higher income spouse can pay, with the lower income spouse paying only principal. In practice, it seems that even a homemaker spouse can share equally in the capital gain since the family home is joint property.

A TFSA is almost always useful since it is a tax shelter that you can use with no risk. Withdrawals are totally flexible. For a large proportion of the Canadian population, the TFSA will become the primary retirement savings vehicle during the early years of the family life cycle and during the last few years before retirement.

Once you have exhausted the basic retirement tax shelters, you put additional savings into unsheltered investments. Shares are preferable, at least from a tax point of view. First, capital gains are taxed at one-half of the rate that interest is taxed. Second, capital gains accumulate untaxed until they are realized. Preferred shares and bonds are priced in the market so that the after-tax yield on dividends and interest are approximately equal for someone in the top tax bracket. If you are in a lower tax bracket, the dividend tax bracket will provide a slightly higher after-tax return than debt instruments of equal risk.

Rental properties are a retirement investment for a significant number of Canadians. Real estate can provide very high rates of return, and it has two significant tax advantages related to deferral and spreading. First, the capital gain accumulates untaxed until the property is sold, just as with securities.

Second, rental properties often operate at low income for income tax purposes, or even a loss during the early years of ownership. Thus, a taxpayer aged 55, at the peak of the earnings curve, could invest in a rental property and pay no tax on the income or even have a loss to deduct from other income. Then, in retirement, when the taxpayer's income and tax bracket are lower, the taxable income from the rental property is higher. This levels the income over time, and defers tax as well.

Two tax aspects create this situation. A taxpayer may claim **capital cost allowance (CCA)** on the building, and deduct it from the rental income along with other expenses. We will not describe the capital cost allowance system in detail in this book, but the reference sources mentioned in Chapters 7 and 8 provide more information. The fundamental tax-spreading aspect is that CCA charges depreciation at higher rates in the earlier years because it is a declining balance system. You can claim up to the maximum rate every year, but need not claim any more than enough to create zero rental income. In the later years, when you are retired, you have less income from other sources, but now the CCA on the rental property is lower and the taxable income is higher. There is one limit to the use of CCA on a rental property. A taxpayer may deduct losses due to cash expenses on a rental property, but may not deduct a loss caused by a CCA claim. Thus, if interest and other expenses are quite high in the earlier years of ownership, the CCA deduction will not be claimed.

A single rental property will usually absorb part or all of a family's savings, and usually requires a mortgage loan at first. The interest on a loan used to buy an income property is deductible from the rental income. As the loan is paid down, the interest portion of the blended principal and interest payments declines, and the taxable income from the property rises. Once again, this pattern offsets the decline in other sources of income in retirement and spreads and defers the tax burden.

INVESTMENT PRINCIPLES

Chapters 14 to 16 provide both practical application and the three basic principles:

1. Risk–return trade-off
2. Diversification
3. Efficient markets hypothesis

The risk–return trade-off when saving for retirement extends over a very long period of time. The k required to meet your goals must be related to the trade-off. For example, if you need to earn a 7% nominal rate of return in order to have a comfortable retirement income, you won't find it by investing in treasury bills.

There are essentially two risks in the long run that you must steer a course between: the risk of not earning a high enough rate of return to accumulate the needed retirement fund, versus the risk of losing part of your capital because of investing in high-risk, high-return investments. Researchers in capital markets have found that the risk of investing in equity for the long term is not as high as the simple measures of risk suggest. Over a long period of time, the higher average return more than compensates for the bad years, and the compounded return is almost certain to outperform the lower, steadier returns in government bonds and bills. This effect is called **time diversification.**

Any portfolio attempting to take advantage of time diversification must be diversified across securities in the class. If it is a portfolio of equities, then numerous different companies must be included. The total value of most RRSPs is too small to allow effective diversification except through a mutual fund. An index fund or an equities fund would be appropriate.

Investment in rental property almost always violates the diversification principle for a single family. A large part of the family's net worth is in a single asset, or perhaps two or three at most. Even if there is more than one property, they are usually in the same area or city. The family probably also has a family home. Thus, the retirement income outside of pensions is dependent on a single volatile market, and this is quite risky.

Rental property also carries another disadvantage. The owner must manage it actively, and this takes time and some skill. For those who have the skill and enjoy the work associated with a rental property, this is not a disadvantage, but others should beware. Investment in a portfolio of securities, or a mutual fund, requires much less management.

There is no numerical method to explicitly compare the tax benefits of investing in rental properties with the risk of insufficient diversification. We prefer to lean more towards avoiding the diversification risk since you could lose a lot by being undiversified, but gain much less from the tax benefit.

SUMMARY

Retirement planning answers three questions:

1. How much do you need? Price the level of consumption you want in retirement, estimate the number of years you will need it for, and calculate the amount needed to finance it at retirement age.

2. How much have you got? Identify and value the present and expected future sources of retirement income. These include government pensions, employer pensions, and family savings in the form of RRSPs, the family home, and unsheltered savings.

3. How do you get from here to there? Using time value calculations, find how much the family needs to save from now until retirement to meet its retirement income goal. The savings should be first in the tax-assisted vehicles — employer pension, RRSP, family home. Then, use the tax advantages of investing in shares or rental property. Be careful to be diversified in securities holdings.

MULTIPLE-CHOICE REVIEW QUESTIONS

1. Anthony Chon, 65, has recently retired. He estimates that he will require $30,000 in after-tax real dollars per year. He does not expect to live beyond 90 years old. All his investments are in government bonds, expecting to yield a nominal rate of 6% per year. His tax rate is 30%, and the rate of inflation is expected to be 3%. How much money does he need today to support his lifestyle?

   (a) $383,501
   (b) $647,413
   (c) $458,910
   (d) $599,692
   (e) None of the above

2. Elaine Rutherford, 55, is contemplating retiring early. She spent $35,000 last year, but she thinks she can cut her expenses by 20% after she retires. Her expenditure will increase at the rate of inflation of 2.5% per year. She expects to live until age 90. Her investment advisor tells her that her investment is expected to earn an average rate of return of 8% per year. How much money does she need today to finance her early retirement? Ignore taxes.

   (a) $449,012
   (b) $326,328
   (c) $438,061
   (d) $547,576
   (e) None of the above

3. Which of the following is not an option for the beneficiary of an RRSP by December 31 of the year in which that person turns 71?

   (a) Buy a term-certain annuity using all the money in the RRSP.
   (b) Withdraw all the funds and pay tax immediately.
   (c) Transfer the funds to a RRIF.
   (d) Buy a life annuity using all the money in the RRSP.
   (e) Transfer the funds to the RRSP of the spouse, provided that the spouse is younger than 71.

4. Which of the following is *not* included in a retiree's taxable income?

   (a) Canada Pension Plan (CPP) payments
   (b) Old Age Security (OAS) payments
   (c) Guaranteed Income Supplement (GIS)
   (d) Withdrawal from Registered Retirement Income Fund (RRIF)
   (e) None of the above

5. The contribution limit of one's RRSP is 18% of one's earned income. Earned income does not include _____.

   (a) interest income
   (b) net rental income
   (c) royalties
   (d) commission
   (e) taxable disability benefits

DISCUSSION QUESTIONS AND RESEARCH PROJECTS

1. Describe or explain each of the following entries:

   discount rates: real discount rate — nominal discount rate — before-tax discount rate — after-tax discount rate / government pensions plans: Canada Pension Plan (CPP) — Old Age Security (OAS) — Guaranteed Income Supplement (GIS) / human capital and pensions / life expectancy / OAS benefits: spouse's allowance — widowed spouse's allowance — OAS clawback / pension plans: defined benefit — defined contribution — indexation — vesting — portability / retirement planning model / Registered Pension Plan (RPP): past service contributions — unfunded liabilities / Registered Retirement Income Fund (RRIF) / Registered Retirement Savings Plan (RRSP): contribution limits — pension adjustment (PA) —unused contribution room — eligible investments — death, dissolution, and maturity — withholding tax / self-administered RRSP / spousal RRSP / time diversification

   The primary information source for the next three projects is Service Canada under Human Resources and Skills Development Canada (HRSDC). You can write, telephone, or visit in person at an office near you or visit their website: <www.servicecanada.gc.ca/eng/home.shtml>.

2. Prepare a two-page summary of the Old Age Security benefits. Your summary should include eligibility conditions, the most recent amount per month, the indexation rules, the rules on claw-back (the government recovers part of OAS from higher income recipients), and any other features you think are important.

3. Prepare a two-page summary of the Guaranteed Income Supplement benefits. Your summary should include eligibility conditions, the most recent amount per month, the indexation rules, and any other features you think are important.

PROBLEMS

4. Prepare a summary of not more than four pages of the most important features of the Canada Pension Plan at retirement age. Your report should include the rules under which the pension is calculated, eligibility, portability, taxation treatment, survivor benefits, indexation rules, and the current maximum pension receivable. Choose the important features for financial planning relevant to most people to stay within the page limit.

PROBLEMS

Note: You can use PlanPlus to assist in solving many of these problems, but the student version is not designed to provide complete solutions.

1. Construct a table like Table 17.2 for males and females who retire at age 60, for probabilities of 50%, 40%, 30%, 20%, and 10%. What are the implications of the results for personal finance?

2. Louise Hammer is a taxpayer who will be in the 40% marginal tax bracket for the next 40 years. She looks at her budget and sees that she will have $2,400 left from her take-home pay, after expenses. She will save everything of this by putting it in an RRSP. The money in the RRSP will be invested in a diversified portfolio of shares. The long-run return on these shares is expected to be 12% p.a. capital gains and 3% p.a. dividends, for a total before-tax return of 15%. At the end of 40 years she will withdraw all the money in a lump sum, and pay tax on it at a rate of 50%.

   Ed Anvil is a taxpayer who has the identical tax situation and budget expectations as Louise. He has decided to invest his savings outside an RRSP to take advantage of the capital gains' lower rate and dividend tax credit. He plans to do this for 18 years, using the same diversified portfolio as Louise. The after-tax dividend yield is 2%. The after-tax capital gains yield is 8%. From year 19 to year 40, he does exactly the same as Louise with his savings. At the end of 40 years he collapses his investments and pays tax as applicable at the rate of 40%. His rate is lower than Louise's because she has put herself into a higher tax bracket by not paying taxes earlier.

   Neither Ed nor Louise has an employer pension plan.

   (a) What does Louise have left in 40 years after paying taxes?
   (b) What does Ed have left in 40 years after paying taxes?
       (*Be very careful! The tax rules have an immediate effect on their savings.*)
   (c) What is the present value of the taxes Louise will pay in 40 years?
   (d) Ed recognizes he can do better than in part (b). He earns $50,000 every year, so his contribution limit is $9,000 p.a. Assume he has seven years of unused contribution. He decides he will contribute $21,000 to his

RRSP in each of years 19, 20, and 21 and get the tax deductions at 40%. He will use part of the accumulated investment pool to provide the cash flow. The rest of the pool will continue to accumulate at 10%. He will contribute the $4,000 based on current income as in part (b), from years 19 to 40. How much will he have after paying taxes at the end of year 40?

(e) When is a capital gain taxed? This question is not related to instalments. When does the 8% after-tax rate of return quoted above assume the capital gain is taxed? How does this affect your answer to part (b)?

3. Elizabeth Maynes wants to plan how much she and her husband Bruce should save for retirement. They have no pension plans because she is an independent consulting economist and he owns his own computer company. Both have contributed the maximum to the Canada Pension Plan so far, and they expect to earn enough to continue to do so. They live in Hamilton, Ontario, and plan to retire in Ontario. They are now 35 years old and would like to retire at age 60, but they are not sure if they will have saved enough. They are willing to work until age 65 if they can get a more secure retirement that way. In retirement, they would like an after-tax income $50,000 p.a., expressed in today's dollars and with no reduction when one of them dies. Elizabeth has $5,000 in an RRSP, which is invested in a GIC. Bruce has $10,000 in a Latin America mutual fund. They each have $15,000 in a TFSA. They plan to keep the TFSAs invested in riskless government bonds that they expect to show a real return of 2% p.a. The TFSAs are their emergency funds; though they expect to spend the money sometime after they retire, they do not want to invest in anything riskier, despite the higher returns that might be possible. They plan to do all of their future saving in RRSPs, but they are unsure of the effects of different investment choices on their retirement and they would like your advice.

Show them the effects of different investment asset mixes for retirement at age 60 and 65 on the amount that they must save each year, in real dollars. Assume that they take CPP and OAS at the normal start date, rather than taking CPP early or delaying the start of either one. Use the 2012 values for CPP and OAS. State your assumptions clearly. They will not receive the age and pension tax credits at age 60. Table 17.1 only applies to a person age 65. Use a tax rate of 12% for age 60–65 in your calculations. Discuss the risk underlying the different choices of asset mix and retirement age.

4. Joan wants to retire in 22 years at age 65 in Yorkton, Saskatchewan. She expects to receive an indexed employer pension of $20,000 p.a. plus 75% of maximum CPP, which is also indexed. She estimates that she will need after-tax pension income of $40,000. She expects to live for 30 years after retirement. Assume a marginal tax rate of 35% for the next 22 years, nominal rate

of return of 10%, and inflation of 4%. Joan has $20,000 in an RRSP now. How much will she have to save each year to reach her goal if

(a) she saves in an RRSP and also contributes the first tax refund due to the RRSP contribution into the RRSP (assume the contribution of the refund occurs at the same time as the original contribution)?

(b) she saves in a TFSA?

5. Mark and Ann are planning to retire in 25 years. Mark makes $65,000 p.a. before taxes and Ann is a housewife with no income of her own. Mark's marginal tax rates are currently at the 38% level, and he anticipates no future increases until his retirement. Mark has no employer pension, but contributes the maximum allowable every year to an RRSP, and uses the tax savings for recreation and entertainment. They figure that they would need an after-tax income of $35,000 in today's dollars at retirement, to live comfortably for 25 years. Their current RRSP has accumulated to $100,000, invested in a balanced mutual fund with an average rate of return of 9% p.a. What do you advise?

6. Jim Scott is 26 years old and has been working for the Ace Manufacturing Company for five years. His gross income in 2010 and 2011 was $23,000 and $26,000, respectively. He is a member of the company's registered pension plan and has contributed $1,100 and $1,200 to it in 2010 and 2011, respectively. The (PA) pension adjustment on his T4 slips showed $2,400 and $2,500 for those two years. The company had no pension plan before 2010. He earned $18,000 in 2007, $20,000 in 2008, and $21,000 in 2009. Jim does not have any RRSP because he never seemed to be able to save any money. In January 2012, he inherited $40,000 from a distant relative. How much can he contribute before March 1, 2012, and get a tax deduction for it?

7. Tracy Qi will be retiring next month following her 65th birthday. She wants to know if she has enough money to support her retirement lifestyle. She has about $300,000 in her RRSP, all invested in treasury bills. She has $55,000 in a term deposit with the Royal Bank, maturing next week. Her home is mortgage free (i.e., totally paid off) and is worth $350,000. She plans to sell it and buy a condominium that would cost $120,000 plus another $10,000 in legal fees, moving expenses, purchases of furniture and appliances, and so on. She does not expect to be able to live beyond the age of 90. She has found out from the government offices that she would receive CPP and OAS benefits of $600/month and $380/month, respectively. It is estimated that her average tax rate will be 15%. She needs $40,000 per year, payable at the end of each year, to maintain the lifestyle she wants after retirement. Assume that the rate of return on treasury bills is 3% p.a. and the rate of return on Canadian equity (i.e., stocks) is 8% p.a. Assume that there will be no inflation.

(a) If she invests all her money in treasury bills, can she afford her retirement lifestyle?

(b) If she invests all her money in Canadian stocks, can she afford her retirement lifestyle?

8. Heather Bloom, 30, is planning to retire after 35 years. She intends to invest $5,000 per year in a mutual fund, which has an expected rate of return of 10%, until her retirement. She is expecting to receive about $20,000 from her family at the end of the fifth year, and she will invest that in a GIC paying 5% interest. On the day she retires, she plans to put all her money in the bank, earning 6% interest. The rate of inflation is assumed to be 2% throughout. She does not expect to live beyond age 95. Ignore taxes.

(a) How much money will she have when she retires
   (i) in nominal dollars?
   (ii) in real dollars?

(b) If she wants to withdraw an equal amount in nominal dollars every year, starting at the end of the first year after retirement, what is the maximum amount she can withdraw?

(c) Suppose her annual withdrawals are unequal. If she withdraws an initial amount, x, at the end of the first year of retirement, and increases all future withdrawals at the rate of inflation, what is the maximum amount of the initial withdrawal?

(d) Suppose she dies after making 20 withdrawals as per part (c). How much money will she leave her estate?

9. Assume a world without inflation. Mr. Littlewood, 35, plans to retire at age 60. His life expectancy is age 87. He wants to live a retirement lifestyle that will cost $30,000 in the first year of retirement, payable at the beginning of the year. Subsequent retirement expenses will grow at a rate of 3% p.a., payable at the beginning of each year. He now has $20,000 in his investment account and plans to invest an equal amount annually for his retirement. The rate of interest that he expects to earn is 5%.

Calculate the following:

(a) the amount that he will need at retirement,
(b) the annual investment that he must make in order to reach his goal in (a).

10. Shahin Safaei is 55 and wants to retire from his job in the Swiss consulate in Toronto at age 65. He is presently earning $120,000 p.a. and he would like to have 75% of that income level in retirement. He wants to provide enough to maintain that standard of living until age 90. He will receive Canada Pension

of $10,000 p.a. in retirement, in today's dollars. He will receive an employer pension of $65,000 p.a., indexed, in today's dollars. He will receive no Old Age Security. His marginal tax rate now is 45%.

He has $100,000 in an RRSP now. He plans to deposit $5,000 p.a. in real dollars into it each year until retirement, which is the limit he can contribute because of his employer pension. He will deposit the tax refund on the RRSP contribution into a Tax-Free Savings Account (TFSA). His quite conservative investment portfolio earns 5% p.a. before tax. He expects the inflation rate to continue at 2% p.a. Assume the deposits into the RRSP and TFSA are made at year-end.

Savings in a TFSA provide no income tax deduction as an RRSP does, but the principal and income in a TFSA are never taxed, even when withdrawn. Therefore, to make the TFSA comparable with the other values in this problem, multiply the accumulated value by 1.3.

(a) Shahin's saving plan will not provide enough to maintain the standard of living he desires if he lives to age 90. How much will be the value of the shortfall in retirement savings at age 65?

(b) How much more must he contribute to his TFSA each year to reach his goal?

CASE STUDIES

1. ### STARTING YOUR RETIREMENT PLAN AT 50
   Alan is 50, Joanne is 51. They have a large house worth $800,000 in Toronto and a cottage worth $200,000 in Muskoka. Mortgage payments on these properties are $42,000 p.a. and they will be paid off in 10 years. They have no other debts, although they just finished paying off a car loan. They each own a recent model car, and they replace their cars every three or four years because they do not want to be seen driving older models. Alan's net income or take-home income was $100,000 last year, after taxes, CPP, EI premiums, medical insurance, etc. Joanne takes home $40,000 p.a. after the same set of deductions and contributions to her employer pension plan. They have two children whom they are currently helping through school, at a cost of $25,000 p.a. This cost will continue for another five years, after which the children are on their own. They are both carrying substantial life insurance and disability insurance, all of the cost of which is deducted from their gross pay in arriving at the net income reported above.

   They have $10,000 in a chequing account and a substantial line of credit at the bank if they need it. Alan has $30,000 in an oil and gas mutual fund. He has no pension plan. Joanne has $20,000 invested in GICs in an RRSP. She expects an indexed pension plan of $25,000 (in today's dollars) if she retires at age 61. They would each qualify for only 80% of maximum Canada

Pension, and that would be further reduced if they start receiving it before age 65.

Alan has been earning gross income over $100,000 p.a. for five years, and he expects the $100,000 net income of last year to be sustainable until he retires. He started saving money only in the last two years. Last year he deposited $15,000 in the mutual fund (this amount is included in the $30,000 balance). Joanne has been contributing $1,000–$2,000 p.a. to her RRSP for 10 years.

They would like to retire in 10 years. Advise them in their retirement planning.

2. HAVE YOU SAVED ENOUGH TO RETIRE?

Etaoin Shrdlu and his wife Qwerty wave goodbye to their daughter Spellcheck as she leaves for the residence at York and her fourth year in the BBA program. After a long shopping trip to replace their depleted stock of linen, soap, liquor, and food, and a trip to the post office to send off a package of pens, pencils, calculator, textbooks, and other trivia she forgot, they get the locks changed on the doors and settle down to plan their retirement. At last, peace and quiet after raising three children!

Etaoin is 54 years old and they want to retire when he is 62. Qwerty is 50. They expect to need 60% of their current income before tax when they retire, and to maintain that amount even for a single survivor. Here is their financial situation:

	Etaoin	Qwerty
RRSP balance	$25,000	$25,000
Company pension balance	nil	100,000
Pay into pension p.a.:		
company gives		3,000
deducted from her pay		3,000
RRSP deposit	5,000	1,000
Gross income	40,000	50,000
Canada Pension Plan pension	6,000	5,000

The Canada Pension Plan (CPP) amount shown is the annual pension each would get in today's dollars if starting at age 62 for him, 60 for her. This projection assumes that each continues to contribute the maximum amount each year. Qwerty's pension plan is defined contribution, invested half in bonds, half in equity. When she retires she will transfer the accumulated amount to a locked-in RRSP. Their RRSPs are invested in money market funds, GICs, and bonds, with an average real return of 2.25% p.a.

They have a house in Thunder Bay and a cottage in Nipigon, both mortgage free. The house is worth $100,000 and the cottage, $25,000. They plan to travel a lot during the winter after they retire. Their initial plan is to continue saving at the rate they have been doing.

(a) By how much will they fall short of their goal of retiring at his age 62 if they continue their current savings plan?

(b) Outline three courses of action that could make the goal achievable.

(c) Do the calculations for the choices suggested in (b).

CHAPTER 18

Maturation of the Retirement Plan

Georgina and Nial retired with lots of money, but Georgina made serious mistakes in her planning, and when she died unexpectedly, Nial was left with very little. Find out how to avoid her mistakes in Example 18.2.

LEARNING OBJECTIVES

➢ *To describe the maturity choices available for different forms of savings at retirement and explain how to match them to a retirement situation.*

➢ *To show how basic principles of risk management, taxation, and investment apply to decisions in retirement.*

➢ *To provide a basic guide to estate planning.*

Financial planning changes once the family retires. The biggest risk is not dying early, but rather living so long that you outlive your money. There are fewer taxation problems to consider, and debt management should be at an end. Budgeting is less important because the family is no longer saving for a distant retirement objective. In some ways, the planning is simpler but also more important because in retirement, the family has no chance to make up for mistakes by earning more in the future.

Shortly before the retirement date of each member of the family, key decisions have to be made, and some of them are irreversible. There are different ways to receive payouts from the retirement income sources like pension plans and RRSPs, and these **maturity options** can affect the family considerably. In this chapter we first provide a description of some specific instruments that we haven't explained in earlier chapters. Then, we examine the different sources of retirement income and the choices available for payment during retirement. We return to some basic principles of goal setting, risk management, tax minimization, and investment to determine how to choose among the different payment forms.

The last part of the chapter discusses estate planning in fairly general terms. Wills, taxation of estates, trusts, the role of an executor, and probate fees are the chief topics. Estate planning becomes a complex matter, beyond the scope of this book in certain situations, primarily when there is a lot of money involved. We give you the outline so that you know what sort of questions to ask the experts.

SPECIAL RETIREMENT INSTRUMENTS

Annuities

Annuities are cash flows with periodic payments. In Chapter 2 we defined them as having equal periodic payments, which allows simple formulas for time value. Annuities may have differing payments per period, however. In this section, we are discussing annuities that are defined by whatever law or contract applies, and so they may have equal or differing payments. The person who receives the payments from an annuity is called the **annuitant**. He pays a principal amount to an insurance company or other insurer and gets regular annuity payments in return. The OAS, CPP, and employer pension plans all pay annuities to their recipients.

A **life annuity** pays the agreed amount to the annuitant until his or her death. A life annuity is a life insurance policy. The risk that the annuitant insures against is outliving his or her money. The insurance company pools a large number of such people's money together. The financial losers are those who die earlier than expected. Their losses provide the extra money to pay the winners, who live longer than expected. Insurance companies have always had to cope with the odd complaint from an heir that the insurance policy "cheated" the annuitant and her heirs when the annuitant dies very soon after buying a life annuity. We can understand that the "losers" and "winners" must balance out, after allowing for the insurer's costs and required rate of profit.

To meet the demand for different patterns of retirement income and risk management, the financial markets have developed the following types of annuities. Generally, they are available with monthly, quarterly, semi-annual, and annual payment options.

Straight life. The annuitant receives the agreed level payment until death, with nothing to the estate. This pays the highest rate of all annuities, per $ of principal.

Life with guaranteed term. The annuitant receives the agreed level payment until death. If the annuitant dies before the end of the guaranteed term, the beneficiary gets the balance. If the spouse is the stated beneficiary, the arrangement may allow the spouse to receive the rest of the payments as scheduled, or to receive the **commuted value** at once. The commuted value is the present value of the future payments at the interest rate set in the policy. The guaranteed period is set by agreement, and is usually five or ten years. The guaranteed period cannot extend beyond the later of age 90 of the annuitant or the annuitant's spouse. Payments are lower than a straight life policy, and decline as the guaranteed term increases.

Joint life and last survivor. This annuity names an annuitant and a second person, usually the annuitant's spouse. If the annuitant predeceases the second person, that person continues to receive payments for life. The annuitant can specify equal payments throughout, or reduced payments after his or her death. A guaranteed term is also possible. Payments from this annuity are lower than straight life on either party.

Substandard health. A person who can demonstrate a sufficiently serious health problem that lowers life expectancy significantly may be able to qualify for an annuity with a higher payment than straight life.

Term certain. This annuity pays a level amount to a specified date. This is not a life annuity and has no insurance aspect to it.

Indexed. An indexed annuity increases the payment each year by an agreed value. The word "indexed" may be misleading because the annuity is not indexed to any inflation measure, it simply increases every year by a fixed percentage. The earlier payments are lower than a straight life annuity and the later payments (if the annuitant lives long enough) are higher. It does provide a reasonable inflation hedge because inflation has been positive for a long time. It helps with taxes, since the higher tax on the higher nominal amount is deferred, relative to taxes on the straight life annuity.

Prescribed. If an annuity is purchased with money on which tax has already been paid, then only the interest portion of the payments is taxable in the future. You will recall from Chapter 2 that the interest portion of any blended payment is higher in the early years. A prescribed annuity is arranged so that the interest portion is level each year to avoid high tax burdens in the early years.

Three factors determine annuity payment amounts. The expected length of time it will be paid is calculated from the mortality tables.[1] The initial amount contributed depends on the annuitant's own savings. The interest rate is set by the marketplace, and since it fluctuates considerably over time, the annuity payments set by contract vary likewise. Average life expectancy of males is lower than females, and hence a man receives a higher payout than a woman of the same age. As a result, a given life expectancy and initial contribution will yield very different amounts depending on when the annuity was purchased. Interest rates in Canada reached very high levels in 1981–82, and people who retired then (or locked their retirement savings into annuities in anticipation of later retirement) received very good incomes. People who retired during the low interest rate period of the 2000s received much lower incomes, in nominal terms. The variation is much less than short-term rates indicate. The insurance companies finance their annuity payouts with very long-term bonds, and hence the annuity rates "match up" the pattern of long-term interest rates.

As a practical matter, retirees who are buying annuities should check with a number of different companies or use an annuity broker to do it for them in order to get the best return.

Registered Retirement Income Fund (RRIF)

All RRSPs must be wound up by December 31 of the year in which the beneficiary turns 71. A **Registered Retirement Income Fund** (**RRIF**, pronounced "riff") is the continuation of an RRSP and its mirror image. The RRSP funds can be partly or wholly transferred to a RRIF. The funds accumulated are withdrawn in

---

[1] The calculations are quite complex for anything other than a straight life annuity, and we do not deal with them in this book.

future years to provide retirement income. Income on the balance in the RRIF accumulates tax-free, but all payouts are fully taxable. A trustee holds the RRIF, and the person whose RRSP created it can either manage the money in a **self-administered RRIF** or use a guaranteed rate RRIF provided by the trustee. The **investment restrictions** on the RRIF are essentially the same as those on an RRSP.

The beneficiary may withdraw as much from a RRIF as desired, but there is a minimum withdrawal required, shown in Table 18.1 The minimum is based on the market value of the assets in the plan at the start of the year.

A person may have more than one RRIF. The income from a RRIF is pension income. The funds in a RRIF in excess of the minimum withdrawal for the year can be used to buy a life annuity. Such an annuity cannot have a guaranteed term extending beyond age 90 of the annuitant or spouse.

Locked-in Pension Funds

What happens to the pension entitlement when a person changes employer? The value in the plan may stay in the plan, or it may be transferred to a locked-in format. These locked-in funds are supposed to provide retirement income, and so they are restricted in much the same way as they would have been in the original pension plan.

The legislation covering a specific pension plan may be federal or provincial, and the terms of the plan itself may affect how the locked-in funds are eventually withdrawn. We discuss the general principles governing locked-in funds, but you must determine the details very carefully for each specific case.

Transfer options vary by jurisdiction, but in general, locked-in pension funds may be transferred from a RPP to one or more of the following:

* Another RPP
* A locked-in RRSP or locked-in retirement account (LIRA)
* A locked-in RRIF (LRIF)
* A life income fund (LIF)
* A prescribed RRIF (PRRIF) (Saskatchewan only)
* A life annuity

Normally, no withdrawal is possible prior to retirement, though that is starting to change under some conditions in some jurisdictions:

* A court may allow withdrawals prior to retirement, or in excess of maximum allowed withdrawals, if the annuitant can show genuine financial hardship.
* Lump-sum withdrawals may be allowed for very small plans.
* Early withdrawals may be allowed for an annuitant who can show significantly shortened life expectancy.
* Withdrawal of the entire amount may be allowed if the annuitant is no longer a resident of Canada.

TABLE 18.1 Minimum RRIF Withdrawal As a % of RRIF Assets	
Age	**Minimum Annual Withdrawal**
65	4.00
66	4.17
67	4.35
68	4.55
69	4.76
70	5.00
71	7.38
72	7.48
73	7.59
74	7.71
75	7.85
76	7.99
77	8.15
78	8.33
79	8.53
80	8.75
81	8.99
82	9.27
83	9.58
84	9.93
85	10.33
86	10.79
87	11.33
88	11.96
89	12.71
90	13.62
91	14.73
92	16.12
93	17.92
94+	20.00

This alphabet soup may confuse you (it confuses us), and the additional complication of differing rules by province makes it worse. Think of it this way. The locked-in RRSP and LIRA are the instruments that you transfer funds into from a RPP while you are still working and don't need a pension. They have much the same investment rules as an RRSP, but you can't get the money out, just like a pension. The rest of the instruments are for the payout phase, when you have started receiving a pension. So, you would then transfer the locked-in RRSP/LIRA into one or more of the other instruments, and relax. However, you must transfer the locked-in funds into one of the payout options by the end of the year in which you turn 71, just as you must transfer an RRSP into a payout option.

LRIF and LIF

Most provincial plans do not allow transfers into these plans before age 55. Both of these have prescribed minimum withdrawals at the same rate as an RRIF. Both have prescribed maximum withdrawals, as well, in order to preserve some capital for age 80. At age 80, the remaining balance in a LIF must be used to purchase a life annuity; the owner may do that earlier if he or she chooses, again, just like an RRIF. The balance in an LRIF may be used at any time to purchase a life annuity, but there is no requirement to do so; in that way, the LRIF is a close substitute for a RRIF. Not all provinces and territories have legislation enabling LRIFs. Saskatchewan's PRRIF replaced the LRIF, but only for that province, and only for pensions under provincial law.

Life Annuity

The conversion to a life annuity has certain limitations. Under all provincial and federal pension law, the annuitant's spouse must also be able to receive a survivor benefit under it. The standard survivor benefit is 66% in Saskatchewan and 60% in all other jurisdictions. If the annuitant does not set up the conversion, it occurs anyway with some minimum requirements:

- The annuity must be guaranteed by a life insurance company.
- The annuity must be payable on a joint life basis if the annuitant has a spouse.
- If the pension contract provides a survivor benefit that is greater than the provincial minimum, the beneficiary may agree, in writing, to a lower benefit, but never less than the provincial minimum.
- No guaranteed period is permitted beyond the annuitant's age 90.

With respect to the last point, requiring a guaranteed period in any life annuity tends to defeat the risk management aspect of it. If what you want to do is minimize your risk of running out of money, then you want the annuity to pay as much as possible per period. A guarantee reduces the amount it will pay because it is sacrificing some of the mortality credits, the benefit that everyone in the pool obtains because half the annuitants in any pool will die earlier than the median age, allowing the others to receive payouts for longer. The only reason to require a guaranteed period is to leave a bequest to children. If there is enough money that there is no risk of running out, then a guarantee is not risky.

If the jurisdiction allows an LRIF, it is the preferable choice in every case because it gives more freedom to decide when and how to pay out, without removing the option of annuitizing.

Income Tax

All of these payout options retain the same characteristics for tax purposes as registered pension plans. All the income paid to the annuitant is taxable, but the income on the unpaid principal continues to accumulate tax-free.

Reverse Mortgage

A **reverse mortgage** is a mechanism for a family to realize part of the equity on its fully paid principal residence while continuing to live in it during retirement.

A reverse mortgage is a loan based on the equity of the house, but it requires no periodic repayments. The interest continues to accumulate and so the loan increases in size. The borrower may repay at any time but must repay when the house is sold. The lender can only recover the loan up to the value of the house.

The benefit of a reverse mortgage is that the retired family is not forced to uproot to a new, smaller home or apartment as long as there is enough value in the house equity. The family may use the funds the reverse mortgage provides for anything. The most important use for some is simply providing additional money for daily living, perhaps with the purchase of a life annuity. In some cases there is an unexpected need for cash to repair the house or buy a car. Some families effectively start distributing the estate early to the children by taking out a reverse mortgage to help them buy their own homes.

The lack of recourse and the indefinite life of the loan make reverse mortgages somewhat riskier than conventional mortgages. In addition, the borrower is no longer earning labour income. In earlier years, reverse mortgages were always sold as a package with a life annuity, and were called **reverse annuity mortgages (RAMs)**, which also provided a bit more security to the lender since there was a guaranteed source of income and the borrower could not squander the money. At the time of writing this edition, reverse mortgages with a one-year term carried an interest rate 1.05% above that posted by the major banks. A number of small financial institutions offer reverse mortgages, but almost all of the business goes through the Canadian Home Income Plan (CHIP).

The amount of the loan is limited by the age of the borrower(s), the type of home, the location, and the market value. If neither partner is over 55, no loan is available, and borrowers under 65 will not usually get more than 30% of the home equity value as a maximum mortgage. Older borrowers may be able to borrow up to 50% of the home equity.

SOURCES OF RETIREMENT INCOME

With the description of the special retirement options complete, we can turn now to the sources of retirement income and how they are paid out during the period of retirement. Table 18.2 summarizes this information. We have discussed most of the sources already with respect to how they are accumulated.

Government Pensions

Under the HRSDC website, the CPP and Old Age Security are both referred to as public pensions. However, technically, the OAS and GIS (an extension of the

TABLE 18.2
Retirement Income Sources and Maturity Options

Source	What It Provides	Maturity Options
CPP	• indexed life annuity	• spousal division • date to start receipt
OAS	• indexed life annuity	• date to start receipt
GIS	• indexed supplement • non-taxable • annual means test	• no choices
RPP	• life annuity • taxable	• % to spouse on death of annuitant
Locked-in RRSP, LIRA	• lump sum • taxable	• LIF or LRIF • life annuity(ies)
RRSP	• lump sum • taxable	• withdraw as needed • annuity(ies) • transfer to RRIF
Home Equity	• lump sum • non-taxable	• trade down or sell • reverse mortgage
Endowment Life Insurance	• lump sum • non-taxable	• annuity
Tax Shelters	• various	• spend as received • annuity(ies)
Regular Savings	• lump sum • capital gains taxable	• spend as needed • annuity(ies)

OAS) are welfare payments, not pensions. They are paid from general government revenue, not from a trusted fund.

CPP is a contributory defined benefit pension, and the pension is indexed. The pensioner has two choices to make. A spousal couple may opt to split their CPP, and if they do so elect, the split must be equal percentages. This allows income splitting, but it has become much less important with the recent tax changes that allow notional spousal splitting of all pension income. A person can choose to start CPP at any age from 60 onwards. The stated pension assumes a start at exactly age

65. For every month earlier than age 65 that the pension starts, the pension is reduced by .6% per month, to a maximum reduction of 36% (12 months × 5 years × .6%) if it starts at age 60. A later start increases it by .6% for each month that the start is delayed beyond age 65, to a maximum increase of 36% if it starts at age 70 for pensions commencing in 2012. In 2013 the increase becomes .7% for each month delayed, to a maximum increase of 42% if started at age 70. A further delay in starting the pension does not increase the payment further.

The federal budget of 2012 made significant changes to the OAS. There is no change for pensioners currently receiving it. The OAS remains an indexed non-contributory benefit for people who have lived most or all of their life in Canada. A person must have lived at least 10 years in Canada after turning 18 to receive any benefit, and can then receive 1/40th of the maximum pension for every year lived in Canada after age 18, up to the maximum. Once a partial pension is approved, the fraction of the maximum will not be increased, except for the indexing.

Two changes affect future pensions. Until the change, OAS eligibility started at age 65. Under the new rules, anyone born before April 1, 1957, will be eligible for OAS upon turning 65. For each two months that a person is born after that date, the starting age of OAS will be increased by one month, up to age 67. For example, a person born July 1, 1959, was born 16 months after the starting point of this change, so she or he will become eligible for the OAS at age 65 years, 8 months, with the first payment due in April 2025.

The second change takes effect in July 2013. A person who is 65 or older and eligible for the OAS but has not yet applied may choose to delay receipt of the OAS for up to five years and get an additional .6% for each month of deferral, to a maximum increase of 36% for delaying the start of the OAS to age 70.

Since GIS is available only to recipients of the OAS, the eligibility date for GIS will be subject to the same later start as the OAS. There is no actuarial adjustment available for delay of GIS receipt since it is means-tested.

Example 18.1: Karim will turn 65 in October 2013. He will have lived in Canada for 14 years since his age 18. If the OAS payment is expected to be $560 per month when he retires, how much will he receive per year if he applies to start at age 65? How much will he receive in 2013 dollars if he opts to delay receiving it for two years?

Answer: If he takes it at age 65, he receives
12 × $560 × 14/40 = $2,352 p.a.

If he defers for two years, he receives
12 × $560 × 16/40 × 1.144 = $3,075.07 p.a. in 2013 dollars.

One specific aspect of the government pensions that many people overlook is the requirement for an application. They are not automatic, and it can take up to six months for them to start. Income Security Programs of Human Resources and Skills Development Canada (HRSDC) provides extensive information on its website, by mail, or by phone (check the Blue Pages of the telephone directory or the Internet for the nearest office). The federal government proposes to start developing a system to enrol eligible seniors automatically in the OAS and GIS, phasing in this new system from 2013–2016.

Employer Pension (RPP)

Some employer plans promise a set percentage of the pension as a survivor pension to a spouse. Other plans allow the employee to choose from several percentages, the most common being 50%–75%. If there is an option, the employee must choose before the pension starts, and the election, or any subsequent change, will require the spouse's signature if the survivor benefit is lower than the legal minimum percentage.

Locked-in RRSP, LIRA

The beneficiary may choose between a LIF or LRIF, in the provinces where they exist, and one of the life annuities. The election must be made before December 31 of the year the beneficiary turns 71.

RRSP

The beneficiary has three choices: withdraw and pay tax, roll over into a RRIF by age 71, or buy one or more annuities. All the annuity choices listed earlier are allowed, or a combination of all three is possible. For example, a couple might withdraw a substantial part of an RRSP the year after retirement to finance a world tour. When they return, they could convert half of the remainder into an annuity that would pay a fixed sum and the other half into a RRIF.

Home Equity

The choices are threefold: sell and move into an apartment; sell and buy a cheaper house; reverse mortgage. The advantages and disadvantages seem to relate more to personal goals than to financial values. The sell and rent option appeals to those who want to avoid shovelling snow and cutting grass or who want to travel without worrying about a house. However, those who are attached to a home could well find themselves very unhappy after a move.[2]

---

[2] We understand that moving seniors out of a home that they have occupied for many years also shortens their life expectancy.

The sell and trade-down options do raise more money, and do save money on operations to some extent. If the trade-down involves a condominium, the fees will eat up a lot of the savings. The value of this option is probably overestimated by most people because they forget all the costs involved. These include real estate agent's commission, legal fees, land transfer tax (in some provinces), and moving costs. A large piece of the expected differential on a trade to a cheaper home may disappear, although there is no tax on the gain. If the move is to an apartment, the automatic indexation of home ownership also disappears, although rent control may help.

With these considerations, a reverse mortgage may be a good compromise, bearing in mind the complexity we have discussed already.

Endowment Life Insurance

Endowment life insurance matures at a set date, usually age 65, providing a lump sum that can be annuitized. The usual annuity options are possible. Since the insurance premiums were not tax deductible, the proceeds at maturity are not taxable.

Tax Shelters

These are so specific to the particular loony piece of legislation that created them that we cannot offer general comments. They do not have a maturity that is connected to retirement date necessarily, though they may coincide. There are no special maturity options. The general option of cashing them in for either spending or annuitization always exists, providing they are liquid enough to permit realization. They are generally structured to minimize tax during working life, and hence may create higher taxable income in retirement when other income is lower.

Regular Savings

There is no required maturity date for unsheltered savings either. In fact, they are the most flexible part of the retirement funds, which makes up for at least part of the tax disadvantage. Since they are in lump-sum form, they can be annuitized or spent at any time. Prescribed annuities might be preferable since only the interest is taxable.

CHOOSING THE RIGHT MATURITY OPTIONS

We have outlined a large array of situations and maturity options. How does a retiree pick a path through this maze? We return to the basic principles of earlier chapters. They provide guidance, but also sometimes conflict, and differing interpretations are possible.

Goals in Retirement

There are three financial goals in retirement:

1. Minimize the risk of outliving your money. That is, minimize the risk that either spouse, a permanent dependant, or the family unit will have inadequate income at any time during retirement.

2. Maximize the income available to the family.

3. Maximize the bequest to the heirs (other than the spouse, whose needs are met in the first two goals).

The definition of a family unit in retirement is spouses plus others (children, parents, etc.) who are permanently dependent by reason of disability or age. The spouses could be same sex, which means that certain legal aspects are different, but the principle is the same. Statute and case law in Canada are changing the status of same-sex couples so that they have more of the rights and responsibilities of traditional marriages. Pension and insurance plans, both private and government, are changing in the same way. The CPP now treats same-sex couples the same as opposite-sex couples. See Chapter 5.

The importance of a bequest to anyone other than spouses and dependants varies greatly among families. We think that it should be of lesser importance in retirement planning except for those families for whom the first two goals are easily met. Since "inadequate income" depends partly on your definition of an acceptable standard of living, we think that most families need to consider the first two goals as the critical ones. One of the authors recommends that the best bequest parents can leave their children is that the children never have to support the parents financially.

Goal one, minimizing the risk of shortfall, is not the same as maximizing retirement income, since there is variation in investment returns. A family might sacrifice the chance of a very high standard of living in order to ensure that the future is at least comfortable. Furthermore, decisions that maximize income for a two-person family may not lead to adequate income for the survivor if one dies prematurely.

Example 18.2: Georgina retired in 2007 after a long and successful career as a restaurant owner. She assured her husband Nial that her retirement income would be more than enough for both of them. Nial's career as an abstract painter had provided no retirement income other than the OAS. For two years, there was plenty of money and they travelled and partied happily. Then Georgina died unexpectedly, and Nial discovered that there was almost no money left for him. She had purchased a straight life annuity with no survivor benefit and no guaranteed term with her RRSP. She had invested the money from the house they had sold and the sale of her business she invested in a high yield U.S. mortgage fund that had evaporated in the financial crisis of 2008. Now he had to live on the OAS plus the survivor benefit from her CPP. Even after the addition of some GIS, he still faced a meagre existence, compared with what he had expected.

This family made serious errors. Most important, the maturity option for the RRSP should have been a joint and last survivor annuity, or a RRIF, so that the remaining principal would provide for the survivor. The investment of the non-registered funds from the house and business should have been properly diversified or else used to buy a joint and last survivor prescribed annuity. They should have planned together so that Nial would have known what to expect. Their retirement plan should have laid out what they could reasonably spend from their means.

Does the Family Have Any Decisions to Make?

The sections that follow this one will not apply to a significant number of retirees. A retired family whose income is a mixture of the OAS, CPP, GIS, and pension from employer pension plans with no discretionary savings will not have much to manage other than the level of spending. The family may not have enough income for a decent standard of living, or it may have far more than enough, but there will be no risks to manage. All those sources of income are defined at retirement date and the only choice the family faces is the date of retirement and commencement of the pensions. If the income is insufficient, one family member at least has to continue working and/or the family has to reduce its consumption. The decision on when to retire is treated in Chapter 17. If a significant portion of the income is unindexed pensions, then inflation may be a problem in the long run. Unless the family is prepared to underspend its income in early years to save some nominal dollars for the future, it will have to reduce the real value of consumption as the purchasing power of the nominal income declines.

The families who have investments in forms they control, like RRSPs, TFSAs, and unregistered savings, do have decisions to make at the date of retirement and beyond. The principles from three of our previous main topics in the textbook recur in different fashions when the family retires: risk management, taxation, and investment. We have changed our treatment of maturity options somewhat from previous editions of the textbook to emphasize risk management, but all three of these major topics affect decisions in retirement; often they are inter-related and cannot be neatly separated into categories. We discuss each one in turn, but they cannot always be resolved as separate decisions.

RISK MANAGEMENT

In one sense, there is only one risk to manage in retirement — not having enough money. We can sub-divide that into six more specific risks in order to determine how to best manage them:

1. The family outlives the money.

2. A survivor spouse or dependant will have insufficient income after the death of the person and loss of pension benefits.

3. Future inflation is materially higher than expected and the family loses purchasing power from any income source not protected against inflation.

4. If the family decides to annuitize wealth and/or is receiving pension income, the annuities may not be secure.

5. If the family decides to manage its discretionary investments without annuitization (sometimes called self-annuitization) and draw money for consumption as required, the family faces investment risk.

6. The family may encounter very large medical expenses (e.g., a permanently disabled child) that are uninsured.

The final piece of the risk management section is a discussion of the family home as an insurance policy.

Avoid Outliving Your Money

We saw in Table 17.2 how long life expectancy is for an individual aged 65 in Canada. For a couple, the probability that at least one of them survives to a given age is even higher. The old biblical three score and ten is no longer the expected limit of someone's life. The biggest single risk for a retired family is living too long. A family may have so much money relative to its consumption that it need not worry, but such families are rare. Thus far in the textbook, we have calculated retirement income as a term-certain annuity. We assume a future date of death rate of return on income-producing investments, and then turn the family's wealth into a term-certain annuity for that period of time. The annual payment is the amount that the family will be able to draw annually. There are complications with income taxes and inflation, but that is the basic model. Very few things are certain in financial planning for long time horizons, but this is particularly fraught with risk because one or more members of the family may live longer than the time horizon we assume. If we assume a long enough time horizon, say death at age 120, we can be sure they won't outlive their money, but we will allow them a very meagre income as a result unless they are so wealthy that there is no risk of running out of money no matter what.

Life annuities are the insurance against running out of money and like any insurance policy there is a trade-off. You give up the ability to leave an inheritance (or perhaps give it up after a specified period of years, called the guarantee period) in return for a guarantee of payments as long as you live. A life annuity offers another very substantial benefit, called mortality credit. Think of the insurance company that issues the annuity. You pay a lump sum to the company in return for a stream of payments until death. The company pools a large number of such contracts together. Because of the law of large numbers, the company will pay the annuity on average to the median age of death. Half of the annuitants will have died by that date and get no further payments, while the others keep getting payments.

Now suppose you are the individual retiree trying to match this. You cannot plan for payments only until your median age of death, since that means there is a 50% chance you will run out of money on that date but still be alive. If you are to plan for a much longer horizon, you will have to draw less each year. Remember, you and the insurance company are both investing the initial lump sum in the same investment markets and getting approximately the same returns. Therefore, the life insurance company can offer you a higher income, guaranteed for life, than you can provide for yourself. The insurance company also has economies of scale in money management that mean it should be able to earn slightly more than all but the most expert individual, simply because it pays a lower percentage amount on the management of the money than does someone hiring a planner or investment advisor, but this is also offset by the insurer's expenses. The net effect is that life annuities offer much higher payments than you can draw from your money if you don't buy an annuity.

Table 18.3 shows a sample of recent life annuity quotes. Each quote shows the best rate offered on March 13, 2012. The amount is the monthly life annuity that $100,000 would buy you. For example, a 65-year-old male could get $582.34 per month for life for a single life annuity with no guaranteed term. This is an annual payout of 7.0% in nominal terms, ignoring the monthly compounding effect. By contrast, if he kept the $100,000 and invested it in a reasonable mix of diversified equity and debt securities, he could only draw about 4% per annum, in real terms, to get a less than 10% chance of running out of money.[3] Given that inflation is about 2.1% per annum when this comparison is being made, the life annuity is a much better deal. It will very likely provide more money and it provides it for sure, no matter how long you live.

---

[3] We draw this conclusion from extensive research over many years with our co-authors, Dr. Moshe Milevsky and Dr. Nabil Tahani. See for example Moshe Milevsky and Chris Robinson (2005), "A Sustainable Spending Rate Without Simulation", *Financial Analysts Journal*, 61(6), 89–100; and Chris Robinson and Nabil Tahani (2010), "Sustainable Retirement Income for the Gardener, the Socialite and the Uninsured", *Financial Services Review* 19(3), 187–202.

Nothing comes for free in personal finance, and annuities also have their disadvantages. We have already mentioned the loss of the bequest, which we do not regard as a reason to avoid annuities. We will discuss the others in the next few sections.

The OAS, CPP, and employer pensions are life annuities, which is part of their attraction. A family that has enough income from these sources doesn't need to annuitize. Most families should consider the annuity option seriously. As we have already stated, adding a guaranteed term reduces the payment, and this shows on Table 18.3. A guaranteed term reduces the effectiveness of the insurance aspect. If the lower income is sufficient for the family, then it should instead buy a life

---

TABLE 18.3
Life Annuity Rates

Monthly income from a single payment of $100,000 from registered funds (e.g., RRIF). The rates shown are quoted by a Canadian insurance company on March 13, 2012. The entire payment is taxable income because the annuitant buys it with registered funds. "Guarantee" means the payments will be made for that length of time, even if the annuitant dies before the end of guarantee period. The joint life values are for a male and female couple of the same age.

A. Fixed Life Annuity

Age at Start	Single Male Guarantee?		Single Female Guarantee?		Joint Life Guarantee?	
	No	20 year	No	20 year	No	20 year
55	$445.67	$412.12	$369.03	$360.16	$322.93	$321.47
60	505.92	450.36	439.82	414.85	383.29	378.75
65	582.34	478.03	502.72	452.76	449.30	435.33
70	690.80	502.50	582.94	482.93	507.46	471.21

B. Life Annuity Indexed at 2% per annum
(The table shows the initial payment, which rises by 2% each year thereafter.)

	No	20 year	No	20 year	No	20 year
55	$312.04	$291.00	$256.73	$248.69	$228.17	$227.17
60	396.21	351.28	311.79	294.06	263.49	260.31
65	481.66	390.91	398.35	357.26	335.91	324.72
70	585.25	418.03	484.72	396.53	415.85	383.67

Source: Courtesy of Ivon Hughes, The Hughes Trustco Group Ltd. <www.lifeannuities.com>

annuity without guaranteed term with a smaller lump sum that produces the same annuity as the guaranteed term annuity. The difference can be kept and invested, and provide an ultimate bequest to the children without giving the insurance company control. This additional sum that is not annuitized also provides flexibility for unexpected expenses, which is one of the weaknesses of annuities.

Survivor Dependant with Insufficient Income

If there is only one member of the family who is going to get a life annuity, then the other member(s) may suffer an unacceptable income drop if the annuity is not joint life. CPP and employer pensions all require that the spouse get survivor benefits and so this is not often a problem any longer. If a large part of the income is coming from an annuity that one member buys from a non-pension source like an RRSP or unregistered savings, then it is essential to make it a joint life annuity. In the case of a permanently dependent child, this is generally not possible. In Chapter 8 we discussed medical expenses and tax measures. A couple who have a child that they know will be dependent on them for a long life and therefore almost certainly outlive them will have to provide using other methods, including an RDSP and additional savings. The death of one spouse may reduce income to an unacceptable level, even with survivor benefits, but this will occur only at quite low income. There is no survivor benefit from the OAS. Furthermore, the loss of the individual tax credit, old age credit, and pension income credit of the deceased spouse may increase the average tax rate for the survivor.

Unexpected and Expected Inflation

Inflation presents a problem for anyone living on a fixed income, and by definition that is what retirement entails. We need to distinguish between expected and unexpected inflation. We have observed positive inflation in Canada every year since the start of World War II, and we expect that to continue. At the time of writing this edition, the expectation for future inflation in Canada is in the range of 2–3% per annum, which is quite moderate. The average over the entire post-war period has been about 4%. Inflation erodes the purchasing power of any annuity that is fixed in nominal terms. This is an entirely foreseeable risk. When inflation is 2% per annum, the erosion is not very large each year, but it accumulates over time. Remember how long you may live in retirement? If you retire at 65, there is a reasonable chance you will live at least to 85. In 20 years' time with inflation of 2% per annum, your fixed pension will buy only two-thirds as much as when you retired.

Example 18.3: John and Anya Banka retire at age 65. They have $18,000 in the OAS and CPP indexed to inflation and $40,000 in unindexed employer pensions. They spend it all every year instead of saving anything. How much purchasing power do they have left at ages 75, 85, and 95, if inflation is a constant 2%, 3%, or 4%?

You solve this problem by calculating the FV in nominal terms of their pension income and the FV in nominal terms of their initial income of $58,000. At age 75 with 2% inflation each year, the OAS and CPP will have inflated to $21,942 and the FV of their initial income will be $70,702. The employer pension plan is fixed in nominal dollars and so it is still $40,000 p.a. when they are 75. Their nominal income will be $40,000 + $21,942 = $61,942. The nominal value of the income they started with is not $70,702. This is how much they would be receiving if their employer pension plan were also indexed. Their purchasing power has declined to 61,942 ÷ 70,702 = 88% of what they had at age 65.

If you perform the same calculations for the other ages and inflation rates, you get the following set of purchasing power values:

Inflation (%)	Age		
	75	85	95
2	88%	77%	73%
3	82%	69%	64%
4	78%	63%	57%

Now suppose the 10-year period was 1972–81, when inflation in Canada was double-digit in three years, and the annual inflation range was 4.9% to 12.2%. Their purchasing power would have declined to 60% of the starting point by age 75.

How do you manage this risk? At least part of your retirement income is indexed to inflation. The CPP and OAS are indexed to inflation. If you are lucky enough to have an indexed employer pension, then most of your retirement income is protected against inflation. However, the majority of Canadians do not have employer pensions, and most of the employer pensions outside government and some groups employed indirectly by governments (teachers, for example) are not indexed. Only defined benefit plans are indexed.

The first way to manage the inflation risk is to plan to consume less in nominal dollars in early years of retirement relative to later years. If a significant portion of your pensions are not indexed to inflation and you don't have a lot of other assets, this requires you to consume less than your entire pension income every year and instead save some of it. Very few people have the discipline to do this. If you don't, you will have no choice but to reduce your consumption in later years. This pattern of consumption does apply to a lot of retired families. In the early years of retirement the family has the energy to travel and be more active. In later years the family will be less active and also stop replacing assets like clothes and furniture, and the real dollar value of consumption may drop to offset the drop in purchasing power of fixed pensions. While this may be the happy result of two opposite effects, the retired family is taking a real risk by not allowing for inflation. Some costs will not decline over time, and some costs like medical expenses and assistance with reduced physical ability to move and do household chores will rise significantly for many families.

One way to try to manage the inflation risk is to invest in assets that will yield higher returns when inflation is high. Now we get to the part about expected versus unexpected inflation. If everyone expects inflation to stay at 2% and it does, then investments will generally incorporate that expectation into pricing. Bonds will offer a yield that allows for that level of inflation. Your investment portfolio will keep pace with inflation. This doesn't necessarily hold when inflation changes, particularly if the change is completely unexpected and is relatively large. As you saw in Chapter 15, the price of bonds drops when the required yield rises, and so if you are holding bonds in retirement, you will suffer a capital loss just when your need for nominal income rises with rising inflation rates. The response of equities to changes in inflation is not predictable. In the long run, equity should return more when inflation is high, but the initial response to a sharp rise in inflation is likely to be a drop in equity prices in order that future expected returns can be higher. An investment in rental real estate is likely to rise in price to match inflation, but as we have explained elsewhere, rental real estate poses a larger set of risks because it is so undiversified relative to a portfolio containing many bonds and stocks.

Life annuities are the answer to the risk of outliving your money, but they are not perfect, and inflation is the main reason. Most life annuities, including pensions, are not indexed. As we said earlier in the chapter, there is an oddity in the way language is used in the annuity market in Canada. An indexed life annuity means that the annuity payment increases by an agreed percentage every year, not that it is indexed to inflation. Nonetheless, this is a reasonable type of annuity to purchase because it will pay less in nominal dollars to start than will a regular life annuity; thus, it will force you to spend a bit less in the early years.

Another choice is an inflation-protected life annuity (IPA), also called a real annuity. Some insurance companies offer real annuities in the United States, but they are not popular, and no insurer sells them in Canada. First, there is a problem for the insurance company in managing its risk. If it is to hedge against unexpected changes in inflation, it needs to invest the lump sum it received for the annuity into assets that are long-run and indexed themselves. There are not a lot of investments that have those two characteristics. Most of them are government bonds that are linked to inflation, but there is not a huge quantity of these securities and they usually have a maturity no longer than 30 years, which will not allow complete hedging of the joint risk of inflation and longevity. Furthermore, the governments and the few companies that sell inflation-linked bonds are themselves taking on inflation risk (although governments also have some influence on the inflation rate) and hence they do not offer attractive yields because they are bearing the extra risk. This means that the insurance company has to take on some extra risk in offering real annuities and get lower yields on the investments it matches them against. As a result, the company has to charge a higher premium in the form of a lower payout than the expected rate of inflation appears to justify on a purely mathematical basis.

Second, a real annuity payment will start at a much lower level than the same lump sum will buy in the form of a fixed annuity. Retirees suffer from **money illusion**. Money illusion is the tendency of people to focus on nominal dollars rather than real dollars or purchasing power. We showed you how to deal with inflation and inter-period comparisons in Chapter 2, but most people have not read this textbook and don't allow for it. Real and indexed annuities start with lower payouts because the payouts will rise over time, but retirees focus on the first year and are not able to recognize the importance of providing for future increases in cost of living.

> *I have always told clients to do their own inflation protection by having the bank automatically transfer 5% of each payment to a savings account. Nice and simple.*
>
> — *Ivon T. Hughes, Hughes Trustco*

Are the Annuities Secure?

The financial failure of the annuity provider is another reason why annuities are not the risk-free solution to avoid outliving your money. Unlike investment risk on the market, you cannot recover from a failed annuity provider or even take action to save yourself if you see the annuity provider running into difficulty because once you have started a life annuity, you cannot cash it in for the market value.

The risk has not been very large in the past. If a life insurance company sold you the annuity, it is regulated very heavily to ensure long-run solvency. Life insurance companies rarely fail, and when they do, the loss is never close to all the value of the liabilities. You can always expect at least part of the annuity payout to continue with another company that takes over the failed insurer. Furthermore, Assuris provides insurance for annuities as set out in Chapter 10. Many pension plans convert the retiree's entitlement at retirement date into an annuity paid by a life insurance company, rather than retaining the funds and paying the pension from the pooled funds of the retirement plan. Assuris covers only the first $2,000 per month of annuity, however, which is not a lot in today's values.

We are not so sure that the future will mirror the past. First, we have seen significant pension plan problems since 2008, and some of the worst problems started well before the 2008 financial crisis. Pensioners who worked for Nortel and GM are suffering losses in their pensions and the post-retirement health care benefits. Almost every defined benefit pension plan in North America has a large deficit in funding to cover future expected payouts. Part of the losses from 2008 was reversed in subsequent equity markets, but there remain large gaps. The demographic shift to a larger portion of the population being in retirement and supported by a smaller percentage of the population working is inevitable. People who are planning for future retirement have to be aware that their pensions are not 100% secure. Defined benefit plans have big funding deficits. Defined contribution plans cannot have a deficit, but they have suffered the same sort of market reverses and hence the pension will be much less in the future than everyone expected.

Self-Annuitization

Self-annuitization is just a fancy term for continuing to manage your investments without buying an annuity. You draw money from your account as you need it, selling investments when there is not enough cash to provide the payment you need. You aim to consume as much as possible every year, principal and income, while still leaving enough in the account to provide your desired standard of living for your lifetime, or for the lifetime of both spouses. Self-annuitization is the alternative to buying an annuity with the capital and receiving the annuity payments for life.

Self-annuitization allows the retired couple more flexibility and liquidity. They can choose to spend a lot more in one year than in another, give a child a large lump sum to buy a house or start a business, etc. A personal portfolio gives more options to protect against inflation than do annuities, although we like the approach that Ivon Hughes takes towards this problem (see quotation in the previous section). Self-annuitization has two serious risks, however. The rate of return on your own investments is risky, although a portfolio invested entirely in government real return bonds is pretty close to riskless. The bigger challenge is how much to take out each month while maintaining the long-run sustainability of the withdrawals for an uncertain life expectancy. A life annuity allows larger withdrawals because of the mortality credits, while providing insurance against living too long.

The retiree can exercise quite a bit of control over the level of consumption, but only limited control over life expectancy and market investment returns. The standard model the financial planner uses assumes a fixed rate of return and a specified date of death. The output is the percentage of the initial portfolio value that can be withdrawn as a fixed amount every year until the assumed date of death. This model is a term-certain annuity solution, because the date of death is assumed to be known. If the planner uses real values, then the percentage translates into an initial dollar value of consumption that should be able to be increased every year by the rate of inflation, thus maintaining a constant standard of living. If the planner uses nominal values, the initial year's consumption will be higher, but it will stay fixed in nominal dollars and thus the standard of living will decline over time.

> *Example 18.4:* Simona is 65 and wishes to allow for a retirement period of 25 years. She has $300,000 invested in a balanced portfolio that she expects will earn 5% p.a. in real terms. Expected inflation is 2%. How much can she consume every year, in before-tax dollars?

The annuity payment from $300,000 at 5% for 25 years is $21,286 p.a. Simona would withdraw this much in the first year. In the second year she would expect to be able to withdraw $21,286 × 1.02 = $21,712. If she instead works with nominal figures, the expected rate of return is (1.05 × 1.02) − 1 = 7.10%. The annual draw would be $25,975 every year in nominal dollars, with no increase expected. In the twelfth year of withdrawals, if she used the real dollar solution, her draw would have grown to $1.02^{11} × $21,286 = $26,466, which is more than she would receive if she had started her withdrawals as a fixed nominal amount. To put it another way, for the first 11 years of retirement she consumes less under the real dollar method than under the nominal dollar method, and then for the rest of her life she consumes more.

The authors of this book and others have conducted extensive research into the question of how much a retiree can consume from an initial retirement portfolio without running out of money before death, allowing for risk. The sustainable consumption or withdrawal rate ranges from 3% to 7% of the initial endowment. In practice, we don't know the date of death or the rate of return. We have modelled this formally in a number of papers, making rate of return, life expectancy, and consumption stochastic variables. *Stochastic* means that these factors can take different values according to reasonable statistical distributions observed in the real world. Table 18.4 shows some results. Each number in the table is the probability that a retiree of the given age will run out of money at the specified real rate of consumption expressed as a percentage of the initial portfolio. A person consumes at a real rate, expressed as dollars for every hundred in the investment portfolio. Consuming at a real rate means the retiree starts in the first year with, say, $4 per $100, or 4% of the portfolio. Each year thereafter the consumption increases by the rate of inflation.

The return distribution depends on the investment choices. We show results for three different portfolios. The low-risk portfolio has a mean real return of 3% with a standard deviation of 1%. You can think of this as a portfolio of Canadian government bonds. The balanced portfolio has a mean real return of 4.5% with a standard deviation of 11%, which is a reasonable expectation for a portfolio of 50% bonds, 40% Canadian equity, and 10% U.S. equity. The all-equity portfolio has a real return of 6% with a standard deviation of 16%, and is a reasonable

TABLE 18.4
How Sustainable Is Lifetime Consumption from a Given Investment Portfolio?

Each entry is the probability of running out of money before death for the given consumption rate, age, and portfolio type.

Panel A: Constant Real Consumption or Draw from the Portfolio

	Consumption Rate (%)											
	Low-Risk Portfolio				Balanced Portfolio				All-Equity Portfolio			
Age	3	4	5	6	3	4	5	6	3	4	5	6
55	6.0	19.0	40.0	61.0	3.0	13.0	28.0	45.0	6.0	15.0	26.0	40.0
60	4.0	13.0	28.0	45.0	3.0	9.0	20.0	34.0	4.0	10.0	20.0	31.0
65	2.0	8.0	17.0	31.0	2.0	6.0	13.0	23.0	3.0	7.0	14.0	23.0
70	1.0	4.0	3.0	10.0	18.0	1.0	3.0	8.0	14.0	1.0	4.0	9.0
75	1.0	2.0	5.0	10.0	1.0	2.0	4.0	8.0	1.0	2.0	5.0	9.0
80	.3	1.0	3.0	5.0	.3	1.0	2.0	4.0	.4	1.0	2.0	4.0

Panel B: Real Consumption or Draw Declines at 1% Per Year, on Average

Age	3	4	5	6	3	4	5	6	3	4	5	6
55	2.0	11.0	27.0	47.0	.5	3.0	12.0	26.0	3.0	10.0	19.0	31.0
60	2.0	7.0	18.0	34.0	.4	2.0	8.0	19.0	2.0	7.0	14.0	24.0
65	1.0	4.0	12.0	22.0	.3	2.0	6.0	13.0	2.0	5.0	10.0	17.0
70	1.0	3.0	7.0	13.0	.2	1.0	4.0	8.0	1.0	3.0	6.0	11.0
75	.4	1.0	4.0	7.0	.2	1.0	2.0	5.0	1.0	2.0	4.0	7.0
80	.2	1.0	2.0	4.0	.1	.5	1.0	2.0	.3	1.0	2.0	4.0

Source: Calculations using the model presented in Robinson and Tahani, op. cit.

expectation for a portfolio of 90% Canadian common shares, 10% U.S. common shares. The equity portfolios are assumed to be widely diversified. These mean returns also assume that the retiree is doing his or her own investment management using ETFs or holding equity and bonds directly through a discount broker. If the retiree pays the very high fees that Canadian mutual funds charge, the returns would be much lower on these portfolios and the risk of running out of money would be much higher than shown in the table.

We show draws of 3%, 4%, 5%, and 6%. At the risk of boring the reader who has already understood what this means, we will explain an example in careful detail.

Example 18.5: Sarah White has a nest egg of $200,000 in addition to her pensions. She wishes to withdraw $10,000 per year from it to supplement the pensions and increase that each year by the inflation to maintain the same standard of living. Let us simplify it by assuming only one withdrawal at the end of each year. In the first year, the total return is 7% and so at year end she has $214,000. After the withdrawal she has $204,000. In the second year the total return is 4% and so at year end she has $212,160. The inflation rate has been 2%. To maintain the same standard of living she must withdraw $10,200 and so she has $201,960 left at the end of two years. This is the process that Table 18.4 shows, except that instead of it being certain what each outcome is, there is a whole distribution of possible returns every year, the consumption can vary a small amount each year, and she can die at any time. This, then, allows us to calculate the probability that she will not run out of money before she dies. This is the probability shown in Panel A of Table 18.4.

Now suppose that Sarah expects her need for money will decline slowly as she ages in retirement. She will not feel like going to the movies as often, she will travel less often, she will need fewer new clothes. Most of a person's expenses in retirement are fixed, and so this reduction will not be very large, but it will affect the sustainability of withdrawals. Panel B of Table 18.4 assumes that Sarah spends 1% less in real terms each year, instead of the same amount each year as in Panel A. What happens if everything in the previous paragraph occurs, but with the reduced spending? We assumed the withdrawal commences at the end of the first year and so those numbers are the same. She starts year two with $204,000. Her spending at the end of year two is reduced by 1% in real terms to $9,900. In nominal terms, this is $10,098, and so she has $202,062. This continues until her death. It is clear that the probability of running out of money is lower in Panel B, with other factors held constant, because she is spending less.

Now let us look at the actual probabilities for Sarah White if she is 65 when she retires and has to determine how she can spend from her savings every year, in addition to her pension. If she has a balanced portfolio and plans to maintain a constant real withdrawal rate of $10,000, she is in the middle column of Panel A, under the 5% withdrawal rate, because the initial real withdrawal of $10,000 is 5% of $200,000. The table shows that she has a 13% probability of not being able to sustain this withdrawal rate for her entire life. The table and this method of analysis do not provide clear-cut answers, but rather give information to help in making decisions. The table can only approximate or estimate risks because the true return distribution is unknown. Sarah must decide among several courses of action.

One possibility is to adjust her portfolio to get a lower probability of shortfall. The table shows this is unlikely to help. An all-equity portfolio yields a slightly higher risk of shortfall, and the low-risk portfolio is even worse.

Another possibility is accept the 13% risk and keep reviewing her position every year to see if the risk is declining or increasing. Most of her income must be coming from pensions, though we have not given the details, and hence she is not going to starve or lose her home if she uses up her savings too quickly.

Another possibility is to adjust her withdrawal rate to 4%, or $8,000 p.a. That rate yields a risk of shortfall of only 6% with a balanced portfolio. If she does better than expected, perhaps in a few years she will be able to increase her consumption again.

Let us look at another example in an early retirement situation.

Example 18.6: Oliver Cheng is 60 and wants to know if he can retire now and have a secure income. He estimates that he needs $55,000 p.a. before-tax real income for life. Oliver is quite active and thinks his requirement will not decline as he ages. He has an indexed employer pension of $20,000, starting at age 60. His OAS and CPP will give him another $15,000 at age 65. For this example, we will ignore the possibility of starting CPP five years early at a reduced rate. He has no debts, and an RRSP balance of $450,000 in a balanced portfolio.

Answer: First, determine how much he needs to draw from the RRSP (which will eventually convert to a RRIF). This is a simple example because all the pensions are indexed.

He needs $55,000 – $20,000 – $15,000 = $20,000 p.a. from the RRSP at age 65. However, he needs to withdraw $15,000 p.a. more from the RRSP for the first five years. The table doesn't handle this situation directly and we need to approximate how much he will have left in the RRSP at age 65 in order to use the table.

Assuming that he draws $35,000 p.a. from the RRSP for five years, how much will he have left at age 65 if he earns 4.5%, which is the return rate used for the balanced portfolio in the table?

PV	$450,000
N	5
PMT	–$35,000
I	4.5%
FV	$369,307

This is not as precise a figure as it looks, since we have not allowed for any risk of earning less than 4.5%, but it is a reasonable procedure. At age 65 he gets the OAS and CPP, and reduces his withdrawal rate from the RRSP to $20,000, which is 5.4% of his RRSP. Looking at the table, Panel A, we see his shortfall probability is somewhere between 13% and 23%.[4] A planner looking at these numbers should advise Oliver that there is a considerable risk of shortfall below his desired consumption for life, if he retires at age 60. The most effective solution is to work. As we saw in Chapter 17, this reduces shortfall in the goal because he delays consuming from his savings while at the same time saving more, and he will then have a larger RRSP balance to provide for a shorter retirement life.

Unexpected Medical Costs

Most costs in retirement are reasonably predictable, but medical costs are not. Retirees are more likely to experience serious medical problems that cost large amounts not covered by universal health care. Only a small percentage of families will incur such costs, but they are more serious because the retiree has no disability insurance from work, may not have family members who can help care for him or her, and has no chance to recover and work to earn money to pay off the bills. Families with a dependent disabled child may face costs that will continue longer than the parents' expected lifetimes.

There are no standard prescriptions for this problem. Long-term care insurance is a common recommendation for retirees, but it is very expensive relative to the

---

[4] We calculated the exact result using the Robinson and Tahani software, and the failure probability is 21%.

coverage provided. For example, Sun Life provides a sample policy that offers a healthy 50-year-old woman long-term care coverage of $500 per week for comprehensive care and $250 per week for facility care for an unlimited period, for a premium of $291.46 per month.[5] Translate these numbers into monthly, and the insurance is a little over $2,000 comprehensive and $1,000 facility expense. To get that coverage this representative woman is paying almost 40% of the monthly benefit as a premium. An occurrence that would trigger this coverage is not a high probability event. Ignoring the time value of money, if she paid 10 years of premiums, the cost would be $35,000. If she then used the comprehensive coverage for 10 years and the facility coverage for another 20 years, she would receive about $480,000, making the premium paid over 7% of the benefit, not allowing for the income the insurance company earns on the premiums. We don't know the exact probability of a 60-year-old woman requiring 30 years of continuous care, but we are quite sure it is a lot less than 7%.

We provided considerable information about the RDSP and other tax relief measures for medical costs, but these are not insurance; the family has to be able to pay the costs in the first place. Retirees with pension plans that provide extended health care benefits may be better protected, but the extended health care in retirement is almost always much less generous than that provided while the person was still employed.

A basic level of care is provided by each province, but it is only worth around $1,000 per month in terms of the level of care, and it is means-tested. Care not subsidized by the province can exceed $5,000 per month for a single occupancy room, and this is still much less space and luxury than the average middle-class Canadian family is accustomed to.[6] Compare this to the $1,000 per month facility insurance in the sample policy we cited, and you can see the limitations of long-term care insurance.

The Family Home Is an Insurance Policy

The family home carries a lot of emotional baggage. We showed how to value a residential property in Chapter 13 and how to analyze the rent vs. buy decision from a financial perspective. We have already told you that a senior forced to leave home before he or she is ready to do so emotionally is likely to have a shortened lifespan. We also discussed extracting the equity from the home via a home equity loan, a reverse mortgage, or trading down to a cheaper residence. The family home also provides excellent insurance against two of the retirement risks.

---

[5] We take these values from a sample policy at <www.sunlife.ca/Plan/Health/Long+term+care+insurance/What+does+long-term+care+cost?vgnLocale=en_CA>. This is a sample policy; it is not an offer of insurance. This Sun Life website provides a lot of information about cost of long-term care in each province.

[6] Op. cit., amounts vary by province.

Shelter is always one of the largest costs of a family. A family living in a home that it owns does not face any inflation risk on the largest part of the shelter cost, the amortized capital cost of the property. Taxes, maintenance, and utilities will rise, but the rent on the capital is already paid and therefore fixed. Unless a family trades down to lower-quality shelter, that cost is fixed in retirement, whereas many of the savings in retirement come from consumables like food, clothing, and transportation. The family home provides relatively more inflation insurance in retirement than it did pre-retirement.

The second insurance policy is insurance against unexpected medical costs. The challenge with allowing for medical costs is that they are serious for only a small portion of the population, but we don't know in advance who will need to save more. As we have already seen, long-term care insurance is expensive and limited. The house works as an insurance policy against the retirees having to go into long-term facility care. Since they no longer live in the house, it can be sold and the funds used to pay for good care for quite a long time. If one goes into care and the other stays in the house, a reverse mortgage will help cover the cost of the long-term care. Conversely, if the retirees never need long-term care or incur other very large medical costs, or their pensions and savings are sufficient to cover the care, the house value remains in the estate and provides a bequest to the next generation.

TAXATION

All of the tax planning principles from Chapter 8 apply: spreading, deferral, splitting, and tax shelters. The opportunities for tax planning are fewer once you are retired, but still important. The most important ones require no planning, just proper completion of the income tax return to take advantage of them.

Spreading

Spreading becomes a two-edged sword. Pre-retirement income is usually higher than retirement income, and occasionally the retiree can avoid moving up a tax bracket by deferring receipt of income until the next tax year, in the year of retirement. The retiree shouldn't cash in RRSPs or RRIFs all at once, either. The withholding taxes constitute an immediate cost for an RRSP withdrawal, and a large withdrawal of RRSP or RRIF funds may raise the tax bracket. Low-income retirees should be very careful how they withdraw any optional, taxable source of income if they are also receiving GIS. In some situations, spreading the income evenly may mean loss of GIS every year. The retiree may actually get more total after-tax cash by withdrawing nothing from an RRSP in one year and then quite a bit the next year in order to receive GIS in the first year. The importance of the TFSA to low-income earners who are still able to save becomes very evident in this situation. Singles or couples who are likely to be receiving GIS in retirement should never save in an RRSP. On the other hand, the clawback of OAS occurs over such a large range of income that taking more income early to reduce clawback in another year will almost never be worthwhile.

One aspect of spreading is the difference between taxable and non-taxable cash flows in retirement, which is not usually an issue while a person is working. TFSAs, proceeds from sale of a principal residence, and the adjusted cost base portion of non-registered savings are all after-tax cash flows. Sale of the family business or farm is partly tax-sheltered, and sale of non-income assets is partly or wholly untaxed. The retiree should balance the use of these sources with taxable sources in order to smooth taxable income and remain at the lowest marginal rate possible over many years. This makes the deferral question more complicated in retirement because deferring a tax saves money, but only if you don't ultimately withdraw the money later at a higher marginal tax rate. Fortunately, the tax brackets are broad enough that absolute precision is not needed in planning how much to draw from each source of retirement income. For people whose income is entirely pensions, there are no choices, but many families have multiple sources. A particularly material time to treat withdrawals with care is the early years of retirement when some pensions may not have started or can be deferred, and the family can use other sources to bridge the gap until the pensions start.

Deferral

Remember that deferring a tax is often beneficial, simply due to the time value of money. Deferral of taxes is possible in retirement, often related to the order in which savings vehicles are liquidated to provide income. The general rule is to use up the funds on which no tax will be payable first. The retiree has no choice with pensions, but discretionary savings can be deferred even further if there is no immediate need for the cash. As we have already noted, there is a balance between deferral and staying in the lowest possible tax bracket.

The first thing to cash is unsheltered saving instruments that have no capital gains or accrued interest. The second thing to cash is unsheltered savings with accrued capital gains or interest. Since capital losses can be offset against capital gains, but not against other income, the two should be matched to use up the losses. The third thing to cash, if it doesn't interfere with other goals, is the family home.

One interesting large deferral is possible for well-off families who own both a cottage and a principal residence. The family can sell the principal residence without tax consequences and make the cottage the principal residence in the future. When the cottage is sold or left in the estate, the capital gains earned on the cottage prior to selling the main home will become taxable, but not before then. This plan only works if the family wants to retire to the cottage and it is suitable for a permanent residence, but many cottages are now better homes than city dwellers had a generation ago.

Another valuable deferral that has recently increased and expanded lies in the start date for receiving CPP and OAS, described earlier in this chapter. Delaying receipt past the normal start at 65 for CPP and 65 but moving toward 67 for OAS provides significant income increases. Deferral of the CPP and OAS start date is worth even more than deferral of RRSP withdrawals because CPP and OAS are indexed. Therefore, it may be worthwhile for a retiree to bridge the gap between retirement date and a late start date of CPP and OAS with RRSP withdrawals and/ or unregistered savings.

Leaving RRSP and RRIF funds to accumulate at the before-tax rate for as long as possible maximizes the after-tax retirement income. The investments outside the RRSP and RRIF were purchased out of after-tax income, and therefore only the net capital gains, dividends, and interest are taxable. TFSA withdrawals attract no tax. However, the entire withdrawal from an RRSP or RRIF is taxable. The longer that tax is delayed, the less it costs. Another deferral tactic is to delay moving funds from an RRSP into a RRIF or annuity for as long as possible. As soon as payouts start, taxes start, too.

Tax Splitting

If both spouses are in the same tax bracket, tax splitting is irrelevant. The common situation of one spouse who stayed home and one who earned a cash income makes tax splitting valuable. The recent tax change to allow splitting of pension income, described in Chapter 8, has changed the tax-planning landscape. In the past, it was essential in a situation of unequal incomes and assets to use mechanisms like a spousal RRSP and having the richer spouse pay all expenses while the lower-income spouse does all the saving. Putting more investment income into the hands of a lower-income spouse prior to retirement still pays off in a lower total tax bill for the family, but it is not necessary for most families post-retirement.

The case where it will matter even post-retirement is in a family with a lot of unregistered assets, including a family business and family cottage. If a family business continues to pay large dividends to a retired founder, for example, that is not pension income and cannot be split for income tax purposes. Even if the unregistered assets are turned into a life annuity, that also is not pension income and cannot be split. Families in this situation are a small minority of the population, but for them, planning to split income and assets prior to retirement and in retirement continues to be important. For the majority whose retirement income is primarily from pensions and RRSPs/DPSPs/RRIFs, the pension income splitting provision is all they need.

CPP cannot be split by a declaration on the tax return; it is not eligible pension income. CPP provides an election in which all CPP payments for both spouses are shared. The percentage shared is equal to the fraction of the years the spouses have been together divided by the number of years they have been contributors.

> **Example 18.7:** Leon and Alana were married for 10 years before they retired. They had contributed to CPP for 28 years. Leon has a CPP of $8,000, and Alana has $5,000. If they elect to share their CPP, how much does each one receive?
>
> **Answer:** Leon gets 18/28 of his CPP plus 10/28 of hers, or
> [(18/28) × $8,000 + (10/28) × $5,000] = $6,929
>
> Alana gets 18/28 of her CPP plus 10/28 of his, or
> [(18/28) × 5,000 + (10/28) × $8,000] = $6,071

A major source of income splitting is the sale of the family home and reinvestment of the proceeds in income assets, divided between the spouses. Both spouses must have contributed to the purchase and maintenance of the home, but the contributions need not be financially equal.

Death of one spouse does create a particularly bothersome tax problem for people with very modest retirement income. The tax credits and deductions for persons over 65, persons receiving pension income, and persons with disabilities disappear on the death of the spouse. At quite low income levels, the death of a spouse doesn't reduce living expenses much, but the lost credits can cost over $1,000, which is a lot for someone already in a low tax bracket.

Tax Shelters

The capital gains shelter and principal residence exclusion continue in retirement. Two additional non-refundable tax credits exist, but the taxpayer need not be fully retired to take advantage of them. Recall that a non-refundable tax credit amount is not a deduction from taxable income, but is added to the total tax credit amount, which is then multiplied by the lowest federal and provincial tax rate to yield federal and provincial non-refundable tax credits that are deducted from federal and provincial tax otherwise payable.

A taxpayer who is 65 or older on December 31 of the tax year may claim a non-refundable *age tax credit* amount up to a specified limit ($6,537 in 2011). If the taxpayer earned more than a specified minimum income ($32,961 in 2011), the allowable claim is reduced by 15% of the income in excess of the limit, until it reaches zero at the upper income limit ($76,541 in 2011). The reader will notice this is the same formula as the OAS clawback, but it starts at a much lower income level.

The *pension income tax credit* allows a tax credit amount of up to $2,000 of eligible pension income for a taxpayer who is 55 or older on December 31. Eligible pension income for someone under 65 is limited to income from employer pension plans and annuity income from an RRSP/RRIF/DPSP arising on the death of the spouse. The definition of eligible pension income broadens at age 65 to include the following:

- Annuity income out of any RRSP or DPSP
- Income from a RRIF
- Interest from a prescribed non-registered annuity
- Income from foreign pensions
- Interest from a non-registered GIC offered by a life insurance company

Note that CPP, OAS, lump-sum withdrawals from an RRSP, and all unregistered investments except life insurance company GICs are not eligible pension income.

In most circumstances, if the taxpayer does not have enough taxable income to use up the refundable tax credits, they can be transferred to the spouse. In order to use up the pension income tax credit, a taxpayer age 65 or older who does not have any pension income should convert enough RRSP/DPSP funds or non-registered funds to an annuity or RRIF as appropriate to get the tax credit.

Taxation of Annuities

An annuity purchased with funds from a registered account is fully taxable because the contributions and earnings in the account were not taxed originally. An annuity purchased with funds from a non-registered account will be taxed only on the interest portion of each payment because the principal portion has been taxed already. If you recall how mortgages annuitize, you will remember that the earlier payments are mostly interest and very little principal. If the payments from an annuity from non-registered funds were to be taxed on the normal amortization schedule, the annuitant would pay a great deal of tax in the early years and it would decline over time. This unfair tax burden is remedied in Canada with a prescribed annuity.

The *Tax Act* prescribes a formula that allocates the interest principal portions equally over the life of the annuity, for income tax purposes only, and hence the after-tax payment remains the same every year. There are a variety of technical steps that must be followed to make sure that an annuity is eligible to be prescribed, and the initial cost of the annuity has to be adjusted if it is a deferred payment annuity, but these details are beyond the scope of this textbook (and the insurance company issuing the annuity will deal with them in any case). The formula for determining the capital portion of an annuity payment is as follows:

Capital portion of a prescribed annuity

$$= \frac{\text{Initial cost of annuity}}{(\text{Total number of payments} \times \text{Amount of each payment})} \times \text{Payment amount}$$

Example 18.8:   Jason buys a five-year annuity with $100,000 from his unregistered investment account that pays out a rate of 2.5% p.a., payable annually. What is the taxable income he reports every year?

Answer: First, calculate the before-tax annuity payment from the insurance company.

PV	$100,000
N	5
I	2.5%
PMT	$21,524.69

Second, calculate the capital portion of each payment:

Capital portion
$$= [\$100,000 \div (\$21,524.69 \times 5)] \times \$21,524.69$$
$$= \$20,000$$

Taxable interest each year
$$= \$21,524.69 - \$20,000$$
$$= \$1,524.69$$

The number of payments from a life annuity is unknown until the death of the annuitant, but taxes have to be calculated every year. As a reasonable but arbitrary approximation, the Income Tax Regulations specify that for a life annuity, the number of payments is assumed to be the life expectancy calculated from the 1971 Individual Annuity Mortality (IAM 1971) tables. These calculations require actuarial mathematics far beyond the scope of this textbook. Men, women, and joint life annuities all have different factors, and each pair of ages of the two parties to a joint life annuity will yield a different expected life of the annuity. Table 18.5 provides the single life values and joint life when the two parties are the same age and there is no guaranteed minimum number of payments.

Example 18.9:   David and Amy Singh are 65 years old and have retired. They wish to convert part of their savings to life annuities to supplement their pensions. They have $250,000 in an unregistered account after paying the capital gains tax when they sold a lot of common shares. They buy a prescribed joint life annuity with no guaranteed period. Using the tables in this chapter, calculate how much they will report each year in taxable interest from the annuity.[7]

---

[7] A practitioner will note a slight inaccuracy here. Life insurance companies pay a tiny bit less for prescribed annuities, presumably because of the extra calculations they have to do. We did not complicate the presentation by including both sets of values in our table showing sample life annuity payouts.

TABLE 18.5			
Life Expectancy Based on 1971 IAM Tables			
	Life Expectancy		
Age	**Male**	**Female**	**Joint Life & Last Survivor**
55	24.71	28.61	32.71
56	23.91	27.71	31.78
57	23.13	26.83	30.85
58	22.35	25.96	29.93
59	21.59	25.10	29.01
60	20.83	24.25	28.10
61	20.08	23.41	27.19
62	19.34	22.57	26.29
63	18.61	21.74	25.40
64	17.89	20.92	24.51
65	17.17	20.10	23.63
66	16.47	19.29	22.75
67	15.77	18.47	21.87
68	15.09	17.67	21.01
69	14.42	16.87	20.15
70	13.76	16.08	19.30
71	13.11	15.30	18.46
72	12.48	14.53	17.63
73	11.86	13.79	16.82
74	11.26	13.05	16.02
75	10.67	12.34	15.23
76	10.10	11.64	14.46
77	9.55	10.97	13.71
78	9.01	10.32	12.98
79	8.50	9.68	12.27
80	7.99	9.08	11.57

Source: Cannex Financial Exchanges Ltd.[8] This table is for annuities with no guaranteed period of payments.

[8] Cannex Financial Exchanges is a useful source of data about products and services from financial institutions. Cannex calculated Table 18.5 for us without charge and provides sample data on its website, <www.cannex.com>, but comprehensive surveys are available only for a fee, and its customers are mostly financial services professionals and companies.

Answer: From Table 18.3, we take the monthly payment on a joint life annuity, no guaranteed period. The payment is for a $100,000 initial cost, so the before-tax monthly payment David and Amy will get is 2.5 × $449.30 = $1,123.25. Next, we calculate the capital portion, using the formula and Table 18.5:

Capital portion = $250,000 ÷ (23.63 × 12) = $881.65

Interest portion = $1,123.25 – $881.65 = $241.60 per month

Annual taxable interest = 12 × $241.60 = $2,899.20

The IAM 1971 table is out of date for any mortality calculation except its prescribed use in the Income Tax Regulations for annuities. You should not use it to estimate life expectancy today.

INVESTMENT PRINCIPLES

How should a retired family invest the funds that now provide the income? Some of the investment decision rests with pension trustees, and the family has no say in the matter. The family's own savings are in its control, however, and the same general principles apply as in Chapters 14–16. We need not repeat ourselves, but we emphasize a few key points.

The most important single principle in investment management is diversification. A simple way to include all elements of diversification within the equity portion of the portfolio is to hold ETFs for Canada and the United States. The weighting should be more to Canadian, but if the family spends a part of the year wintering in a U.S. sun state, then a significant holding of U.S. equity is reasonable, say as much as 30%. Holding a diversified U.S. ETF is sufficient to get all the international diversification you need, because so many of the large U.S. companies own operating subsidiaries around the world. The one weakness of the Canadian equity market is its concentration in financials and resource shares. U.S. diversification brings in every sector that an investor can buy.

If we are recommending broad market ETFs, then we are also making a statement that says 40–60 shares, across all industries, is a suitable level of diversification. Holding shares in five Canadian banks, five Canadian oil companies, two food retailers, and three mines is not sufficient diversification.

The critical question that confronts the retiree is how much equity and how much debt or low-risk income assets is suitable. There is an old rule of thumb that says your bond holding should equal your age, but that is not a valid rule. It depends on the person's goals, which means primarily the desired level of consumption from the portfolio, and the person's age. When that rule of thumb was created, life expectancy was much lower. We know that on average equity has a higher return, but in order to avoid too much risk in equity, the investor needs a long time horizon for time diversification to take effect. If a family has a low enough draw from its savings, say 3% p.a., then a portfolio almost entirely composed of government bonds is the right answer because it is virtually certain to be enough. A family wanting to consume 4% or 5% will need a balanced portfolio, around 50–60% bonds. As the family ages into the late 70s and 80s, the sustainable withdrawal rate as a percentage of the assets rises, and the family can check if it can stick with a lower ratio and move all the portfolio into bonds, or whether it needs to stay with a more balanced portfolio. If the family seems to be able to get a sustainable draw only with very risky assets, this is a signal that the family should try first to reduce consumption.

In retirement, the family has less flexibility in financial terms. There is no more earned income, just income from various investments. If the family needs a short-term increase in income, say for a trip, or a large lump sum, it can be difficult to manage if the investments are not liquid. You cannot draw on future pensions, and banks won't lend on them as security because they can't seize them. Therefore, some of the unsheltered investments must be in a form that can be liquidated readily. As well, some of the investments must be ready for sale each year in a RRIF in order to be able to make the minimum withdrawal.

Most shares listed on major stock exchanges in Canada or other developed countries, bonds of governments and large companies, treasury bills, and bank and trust company deposit accounts and instruments are highly liquid. The principal investments that are illiquid, or at least require more than a few days to realize, are securities of private companies, direct interests in unincorporated businesses, real estate, and collections (stamps, coins, art, etc.). A retiree with most of her assets in these illiquid categories may never have a problem, but if a sudden need for a substantial sum of cash arises, it may be very difficult to meet. These illiquid assets are frequently in large units so that division of them to provide only partial realization is impossible. Listed securities can be divided easily into 100 share, or even single share, lots, by contrast.

Modern financial intermediation is providing some relief from liquidity problems for persons just as they have for many years for corporations. People with identifiable valuable assets (including the value of future income implicit in valuable human capital) can get a personal line of credit, credit cards, and loans based on home equity. All of these allow the family to spend money it doesn't have in the short term, but money that it expects to receive in the long term.

ESTATE PLANNING

Most people don't like to talk about death, particularly their own. About half of all Canadians do not have a will. Many people with wills have not had them professionally reviewed in the past three years.

Dying without a will or with one that is out of date risks needless taxation, legal challenges, delays, and family strife that may last for years. Many Canadians believe that estate planning is only needed by the wealthy. But even individuals with a modest or straightforward estate can benefit from planning. Everyone should have a will that reflects the current situation to ensure that his or her wishes will be followed, and that assets will be passed on in a timely, tax-effective manner.

In this chapter we provide an overview of will and estate planning and the duties of an executor. This is not a complete guide. As the laws pertaining to estate planning and administration are complex, substantial professional training is required to prepare and execute estate plans. Furthermore, the many gray areas in which professional judgment is required make it impossible to set out precise rules. However, this overview introduces the important issues and the various techniques for resolving them. We also explain the use of two important powers of attorney that should accompany a will and be updated regularly.

This part of the chapter contains a lot of new terminology. A glossary at the end of the chapter defines these terms. Let us start by outlining the most fundamental things you need to know to understand estate planning.

A will is a legal document that allows one person's property at date of death to be passed to one or more other persons or organizations, called beneficiaries. A trust is a distinct legal entity that hold assets for you or for the benefit of others. One or more trustees are responsible for managing the assets in the trust in accordance with the instructions of the person who created the trust. Whenever a person dies, an estate is created automatically even if the person did not write a will. The estate is a trust whose property is the debts and the assets of the person who died, with some special exceptions. The **estate trust** may also contain some assets and debts that are caused by the death of the person, such as payouts from life insurance policies and income tax liabilities that become payable on the death of the person.

A trust has to have a trustee and a set of rules to determine what happens to the property of the trust. If the person who died made a valid will, that will appoints one or more persons or companies to be the trustees — called **executor**(s) — and also says what is to happen to all the assets in the estate after the debts have been paid. The person who wrote the will is called the **testator or testratix** (feminine). If the deceased did not make a valid will, then he or she dies **intestate**. The estate trust is still automatically created on the death of the person, but a court will appoint an **administrator** as the trustee and the disposition of the estate will be according to a law specific to each province.

Once the executor has completed all the actions required by the will, and paid all taxes that the estate trust owned, the estate trust is no longer necessary and will be terminated. Note that the will may have created one or more **testamentary trusts** that continue after the estate trust has ended.

What Is Estate Planning?

Estate planning is a process that ensures testators' assets are distributed in accordance with their wishes for the maximum benefit of the heirs. On a more practical level, estate planning provides the spouse and other dependants with sufficient income to meet their needs, both immediately and in the long run.

In this chapter we deal primarily with the issues related to assets that pass through an estate under the terms of a will. This is the most common way Canadians choose to pass on a property to a surviving spouse or other family member. There are six different ways property can be transferred to beneficiaries:

1. Gifts during the testator's lifetime
2. Living (*inter vivos*) trusts
3. Non-probatable assets (that is, not through the will)
4. Directly through a bequest in a will
5. Indirectly through a testamentary trust created in a will
6. According to provincial law if a person dies intestate (see Table 18.7 on page 539)

Each method of passing on assets has advantages and disadvantages. Gifting property during your lifetime may have some tax benefits, but it means relinquishing control over the asset (e.g., family cottage or business). Establishing a living or *inter vivos* trust, a trust that is established during your lifetime, may enable you to retain some control over the asset, but it could have some unfavourable tax implications unless properly structured by a trust professional. A trust requires annual reporting and a trustee, and thus spends some of the money you are trying to preserve for your heirs. Registering assets as joint tenants with another individual so that upon your death ownership passes directly to the other individual without forming part of your estate (i.e., a non-probatable asset) may save executor and probate fees, but it could create unintended income tax problems. It also limits your control of the asset.

All six methods of passing on assets may be part of any estate plan. However, most individuals wish to retain control and direct ownership over their property for as long as possible and very often want to keep their intentions regarding the disposition of their property confidential until their death. The only way to ensure this happens is to write a valid will.

Estate Planning Considerations

Table 18.6 lists some of the areas to consider when developing the estate plan. Proper estate planning requires careful consideration of many factors given the wide range of objectives the testator may wish to achieve. Often, in an effort to minimize taxes or avoid probate fees, another objective is thwarted. It is therefore important to weigh and balance the costs and benefits of different courses of action.

TABLE 18.6
Estate Planning Considerations

Record of personal affairs
Gifts to family members
Planned giving to charity
Joint property
Living trusts
Life insurance
Preparation of a valid will
Letter of wishes
Taxes
Incapacity — power of attorney and living wills
Pre-planned funeral arrangements

Record of Personal Affairs

It is in the best interests of the family that the executor be able to act quickly to protect the assets. To assist the executor with this task, a complete estate plan should include a complete listing of the testator's financial affairs:

- Location of original will (not a copy)
- Location of trust documents
- Social Insurance Number
- Human resource department or other relevant link to notify the employer and claim any benefits
- List of advisors with current communication links to them
- Information on pre-planned funeral arrangements
- Birth and marriage certificates
- Bank accounts/GICs/safety deposit boxes
- Insurance policies
- Pension plans
- Real estate titles
- Investment portfolio records
- Security certificates (sometimes forgotten, but they still exist in this day of electronic records)
- Loans
- Credit cards
- Club memberships

Gifts to Family Members

The most straightforward method of accomplishing a number of estate planning goals is to give assets to your potential heirs during your lifetime. A gift of property does not incur executor or probate fees nor is it taxed in the hands of the recipient. However, you will give up ownership and control and in some situations where the recipient is either your spouse or is under age 18, any income from the property could be attributed back to you and taxed in your hands. If you give an asset to any person, except your spouse, you are deemed to have received proceeds of disposition equal to the fair market value of the asset and you must report any resulting capital gain or loss. In other words you might be taxed as though you sold the asset at fair market value even though it was a gift! This is not an issue with ordinary gifts under $1,000, nor does it create tax problems if it is a personal asset worth much more than $1,000, but still less than you paid for it originally, like a car.

Gifts of sentimental property such as jewellery, art, or furniture can also lead to conflict between beneficiaries if the property is also listed in the will. Disputes can occur between beneficiaries over whether the deceased really intended to give away the property during his or her lifetime.

Planned Giving to Charity

Planned giving is when a charitable gift is made in a way that maximizes the tax and estate planning benefits. Planned giving has become quite sophisticated in recent years, partly because of deliberate changes to the Income Tax Act to make it more attractive, and partly because charities have had to become much more clever because there is such great competition for donations and Canadians are not very generous donors on average.

Any donation of valuable property to a registered charity[9] creates a non-refundable tax credit for the value given. The first $200 of donations in a year attracts a tax credit at the minimum tax rate of 15% federally plus the minimum provincial rate. Any donations beyond $200 receive tax credit at the maximum tax rates. We are discussing this under estate planning because estates may have very large accumulated tax deferrals that come due all at once on the date of death, or on the date of death of the second spouse. All this gets taxed at the top marginal rate. The person with all the wealth could donate some every year instead of putting it all in the will, but many people do not want to lose control of any of their wealth during their lifetime. There are two important aspects to planned giving as part of estate planning.

---

[9] A charity must register with the Canada Revenue Agency and follow prescribed rules and provide its registration number on every receipt in order for the doner to get the tax benefits.

If the estate has substantial investment assets with accumulated capital gains, they will all be triggered on the date of death, unless the beneficiary is the spouse. The 2006 Federal Budget and subsequent provincial budgets made special provision for a donation in kind of securities. The taxable capital gain on such a donation is not added to taxable income, but the tax credit on the full value of the donation is still claimable. This provision applies for any donation in kind of publicly traded securities and government bonds, either while the donor is living or through a will.

Another technique in estate planning is to take out a term life insurance policy and make the beneficiary a charity, and make that beneficiary designation irrevocable. In this situation, the premiums the policyholder pays become a charitable donation subject to a refundable tax credit. When the insured dies, the charity gets the face value of the policy and this amount is not part of the estate.

Joint Property

There are two ways of registering legal ownership of property. One is as "joint tenants"; the other is as "tenants-in-common". There is a distinction between the two at death. In the case of joint tenants, the deceased's ownership automatically goes to the survivor without forming part of their estate. In the case of tenants-in-common, the deceased's interest in the property forms part of the estate. The above applies not only to real estate but also to bank accounts, GICs, investment portfolios, etc.

Registering property as "joint tenants" is a useful way of avoiding the estate process as the property automatically goes to the survivor. This helps reduce probate fees and estate administration costs but can lead to other problems. This is discussed in more detail in a later section.

Living Trusts

A trust is created when a **settlor** transfers property to a **trustee** who holds property for the benefit of a **beneficiary**. In its simplest form, a trust merely involves the holding of property by one person for the benefit of another person. A trust may be either **testamentary** (i.e., arising upon your death), or *inter vivos* or **living** (i.e., established during the person's lifetime). In this section we focus on living trusts. Testamentary trusts are discussed in a later section.

A living trust can be a flexible financial tool to transfer beneficial ownership of assets to an intended heir while the settlor maintains control over the asset. For example, you can provide a beneficial interest in the income of a trust to your spouse while retaining control via the express terms of the trust as to who will ultimately receive the capital. There are a number of reasons for considering a trust during your lifetime. Some of these reasons are for estate planning purposes only, while others also provide a benefit from a tax planning perspective. Typical uses include the following:

- To provide long-term income and protection for minor children or dependants who are not able to look after themselves or handle financial matters.
- To provide protection of family assets for professionals (e.g., doctors) who may be exposed to lawsuits in excess of insurance limits.
- To create a trust for charitable purposes.
- To avoid probate and provide secrecy on death.
- As part of an estate freeze structure where asset value is "frozen" and future asset growth is transferred to the next generation.
- To achieve income splitting with adult family members with lower marginal tax rates to the extent that attribution rules allow.

Often, parents will hold some assets for their children or grandchildren "in trust" without ever having created a formal trust structure, which includes annual reporting and a trustee. Banks keep many such accounts for parents and children. This is a somewhat grey area in the law, but for efficiency and convenience everyone ignores the lack of a formal trust structure when the amounts are not large and a formal trust would waste too much money on administration.

Life Insurance

Life insurance can serve the following purposes:

- Provide liquidity in an estate to pay off liabilities such as tax or mortgages. This will ensure non-liquid assets like a cottage or business do not have to be sold, but can be left to an heir.

- Establish a fund to provide income for an individual you wish to support (e.g., spouse, children, or grandchildren).

Think back to Chapter 9, where we discussed life insurance. The primary purpose of life insurance is risk management. The insured wishes to avoid an unacceptable drop in the living standard of his or her dependants in the case of premature death. Alternatively, you can consider life insurance to be a replacement of the net human capital value of the insured. Life insurance agents will sell any amount they can, because of the commissions, but you should remember the purpose of life insurance. Buying life insurance in order to leave the beneficiaries better off than they would be if you lived out your normal lifespan is not a wise use of resources.

The first use mentioned, to pay taxes, is important only when the asset is something that needs to be kept in the family, like a family business or a cottage. These are illiquid assets, and not divisible. Buying life insurance simply to pay the tax on capital gains on a portfolio of traded securities is simply a pre-payment of taxes, and in the long run may cost the heirs since the accumulated insurance premiums might amount to more than the present value of the income tax the estate would have to pay.

The benefits paid from life insurance are generally not subject to tax whether they are left to the estate or to a named beneficiary. However, if the estate is the beneficiary, the benefit will be subject to provincial probate fees and executor fees.

Letter of Wishes

A letter of wishes can be a valuable part of your estate plan. It can provide assistance to your executor and heirs in explaining your wishes and desires, provide comfort to the family, and assist your executor in finding assets. A letter of wishes is not legally binding and cannot override your will, which is the official document that is probated by the court. Contents of the letter can include your wishes regarding funeral services, reasons why certain assets were given to a particular individual, or how you would like to see a cherished family asset such as the cottage, farm, or business handled in the future.

Taxes

A key estate planning objective is to reduce or defer the tax that would otherwise be payable at death. Currently, the federal and provincial governments do not impose estate taxes or succession duties. In the year of death, your taxation year would run from January 1 to the date of death. A final or "terminal" return would have to be filed by your executor. All income earned to the date of death must be reported. This includes interest, rents, annuities, employment income, and other amounts due but not paid. Also included are taxable capital gains or losses realized prior to death and not included in income in a previous year.

In addition, the deceased is deemed to have disposed of all capital property immediately before death. Any net gains (gains less losses) are to be included as capital gains in the individual's final tax return. In other words, even though there had not been an actual sale of property, your estate will be taxed as though your property had been sold just prior to death. For individuals with assets that have accrued capital gains (e.g., cottage, business, stock portfolio) the potential tax liability can significantly affect their plans. Fortunately there are some planning techniques that can help reduce these taxes. Since tax law is very complex, it is strongly recommended you seek professional advice:

1. *Spousal rollover of unregistered property.* The *Income Tax Act* allows a tax deferral when property is transferred from the deceased to his or her spouse. The surviving spouse will take ownership of the property at the deceased's adjusted cost base and will not have to pay capital gains tax until the property is disposed of or until the surviving spouse dies.[10]

---

[10] In some circumstances the spouse can elect to transfer the property at market value, and there may be situations when this is beneficial.

2. *Spousal rollover of registered property (RRSP, RRIF, DPSP, registered pension plan).* The *Income Tax Act* also allows registered accounts to be rolled over to the surviving spouse's RRSP or RRIF in a locked-in form, or used to purchase an annuity without triggering any immediate tax liability for the entire amount. Careful consideration should be given to the named beneficiary on RRSPs and RRIFs. If the named beneficiary is not the spouse, the estate is responsible for the tax liability upon deregistration of the entire fund while the beneficiary receives the entire amount without paying taxes. In some cases, a registered account can be rolled over or partially deferred to a financially dependent child or grandchild. This provision is most useful when the dependant is disabled and would be dependent for his or her entire life.

3. *Spousal trust.* A trust can be established that would provide your spouse with income for life but leave the capital for other beneficiaries (e.g., children or grandchildren). The *Income Tax Act* allows the transfer of property from the deceased to a spousal trust on a tax-deferred basis. This would be an option to consider if you did not want to distribute outright to your spouse.

4. *TFSA.* A TFSA allows some alternatives if a beneficiary for the TFSA is explicitly named as the recipient in the will, or else as the beneficiary in the TFSA contract with the financial institution managing it. The beneficiary can keep the TFSA or move the assets into his own TFSA without reducing his contribution room in his own TFSA. Designated beneficiaries can include the spouse, former spouses, children, and qualified donees. If the TFSA is not specifically allocated in the will and there is no beneficiary designation in the contract, the executor will liquidate the assets in the TFSA, add them to the estate assets, and distribute them according to the provisions of the will. There is no tax on the liquidation because it is a tax-free account, but the tax-free status of future income on the funds is lost. If it is properly written, a beneficiary designation in the will over-rides the beneficiary designation on the TFSA contract. Provincial rules have some variations on how a TFSA is handled on the death of the holder.

5. *Final tax returns.* The filing of a deceased taxpayer's income tax returns can be a complicated matter. There are special rules relating to prior years' returns, the "Terminal Return", and up to three separate "optional returns" depending on your assets and circumstances. Knowledge of these rules and the various elections available can result in considerable tax savings to your estate.

Planning for Incapacity

■ POWER OF ATTORNEY

You should also give consideration to how your affairs would be handled in the event you become incapacitated. The best method is an **enduring** or **continuing**

power of attorney. The words "enduring" and "continuing" are interchangeable. The law governing power of attorney is provincial and the laws vary somewhat, as does the choice between the words "enduring" and "continuing."[11]

A power of attorney is a legal document that gives one or more people the power to manage your financial affairs (not necessarily your lawyer) while you are alive. A power of attorney can be "general" (covering all aspects of your financial affairs) or "limited" in the scope of the powers given to the attorney(s). Normally it will only be valid while you are mentally competent and is used to give someone temporary powers or power over some specific task, like making trades on the stock market for you. However, if you have an enduring power of attorney prepared, it will continue to be valid in the event you become incapacitated. It is important to note that all powers of attorney terminate if a court-ordered committee or guardian is appointed, or if the person you appoint as attorney dies, or upon your death. You can revoke a power of attorney at any time if you are mentally competent.

It is important to seek legal advice before preparing a power of attorney. The attorney has broad powers and a person should understand the nature of the document. Limitations can be included to prevent many problems from occurring.

■ LIVING WILL OR POWER OF ATTORNEY FOR PERSONAL CARE

Living wills express individuals' wishes on what kind of medical treatment they wish or do not wish to receive when they are not able to speak for themselves. Living wills are not binding at the present time in all provinces but should be discussed with your doctor and family so they are aware of your wishes. A lawyer can assist you with the preparation of a living will and advise you of the limitations that may apply in your province.[12]

How to Establish the Estate Plan

There are three basic steps to establishing your estate plan:

1. Identify estate planning objectives.
2. Prepare an inventory of assets and liabilities.
3. Prepare a will and powers of attorney.

Identify Your Estate Planning Objectives

Your objectives will depend on a number of factors, including the following:

• Your age
• The ages of your family members and other beneficiaries

---

[11] For an example of the Ontario version, see <www.attorneygeneral.jus.gov.on.ca/english/family/pgt/incapacity/poa.asp>.
[12] For an example of the Ontario version, see ibid.

- The needs of your beneficiaries
- The current value of your estate
- Your beneficiaries' ability to handle their own financial affairs
- Your tax situation

Every situation is unique. A young couple with children will have different concerns from a wealthy widow or widower without children. Most people have estate planning objectives that can be broken down into things they want to "achieve" and things they want to "avoid". Some common estate planning objectives are listed below. Things people want to achieve:

- Maximizing estate proceeds for heirs
- Providing some immediate cash for dependants while the estate is going through probate
- Distributing assets in accordance with wishes
- Ensuring adequate liquidity in the estate to pay taxes and any liabilities
- Ensuring guardian of person and property for minor children

Things people want to avoid:

- Needless taxation
- Family strife
- Delays in settling the estate
- Costly legal challenges
- Probate fees charged by provincial courts
- Forced sale of family assets that the family wants to keep, such as cottage property, farm, or family business

Prepare an Inventory of Assets and Liabilities

We have already explained how to do this in Chapter 4. An important issue is the tax liability created by the deemed disposition of assets at death. It is also important to list how various assets are registered (e.g., joint tenants or tenants-in-common) and to list the beneficiaries of life insurance policies and retirement plans, etc.

Prepare Your Will

A **will** is a written document in which the **testator**, the person making the will, directs how his or her estate is to be distributed after his or her death. A will becomes effective and public upon the death of the testator. Until then, a mentally competent testator can change the terms or revoke it. You should review your will at every change in the family life cycle — marriage, birth of a child, retirement, etc., and any time there is a change in the relevant laws or a large change in your financial situation. Sometimes, an out-of-date will can be worse than no will at all.

Why Is a Will Important?

- It is the only way of ensuring your property will be distributed according to your wishes. If you die without a will your assets may be distributed according to a government formula (see Table 18.7).

- It is important to note that the definition of spouse in the provincial *Family Law Act* may not yet include unmarried partners, and hence without a will, these spouses might be completely disinherited.

- It names your executor, the individual or institution who will act on your behalf and carry out your wishes. Without a will the courts will appoint someone as an administrator of your estate who may not be the exact individual you would have chosen.

- Your choice of guardian for minor children will be clearly stated and considered by the provincial courts, who make the ultimate decision.

- It helps ensure that sufficient income is provided for your spouse and children.

- It helps ensure tax saving strategies are considered and can be implemented by your executor.

Table 18.8 summarizes the contents of a basic will.

Types of Wills

A **holographic will** is entirely handwritten by the testator and signed and dated by the testator. No witness is necessary. Most provinces recognize holographic wills. In exceptional cases, a piece of correspondence has been found to be a valid holographic will, because the intention to make a bequest was evident. In a celebrated English case, the words "All to mother" scrawled by a dying man were decided to constitute a valid will. The author of a holographic will is not taking legal advice, however, and many problems can arise.

An **English form** or **standard** (**notarial will** in Québec) will is typed or handwritten and dated, and then signed at the end of the last page in the presence of at least two witnesses. The usual practice is to initial each page of the will. Neither witness can be one of the beneficiaries or their spouse. Most formal wills are drafted by lawyers because they are trained to ensure the legal drafting of your will meets your needs. The cost of the lawyer is modest compared with the costs that can arise if the will is ambiguous or contested.

Testamentary Trusts in Your Will

Living (or *inter vivos*) trusts are established while you are alive, while testamentary trusts take effect upon your death. The legal clauses for the establishment of a testamentary trust are included in your will. These clauses will indicate what assets are to go into trust, who the trustee(s) will be, and who the beneficiaries will

TABLE 18.7
This Is What Happens If You Die Without a Will

Province	Spouse Only	Spouse, Relative(s) But No Children	Child or Children Only	Remaining Family — Spouse and One Child	Remaining Family — Spouse and Children	No Spouse or Children
Alberta	All to spouse	All to spouse	All to children[1]	1st $40,000 to spouse; rest split equally[1]	1st $40,000 to spouse; rest 1/3 to spouse and 2/3 to children[1]	All to closest next of kin, usually in this order: parents; if neither survives, brothers/sisters;[8] if none survive, nephews/nieces; if none survive, next of kin. If there is no traceable next of kin, it all goes to the government.
British Columbia	All to spouse	All to spouse	All to children[1]	1st $65,000 to spouse[3]; rest split equally[1]	1st $65,000 to spouse[1]; rest 1/3 to spouse[3] and 2/3 to children[1]	
Manitoba	All to spouse	All to spouse	All to children[1]	Either (i) all to spouse[5] or (ii) greater of $50,000 or half of estate to spouse[10]; rest 1/2 to children[6]	greater of $50,000 or half of estate to spouse and 1/2 to children[6]	
New Brunswick	All to spouse	All to spouse	All to children[1]	Marital property to spouse; rest split equally[1]	Marital property to spouse; rest 1/3 to spouse and 2/3 to children[1]	
Newfoundland/ P.E.I	All to spouse	All to spouse	All to children[1]	Split equally[1]	1/3 to spouse; 2/3 to children[1]	
Nova Scotia/ NWT/Nunavut	All to spouse	All to spouse	All to children[1]	1st $50,000 to spouse[2]; rest split equally[1]	1st $50,000 to spouse[2], rest 1/3 to spouse and 2/3 to children[1]	
Ontario	All to spouse	All to spouse	All to children[1]	1st $200,000 to spouse; rest split equally[1,4]	1st $200,000 to spouse; rest 1/3 to spouse and 2/3 to children[1,4]	
Quebec	All to spouse	2/3 to spouse; 1/3 to privileged ascendants or privileged collaterals[9]	All to children[1]	1/3 to spouse[7]; 2/3 to child[1]	1/3 to spouse[7]; 2/3 to children[1]	
Saskatchewan	All to spouse	All to spouse	All to children[1]	1st $100,000 to spouse; rest split equally[1]	1st $100,000 to spouse; rest 1/3 to spouse and 2/3 to children[1]	
Yukon	All to spouse	All to spouse	All to children	1st $75,000 to spouse; rest split equally	1st $75,000 to spouse; rest 1/3 to spouse and 2/3 to children[1]	

Notes: (a) In some cases provincial *Family Law Acts* can override these distribution formulas.

(b) The formulas on the chart are based on provincial laws in effect at time of printing.

[1] Divided equally. Issue of a deceased child (grandchildren, great grand-children) take that child's share.
[2] Spouse may elect to receive house and contents in lieu of $50,000.
[3] Plus household furniture and life interest in family home.
[4] Subject to possible equalization claim under *Family Law Act*.
[5] If all the children are also children of surviving spouse.
[6] If any of the children are *not* also children of surviving spouse. Children of deceased child (grandchildren) share in the estate.
[7] Subject to provisions of Bill 146 [Economic Equality between spouses].
[8] Children of deceased brothers and sisters share their parent's share.
[9] Privileged ascendants are the deceased's parents. Privileged collaterals are the deceased's brothers and sisters and their descendants in the first degree.
[10] Life interest in the home plus a possible equalization payment under the *Marital Property Act*.

TABLE 18.8
What's in a Will?

A will requires careful planning to ensure all aspects are covered. The chart below outlining the contents of a basic will clearly demonstrates this point.

Common Clause	Purpose of the Clause
Identification and Revocation Clause	Identifies you and your residence. Declares that this is your last will, which revokes all prior wills.
Appointment of Executor(s)	Designates the individual or institution you appoint as your executor. May also designate alternate and successor executors if your original executor cannot act. The clause may provide compensation to the executor.
Payment of Debts	Directs your executor to pay all debts.
Payment of Taxes and Fees	Authorizes your executor to pay income tax and probate fees.
Specific Bequests	Outlines the distribution of specific personal property such as furniture, jewellery, cars. May also refer to your RRSPs, RRIFs, and pensions.
Legacies	Directs specific cash amounts to be paid.
Residual Estates	Outlines the distribution of your remaining property after all the specific bequests have been made.
Trusts	Sets out the terms of any trust created by your will.
Power Clauses	Enables your executor to exercise various powers in the management of your estate without the approval of the court.
Life Interest Clause	Used when you want to leave someone the income or the enjoyment of the asset, rather than the asset itself. Upon the life tenant's death, the asset would pass on to another beneficiary.
Encroachment Clause	Used in a trust when you want the trustee to be able to give the life tenant or a capital beneficiary additional funds for special circumstances or needs.
Common Disaster Clause	Outlines the distribution of your assets if an intended beneficiary dies at the same time as you.
Survival Clause	States that a beneficiary must survive you for a set period of time (often 30 days) before he or she can benefit from your estate.
Guardian Appointment	Names the individual(s) who would be appointed guardian of your minor children. Also names guardians of property of any beneficiaries who are minors.
Testimonium and Attestation Clauses	These clauses are found at the end of your will. They ensure the legal requirements for a validly executed will are met.

be. The will may give specific rules for the management and distribution of the trust assets or leave part of this to the discretion of the trustee.

A testamentary trust enables you to earmark assets for specific family members, and place restrictions on how the money is to be used. It also ensures that the money will be managed professionally by a competent trustee — an individual or trust company of your choice. Many people set up a trust to ensure that the money being left to a spouse is properly managed, and that adequate income is provided in later years. When the spouse dies, the remaining capital passes outright to children or grandchildren. If you have minor children to whom you want to leave money, a trust is required to hold and manage their inheritance, at least until they reach the age of majority. If you fail to name a guardian or trustee of the inheritance of a minor child, the provincial law may not recognize the child's guardian as the trustee, and the court or the province may place the money in trust with a provincial body set up for this purpose.

But many people leave assets in trust for older children as well. Trusts can provide for a child's education, assist in purchasing a first home, or any other valid purpose. Some people want to accustom their children to handling money gradually. So they set up a trust that turns over part of the inheritance when the child reaches certain ages. For example, a child could receive a third of the inheritance at age of majority, another third at 25, and the balance at 30. Provincial laws are structured such that you can keep assets in your family for an extended period. However, for trusts that last longer than a beneficiary's lifetime, it's best to consult an estate and trust professional to ensure tax implications are considered.

If a beneficiary is a disabled person who is not likely to be able to work, the testator should consider an **Absolute Discretionary Trust**, popularly called a **Henson trust**, after Leonard Henson, who created the first one whose legality was established in a series of court battles in Ontario. We discussed tax issues related to disability in Chapter 8. A further consideration is the support the provincial government provides to a disabled person. This support, like GIS, is related to the income and assets of the disabled person. If a will creates a Henson trust, the money in the trust will not be counted as an asset of the beneficiary and will therefore not reduce the disability benefits from the government. The most important requirement of a Henson trust is that the trustee has complete discretion as to how the money is spent and when it is spent; the beneficiary has no power to direct the spending. As long as the money taken from the trust is spent appropriately for the necessary support of the disabled person, the provincial benefits are not lost. Henson trusts are legal in British Columbia, Saskatchewan, Manitoba, Ontario, New Brunswick, Nova Scotia, and Prince Edward Island.

Probating a Will

Probate is a legal process that confirms a will. The executor applies to a provincial court for approval of the will. The court will issue a **Grant of Probate**, or **Letters Probate**, confirming that the will is valid. The executor must have both

TABLE 18.9 Provincial Probate Fees†	
Province	**Probate Fee**
Alberta	Up to $250,000, a maximum of $300. Over that, a maximum of $400.
British Columbia	0.6% for estates of value $25,000 to $50,000; and 1.4% over $50,000. No maximum fee.
Manitoba	$70 flat fee plus 0.7% on value over $10,000. No maximum fee.
New Brunswick	Up to $100 at $20,000 plus 0.5% on value over $20,000. No maximum fee.
Newfoundland	$60 plus 0.5% on value over $1,000. No maximum fee.
Northwest Territories	Up to $250,000, a maximum of $300. Over that, a maximum of $400.
Nova Scotia	Up to $902.03 for estates of $100,000 plus 1.523% on value over $100,000. No maximum fee.
Nunavut	Up to $250,000, a maximum of $300. Over that, a maximum of $400.
Ontario	0.5% for estates of $1,000 to $50,000; 1.5% on value over $50,000. No maximum fee.
Prince Edward Island	Up to $400 at $100,000 plus 0.4% on value over $100,000. No maximum fee.
Québec	$99 for wills made by natural person, $111 by legal person.
Saskatchewan	0.7% of estates. No maximum fee.
Yukon	$140 for estates over $25,000.

† Based on information available at time of printing. Probate fees are subject to change.

the Grant of Probate and a notarized copy of the will in order to demonstrate he has the authority to carry out his actions as trustee of the estate. For example, financial institutions will not release assets of an estate to an executor unless they receive a Grant of Probate. Provincial probate fees at the date of writing are shown in Table 18.9. The estate must pay these fees to the court when it makes the application for probate, which creates a Catch-22 because the executor doesn't have the power to take any money from the estate until probate is granted. Usually the financial institutions will release sufficient funds to cover probate fees, upon presentation of a notarized will that names the executor.

Reducing Probate Costs

Many people seek ways to reduce the amount of their assets that fall into their estate and are distributed according to the will, where they would be subject to probate fees. The lower the total value of the assets that become part of the estate, the lower the probate costs. This strategy is most relevant in Ontario and BC, which have quite high probate fees. Reducing the size of an estate also cuts executor fees, which are normally 3% to 5% of the estate's value, depending on the province of residence. Many of these methods of transferring assets outside the will get the funds into the hands of the beneficiaries faster, avoiding liquidity problems. These are the most common strategies:

- Make the spouse the RRSP/RRIF beneficiary. The assets in the retirement plan pass directly to the spouse's plan without tax, and without becoming part of the estate and incurring probate costs.

- Name an adult person, not the estate, as beneficiary of life insurance policies and annuity contracts. Make sure the insurance proceeds are not "earmarked" for specific purposes, e.g., meeting a tax liability or funding a specific gift. If they are, then they should be left to the estate.

- Hold real estate as joint tenants. This allows your home, cottage or other property to pass directly to your surviving joint tenant on your death.

- Have bank accounts and other investments under joint tenancy agreements, with a right of survivorship. Here again, the assets will automatically pass to the surviving owner if one dies, without falling into your estate. Danger: Joint ownership means joint control; make sure you and your spouse (or any other joint owner) share the same financial objectives.

- Set up a living trust. Assets held in a trust do not fall into your estate after death. A trust is an effective estate-planning device that can be tailored to your needs. For example, the trust could allow you access to its capital or income during your lifetime. On your death, assets pass to your intended beneficiaries as per the terms of the trust document — not your will. However, you should investigate the tax implications before you act.

Beware

Transferring assets into joint names and other techniques may have other implications Below are some factors to examine:

Estate taxes and liabilities. There will probably be some taxes to be paid upon death, no matter how well you structure your affairs. Make sure the estate will have adequate funds to cover these taxes; otherwise the CRA will go after the beneficiaries for the money. Remember, too, that taxes on assets passing outside the estate will be borne by the estate's beneficiaries or paid immediately by the person transferring the asset — reducing the net proceeds. This factor must be considered in estate planning.

Consider family law. Provincial family laws can also upset your estate planning when you try to reduce probate costs. For example, suppose you and your spouse jointly own a cottage. If you die, the cottage passes directly to your spouse without probate. If your spouse then remarries, the new husband or wife may have a claim on the value of the cottage and it will bypass your children. Consider the impact of family law before you decide. A spouse who is separated cannot use a will to leave money to someone other than the former spouse in order to thwart the spouse's entitlement under the Family Law Act of the province. A separation has no effect on a will; however, a divorce nullifies any provisions of a will that deal with the former spouse. The rest of the will remains valid, but the effect of the invalid clauses may render the will invalid or incomplete, requiring a new will.

Tax consequences. Transferring property into joint ownership with someone other than a spouse may trigger taxable capital gains or losses that cannot be used immediately. Also, income attribution will apply if property is held jointly with a spouse or minor child.

Remember also that if you appoint a family member to act as executor without payment of a fee, the size of the estate doesn't affect directly the management fees the estate pays, since any experts the executor hires will charge hourly fees. The highest probate fee is only 1.5% of assets, and some of the ways of reducing probate fees entail risks or costs much greater than the probate fee.

Executors

An executor (executrix, if female) is the individual or institution named in the will who is responsible for administering the estate, and that person has all the powers and responsibilities of a trustee. It is possible to name more than one executor, and also to name alternate executors in the event that the preferred executor is unable or unwilling to accept the appointment. Co-executors are often appointed when an individual wants to combine professional estate administration expertise (e.g., trust company) with someone who is knowledgeable about the personal and family situation (e.g., spouse or child). Both the testator and the potential executors must understand the extensive responsibilities required of an executor, in order that only someone who is capable of doing it is appointed. An executor always has the authority to hire and pay experts to assist in the administration of the estate, and hence an executor does not need to have expert knowledge of every aspect of managing the estate. An executor who does not live in the province where the will is probated may be required to post a bond equivalent to the estate value.

Duties of an Executor

Table 18.10 lists some of the more common duties executors must perform. These duties will vary depending on the complexity of your estate. However, even the simplest of estates require great care and skill from your executor for a wide range of duties.

Executor Duties — Tax Returns

When an individual dies, three different "taxpayers" may have to file a return and pay taxes:

1. The deceased
2. The estate of the individual between the date of the death and the date when assets were distributed
3. Any trusts set up under the terms of the will

It is the responsibility of the deceased's executor and trustee, if there is a trust, to file tax returns within the time parameters set out under the *Income Tax Act*.

Tax Returns for the Year of Death. A final tax return must be filed for the period beginning January 1 to the date of death. Special rules apply upon death relating to the following:

• Deemed disposition of capital property
• Spousal rollover of property
• Collapsing of RRSPs/RRIFs or transferring to a spouse
• Income accrued to the date of death
• Medical and charitable deductions

Tax Return for Year Prior to Death. If an individual dies after December 31 and before filing a return for the preceding year, the executor of the estate will have to file one on that individual's behalf in addition to the terminal return mentioned above.

Tax Return for "Rights or Things". Executors may also choose to file a separate return for amounts owed to the deceased at the time of death but not received. Such "rights or things" include income, such as matured but uncashed bond

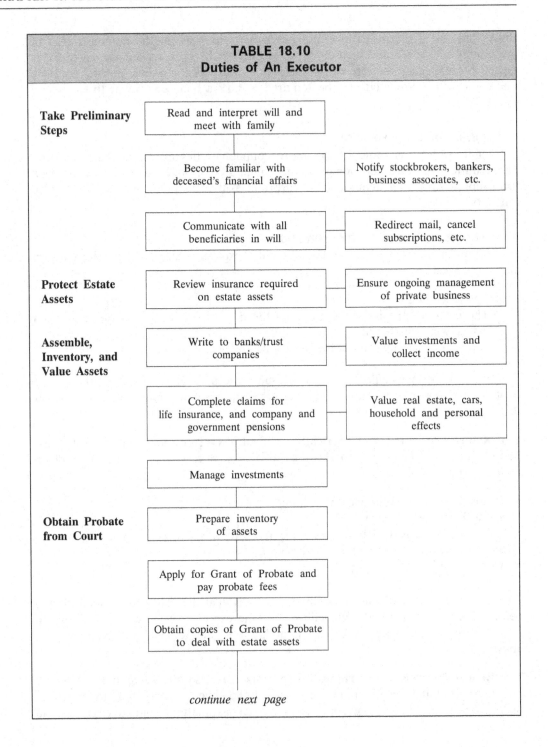

TABLE 18.10
Duties of An Executor

Take Preliminary Steps
- Read and interpret will and meet with family
- Become familiar with deceased's financial affairs → Notify stockbrokers, bankers, business associates, etc.
- Communicate with all beneficiaries in will → Redirect mail, cancel subscriptions, etc.

Protect Estate Assets
- Review insurance required on estate assets → Ensure ongoing management of private business

Assemble, Inventory, and Value Assets
- Write to banks/trust companies → Value investments and collect income
- Complete claims for life insurance, and company and government pensions → Value real estate, cars, household and personal effects
- Manage investments

Obtain Probate from Court
- Prepare inventory of assets
- Apply for Grant of Probate and pay probate fees
- Obtain copies of Grant of Probate to deal with estate assets

continue next page

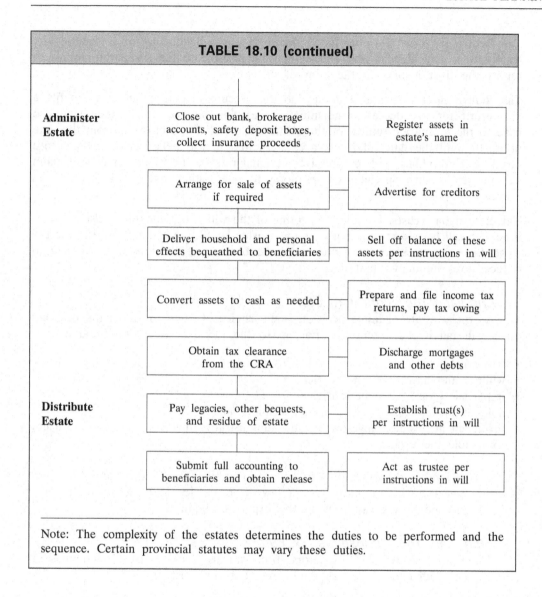

TABLE 18.10 (continued)

Administer Estate	Close out bank, brokerage accounts, safety deposit boxes, collect insurance proceeds	Register assets in estate's name
	Arrange for sale of assets if required	Advertise for creditors
	Deliver household and personal effects bequeathed to beneficiaries	Sell off balance of these assets per instructions in will
	Convert assets to cash as needed	Prepare and file income tax returns, pay tax owing
	Obtain tax clearance from the CRA	Discharge mortgages and other debts
Distribute Estate	Pay legacies, other bequests, and residue of estate	Establish trust(s) per instructions in will
	Submit full accounting to beneficiaries and obtain release	Act as trustee per instructions in will

Note: The complexity of the estates determines the duties to be performed and the sequence. Certain provincial statutes may vary these duties.

coupons and declared but unpaid dividends. Filing a separate return for these rights or things may entitle the deceased taxpayer to additional tax credits for the year of death and attract a lower marginal tax rate.

Tax Return for Business Income. If the deceased taxpayer had an interest in a proprietorship or partnership it may be possible to file a separate return to report business income earned to the date of death.

Tax Return for Trust Income. If the deceased was a beneficiary of a testamentary trust with a non-calendar year end, it may be possible to file a separate return to report the trust income to the date of death.

Tax Return for the Estate. Not only do the executors of an estate have to file a tax return for the deceased individual up to the date of death, they will also have to file a separate return for the estate trust itself for every year from the date of death until the date all assets are distributed to the beneficiaries. Estates are taxed like individuals, with progressive marginal rates of taxation, but cannot claim personal tax credits. Special tax rules apply to estates that may enable taxes to be reduced.

Tax Return for Trusts. If under the terms of the will a testamentary trust is established, it will be the responsibility of the trustee to file annual tax returns for the trust. Like estates, special tax rules apply to trusts, and elections are available to reduce taxes in many situations.

Choosing the Right Executor

A crucial estate planning decision is the choice of executor. Even the best-laid plans will fail if the executor is not up to the job. An executor should be

- trustworthy;
- willing, and have the time to act;
- impartial toward all beneficiaries;
- able to make decisions in a timely fashion; and
- proficient in business, investment, and administrative matters at a level sufficient to handle the estate.

It is helpful if the executor also knows something about estate and trust law, but the executor will ordinarily hire a lawyer for advice and execution of some actions, and the lawyer can provide the expertise required.

Who Can You Choose as Executor?

There are two types of executors: professionals, such as trust companies or lawyers, and individuals, such as family members or close friends.

■ INDIVIDUAL EXECUTORS

It may seem that naming a family friend or relative as your executor is like bestowing an honour on them. In reality it is a heavy imposition. They will be required to devote substantial time and effort to the task. In addition, they can encounter many potential problems, such as the following:

- Personal liability for mistakes made while administering the estate. For example, this can happen if they distribute proceeds of the estate and then find out a creditor has a legal claim. Or they can be liable for taxes if they distribute the estate before obtaining tax clearance from the CRA and then find out additional taxes are due.

- Personal criticism from family members and friends who disapprove of how things have been handled, no matter how well intended the executor's actions were.

- Challenges from family members excluded under the will.

- Conflict of interest from being appointed executor and also being a beneficiary or business partner.

- Difficulty in administering the estate due to location, lack of time, or ability.

- Difficulty handling financial matters at such an emotional time.

Appointing your spouse or children as executor is appropriate if you are convinced that they are capable of handling the duties and can act in an unbiased manner to all beneficiaries and can be available. If your estate is fairly straightforward, it is likely they can attend to most matters by themselves or can seek out professional legal and accounting advice at a reasonable cost. It is important to remember that all executors, even family members, are entitled to be paid for their work. However, payment as an executor is taxable income, and so paying a beneficiary who would otherwise receive the money as part of the inheritance actually reduces the net amount the executor receives. One way to circumvent this is to leave an additional bequest to the executor.

■ PROFESSIONAL EXECUTORS

Given the complexities and responsibilities of executorship, many individuals appoint a lawyer or trust company to act as their executor. Below are some of the more common reasons why you might want to choose a professional executor:

- You do not wish to burden family members or friends.
- You do not have immediate family members living close by or do not wish to have them involved.
- The family members you would consider do not have the time or expertise to administer your estate.
- The individual you are considering would likely pre-decease you.
- You are concerned family members appointed as co-executors would not get along and have difficulty making decisions.
- You are in a second marriage and you want an impartial executor who will balance the needs of your second spouse and the children from your first marriage.
- Your will provides for the establishment of a trust which requires professional management by a permanent trustee.

In some situations it may be appropriate to appoint a lawyer or trust company as co-executor along with a family member. This would combine the expertise of the professional executor along with the knowledge of your family situation by one of its members.

The fees charged by a professional executor are the same as can be charged by an individual (set by provincial legislation). Executor fees are paid out of the proceeds of your estate on the basis of time and effort required to settle your estate. Often, these fees can be more than offset by savings in income tax and legal fees, which may be incurred by less experienced individuals. In many cases, where a professional executor is involved, and where provincial legislation permits, the fees can be set out in an agreement that is signed by you. In this way you will know in advance what the cost to your estate will be.

Glossary of Terms for Estate Planning

Administrator: The person appointed by the court to administer the estate when there is no will, the will did not name an Executor, or the named Executor has died or is unwilling to act. Also referred to as a "personal representative".

Agent for Executor: Where a trust company like Royal Trust is hired by the named Executor for a fee to provide advice and administration services.

Alternate Appointment: An alternate Executor appointed if the first named Executor cannot or will not act.

Beneficiary: A person who receives a benefit or gift under a will, an insurance policy, or a trust account, or a person for whose benefit a trust is created.

Codicil: An amendment to a will that makes changes or additions. It's executed with the same formalities as a will.

Estate: The right, title, or interest that a person has in any property.

Executor: The person or trust company named in a will responsible for the management of the deceased's assets and the ultimate transfer of the property; also commonly referred to as a "personal representative".

Fiduciary: An individual or institution under a lawful duty to act for the benefit of another party.

Grant of Probate: A certificate confirming the authority set out in a will to administer a particular estate; issued to an Executor by the court. Also called Grant of Letters Probate and Letters Probate.

Guardian: The person named to be legally responsible for the minor children should both parents die.

Inter vivos **Trust:** Also known as a living trust, *inter vivos* trusts come into effect during the lifetime of the settlor.

Intestate: A person who dies without a will. A partial intestacy is where a valid will does not dispose of the whole of the estate.

Irrevocable Trust: A trust that cannot be revoked (cancelled) by the person who created the trust (settlor).

Issue: All persons who have descended from a common ancestor. It is a broader term than "children", which is limited to one generation.

Joint Tenants: A form of joint ownership in which the death of one joint owner results in the immediate transfer of ownership to the surviving joint owner or owners.

Probate of Will: Formal proof before the proper officer or court that the will offered is the last will of the testator and confirming the Executor(s) named. (See also: Grant of Probate)

Revocable Trust: A trust that gives the settlor the power to revoke the trust.

Settlor: The individual who establishes a trust.

Tenants-In-Common: A form of joint ownership in which two or more persons own the same property in equal or differing proportions. At the death of a tenant-in-common, ownership of the deceased's share transfers to that person's estate, not to the other joint owner.

Testamentary Trust: A trust set up in a will that only takes effect after death.

Testate: A person who dies having left a valid will.

Testator/Testatrix: The individual who makes a will.

Trust: A legal arrangement in which one person (the settlor) transfers legal title to a trustee (a fiduciary) to manage the property for the benefit of a person or institution (the beneficiaries).

Trustee: The person or trust company that manages property according to the instructions in the trust agreement and the laws governing trustees.

Will: A legal document, prepared by a person in compliance with formal requirements, which takes effect on his/her death and which states what he/she wants to happen to his/her property on death.

SUMMARY

The family has three goals when it comes time to use its retirement savings to provide retirement income. In order of priority, they are as follows:

1. Minimize risk of inadequate income for the family at any time, including after the death of a member.

2. Maximize income.
3. Maximize the bequest to the heirs who are not dependent members of the family.

The family has a variety of sources of retirement income — government pensions, employer pensions, home equity, and its own savings in tax shelters and unsheltered investments. The family must choose among the various maturity options to maximize its chance of meeting the three goals. Risk management is by far the most important factor to consider, but the family must also deal with investment, taxes, and liquidity in its retirement plan.

Estate planning requires attention to a lot of detail. The most important aspect is the preparation and maintenance of an up-to-date will that arranges for each adult family member to distribute his or her assets according to his or her goals. Issues around the will and estate planning include taxes, selection of an executor, incapacity of one of the adults, and probate fees.

MULTIPLE-CHOICE REVIEW QUESTIONS

1. Which of the following is *not* a source of retirement income?

   (a) Reverse mortgage on the home
   (b) Locked-in RRSP
   (c) OAS (Old Age Security)
   (d) Employer pension
   (e) None of the above

2. To meet the demand for different patterns of retirement income and risk management, the financial markets have developed many types of annuities. Which of the following has *not* been developed?

   (a) Fully indexed (to some inflation measure) annuity
   (b) Straight life annuity
   (c) Term-certain annuity
   (d) Life with guaranteed term annuity
   (e) None of the above

3. Which of the following will *not* affect the optimal asset allocation of investment funds for retirees?

   (a) Gender of the retiree
   (b) Initial wealth
   (c) Annual consumption
   (d) Rate of return on investment
   (e) All of the above affect optimal asset allocation

4. Which of the following is *not* a way to transfer assets to your beneficiaries?

   (a) Selling of properties to your beneficiary at fair market value
   (b) Gifts to the beneficiaries during your lifetime
   (c) Assets transferred directly through a bequest in a will
   (d) Assets transferred according to provincial law if you die intestate
   (e) Assets transferred through "inter vivos"

5. If one dies intestate, without any surviving spouse or children, the estate will go _____.

   (a) all to the brothers and sisters
   (b) all to the next of kin
   (c) all to the government
   (d) half to the parents and half to the next of kin
   (e) all to the charitable organizations approved by the government

DISCUSSION QUESTIONS

1. Describe or explain each of the following terms:

   annuitant / annuities types: indexed — joint and last survivor — life with guaranteed term — registered — straight life — substandard health — term certain / commuted value / estate planning / estate planning considerations: record of personal affairs — gifts — trusts — taxes — power of attorney — wills — executor — probate costs / Locked-in Pension Funds: Life Income Fund (LIF) — Life Retirement Income Fund (LRIF) — locked-in RRSP — Locked-in Retirement Account (LIRA) / maturity option considerations: goals — risk — taxation — deferral — splitting — spreading / optimal asset allocation / Registered Retirement Income Fund (RRIF): self-administered — guaranteed rate / Reverse mortgage: equity of redemption — reverse annuity mortgage (RAM) — term or straight / sources of retirement income

2. A debate has arisen over the reasonableness of the OAS being paid to tax-payers with substantial income from other sources. Do some research and discuss this issue. You should find out the current level of "claw-back" of OAS, and consider both the ethical and practical issues in the context of increasing government deficits.

3. How would you protect your family at retirement from the risk of failure of financial institutions?

4. What are the two situations in which the deceased's assets go directly to a beneficiary independent of her will?

5. What would happen to your estate if you were to die intestate?

6. How did you choose your executor/executrix? Do you think this person is the best choice in light of what you have read in Chapter 18? If you do not have a will, explain how you would choose an executor/executrix. If you don't have enough assets for a will to be necessary, then answer this question from the point of view of one of your parents, or some other person for whom a will is relevant.

PROBLEMS

1. Claudette and Onesime are planning to retire soon. Claudette will be 59, and Onesime, 64, when they retire. Both have lived in Canada all their lives. Neither one has an employer pension. Claudette has an RRSP of $50,000, and has a full CPP entitlement. She will defer taking her CPP until she reaches age 65. Onesime has $100,000 in his RRSP, and full CPP entitlement. Assume that both RRSPs will continue to earn a 6% real rate of return. At age 71, they convert their RRSPs into RRIFs, and start withdrawing the minimum amount.

   (a) Estimate their pre-tax retirement income for the following years: first year of retirement, Onesime's age 65, Claudette's age 65, Onesime's age 71, Claudette's age 71.
   (b) Estimate their after-tax retirement income at each point in time.

2. Refer back to Example 18.6 about Oliver Cheng. Oliver's response to the analysis is to decide to retire at age 62 as a compromise. During the next two years he will take extra unpaid holidays and travel a lot, so he will save nothing more in his RRSP. Expressing everything in real dollars, his CPP and OAS entitlements and his annual retirement income requirement are unchanged, and his employer pension will increase to $24,000 p.a. in today's dollars but at age 62.

   (a) Will this plan work for him if he continues to self-annuitize with a balanced portfolio?
   (b) How would you advise him to manage his money with annuities instead at age 62, assuming rates stay the same as in Table 18.3 and you can use linear interpolation to get a rate for him at age 62? He will use straight life with no guarantee. A three-year term-certain annuity yields 2.3% nominal and five-year yields 2.5%. You will have to consider how to handle inflation.
   (c) Can he retire at age 60 if he converts the RRSP entirely to annuities?

3. Running Bear has $200,000 in savings bonds, a house worth $80,000, and three dependent children. Running Bear has an insurance policy of $100,000

payable to his estate. His wife, Judy Ermineskin, has a spousal RRSP of $10,000, with one of the children named as the beneficiary. The house is listed in his name only. They live in Yorkton, Saskatchewan.

(a) If Running Bear dies intestate, how will the estate be divided?

(b) If Running Bear and Judy made wills and took other actions, what would be the minimum probate fees they could arrange to pay on the death of either of them?

(c) Answer parts (a) and (b) as if they lived in Fernie, British Columbia.

4. Kenneth Wallingford died without a will in Prince Edward Island, at the age of 60. He is survived by his wife, Jill, and three adult children: John, Janet, and Bill. He left behind the family home, which he bought 40 years ago and which is now worth $200,000. The house is registered in Kenneth and Jill's names as joint tenants. He also left behind a portfolio of shares with a current market value of $400,000 and an adjusted cost base of $150,000. He was entitled to full CPP at age 65, and would have been entitled to OAS. Jill is also 60 years old.

(a) How much will Jill and each of the children inherit, after probate fees and income taxes? Assume the estate pays executor and legal fees of $5,000.

(b) Answer part (a) as if they lived in Corner Brook, Newfoundland.

CASE STUDIES

1. **MIKE AND BETTY GORDON**

   Mike and Betty Gordon are both 66 years old. Mike will retire January 1 from his position as a professor of radical social thought. He will be eligible for a pension of $50,000 p.a., indexed to the Consumer Price Index. He will receive maximum CPP, and is already receiving full OAS. He has $200,000 invested in ethical mutual funds (adjusted cost base $150,000). Assume Mike will receive about $5,000 in dividends from the mutual fund and $2,000 in realized capital gains. Betty has no pension, but is receiving full OAS. Betty has $100,000 in a spousal RRSP, invested in Canada Trust GICs. They jointly own a condominium in Toronto worth $250,000 (no mortgage). Their planned donations for this year include $2,000 to registered charities, and $200 to a registered federal political party. They have two children. One of the children is married, with three children of his own.

   (a) How should they structure their retirement planning, both now and for the rest of their retirement? There are some decisions they must make now, and others that will have to be made within the next six years.

(b) What will be their marginal and average income tax rates? Assume that they take no payments from the RRSPs into income in this year and do not sell any mutual fund units. Other than that assumption, assume that you have done the best job of planning in (a). To do this question, you must calculate taxable income for each one of them.

2. **THEODORE AND ASTRID HORSTMANN**
Theodore Horstmann is 65 years old and will retire in six months' time. He and his wife Astrid (60 years old) currently live in a three-bedroom house in Calgary that is worth $450,000. The house has been totally paid off. Theodore has in his name a bank account of $5,000, RRSPs of $75,000, GICs of $75,000, stock mutual funds of $20,000, and a solarium containing $10,000 in orchids. Astrid has a spousal RRSP worth $50,000. Astrid's RRSP is invested in an index mutual fund at the Toronto Dominion Bank. All the other financial assets are at a local trust company. Their two children, David and Mary, are working in Montreal and are financially secure and independent. The Horstmanns currently spend about $27,000 a year, categorized as follows in monthly amounts:

Property taxes	$ 250
Insurance	30
Utilities (water, gas, hydro)	200
Cable	30
Phone	50
Food and grocery	600
Clothes	200
Transportation (five-year-old Ford)	200
Gifts	100
Entertainment	200
Medicine and health care	100
Books, subscriptions	50
Miscellaneous	200
TOTAL	$2,210

Theodore will not have a company pension, but he will be eligible for maximum CPP and OAS. Astrid has no pension credits. They wish to travel during their retirement, and estimate that trips would cost $10,000 annually. You may assume that expected inflation is 4%, GICs earn 5.5%, and stock mutual funds are expected to return 11% after management fees. The Horstmanns don't wish to plan for living beyond age 90 for either of them.

Required:
Analyze the Horstmanns' financial situation in retirement and make recommendations. Be thorough. State any further assumptions you make.

3. **ARCHIE GOODWIN**

Archie Goodwin is 68 years old and retired. He has indexed pensions of $15,000 p.a. and $300,000 in GICs inside RRSPs at a bank and a trust company. He owns a two-bedroom condominium that he lives in, and another unit in the same building that he rents out for $1,000 per month, net of all expenses. He bought the condominiums two years ago for $150,000 each, and he could sell them for that now, after legal and real estate fees. He is currently living on an income of $50,000 p.a.: $15,000 pensions, $12,000 net rent, and $23,000 withdrawal from the RRSP. Next year he will move the RRSP into a RRIF. He has no dependants and no wish to leave a bequest to anyone. Advise him how he should invest his retirement wealth.

4. **JANET AND JOSEPH**

Janet retires next month at age 63. She has been divorced for many years, and receives no support payments from her ex-husband. Her severely handicapped son, Joseph, lives with her. She will receive an employer pension of $50,000 p.a., unindexed. There is no way to provide for a survivor pension for Joseph. She is entitled to full CPP and OAS. She has a house in a nice Kelowna neighbourhood worth about $250,000. It has been specially adapted so that Joseph can live in it comfortably. She has an RRSP with $40,000 in it, and mutual funds worth $10,000. Joseph has a trust fund of $200,000, all invested in GICs of the trustee, a local trust company.

Joseph's handicaps are physical, and he will never be able to earn a living. He has completed high school, and is fully competent to make decisions. However, he will have to have constant physical care for as long as he lives. The medical advice is that he can expect to live to his 50s. However, a few people with his disabilities have lived into their 70s. He is 30 years old.

Janet estimates that she needs $25,000 p.a. after-tax, in today's dollars (i.e., real dollars) for her own needs in retirement, as long as they live in the house. Although she can now provide care for Joseph to a greater extent in retirement than she did when working, she is also growing older and will not be able to do so forever. Furthermore, she needs quite a bit of time away, because of the draining nature of the care required. Accordingly, she estimates that she will need another $25,000 p.a. after-tax to care for him. In the event of her death, she would like him to be able to receive care in a good institution, at a cost in today's dollars of $40,000 p.a.

Required:

Provide advice to Janet and Joseph on all aspects of the maturation of her retirement plan, including his trust fund.

Appendices

APPENDIX A1
Present Value of $1 Received *n* Periods in the Future

$$PVIF = \frac{1}{(1+k)^n}$$

Period	1%	2%	3%	4%	5%	6%	7%	8%	9%	10%	11%	12%	14%	16%	18%	20%	25%
1	0.9901	0.9804	0.9709	0.9615	0.9524	0.9434	0.9346	0.9259	0.9174	0.9091	0.9009	0.8929	0.8772	0.8621	0.8475	0.8333	0.8000
2	0.9803	0.9612	0.9426	0.9246	0.9070	0.8900	0.8734	0.8573	0.8417	0.8264	0.8116	0.7972	0.7695	0.7432	0.7182	0.6944	0.6400
3	0.9706	0.9423	0.9151	0.8890	0.8638	0.8396	0.8163	0.7938	0.7722	0.7513	0.7312	0.7118	0.6750	0.6407	0.6086	0.5787	0.5120
4	0.9610	0.9238	0.8885	0.8548	0.8227	0.7921	0.7629	0.7350	0.7084	0.6830	0.6587	0.6355	0.5921	0.5523	0.5158	0.4823	0.4096
5	0.9515	0.9057	0.8626	0.8219	0.7835	0.7473	0.7130	0.6806	0.6499	0.6209	0.5935	0.5674	0.5194	0.4761	0.4371	0.4019	0.3277
6	0.9420	0.8880	0.8375	0.7903	0.7462	0.7050	0.6663	0.6302	0.5963	0.5645	0.5346	0.5066	0.4556	0.4104	0.3704	0.3349	0.2621
7	0.9327	0.8706	0.8131	0.7599	0.7107	0.6651	0.6227	0.5835	0.5470	0.5132	0.4817	0.4523	0.3996	0.3538	0.3139	0.2791	0.2097
8	0.9235	0.8535	0.7894	0.7307	0.6768	0.6274	0.5820	0.5403	0.5019	0.4665	0.4339	0.4039	0.3506	0.3050	0.2660	0.2326	0.1678
9	0.9143	0.8368	0.7664	0.7026	0.6446	0.5919	0.5439	0.5002	0.4604	0.4241	0.3909	0.3606	0.3075	0.2630	0.2255	0.1938	0.1342
10	0.9053	0.8203	0.7441	0.6756	0.6139	0.5584	0.5083	0.4632	0.4224	0.3855	0.3522	0.3220	0.2697	0.2267	0.1911	0.1615	0.1074
11	0.8963	0.8043	0.7224	0.6496	0.5847	0.5268	0.4751	0.4289	0.3875	0.3505	0.3173	0.2875	0.2366	0.1954	0.1619	0.1346	0.0859
12	0.8874	0.7885	0.7014	0.6246	0.5568	0.4970	0.4440	0.3971	0.3555	0.3186	0.2858	0.2567	0.2076	0.1685	0.1372	0.1122	0.0687
13	0.8787	0.7730	0.6810	0.6006	0.5303	0.4688	0.4150	0.3677	0.3262	0.2897	0.2575	0.2292	0.1821	0.1452	0.1163	0.0935	0.0550
14	0.8700	0.7579	0.6611	0.5775	0.5051	0.4423	0.3878	0.3405	0.2992	0.2633	0.2320	0.2046	0.1597	0.1252	0.0985	0.0779	0.0440
15	0.8613	0.7430	0.6419	0.5553	0.4810	0.4173	0.3624	0.3152	0.2745	0.2394	0.2090	0.1827	0.1401	0.1079	0.0835	0.0649	0.0352
16	0.8528	0.7284	0.6232	0.5339	0.4581	0.3936	0.3387	0.2919	0.2519	0.2176	0.1883	0.1631	0.1229	0.0930	0.0708	0.0541	0.0281
17	0.8444	0.7142	0.6050	0.5134	0.4363	0.3714	0.3166	0.2703	0.2311	0.1978	0.1696	0.1456	0.1078	0.0802	0.0600	0.0451	0.0225
18	0.8360	0.7002	0.5874	0.4936	0.4155	0.3503	0.2959	0.2502	0.2120	0.1799	0.1528	0.1300	0.0946	0.0691	0.0508	0.0376	0.0180
19	0.8277	0.6864	0.5703	0.4746	0.3957	0.3305	0.2765	0.2317	0.1945	0.1635	0.1377	0.1161	0.0829	0.0596	0.0431	0.0313	0.0144
20	0.8195	0.6730	0.5537	0.4564	0.3769	0.3118	0.2584	0.2145	0.1784	0.1486	0.1240	0.1037	0.0728	0.0514	0.0365	0.0261	0.0115
25	0.7798	0.6095	0.4776	0.3751	0.2953	0.2330	0.1842	0.1460	0.1160	0.0923	0.0736	0.0588	0.0378	0.0245	0.0160	0.0105	0.0038
30	0.7419	0.5521	0.4120	0.3083	0.2314	0.1741	0.1314	0.0994	0.0754	0.0573	0.0437	0.0334	0.0196	0.0116	0.0070	0.0042	0.0012
35	0.7059	0.5000	0.3554	0.2534	0.1813	0.1301	0.0937	0.0676	0.0490	0.0356	0.0259	0.0189	0.0102	0.0055	0.0030	0.0017	0.0004
40	0.6717	0.4529	0.3066	0.2083	0.1420	0.0972	0.0668	0.0460	0.0318	0.0221	0.0154	0.0107	0.0053	0.0026	0.0013	0.0007	0.0001
45	0.6391	0.4102	0.2644	0.1712	0.1113	0.0727	0.0476	0.0313	0.0207	0.0137	0.0091	0.0061	0.0027	0.0013	0.0006	0.0003	*
50	0.6080	0.3715	0.2281	0.1407	0.0872	0.0543	0.0339	0.0213	0.0134	0.0085	0.0054	0.0035	0.0014	0.0006	0.0003	0.0001	*
60	0.5504	0.3048	0.1697	0.0951	0.0535	0.0303	0.0173	0.0099	0.0057	0.0033	0.0019	0.0011	0.0004	0.0001	*	*	*

* less than .0001

APPENDIX A2
Future Value of $1 Compounded for *n* Periods

$$FVIF = (1 + k)^n$$

Period	1%	2%	3%	4%	5%	6%	7%	8%	9%	10%	11%	12%	14%	16%	18%	20%	25%
1	1.0100	1.0200	1.0300	1.0400	1.0500	1.0600	1.0700	1.0800	1.0900	1.1000	1.1100	1.1200	1.1400	1.1600	1.1800	1.2000	1.2500
2	1.0201	1.0404	1.0609	1.0816	1.1025	1.1236	1.1449	1.1664	1.1881	1.2100	1.2321	1.2544	1.2996	1.3456	1.3924	1.4400	1.5625
3	1.0303	1.0612	1.0927	1.1249	1.1576	1.1910	1.2250	1.2597	1.2950	1.3310	1.3676	1.4049	1.4815	1.5609	1.6430	1.7280	1.9531
4	1.0406	1.0824	1.1255	1.1699	1.2155	1.2625	1.3108	1.3605	1.4116	1.4641	1.5181	1.5735	1.6890	1.8106	1.9388	2.0736	2.4414
5	1.0510	1.1041	1.1593	1.2167	1.2763	1.3382	1.4026	1.4693	1.5386	1.6105	1.6851	1.7623	1.9254	2.1003	2.2878	2.4883	3.0518
6	1.0615	1.1262	1.1941	1.2653	1.3401	1.4185	1.5007	1.5869	1.6771	1.7716	1.8704	1.9738	2.1950	2.4364	2.6996	2.9860	3.8147
7	1.0721	1.1487	1.2299	1.3159	1.4071	1.5036	1.6058	1.7138	1.8280	1.9487	2.0762	2.2107	2.5023	2.8262	3.1855	3.5832	4.7684
8	1.0829	1.1717	1.2668	1.3686	1.4775	1.5938	1.7182	1.8509	1.9926	2.1436	2.3045	2.4760	2.8526	3.2784	3.7589	4.2998	5.9605
9	1.0937	1.1951	1.3048	1.4233	1.5513	1.6895	1.8385	1.9990	2.1719	2.3579	2.5580	2.7731	3.2519	3.8030	4.4355	5.1598	7.4506
10	1.1046	1.2190	1.3439	1.4802	1.6289	1.7908	1.9672	2.1589	2.3674	2.5937	2.8394	3.1058	3.7072	4.4114	5.2338	6.1917	9.3132
11	1.1157	1.2434	1.3842	1.5395	1.7103	1.8983	2.1049	2.3316	2.5804	2.8531	3.1518	3.4785	4.2262	5.1173	6.1759	7.4301	11.6415
12	1.1268	1.2682	1.4258	1.6010	1.7959	2.0122	2.2522	2.5182	2.8127	3.1384	3.4985	3.8960	4.8179	5.9360	7.2876	8.9161	14.5519
13	1.1381	1.2936	1.4685	1.6651	1.8856	2.1329	2.4098	2.7196	3.0658	3.4523	3.8833	4.3635	5.4924	6.8858	8.5994	10.6993	18.1899
14	1.1495	1.3195	1.5126	1.7317	1.9799	2.2609	2.5785	2.9372	3.3417	3.7975	4.3104	4.8871	6.2613	7.9875	10.1472	12.8392	22.7374
15	1.1610	1.3459	1.5580	1.8009	2.0789	2.3966	2.7590	3.1722	3.6425	4.1772	4.7846	5.4736	7.1379	9.2655	11.9737	15.4070	28.4217
16	1.1726	1.3728	1.6047	1.8730	2.1829	2.5404	2.9522	3.4259	3.9703	4.5950	5.3109	6.1304	8.1372	10.7480	14.1290	18.4884	35.5271
17	1.1843	1.4002	1.6528	1.9479	2.2920	2.6928	3.1588	3.7000	4.3276	5.0545	5.8951	6.8660	9.2765	12.4677	16.6722	22.1861	44.4089
18	1.1961	1.4282	1.7024	2.0258	2.4066	2.8543	3.3799	3.9960	4.7171	5.5599	6.5436	7.6900	10.5752	14.4625	19.6733	26.6233	55.5112
19	1.2081	1.4568	1.7535	2.1068	2.5270	3.0256	3.6165	4.3157	5.1417	6.1159	7.2633	8.6128	12.0557	16.7765	23.2144	31.9480	69.3889
20	1.2202	1.4859	1.8061	2.1911	2.6533	3.2071	3.8697	4.6610	5.6044	6.7275	8.0623	9.6463	13.7435	19.4608	27.3930	38.3376	86.7362
25	1.2824	1.6406	2.0938	2.6658	3.3864	4.2919	5.4274	6.8485	8.6231	10.8347	13.5855	17.0001	26.4619	40.8742	62.6686	95.3962	264.6978
30	1.3478	1.8114	2.4273	3.2434	4.3219	5.7435	7.6123	10.0627	13.2677	17.4494	22.8923	29.9599	50.9502	85.8499	143.3706	237.3763	807.7936
35	1.4166	1.9999	2.8139	3.9461	5.5160	7.6861	10.6766	14.7853	20.4140	28.1024	38.5749	52.7996	98.1002	180.3141	327.9973	590.6682	2465.2
40	1.4889	2.2080	3.2620	4.8010	7.0400	10.2857	14.9745	21.7245	31.4094	45.2593	65.0009	93.0510	188.8835	378.7212	750.3783	1469.8	7523.2
45	1.5648	2.4379	3.7816	5.8412	8.9850	13.7646	21.0025	31.9204	48.3273	72.8905	109.5302	163.9876	363.6791	795.4438	1716.7	3657.3	22958.9
50	1.6446	2.6916	4.3839	7.1067	11.4674	18.4202	29.4570	46.9016	74.3575	117.3909	184.5648	289.0022	700.2330	1670.7	3927.4	9100.4	70064.9
60	1.8167	3.2810	5.8916	10.5196	18.6792	32.9877	57.9464	101.2571	176.0313	304.4816	524.0572	897.5969	2595.9	7370.2	20555.1	56347.5	652530.4

APPENDIX A3
Present Value of an Annuity of $1 Per Period for *n* Periods

$$PVIFA = \frac{1 - \frac{1}{(1 + k)^n}}{k}$$

Period	1%	2%	3%	4%	5%	6%	7%	8%	9%	10%	11%	12%	14%	16%	18%	20%	25%
1	0.990	0.980	0.971	0.962	0.952	0.943	0.935	0.926	0.917	0.909	0.901	0.893	0.877	0.862	0.847	0.833	0.800
2	1.970	1.942	1.913	1.886	1.859	1.833	1.808	1.783	1.759	1.736	1.713	1.690	1.647	1.605	1.566	1.528	1.440
3	2.941	2.884	2.829	2.775	2.723	2.673	2.624	2.577	2.531	2.487	2.444	2.402	2.322	2.246	2.174	2.106	1.952
4	3.902	3.808	3.717	3.630	3.546	3.465	3.387	3.312	3.240	3.170	3.102	3.037	2.914	2.798	2.690	2.589	2.362
5	4.853	4.713	4.580	4.452	4.329	4.212	4.100	3.993	3.890	3.791	3.696	3.605	3.433	3.274	3.127	2.991	2.689
6	5.795	5.601	5.417	5.242	5.076	4.917	4.767	4.623	4.486	4.355	4.231	4.111	3.889	3.685	3.498	3.326	2.951
7	6.728	6.472	6.230	6.002	5.786	5.582	5.389	5.206	5.033	4.868	4.712	4.564	4.288	4.039	3.812	3.605	3.161
8	7.652	7.325	7.020	6.733	6.463	6.210	5.971	5.747	5.535	5.335	5.146	4.968	4.639	4.344	4.078	3.837	3.329
9	8.566	8.162	7.786	7.435	7.108	6.802	6.515	6.247	5.995	5.759	5.537	5.328	4.946	4.607	4.303	4.031	3.463
10	9.471	8.983	8.530	8.111	7.722	7.360	7.024	6.710	6.418	6.145	5.889	5.650	5.216	4.833	4.494	4.192	3.571
11	10.368	9.787	9.253	8.760	8.306	7.887	7.499	7.139	6.805	6.495	6.207	5.938	5.453	5.029	4.656	4.327	3.656
12	11.255	10.575	9.954	9.385	8.863	8.384	7.943	7.536	7.161	6.814	6.492	6.194	5.660	5.197	4.793	4.439	3.725
13	12.134	11.348	10.635	9.986	9.394	8.853	8.358	7.904	7.487	7.103	6.750	6.424	5.842	5.342	4.910	4.533	3.780
14	13.004	12.106	11.296	10.563	9.899	9.295	8.745	8.244	7.786	7.367	6.982	6.628	6.002	5.468	5.008	4.611	3.824
15	13.865	12.849	11.938	11.118	10.380	9.712	9.108	8.559	8.061	7.606	7.191	6.811	6.142	5.575	5.092	4.675	3.859
16	14.718	13.578	12.561	11.652	10.838	10.106	9.447	8.851	8.313	7.824	7.379	6.974	6.265	5.668	5.162	4.730	3.887
17	15.562	14.292	13.166	12.166	11.274	10.477	9.763	9.122	8.544	8.022	7.549	7.120	6.373	5.749	5.222	4.775	3.910
18	16.398	14.992	13.754	12.659	11.690	10.828	10.059	9.372	8.756	8.201	7.702	7.250	6.467	5.818	5.273	4.812	3.928
19	17.226	15.678	14.324	13.134	12.085	11.158	10.336	9.604	8.950	8.365	7.839	7.366	6.550	5.877	5.316	4.843	3.942
20	18.046	16.351	14.877	13.590	12.462	11.470	10.594	9.818	9.129	8.514	7.963	7.469	6.623	5.929	5.353	4.870	3.954
25	22.023	19.523	17.413	15.622	14.094	12.783	11.654	10.675	9.823	9.077	8.422	7.843	6.873	6.097	5.467	4.948	3.985
30	25.808	22.396	19.600	17.292	15.372	13.765	12.409	11.258	10.274	9.427	8.694	8.055	7.003	6.177	5.517	4.979	3.995
35	29.409	24.999	21.487	18.665	16.374	14.498	12.948	11.655	10.567	9.644	8.855	8.176	7.070	6.215	5.539	4.992	3.998
40	32.835	27.355	23.115	19.793	17.159	15.046	13.332	11.925	10.757	9.779	8.951	8.244	7.105	6.233	5.548	4.997	3.999
45	36.095	29.490	24.519	20.720	17.774	15.456	13.606	12.108	10.881	9.863	9.008	8.283	7.123	6.242	5.552	4.999	4.000
50	39.196	31.424	25.730	21.482	18.256	15.762	13.801	12.233	10.962	9.915	9.042	8.304	7.133	6.246	5.554	4.999	4.000
60	44.955	34.761	27.676	22.623	18.929	16.161	14.039	12.377	11.048	9.967	9.074	8.324	7.140	6.249	5.555	5.000	4.000

APPENDIX A4
Future Value of an Annuity of $1 Per Period for *n* Periods

$$FVIFA = \frac{[(1 + k)^n - 1]}{k}$$

Period	1%	2%	3%	4%	5%	6%	7%	8%	9%	10%	11%	12%	14%	16%	18%	20%	25%
1	1.000	1.000	1.000	1.000	1.000	1.000	1.000	1.000	1.000	1.000	1.000	1.000	1.000	1.000	1.000	1.000	1.000
2	2.010	2.020	2.030	2.040	2.050	2.060	2.070	2.080	2.090	2.100	2.110	2.120	2.140	2.160	2.180	2.200	2.250
3	3.030	3.060	3.091	3.122	3.152	3.184	3.215	3.246	3.278	3.310	3.342	3.374	3.440	3.506	3.572	3.640	3.813
4	4.060	4.122	4.184	4.246	4.310	4.375	4.440	4.506	4.573	4.641	4.710	4.779	4.921	5.066	5.215	5.368	5.766
5	5.101	5.204	5.309	5.416	5.526	5.637	5.751	5.867	5.985	6.105	6.228	6.353	6.610	6.877	7.154	7.442	8.207
6	6.152	6.308	6.468	6.633	6.802	6.975	7.153	7.336	7.523	7.716	7.913	8.115	8.536	8.977	9.442	9.930	11.260
7	7.214	7.434	7.662	7.898	8.142	8.394	8.654	8.923	9.200	9.487	9.783	10.090	10.730	11.410	12.140	12.920	15.070
8	8.286	8.583	8.892	9.214	9.549	9.897	10.260	10.640	11.030	11.440	11.860	12.300	13.230	14.240	15.330	16.500	19.840
9	9.369	9.755	10.160	10.580	11.030	11.490	11.980	12.490	13.020	13.580	14.160	14.780	16.090	17.520	19.090	20.800	25.800
10	10.460	10.950	11.460	12.010	12.580	13.180	13.820	14.490	15.190	15.940	16.720	17.550	19.340	21.320	23.520	25.960	33.250
11	11.570	12.170	12.810	13.490	14.210	14.970	15.780	16.650	17.560	18.530	19.560	20.650	23.040	25.730	28.760	32.150	42.570
12	12.680	13.410	14.190	15.030	15.920	16.870	17.890	18.980	20.140	21.380	22.710	24.130	27.270	30.850	34.930	39.580	54.210
13	13.810	14.680	15.620	16.630	17.710	18.880	20.140	21.500	22.950	24.520	26.210	28.030	32.090	36.790	42.220	48.500	68.760
14	14.950	15.970	17.090	18.290	19.600	21.020	22.550	24.210	26.020	27.970	30.090	32.390	37.580	43.670	50.820	59.200	86.950
15	16.100	17.290	18.600	20.020	21.580	23.280	25.130	27.150	29.360	31.770	34.410	37.280	43.840	51.660	60.970	72.040	109.700
16	17.260	18.640	20.160	21.820	23.660	25.670	27.890	30.320	33.000	35.950	39.190	42.750	50.980	60.930	72.940	87.440	138.100
17	18.430	20.010	21.760	23.700	25.840	28.210	30.840	33.750	36.970	40.540	44.500	48.880	59.120	71.670	87.070	105.900	173.600
18	19.610	21.410	23.410	25.650	28.130	30.910	34.000	37.450	41.300	45.600	50.400	55.750	68.390	84.140	103.700	128.100	218.000
19	20.810	22.840	25.120	27.670	30.540	33.760	37.380	41.450	46.020	51.160	56.940	63.440	78.970	98.600	123.400	154.700	273.600
20	22.020	24.300	26.870	29.780	33.070	36.790	41.000	45.760	51.160	57.270	64.200	72.050	91.020	115.400	146.600	186.700	342.900
25	28.240	32.030	36.460	41.650	47.730	54.860	63.250	73.110	84.700	98.350	114.400	133.300	181.900	249.200	342.600	472.000	1055
30	34.780	40.570	47.580	56.080	66.440	79.060	94.460	113.300	136.300	164.500	199.000	241.300	356.800	530.300	790.900	1182	3227
35	41.660	49.990	60.460	73.650	90.320	111.400	138.200	172.300	215.700	271.000	341.600	431.700	693.600	1121	1817	2948	9857
40	48.890	60.400	75.400	95.030	120.800	154.800	199.600	259.100	337.900	442.600	581.800	767.100	1342	2361	4163	7344	30089
45	56.480	71.890	92.720	121.000	159.700	212.700	285.700	386.500	525.900	718.900	986.600	1358.2	2591	4965	9532	18281	91831
50	64.460	84.580	112.800	152.700	209.300	290.300	406.500	573.800	815.100	1164	1669	2400	4995	10436	21813	45497	280256
60	81.670	114.100	163.100	238.000	353.600	533.100	813.500	1253	1945	3035	4755	7472	18535	46058	114190	281733	2610118

APPENDIX B
Canada, Life Tables[1]

The tables provide the number of deaths expected during any year of life for a hypothetical cohort of 100,000 Canadians, based on 2007 statistics.

The first column, Age, is the starting age for the given year. Thus, the first line covers the year from birth to immediately before the first birthday.

The second column, Alive at Start of Year, shows how many of the cohort were alive at the start of the year of the age shown in column 1. For example, looking at Appendix B1 for Canadian females, we see that on their fifth birthday, 99,450 of the original cohort were expected to be living.

The third column, Deaths During Year, records the number of deaths expected to occur during the year starting on the birthday in Column 1. Thus, again looking at Appendix B1 for Canadian females in the year starting with their fifth birthday, we see that on average, 14 of the 99,450 alive on their fifth birthday are expected to die before their sixth birthday. The entry for Column 2, Alive at Start of Year, Age 6, is equal to Column 2 minus Column 3 from the previous line, Age 5.

Column 4, Probability of Survival, is calculated as (Column 2 – Column 3) ÷ Column 2, rounded to five decimal places. Thus, a five-year-old girl has a .99986 probability of living to her sixth birthday.

Column 5, Probability of Death, is calculated as Column 3 ÷ Column 2, rounded to four decimal places. Thus, a five-year-old girl has a .00014 probability of dying before her sixth birthday.

[1] *Canadian Human Mortality Database*. Department of Demography, Université de Montréal (Canada). Available at <www.demo.umontreal.ca/chmd/> (data downloaded on 2011-12-04).

APPENDIX B1
Standard Mortality Table — Canadian Females

Age	Alive at Start of Year	Deaths During Year	Probability of Survival	Probability of Death
0	100,000	476	0.99524	0.00476
1	99,524	29	0.99971	0.00029
2	99,495	19	0.99981	0.00019
3	99,477	10	0.99990	0.00010
4	99,467	10	0.99990	0.00010
5	99,457	14	0.99986	0.00014
6	99,443	13	0.99987	0.00013
7	99,429	14	0.99986	0.00014
8	99,415	9	0.99990	0.00010
9	99,406	10	0.99990	0.00010
10	99,395	7	0.99993	0.00007
11	99,389	8	0.99992	0.00008
12	99,380	11	0.99989	0.00011
13	99,369	11	0.99989	0.00011
14	99,359	18	0.99982	0.00018
15	99,341	21	0.99979	0.00021
16	99,319	19	0.99980	0.00020
17	99,300	26	0.99974	0.00026
18	99,274	33	0.99966	0.00034
19	99,241	31	0.99969	0.00031
20	99,210	29	0.99970	0.00030
21	99,181	28	0.99972	0.00028
22	99,153	31	0.99969	0.00031
23	99,122	29	0.99971	0.00029
24	99,093	30	0.99970	0.00030
25	99,063	35	0.99965	0.00035
26	99,028	30	0.99969	0.00031
27	98,997	30	0.99970	0.00030
28	98,968	33	0.99967	0.00033
29	98,935	33	0.99967	0.00033
30	98,902	36	0.99964	0.00036
31	98,866	34	0.99965	0.00035
32	98,832	51	0.99949	0.00051
33	98,781	40	0.99959	0.00041
34	98,741	46	0.99954	0.00046
35	98,695	47	0.99953	0.00047
36	98,649	48	0.99951	0.00049
37	98,600	70	0.99929	0.00071
38	98,530	57	0.99942	0.00058
39	98,473	73	0.99926	0.00074
40	98,400	77	0.99922	0.00078
41	98,322	92	0.99906	0.00094
42	98,230	105	0.99893	0.00107
43	98,125	103	0.99895	0.00105
44	98,022	113	0.99885	0.00115
45	97,909	149	0.99848	0.00152
46	97,760	155	0.99841	0.00159
47	97,605	175	0.99821	0.00179
48	97,430	180	0.99815	0.00185
49	97,250	201	0.99793	0.00207
50	97,049	217	0.99776	0.00224
51	96,832	225	0.99767	0.00233
52	96,606	265	0.99725	0.00275
53	96,341	277	0.99712	0.00288
54	96,064	293	0.99695	0.00305
55	95,771	316	0.99670	0.00330

APPENDIX B1
Standard Mortality Table — Canadian Females (continued)

Age	Alive at Start of Year	Deaths During Year	Probability of Survival	Probability of Death
56	95,456	357	0.99626	0.00374
57	95,098	390	0.99590	0.00410
58	94,708	427	0.99549	0.00451
59	94,282	441	0.99532	0.00468
60	93,840	514	0.99452	0.00548
61	93,327	507	0.99457	0.00543
62	92,820	555	0.99402	0.00598
63	92,264	639	0.99307	0.00693
64	91,625	726	0.99208	0.00792
65	90,899	755	0.99169	0.00831
66	90,144	818	0.99093	0.00907
67	89,326	920	0.98970	0.01030
68	88,406	1,023	0.98843	0.01157
69	87,383	1,048	0.98800	0.01200
70	86,335	1,190	0.98622	0.01378
71	85,145	1,298	0.98475	0.01525
72	83,847	1,383	0.98350	0.01650
73	82,463	1,454	0.98236	0.01764
74	81,009	1,628	0.97991	0.02009
75	79,381	1,720	0.97833	0.02167
76	77,661	1,872	0.97589	0.02411
77	75,789	2,069	0.97270	0.02730
78	73,719	2,181	0.97042	0.02958
79	71,539	2,439	0.96591	0.03409
80	69,100	2,583	0.96261	0.03739
81	66,517	2,757	0.95855	0.04145
82	63,760	3,107	0.95128	0.04872
83	60,653	3,172	0.94770	0.05230
84	57,482	3,545	0.93833	0.06167
85	53,936	3,796	0.92962	0.07038
86	50,140	3,886	0.92250	0.07750
87	46,254	4,185	0.90953	0.09047
88	42,069	3,955	0.90598	0.09402
89	38,114	4,234	0.88892	0.11108
90	33,881	4,048	0.88052	0.11948
91	29,832	4,186	0.85967	0.14033
92	25,646	3,985	0.84461	0.15539
93	21,661	3,659	0.83109	0.16891
94	18,002	3,409	0.81064	0.18936
95	14,593	2,981	0.79573	0.20427
96	11,612	2,598	0.77626	0.22374
97	9,014	2,200	0.75592	0.24408
98	6,814	1,807	0.73483	0.26517
99	5,007	1,436	0.71316	0.28684
100	3,571	1,103	0.69108	0.30892
101	2,468	817	0.66878	0.33122
102	1,650	583	0.64646	0.35354
103	1,067	401	0.62432	0.37568
104	666	265	0.60256	0.39744
105	401	168	0.58135	0.41865
106	233	102	0.56085	0.43915
107	131	60	0.54121	0.45879
108	71	34	0.52253	0.47747
109	37	18	0.50490	0.49510
110+	19	19	0.00000	1.00000

APPENDIX B2
Standard Mortality Table — Canadian Males

Age	Alive at Start of Year	Deaths During Year	Probability of Survival	Probability of Death
0	100,000	561	0.99439	0.00561
1	99,439	33	0.99967	0.00033
2	99,407	24	0.99976	0.00024
3	99,383	18	0.99982	0.00018
4	99,365	11	0.99989	0.00011
5	99,354	10	0.99990	0.00010
6	99,344	12	0.99988	0.00012
7	99,332	13	0.99987	0.00013
8	99,319	10	0.99990	0.00010
9	99,310	10	0.99990	0.00010
10	99,300	9	0.99991	0.00009
11	99,291	11	0.99989	0.00011
12	99,280	15	0.99985	0.00015
13	99,265	17	0.99983	0.00017
14	99,248	24	0.99976	0.00024
15	99,224	29	0.99971	0.00029
16	99,195	38	0.99962	0.00038
17	99,157	61	0.99939	0.00061
18	99,097	73	0.99927	0.00073
19	99,024	88	0.99911	0.00089
20	98,936	96	0.99903	0.00097
21	98,839	78	0.99921	0.00079
22	98,762	78	0.99921	0.00079
23	98,683	76	0.99923	0.00077
24	98,608	81	0.99918	0.00082
25	98,527	76	0.99922	0.00078
26	98,451	81	0.99918	0.00082
27	98,370	80	0.99919	0.00081
28	98,290	72	0.99927	0.00073
29	98,218	87	0.99912	0.00088
30	98,132	79	0.99920	0.00080
31	98,053	80	0.99918	0.00082
32	97,973	74	0.99925	0.00075
33	97,899	85	0.99913	0.00087
34	97,814	95	0.99903	0.00097
35	97,719	105	0.99892	0.00108
36	97,614	110	0.99887	0.00113
37	97,504	107	0.99890	0.00110
38	97,396	119	0.99878	0.00122
39	97,278	133	0.99863	0.00137
40	97,145	131	0.99865	0.00135
41	97,013	153	0.99842	0.00158
42	96,860	153	0.99842	0.00158
43	96,707	173	0.99821	0.00179
44	96,534	182	0.99811	0.00189
45	96,352	204	0.99788	0.00212
46	96,148	220	0.99771	0.00229
47	95,928	256	0.99733	0.00267
48	95,671	260	0.99728	0.00272
49	95,411	288	0.99698	0.00302
50	95,123	333	0.99650	0.00350
51	94,791	351	0.99630	0.00370
52	94,440	411	0.99565	0.00435
53	94,029	429	0.99544	0.00456
54	93,600	467	0.99501	0.00499
55	93,133	510	0.99453	0.00547

APPENDIX B2
Standard Mortality Table — Canadian Males (continued)

Age	Alive at Start of Year	Deaths During Year	Probability of Survival	Probability of Death
56	92,623	553	0.99403	0.00597
57	92,070	630	0.99316	0.00684
58	91,440	634	0.99306	0.00694
59	90,806	686	0.99244	0.00756
60	90,119	830	0.99079	0.00921
61	89,289	792	0.99114	0.00886
62	88,498	870	0.99017	0.00983
63	87,628	984	0.98877	0.01123
64	86,643	1,063	0.98773	0.01227
65	85,581	1,155	0.98650	0.01350
66	84,425	1,207	0.98570	0.01430
67	83,218	1,348	0.98380	0.01620
68	81,870	1,520	0.98144	0.01856
69	80,350	1,632	0.97968	0.02032
70	78,718	1,706	0.97832	0.02168
71	77,011	1,810	0.97649	0.02351
72	75,201	1,945	0.97414	0.02586
73	73,256	2,141	0.97077	0.02923
74	71,115	2,296	0.96771	0.03229
75	68,819	2,446	0.96446	0.03554
76	66,373	2,538	0.96177	0.03823
77	63,835	2,807	0.95602	0.04398
78	61,028	2,897	0.95252	0.04748
79	58,131	3,129	0.94617	0.05383
80	55,001	3,193	0.94194	0.05806
81	51,808	3,219	0.93786	0.06214
82	48,589	3,502	0.92793	0.07207
83	45,087	3,600	0.92016	0.07984
84	41,487	3,638	0.91231	0.08769
85	37,849	3,705	0.90210	0.09790
86	34,144	3,536	0.89644	0.10356
87	30,608	3,749	0.87750	0.12250
88	26,859	3,518	0.86903	0.13097
89	23,341	3,433	0.85291	0.14709
90	19,908	3,150	0.84177	0.15823
91	16,758	2,950	0.82395	0.17605
92	13,807	2,654	0.80781	0.19219
93	11,154	2,316	0.79236	0.20764
94	8,838	1,965	0.77769	0.22231
95	6,873	1,679	0.75565	0.24435
96	5,194	1,368	0.73655	0.26345
97	3,825	1,083	0.71696	0.28304
98	2,743	831	0.69701	0.30299
99	1,912	618	0.67683	0.32317
100	1,294	444	0.65658	0.34342
101	850	309	0.63641	0.36359
102	541	207	0.61645	0.38355
103	333	134	0.59686	0.40314
104	199	84	0.57776	0.42224
105	115	51	0.55927	0.44073
106	64	29	0.54149	0.45851
107	35	17	0.52450	0.47550
108	18	9	0.50836	0.49164
109	9	5	0.49314	0.50686
110+	5	5	0.00000	1.00000

APPENDIX C
The Normal Distribution

$$Z = \frac{X - \mu}{\sigma} \quad \text{(standardized normal)}$$

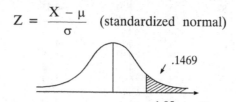

.1469

z = 1.05   Z

z	.00	.01	.02	.03	.04	.05	.06	.07	.08	.09
0.0	.5000	.4960	.4920	.4880	.4840	.4801	.4761	.4721	.4681	.4641
0.1	.4602	.4562	.4522	.4483	.4443	.4404	.4364	.4325	.4286	.4247
0.2	.4207	.4168	.4129	.4090	.4052	.4013	.3974	.3936	.3897	.3859
0.3	.3821	.3783	.3745	.3707	.3669	.3632	.3594	.3557	.3520	.3483
0.4	.3446	.3409	.3372	.3336	.3300	.3264	.3228	.3192	.3156	.3121
0.5	.3085	.3050	.3015	.2981	.2946	.2912	.2877	.2843	.2810	.2776
0.6	.2743	.2709	.2676	.2643	.2611	.2578	.2546	.2514	.2483	.2451
0.7	.2420	.2389	.2358	.2327	.2296	.2266	.2236	.2206	.2177	.2148
0.8	.2119	.2090	.2061	.2033	.2005	.1977	.1949	.1922	.1894	.1867
0.9	.1841	.1814	.1788	.1762	.1736	.1711	.1685	.1660	.1635	.1611
1.0	.1587	.1562	.1539	.1515	.1492	.1469	.1446	.1423	.1401	.1379
1.1	.1357	.1335	.1314	.1292	.1271	.1251	.1230	.1210	.1190	.1170
1.2	.1151	.1131	.1112	.1093	.1075	.1056	.1038	.1020	.1003	.0985
1.3	.0968	.0951	.0934	.0918	.0901	.0885	.0869	.0853	.0838	.0823
1.4	.0808	.0793	.0778	.0764	.0749	.0735	.0721	.0708	.0694	.0681
1.5	.0668	.0655	.0643	.0630	.0618	.0606	.0594	.0582	.0571	.0559
1.6	.0548	.0537	.0526	.0516	.0505	.0495	.0485	.0475	.0465	.0455
1.7	.0446	.0436	.0427	.0418	.0409	.0401	.0392	.0384	.0375	.0367
1.8	.0359	.0351	.0344	.0336	.0329	.0322	.0314	.0307	.0301	.0294
1.9	.0287	.0281	.0274	.0268	.0262	.0256	.0250	.0244	.0239	.0233
2.0	.0228	.0222	.0217	.0212	.0207	.0202	.0197	.0192	.0188	.0183
2.1	.0179	.0174	.0170	.0166	.0162	.0158	.0154	.0150	.0146	.0143
2.2	.0139	.0136	.0132	.0129	.0125	.0122	.0119	.0116	.0113	.0110
2.3	.0107	.0104	.0102	.0099	.0096	.0094	.0091	.0089	.0087	.0084
2.4	.0082	.0080	.0078	.0075	.0073	.0071	.0069	.0068	.0066	.0064
2.5	.0062	.0060	.0059	.0057	.0055	.0054	.0052	.0051	.0049	.0048
2.6	.0047	.0045	.0044	.0043	.0041	.0040	.0039	.0038	.0037	.0036
2.7	.0035	.0034	.0033	.0032	.0031	.0030	.0029	.0028	.0027	.0026
2.8	.0026	.0025	.0024	.0023	.0023	.0022	.0021	.0021	.0020	.0019
2.9	.0019	.0018	.0018	.0017	.0016	.0016	.0015	.0015	.0014	.0014
3.0	.0013	.0013	.0013	.0012	.0012	.0011	.0011	.0011	.0010	.0010

Note: The table plots the cumulative probability $Z \geq z$.

APPENDIX D
Nominal Returns of Asset Classes, 1957–2010 (in %)

Year	CPI	T-bill	Bonds	S&P/TSX	S&P 500	World
1957	1.72	3.76	7.94	−20.64	−8.61	
1958	2.82	2.25	1.92	30.67	36.15	
1959	1.10	4.81	−5.07	2.28	10.38	
1960	1.63	3.20	12.19	1.49	4.41	
1961	0.00	2.81	9.16	34.09	30	
1962	1.60	4.05	9.03	−7.56	−3.1	
1963	2.11	3.56	4.58	14.18	21.15	
1964	2.06	3.75	6.16	24.69	14.99	
1965	3.03	3.98	0.050	5.750	12.450	
1966	3.43	5.02	−1.05	−7.07	−9.00	
1967	3.79	4.58	−9.48	18.09	22.05	
1968	4.11	6.44	2.14	22.45	10.30	
1969	4.82	7.11	−2.86	−0.81	−8.39	
1970	1.26	6.70	15.39	−3.87	2.11	−4.80
1971	4.96	3.81	14.84	8.01	13.04	17.66
1972	5.12	3.55	8.11	27.38	16.98	20.99
1973	9.36	5.11	1.97	0.27	−14.22	−13.86
1974	12.3	7.83	−4.53	−25.93	−25.95	−24.32
1975	9.45	7.41	8.02	18.48	38.71	36.60
1976	5.85	9.28	23.64	11.02	21.38	13.43
1977	9.47	7.65	9.04	10.71	0.96	10.20
1978	8.41	8.34	4.10	29.72	15.67	26.13
1979	9.76	11.41	−2.83	44.77	15.58	10.61
1980	11.11	14.97	6.57	30.13	31.62	27.89
1981	12.18	18.41	4.20	−10.25	−4.59	−2.84
1982	9.24	15.42	35.36	4.14	24.64	15.97
1983	4.60	9.62	11.53	37.31	22.31	22.73
1984	3.69	11.59	14.66	−2.39	12.48	12.03
1985	4.38	9.88	21.23	25.07	35.82	42.76
1986	4.19	9.33	14.70	8.95	16.98	36.47
1987	4.15	8.47	4.04	5.88	3.57	12.34
1988	3.99	9.41	9.79	11.08	7.06	13.46
1989	5.23	12.36	12.81	21.37	25.11	13.35
1990	4.97	13.48	7.54	−14.80	−1.28	−13.89
1991	3.79	9.83	22.13	12.02	27.56	17.81
1992	2.13	7.08	9.84	−1.43	17.41	5.18
1993	1.69	5.51	18.14	32.55	13.81	25.73
1994	0.20	5.35	−4.31	−0.18	7.19	11.53
1995	1.75	7.39	20.67	14.53	30.01	16.90
1996	2.20	5.02	12.26	28.35	21.72	13.71
1997	0.75	3.15	9.63	14.98	34.84	20.30
1998	1.02	4.79	9.18	−1.58	37.70	33.65
1999	2.58	4.66	−1.14	31.71	14.160	18.200
2000	3.23	5.49	10.25	7.41	−5.520	−9.490
2001	0.72	4.72	8.08	−12.57	−6.46	−11.38
2002	3.80	2.52	8.73	−12.44	−22.74	−20.20
2003	2.08	2.97	6.69	26.72	5.29	9.44
2004	2.13	2.33	7.15	14.48	3.25	7.33
2005	2.09	2.56	6.46	24.13	1.61	6.58
2006	1.67	4.00	4.06	17.26	15.74	20.58
2007	2.38	4.34	3.68	9.83	−10.55	−7.10
2008	1.16	3.13	6.41	−33.00	−21.92	−26.05
2009	1.32	0.49	5.41	35.06	8.08	11.78
2010	2.35	0.39	6.74	17.61	9.35	6.76
Arithmetic Mean	3.98	6.39	7.87	10.74	10.58	10.35
Geometric Mean	3.94	6.32	7.59	9.37	9.40	9.07
Standard Deviation	3.15	3.84	7.99	17.03	15.91	16.43
Year of Data	54	54	54	54	54	41

Sources: Scotia McLeod Inc., Morgan Stanley Inc., provided by PlanPlus Inc.

APPENDIX E
Real Returns of Asset Classes, 1957–2010 (in %)

Year	T-bill	Bonds	TSX	S&P	World
1957	2.01	6.11	−21.98	−10.16	
1958	−0.55	−0.88	27.09	32.42	
1959	3.67	−6.10	1.17	9.18	
1960	1.54	10.39	−0.14	2.74	
1961	2.81	9.16	34.09	30.00	
1962	2.41	7.31	−9.02	−4.63	
1963	1.42	2.42	11.82	18.65	
1964	1.66	4.02	22.17	12.67	
1965	0.92	−2.89	2.64	9.14	
1966	1.54	−4.33	−10.15	−12.02	
1967	0.76	−12.79	13.78	17.59	
1968	2.24	−1.89	17.62	5.95	
1969	2.18	−7.33	−5.37	−12.60	
1970	5.37	13.95	−5.07	0.84	−5.98
1971	−1.10	9.41	2.91	7.70	12.10
1972	−1.49	2.84	21.18	11.28	15.10
1973	−3.89	−6.76	−8.31	−21.56	−21.23
1974	−4.01	−15.01	−34.06	−34.08	−32.63
1975	−1.86	−1.31	8.25	26.73	24.81
1976	3.24	16.81	4.88	14.67	7.16
1977	−1.66	−0.39	1.13	−7.77	0.67
1978	−0.06	−3.98	19.66	6.70	16.35
1979	1.50	−11.47	31.90	5.30	0.77
1980	3.47	−4.09	17.12	18.46	15.10
1981	5.55	−7.11	−19.99	−14.95	−13.39
1982	5.66	23.91	−4.67	14.10	6.16
1983	4.80	6.63	31.27	16.93	17.33
1984	7.62	10.58	−5.86	8.48	8.04
1985	5.27	16.14	19.82	30.12	36.77
1986	4.93	10.09	4.57	12.28	30.98
1987	4.15	−0.11	1.66	−0.56	7.86
1988	5.21	5.58	6.82	2.95	9.11
1989	6.78	7.20	15.34	18.89	7.72
1990	8.11	2.45	−18.83	−5.95	−17.97
1991	5.82	17.67	7.93	22.90	13.51
1992	4.85	7.55	−3.49	14.96	2.99
1993	3.76	16.18	30.35	11.92	23.64
1994	5.14	−4.50	−0.38	6.98	11.31
1995	5.54	18.59	12.56	27.77	14.89
1996	2.76	9.84	25.59	19.10	11.26
1997	2.38	8.81	14.12	33.84	19.40
1998	3.73	8.08	−2.57	36.31	32.30
1999	2.03	−3.63	28.40	11.29	15.23
2000	2.19	6.80	4.05	−8.48	−12.32
2001	3.97	7.31	−13.19	−7.13	−12.01
2002	−1.23	4.75	−15.65	−25.57	−23.12
2003	0.87	4.52	24.14	3.14	7.21
2004	0.20	4.92	12.09	1.10	5.09
2005	0.46	4.28	21.59	−0.47	4.40
2006	2.29	2.35	15.33	13.84	18.60
2007	1.91	1.27	7.28	−12.63	−9.26
2008	1.95	5.19	−33.77	−22.82	−26.90
2009	−0.82	4.04	33.30	6.67	10.32
2010	−1.91	4.29	14.91	6.84	4.31
Arithmetic Mean	2.33	3.83	6.59	6.46	5.75
Geometric Mean	2.30	3.51	5.23	5.26	4.47
Standard Deviation	2.76	8.17	16.59	15.68	16.00
Year of Data	54	54	54	54	41

Source: PlanPlus Inc.

Index

About the Authors

KWOK HO is Associate Professor of Finance and Finance Area Co-ordinator, School of Administrative Studies, York University, where he teaches personal and corporate finance. He received his Ph.D. in finance from the University of Toronto in 1982, his Certified Management Accountant designation in 1985 and his Certified Financial Planner® designation in 1999. Prior to his academic career, he gained extensive business experience in Hong Kong, China, Japan, and Canada. Writing with Moshe Milevsky and Chris Robinson, he has won a number of best paper awards for his research in retirement planning. His research has appeared in journals such as *Financial Services Review*, *Review of Quantitative Finance and Accounting*, *International Review of Financial Analysis* and *Canadian Investment Review*. His current research interests include personal finance, dividend policy and capital structure.

CHRIS ROBINSON is Associate Professor of Finance, School of Administrative Studies, York University, where he teaches personal finance, financial statement analysis, ethics, security valuation, and corporate finance. In 2011, he was named one of the inaugural Fellows of the Financial Planning Standards Council for his contributions to the financial planning profession in Canada. He articled with Thorne Riddell (now KPMG) and received his Chartered Accountant designation in 1977. He received his Ph.D. in finance from the University of Toronto in 1985 and his Certified Financial Planner® designation in 1999. His research has appeared in journals like *Financial Services Review*, *Financial Analysts Journal*, *Journal of Corporate Finance*, *Canadian Journal of Administrative Science*, *Review of Quantitative Finance and Accounting*, *North American Actuarial Journal*, *International Review of Financial Analysis* and *Canadian Investment Review*. He was a contributing editor to *The Financial Post*, *International Accounting Bulletin* and *World Accounting Report* during the 1980s. He has won several best paper awards for his research in personal finance, with a variety of co-authors. His current research interests include personal finance, alternative and critical perspectives on finance and accounting, dividend policy, regulation of payday lending, financial exclusion and estimation of life insurance requirements.